New Dimensions of Confucian
and
Neo-Confucian Philosophy

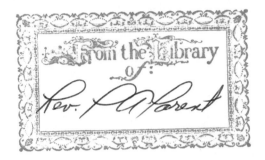

SUNY Series in Philosophy
Robert Cummings Neville, Editor

New Dimensions of Confucian
— and —
Neo-Confucian Philosophy

by

Chung-ying Cheng

State University of New York Press

Published by
State University of New York Press, Albany

© 1991   State University of New York

Production by Marilyn Semerad
Marketing by Dana E. Yanulavich

For information, address State University of New York
Press, State University Plaza, Albany, N.Y., 12246

Library of Congress Cataloging-in-Publication Data

Ch'eng, Chung-ying, 1935-
   New Dimensions of Confucian and Neo-Confucian philosophy / Chung-ying
Cheng.
      p.   cm.—(SUNY series in Philosophy)
   Includes bibliographical references.
   ISBN 0-7914-0283-5.—ISBN 0-7914-0284-3 (pbk.)
   1. Philosophy, Confucian.   2. Neo-Confucianism.   I. Title.
II. Series.
B127.C65C495   1991   89-19655
181'. 112—dc20   CIP

10 9 8 7 6 5 4 3 2 1

Contents

Part III. Neo-Confucian Dimensions

Preface

This book consists of my essays, written in different periods of time, covering a span of twenty years, roughly from 1965 to 1985. The earliest essay "Rectifying Names (*cheng-ming*) in Classical Confucianism" dates back to 1965 and the latest essay "Confucius, Heidegger and the Philosophy of the *I Ching*" to 1985. These two essays represent two focal points of my inquiry, an early-stage analytic-reconstructive inquiry into the microscopic structures in the Confucian philosophy and a later-stage philosophic-hermeneutic inquiry into the macroscopic paradigms in the Confucian framework. In between these two terminal points I have undergone a process of growth and development in both depths of understanding and scope of interest. I have come to see Confucianism as a multi-dimensional structure and a multi-stage process of creative change and creative transformation that includes heights of innovation and near-heights of renovation. Therefore my interests include not just the classical Confucian scenario but encircle the pre-Confucian origins of Confucian thinking and other related schools of thought in the classical period as well as the latter development of the classic Confucian system into the Neo-Confucian philosophy.

For me, Neo-Confucian philosophy is a creative advance on the classical Confucianism in terms of meeting a vast challenge from the outside and, therefore, represents a deepening and maturing of the Confucian philosophy. In particular, it has brought out the outstanding cosmological-ontological perspective of the *I Ching*, which commands a contemporary significance. The whole phenomenon has an architechtonic prospect that preserves its primary identity in the moral and ethical inspirations of the classic Confucianists. The thrust of this study on Confucian and Neo-Confucian philosophy therefore becomes the embedding of the Confucian ethical philosophy in a metaphysical and methodological context and the development of a metaphysics and a methodology for the illumination of human creativity in Confucian morality. In this sense, the final justification of this study is to be found in the organic interdependence and unity of threads of various levels and dimensions of Confucian and Neo-Confucian philosophy in a temporal and dialectical development of pristine insights, which provides both drama and logic to the formation of a great philosophical enterprise and tradition.

To provide a "thread of unity" for the underlying thinking in all these essays written in different times for different purposes, I have written a comprehensive introduction to this volume that explains my views on East-West or Chinese-West comparative philosophy as well as my views on the rise, development, and prospect of the Confucian and Neo-Confucian philosophy. My Introduction is intended also to provide a methodological backdrop and justification for my themes in the volume as well as to offer a rationale for evaluating the philosophical worth and meaningfulness of my inquiries. Since my Introduction is comprehensive enough to include some recent reflections on my earlier studies, I hope that I have given both a substantive self-containedness as well as a formal consistency to the essays in this volume. For these reasons, I do not have more things to say in concluding these essays as a unity. Hence, I withhold from writing a conclusion to these essays, believing each essay presents a conclusion of its own and at the same time enhancing the conclusions of other essays, as I have indicated in the Introduction.

In preparing this volume for publication, I wish to thank my friend and colleague Professor Robert Neville for his warm encouragement as well as for his very thought-provoking Foreword.

Foreword

G ood fortune, not my worthiness, brings me the honor to introduce this collection of essays by Professor Chung-ying Cheng. Though I have long endeavored to practice philosophy in ways that are open to learning as much from the traditions of China as from the West, Professor Cheng has accomplished what I merely try. Educated both in China and at Harvard, he has long thought and written about philosophical topics in ways that demonstrate the relevance and usefulness of Chinese thought in the contemporary scene. More than anyone else I can think of—and the field embraces many very distinguished scholars—Professor Cheng has developed the institutions and academic habits that bring Chinese philosophy to contemporary readiness. He was the founder of the International Society for Chinese Philosophy, which has gathered for rich intellectual discussion not only specialists in Chinese thought but also thinkers in the Western tradition who are open to the traditions of China. The same openness to Western thinkers appreciative of Chinese thought characterizes the *Journal of Chinese Philosophy,* which he founded and edits. To introduce this volume of his essays, thus, provides the opportunity to express gratitude for his effective contributions to our intellectual life.

The first point to understand about these essays is the catholic position of their author. Because of the important need to get some orientation points in Chinese philosophy, Western scholars from the beginning categorized it into schools: the Confucian, Taoist, Buddhist, Legalist, Moist, Neo-Confucian, and so forth. Those of us who have benefited much from Wing-tsit Chan's *Source Book of Chinese Philosophy*, are deeply appreciative of the categories he and others such as Fung Yu-lan have provided. Yet it is a mistake to believe that Chinese thinkers through the centuries have operated as if they were identified exclusively with a school, or thought within it as if the other schools did not count. "Confucianism" did not consistently think of itself as a school in oposition to Buddhism and Taoism until the eighth or ninth centuries in the work of scholars such as Li Ao and Han Yu; was Wang Pi less a Confucian because he wrote about the *Tao Teh Ching?* By the time Neo-Confucianism was becoming self-conscious the philosophic practice of the "Three Schools" was flourishing, as Judith Berling has shown. True, the Neo-Confucians, in their polemics, used to call each other "Buddhistic" as a means of criticism. But there generally was good reason for that: the Neo-Confucian scholars had learned a great deal from Buddhism, as from Taoism. Chinese thinkers of all schools read widely and took all the traditions as their sources, even when adhering to the intellectual bent or politics of one or the other.

Professor Cheng is a Chinese thinker in this catholic sense. His sources in this volume range from the *I Ching* through classic Taoist, Confucian, and Buddhist texts up through twentieth century Chinese thinkers. If forced to say what he "is," I suppose he would admit to being a contemporary Confucian. But that's because accepting labels is a Confucian rather than Taoist enterprise. He would certainly not denigrate the Taoist texts nor criticize them for romantic naturalism.

The second remark to make about these essays is that they are about contemporary philosophy as that is defined by the philosophic needs of our world. This is significant because most of our philosophers write about the problems of philosophers. Two motives, I believe, impell Professor Cheng toward making philosophy relevant. One is his thorough education in contemporary Western philosophy and his continued professional participation in the academic associations of American philosophy. He knows where contemporary philosophy has found its problems, and these essays show that sensitivity. The other motive is the practical orientation of Chinese philosophy itself. Mou Tsung-san and Tu Wei-ming's phrase "moral metaphysics" can be applied to the whole of the Chinese set of traditions, and especially to Professor Cheng's work.

The third point I want to make about these essays is that, in addition to their erudition and scholarship, they embody a splendid speculative imagination. Is it insulting to suggest that the flair of Professor Cheng's imaginative intelligence is more American than Chinese? I hope not. This is a time when philosophy's greatest challenge is to rethink the inherited categories (whencever inherited) and to construct new perspectives capable of understanding the encounter of world cultures, the effects of modernization, and the rise of cultural traditions that have so far not been dominant. Speculative imagination is the tool for this, and Professor Cheng's retrieval of Chinese philosophy has the effect of calling forth a rethinking of philosophy East and West.

This volume is to be appreciated on many levels. It is a work of scholarship in Chinese philosophy. It is a work of comparative scholarship, bringing Chinese philosophy into productive dialogue with Western ideas. It is a work of contemporary speculative imagination. But most of all it is a work of belles lettres, and therefore fun. I hope the readers will enjoy this volume as much as I have, on all these levels.

ROBERT CUMMINGS NEVILLE

Boston University

Introduction
Chinese Philosophy and Confucian/ Neo-Confucian Thinking: Origination, Orientation, and Originality

Unity of Human Experience and Human Thinking

L ike other traditions of philosophy, Chinese philosophy has its origin in the unity of human experience and human reason. But, as a tradition of philosophy, Chinese philosophy has unique orientations that make it different from other traditions of philosophy in the world in important ways. In an earlier article, [1] I explained the differentiating characteristics of Chinese philosophy in terms of intrinsic humanism versus extrinsic humanism, organismic naturalism versus mechanistic naturalism, concrete rationalism versus abstract rationalism, and self-cultivational pragmatism versus utilitarian or instrumental pragmatism. However, I did not make efforts to explain how these characteristics are interrelated and rooted in the common source of human experience and human reason. Now, with deeper explorations into the historic sources of Chinese philosophy and given understanding of the wider scope of development of schools of Chinese philosophy, I may show that all these characteristics of Chinese philosophy are reflections of a unity of fundamental experience and thinking on humankind, nature and the human relation to it, experience being the human feeling or perception, and thinking being the natural response of natural human reason. This is what the Great Commentary of the I Ching refers to as *kan-ying* (feeling-response) between humankind and the world. The *Great Appendix* of the *I Ching* says: "Quiet and being unmoved, when feeling is incurred, it gives rise to understanding of all principles of the world."[2]

How this unity of experience and thinking started cannot be precisely determined, just as how humanity started to become human cannot be precisely pinpointed. The important thing to remember is that this funda-

1

mental experience and thinking on the human relation to nature leads to a *configuration and culture of experience and thinking* that represents humanity as the existence of agency and nature as existence of change. This suggests that the term *human experience* and the term *human thinking* each has an epistemologic and an ontologic significance; namely, the terms human experience and human thinking suggest the way in which a human being experiences and thinks of the world or nature as well as the way in which the world and things in the world are experienced and thought of.

In Chinese philosophy, a human being experiencing and thinking of the world and the world being experienced and thought of by a human being constitute real processes and natural relationships that function as rationales for being real and natural. In other words, it is in terms of the reality of the process of a human experiencing and thinking of the world and the resulting relationship that both the human and the world become fully and simultaneously realized. In the *Analects* Confucius speaks of humankind being capable of "substantiating the *tao*,"[3] whereas in the *Tao Te Ching* Lao Tzu suggests humankind's following and embodiment of the *tao*[4] as a way of preserving and strengthening human existence. Although Confucianist and Taoist adopted different approaches to evaluating the experienced relationship between a human and the world, that they have not for a single moment doubted that the human and the world or the *tao* are in a constant process of interaction, in an intimate relationship of interchange and that this is a common experience. In fact, for them as for all different schools of philosophy throughout the history of Chinese philosophy, unity of human experience and human thinking is both a source and a result of the human being's encounter with nature and the human reflection on the human place in nature.

Before we elaborate further on the nature of human experience and human thinking in Chinese philosophy, it is well to remember that human experience has two levels, the individual and the community, each of which presents human experience and human thinking in a holistic unity of organic totality. Although distinct in scope, these two levels also are intimately related in the sense that the individual experience and individual thinking contribute to the experience and intellectual consciousnesss of community in so far as the community is a form of cultural sharing and value sharing in the practical life of individuals. The experience and intellectual consciousness of the community not only are the depository of individual experiences, but also transmit experience and mold individuals in the community. It is in this sense that Confucius speaks of himself as the transmitter but not the creator of his philosophical thoughts. For it is in this sense that Confucius has inherited the best of his community experience and community thinking from the ancient tradition of Chinese culture and Chinese values.

By way of experiencing and articulating this tradition and giving it new form and new meaning he also molds this community as it is his own.

Community experience and community thinking as a historically evolved common form of individual experience and individual thinking are the very basis for the development of intersubjectivity of individual consciousness as a subjective subject, not merely as an objective object. In light of this understanding, when we speak of human experience and human thinking in Chinese philosophy, we do not merely mean experience and thinking of an individual philosopher, but also the experience and thinking of a community with a historic origin. In this sense, individual experience and individual thinking both shape and are shaped by a community experience and a community thinking. That Chinese philosophy has its origin in the unity of human experience and human reason or thinking thus cannnot be understood independently of the formation of the community experience and the community thinking of China as reflected in Chinese history, Chinese literature, and other forms of cultural creativity such as art and medicine.

Another important observation concerning human experience and human thinking as the ultimate source of Chinese philosophical insight is a distinction between conditions of human experience and human thinking and nature of human experience and human thinking itself. What would account for the emergence of human experience and human thinking that mold a tradition of philosophy? My reply to this question is this: Because the human experience and human thinking that lead to a philosphic position and view form an organic unity, they should embrace and reflect all factors relevant to that experience. Human experience and human thinking are possible on the basis of nature, climate, circumstances, human culture and human creativity. In a sense, human experience and human thinking present a configuration of all ingredients and elements in the human environment, be it natural, human, or social. In this sense, human experience and human thinking reflect a whole lifeworld of humanity. They cannot be conceived simply as thinking of the subject or the experience of the object, as already indicated. They also reflect an experience of the subject and the thinking of the object. Human experience and human thinking in so far as they represent or lead to a philosophic position or view has an emergent quality not to be reduced to a trait of the subject or a feature of the object. They can be understood in terms of the philosophy they give rise to. Perhaps, they also can be understood in terms of the natural conditions under which they rise.[5] This means that Chinese philosophy did not develop accidentally but instead evolved from a cultural and ecological complex of reality and environment in which relations and interactions of human beings, with themselves, and with the world are basically defined.

What then is the nature of human experience and human thinking that form the root of Chinese philosophy as manifested in Confucianism, Taoism, and other schools of philosophy in the pre-Chin period? The best way to answer this question comes from a general contrast between the origination and orientation of Western philosophy, on the one hand, and the origination and orientation of Chinese philosophy on the other. What I have suggested as characteristics of Chinese philosophy in my earliest article can be regarded as descriptions of the nature of human experience and human thinking leading to development of Chinese philosophy. But, in that article, I have not indicated nor described the process by which these characteristics of Chinese philosophy are reached. By the same token, the contrasting characteristics of Western philosophy also fail to reveal the process by which they are reached. Hence, the nature of human experience and human thinking that embed and nourish the development of Chinese philosophy cannot be said to be fully disclosed. To bring out the full nature of human experience and human thinking that orient and differentiate the different philosophic traditions, we must discern the subtle tendencies that different types of human experience and human thinking embody and that are conditioned as well as consummated by reality and thus exhibit both the creativity and receptivity of human consciousness.

Contrasting Modes of Origination and Orientation

In light of a synthetic examination of major philosophical texts, language forms, art, and culture forms, medical practice, and practical forms of life including political, economic, moral, and social customs in both structural and generative contexts, we suggest a hypothetical characterization of the nature of human experience and human thinking underlying Chinese philosophy in terms of the mode of origination and orientation called *natural naturalization* and *human immanentization*. In contrast, we suggest a hypothetical characterization of the nature of human experience and human thinking underlying Western philosophy in terms of the mode of origination and orientation called *rational rationalization* and *divine transcendentalization*. This contrast between the two modes of origination and orientation for two types of human experience and human thinking is important, for it is against this contrast that the Eastern and the Western types of experience and thinking can be better understood. Although a full study of this contrast cannot be given here, some basic items of contrast and their possible integration is exhibited in the table and will be explained here as a background for understanding the basic motivating force of Chinese philosophy and its representation in Confucian thinking. Perhaps, we

Chinese Philosophy and Western Philosophy:
Contrast in Development and Possible Integration

Chinese Philosophy	Western Philosophy
Basic Orientations	
1. Harmonizing human experience with human thinking	1. Overcoming human experience by human thinking
2. Nonreductive naturalism	2. Reductive rationalism
Development and Possible Integration	
1. Naturalization (nature and naturality in Chinese philosophy: *I Ching/ Tao Te Ching*)	1. Rationalization (reason and rationality in Greek philosophy: Socrates/ Plato/Aristotle)
2. Humanization (classical Confucianism)	2. Transcendalization (Judeo-Christianity)
3. Interplay between naturalization and humanization (Neo-Confucianism)	3. Interplay between rationalization and transcendentalization (modern science and modern rationalistic philosophy)
4. Future development in light of interaction with Western orientation	4. Future development in light of interaction with Chinese orientation
5. Possible rationalization of naturalization	5. Possible naturalization of rationalization

can first explain the originating and orientating experiences of *rational rationalization* and *divine transcendentalization* in the West in order to appreciate the ground-laying experiences of *natural naturalization* and *human immanentization* in Chinese philosophy.

Rationalization is the process of achieving rational knowledge of reality and performing rational action according to this rational knowledge of reality. To be rational is to think and act independently of influences of imagination and desires but in accordance with a perception of reality. It is the process based on a distinction between the knowing one's self and the known reality for the purpose of knowing one's self knowing reality. What makes this distinction necessary is the need for survival under certain objective conditions of nature and society. However, there is no ultimate cause for such rationalization to be unilaterally conceived. The totality of circusmtances for a given placement of a human being in nature and society codetermine the dynamics of formation of human experience and human thinking for both the individual and the community. Thus, the call for reason and rationality as a way of knowing reality and controlling action is premised on such a totality of circumstances in which one finds oneself when one becomes aware of one's own existence. In this sense both reason and rationality are existential qualities emerging from development of an individual in relation to his or her environment, reason being an ability to think independently of oneself for reality, rationality being a state of mind created by use of reason. Both reason and rationality are developed for fulfilling the human need to adapt to the environment and to transform the environment into a fulfilling state of human life. Rationalization is a process of initialization of use of reason and pursuit of rationality. *But to make rationalization an exclusive ideal and goal in all aspects of life and therefore to make reason and rationality a systematic pursuit and absolute value is what I refer to as rational rationalization, which therefore can be regarded as a radical development of reason and rationality.*

Given this description of *rationalization* and *rational rationalization*, it is clear that Greek philosophy beginning with the Greek cosmologists illustrates the development of reason and rationality in humankind and hence typifies the process of rationalization in the formation of culture and personality. Without going into detail about the origination of Greek philosophy and its development, it suffices to point out that the Greek cosmological speculation exemplifies the first attempt to rationally describe the real and the naturally given. It also is an attempt to make essential attributes out of the given nature as well as an attempt to characterize nature in terms of clear-cut conceptual paradigms. In this sense, to rationalize or to think rationally is to objectify nature and consequently to conceptualize nature. This implies a separating of the subject from the object. How the Greek came to this turning point of rational thinking is a matter of cultural and environmental development.[6] For, in light of total situational considerations, the striving for survival and prosperity of the Greeks in Asia Minor and the development of maritime trade and war in the period of the Homeric epic provided a cultural and ecological backdrop for the origination and protrusion of rational thinking as a mode of thinking and perception. One need not to mention that from Greek cosmologists to Socrates and then to Plato and Aristotle one witnesses a maturing process of reason and rationalization as the Greek way of thinking, a process that not only reached a height of systematization, but provided essential and conceptual definitions of humankind and world and the human relation to the world under the guidance of rational criteria and demands. This is the beginning of the process of *rational rationalization*, which for the first time becomes a process of conscious and conscientious search for rational method and methodology toward truth and knowledge.

Heidegger has criticized Greek philosophy as essentialist and as covering up Being in metaphysical concepts of substance and attribute, idea and matter.[7] This criticism can be construed as a critique of rationalism as conceived by the Greeks: It is not only that rationalization in the Greek philosophy is criticizable, but that any rationalization in any tradition is criticizable, for according to Heidegger any rationalization produces a conceptual blockade that obscures our experience of Being. The significance of Heidegger's critique is that Greek philosophers are responsible for starting the process of rationalization as a way of philosophical thinking and this process leads to its radicalization in the form of what I call *rational rationalization.* In this light Heidegger not only intends his criticism as a criticism of Greek philosophy, but as a criticism of the European-based and European-centered philosophy from the Greek sources, inclusive of the Roman development, medieval development, and modern Western development. For him, all Western philosophies up to the modern times have been committed to a Being-hiding and Being-forgetting way of thinking, which he characterizes as *onto-theo-logik*[8] which I refer to as *rational rationalization*, in which the totality of Being, the individuality of human existence, and the possibility of creativity and creativeness of experience and thinking are reduced to the form and order of universal law and thinghood.

It is only fair to point out that although rationalization does not lead to permanent disclosure of Being, it does satisfy the practical purpose of controlling the human environment for the needs of human survival. In other words, one should not forget that the origin and incentive for rationalization are practical and pragmatic: It is not intended as ultimately ontological or axiological or soteriological. It always should be considered a means rather than an end. Only when it is considered or taken to be an end rather than a means, or when it is absolutized as the exclusive method of approach to all problems of life, does it become a block and an obscuration. Besides, rationalization or the use of reason at any time or during any period results only in a finite number of concepts of explanation that have applications only for situations of finite space and finite time. There is no rational proof that a rational system must be valid at all times and in all places. To assume this is merely a matter of faith, not a matter of reason.

From experience and history one must see that all rational systems and all rational methods have intrinsic limitations to their validity that eventually must be transcended by new experiences and new circumstances. That time and experience can be innovative and indefinitely open is an understanding not based on any closed concept of rationality but on an open concept of rationality. Hence, every rational system and rational method must exhaust itself, transcend itself, and thus renew and transform itself. In this fashion, rationalization as an open process and as a process embedded in the total process of life-formation and life-transformation will have its validity and usefulness, which need not conflict with the ontological interest in understanding Being and life.

Another point to be made in connection with the Heideggerian criticism of rationalization is that the technological origins of science and the scientific origins of technology in modern Western society serve an important purpose for modern humans in the context of modernization or rationalization (to use Max Weber's paradigm) and this represents the modern development of rationalization in the form of scientific and technological reason, which is another case of rational rationalization. Although Heidegger's critique of science and technology has an ontological message, we must not forget that Alfred Whitehead and Henri Bergson in the beginning of the twentieth century also made similar critiques and even constructively proposed revamping and enlarging scientific rationality in highly innovative ways, pursuing cosmological and ontological objectives.

We must note, finally, that despite the critiques of rationalization and rational rationalization in the West by Heidegger and others, the process of rationalization or rational rationalization will not cease in human thinking, because not only is there a practical need for rationalization but because rationalization is grounded in human experience in relation to the human environment. Our problem regarding this process is not to stop it, but to contextualize it in the total understanding of reality and the total development of humanity. Thus, we need to look into other philosophical traditions for other significant philosophical principles based on human experience and human encounter with the world-environment. A harmonization and balancing of all philosophical priniciples based on consideration of all human experiences and comparison of the major orientations of human thinking would induce both innovative and renovative development toward a human use and humane control and discipline of rationalization and rationalism in the world today.

With such understanding of all important traditions of philosophy as a starting point and as a reference framework, no talk of critical reason and deconstruction of reason can do justice to the positioning of reason in humanity. It might even run the risk of rationalizing *derationalization* and therefore becomes a victim of rationalization in disguise. This should be a warning for the direction of development of critical or philosophical hermenentics in contemporary West vis-à-vis the analytical and scientific philosophy.

The second foundational principle explanatory of Western philosophy derived from Western experience and Western thinking is that of *divine transcendentalization*, which is the tendency and effort to go beyond worldly things for a transcendent subject or object as ultimate goal or source of values. The transcendent subject or object is conceived as qualitatively different from the mundane world and yet is the ultimate cause or source of meaning and value in things in the world. This mode of thinking, of course, has its origin in the Judeo-Christian religiosity, which combines a form of religious experience with a religious faith inspired by the Judeo-Christian religious experience and cultural tradition. Recent studies of the

Jewish culture suggest that there was a strong desire for justice and equity among the ancient Jewish people that leads to the positing of a god of justice.[9] It is apparent that both the hope and the demand for justice amidst a people desperately seeking emancipation from oppression and the bondage of slavery created a deep vision of a divinity who would condemn the unjust and reward the just and oppressed. One may indeed suggest that the very idea of transcendence comes from the divine in the first place in the Judeo-Christian tradition and then provides a model and cause for transcendence in later development of religion and philosophy. It is interesting to note that, whereas the sense of the divine has led to the transcendent, the sense of the transcendent also tends to lead to the sense of the divine in philosophical thinking. This is true even of Kant in his practical-critical approach to the noumenal. In general, Western philosophy since the medieval period is guided by the two principles just mentioned and their combination and synthesis. In Descartes we see the beginning of the tendency to transcendentalize human reason as against the human body, which leads to the bifurcation of mind and matter or body, that dominates later Western way of thinking. Even though the difficulties of this dualistic view have been discussed again and again, the fact remains that rationalization seems to require a transcendent justification, and transcendentalization seems to require a rational illumination. The dialectical tension between the two produces a creative power for philosophical thinking that manifests itself in constant quest and reformulation of philosphical methodology and metaphysics, and consequently constant critique and rejection of them or their limitations. Even in today's analytical philosophy, we see a radical rationalization in conceptual language analysis. We also see the transcendental *aufheben* of practical moral issues in reality of life into the metalinguistic and metaethical issues.

Natural Naturalization and Human Immanentization

In contrast with the foundational principles underlying experience and thinking in the Western philosophy, the foundational principles underlying experience and thinking in Chinese philosophy present quite different philosophical orientations, which I would describe as *natural naturalization* and *human immanentization*. This difference is to be accounted on many factors, including both environmental and social considerations. It should be noted that in the beginning of Chinese philosophy as exhibited in the *Book of Changes (I Ching)*, the *Book of Documents (Shang Shu)*, and the *Book of Poetry (Shih Ching)* both principles are presented. Even though heaven (*t'ien*) originally was conceived as a supernatural moral and existential creator-judge with personalistic characteristics, heaven has not been fully personalized as in the case of the Jewish Jehovah or the Christian God. Heaven is closely related to the real world as we perceive it and therefore does not transcend it. Perhaps, the phrase "not mixed with nor separated from" (*pu-tsa pu-li*)[10] could be used to describe this nontranscending and nonidentical relation of heaven-in-the-world.

Confucianists often speak of "unity and unification of man and heaven," whereas Taoists often speak of "unity and unification of man and heaven in *te* (virtue) or in *tao* (way)." In both cases heaven and man are considered closely related in both a cosmological and an axiological sense. In other words, heaven and man are not far apart as a matter of given fact. But heaven and man can be fully identified in terms of their essential natures when man cultivates himself into a refined state of understanding and creativeness that defines virtue. It can be said that in actuality man is always part of nature as he has been generated and conditioned by Heaven. But in an ideal form of development man can make heaven a part of himself. Therefore, there are two senses of unity and unification of man and heaven, a descriptive sense and a prescriptive sense. There is a possibility of movement from the description to prescription by way of development, cultivation and transformation of man. For this conception of unity and unification of heaven and man implies that man is the crossing of the two dimensions of existence, the temporal and the nontemporal, which constitute a holistic structure of reality to be represented in the idea of the great ultimate (*t'ai-chi*) in the philosophy of the *I Ching*.

According to the philosophy of the *I Ching*, the world is the dynamic unity and unification of the *yin* and the *yang*, where the *yin* represents the receptive and the potential and the *yang* represents the creative and the actual. One can readily see that in time (the temporal) there is creative realization of being, whereas in being there is great potentiality for individuating development and innovative ontogenesis. Hence we can conceive of time as a matter of the *yang* and being as a matter of the *yin*. The Heideggerian categories can be seen to implicitly conform to the ontocosmological thinking of the *I Ching*, and their relationship can be better understood in terms of the dynamic unity and unification of the *yin* and the *yang*; that is, in terms of the transformation of *yin* into *yang* and the transformation of *yang* into *yin* in a continuously creative upgrading (in a certain human perspective) of structure of reality.[11] Similarly, time can be said to transform itself into being to be hidden and potentialized and being to transform itself into time to be disclosed and actualizated. Their mutual transformation produced a historic world of human development and a moral world of human growth.

In light of this unity of time and being based on the unity of paradigmatic *yin* and *yang*, we will see a new meaning or new intepretation of the unity and unification of heaven and humanity and following from it an introduction to the foundational principle of *natural naturalization* in Chinese philosophy. First, regarding heaven and humanity, it is apparent that heaven has played the ontogenetic role of time in the beginning, whereas the human is the being to be disclosed or to emerge as the result of creative advance of time. But given humans being capable of creating their own surroundings, humans can temporalize themselves into timely agents for creating either the human associations or human society or choosing to be isolated individuals. Hence, the process or stage of heavenization is where heaven creates humans and the process or stage of humanization or development of human being is where humans create heaven: The unity and unification of heaven and humanity in the Confucian sense underscores the second process, whereas unity and unification of heaven and humanity in the Taoistic sense underscores the first process. As these two processes can reciprocate with each other and transform back and forth into each other, the dynamics of transformation also underscores the distinction between the dimension of natural inclusion on Taoistic grounds and the dimension of moral transcendence on Confucian grounds. In this sense there is unity and balance of the Confucian and Taoistic views.

What then is the principle of *natural naturalization*? To answer this question briefly in light of the ontocosmology of the *I Ching*, the principle can be said to be respectively understood as the principle of preserving heaven for humanity; namely, it is the principle of the heavenization of humans. On the other hand, this principle is to be enriched by a reciprocal principle of humanization. Hence the principle of natural naturalization is a twofold principle that accentuates the importance of balance, harmony, and totalization. Perhaps, it is with this understanding that the foundational experience of the world by the Chinese is one jumping-forward toward totality, harmony, and balance as well as mutual transformation. What is regarded as natural is the action or event conforming to the paradigmatic attribution of harmony and balance, whereas nature is the result of the naturalization—*to-make-natural*—and this process serves the best purpose of human existence.

That naturalization represents a process of harmonization, balancing, and totalization of elements in the world makes it radically different from rationalization, which depends on a recognized functioning of the rational faculty of man. This rational faculty called *reason* or *rationality* is an ability to discover and cognize the world in terms of abstract laws and represent them in abstract concepts. It also is the ability to formulate knowledge in a consistent system and attribute universal validity to it. We have already indicated that this rational ability and activity are instrumental for the practical purposes of human beings to explore and exploit the world. This rational ability leads to abstract principles of logical reasoning, on the one hand, and to the invention of skills and technology, on the other hand. When one applies the same rational ability to moral and practical affairs, morality and ethics then would be transformed into a system of rational rules that commands action unconditionally as required of Kant's practical reason.

The human rational ability becomes so established and outstanding a feature of humankind that it leads Aristotle even to speak of it as the defining human attribute. That from the earliest period of Western philosophy reason was singled out for attention and cultivation is a matter of cultural and social conditioning we have generally explained as result of the interaction between human experience and human thinking. By the similar process of interaction between human experience and human thinking, we also may explain how rationality as a generalized faculty can become differentiated and ramified into apparently unrelated areas of formal logic, science and technology, and ethics and law. It is an undeniable fact that in Western philosophy reason dominates as the fundamental cognitive and the practical principle: It is through reason (abstraction and systematization)that we know the world, and it is through high axiological valuation of the rational in conduct and life that reason also becomes a deontological principle—it is rational to obey reason or to follow rational principles in one's actions. Another important characteristic of rationality, apart from universality and conformity to objectivity, the rational as a cognitive principle is often reductivistic. This is because in abstraction the rational only recognizes general concepts for explanation and requires simplicity over complexity. This certainly leads to reductionism and the rational methodology presented by Descartes in his treatise on method which can be said to typify this circumstance. To look for simple, universalistic principles of moral action also is basically a result of reduction, for it neglects a rich context of particulars.

In contrast, *nature (hsing)* or *naturality* (a term I invent to contrast with *rationality* in describing what conforms to the power of nature or what is natural) finds its interest in recognizing the play and display of different elements in human experience and in coordinating and harmonizing them for the benefit of the whole. Although the rational will still play an important role for such coordination and harmonization, natural forces of different given elements also are well channeled, but not simply controlled or manipulated, for a dominating rational plan or vision. In other words, in the work of nature or naturality, reason or rationality is not regarded as an external authority to be imposed on the natural elements of a given entity but as an internal capacity for preserving and sustaining the whole without sacrificing its parts. What is natural therefore is not to let the rational dominate among all constitutive factors of human existence but to let the rational to contribute to a concrete reality of harmony of a variety of differences. In doing this, nature or naturality does not provoke an exterior design or scientific calculation in an abstract manner nor adopt a reductivistic program for reconstruing and regimenting human experience according to an ontology of abstract entities. Instead, nature or naturality stresses naturalness and spontaneity from given natural existence and displays and fulfills itself in concreteness and particularity. The key ingredients for nature or naturality is totality, naturalness, nonreductiveness, and concreteness, in contrast with partiality, dominance, externality, reductionism, and abstractness as key ingredients for reason and rationality. Whereas rationality denies a role of naturality and therefore substitutes a designed context for a given natural context or disregards the latter completely, naturality does not deny a role to the rational but puts it to the right use at right place at right time. Hence, the guiding light for naturality is concrete harmony, whereas that for rationality is abstract order.

Naturalization via nature or naturality in Chinese philosophy normally takes the form of presenting and explaining reality in terms of opposites and their unity and unification in the spirit of the philosophy of the *I Ching*, which provides a naturalistic mode of thinking and represents a naturalistic form of experience. Naturalization as a process also tends to transform or interpret what is transcendent, external, and personalistic into what is immanent, internal, and nonpersonalistic, because in the light of need for the harmony of totality, the preset narrow concept of personalistic and transcendent force will lose its place in the organic unity of the whole. Thus, the concept of *shang-ti* (supreme ruler on high),which was more or less a personalized god for the Hsia and Shang people before around 1200 b.c. as presented in classical texts, was transformed into the concept of *t'ien* (heaven), which becomes a less personalized concept of god for all peoples under the Chou rule around 1200 b.c. Until the time of Confucius, the personalistic character of heaven was still appealed to. But even before and during the time of Confucius, the concept of heaven became less and less personalized, and an even more pervasive and universal concept of reality was introduced: This is the concept of the *tao* (the way). In fact, the *tao* as presented in the *Tao Te Ching* was not personalistic at all. When heaven becomes depersonalized and desubstantiated, heaven becomes the *tao*, the ultimate source of existence and value. Since the time of Taoist philosophy around 500 b.c., the *tao* has become the ultimate ontological category for Chinese philosophy up to the present time. This is a typical example of naturalization in Chinese philosophy. It also is clear that in this process of naturalization *tao* is interpreted to have two forms of movement, the *yin* and the *yang*, that form a unity of complementary opposites, as already indicated in the *Commentaries* of the *I Ching*.

In the whole context of classical Chinese philosophy, even where *t'ien* is fully transformed into the *tao*, it nevertheless forms a unity of metaphysical import in which the personalistic implication of *t'ien* is diluted. Another form of naturalization is the development of nearly opposite and complementarly concepts in the account of human existence. Crucial to this development is the concept of nature (*hsing*) of being human. What is the nature (*hsing*) of being human? The *Chung Yung* says: "That which is endowed by heaven is called *hsing*." *Hsing* can be said to have three basic elements for its codetermination: First, it is a given mode of existence for an entity that presents a place in the scheme of things in the world. Second, it constitutes the given potentiality of an individual entity that both opens up the possibility of development and delimits its possible development. Third, it is the source of the entity's activity and creativity that forms the basis for its freedom and value. When we understand nature with this complex background of meaning, we can see that *hsing* can be contrasted with the faculty of actualization and consciousness that finds its presence in the concept of hsim (*heart-mind*). Hence, there is a unity of opposites in *hsing* and *hsin*. *Hsing* can be further contrasted with emotional and existential states of a person that finds its presence in the concept of feeling-emotion (*ching*). Hence, there is the unity of opposites in *hsing* and *ching*. Finally, we can also contrast *hsing* with *ming*, which is external determining conditions imposed on a person beyond that person's own will and capacity and which therefore forms the prior determinations or casually present limiting factors for the life of the person. In this sense we can see human life and even human experience as a unity of *hsing* and *ming* in interplay and mutual determination. Similarly we can see that *hsin* and *shen* (body) form a unity of opposites in the individual's personal identity, and *t'ien* and the person form a unity of opposites in the actual and ideal development of human existence as indicated earlier.

In connection with this discussion of *hsing* of being human, we can see that our use of the term *naturality* has a special significance. For this term suggests not only what is given as nature but that this nature is a force or power that will develop actively in a certain manner just like rationality in human composition. This development of nature is indicated in the process of reaching a harmony, balance, and totality of existence pertaining to the nature of a given form of reality. The process of realizing nature and hence the naturality of a form of a thing is then the process of naturalization.

In Chinese Buddhistic philosophy and Neo-Confucian philosophy, the tradition of depersonalization and naturalization continues with further development of the *li* and *ch'i* concepts, on the one hand, and the *hsin* and *hsing* concepts on the other. Both pairs of the concepts form a unity of complementary opposites after the manner of the unity of *yin* and *yang* in the *tao*.[12] Hence we can conclude that naturalization in the paradigm of the *I Ching* mode of thinking is a universal feature of Chinese philosophy. We can make the same point by saying that the naturalization of Chinese philosophy takes the *I Ching* mode of thinking as its paradigm. It must be pointed out that naturalization contains rationalization in a relative sense; namely, in the sense that what is natural is rational, if being rational means having a proper place and an ontological reality in the total order of the world. This is the meaning of rationality in the Neo-Confucian concept of *li*.

In fact, in light of the Neo-Confucian philosophy, what is natural is equivalent to the *ch'i*, which is the dynamic energy inherent in as well as constitutive of everything in the world, and what is rational is equivalent to *li*. As Chu Hsi says, "Under heaven there is no *ch'i* without *li*, and there is no *li* without *ch'i*."[13] Hence, what is rational and what is natural are not separable, and together they form the actuality of things in the world. This is a relationship of interpenetration and harmonization that is different from the deductive order of rationalization in the Western philosophical tradition. Apart from what we have said about rationalization as a guiding principle of Western philosophy, it also may be pointed out that reason or rationality as an original and primary character of human being has an axiological significance that would belong exclusively to human beings. Hence, the natural world cannot be said to be rational in the sense in which human intellect can be said to be rational. If the world can be said to be rational in any sense, its rationality is attributed by and founded on the human rational mind. This would be the position of Kant. In the strict sense of rationality, there is always a bifurcation and contrast between what is rational and what is natural, which can be nonrational or even irrational. This is basically the position of the dualism of mind and body since Descartes. After classical physics discovered mechanical laws in nature, philosophers came to consider physical science but not metaphysics the rationale for rationality, and this proclivity leads directly to a physicalistic position that would represent and explain mind and intellect in physical-scientific terms. This is a typical example of the reductionism that characterizes much of the modern philosophy in the West.

Beside dualism and reductionism in the account of rationalization in the West, there also is an idealism that could see the world in an ideal sense of rationality consistent with human intellect and ideal. For example, we find in Hegel the proposition that what is rational is real and what is real is rational. But a proper understanding of this proposition shows that the real and the rational are primarily attributes of the fully realized Absolute Geist. Similarly, if we consider the world as a creation of rational god, the world also can be regarded as having the attribute of rationality based on god. This is how the insistence on the pervasiveness of rationality is premised on the idealistic thesis of the prior existence of an overarching spirit or god.

In contrast with the Western view on rationalization, in Chinese philosophy there is no dualistic, reductionalistic, or idealistic explanation of rationalization. Rationalization as part of naturalization is inherent in the nature of things, not just in the nature of humankind. This is why Neo-Confucianists say that they find *li* or rationality in all things and one need only investigate things for genuine knowledge. This concrete and equalitarian concept of rationality is stated even better in Chang Tsai: *li* is simply the concrete pattern in the activities of *ch'i*. Hence *li* is confined and contextualized in *ch'i* and particularities of things, which would make *li* more particularistic than universalistic, not as in the case of the Western philosophy. For the Taoist Chuang Chou, when asked where we can find the *tao*, he replied that the *tao* can be found in anything and everything including the lowest of things. This can be seen as seeing rationality in any- and everything, and therefore nothing in the world is without value or without an inner reason for existence. But then one finds in Chuang Chou, as one finds in Chang Tsai an interesting identification of the natural and the rational that bespeaks the best formation of the principle of naturalization in Chinese philosophy. As this principle develops in a spontaneous and natural fashion in Chinese philosophy, it can be thus described as the principle of *natural* naturalization. One also can easily see as a consequence that both the human mind and the human body have their own respective rationalities.

Now we can come to the principle of human immanentization in Chinese philosophy. Unlike the principle of natural naturalization, the principle of human immanentization is easier to explain and easier to understand. In contrast with divine transcendentization, which consists in positing an external creator, sustainer, deliverer, supporter, and justifier such as God over and above the world and thus providing a transcendent basis and foundation for the world and the meaning of life of human beings, human immanentization consists in pointing to the inherent source and resources of creation and creativity in the nature of human beings as well as in the nature of the world for the meaningful fulfillment of human life and for the valid explanation and justification of existence and value of the world. In this sense the idea of immanentization depends on the concept of the nature or naturality of humankind and the world, and one can see that nature or naturality stands for the immanent source and resources of existence and the value of humanity or the world. Because of the presence of nature or naturality, there is no need nor reason for positing an external transcendent source of creative power or value. Nature or naturality is itself the creative power, and when generalized over, it is the *tao*, the concrete universal creative and transformative power that is indeterminate in form but is determinative of every form. For both Confucianists and Taoists, the *tao* as the concrete universal and ultimate ontological source of creativity is in the nature of all things that relates everything together in the organic network of all things, on the one hand, and individuates each thing of each type on each level, on the other. However, as pointed out earlier, whereas the Taoists would consider going (back) to the *tao* and imitate and embody the *tao* as the general and ultimate way of fulfilling the life of human beings, the Confucianists would consider developing and cultivating one's nature as the correct way of fulfilling one's nature as well as the correct way of consummating and illuminating the *tao*. Hence, the immanentization principle prescribes not only that all truth and value of being are innate and inherent in the nature of things and human beings, but that nature has the cultivatable power to reveal, fulfill, and substantiate the *tao*. This is considered meaningful not only for the individual persons or things themselves but for the *tao* itself.

The beginning of such a process of immanentization in Chinese philosophy can be traced to the human organismic experience of congeniality and consanguinity of the whole universe, in which one would see or feel the presence of the whole and every part of the whole in each part of the whole. Of course, this is merely a hypothetic observation regarding the collective consciousness of a people, yet this observation does become transcribed as the principle of comprehensive interpenetration (*chou-pien han-yung*) in both Chinese Hua Yen and T'ien Tai Buddhistic philosophy and the Neo-Confucian philosophy of the Sung and Ming eras. Historically speaking, when the symbolism of the *I Ching* was first formulated in 1200 to 800 b.c., there already was a comprehensive interpenetration of the subject and the object, the world and the human, the part and the whole of reality in the human experience and human thinking of the time. In the Chou dynasty and earlier records of political-moral statements of the sagely kings in *Shang Shu*, one also sees the internalization of cause and reason for power and substance of rule in the virtue, character, and conduct of individuals. The ruler particularly is made to see that his mandate of heaven rests with his virtues of reverence, care and benevolence toward people. He also is charged with the moral responsibility to educate and inculcate people toward virtuous life; that is, toward a life based on self-restraint and community piety. One can readily see that the Confucian ethical philosophy of virtues grew out of this fundamental experience. To put this point in brief, the concept and principle of *te* (virtue and virtuous cultivation of self-control and community regard) can be seen as the first explicit formulation of the human immanentization principle.

Another evidential source for human immanentization is indicated in the use of the following genres of poetry in the *Shih Ching*: the form of *hsin* (arousing), the form of *pi* (analogizing), and the form of *fu* (display). In all these forms, any item in the world could provide an occasion for relating to something else, particularly for exhibiting the poetic justice of criticism, irony, or the imaginative fulfillment of wishes and dreams. Clearly this would be impossible if there is not presupposed through human experience or human thinking, the organismic and holographic ontology of the world in which everything is related to everything else on a deep level.

In light of the meaning of immanentizing sources and resources of creativity and transformation in human nature, this principle can be formulated both as the principle of immanentization of humanity and the principle of humanization of the immanent *tao*. In the first formulation stress is put on the fact that, whatever virtues humankind can develop are based on and derived from the human nature. This clearly is the position developed by Mencius. In the second formulation stress is put on the fact that the profound *tao* inherent in all things can be made of human use and used to transform or fulfill human relationships and the higher purposes of the human community, depending on whether the orientations of the human experience are Confucianist or Taoist. Even for Mencius, there is no simple limitation of his position to the principle of immanentization of humanity, but one must see how he goes beyond the first formulation of the immanentization principle and reaches for the second one: When he says that "all things are complete within me, and I will realize this by reflecting on myself,"[14] he is speaking of a possibility of reaching for the inner unity with the *tao* and all things in the world as a human being. In this manner a human being can become "great" (*ta*), "sagely" (*sheng*), and "divine" (*shen*).[15] The humanization of the *tao*, of course, becomes equivalent to the tao-ization of humanity, which is not simply a matter of immanentization but a matter of explicit existential realization or "form-embodiment" (*chi'en-hsing*) of the *tao*.[16]

The human immanentization finds its most illuminating realization in the ethical sublimation of the human religious need in Chinese philosophy. When one fulfills onself in developing one's nature and relating to others in the community by virtue—that is, by contributing to the fulfillment of the lives of others in the community—one has reached and established an immanent immortality of virtue (*li-te*),[17] and one's religious need for reaching the ultimate becomes satisfied as well. One may say that in fulfilling humanity one dissolves the religious need for the ultimate and the transcendent, if this need is so interpreted. The point is that the fulfillment of humanity is the way for satisfying the need for the ultimate and the transcendent, and in the ultimate sense the human is the ultimate and the immanent is the transcendent. Certainly, this view can be sustained only when under optimum conditions the equivalence can be made between the human and the ultimate and between the immanent and the transcendent. It is clear that both Confucianists and Taoists argue and believe in obtainability of such conditions. Under such conditions, which are basically interpreted under the principle of naturalization, problems of life and death both as a matter of total fulfillment of value and as a matter of temporalizing the eternal and eternalizing the temporal become dissolved; in other words, they become nonproblems. In fact, because of the interdependence and interpenetration of things in the world and in human life, fulfillment of life is simultaneously the resolution or forgetting of the problem of death. The power of creative transformation for the human integrates and breaks through the problems posed by life and death and presents a transcendent deliverance in identifying a larger background reality or higher level of reality for human life. We must concede, however, that this theoretical possibility of satisfying the human religious need in Chinese philosophy, which obtains in a large measure among Chinese intellectuals, may not always become actualized or actualizable because of the lack of optimum conditions. In fact no matter how an individual tries, he or she still may be limited by the *ming* (unavoidable determinations of life), which sometimes may be manifested as circumstances of time and locality that cannot be avoided or transformed. Hence, the religious need for transcendence may arise in spite of the Taoist and Confucianist arguments in the history of China. Yet one still can observe that the tendency to immanentize the transcendent and the tendency to humanize the divine always is at work in history, due to orientation of human experience and human thinking in the beginning of Chinese philosophy as presented in both Confucianism and Taoism.

The extreme form of human immanentization is to identify all reality and value with activities of the heart-mind (*hsin*). This is the position attributed to Mencius by Lu Hsiang-shan and strongly held by Lu Hsiang-shan and Wang Yang-ming, who have been called the *idealistic Neo-Confucianists* in contrast with the so-called *realistic Neo-Confucianists* Ch'eng Brothers and Chu Hsi. Although there are essential differences between these two schools, to contrast them as idealists and realists may miss the point. The first major difference between the two schools is the onto-epistemic difference between the *hsin* (heart-mind) and the *hsing* (nature). The second major difference is that between mode of identification of *hsin* with the world and the mode of identification of *hsing* with the world. For Lu Hsiang-shan, *hsin* is the substance of all things and there is no *hsing* apart from *hsin*: *Hsin* in the original form (called *pen-hsin*) contains all principles of things and therefore in exercising one's mind one comes to understand the fundamental truths of all things. The autonomy of *hsin* of a person and the illumination of the universe in *hsin* is what constitutes the most important activity of *hsin*. Whether or how *hsin* is to be ontologically founded is not an important question. In this regard the Ch'anist (Zen) philosophy of *hsin* as the center of universe of the basis for reality may come to mind. But as Lu never wishes to say that things are constituted by projection and transformation of consciousness, he can be assumed to subscribe to the basic ontology of the Confucian school, which allows that the world and the human being are parts of the great ultimate and its transformation.

For Wang Yang-ming, *hsin* becomes more ontologized than epistemologized, for *hsin* now assumes the form of *liang-chih-pen-ti* (original substance of innate knowledge of goodness) that by its nature is both truth-illuminating and existence-contextualizing. In light of *hsin*'s role of contextualizing existence, Wang Yang-ming holds that *hsin* is *li* (heart-mind is ultimate reality) in contrast with Ch'eng I's and Chu Hsi's thesis that *hsing* is *li* (nature is ultimate reality). In this sense Wang has absorbed nature into mind just as Chu Hsi has absorbed mind into nature. For Chu Hsi nature is ontologically given and the mind is epistemologically given: Although the mind is embedded in nature so that the mind can seek guidance from nature, nature has its fulfillment in the mind as the mind directly controls human action. For him identification of the human with heaven will inevitably take the form of identification of nature of being human with reality or *li* (principle), but not that of identification of the human mind with *li*. This is because the mind could be subject to influence of the body and desires and therefore may not be able to respond to the ultimate truth of reality. Besides, nature as the ontological fountainhead of human reality will provide a basis for a process of transformation and cultivation of the human person.

In spite of these differences between *hsin* and *hsing*, it is clear that they share a common ground in their identification with heaven; namely, perfection of humanity and fulfillment of human life are attained in the identification that is the goal of human immanentization, the experience of the unity of the individual with heaven. Perhaps the mode of identification with heaven *à la* mind is a state of perception and illumination, whereas the mode of identification with heaven *à la* nature is a state of feeling and contemplation. Perhaps the the best way to resolve their differences is still to be found in Mencius, where Mencius suggested that one must first exhaustively fulfill one's mind (*chin-hsing*), then one can come to know one's nature (*chih-hsing*) and finally come to know heaven (*chih-ti'en*).

In the preceding, I have characterized the two orientational principles of human experience and human thinking for the beginning and development of Chinese philosophy. It should be clear that these two principles are not intended to explain all ramifying and diversifying strains of Chinese philosophy but rather the centralizing and converging strains. They should provide a basic framework of the tradition of Chinese philosophy as well as a framework for interpreting Chinese philosophy, particularly in comparison with Western philosophy. It should be noted that these two principles alone do not present a total picture of Chinese philosophy although they are useful for understanding and interpreting its tradition, their interaction and interplay that reinforce and overcome each other on various occasions make not only possible but fruitful a genuine understanding and interpretation of individual instances in Chinese philosophy. However, for an analysis and synthesis of a thesis in Chinese philosophy, from a metaphilosophical and comparative philosophical point of view, these two principles must be combined with the two contrastive principles from Western philosophy, rational rationalization and divine transcendentization. We can ask to what a degree the two Western orientating principles have been manifested in some cases and to what a degree they have been far-reaching, as similar questions can be asked for Chinese philosophy. In an integrative systematic reflection, the two Chinese principles and the two corresponding Western principles could form a system of complementary opposites that can be unified on higher levels and in larger processes. Perhaps the *I Ching* model of the *tai-ch'i* (the great ultimate), *liang-yi* (two norms), and *shih-hsiang* (four forms) could be appropriated for giving a place to each principle and for the transformation of each principle. With regard to this possibility, we are not to speak of Chinese philosophy anymore, but of a world philosophy in the making, to which both Chinese philosophy and Western philosophy could make their unique contributions.

Another important consequence from understanding Chinese philosophy on the basis of these two principles is that it will explain why Confucianism and Neo-Confucianism became the dominating trends and forms of Chinese philosophy, not by accident but by the inner logic of history of Chinese philosophy. To say this is to say that Confucian and Neo-Confucian philosophy are essentially related to the primary orientations of Chinese philosophy in terms of the principles of natural naturalization and human immanentization. In the following text, I shall indicate how this Confucian

philosophy continues and manifests the orientations embodied in the beginning of Chinese philosophy and then how Neo-Confucian philosophy continues and enriches this tradition after meeting the challenges of Taoism
and Buddhism.

Two Senses of Confucian Philosophy as the Mainstream

There are two senses in which Confucian philosophy can be said to be
the mainstream in Chinese philosophy. In one sense, which is well known
to all historians of Chinese philosophy, Confucian philosophy was instituted as the dominating political and educational ideology for government
policy making and official academic studies during the period 136-135 b.c.
in the reign of Han Wu-ti (Emperor Wu in the Early Han dynasty). This was
made possible through the personal faith in Confucianism by Wu-Ti, which
was inspired by the views of the distinguished Confucian scholar-thinker
Tung Chung-shu (197-104 b.c.) Tung wrote his famous *Proposals for
Recruiting Worthy and Virtuous Men (Hsien-liang tui-tse)* in response to
Wu-ti's quest for guiding ideas. In this piece of writing Tung proposed that
government policies should follow the mandate of heaven, should guide
the people by edification and education, and should control the desires of
people by proper institutions. It is apparent that Tung's ideas are derived
from the Confucian tradition, and specifically from his study of the *Kung-
yang Chun-chiu*, a reform-oriented and forward-looking commentary on
the *Annals* of the Lu (home state of Confucius) that Confucius had edited.
Tung also proposed that all schools of thought apart from Confucianism
should be rejected and not advanced in the government. Tung's basic proposals including the last suggestion was accepted wholeheartedly by Wu-ti,
and consequently Confucianism was pronounced the orthodox ideology
for government. Since then it has occupied a dominating and authoritative
position in government policy making, ethical edification, and examination
core materials for succeeding dynasties through the very end of the Ching
dynasty in the beginning of this century.

Although the way in which Confucianism became a dominating ideology influencing society and people in powerful ways was not accidental,
the reason why Confucianism could form an appealing philosophy for political rule and social and cultural control has to be found in the Confucian
doctrines themselves. In particular, that Tung was a scholar of the Kung-
Yang studies is not to be ignored. From this background perspective, one
can see that Confucianism is a philosophy of political reform based on a
political idealism regarding what people ultimately wish for. The official
endorsement of Confucian ideology also underscores the fact that Confu-

cianists, perhaps beginning with Confucius, always depend on a sagely king for instituting and implementing their reform views. This political conjunction or partnership did not happen to Confucius but did happen to Tung Chung-shu and his colleague Kung-sun Hung (200-121 b.c.). This led not only to the consequence that Confucianism became officially embedded in the government and educational processes, but to the dependence of the interests of Confucian rule on the self-interests of rulers and thus made them subject to the arbitrary whims of the traditional emperors. Even though this may have had a restraining effect on the rulers, the rulers also could manipulate Confucianism to their self-interests. From this point of view, all the evils and ills of past feudalist rulers also became attributable to Confucianism. The political use of Confucianism in the past has given it a fixed image and a fixed role, which causes Confucianism to stand as a symbol for close-mindedness and conservativism of the ruling class and the politically privileged. This image and this role, together with its philosophical justification, provoked the vehement criticism and rejection of the Confucian past in the May 4 Movement of 1919 in modern China. It is also in reference to this image and role that Levenson speaks of the "Confucian China and its Modern fate," in his book of the same name.[18]

The second sense in which Confucian philosophy is the mainstream in Chinese philosophy is to be understood from a depth-structure point of view. Although not well articulated, it is the sense in which Confucian philosophy can be said to manifest and consummate the Chinese experience and Chinese thinking at their roots and in their very beginnings. Of course, I have no desire to simplify the process of development of philosophical ideas and categories before Confucius articulated and taught his views. But, at the very least, it is clear that the Six or Five Classics he later edited provided matter and form for his philosophical and ethical thinking. What he saw and experienced in his life in connection with the Lu court and the larger, changing society also gives impetus to his formulating a goal of reform and a philosophy of life consistent with his goal of reform. His approach is totalistic and thoroughgoing, for he formulates the ideal ends of state, society, and the human individual as well as the ideal means toward these ends. What he proposes about how to reach these ends clearly is based on a totalistic reflection on the nature of life, humanity, state, and society. This totalistic approach to both the end and the means marks out his philosophy as unparalleled in his time and also innovative, even though it is based on history and tradition. Thus, his testimony on his own growth and his description of what he normally taught shows a process of development that has links to the past but includes his own contributions. We therefore may say that on different levels and for different times Confucius both reflected and integrated, both illuminated and transcended, the best comprehensive experience and ways of thinking from the Hsia-Shang-Chou dynasties in the last millennium. Specifically, we could argue that Confucian philosophy closely embraced and embodied the two orientations of Chinese philosophy, *natural naturalization* and *human immanentization*, discussed earlier. We indeed can say that in Confucius these two processes begin to deepen.

In connection with the principle of natural naturalization, Tzu Kung, the disciple of Confucius, says in the *Analects* that "I have never heard the Master talking about *hsing* (nature) and *t'ien-tao* (way of heaven)." [19] But Confucius did speak of nature at least once in the *Analects*: "The nature of men is close, but habits make men far apart." [20] He also speaks of *t'ien* no less than sixteen times and of *tao* no less than sixty times. However, it is clear that Confucius always has seemed to avoid talking about metaphysical and supernatural matters. His interests are connected with how human beings could become better and more humane human beings in human ways. He is concerned with establishing a good person, a good society, a good human relationship, a good state, and a good world; and good means benevolence, righteousness, decency and elegance, wisdom, and trustworthiness as connoted by the concepts of virtues such as *jên, yi, li, chih*, and *hsing*. However, this does not mean that he lacks a metaphysical faith and religious beliefs. In moments of personal grief, righteous self-assertion, or lamentative self-expression, Confucius did address himself to heaven as a personal spiritual entity. Again, the contexts of his *t'ien*-addressing show that he did not rely on *t'ien* as a foundation of his moral, political, or educational philosophy. He was said not to speak of anything transnormal, strange forces and weird spirits. Even in matters of offering sacrificial rites, he advises a sincere attitude rather than a rigid belief. As regarding his views on the *tao*, it is also clear that in most uses of the term *tao* he means the way of human beings, or the way of a ruler, or the way of good government. On one or two occasions that *tao* can be given a metaphysical connotation, but even on these occasions, such as the fulfillment of the *tao* by human beings, he was not speaking about a transcendent subject or object but something near at hand.

Hence, the tendency toward natural naturalization is obvious in Confucius's philosophical discourse. Although Confucius may not immediately submit to a philosophy of natural cosmology like the *Lao tzu* and the *I Ching*, his way of thinking in terms of harmony, balance, and unity of virtues, feelings and intellect, individual and community, style and substance — all these indicate that he has been under the influence of the totalistic and harmonistic way of the *I Ching* and therefore exhibited a great measure of natural naturalizatIon as an organizing and guiding principle for his thinking and evaluation.[21]

In the *Analects* Confucius mentioned the *I Ching* only once and quoted from the *I Ching* only once. In Chapter 7, section 17, of the *Analects*, Confucius says that "If I were given more years, I would study the *I* at age fifty, and I would not have made any serious mistake." Despite that many scholars doubted about the reference of this passage as to whether Confucius did mention the *I* any all, there is still the possibility that Confucius has given very serious thought to the study of the *I Ching*. This can be understood as a matter of what he thought about being fifty. He said in his description of his life career that at age fifty he would know the mandate of heaven (*t'ien-ming*). [22] It might be suggested that the *I Ching* has a connotation for *t'ien-ming*, because *t'ien-ming* can be understood as way of change or transformation if we understand the *t'ien* as the way of total nature and *ming* as a matter of necessary conditions of change in accordance with the principle of natural naturalization. Therefore, there is a good reason for giving truth to what Confucius says in that passage about the *I*. In *Historical Records (Shih Chi)* of the Grand Historian Ssu-ma Chien, Confucius is said to love the study of the *I* in his late years and he in fact broke the bamboo pages of the *I* three times in reading it.

As a historic-hermenenutic insight, one also can point out that the development of Confucianism after Confucius, in the writings of Tsu Ssu (the *Chung Yung*) and Mencius as well as in the Commentaries of the *I Ching* such as *Wen Yen* and the *Hsi Tzu*, has a great deal to do with philosophical interpretations of the *I* text that must be explained on the basis of the Confucius's study and teaching on the *I* in accordance with the principles of natural naturalization and human immanentization. I would hold that not only has classical Confucianism benefited greatly from absorbing the wisdom and way of thinking of the *I* as a philosophical text, but also that the way Confucius developed his views is a naturalistic, humanistic way of applying the philosophy of the *I*, for the implicit in-depth guiding principle is to see humanity as capable of transformIng itself into goodness and virtue, which must be founded on the comprehensive harmony and interrelatedness of things, for goodness is no other than achieving creative harmony and virtue is no other than timeliness (*shih-chung*) in performing good actions. The creative energy for transformation by cultivation of one's character and the achievement of harmony and timeliness by formation of virtues can be explained on the basis of the philosophy of the *I Ching* and also give an interpretative edge to the naturalized and humanized understanding of the *I Ching*.

The development of immanentization of values and powers is no less a significant feature of the ideas in the *Analects*. Confucius himself pronounced that "Heaven has given me virtue (*te*) by birth, what harm can Huan Tui do to me?"[23] Confucius also says that "Is benevolence (*jên*) far away? If I desire *jên*, *jên* will be right here."[24] For Confucius, human beings are born morally equal and thus all deserve to be treated with benevolence (*jên*), righteousness (*yi*), and propriety (*li*). This equality of moral worth also is derived from the implicit metaphysical belief that individuals are endowed with innate capacities to transform themselves and induce the transformation of others in the domain of moral relationships and moral virtues. This means that one has the great virtue inherent in oneself that is rooted in the ultimate reality and enables one to reach for individual moral perfection, which is implicitly a matter of ontological perfection as well, and reach for universal brotherhood of humanity by way of extension of human relationships and benevolent government. In this sense Confucius has created a humanistic model for understanding the unity of human and heaven even though he never explicitly spoke of it.

Human immanentization of values and powers gives both content and creativity to the philosophical teachings of Confucius, just as naturalization of nature gives a rational strain to the arguments or discourse of Confucius. Classical Confucianisms became well formed and well developed because of these two principles and their interplay. In the process of developing ethics and metaphysics, which is a totalistic process from the beginning, ethics, political philosophy, and metaphysics became well interwoven and interfused and a total picture of the ultimate reality, universe, individual, and society and state emerged in order and harmony with inner dialectics of the organic links and relationships of mutual interdependence. This is the historical development of Confucianism from Confucius to the *Ta Hsueh* and the *Chung Yung* to the *Mencius* and the commentaries of the *I Ching* in the fifth century to third century B.C. In this context of development under the totalistic vision of humankind and the world, even Hsun Tsu would be recognized as a strongly humanized and naturalized advocate of Confucianism. In other words, we can see in Hsun Tzu the radical application of the principles of natural naturalization and human immanentization. For him, nature at large can be understood in a lawlike fashion and utilized by humanity, whereas humanity is completely malleable by education and edification, because human reason as a nature-rooted, empirically reinforcable faculty can be developed to benefit both the individual and the community.[25]

Given the preceding description and analysis of Confucianism, we can conclude that Confucianism became the mainstream of Chinese philosophy not by accident or political orthodoxy, but also by its continuation of a basic humanistic tradition from the past and its creative absorption and interpretation of new experience and new thinking (as evidenced in the interpretation of moral personhood in the notion of *chun-tzu* and integration of virtues and metaphysicalization of the texts of the *I Ching*). It was destined to become the mainstream, because of its totalistic vision and practical orientation as well as its historic base. It gave a creative and natural play to the principles of naturalization and humanization that suited the needs and feelings of the people in that period. As pointed out, the implicit philosophy of transformation and timeliness of the *I Ching* played a determining role, and this became even more important when Confucianism was confronted by challenges from competing Taoism and Legalism or a foreign tradition such as Buddhism. In both cases, the vision and methodology of *I*-thinking provided an inspiration and insight for reorganization, reintegration, and reconstruction. It also is the basis for deconstruction in so far as it is capable of providing space and freedom for new structures and new processes. This is typically the case with the development of Neo-Confucianism in the Sung and Ming times, in which the systematic philosophy of Chu Hsi and the intuitionalistic philosophy of Wang Yang-ming provide paramount examples of the comprehensive naturalization and the comprehensive immanentization in regard to the metaphysical categories of *li* (principle), *ch'i* (breath and energy), *hsin* (heart-mind) and *hsing* (nature). The resources of the philosophy of the *I Ching*, as first experienced and thought of in the classical period, once more became the source of philosophical insights and life-creativity, which enriched and continued the mainstream of the Confucian thinking.

Understanding Methodology and the Methodology of Understanding

In *Truth and Method*,[26] Hans-Georg Gadamer makes a distinction between truth and method to the effect that truth, if fulfilled, will not depend on method and method, on the other hand, will hide or obstruct presentation of truth. In making this distinction, Gadamer shows that he follows his tutor Heidegger very closely in his conceptions of truth and method. Although there is no elaboration on what precisely is meant by *truth* and *method*, it is clear that truth basically is a clearing or disclosure (*aletheia*) of Being and method is a rational conceptualization that falls away from Being. Given the Heideggerian framework, the Gadamerian criticism of applying a method for understanding truth is fully understandable. Yet one can still raise the question as to whether truth and method must exclude each other on all levels of human experience and human thinking. It might be true that in the human and social sciences, using a method, particularly

a method originating in natural sciences, amounts to reducing the richness and individuality of reality of humanity and society to a lower level of
abstraction and generalization. But this is no denial of the fact that in
natural sciences the scientific method has enabled human beings to reach
for a certain well-defined and well-controlled reality of nature. For understanding truth of being in humanity and society the important requirement
rather seems to be such that categories and abstractions should arise from
the contexts of lived experiences pertaining to humanity and society. In
other words, they should arise internally from experiences on the same
level. In this sense, a method for human and social sciences can be
sanctioned by human sciences and social sciences. It is precisely in this
sense that Dilthey has argued for life-categories for human and historical
sciences. Besides, any method has a limitation for properly pursuing truth
and should be not overused for external purposes. To extend a method,
which has become rationally normalized and rigid, or to apply it from one
field to another, cannot avoid the risk of reductionism or impoverishment
due to overrationalization; and thus it will face difficulties in envisioning
the total and living context of human experience and human thinking proper
to a given subject matter. In light of this discussion, it seems reasonable to
assume that truth could include method and method could lead to truth if a
preunderstanding of truth gives rise to a method from inside its being that
would bring a full bloom of truth. By conforming to truth and in the full
realization of truth, the method will dissolve itself as part of truth.

In achieving an understanding of Chinese philosophy we therefore need
a proper understanding of the methodology for understanding Chinese philosophy as well as a proper understanding of the general methodology of
understanding. In both these efforts, the question of what is understanding
must be answered. To answer this question, we have no other choice than
inquiring into the history of hermeneutics, which deals with the problem of
understanding. Two fundamental principles immediately suggest themselves:
the principles of the autonomy of understanding and the totality of understanding. The principle of the autonomy of understanding requires that
understanding not be identified with knowledge or information. In this sense,
understanding will be seen as a state of mind as well as an act of mind or
intention. The principle of totality of understanding requires what is understood to exist as a whole that penetrates into its parts. This is the well-
known principle of the hermeneutical circle. The first principle can be said
to derive from the hermeneutic philosophy of Schleiermacher, which holds
that understanding results from a modification of a person's life-process
and that understanding requires the coherence and correlation of various
moments of modification of the person. This means that understanding

is a unique product of two activities related to a process, the inner thinking of a person and the language used in the form of speaking. As such, understanding cannot be reduced to anything that does not have a natural place in the language and mind of a person, and thus need not be explained as a teleological process (such as in Hegel or Marx) or as a reference to a world of empirical data (such as in Ranke or Schlick).[27]

But precisely how the inner thinking of a person is to be described is left open, and it is not until Dilthey that the full autonomy of understanding as an inner experience of a person is fully explored and asserted. Dilthey was devoted to the establishment of the epistemology and methodology for the human sciences. He saw that the human sciences form a totality of knowledge independent of the totality of knowledge for the natural sciences. Taking Kant as a model in providing a methodological basis for knowledge in natural sciences, Dilthey tried to develop a set of paradigms and categories for the human sciences to provide for them a methodological foundation. In his view, understanding in human sciences is rooted in the lived experiences of people and hence is a primary category and manifestation of life. With this understanding of understanding, understanding gains a deeper grounding than simply the language and thinking of a person. In fact, both language and thinking can be regarded as the realization of understanding as a life process, and therefore understanding should be conceived as a three-dimensional entity of human existence: Human thinking and human language are embodied and unified in the intensity of a certain form of human experience, namely, the experience of value and purpose.

The principle of the hermeneutical circle was stated clearly in the writings of Schleiermacher, and since then has become a universally recognized characteristic of the hermeneutical process. But to explain how understanding involves a totality and to specify the nature of this totality require philosophical elaboration. One may even see that the autonomy of th hermeneutical process already presupposes the totality of a hermeneutical object. This totality, I believe, was not made specific until Humbodt, for there we find the primary concern with the preestablished correspondence between a comprehending subject and an object to be comprehended, particularly with regard to historic inquiries. In a sense Humbodt was influenced by both Leibniz and Hegel in seeing the world as a unity to be shared by the subject and the object of inquiry. Whereas Leibniz saw a preestablished harmony of all monadic individuals in the world, Hegel prescribed an inner spirit inhering in all things that moves the world of things toward a higher plane. In both we see a good reason for justifying the necessity of hermeneutical circle in the interpenetration of parts and whole. For my purpose I would consider the circle from a concrete naturalistic point of view, which should take the harmony of reality without the preestablishedness and the inner moving spirit of the world without the mechanics of conflict in the Hegelian-Marxist dialectics as two components of the experienced totality of reality. This amounts to suggesting the principle of natural naturalization as the onto-epistemological foundation of the hermeneutical circle. Both ontologically and epistemologically speaking, the hermeneutical circle is an *organically established harmony of transformations* among all things and hence both an ontological and an epistemological circle.

Given the autonomy and totality of understanding, there also is the totality and autonomy of reality as realized by understanding, which should be distinguished from experiences not characterized by such autonomy and totality. As internal features of understanding, autonomy and totality are found in the Gestalt perception of a person, but they also are found in the formation of new forms or new levels of reality. In fact we could consider any new type of entity or even any new instance of entity as a base for the realization of the autonomy and totality of understanding. This means that understanding involves a stand in the world of things and a point of view from which to see the world of things. This is brought out no better than by Chuang Tzu in his discourse on the equality of things (*ch'i-wu*): All living things, not just human beings, have their own fears and joys, their likes and dislikes, which are different from each other, yet they are equally valid points of view located on the circle of the all-comprehensive and all-transforming reality called the *tao* (the way). That understanding is specifically human and pertains to human existence is made possible by human existence, for in the proper use of the term *understanding*, understanding is precisely human understanding, which requires the presence of a human mind and a human point of view ingrained in human existence. Despite the equality of things in the Taostic sense, it can be said that the *organically established harmony of things* presents levels of beings or things that can be understood hierarchically. Aristotle has pointed to a hierarchy of forms and substances in one sense of hierarchy. Even though we need not think of a hierarchy as a teleological structure in the Aristotelian sense, the modern perception of ecological interdependence among forms of life reveals the large nature as containing an organic hierarchy of functions and transactions of life.

Another important sense of hierarchy comes from observation and reflection on the meanings of human language and human experience. Human language and human experience give rise to different levels of meaning and understanding, and this is obviously due to the existence of levels of organization of language and understanding. It cannot even be said that human understanding is exactly embodied in human language, language on its different levels of organization can be a vehicle as well as a catalyst for energization of understanding. In Ch'an/(Zen) literature it is clear that language leads to transcendence beyond language, which represents a higher level of understanding than any ordinary understanding in language, but which results from a challenge to the ordinary understanding presented in a specific form of language.

Levels of meaning and understanding have a polarity in the human mind apart from the polarity in language and expression. But the human mind is not simply human rationality as the rationalistic tradition would have it. In both Greek and modern Western philosophy, there is a strong tendency to rationalize the human mind and see it as a function of thinking. But in the Chinese tradition the human mind is not simply the mind alone but comprises both the mind and the heart, both of which are rooted in the nature of being human. This follows from the primary experience of *natural naturalization* of human existence, for the human mind must be based on the primary nature of human existence, which is part of the natural whole and also forms a level of existence with its autonomy and totality of being in the totality of beings. Thus, when we speak of understanding as a happening of the human mind, it is not a matter of rational explanation nor a matter of conceptual knowledge or factual information. In fact, it is an experience of human existence defined by a totality and autonomy, which should be explained not only by the transformation and interdependence of all things in the world in relation to human existence, but also by the creative potentiality of human existence as part of the open world. In other words, the human mind is a creative agency and its creativity derives from human existence, which gives rise to human experience in the world of transformations.

In Western philosophy Dilthey has explicitly and systematically inquired into understanding as a deep form of human experience that involves not only rational thinking but human life. For him, to understand human life and human history, one needs to experience deeply human life and human history. This deep experience apparently is an experience of human existence as a whole, and hence as a totality, and as an emergent autonomy. He calls such experiences Erlebnis, the embodiment of life and time. This is a proper way of characterizing the nature of human understanding insofar as human understanding must derive from the lived experience of human existence. This experience not only signifies the temporal flow of life, but also signifies the depth structure of human existence as a whole world; and therefore it reveals a level of being pertinent only for human existence. For Dilthey, all basic concepts related to modes of human activities and proper explanations of human life are derived from the process of *erleben* or "living through," and therefore should reflect the structure of human existence as a totality and an autonomy. It is on this basis that Dilthey wishes to develop his "categories of life" for human and social sciences. It is clear that for his categories of life to be adequate for their designated purpose, they always must be linked to the basic understanding of human existence and its nature, and they must be allowed to identify various instances of human experience whenever and wherever they occur. In addition, levels of such experiences regarding their values and purposes also should be recognized.

The preceding discussion should lead us to formulate a principle of hierarchy for understanding in addition to the principles of totality and autonomy. According to this principle, understanding always reveals a level of reality pertaining to human existence, depending on how much and what aspect of human existence is involved. Understanding also can be conceived as forming a progression of levels and circles in terms of its depth or height and scope, even though each level of understanding has a totality and autonomy. From an ideal point of view, the understanding that includes all circles and levels and integrates them as a totality and autonomy is the ultimate understanding one could aim for in one's pursuit of truth and value. It must be understood that different levels of understanding could be related in terms of conditional dependency, so that one level of understanding can lead to another, higher level under proper conditions or on proper occasions. In this sense we may appeal to Michael Polanyi's theory of emergent levels as an explanation. According to Polanyi's theory,[28] conditions of existence of a type of reality is not the same as parts of the type of the reality and thus the type of an entity is always an irreducible emergence from the given conditions. In this way, we can perceive trees apart from perceiving sense-data of trees and we can perceive the meaning of the trees apart from perceiving the trees. When we speak of human understanding, understanding can be conceived as a world of seeing, feeling, and thinking integrated from our life-experiences and achieving a form of unity and harmony. In fact, in light of the two polarities of understanding via the mind and via language, we may regard this form of unity and harmony as one of language and the mind; namely, a unity and harmony of language and mind in the copresentation of reality. Or, we may put in a different way: Understanding in this sense is unity and harmony of the mind and language in a fulfilling form of reality, which is equivalent to pointing to the emergent fusion of language, the mind, and reality based on the experience of human existence as a whole.

Given the exposition of understanding as life-experience or experience of human existence presented in the form of unity and harmony of the mind and language, it is not difficult to see that understanding is basically existential and ontological and not simply epistemological. In light of this understanding, Heidegger presents understanding as the Being of human being or Dasein; and following this, Gadamer speaks of understanding as ontological. In regard to the analytical theory of fundamental ontology of Being, Dasein, and beings in the philosophy of Heidegger, understanding in this sense receives an important illumination. Understanding is not a matter of rational discourse, but always represents a point of view or standpoint of being and specifically the being of a human person, the Dasein. The point of view for the understanding determines the scope and depth of understanding and therefore reveals a whole world of reality from that point of view. Hence Heidegger calls understanding the "disclosedness" of the Being-in-the-world that is the world seen as fundamental reality. In this disclosedness understanding becomes the meaningful presentation of Being or presentation of Being in meaningfulness. In so far as Heidegger speaks of a state of mind and human language as forms of Dasein, it is clear that understanding can be seen as disclosedness of the world or Being in the meaningful unity of the mind-state and the use of language that defines the content of the meaningfulness of the presentation.

In understanding *understanding* as the being of a human person, the dynamics of being a person or Dasein becomes closely relevant. Being a person or human-being is not only confronted with a world as experienced by the person, but one is given the ability to see possibilities of the future and transformations of time, and one is made aware of the potentiality for change and transformation in the world of things.[29] Understanding hence becomes an existential world-horizon for a person in terms of which one can assert one's own identity relative to the world as well as show concern with things and others in the world. It becomes an insight of a person that serves as a guide for projecting action and forming judgment and even for reaching a view on a particular matter in the world. In this sense, understanding constitutes the fore-having, fore-seeing, and fore-thinking of a person. Perhaps, what Gadamer called *tradition* and *prejudice* also can be understood as understanding in this ontological sense. To put in a different manner, one may indeed consider understanding as Being as the integrated state of a person insofar as one's being, thinking, self-knowing, and world-knowing are fused in a state of consciousness of being as well as a state of being of consciousness.

In understanding as Being, understanding is disclosed in Being as Being is disclosed in understanding, whether in a primary state or in an evolved state. Clearly, the criterion for such disclosure is our sense and experience of relatedness of the self to the world in harmony and freedom in which both totality and autonomy of being must be experienced. This state also exemplifies the natural naturalization of a person that embodies rationalization or rationality as an implicit part. This means that understanding need not be considered as rationalization or relying on reason as the only guiding light. In fact, in understanding, reason never dominates but instead subscribes to an existential insight that fuses thinking and feeling and even willing. One good word from Heidegger describes this state of being very well, let it be, or *gelassen*.[30] Reason or rationality is not to let go or let be things but instead demands consistent and systematic explanation and characterization.

Following Heidegger on this natural state of understanding as being, we can make the distinction between interpretation (*Auslegung*) as understanding that naturally involves the world-being and interpretation (*Interpretation*) as rationalization that relates a given state of being to a particular purpose or project or idea or ideal.[31] In the latter case, we can see the possibility of generating new meaning and new relevance for a given world-being, which consequently acquires a new configuration of being and a new structure of relationships of things in the world. That interpretation as rationalization is possible is due to reason capable of discerning and hence disclosing the implicit relations of things in the implicit totalities of things, which, as we have seen, exist in an organically established harmony of being. In this process of relating, meanings become articulated on the basis of the given being and hence the interpretation as rationalization is based no less on the understanding existing as the prehaving, preseeing, and preconceiving state of Dasein. From interpretation as rationalization, one can come to see not only the relation between understanding as a primary state of being and understanding as an active force of reason within the state of being, but how the former lends itself to the latter and hence is presupposed in the development of the latter. We may call this understanding as Being as the principle of being for our understanding of understanding.

Finally, we come to the act of mind or consciousness as a principle characterizing understanding. It is well known that Husserl developed his phenomenological method in terms of a presupposition-free reflection on the noetic-noematic processes of mind or consciousness.[32] According to Husserl, intuition of the meaning of an expression is essential to the understanding of an expression, but the so-called meaning of an expression (the understood sign) is to be conferred by an act of mind in the first place. This is what he calls the *meaning intention* for an expression. But meaning is not simply a result but rather a process that involves more than the meaning-conferring acts of the mind to fulfill the meaning intentions under a given interest or in a given context. By the meaning-fulfilling act, an expression comes to express its meaning and actualize or confirm its reference to the noematic object of the expression. The unity of the sign and the object signified will result from the fusion of the process of meaning conferring and meaning fulfillment of our intentional acts, and thus present intuitively a lived world constituted of the acts in unity. It is clear that the phenomenological constitution of the world brings about an important aspect of understanding; namely, understanding is a creative and active process rooted in the cognitive function of the mind, and what is understood is not simply something given but something to be constituted in the process of understanding, or the meaning-formative process of mind.

In early Husserl (via *Logical Investigations*), this phenomenological constitutive process focuses on the establishment of the objective basis for logic and mathematics; but in his later work such as *The Crisis of European Sciences and the Task of Phenomenology*,[33] the meaning-formative process unifies the acts of the mind with the whole scenario of the presented world called *life-world* as its constitution.[34] This is revealing on two scores: First, it reveals the world as a continuous presentation with its possible transformations under a meaning-formative process; that is, the world is an interpretation and is always part of a whole of which the mind is the other part. It also reveals the profound potentiality of mind, not just as an act or possible acts of consciousness, but as a source of order, structure, and meaningfulness to be realized in our concept of value. The net result of such understanding is that the world and the mind form a hermeneutical whole that presents reality as a whole. Hence I call this an *onto-hermeneutical whole* to be realized on different levels or in different realms based on the attainment of the totality and autonomy of experience. This process in understanding also shows how meaning and reference are possible: They are possible because of the organically evolved relationship of mind and world and hence, because of being derived from specific circumstances demonstrating this relationship. Understanding, hence, is clearly seen as a process of creative constitution that presents the mind and world both as participators. It can have levels and stages, just as meaning-formation can have levels and stages.

In connection with this phenomenological method, it can be pointed out that the method of logical analysis or linguistic analysis in contemporary British and American philosophy can be said to have a phenomenological aspect. This is because, in conducting such an analysis, a certain structure unfolds in accordance with a given logical or semantic-linguistic consciousness. The only difference is that such logical or semantic-linguistic consciousness may be said to be cultivated rather than spontaneous. But this difference can be regarded as a matter of degree. In addition, under a Chomskian conception of internal grammar or under a Heideggerian conception of preunderstanding, the process of analysis would acquire a naturalness or spontaneity as part of the analytic mind, particularly in contexts specifically calling for such analysis. On the other hand, we also may regard the phenomenological process of constitution of concepts and even objects by acts of consciousness as a process of logical or linguistic analysis, even though in using the words *logical* or *linguistic*, we do not have to presuppose any known specific forms of logic. The question of alternative logics long has been raised.[35] But it is also possible to regard any rational process of concept-constitution as capable of defining or revealing a unique logic or a logical criterion of validity. From this discussion, I wish to suggest that our conception of logical analysis or linguistic analysis could be broadened in scope and that the principle of acts of consciousness could include a principle of logical analysis.

What I have said about the significant implications of the phenomenological method does not necessarily reflect Husserl's own view of the matter. But it does reflect how his method could contribute to our understanding of understanding in light of understanding the problem of understanding. If we put together all the principles of understanding discussed earlier, we can gather a clear but enriched conception of understanding that has not been discussed in contemporary literature but that should illuminate the nature of understanding as both a methodological notion and an ontological notion. If we see understanding as involving the five principles discussed earlier — namely, those of *totality, autonomy, hierarchy, being, and act* — we should be able to see how understanding defines a methodology in which an ontology is to be understood as well as defines an ontology in which a methodology is to be understood. In other words, understanding as both the disclosure of a world and the world disclosed is clearly ontologically rooted and ontologically presented: It is the mentally illuminated totality of world for a person that is the self-determined and self-contained emergent level of Being. But the components and the procedure for bringing about understanding as a level of being makes understanding as a methodology possible. Understanding can begin with either disclosure of being or conscious acts of analysis. In the former case the world of being as disclosed could be shown to be rationally constituted by reflection and analysis. In the latter case, rational acts of analysis should lead to the emergence of a world of being either by way of the necessity of emergence of a level of being under proper conditions or by the inherent hermeneutical circle of total integration that corresponds to the ontological circle of total comprehension, as the principle of totality suggests.

With the level of being thus configurated, concretion and differentiation of meaning occur as a matter of the existing harmony between the mind and reality, and this is how the principle of autonomy that demands consistency and self-containedness of meaning is conceived. In both cases, the principle of totality or the onto-hermeneutical circle (the totality of wholes and parts of correspondence and coherence between the hermeneutical and ontological circles) is the underlying ground and the motivating force for the successful development of understanding. Insofar as understanding requires a process of reality or acts of mind, it is methodological, for rational description and characterization of such a process or acts always are possible as a result of rational reflection. Further, to understand such a process or the acts involved will enable us to reach for a genuine case of understanding with rational justification. Because understanding is involved or presupposed naturally in the appropriation and achievement of a form of understanding, understanding cannot be fully rationalized and enclosed in rational conceptualization without an ontological reference. This means that understanding must be ontological in the first place and will become transformed into rationality and methodology for analytical or inquisitive purposes, which again defines a level of being. This also means that, whereas ontology of understanding can be self-reflectively methodological, methodology of understanding rationally defined and constructed also has to be ontological in terms of the emergence of a level of being.

If we conceive understanding as ontology, understanding is the total disclosure of a world of being informed by meaningful acts of mind or consciousness as seen in the human existence. Hence, relationality must be realized as well. If we conceive understanding as methodology, understanding is the procedure and process or acts to be used for rational constructive or reconstructive thinking of a human person that reveal a level of being. Hence ontology must be consequently realized. This suggests that methodological understanding implies ontological understanding and vice versa in an onto-hermeneutical circle, which is both ontologically and methodologically understandable. In this sense methodology and ontology together constitute a duality of understanding, and there is no methodology without a possible ontological image or a world of being to be disclosed correspondingly, and there is no ontology without a possible methodological image or procedure to be formulated correspondingly. This duality, relationality, and consequent relativity provide a full picture of understanding of any issue or problem in philosophy. We therefore can conceive the methodology of understanding as consisting of the principles of totalization, autonomization, concretization of meaning, disclosure of a world of being, and constitution of analytic acts to be applied to a text or an issue for understanding.

Corresponding to this methodology of understanding, we also can conceive understanding as the unfolding of being in terms of the five principles and their internal coherence, organic interaction and interdependence that define understanding as an ontology. Specifically, to understand methodology is to understand rationality and reason as necessarily involving the five principles that can be applied to both ontology and methodology. In light of this full analysis of understanding, we can now conclude that there is no conflict between truth and method in understanding a philosophical issue or a philosophical text, as Gadamer conceived there is. There are only degrees of adequacy of understanding to be achieved. Also, truth can have a methodical or methodological image as a method or methodology may have its ontological validity, however limited it may be. A method or a methodological system may serve a specific purpose, even in disclosing truth under a specific purpose. But it cannot serve all purposes or even its specific purpose at all times. This is why a method or even a methodology has to be surpassed or transcended in the course of time. The whole history of philosophy in the West from the time of Socrates and Plato to the time of Heidegger and Derrida illustrates amply the continuous process of creating or formulating methods and then surpassing and transcending them. I mentioned Derrida because even his deconstructive thinking is a method or methodological system and is subject to deconstruction or being transcended on its own. Our discussion on the methodology of understanding does not produce any rigid method or require a regimentation of rigid application: Its essence consists in its having a methodological openness as well as an ontological indeterminateness.[36]

Intrinsic to this conception of understanding are always the possibilities of transformation of methodology in light of ontological space and those of transformation of ontology in light of methodological relevance. The duality and polarity of both provide a fountain of mutual restriction and mutual enhancement toward realization of the truth to be understood. In light of this duality of method and truth or duality of methodology and ontology, we also are able to develop a broader and richer concept of reason or rationality on the basis of which methodology is founded. No single given concept of reason and rationality is absolute. Reason and rationality must have a specific level as well as a specific scope or structure according to the subject matter and experience under the purview of truth or ontological understanding. We therefore could speak not only of logical reason, scientific reason, technological reason, and critical reason in the traditional sense, we also could speak of hermeneutical reason, communicative reason, deconstructive reason, and so forth in a nontraditional sense.

In connection with conceiving understanding as methodology, one matter finally needs to be briefly dealt with; namely, the distinction we make between understanding as a disclosure of being and understanding as a creative act toward such a disclosure of being. This is highly comparable to the distinction between "sudden enlightenment" (*tun-wu*) and "gradual enlightenment" (*ch'ien-wu*) in the history of Chinese Ch'an (Zen) Buddhism. Sudden enlightenment consists in fully disclosing a world of reality that is an all-comprehensive and yet all-transcending nonreality without any process. On the other hand, gradual enlightenment requires a process of cultivation and fermentation toward achieving the full state of enlightenment. Are they incompatible approaches toward the desired Buddhistic goal of enlightenment? Or, are they two parallel roads leading to the same destination? In light of our discussion of understanding, it is clear that there is no incompatibility between the two, even though the striving in one may differ from that in the other. But, if we reflect on the differences, we can say that one stresses level emergence, whereas the other stresses act constitution. With the full scope of understanding in view, it is not difficult to conclude that controversies of such a kind could be resolved by the full understanding of the methodology of understanding.

Topics in Confucian and Neo-Confucian Philosophy

Earlier, I delineated and elaborated a methodology of understanding based on my reflections on both Chinese and Western philosophy. Also this is the methodology of understanding that I have developed and applied in my studies of Chinese and Western philosophy over the last twenty years. Specifically, I have applied this methodology to the study of major schools and major issues in Chinese philosophy. In order to transcend other methods in the past and bring new light and new life into Chinese philosophy, it is important to look into both the methodological basis and the metaphysical content of Chinese philosophy. The methodology of understanding is a natural choice for such a task. Indeed, due to my efforts to disclose the methodological and ontological structures of Chinese philosophy as well as to reveal the duality and codetermining relationality of these structures, that the methodology of understanding evolves and presents, I find useful to formulate this methodology in the context of contemporary philosphy in the West. In a certain sense, Chinese philosophy is strongly hermeneutical from the very beginning, as testified by the tradition of writing commentaries. Even though no strict methodological discipline of philosophical hermeneutics comes out of the textual or exegetic hermeneutics, the display of hermeneutic self-reflection in the genesis of enriched notions of philosophical importance or centering of new categories of philosophy is itself a philosophical scenario that has both methodological and metaphysical significance. Whether in Confucianism or Taoism, there are efforts to achieve understanding of the totality of reality based on considerations of totality, autonomy, level, and act. This is made possible by the model of thinking underlying the *I Ching* that, as a philosophy of method or as a philosophy of cosmic reality, can be described best as totalistic, self-contained, level-emergent, ontologically disclosive (whether as a whole or as a part in terms of believed divinatory practice), act-constitutive, and therefore analytic (whether through its traditional numerology or modern algebraic or logical modeling). We have no time to develop a detailed description of this mode of thinking in its own terms and its illustration in classical Confucian or Neo-Confucian philosophy. But it leaves no doubt that the methodology of understanding I have just described is a reflection of the *I Ching* mode of thinking, which I discussed on another occasion.[37]

Given the methodology of understanding and the predominance of Confucian philosophy in the history of Chinese philosophy, my study of Confucian and Neo-Confucian philosophy presented in this book is intended to illustrate and illuminate the methodological and metaphysical dimensions of Confucian and Neo-Confucian philosophy and to use them to stimulate and develop methodological and metaphysical thinking in general. What I have done specifically in terms of particular topics that have key importance for understanding Chinese philosophy or Confucian-Neo-Confucian philosophy can be said to be an onto-analytical reconstruction of the Confucian-Neo-Confucian philosophical enterprise. The methodology of understanding is focused on a rational and analytical understanding of the philosophical issues in light of a whole reality of philosophical thinking and human experience of reality. Hence, it is not only analytically conceptual but also hermeneutically ontological. Thus, to characterize it as onto-analytical would be appropriate. But one can also see that other principles of understanding still apply, for I always stress and use totality and autonomy of self-contained meaningfulness as a rationale or criterion for defining a world of being or a level of reality to be realized or appreciated. This is because of the underlying and subsisting interrelated network of meaning in the whole tradition of Chinese philosophy in general and in the whole tradition of Confucian-Neo-Confucian philosophy in particular. This characteristic tradition forms both a hermeneutical circle of understanding and an ontological circle of disclosure; hence, it can be called the *onto-hermeneutical understanding* that is the essence of the methodology of understanding. My study in Confucian and Neo-Confucian philosophy provides a basis for opening-methodological and metaphysical understanding of Chinese philosophy as a whole, not just a methodological and metaphysical understanding of Confucian and Neo-Confucian philosophy alone. It also should point to the beginning of a fusion of horizons between Chinese philosophy or Confucian-Neo-Confucian philosophy with some salient but relevant philosophical traditions from the

West. This is possible because we find the common ground for understanding in terms of a framework of onto-hermeneutics of understanding.

There are three parts to the presentation of essays in this book. In the first part, I present Chinese philosophical orientations in a general methodological and metaphysical context and as the background of Confucian and Neo-Confucian thinking. In fact, these Chinese philosophical orientations further provide certain basic categories or principles of interpretation in terms of which understanding of Confucian and Neo-Confucian philosophy can be facilitated. Thus, in the essay "Chinese Philosophy: A Characterization," I offer a synthetic characterization of the classical Chinese tradition in terms of an analytical reconstruction of its main themes and thrusts. Specifically, I discussed the intrinsic humanism, concrete rationalism, organic naturalism, and pragmatism of self-cultivation and their interrelations as inherent and dominating features of Chinese philosophy, to be contrasted with the extrinsic humanism, abstract rationalism, mechanic naturalism, and pragmatism of utility and their interrelations as main features of Western philosophy as a whole. This serves as a basis for my commentary on the fundamental distinction between Chinese philosophy and Western philosophy in terms of the tendencies toward natural naturalization and rational rationalization.

In "A Model of Causality in Chinese Philosophy: A Comparative Study," I choose a basic problem in philosophy—the problem of causality—for critical close analysis and reconstruction in the context of Chinese philosophy. I first examine the Humean definition of causation in empirical and phenomenal terms and find it provides a common ground for redefining and redescribing the form and content of the principle of causation. My exploration into an alternative model in Chinese philosophy to the scientific-theoretical model gives me an opportunity to bring out the salient points of both Confucian and Taoistic methodological and metaphysical thinking and observation. Specific reference is made to the metaphysical framework of the *Commentaries* of the *I Ching* which articulate most clearly the organismic and holographic principle of generation and transformation of things, leading to a vitalistic and holistic understanding of causation as a cosmological principle. This essay again provides a useful illustration of the natural-naturalization way of thinking conforming to the methodology of understanding described in the preceding section.

In "The Nature and Function of Skepticism in Chinese Philosophy," I again explore the methodological and metaphysical differences between Chinese and Western philosophy with regard to the epistemological issues of skepticism. First I discuss the self-defeating nature of negative skepticism that seems to predominate in the Western tradition. Then I discuss the positive or constructive skepticism in Taoism, Ch'an Buddhism, and Confucianism as the road toward dialectically achieving a higher level of understanding truth. In this regard, skepticism is employed as a methodological doubt to bring about metaphysical disclosure and accentuate the underlying unity of the subject and object in the world of being.

In "Conscience, Mind, and the Individual in Chinese Philosophy," I attempt a critical construction or reconstruction of the notions of *conscience*, *mind*, and *individual* in terms of Confucian and Neo-Confucian philosophy. The focus of this study is the Mencian concept of *liang-chih* (the so-called innate knowledge of goodness), which is compared to conscience as conceived by the moral philosophy of eighteenth century England. Although I make no case for the historical affinity between Chinese moral philosophy and eighteenth century European moral philosophy of enlightenment, it is clear that the moral philosophy of conscience and the philosophy of *liang-chih* provide a common ground for both the naturalization tendency and the rationalization tendency described earlier.

Finally, in the last essay of the first part, I offer my critical reflections on the methodological and metaphysical differences between Chinese and Western philosophy (and also between the former and the Indian philosophy) in terms of examination and formulation of dialectical thinking or thinking involving being and time, transcendence and immanence. The basic point of departure is Chinese views on harmony and conflict, a pervasive and important part of the Chinese philosophical tradition. I formulate and construct the dialectics of harmonization as the basic theme of methodology and metaphysics or ontology for Chinese philosophical thinking, which I now call the *onto-hermeneutical* way of thinking or *onto-methodology*. In contrast, I suggest the dialectics of conflict for the modern Western philosophy related to Hegel and Marx and the dialectics of negation for the Indian and Buddhistic philosophy. These discussions should provide a context and ground for further explorations into the methodological and metaphysical differences between the Chinese and Western or other traditions. They also provide a foundational approach to the problem of harmony and transformation as shown in the philosophy of the *I Ching*, which is the point of return and source of inspiration for the Neo-Confucian philosophy, if not the classical Confucian philosophy outright.

In the second part of this book I present several essential dimensions of Confucian philosophy which are both methodologically and metaphysically significant. First, rectifying names (*cheng-ming*) may be said to embody in a nutshell all main ideas of Confucian philosophy, for it presents the Confucian humanistic ideal of achieving good government on the basis of individual moral self-cultivation and social ethical edification. Confucius hoped that a ruler would set a moral personal example for people to emulate so that the ruler would sit facing the south like the pole star and the people would behave themselves in good order. This is a kind of "doing nothing" (*wu-wei*) but with the ruler as an "unmoved mover," not the *tao*, which in any case is not confined to a particular person nor simply unmoved but instead spontaneously self-moving. To rectify names combines both the implicit appeal to "doing nothing" and the explicit appeal to "doing something" for creating and maintaining good government. To rectify names is to put everyone in a proper place doing proper things in a world of well-conceived social and socially determined moral relationships. For Confucius, the first step for founding a human society is to recognize that there are inherent virtues among human persons that form a stable and socially meaningful relationship. Thus there are the virtue of kindness and filial piety between parent and child and the virtue of respect and obedience between a ruler and a people. However, these virtues will not take place if the concerned individual does not recognize these relationships and cultivate the ability to develop and preserve them. In doing so, individuals consequently fulfill three functions: the fulfillment of their moral development as persons, the fulfillment of their social development as members of a society, and the fulfillment of their political development as members of government. Rectifying names implies all three kinds of development of a person as well as the social objectification of these developments in terms of concepts and norms codified in language. However, this is possible only when the ruler as a moral paragon can publicize and socialize moral standards and moral ideal norms in society. Both the political and moral authorities of the ruler are presupposed. A name to be rectified is a name of a value and at the same time a norm, for value is a goal for emulation and cultivation and a norm is the requirement implicit in the naming of the value. But both value and norm are derived from virtue, which is the actually cultivated ability and power of one to do good to others and oneself. Hence, to rectify names is to require that actual individuals live up to the required virtues governing the relationships of individuals in society.

The interesting question raised, which was not raised in the article "Rectifying Names in Classical Confucianism," is whether rectifying names is simply a moral demand without implying any institutional and legalistic reform. My reply to this question is that there could be two interpretations, a strictly moral interpretation that leads to Mencius's theory of human nature and a possible institutional-legalistic interpretation that manifests itself in Hsun Tzu's philosophy of institutional control. For the former, moral values are rectified when the development of human nature as embodiment of goodness is encouraged by good example and self-reflection, whereas, for the latter, moral norms are rectified when human nature as the embodiment of selfish desires is disciplined by intellectual learning and social conditioning. As rectifying names in Confucius provides a basis for discussing various moral, political, and moral-to-political-transformational problems, this theme should open up an important issue for discussing the overall feature of classical Confucianism as a moral political philosophy.[38] It also affords a forum for verifying the process of natural naturalization versus the process of rational rationalization in the political philosophy of balance of powers and government by law in the West.

In connection with the institutional-legalistic approach to rectifying names and government, "Legalism versus Confucianism: A Philosophical Appraisal" shows how Hsun Tzu was still more a Confucianist than a Legalist because he combined a naturalistic theory of language origins and a moralistic theory of rectification of names for the purpose of social ordering. He did not adopt a strict legalistic point of view based on infinite consideration of the interests of the ruler and the state as Han Fei did. Beside, the stress Hsun Tzu put on education and learning undoubtedly marked the Confucianist orientation of his philosophy. But unlike Mencius, Hsun Tsu did speak of institutionization of *li* (propriety) for government, and his description of *li* takes on a lawlike and rationalizing function for social ordering and social engineering. This apparently causes *li* to lose its aesthetic appeal. Hence, the transformation of *li* into *fa* (law) in Han Fei could be easily effected when the interests of the ruler—not the people, not the state, not the society—are taken to be the departing point. The essay specifically points out the politically oriented fallacy of interpreting Hsun Tzu as legalistic by some mainland Chinese scholars during the later Great Cultural Revolution period.

A second dimension of classical Confucianism concerns the meaning and nature of Confucian moral philosophy and ethics. Although much discussion has been made on this dimension of classical Confucianism, little attention was paid to the development of the Confucian morality as a dialectical process that shows growth and dynamics. In this process one can see that the Confucian morality is essentially a philosophy of human self-transformation, self-transcendence, and self-delivery, and thus a philosophy of human self-understanding and self-perfection rooted in the fundamental experience of being human. It also reflects a process of self-orientation and self-choice in human life that leads to creation of a unique life-world of human existence. With this understanding as explained in the essay "Dialectic of Confucian Morality and Metaphysics of Man: A Philosophical Analysis," I initiate fresh insights into the nature of the Confucian morality and ethics. In the first place, although *jên* (benevolence) is the most basic and most dominating virtue (value and norm) in classical Confucianism and generally better understood than any other virtues, *yi* (righteousness) as the virtue Mencius singled out for close attention has not been adequately explained or adequately understood. The question lies in how to formulate the principle of *yi* as well as how to cultivate and apply *yi*. It seems to me that the development from Confucius to Mencius can be captured in the development from a philosophy of *jên* to a philosophy of *yi*, which represents not only a concretion of *jên* but a deepening of the understanding of *jên*. In this development, we can see that, being rooted similarly in human nature, *jên* and *yi* have to be understood and applied side by side not only for a more balanced cultivation of the good individual, but for a more substantial development of a harmonious society. In this context, *yi* is seen not only as the virtue of righteous conduct or a just attitude, but a benevolence-relevant recognition of a universal principle for specific application to secure or create a good and just human personhood in a good and just human society.

In the essay "On *yi* as a Universal Principle of Specific Application in Confucian Morality," I also develop the Mencian point of relating *yi* to the human-cosmological relationship in moral cultivation of *yi*. This should lead to a holistic cosmology of moral virtues in which *jên* and *yi* become both human and cosmological virtues or powers. This reveals how the Confucian morality is not conventional but rather creative on the part of the individual moral person, for in *yi* one sees how an individual could shoulder a cosmic load of moral responsibility and therefore acquire a cosmological abundance of moral dignity.

Given this understanding of Confucian morality, we can see another holistic requirement in Confucian morality; namely, the unification of theory and practice. For Confucius as for other classical Confucianists, morality is not abstract understanding alone. It is the practice and embodiment of virtues in daily work and life. It is a conscious and conscientious effort to create a human work-world and human life-world in which the value of ideal humanity becomes implementable. Concretion and implementation of morality for Confucianists are intrinsically fulfilling and not means to an external purpose. Even the political objective of a good government is directed toward this intrinsic end and nothing else. This is implied in Confucius' remark on educating people after multiplying them and making them rich.[39] It is clear that the ultimate education for Confucius is moral education, which consists in making people realize and cultivate their moral natures. The concrete development and practice of Confucian morality become Confucian ethics codified in the five social norms (*wu-lun*), widely followed as basic tenets of Confucianism in Chinese society. The interest ing thing to note is that, in the presupposed metaphysical nature of moral understanding, the theoretical visions of virtue and the moral person must lead to the practical achievement of these visions. With these holistic visions as given premises, one also can see how theory and practice in general form a self-generating creative unity in Confucianism. It becomes an internal principle of thinking derived from both the metaphysical and moral experiences of human beings in Confucianism. "Theory and Practice in Confucianism" has made some primary inquiries into all these important issues.

The third dimension of Confucianism is metaphysical. Given both the moral and moral-to-political philosophizing in Confucianism, we can see how the metaphysical is naturally implicit and required in such philosophizing. A holistic understanding of Confucianism also makes a metaphysical understanding of Confucianism imperative. Earlier I indicated how the dialectical development of Confucianism leads to a metaphysics of man. To further pursue the metaphysical theme, in "Some Aspects of the Confucian Notion of Mind,", I inquire into the Confucian notion of the mind as embodied in the *Doctrine of the Mean* (the *Chung Yung*) and show how a potential holistic unity of mind and reality is required and presupposed in the process of Confucian moral self-cultivation. In fact, both goodness and creativity of human will must depend on this unity to provide self-reliant energy and confidence for cultivation and growth. Besides, the mind is not to be understood simplicistically, it must be understood as feelings, consciousness, and ability all at once. In this sense, we can conceive the Confucian mind as heart-mind, on the one hand, and mind-nature, on the other. The self-cutivational process in the Confucian mind also can be understood as a process reflecting the cosmological process of creativity, harmonization, and equalization that gives rise to creativity again. This is a deeper side of holistic organic philosophy of Confucianism indicated in the *Chung Yung* and *Commentaries* of the *I Ching*. An understanding of the latter cannot be philosophically separated from any adequate understanding of Confucian morality and moral self-cultivation.

To explore the ontological-cosmological foundation of the Confucian philosophy of humankind, I have undertaken the task of interpreting Heidegger's philosophy of Dasein in terms of the Confucian philosophy of nature (*hsing*) understood in the context of the *Chung Yung* proposition *t'ien-ming chih wei hsing*" (what heaven commands is nature). This is an onto-hermeneutical attempt to understand Heidegger and Confucianism side by side in a mutually interpretive context. In this context the relevance of the philosophy of *I Ching* becomes obvious. Hence, "Confucius, Heidegger and the Philosophy of the *I Ching* provides an innovative approach to the understanding of the metaphysical insights of Confucius that should vindicate the contemporaneous meaningfulness of Confucian philosophy as a whole. In this essay I also make clear that behind the moral experience of humanity is always the metaphysical experience of humanity and behind the metaphysical experience of humanity is even the transmetaphysical experience of being and becoming of human existence.

Finally, we come to the methodological dimension of Confucianism. In my view, metaphysics cannot escape from methodology just as methodology cannot escape from metaphysics. A close analysis of Confucian morality and its metaphysical background and implications should reveal a welter of methodological insights in the Confucian approach to issues of humankind and the world. I have not carried out a complete analysis of this nature in the book, but in "Confucian Methodology and Understanding the Human Person" I inquire into how the organic and holistic image of humans leads to the formation of the moral and metaphysical development of humans and the metaphysical justification of such a development. The Confucian methodology is both conceptual and nonconceptual insofar as practice is required. It is essentially one of sympathetic understanding of creative transformation and creative transcendence, again rooted in a rich body of concrete experience of the individual as a whole entity. Further, this methodology already has two sides, the moral-practical side and the metaphysical-theoretical side, which also form a dialectical unity. One cannot understand this methodology without simultaneously understanding the moral and metaphysical content of the Confucian philosophy.

The third part of this book deals with the Neo-Confucian philosophy. From a historic perspective Neo-Confucian philosophy is a creative extension and interpretation of classical Confucian philosophy in terms of absorbing the latter into an architectonic structure, such as in the case of Chu Hsi, or in terms of elaborating deeply felt ontological insights and paradigms, such as in the case of Wang Yang-ming. What is important to see is that Neo-Confucianism has an inner life and energy that seek to articulate themselves in an essentially similar cultural and social or political environment. In other words, the social-cultural-political continuity from past was not challenged nor cut short, hence the intellectual roots and moral and cultural visions of the past could provide both support and resources for the development of current philosophical thinking in terms of its needs and in regard to external challenges and critiques. In this regard, Neo-Confucianism is a revitalization and reconstruction of Confucianism with both an inner life and an outer form based on reflections of the challenges.

The challenges to the Confucian point of view basically are Buddhism and Taoism, and the latter two also challenge each other. It may be pointed out that the origins of the challenges actually started with Buddhism, which was introduced to China as early as third century. The process that led to Neo-Confucianism is complicated. It suffices to say that Taoistic philosophy provided the medium for anchoring Buddhism in China as an intellectual discipline and a social religion. Notwithstanding their mutual challenges, Taoism and Buddhism together provided challenges to Confucianism in regard to metaphysical issues, philosophical methods, and fundamental concepts or categories. The question is whether Neo-Confucianism is influenced more in spirit or more in form by Taoism and Buddhism. Another question is whether Neo-Confucianism is influenced more by Buddhism or by Taoism. Judging from the objections Neo-Confucianists wedged against both, it can be said that it is influenced equally by both and perhaps influenced equally in both spirit and form in the formation of Neo-Confucian system and the origination of Neo-Confucian insights.

In more concrete terms, we may say that the Buddhistic and Taoistic influences on Neo-Confucian philosophy come strongly in regard to metaphysics and methodology. Generally speaking, both the awareness of major explicit metaphysical issues and the development of major metaphysical categories in Neo-Confucianism are prompted or mediated by Buddhistic and Taoistic thought. For example, the basic concepts of *tao* (way) and *li* (principle), which become the core ideas of Neo-Confucian metaphysics, are centralized first in Taoism and Hua-yen Buddhism, even though they were used earlier (but not centralized) in classical Confucian texts such as *Mencius* and the *Chung Yung*. Their metaphysical content in both its breadth and depth are immensely enriched by the Buddhistic and Taoistic backgrounds.

Similarly, in regard to methodology, both structural conceptualization and dialectical or rational argumentation acquire a higher level of sophistication in Neo-Confucianism than any Confucian system. In this regard, Neo-Confucian methodology is comparable in its self-reflexive all-aroundness to Chinese Buddhism but has achieved a level of expressional simplicity and directness not paralleled by Buddhistic texts. What Neo-Confucian philosophy aims at is a totality and consistency of thinking in many dimensions and on many levels that illuminate a life-world of human fulfillment for an individual and for a community and that can be used to justify and direct human life. The Neo-Confucianist is interested in constructing the order of things in this totalistic perspective and in realizing this totality for the cultivation of an individual nature or individual mind. In light of this, one can say that any single concept embodies a methodology of the totalistic suggestiveness, for only in reference to a network of concepts does a single concept become genuinely meaningful. Thus, the fundamental method of thinking is that of *hermeneutical circling* in the sense of building the network of meaning by relating various experiences and ideas to a central core of concepts such as *li*, *ch'i* (vital energy), *hsin* (heart-mind), and *hsing* (nature). The more experiences and more reflection one has, the more one will be able to develop this *hermeneutical circling*. In this sense, *hermeneutical circling* as a way of thinking is integrative thinking based on integrating both subjective and objective experiences of a human individual with both the subjective and objective conceived as infinitely expandable worlds of truth and being. Hence *hermeneutical circling* is not simply aiming to produce a hermeneutical circle of meanings but a hermeneutical circle of experiences and reality of ever-growing nature. This is what I call the *onto-hermeneutics* for understanding. In this light, it is clear that my inquiry into the Neo-Confucian methodology and metaphysics gives rise to the idea of onto-hermeneutics, and therefore we may be equally entitled to characterize onto-hermeneutics as the fundamental way of thinking in Neo-Confucian philosophy.

As human experiences always are open and fresh for an individual, and as *hermeneutical circling* is an indefinitely refreshing and creative process for any thinking mind, the right way to achieve philosophical understanding is to continually cultivate oneself and do so not only on a daily basis but in reference to the commonest affairs of daily life. This is why Chu Hsi titles his anthology of earlier Neo-Confucian masters *Reflections on Things Close at Hand (Ching Ssu Lu)*, based on a mottolike saying from the *Analects*.[40] The way of thinking I call *hermeneutical circling*, in fact, can be found in all classical Confucian texts, commonly called the *Four Books*, which a careful reading will reveal. As there is no ending to this process of thinking and as this thinking always requires concretion in common life and interaction with community, human life and human thinking should form a dynamic, dialectical unity of mutual enrichment and growth, the goal of which is the idealized form of perfection of all virtues including understanding reality. This goal is titled by Neo-Confucianists *sagehood (sheng)*.

It needs be added that there is the obvious difference of breadth and depth of thinking between classical Confucian and Neo-Confucian philosophy. This is because the Neo-Confucian thinking as an example of methodological and metaphysical exercise is uniquely outstanding and not to be matched by the classical Confucianists. This difference lies precisely in the marked presence and effort-making for the presence of metaphysics and methodology in Neo-Confucianism, which are not found in classical Confucianism. It is most important to point out, however, that if we consider classical Confucianism as a corpus including the metaphysical and methodological thinking found in the *Commentaries* of the *I Ching*, the *Chung Yung*, the *Ta Hsueh*, and the *Mencius*, then we must see that the basic framework and paradigms of thinking in classical Confucianism, whether metaphysical and methodological, are the very inspiring source, form, and resource for insight and points of accentuation in Neo-Confucianism. This is true of Chu Hsi with regard to the *Ta Hsueh* doctrine of investigation of things (*ke-wu*) and extension of knowledge (*chih-chih*). It also is true of Wang Yang-ming with regard to his Mencian doctrine of fulfilling the innate knowledge of goodness (*chih-liang-chih*). But in Chu Hsi, as in Wang Yang-ming, one clearly can detect a metaphysical and methodological sophistication that is not as detectable in the *Ta Hsueh* and the *Mencius*.

One must point out that the universal and perennial source and resource of metaphysical and methodological thinking *pro forma* in the Neo-Confucian philosophy come from the philosophizing about the *I Ching*. For the Neo-Confucianists, the *I Ching* presents the pristine insights into the ceaseless creativity and transformation of things that explain the changes of things in the world, their relationships of interdependence and interpenetration, and their renewable life, innovativeness, and richness. The *I Ching* system therefore becomes in my opinion the infinite storehouse of philosophical inspiration and invigoration. It also becomes the basis for anticipating change and integrating the past and therefore a methodological and metaphysical vehicle of philosophical integration and comprehension. Without reference to the *I Ching* there could be no foundation of initial themes in Chou Tun-i, Ch'eng Hao, Ch'eng I, Chang Tsai, and Shao Yung, whose independent works contribute to the development of the architectonic system of Chu Hsi and those who came after him. It is no exaggeration to say that Neo-Confucianism became methodological and metaphysical as a result of thinking by way of and on the basis of the *I Ching*. Of course, the relation between Neo-Confucianism and the philosophy of the *I Ching* again is ontohermeneutical; that is, the *I Ching* became a methodology and a metaphysics because of the Neo-Confucianists' responses to it, and this is possible because the *I Ching* contains the methodological and metaphysical insights to be occasioned by the challenges of Buddhism and Taoism.

A final observation concerning the Neo-Confucian development is that even though metaphysics and methodology become its dominating features, the moral and ethical component of the Neo-Confucian philosophy stays very close to the classical Confucianism. One does not see much introduction of novel ideas in moral philosophy in the Neo-Confucian framework, even though the Confucian ethics and moral philosophy become more systematized and metaphysicalized, as is seen in the essay "Western Inscription" (*Hsi-ming*) of Chang Tsai. Perhaps, one or two concepts from the classic Confucian context are singled out to embody a deep sense of cosmic relevance or a deep sense of moral psychological relevance. In this connection I have in mind *jên* as life creativity and *ching* (reverence) as moral alertness, both carrying an epistemological and an ontological implication. The moral and ethical centrality in Neo-Confucian philosophy not only marks out the continuity of Neo-Confucianism from Confucianism but also the creative mindedness of Neo-Confucianism from the Confucian tradition, for in the markedly profound contexts of metaphysical and methodological thinking even the Confucian moral and ethical component has undergone a subtle transformation to answer the needs and challenges of the times. The Neo-Confucian must act or not act within methodological and metaphysical perspectives that the classical Confucian does not conscientiously have.

This last observation leads to a retrospective reflection regarding the problem of the modern fate of the transformation of Neo-Confucianism. This is the problem of how to transform and organize Neo-Confucian philosophy metaphysically and methodologically under the needs and challenges of modern times, which include the problem of both integrating and transcending the challenges from the West and social changes inside China. The methodological and metaphysical reconstruction may be so great that the Neo-Confucian insights in moral philosophy and ethics will lose their relevance and meaningfulness. On the other hand, it may be that the methodology and metaphysics of Neo-Confucianism have to yield to a new form and new content so that the Confucian ethics and moral philosophy can become relevant and meaningful. In either case, the transformation and modernization of Neo-Confucianism today means a radically different, and unprecedented challenge.

In "Method, Knowledge and Truth in Chu Hsi," I provide a systematic elucidation and justification of Chu Hsi's views on method, knowledge and truth from a totalistic hermeneutic point of view. I inquire into the organic interrelatedness of Chu Hsi's epistemology and methodology of *ke-wu* (investigation of things) and exhaustion of principles (*chiung-li*) in relation to the ontology of the human mind and the ontology of the world of principles. This amounts to determining the architechtonic structure of the concepts of *tao*, *hsing*, *hsin*, and *chih*. In fact, in light of the organic contexts of these concepts, the metaphysical and methodological meanings of *li* as principle and ordering will stand out as insightful. This again demonstrates that an ontology of understanding and an understanding of ontology go hand in hand, which codetermines the origin of a life-world of the Neo-Confucian harmony between the nature and human nature, between value and fact, and between truth and knowledge. This last point regarding the relationship between truth and knowledge is instructive, for it directly leads to the issue of whether knowledge defines truth or truth defines knowledge, which are respectively the idealistic and realistic approaches in modern Western philosophy. The interesting suggestion from Chu Hsi is that they mutually determine each other so that there is no single linear way of determination for knowing and truth. The crucial medium is the human mind, which has the potentiality for awakening to the total truth in terms of empirical knowing and learning.

In "Unity and Creativity in Wang Yang-ming's Philosophy of Mind," I analyze and reconstruct Wang Yang-ming's philosophy of mind in terms of an organic unity of concepts, which furthers creative insights into human nature and the human mind and which inspires human moral actions. Again, for Wang Yang-ming as for Chu Hsi, the basis for moral commitment and moral action lies deep in the metaphysical experiences of reality and self as a unity. For Wang Yang-ming this means the unity of subjectivity and objectivity that reveals the life-creative and life-comprehending cosmic and ontic truth of being he called *liang-chih* (innate knowledge of goodness) and *pen-hsin* (original mind). The important lesson, methodologically speaking, is that any organic unity of experiences presents insight into reality, and moral experience is an organic, most profound experience of reality and represents a most profound insight into reality. For Wang Yang-ming this reality, such as revealed by one's *liang-chih*, need not itself be called *moral*, for in this way it would become limited in its scope of creativity. But when the reality is revealed via the original mind of an individual, it is what emerges as a morally significant experience that leads to formulation of value and commitment to practice. In other words, the context of human life and human needs renders the real into the moral, but again human moral insight enables us to see reality as creative. Thus, for Wang Yang-ming the morally experiential or the mind (as *hsin*) is the real (as *li* or the principle) and the cultivation of one's nature becomes the enlightening discovery or rediscovery of the mind and reality in the interactive relationship of unity between mind and reality. Unlike Chu Hsi who stressed the rational process of investigation and extension, Wang Yang-ming stressed the Ch'an-like grasp or intuition of the vital essence of reality and the mind that is the creative force of action for change and meeting a challenge. It also may be regarded as a moral force for transcendence and innovation, which emancipates an individual from bondage of conventions and conceptual trappings. It is clear that Wang's Neo-Confucian philosophy is not necessarily architechtonic like Chu Hsi's, but nevertheless it shares with Chu Hsi the deep involvement with classical Confucian ethics in that it wishes to make it a dynamic force for commitment and action in a world of transformation. Whereas Chu Hsi's philosophy is space-oriented, stressing understanding and cultivation, Wang's philosophy is time-oriented, stressing commitment and action. In this regard, they can be analogized to the northern school of gradualistic Ch'an Buddhism and the southern school of suddenistic Ch'an Buddhism; and they can be said to be complementary to each other rather to be opposite to each other, as their respective followers and many later scholars of Neo-Confucianism make them to be. In this sense, Wang needs not be characterized as idealistic in any useful sense. As I indicated elsewhere, Wang and Chu Hsi need to be understood in a larger system of integration of Neo-Confucian insights.

Although Wang did not explicitly and systematically inquire into the philosophy of the *I Ching*, as did Chu Hsi, he can be said to apply directly the spirit of creative transformation in the philosophy of the *I Ching* to the daily life and political affairs of his times.

The implication and influence of Wang's philosophy of mind, understood as a philosophy of creative unity of subjectivity and objectivity, are immense and deep, not simply because he has actively taught many disciples in his career, but because his philosophy of mind contains a metaphysics and methodology that is not fully spelled out by him but needs to be spelled out for justifying its impact and attraction. Thus, his latter-day teaching of the "four-sentence teaching" (*shih-chu-chiao*) provides a focal point for the articulation of both the metaphysics and the methodology of Wang's philosophy of mind. In "The Consistency and Meaning of the Four-Sentence Teaching in *Ming Ju Hsueh An*," I argue not only for the consistency of this later view of Wang Yang-ming with his earlier views on the mind and *liang-chih*, but for the logical necessity of the ontological development of his philosophy of moral action as a unity of theory and practice, which should give rise to a solution to the problem of how to fulfill one's innate knowledge of goodness. For the teaching of the "four-sentences" indicates that *liang-chih* cannot be understood isolatedly but as layers of reality of will rooted in a creative but invisible *pen-ti* (original substance). The reference to *pen-ti* opens up not only the fundamental question of fundamental ontology but the relation of creative transformation and creative unity between being and moral valuation. For Wang and many of his important disciples, the relation is to be realzied and fully enacted in the mind of an individual if the individual acts according to his or her *liang-chih* and that *liang-chih* develops according to the individual's moral practice.This is an onto-hermeneutical circling that focuses on that unity of knowing and acting as well as on the unity of ontology and morality.

This discussion provides an important distinction between two contrasting (though complementary, as I indicated) positions in Neo-Confucian philosophy; namely, between the understanding-oriented philosophy of Chu Hsi and the action-oriented philosophy of Wang Yang-ming. This distinction essentially also is a distinction between nature (*hsing*)-based thinking and mind (*hsin*)-based thinking in Neo-Confucianism as well as a distinction between *li* (principle)-accentuated way of thinking and *ch'i*-accentuated way of thinking in the moral philosophy and metaphysical philosophy of Neo-Confucianism. To say that Chu Hsi's philosophy is understanding-oriented, nature-oriented, and *li*-accentuated is not to say that Chu Hsi does not consider moral practice as part of his philosophy of moral understanding, or Chu Hsi does not consider the mind as an essential component of his view of human nature endowed a priori, or Chu Hsi does not consider *ch'i* as one of the two building blocks of a cosmo-ontology, the other being *li*. But, the general tendency and character of Chu Hsi's philosophical approach is to play up the importance of understanding, nature, and principle for full development of an individual. Understanding (*li-hui*)[41] includes the extension of knowledge as a condition but goes beyond the extention of knowledge in that it represents the total and ultimate grasp of, and therefore awakening to, a universal reality of truth and being as represented by the concept of *li*, by the mental power that is again informed by *li* and activated by *li*. Hence, understanding is *li*-constructive and *li*-active, presenting a unity of the ontology of *li* and the epistemology of mind-nature as well as a unity of the subjective activity of the mind and the objective ordering of *li*. For Chu Hsi, understanding also is a process of investigation and reflection that requires simultaneous intellectual effort and moral control, and this means that understanding is to be achieved on the basis of an underlying nature that activates and sustains the process of understanding. In light of this underlying nature, not only does a process of understanding become actually realizable but initiation of the process becomes explainable. The mind consequently becomes a faculty of this nature that, on the other hand, is rooted in the ultimate reality in which objective knowledge is equally rooted. In Chu Hsi there is the unity of the mind and *li* because there is the unity of the mind and nature, on the one hand and the unity of *li* and nature on the other.

In contrast with Chu Hsi, Wang Yang-ming does not treat nature as a separate entity from the mind, which is characterized as active and creative in being able to present the awareness of goodness and will toward goodness at the same time. This is why *liang-chih* is considered to be the concretion of moral value, on the one hand, and disclosing reality on the other. In this sense, one's nature is the naturing of one's mind, and one's mind is the minding of one's moral commitment to value-realizing action. Hence moral understanding is achieved all at once and need not depend on a process linked to the moral understanding as an achievement. What makes this possible is the *ch'i*-activity of mind as both awareness and will. But this is not to deny the relevance of *li* either, just as this is not to deny the relevance of understanding and nature. *Li* becomes vitally relevant in the action of the mind as well as in the action resulting from the mind. *Li* is basically understood as morally significant even though it is ontologically significant on a different level according to the the "four-sentences" teaching and is to manifest itself from being inside the *ch'i*-activity of the mind and *liang-chih*.

The comparison of Chu Hsi and Wang Yang-ming suggests a comparison between Hsun Tsu, who stressed the badness of human feelings and desires and *ch'i* as an element of human activities, and Mencius, who stressed the goodness of human feelings and *ch'i* of one's heart and body in so far as they issue from one's original nature and in so far as one opens up to the reality of the cosmos as an life-active reality of harmony and truth. It also suggests a comparison between the *ch'ien-wu* (gradualist) approach of the northern Ch'an Buddhism and the *tun-wu* (suddenist) approach of the southern Ch'an Buddhism, a comparison mentioned earlier. Both comparisons should provide a useful, focused understanding of two essentially different metaphysics and methodologies within a common framework of moral and ethical concerns in the Neo-Confucian tradition. They can be said to represent two basic dimensions of Neo-Confucian totalistic and organic thinking, one leaning toward *li* and the other leaning to *ch'i*.

In earlier stages of the development of Neo-Confucian philosophy prior to Chu Hsi, there is a *li*-dominated system such as Ch'eng I's and also a *ch'i*-dominated system such as Chang Tsai's. In addition, there are philosophical positions that pay equal attention to *li* and *ch'i* but may not fully develop these basic categories to a complete system, such as Chou Tun-i and Ch'eng Hao. Considering all the basic issues and needs, it is obvious that the ideal goal for a totalistic philosophy in the Neo-Confucian terms is to integrate all the basic concepts and themes in a coherent and organic unity and, in this light, a balanced consideration of the roles and limitations of *li* and *ch'i*, on the one hand, and mind and nature, on the other. This is not to suggest a dualism of any sort, but to suggest that the duality and polarity of concepts and experiences should be recognized and used as a base for constructing a full, total picture of humanity and reality. This also is to suggest that one should not overplay *li* alone, as *li* will play a better role in the context of the duality of *li* and *ch'i*. Above all else, Chu Hsi seems to come close to this ideally balanced position on the cosmological level, but he also has failed to develop a viable internal relationship between the object and subject.

After Wang Yang-ming and his popular school, the Neo-Confucian philosophy of *li* and *hsin* continued to spread and develop. In so far as Wang Yang-ming is considered a critic of Chu Hsi, philosophers in succeeding generations took side either with Chu Hsi or with Wang Yang-ming or attempted to synthesize the two. Many philosophically stimulating arguments took place, and new concepts bearing on the mind such as *yi* (intention) and *shih* (consciousness) were elaborated. This historic dimension of Neo-Confucianism indeed requires a close separate study. But the overall fact remains that more and more attention is paid to the integration of *li* and *ch'i* as methodological as well as metaphysical concepts. On the moral and ethical levels, the philosophy of *li* in particular is seen as contributing to more moral injustice and inequity, because *li* was used to suppress normal expression and the satisfaction of natural desires. This incisive criticism was expressed by the eighteenth century philosopher Tai Chen regarding "using *li* to kill people" (*yi-li-sha-jên*).[42] The basic issue involved was how to develop a correct relationship between *li* and *yu* (natural desires) for a healthy and open ethics of individual, society, and state.

Another important tendency is to criticize both Chu Hsi and Wang Yang-ming and their schools for failing to bring effective action and changes to improve the state and society. This lead directly to the various action-oriented moral philosophies in the late Ming period. Apart from stressing the importance of action versus understanding, the basic categories of *li*, *ch'i*, *hsin*, and *hsing* are given enriched and innovative interpretation and elaboration. One good example is Yen Yuan's interpretation of *ke-wu* as having an active impact on things to obtain lively and useful knowledge of things rather than their perceptual and contemplative investigation. Another good example is Wang Fu-chih's notion of *li*, not as a passive static principle but one of activation, transformation, and growth. These innovative and critical Neo-Confucian philosophical developments may be titled *critical* or *pragmatic* Neo-Confucian philosophies, which even have their appeal to many Chinese philosophers today. The basic historic transformation and development of Neo-Confucian philosophy are depicted in "*Li-ch'i* and *li-yu* Relationships in Seventeenth-Century Neo-Confucian Philosophy" and "Practical Learning in Yen Yuan, Chu Hsi and Wang Yang-ming."

Apart from the systematic (which includes the moral, the metaphysical, and the methodological) and the historic dimensions of Neo-Confucian philosophy, including the *li*-systematic, the *hsin*-systematic, the *ch'i*-systematic, the critical, and the pragmatic discussed earlier, another dimension of Neo-Confucian philosophy is worthy of special attention. It is the religious dimension, which one may see in the expressions articulating profound feelings for the destiny, mission and intrinsic purposefulness of human life and profound experiences of a spiritually profound reality. One finds such expressions in Lu Hsiang-shan, Chang Tsai, and Ch'eng Hao. Even in otherwise rational writings, one finds the philosophical poetry of Chu Hsi and Wang Yang-ming that bespeak a lived understanding of life and reality fused with personal conviction on ultimate truth. One may suggest that this religious dimension is necessary and the natural result of a systematic philosophy founded on both personal cultivation of the self and a deep reading of the Confucian tradition with its concept and experience of the *t'ien-ming* (mandate of heaven) as an integral part. As indicated earlier, *t'ien-ming* has been gradually naturalized and humanized in the development of classical Chinese philosophy. But nonetheless, the overtones and underlying feelings of *t'ien-ming* assumed a totalitic form in the Neo-Confucianist understanding of reality, life, and moral action. In other words, the religious as the profound experience of the profound, the total, the ultimate is the generally shared common feature for both *li*-oriented and *ch'i*-oriented philosophers in Neo-Confucianism. In fact, this expression of the experience of the profound that relates to one's life and the life of the universe shows a basic approach to the problem of religious understanding inherent in the Confucian tradition. This approach fuses the moral with the cosmic, the experiential with the ontic, the personal with the universal, the understanding with the practice so that we will reach a genuine and dynamic unity of individual and heaven. One can see that Wang Yang-ming's philosophy is basically such a philosophy of unities with the unity of humanity and heaven as the ultimate justification and ultimate goal. It is a statement of the religion of divine humanity and a religion of immanentization of divinity in humanity. It is a religious consciousness radically different from that of the transcendent religion in the West. In "Religious Reality and Religious Understanding in Confucianism and Neo-Confucianism," I explore this Neo-Confucian religiousness and its Confucian roots and show how it can provide a new model and new paradigm of religious understanding unlike that expressed in the paradigm of the numinous formulated by Otto and meaningful for a universal human self-understanding.

As in Part II on the Confucian dimensions, where I include an essay discussing the Confucian philosophy from a comparative point of view, I also include an essay discussing the Neo-Confucian dimensions from a comparative point of view in Part III on the Neo-Confucian dimensions. In "Categories of Creativity in Whitehead and Neo-Confucianism," a philosophical discussion of the fundamental categories bearing on creativity on the cosmological-ontological plane is made in reference to Whitehead and Chou Tun-i and other important Neo-Confucain philosophers. The reason why Whitehead was chosen for this comparative purpose is obvious: Like Heidegger, Whitehead is one of the most systematic contemporary philosophers in the West who understands reality as a totality and as a transformation and who articulates his understanding in a comprehensive and consistent way. As far as the Neo-Confucian metaphysics is an articulation of the cosmological and ontological totality and creativity inspired by the philosophy of change and transformation in the *I Ching*, there are interesting points of intersection that form a framework for comparison, mutual interpretation and reciprocal interaction. But this comparative study not only illuminates but also reconstructs and rethinks the Neo-Confucian philosophy in a large and open up-to-date perspective. In this context, Neo-Confucianist philosophy as a deeply meaningful tradition can be infused with a new vitality and a modern interest.

Notes

1. See my paper "Characteristics of Chinese Philosophy," the first chapter in this book, first published in *Invitation to Chinese Philosophy*, ed. Arne Naess, 1972, pp. 141-167. Oslo.
2. See the *I Ching*, the *Great Appendix*, first part, Section 10. The translation is mine.
3. See the *Analects*, Chapter 15-29.
4. See the *Tao Te Ching*, Chapter 25, where it says that "Man follows the earth, earth the heaven and heaven the *tao*, and the *tao* the natural"; also see Chapter 21, where it says that "The manner of great virtue [for man] is to closely follow the *tao*".
5. There are two levels of understanding, which should not be confused: understanding in terms of the intrinsic structure of a given subject matter and understanding in terms of the extrinsic conditions that, in one way or another, can be said to give rise to the instrinsic structure of the given subject. This distinction can be likened to the distinction between the teleological cause and the material cause of an existing object.
6. See Francis Cornford, *From Religion to Philosophy: A Study in the Origins of Western Speculation*, New York, 1957; see also his *Principium Sapientiae, the Origins of Greek Philosophical Thought*, Cambridge, England 1952.
7. See Martin Heidegger, *An Introduction to Metaphysics*, trans. Ralph Manheim, New York, 1961, 81 ff; see also *Being and Time*, trans. John Macquarrie and Edward Robinson, New York, 1962, Introduction, 49 ff.
8. See Martin Heidegger, *Identity and Difference*, trans. Joan Stambaugh, 1969, New York.
9. See Georg Fohrer, *History of Israelite Religion*, trans. David E. Green, Nashville, 1972. See also Johannes Pederson, *Israel: Its Life and Culture*, 4 parts, trans. Aslang Moller and Annil Fausboll, Oxford, England, 1926-1947. Reprinted 1959.
10. This phrase has been generally used by modern-day Chinese Neo-Confucian scholars to describe the relative autonomy of *li* and *ch'i* and their interdependence in the philosophy of Chu Hsi.
11. Although human beings have made great advances in science and technology, which has progressively transformed human society and forms of human life,

the human ecological environment however has deteriorated to a considerable extent. This does not mean that there is no progress, but only that all progress is counterbalanced by a certain counterprogress and the total result of progress and counterprogress forms a unity of compensation, which should lead to a unity of balance supportive and productive of continual creativity.

12. Here we cannot discuss in detail the structure of the unity of opposites in *li* and *ch'i* and *hsin* and *hsing*. For such a discussion see my article, "Preliminary Inquiries into Philosophical Categories in Chinese Philosophy" (in Chinese) in *Chung-kuo-che-hsueh-fan-chau-lun-wen-chi* (Essays on Chinese Philosophical Categories), ed. Tang Yijie, Beijing, 1986, pp. 40-96.

13. See *Chu Tzu Yu Lei* (Classified Sayings of Chu Hsi), *chuan* 1

14. See the *Mencius*, Chapter 7a-4. The translation is mine.

15. See ibid., Chapter 7b-25.

16. See ibid., Chapter 7a-38.

17. It is said in *Tso Chuan*, Duke Hsiang, twentyfourth year that "In the ancient time, there were (sages) who established virtues (*li-te*), there were (sages) who established deeds (*li-kung*), and there were (sages) who established words (*li-yen*)."

18. Joseph Levenson, *Confucian China and Its Modern Fate*, Berkeley, Calif., 1958.

19. See the *Analects*, Chapter 5-13.

20. See ibid., Chapter 17-2.

21. See my article "Harmony as Transformation," in *Harmony and Strife*, ed. Shu-hsien Liu and Robert Allinson, Hong Kong, 1988, pp. 225-249.

22. See the *Analects*, Chapter 2-4.

23. See ibid., Chapter 7-23.

24. See ibid., Chapter 7-30.

25. Here we have no time to dwell on the details of the naturalization, humanization, and immanentization processes in the well-known writings of classical Confucianism.

26. Trans. Joel C. Weinsheimer, New York, 1985.

27. See selections from Friedrich Daniel Ernst Schleiermacher in *The Hermeneutics Reader*, Kurt Mueller-Vollmer,The Hague 1988, 74 ff.

28. See Michael Polyani, *Knowing and Being*, London, 1968. See also Polanyi, *Meaning*, Chicago, 1975; *The Study of Man*, Chicago, 1959.

29. Heidegger says that "Understanding is the existential Being of Dasein's own potentiality-for-Being; and it is so in such a way that this Being discloses itself what it as Being is capable of." *Being and Time*, Section 31.

30. See Martin Heidegger, *Gelassenheit*, Pfullingen, 1959, first essay.

31. See Heidegger's *Being and Time*, translators' footnote 3 on page 1 in regard to Heidegger's statement "Our provisional aim is the Interpretation of time as the possible horizon for any understanding whatsoever of Being." See Part 1, Chapter 5 and after, and Part 2, Chapter 2 and after.

32. The mind for Husserl is cognitive consciousness experiencing the world in a nonactive manner, and everything else is constituted out of the noetic-noematic-processes of consciousness.

33. Husserl started to write this book in 1934, and it was first published posthumously in 1954.

34. Roman Ingarden has applied this broader scope of phenomenological method to the reconstitution and interpretation of the literary world presented in arts and literature, whereas Heidegger deepens this process for disclosing and understanding the being of human existence—the Dasein as indicated in my earlier statement of the principle of understanding as Being. See Mueller-Vollmer, *Hermeneutical Reader*, pp. 28, 30-32, 187-213.

35. Cf. Susan Haack, *Deviant Logic: Some Philosophical Issues*, London and New York, 1974.

36. The methodological openness of this methodology of understanding is due to the principles of autonomy and creative acts of constitution, whereas its ontological indeterminateness is due to the principles of level emergence and Being.

37. See note 21.

38. Not simply a moral and a political philosophy, the integration of moral and political considerations is a characteristic of Confucianism.

39. See the *Analects*, Chapter 13-9.

40. See ibid., Chapter 6-30.

41. Chu Hsi uses this term to indicate the understanding of reality or a problem in terms of the principles inherent or presupposed in reality or the problem in question. In other words, *li-hui* (meeting of principles) consists in awakening to principles and reality that brings enlightenment and truth to mind. This notion of understanding is obviously holistic and onto-hermeneutical. See *Chu Tzu Yu Lei*, chuan 5, for Chu Hsi's use of this term.

42. See my book, *Tai Chen on the Origin of Goodness*, University Press of Hawaii, Honolulu, 1969.

Part I

---

*Chinese Philosophical
Orientations*

1. Chinese Philosophy: A Characterization

Fallacies in Early Studies in Chinese Philosophy

Early studies in Chinese philosophy in the European languages have led to many confusions and misunderstandings concerning the true nature of Chinese philosophy. Four such confusions and misunderstandings are common in many writings on Chinese philosophy. There is, first of all, the belief that Chinese philosophy is irrational and mystical and merely to be grasped by some form of intuition. On the basis of this belief it is naturally assumed that Chinese philosophy is so radically different from Western modes of thinking that it is impossible to convey Chinese philosophy in Western terms. This assumption and its presupposed belief are fallacious and misleading, for in fact there are conspicuous traditions of naturalism and rationalism in Chinese philosophy, as well as other universal elements which should make comparisons and contrasts between Chinese philosophy and Western philosophy not only intelligible but profitable.

In direct contrast with the fallacy of the attribution of mysticism is the fallacious belief that there is nothing new and original in Chinese thinking and that everything which is contained in Chinese thought has been dealt with in the Western tradition. This latter view is characteristic of the critics of Chinese culture in early nineteenth-century Europe, just as the former view is characteristic of the admirers of Chinese culture and philosophy in twentieth-century America. Certainly this second view is not true, for a thorough understanding of Chinese philosophy will reveal many fundamental concepts of Chinese philosophy which are not to be found in the Western tradition. Even though there are of course many similarities between Chinese philosophy and some philosophical thought in the West, it must be pointed out that similarities can he profoundly significant and inspiring in philosophical inquiries. In fact, a dialogue between Chinese and Western philosophies can be conducted and developed only when similarities and differences between them are not limited to surface observations. To develop a dialogue between Chinese and Western philosophy, one has to understand first of all the languages of both traditions and be able to translate one language into another in a constructive fashion. To do this, it is evident that one has to have creative insights so that one can see the philosophical problems and solutions presented in a different tradition and then be able to conceptualize them in one's own native system.

The beneficial consequences resulting from a dialogue between Chinese philosophy and Western philosophy can be many. Among others, the most relevant would be a better understanding of one's own position. If it is one of the functions of philosophy to uncover the presuppositions of an accepted view and to explore new ways of thinking and argumentation; the dialogue in question will certainly provide new light for such discovery and exploration. No improvement in self-understanding is possible without such discovery and exploration.

Related to the second fallacy mentioned above is the general erroneous tendency toward crude generalization of many of the Marxist-oriented studies on Chinese philosophy. Crude generalizations on the nature of Chinese philosophy are reflected in the facile classification of all Chinese philosophers into idealists and materialists, objectivists and subjectivists, proletarianists and aristocratists. On the basis of these classifications pretentious value judgments are then drawn which cannot but throw a veil on the true nature of the school under examination. This approach toward the study and evaluation of Chinese philosophy is unacceptable and undesirable, as it is based on dogmatic premises which are not open to criticism. Furthermore, the classifications in use are too general and vague to capture the individual merits and demerits of specific schools or thinkers. They naturally lead to a distorted picture of Chinese philosophy rather than to a clarification of it. A lesson which one can learn from this fallacy is that one has to be critical of one's own conceptual tools of study and evaluation before one embarks on a study and evaluation of Chinese philosophy. There can be no adequate understanding of a subject, be it Chinese or any other philosophy, if there is no adequate conceptual tool for uncovering and formulating an adequate understanding. Generalizations are usually necessary for the purpose of understanding, but we should remember nevertheless that generalizations must be reached as conclusions based on a detailed study, analysis, and reconstruction, and must also be considered as instigations to further critical studies. It is with this view of generalization in mind that I shall present a general picture of Chinese philosophy as a whole.

A final fallacious view prevalent in the study of Chinese philosophy is that Chinese philosophy can he explained in terms of socio-political or socio-economic, or even socio-psychological, conditions and features of the thinker and his times. The Marxist has of course developed a systematic method for relating philosophy to the socio-economic conditions of a time period. The undesirability of dealing with Chinese philosophy on this basis has been indicated in the discussion of the third fallacy in the study of Chinese philosophy. What I am now referring to are the non-Marxist intellectual historians who commit themselves to explaining Chinese philosophy in terms of historical events without developing any systematic methodology or theoretical justification. The result of this approach to the study of Chinese philosophy is that many significant philosophical ideas are reduced to specific historical referents and are therefore divested of their universal meanings and truth-claims. This is the fallacy of historical reduction. As with any form of reduction, it is bound to impoverish the rich content of philosophical thought in China and will mislead people to disregard the independent philosophical character of Chinese philosophers.

Before we engage ourselves in a general discussion of the over-all characteristics of Chinese philosophy, it is important to do two things: first, we should explicitly state our method of study and evaluation; secondly, we should actually apply our method to bear upon our historical review of the major trends and traditions in Chinese philosophy. The methodology which we are to adopt to characterize Chinese philosophy is one of analysis and reconstruction, which we may call briefly the method of analytical reconstruction. This method consists, first, in analyzing various basic views in Chinese philosophy in an attempt to display and reveal the intricate implications and relationships of concepts involved in these views. It will, furthermore, be directed toward making explicit the presuppositions and consequences of these views. Finally, it will lead to a systematic and critical explication of the concepts and views under analysis. It seems deplorable that in the past no such method has been applied to the study of Chinese philosophy and little attempt has even been made to state views and concepts in Chinese philosophy in clear and systematic philosophical language. A consequence of this is that Chinese philosophical ideas, couched in the classical language, gradually lose their direct appeal to the philosophical mind of modern man. This is due to a conceptual block and to the lack of linguistic criticism. In the following, our discussion of Chinese philosophy will be based on the methodology of analytic reconstruction, and will be conducted in such a way that the relevance of Chinese philosophy to modern philosophers and modern man will become manifest, and a comparison of Chinese philosophy with Western philosophy possible.

Archetypal Ideas in the Pre-Confucian Period

Historically speaking, Chinese philosophy begins with a tradition which is not characterized by any systematic mythology or dogmatic personalistic religion, but instead by a sentiment of the consanguinity of man and nature, a sense of historicality and continuity of life in time, and finally a faith in the reality and potential perfectibility of man and this world. In the Shang and Chou times, long before Confucius was born, there were already developed archetypal ideas concerning ultimate reality and its determining authority, the potentiality of man for achieving goodness, the external limitation of man's existence and the need for establishing a relationship of unity and harmony between man and reality in well-tuned behavior patterns. There are ideas of *t'ien* (heaven), *ti* (lord on high, ancestral god of man), *hsing* (nature of man), *ming* (mandate, destiny and necessity), *te* (power, potentiality, virtue) and *li* (rites and proprieties). The ideas of *ti* and *t'ien* are specifically related to the practice of ancestral worship in ancient times: the ancestors of men were identified with ultimate reality and regarded as a perennial source of life. This view had profound philosophical significance. Later, the more personalistic notion of *ti* was replaced by the less personalistic notion of *t'ien*, as the latter represents a more general notion open to acceptance by a broader group of people. In a sense, we may regard *t'ien* as a generalized notion of *ti*, developed from the need to unify the ancestral worships of different groups of people. Thus *ti* may be regarded as the ancestor of a specific people, *t'ien* as the ancestor of all peoples. In this fashion *t'ien* becomes less personalistic than *ti*, because it is divested of the specifically personalistic characteristics of *ti*, even though *t'ien* still retains the special and moral powers of *ti*.

Apart from all this, *t'ien* is primarily a spatial notion, while *ti* is primarily a temporal notion. The development from the idea of *ti* to that of *t'ien* indicates an awareness of the physical proximity to man of the ultimate reality and supreme authority. This proximity is further indicated in the fact that *t'ien* has a close and deep concern with the well-being of people. The existence of government and ruler is made possible through the desire of heaven to raise people in happiness. Because of this concern of *t'ien*, a ruler is responsible for seeing that his people are well-nourished and well-ordered. Also because of it, the will of heaven is identified with the will of the people, so that the dissatisfaction and unrest of the people can be interpreted as a sign of heaven's withdrawing of a ruler's appointment as ruler due to his loss of virtue or goodness. The virtue and goodness in question are nothing but powers for carrying out the intentions of heaven in fulfilling the potentiality of one's life. This *te*, which in a sense is inherent in man, and which one can cultivate so as to fulfill oneself in accordance with the will (or mandate) of heaven—this potentiality of man and his ability to cultivate this potentiality—is called the nature (*hsing*) of man. It is clear from the fact that man is closely related to heaven—the source of his life and his model for greatness—that he must have his nature cultivated to realize *te*. Furthermore, since the order of man is based on the order of nature, the principle which should preserve the order of man is a practical concern of man. It is from this concern that li), governing relationships among men and between men and spirits, are developed and valued as most fundamental and essential for the development of man, as well as for maintaining the well-being of society.

To conclude, the archetypal ideas of the pre-Confucian period have profound philosophical significance. They are interrelated and founded on a sentiment of the original consanguinity between man and nature, and on a sentiment of man's existence as a potential entity capable of development. Thus the existence of virtue in man is his ability to conscientiously pursue and attain, or realize, the unity of man and reality. In the following we shall see how, on this general basis, the main trends and traditions of Chinese philosophy develop and diversify.

The Tradition of Confucianism

The Confucian age begins with Confucius's explicit recognition that the external *t'ien* (heaven) has an essential link with the internal *te* (virtue, power) of man and that man should extend himself in a graded love toward other men and thus achieve the universal humanity inherent in us. We may say, therefore, that Confucianism as represented by Confucius is an awakening of man in regard to his relationships to heaven, to other men and to himself. The relationality of man is to be realized in the practice and perfection of virtues such as *jên* (love and benevolence), *yi* (or *i*) (righteousness), *li* (propriety) and *chih* (wisdom in distinguishing good from bad). *Jên* is the universality of man. *Yi* is the necessity and actual application of *jên* to a diversity of situations and relationships. *Li* is the proper way of expressing oneself in fulfilling one's *jên* by means of *yi*. If *li* is the exterior behavior pattern of a man toward another man in a situation, *yi* is the principle which confers propriety on the behavior pattern in question, and *jên* is the natural desire for fulfilling *li* in the spirit of *yi*. Thus *jên* is most fundamental for making a man a man. For it is on the basis of *jên* that a man will seek to fulfill others in order to fulfill himself, as well as to fulfill himself in order to fulfill others. It is on this basis that a man can relate to other men and become himself.

A man who sets his mind in pursuing *jên* is called a superior man (*chün-tzu*), a man who has come to the awareness of *jên* and his ability and necessity to fulfill himself by *jên*. When he succeeds in achieving the perfection of *jên*, so that he may act in total freedom and yet according to strict principles of *yi* and *li*, he is not only a *chün-tzu*, but a sage (*shen-jên*). Thus *jên* can also represent the ideal perfection of man in Confucian thinking. It is to be identified with both the totality of all virtues (*te*) and the essence of all virtues.

When *t'ien* is regarded as related to the internal *te* of man, *t'ien* is a source of moral courage and moral wisdom in a superior man. But, on the other hand, *t'ien* in Confucius, and later in Mencius, is regarded not merely as an internal source of one's potentiality, but also as an external limitation and necessity which puts life to trial and limits life. In understanding this phase of *t'ien*, a superior man will have to accept many determined facts of life, such as death, misfortune, etc. These determinations are possible because man has his object-nature—that is, he is an object. But Confucius and Mencius recognize that besides this object-nature of man, according to which man is determined by external causes, man has a dynamic subject-nature—that is, man is a subject capable of cultivating himself in the path of virtue and therefore of determining himself in the direction of achieving the full autonomy and independence of his nature. This is how man may realize his spiritual freedom despite the external determination and limitation imposed upon him as an object. The importance of Confucius is his insistence that man can become a full subject, and that his life is meaningful because he has a subject-nature and thus the power to pursue perfection in the actual conduct of himself in a network of relationships.

Confucianism after Confucius was greatly developed in the classical period in Mencius, Hsun Tzu, and in the works of the *Great Learning* and the *Doctrine of the Mean*. Mencius explicitly forms the doctrine of the goodness of human nature as a foundation for man's capacity for self-cultivation toward perfection. He appeals to the natural sentiments of man, such as compassion, shame, modesty, reverence, and like and dislike, as the bases and beginnings of virtues such as *jên, yi, li* and *chih*. Thus it is asserted in Mencius that virtues have a natural foundation in man and that the nature of man is nothing other than the ability to pursue virtues. The goodness of human nature is therefore nothing but a fulfillment of the inherent nature-virtue in man, whereas badness is but the abandonment and deviation of one's natural sentiments and nature under circumstances which dominate man. But man cannot really lose his inherent goodness and his innate ability to know and see what he needs for the preservation of his goodness. Thus Mencius is fond of talking about 'collecting oneself in return to goodness'. His doctrine of government by the love of people and by becoming a good example in the person of a ruler is based on this doctrine of the goodness of human nature.

Though Hsun Tzu, as a later Confucianist than Mencius, argues that human nature is bad and that man's goodness is only man-made and is not natural, he nevertheless remains a staunch Confucianist in his faith in man's ability, potential, and initial willingness to better himself. For Hsun Tzu, human nature is bad because it is seen to consist basically in desires which know no proper limitation and which mean only self-profit. But this is not the whole of Hsun Tzu's view of man's nature, for he recognized the power of the human mind or reason to be inherent in that nature too. By experience man must come to use his mind and reason for the benefit of himself and others. Thus Hsun Tzu argues for the importance of education and training in terms of *li*, which are regarded as principles for ordering and organizing human behavior and efforts in society and the State. *Li* in this sense is the creation of reason, and is the fundamental saving virtue of man.

Confucianism in later ages has received various formulations, but basically the minimal and necessary principles of self-cultivation of virtue, unity of man and heaven, and relevance of social order and political harmony for individual self-realization, are never abandoned and are universally affirmed from the Han to the Sung-Ming period. Even though Sung-Ming Confucianism (called Neo-Confucianism) was deeply involved with metaphysical speculations over the problems of *li* (principle of being and reason) and *ch'i* (vapor, substance, and material), *li* and chi have also been used to explain the essentially good nature of man, the potential unity between the nature of man and the nature of heaven all things in reality, and, not least of all, why man by cultivating himself can actualize what is inherent in him.

The Tradition of Taoism

Another important tradition in Chinese philosophy is Taoism. It may be suggested that Taoism represents the stage of development of the concept of *t'ien* to that of *tao* in the classical period. It is true that the term *tao* has been used in Confucian writings, but it is Taoists such as Lao Tzu and Chuang Tzu who formulate an exclusive philosophy of *tao*. The concept of *tao* is altogether different from the concepts of *t'ien* and *ti* in being a completely non-personalistic concept of ultimate reality. It is more generalized in scope than *ti* and *t'ien*, because it comprehends everything in the world. There is, however, one respect in which *tao* shares something in common with the earlier concepts of *ti and t'ien*. *Tao* is internally related to man just as *ti* and *t'ien* are internally related to man in Confucianism. In a sense, *tao* is regarded as the primordial being of man. In saying this we must bear in mind that *tao*, unlike *ti* or *t'ien*, is not regarded as being in a position to dispense a special favor to man or as deeply concerned with man's well-being, for *tao* is impartial to everything as it generates, comprehends, transforms and preserves all things. It is with regard to this impartiality of *tao* that all things can be regarded as being ontologically equal. In Lao Tzu this concept of ontological equality is implicit in the very notion of *tao*, while on the basis of this same concept, Chuang Tzu goes a step further in developing a new sense of the ontological equality of all things.

Things are ontologically equal, according to Chuang Tzu, because they are formed by a process of self- and mutual transformation. There is no substance to individual things nor to their individuality, for all individual things are only relatively determined in the totality of the self-and mutual transformation of things. Thus things are ontologically equal also in the sense of being both self-activating and mutually determining.

There are several important characteristics of the philosophy of *tao* which must be mentioned. First, *tao* is a totality which is basically indefinable and unnameable. A proper interpretation of this indefinability and unnameability of *tao* is that *tao* cannot be limited by any object or be finitely characterized. This means that no object and no character can stand for *tao* without creating a partial and misleading conception of *tao*. Because *tao* cannot be characterized by any finite character, it can be contrasted with things which are finitely characterizable. If things which are finitely characterizable are called 'being', then *tao* would be the opposite of being, and is in fact called by Lao Tzu the non-being, or the void (*wu*). Thus, *tao* for Lao Tzu is not a reality merely negatively conceived, but is instead something which can only be conceived as the indeterminate, as the source and origin of all things. Although 'void' is the concept conveyed by Lao Tzu to capture the virtue of *tao*, it is better to use the terms 'indeterminate' or 'ultimateless' to suggest the possibility of *tao* actually generating things and men. Indeed, Lao Tzu has specifically maintained that it is *tao* which gives rise to all finite things that are related to us in any way, and that it is the void or the indeterminate which one has to understand and to take into consideration in the understanding of *tao*.

Another point about Taoism is that *tao* is not conceived as a static or unchanging substance, but as a process of movement and change. This means that all things comprehended in *tao* are in a process of change and movement. Now there are two questions to be answered in this connection: By what operation does *tao* give rise to all things in being? How is *tao* as a process of change and movement to be described? The answer to the first question is that *tao* gives rise to everything by way of differentiation and self-realization. There is an apparent paradox in the process of generation by *tao*, which should be resolved from a dialectical point of view.

Tao, as we have seen, is void and yet produces everything. This is so because *tao* is the principle by which the negative can become the positive, the potential can become the actual, the void can become the substantive, and the one can become the many. It is by the very negativity and potentiality of *tao* that everything positive and actual is created and preserved. But at the same time, when the potential becomes the actual, the negative becomes the positive, the void becomes the substantive, and the one becomes the many, the converse process takes place as well. *Tao* in this sense is inexhaustible, and its workings define change in terms of dialectical oppositions and complementation. This notion of *tao* is insisted upon by Taoists as representing the most fundamental wisdom of life, which, the Taoists hold, is basically experienceable in a careful reflection on life and reality.

Because *tao* is change, and change is always change from something to something else, *tao* itself is a unity of two opposites. The two opposites of *tao* are respectively called *yin* and *yang*, the feminine force (or principle) and the masculine force (or principle). In Lao Tzu it is clear that the *yin-yang* forces represent two aspects of a unity, be it an individual or the totality of *tao*. *Yin* can be identified with the negative, the potential, the subjective, and the preservative, while *yang* can be identified with the positive, the actual, the objective, and the creative. In a sense, *yin* represents *tao* as an inexhaustible source from which every form of energy or activity is derived, whereas *yang* represents *tao* as a form of activity which is ever creative, but which has a beginning and an ending and therefore remains exhaustible. When the *yang* force exhausts itself, it will fade into the *yin*, but when *yin* dominates, there is then great promise of *yang* activity. In the process of change which is constituted by the interchange of the two forces in the twofold movement of *tao*—actualization of *yin* by *yang* and potentialization of *yang* by *yin*—Lao Tzu has specifically emphasized the notion of return (*fu*). Return is return to *tao, the indeterminate* and *the inexhaustible*. It is an emphasis on *tao* as a *yin* force. But this is no denial of the *yang*, for one thing cannot return to *yin* except by way of exhausting the *yang* activity in the thing itself. Thus, as in explaining the cosmological principle of the generation of all things by *tao*, Lao Tzu also made explicit the cosmological principle of the destination of all things.

Lao Tzu has applied his cosmological principles of generation and destination to man, as the world of man is not separate from the world of nature. According to these principles, the well-being of man consists in his ability to follow the *tao*, and this means his ability to preserve potentiality for action but not actually acting out this potentiality. This is so because man is a part of *tao* and part of the production of *tao*; when he exerts himself to act and exhausts himself, he will be simply tossed away as a product of the *tao*, which can be explained as frustration and exhaustion resulting from too much effort. Thus a better way to deal with life is not to exhaust oneself and to become an object. Instead one should try to potentialize the actual and remain one with the source which *tao*. To do this one must become aware of *tao* and cultivate the *tao* in the sense of imitating the action of the non-action of *tao*, so that man will become infinitely creative and free himself from domination by destructive forces. It is in this state that one's life will flow naturally and spontaneously, and everything will be preserved in a similarly natural and spontaneous way. This doctrine has been aptly described as 'doing everything by doing nothing'. Doing nothing means doing nothing specific, while doing everything means allowing everything to flow from *tao* on its own. Lao Tzu has used many images and analogies to convey the importance of preserving the potential of life and remaining effortless and natural in the conduct of life. It is not difficult to see Lao Tzu's point if we reflect on the nature and strength of such things as water, a valley, an uncarved block of wood, a child, a mother, and the female.

In regard to the movement of *tao*, and in regard to the attainment of the well-being of life, Chuang Tzu differs fundamentally from Lao Tzu. In the first place, Chuang Tzu does not stress the idea of a return to *tao* as the source and origin of everything. For him *tao* is a universal presence and the total activity of all things. It is revealed, in particular, in the relativity and relationality of all things. Chuang Tzu has put a special stress on these ideas. The relativity and relationality of things are twofold; things are relative and relational to each other, and furthermore relative and relational to the totality of things which is *tao*. They are relative and relational to each other in the sense that each thing is a 'this' and a 'that', and thus are relatively and relationally determined and defined. Things are different from one another, but are interdependent for their individuality. Thus nothing is an absolute or center of the world, because everything is an absolute and a center of the world. Things are relative and relational to *tao* in the sense that they, each of them, are part of *tao* and each of them come about by way of self- and mutual transformation. On the basis of *tao* there is no limitation to the process of self- and mutual transformation, and *tao* is itself a whole which exemplifies self- and mutual transformation. Because of this, no individuation and differentiation of things is absolute and yet there is no simple undifferentiated homogeneity.

From the point of view of *tao*, an individual is both *tao* and not *tao*. It is *tao* because it is an exemplification of the self-transformation of *tao*; it is not *tao* because it is not the totality. This principle of self- and mutual transformation, as we have indicated earlier, establishes the fundamental equality of things. It applies, furthermore, to the life of man. On recognizing the relativity and relationality of things, man could detach himself from any specific perspective of things and thus open his mind to all the possible perspectives and possibilities which are manifested in things. This attitude will lead him to a natural and spontaneous life, even when facing hardships and disasters. Chuang Tzu does not regard this attitude as one of recession and passivity, but rather as a natural positive result of understanding *tao*. To positively understand *tao* is to become *tao* and to adopt the perspective of *tao*, and thus to realize the centrality of everything. In this manner one will become creative, in the sense that one is open to all possibilities of becoming, and free, in the sense that one will not be attached to any single fixed position. We might suggest that the Taoism of Chuang Tzu has made freedom and creativity the goal of man's life, besides naturalness and spontaneity.

The Tradition of Chinese Buddhism

A third important tradition in Chinese philosophy is Chinese Buddhism. We must distinguish Chinese Buddhism from Buddhism in China. The latter is an Indian importation, but the former is the product of the native intelligence of the Chinese in the later stages of the development of Buddhism in China. An interesting fact, often overlooked in the discussion of Chinese Buddhism, is that there are two schools of Chinese Buddhism which have corresponding Indian predecessors, whereas there are two other schools of Chinese Buddhism which do not have corresponding Indian predecessors and which can be regarded as having developed or evolved from the two other schools, transcending them in significance and profundity. The first two schools of Chinese Buddhism are the Madhymika and Yogacara, and the second two, the T'ien-t'ai and Hua-yen. We shall first discuss briefly how the two later schools overshadow the two earlier ones by advancing concepts which are typical of Chinese Buddhism, and then how these two schools can be considered to combine theoretically to lead to a novel position which has exercised a powerful influence in later ages, especially on the Ch'an Buddhism of Hui-neng and the other Ch'an masters after him.

In Madhymika, the essential idea is that one has to go beyond both affirmation of this and the affirmation of not-this in order to reach the state of non-attachment and transcendence characteristic of Buddhist wisdom. But this logic of the denial of the four terms (this, that, this and that, neither this nor that), when applied to ontology, will entail a concept of constant and infinite detachment and negation. This process, however, is difficult to reconcile with the actual experience of order and stability in which man finds himself. T'ien-t'ai was apparently developed from a concern with this type of problem, namely, a concern with the problem of man's relationship with this world.

In the T'ien-t'ai literature the negative attitude of constantly transcending this and that is combined with a positive attitude toward seeing the meaningfulness of affirming this and that. The proposition that this world is nothingness and thus to be denounced is supplemented with the proposition that nothingness is this world, and thus to be accepted in this world. The upshot of this, as far as the T'ien-t'ai Buddhist thinker is concerned, is that to denounce the world is to accept the world and that to accept the world is to denounce it, for one can denounce what is denounceable of the world and one can accept what is acceptable of the world. The world is thus seen as both denounceable and acceptable, both affirmable and negatable. It is thus held that truth is twofold and yet remains one unity. Now we must ask how this is possible. The answer is very simple, for the world is seen from a dialectical point of view, and therefore is seen as a dynamic unity of two opposing and yet complementing polarities. One may note that classical Chinese philosophy provided a model for this dialectical thinking in Taoism and the *Book of Changes*.

The course of the theoretical development from the Yogacara school to the Hua-yen school seems to follow a similar pattern. In the original teaching of Yogacara the whole world is regarded as a projection of the ideational activity of a trans-this-worldly mind or potential consciousness called *alaya*. The assumption of this all-powerful mind or consciousness goes together with the assumption of the ideational attachment of this mind, which accounts for the existence of the world. In other words, the world is regarded as a concomitant reality resulting from the activity of mind. Thus the cycle of life and death will not cease if the ideational activity of mind continues and persists. One of the ultimate goals of the Yogacara doctrine is to show ways of terminating the activities of life and death by terminating the activities of mind, and to show ways of withholding the reality of the world by withholding the reality of mind. Now this view is again incompatible with the human experience of the goodness of life, as well as that of the continuity of the world's existence. Perhaps it is because of a need to resolve this incompatibility that the school of Hua-yen comes to advance the doctrine that the world can be seen in a manifold of ways and that wisdom and true salvation consist in actually seeing the world in a manifold of ways.

Thus, according to Tu Shun, the first master of the Hua-yen school, the world is simultaneously a unity of every principle with every particular, a unity of every principle with every principle, a harmony of particulars, and finally a unity of every particular with every particular. All this means that the world is infinitely rich and real at the same time, and that mind should open its eyes to this rich and real world which is not bound by the attachment of ideation. By further holding that all is in one and one is in all, it is clear that the Hua-yen school must regard mind as a principle and as a particular which is present in all other principles and all other particulars, and vice versa. This principle of ontological interdependence and interrelationship thus serves to restore reality to both mind and world by restoring the primordial unity of the two. This principle has also the implication that the subjective and the objective must be interdependent in a reality of infinite harmony, so that both necessarily contribute to a knowledge of the real. The possibility of this thinking again has to be understood in the light of the dialectical point of view developed in Taoism and the *Book of Changes*.

Next we come to the development of Ch'an Buddhism in Chinese philosophy. As we have indicated, and to express it from the viewpoint of analytical reconstruction, Ch'an Buddhism can best be described as the final and finest product of the tradition of Chinese Buddhism preceding it. This means that Ch'an has the best of the T'ien-t'ai tradition on understanding the problem of nothingness (*kung*, sunyata), and the best of the Hua-yen tradition on understanding the problem of mind (*hsin* or consciousness) . . . In the above we have explained the fundamental points of these two schools. From this explanation one can readily see that the T'ien-t'ai school has developed an ontology of nothingness which nevertheless confers meaningfulness on the existence and reality of this world and preserves the phenomenological reality of mind, whereas the Hua-yen school has developed a phenomenology of mind or consciousness which recognizes and affirms the ontological reality of the world. Both have indicated a possibility of unifying ontology and phenomenology in regard to the reality of this world and of the mind of man. They point to the same direction, even though they begin from the different points of view of their respective background philosophies.

This possibility of unifying ontology with phenomenology with regard to the reality of the world and man, that is, of unifying the ontological reality of the world and the phenomenological activity of mind, is actually and explicitly realized by the teachings and practice of Ch'an Buddhism. For according to the teachings and practices of Ch'an, when one sees the true nature and the original mind of oneself, one will realize ultimate reality and becomes enlightened, in the sense of ceasing to be bound by attachment, prejudice, and illusion of any kind. This of course does not mean that one loses one's mind or denies the existence of the world. On the contrary, it is important to keep one's mind and to affirm the existence of the world in order for a Ch'an Buddhist to achieve enlightenment. For it is only by holding to one's mind and affirming the existence of the world that one will be free from the bondage of one's mind and of the world. To use the Buddhist idiom, there is *nirvana* (freedom) in one's actual life, and there is actual life in *nirvana*.

The above dialectical combination is not only realized in an act of enlightenment, it is also embodied in the practical performance of one's life. Or, to put it another way, the act of enlightenment is not, and cannot be, separate from the actual living of one's life. Even language cannot be considered intelligible in its own terms apart from living contexts. In fact, for the Ch'an Buddhist, use of language represents many aspects of reality and results from the interaction of all possibilities in reality. Thus language and its uses have many functions apart from that of stating, arguing, or making a verbal point. While language can normally make a point by stating a point, it can be used to make a point by not stating a point, or by verbally denying that point which it is making. The complex ways in which Ch'an masters use language to express enlightenment or to awaken enlightenment deserves careful analysis and explication. Such an analysis and explication will not only be significant for revealing the simple and yet profound character of Ch'an thinking, but will testify to the potential nature of language and its use. In fact, for the Ch'an masters, use of language is not the only way to induce or express enlightenment; many other ways, such as various physical bodily actions, can be the inspiration.

What is important to note in connection with this is that every action of man has an ontological meaning which is phenomenologically transparent and a phenomenological meaning which is ontologically hidden. The insight of Ch'an is to reveal the hidden and to assimilate the transparent in the simple ways of creative living and self-awareness. There is really nothing mystical or irrational in it, as sometimes claimed by outsiders who have only a superficial grasp of the spirit of Ch'an Buddhism and its historical background. What is relevant here is the natural wish to preserve the world but without confining the meaning of the world to one level of categorial understanding, which is also a message conveyed in both Taoism and the *Book of Changes*.

Man, being essentially an embodiment of *tao* or Buddha-nature, has every reason to claim an ability to realize and achieve *tao* and/or Buddha-nature in his conscious active life. The ontological relationship between knowing and doing or acting should easily lead to the doctrine of instantaneous enlightenment in Ch'an Buddhism. The instantaneousness of enlightenment is a dynamic unification of the objective with the subjective, that is, of the known object with the knowing subject.

Marxism in Contemporary China

Finally we come to the position of Marxism as a representative school of thought in contemporary China. Since China entered the twentieth century there has been a constant search among Chinese intellectuals for an enduring philosophy which will accommodate and adjust the Chinese mind, life, and culture to the needs of the modern world as shaped by Western science, religion, and technology with all its merits and drawbacks. In the turmoil of political, economic, and social upheavals in China, there was little time for analysis and evaluation of the past and for planning, construction, and anticipating the future. There was, in addition, little time for synthesizing the past with the present, the West with the East. There was time only for growing discontent with the past and for rejecting it in favor of something which could become an agent of practical change and transformation. This should suffice to explain the rise of Marxism in China in the early twenties and the general failure of the Chinese intellectuals to make the transition from the past to the future a smooth one.

Clearly, Chinese Marxism is a breakaway from traditional Chinese philosophy as we have discussed it under Confucianism, Taoism, and Chinese Buddhism. Yet it shares with the traditional views its pragmatic orientation toward social and political actions. With the rise of Marxism in contemporary China, the reconciliation of Marxist principles with past philosophical traditions becomes a theoretical-ideological problem as well as a cultural-realistic problem. Though we cannot probe here the problem of intellectual continuity in contemporary Chinese thinking, one thing is increasingly clear—Chinese Marxists have made sporadic yet systematic efforts to interpret or re-interpret Confucianism, Taoism, and Chinese Buddhism in terms of the Marxist ideology, and to evaluate them accordingly. In doing this, however, they have also exposed themselves to doctrines of the past which are bound to renew their influences on current thinking. In other words, in the present context, the language and mentality of earlier doctrines in Chinese philosophy will continue to function and interact with the language and mentality of Marxism. What will ensue from this type of interaction is something which is difficult to predict. Perhaps with a reassertion of what is best in the past, the significance of Chinese philosophy for the modern world will be gradually recognized. Chinese Marxism, therefore, at the present stage represents a test and trial of the true potential of Chinese philosophy to meet the needs of man.

Four Characteristics of Chinese Philosophy

In light of our discussion we can now formulate four distinctive characteristics of Chinese philosophy. Our problem is not to evaluate Chinese philosophy, but to describe it in the most relevant terms. This description and characterization of Chinese philosophy can be regarded as a conclusion based on a comprehensive reflection on the nature of Chinese philosophy. It may also be regarded as a result of our reconstructive analysis of the important traditions in Chinese philosophy. They are formulated here to represent only the major, not all, the characteristics of Chinese philosophy. They are sufficient, however, to provide a basis for further inquiry into the nature and significance of Chinese philosophy, and to capture and manifest both the dialectic and problematic of Chinese philosophy as a whole.

Chinese Philosophy as Intrinsic Humanism

Although there can be many versions of humanism, humanisms can be conveniently divided into the extrinsic and the intrinsic. Most humanistic thinking in the West is extrinsic, whereas the humanism in Chinese philosophy is intrinsic. In Greek as well as Renaissance philosophy the existence of man and his power of reason are given a unique place in the scheme of things. But with the background of a transcendental religion (be it Orphic or Christian) and a speculative metaphysics (be it Platonic or Thomist) which distinguishes between the natural and the supernatural, man and God, the subjective and the objective, mind (or soul or spirit) and body in an absolute sense, the affirmation of the value of man tends to be made at the expense of the value of that which is contrasted with man, be it the natural or the supernatural. That is, the affirmation of the value of man entails either a denunciation or a neutralization of the value of that which is contrasted with man or the value of man.

Thus, as a consequence of Renaissance humanism, the Western mind is guided by an interest in the exaltation of man toward exploring, utilizing, and controlling nature as an inanimate object and as a means for achieving human power, thus contributing directly to the development of modern science. But when science has grown to a respectable stature, humanism is regarded as too subjective and limited in dealing with nature and thus, dispensable in virtue of truly scientific interests. This is so because in the light of scientific achievement, not only has nature been deprived of human meaningfulness and considered value-neutral, but human beings are themselves treated as objects of scientific investigation, subject to a methodology which regards value purely as an invention of man. This is the unavoidable result of a humanism which begins with the extrinsic assumption that man and nature are different and therefore in opposition.

The modern revolt against this scientific mentality in existentialism is no less extrinsic, for it stresses the absolute subjectivity of man as a humanistic principle to the exclusion of objective and physical nature. This leads to a depth-psychology of man which is no less frustrating and humiliating.

The philosophical assumption that nature is intrinsic to the existence of man and man intrinsic to the existence of nature, is the foundation of Chinese humanism. Here there is no such absolute bifurcation between the objective and the subjective, mind and body, man and God. The reason for this is not, of course, that the bifurcation has failed to be made, but that it should not be made from the viewpoint of Chinese philosophy. In all the major traditions and schools of Chinese philosophy it is considered important that man and nature or reality should be seen as forming a unity and harmony, just as man himself is a unity and harmony of mind and body. There is, furthermore, no separation of the natural from the supernatural, if indeed we can regard the pre-Chin conceptions of *ti* (lord on high), *t'ien* (heaven), and *tao* (the way) as supernatural conceptions at all. Body and mind mutually determine and define each other to constitute the existence of man, who interacts with everything else in the world, to grow and develop into an ideal perfection which has both anthropological and cosmological significance. Perhaps because there is no fundamental division between mind (or soul) and body in man, the fundamental category relating to the existence of man and to the value of his existence is 'life' (*sheng*), which applies to nature as well as to the creative activity of *tao* or heaven.

Chinese Philosophy as Concrete Rationalism

Rationalism is the belief that truth can be obtained by man through use of his reason. In fact, the rationalistic tradition in Western philosophy has distinguished truths of reason from truths of fact. Truths of reason are truths known independently of experience and therefore *a priori*, whereas truths of fact are founded on sense experience and therefore *a posteriori*. Now, this conception of truths of reason is related to two basic suppositions in rationalistic philosophy: first, reason is innate in man and man will naturally come to understand the truths of reason through rational reflection, since these truths are inherent in reason; and secondly, truths of reason are considered more certain and noble than truths of fact and are therefore considered paradigms of human knowledge. Logic, mathematics and even theoretical physics are taken as examples of truths of reason in Western rationalism. Even in ethics and metaphysics truths of reason have been the focus of attention, and only relatively recently has rationalism in the above sense been subject to severe criticism and doubt.

It is clear that the most significant characteristic of Western rationalism is the belief that man's rational faculty of abstraction and deduction is able to establish abstract and universal principles of knowledge. As the faculty of reason is fundamentally discrete from experience, so truths of reason are fundamentally discrete from truths of fact or experience. Western rationalism may therefore be called a rationalism of abstract reason, or of reason in its abstract use.

Chinese philosophy, on the other hand, is rationalistic not in an abstract, but in a concrete sense. The Chinese philosopher recognizes man as a rational being who is endowed with a rational faculty for knowing truths. This derives from the belief that man is in unity with nature and that nature in its development culminates in man as a being full of creative potential. That man may naturally come to know reality, or the way, is just a step in the development of the creative potential of man. Reality, in the sense of heaven or the Way, as man sees it, is a rational order displayed in concrete things which can be seen and understood by man in his inquiries. Since there is no original demarcation between the objective and the subjective, the subjective in man naturally corresponds to the objective in nature. This may be regarded as a metaphysical article of faith, but it has the virtue of ruling out epistemological puzzles about knowledge of the external world and other minds. Hence there are no doctrines of solipsism and scepticism in Chinese philosophy.

There are three fundamental senses in which we may define the concrete use of concrete reason in Chinese philosophy. In the first place, man has to open his eyes to reality and observe activities and patterns of things. It is on the basis of empirical observation and experience at large that the philosophy of change, in terms of interchange of *yin* and *yang*, is developed in the *Book of Changes*. Furthermore, one can see from the use of language in the Classics that the terms for ultimate reality, such as *t'ien* and *tao*, are not general and abstract terms capable of logical definition, but terms with a universal yet concrete content, to be understood by means of direct and diverse experience.

Similarly in ethics, we see that in Confucianism ideas of virtue are closely related to the experience of basic sentiments. If we compare Mencius's doctrine of immediate feelings as the beginnings of virtues with Kant's doctrine of the categorical imperative, we can readily see that sentiments of virtue are concrete realizations of experience in concrete situations, whereas commands of the categorical imperative are abstract deductions of reason. Thus, whereas there is no practical problem of applying Confucian virtues, applying the Kantian categorical imperative to concrete situations does present a difficult problem. But on the other hand, whereas Kantian ethics has a deductive structure and a rational justification, there is comparatively little systematic organization for the moral insights in the Confucian writings. Even though Mencius speaks of man's innate knowledge of goodness (the so-called *liang-chih*), *liang-chih* is not taken to be a faculty which enables man to arrive at moral injunctions, but an ability to distinguish between good and bad in concrete situations. Thus concrete reason in Confucian philosophy does not straightforwardly correspond to Kantian practical reason, nor for that matter, does Confucian abstract reason correspond straightforwardly to Kantian pure reason, for concrete reason, as typified in Chinese philosophy, not only deals with practical problems but guarantees the ultimate connection of reason with practice. This leads to the second sense of concrete rationalism.

Chinese philosophy is generally oriented toward action and practice in society and government, and aims at the reform and perfection of man and the world. It stresses, furthermore, that theory must be applied to practice or be considered merely empty words. In the extreme case of Wang Yang-ming, theory and practice are considered two ends of the same thing. This means that theoretical understanding must entail practical doing, and in practical doing of any kind one will acquire knowledge and wisdom of oneself and the world. In light of this characteristic of Chinese philosophy, which we shall discuss more below, concrete rationalism simply means that one has to attain moral perfection through a process of self-cultivation and of concrete realization of knowledge in practice. In practice, this process is not merely a rational activity of reason, for it manifests reasonableness in life and in the attainment of an ideal of perfection. Indeed, contrasting the ideal of pure rationality in abstract reason with that of natural reasonableness in concrete reason is a way of accentuating the characteristic of Chinese philosophy under discussion.

Finally, the third sense of concrete reason in Chinese philosophy is that it is primarily directed toward moral and political goals. Even ontological and cosmological speculations are not without moral and political significance. *Li* (principle, reason), in Neo-Confucianism for example, is a concretely rational ideal and idea. *Li* is not something divorced from man's basic life-experience in relation to himself, other men, and things; it is taken to be the basis for achieving social harmony and administering political order.

Perhaps it is the lack of any differentiation between the abstract principles of rationality and concrete instances of reasonableness in Chinese thinking that has prevented the abstract cultivation of such pure sciences as logic and mathematics, and explains why Chinese thinkers do not consider philosophy itself a deductive rational activity but a synthetic moral achievement capable of influencing the actions of men.

Chinese Philosophy as Organic Naturalism

Naturalism is an important feature of Chinese philosophy, since the Chinese world-view is basically this-worldly rather than other-worldly. In fact, as noted earlier, the dichotomy between man and God, the natural and the supernatural, does not exist in Chinese philosophy. There are, consequently, no arguments between transcendentalism and immanentism in Chinese philosophy. Every form of reality is considered a process of change and development in nature. As we have seen in the case of Taoism, the potentiality for change and transformation is in the nature of things, which means that individual things do not have static substances, and are not unrelated to one another as individual entities, but mutually determine and define one another in a dynamic process of change within the context of organic relationships.

Organic naturalism in Chinese philosophy is perhaps better described in consideration of the relation between the objective and the subjective, and between the physical and the mental. Chinese philosophers consider these in terms of natural correspondence, interdependence, and complementation, in which life and understanding can be achieved and preserved. In fact, the relationships in question might even be thought of, from a general viewpoint, as continuities, for there is no real break between physical and mental, objective and subjective. Ontologically and cosmologically speaking, the objective and the subjective, and the physical and the mental are transparent to *tao* as the ultimate reality and therefore parts of a total dynamic process.

The organic relationships between man and society and State constitute further evidence for organic naturalism in Chinese philosophy. In Confucianism, man is a relational being who depends upon other men for the cultivation and perfection of himself. In Taoist, and even in Chinese Buddhistic doctrines, man is relational to all things, but has to interact with and participate in the activities of *tao* in order to be good and perfect. He is not simply to identify himself with *tao*. In this context of organic relationships among men and between man and things, harmony and harmonization are the key words, and harmony and harmonization are possible only if there are organic relationships of unity in variety. Chinese philosophy provides a serious elaboration of such relationships as a basis upon which 'goodness' can be conceived as essentially the ability to achieve and preserve harmony.

Chinese Philosophy as the Pragmatism of Self-Cultivation

As has been generally indicated, Chinese philosophy has been concerned from the very beginning with the practical question of advancing the well-being of the individual and the order and harmony of society and State. The moral ideas of Confucius and other Confucian thinkers clearly manifest this mentality. Even in the Taoist philosophy of Lao Tzu there is a concern for the best form of governnment. The principle of doing everything by doing nothing is both a cosmological principle of the *tao*, and a political principle of a *tao* inspired ruler. The practicality of Chinese Buddhism and Chinese Marxism in the contemporary scene needs no special elaboration, for it is clear that Chinese Buddhism has aimed at the practical solution of fundamental problems in life, and that Chinese Marxism has aimed at the practical solution of social and political problems in China. What is noteworthy is that no philosophical school and no philosophical thinker in China regards philosophy as a mere speculative activity. Chinese philosophy has a special dimension which we may call 'self-realization by means of philosophical self-cultivation'.

In both Confucianism and Taoism a special branch of studies has been developed which may be called 'theory of self-cultivation' or 'theory of self-realization'. In the Confucian writings specifically, the *Great Learning (Chung Yung)* has formulated eight steps of self-cultivation, with harmonization of the world as its ultimate goal. The first two steps, investigating things and extending knowledge, are directed toward the goal of understanding the world. The next three steps, making sincere one's intentions, rectifying one's mind and cultivating or improving one's person, are directed toward the goal of perfecting oneself within, so that one can be ready for social and political responsibility in order to better others. The last three steps, regulating a family, governing a State well, and pacifying the world, are directed toward extending one's virtues among men so that one can be said to realize one's potentiality in a reality of relationships.

There are two essential features in this process of self-cultivation and self-realization. First, the process is one of extension from individual perfection to the perfection of all men; secondly, it is one of unifying one's internal attainment with one's external efficaciousness. This process has been termed the unification of 'sageliness within and kingliness without' (*nei-sheng wai-wang*). It seems clear that Confucianism has perfectly exemplified this ideal of self-cultivation with reference to the perfection of others. It is not so clear how Taoism and Chinese Buddhism can be said to be pragmatic in this regard. Chinese Buddhism offers pragmatic instructions for attaining the salvation of the whole through the self-cultivating efforts of the individual. Although Taoism remains basically individualistic, nevertheless in the case of Lao Tzu, the ideal ruler who preserves the well-being of all must be a follower of *tao*. It is also an historical fact that Taoist principles have suggested to later political craftsmen various practical measures in dealing with the problems of State and society, as exemplified in the writings of Han Fei Tzu.

It is generally held that in Chinese philosophy man is capable of reaching the ultimate and highest state of perfection, be it called sagehood, true manhood, or Buddhahood. In other words, man is capable of generating the highest form of good without needing to look beyond and transcend his own world. Thus, the pragmatism of self-cultivation in Chinese philosophy provides a substitute for the worship and dependence upon a supreme god. The moral philosophy underlying this pragmatism of self-cultivation can thus be said to perform for the Chinese mind the function performed in the West by religion, but without suffering from the dogmatism of Western religion. The religious import and autonomy of morality in this pragmatism of self-cultivation is possible also on many other grounds, none of which is not covered, however, by what we have said about the intrinsic humanism, concrete rationalism, and organic naturalism of Chinese philosophy.

Conclusion

In the preceding, we have made a synthetic characterization of Chinese philosophy based on an analytical reconstruction of its main traditions and thought. There are three main traditions in Chinese philosophy: Confucianism, Taoism and Chinese Buddhism. All three have interacted and shared something in common in their historical and theoretical developments. We have noted that Chinese Marxism developed as a result of the Western impact upon China in recent times. In light of our discussion of the archetypal ideas in the pre-Confucian period, we can see that Confucianism and Taoism have in fact shared the same origin and source, and in a sense mutually define and complement each other. This view should fit well with the dialectical metaphysics of *yin* and *yang* accepted by both Confucianism and Taoism.

We have described four characteristics of Chinese philosophy. The first and the last, intrinsic humanism and the pragmatism of self-cultivation, deal primarily with moral, social, and political aspects of Chinese thinking, whereas the second and third, concrete rationalism and organic naturalism, deal primarily with the metaphysical and epistemological aspects. But we must remember that the moral and socio-political aspects of Chinese thought are internally and dialectically intertwined, for the moral and socio-political thinking has metaphysics as its basis, whereas metaphysical and epistemological thinking, on the other hand, always has moral practice and socio-political improvement as its goal. It is clear from our discussion that these four features of Chinese philosophy are interrelated and mutually supporting, and are thus best understood in the context of one another.

We have not dealt with every branch of Chinese philosophy. Thus we did not dwell on Neo-Confucianism as a special development of Classical Confucianism under Chinese Buddhistic influences. But if we looked into

Neo-Confucianism, we would see that, like the other main traditions of Chinese philosophy, it possesses the same four features.

Something else we have omitted is a discussion of the philosophical problems resulting from the acceptance of the perspective of Chinese philosophy as we have characterized it. If Chinese philosophy can be said to be broadly based on the principles of the unity of man and nature, of reality as a process of dialectical interchange between *yin* and *yang*, of the non-bifurcation between objective and subjective, mind and body, and abstract and concrete, and of the perfection of the totality through the self-cultivation of the individual, there are bound to be questions regarding how Chinese philosophy is to face the problems of the need for transcendence, the origin of evil, and the nature of logic and of theoretical knowledge in science. We will also be led to ask how Chinese philosophical principles can be reconciled with existing doctrines of transcendence, evil, logic and theoretical knowledge in the Western tradition. Our discussion has deliberately left these questions open. If Chinese philosophy serves to make us critically aware of these problems and to provide alternative ways of thinking, we are more than justified in presenting it as a philosophy of universal concern and comprehensive significance.

2. A Model of Causality in Chinese Philosophy: A Comparative Study

Two Levels of Understanding

Causality, like other related terms such as 'law', 'time', 'space', 'motion' and 'force' in philosophy of science, is a difficult concept. Even after philosophical discussion on it has been carried on for over two millennium, no ready, explicit and uniformly accepted definition or description of the concept has been reached. A very recent symposium on causation has revealed much disagreement on the explaining of causality.[1] I believe that part of the difficulty of defining or describing causality stems from the fact that two levels for understanding causality are not always clearly distinguished.

The two levels for understanding causality are, on the one hand, the phenomenal or experiential level where causality can be understood as a certain experiential or observable relation, and, on the other, the theoretical or conceptual level where causality can be understood only subject to a theory or theoretical philosophy which serves to explain as well as justify causality in an observational or experiential sense. When Hume suggests his view on causality—"We may define a cause to be an object followed by another, and where all the objects, similar to the first, as followed by objects, similar to the second. Or, in other words, where, if the first object had not been, the second never had existed."[2]—he seems to confuse two senses of causation without knowing it. In the first definition he offers a phenomenal or observational concept of causation, but in the second definition, which he thinks is equivalent to the first, he has implicitly introduced a theoretical explanation of causation understood in the observational sense. He attempts to challenge metaphysical views on causality with his empirical-phenomenal definition of causality, but leaves his own theoretical concept of it unexplained. Of course, he has an explicit psychological explanation of causation, which, however, is not intended to explain the second definition of causation, but rather to explain a third view of causation, namely, what we ordinarily experience as causation as exemplified by one object causing another to move or change in a certain fashion, as if the cause has the moving power. This third view can be rephrased as suggesting that causation is causal efficacy inherent in the nature of objects. This view is the traditional Western view dating back to Aristotle. It is the view that causation is the process where one object acts on another and efficiently creates a new state for the other. The first object (or rather the action of the first object) is called the efficient cause of the causation and the created new state of the second object is called the effect of causation.

Granted Hume's observation that causation is nothing more than the constant conjunction of two ideas, it is natural and reasonable to ask whether there is any objective or rational basis for such a conjunction. In fact, Hume is open to two kinds of challenges. The first challenge asks: Is causal efficacy merely a matter of psychological propensity toward the association of two constantly conjuncted ideas? The second challenge raises the question of the importance of psychological causation independently of psychological explanation.

It seems that the datum of constant conjunction must be explained so that one may say that not any sort of thing may be constantly conjuncted with any other sort. Either our experience of the world or the structure of the world or both must provide a restricting condition for the actual conjunction of things which our experience has discovered. This is certainly not an irrational demand. In fact, Hume himself has subconsciously answered to this demand by providing a second definition of causation in the passage we have quoted. After Hume, there are many philosophers who have provided objective and/or subjective conditions for causation. Notably, Kant has explained causation as a category of human understanding which is not a psychological state but a transcendental condition of the intelligibility of scientific knowledge. Whitehead and others[3] have pointed out that we not only observe causation as a matter of conjunction between objects of two similarity classes, but also we observe the relation of causation as real. This relation is one of acting on impact, or efficient inducement, such as one witnesses in the striking of the match to cause fire. What is observed in such cases is aptly described by Whitehead as the mode of *causal efficacy*.

In this article it is not my purpose to examine various explanations of causation in the post-Humean tradition of Western philosophy. My purpose is to bring about, explicate and explain causality from the point of view of

Chinese philosophy, particularly from the point of view of classical Chinese thought. What I have said earlier is relevant for achieving this purpose, for I assume that Hume's empirical and phenomenal definition of causation is quite compatible with that of the Chinese philosopher. This provides a common denomination for a comparative philosophical study on causality. Given this, one will be able to see that there exist important and great gaps between Chinese philosophy and Western philosophy in their respective theoretical explanations of causation. As the Chinese view is no less a theoretical view than any of the Western ones, the merits of each must be justified in some objective terms in a comprehensive framework. In my discussion I will use the term "causality" as indicating theoretical explanations and interpretations of causation in an empirical and observational sense, thus causality entails causation but not vice versa.

Standard Model of Causality in Western Philosophy

For the purpose of contrasting the Chinese approach to causality, I will sketch a standard model of causality (theory of causation) in Western science in the eighteenth century. This model is called standard because it seems to underlie the mechanistic physics as developed by Newton, which in that period was generally accepted by the scientific community as the paradigm of natural knowledge. This model seems also to underlie the scientific thinking of most scientists today and the common sense world view of the Western laymen. The latter is true, because, as we shall see, it is derived from the same background source from which modern mechanistic science has derived its own inspiration. This same source forms a metaphysical background for the common sense outlook of the world. One may even suggest that modern science and its model of causality are expressions of the refined product of the main trends of Western metaphysics and civilization.

The standard model of causality in the Western philosophy of science has the following constituents:

1. The world in which causality prevails consists of numerous discrete individual objects or substances which, if conceived statically, are independent of one another.
2. The world in which individual objects or substances reside can be identified with the conjunction of absolute time and absolute space of Newtonian physics. But time and space are not integrated as a manifold as in Einstein's relativity.
3. Motion of objects in the world is possible when external force is applied from one object to another.

4. It is assumed that there are motions in the world which follow strict and precise laws quantitatively describable by physics.

Given this model, we may describe the law of causality as requiring that (A) every object in the world is causally determined by things prior to it in time. This means that these other things prior to a given thing are conditions for the existence of the given thing; and that (B) every given motion is made possible by a temporally prior motion. Both (A) and (B) can be made more precise. Regarding (A), one can distinguish between necessary and sufficient conditions for the existence of a thing. A thing X is a necessary condition for the existence of another thing Y, if given Y there must be X, or without X the existence of Y is impossible. A thing X is a sufficient condition for the existence of another thing Y, if the existence of X entails the existence of Y, or without Y the existence of X is impossible. Thus it has been generally suggested that we can define the cause of a thing as follows: the cause of a thing E is that set of conditions (things), which within the totality of those other conditions, existed as individually necessary and jointly sufficient for E[4]. This logical way of describing causation in terms of necessary and sufficient conditions of cause apparently does not exhaust the meaning of the law of causality, for it does not tell us how a set of conditions becomes the cause of a thing. Thus we must recognize the relevance of the motion or power of motion which enables one set of conditions to he necessary and sufficient for the *bringing about* of another thing. This is the intent of (B). (B) can be reformulated as requiring that in order for a set of conditions to be a cause, it must be individually necessary and jointly sufficient to produce a motion (or impact) or to act on another thing to produce a motion. A cause must cause its effect through some form of motion which is prior in time to the formation of its effect.

The law of causality thus can be said to involve at least three things: (1) sufficiency and necessity of conditions; (2) efficacy (of motion and force); (3) priority in time.[5] This standard model of causality seems to require that each causation can be subsumed in a general law and that all things in the world are related or ordered by such general laws. In fact these laws are considered to characterize the nature of things in the world, even though things themselves are so many kinds or types of irreducible individual substances or objects. This model further holds that it is the function of scientific investigation, experimentation and observation to discover these causal laws of things and that we are able to make these discoveries. It is not difficult to see that one can talk of events instead of objects, and of the occurrence of events instead of the existence of objects in the account of laws of causation.

Ontological Presuppositions of Laws of Causation

From the above analysis we can see that the standard model of causaltry involves a description of causal laws (or laws of causation) and a world picture in which the laws of causation hold. One might conclude from this that this model is predicated on the following philosophical principles which form the ontological background of this model. (1) Principle of discreteness: Substances are discrete entities. (2) Principle of externality: Laws of causation are laws externally governing things. One would say that things conform to laws or are determined by laws. Laws are not exactly what things are. (3) Principle of external source of motion: If the world is not a static one and motions are actual, not merely possible, the laws of causation lead to the positing of an ultimate cause, which has been called by Aristotle the Unmoved Mover. The Unmoved Mover or God is the source that gives initial movement to things. Later Western philosophers have alternatively conceived that God provides the continual motion of things. But even without this assumption it seems that the initial motion or energy as imparted by God is sufficient to explain the movement of things according to causal laws, as the principle of the conservation of energy in mechanics may sustain the given motions without losing energy.

Combined with the picture of an Unmoved Mover, the model of causality, as one can now see, is made possible simply because God has created a world of things governed by laws of causation. God can be made responsible for the creation of such laws. Thus the ultimate explanation of the model, the world, the causal law, and the motion may be traced to God as an infinite existence. Yet this notion of God implies that God is no less a principle of externality to things than are causal laws. For God is not governed by causal laws nor is he a member of the things in the world.

It is clear from the above that the transcendental theology of the Judeo-Christian tradition and the Democritean mechanistic model of atoms combined together to form a standard model of causality which underlies modern science. I will not try to explain how these two traditions—perhaps, plus the Roman Law tradition as another principle of externality—provide historical-genetical grounds for the development of this standard model. I will assume that science would not be possible in the West without these cultural traditions as its intellectual background. One can also see that, when the model of causality is fully formulated, one perhaps need not pay attention to the existence of God. This explains the development of nineteenth-century materialism based on this model of causality. According to this philosophical development, the sources of energy and motion are to be sought in the discrete things themselves.

Model of Causality: A Chinese Approach

A fundamental assertion in Chinese metaphysical thinking is that all things arise from one source in a natural and spontaneous way. The dominating question for all Chinese philosophical schools is to explain how things and human beings are properly placed in the scheme of the totality of things which arise from the same origin. These concerns may appear to be simple enough to understand, but also they bear profound consequences for the ontological and methodological orientation of Chinese philosophy and the Chinese mind in general. One of these consequences is that Chinese thinkers as a whole have not developed the atomistic-mechanistic model of causality of the Western philosophical tradition, nor have they evolved any idea of causal law like the Western scientific and philosophical descriptions. But this does not entail that the Chinese thinkers have not developed or evolved any views regarding causality in an empirical and observational sense. On the contrary, Chinese thinkers have concentrated so much on causality in the empirical and observational sense that they have evolved and developed their theoretical and metaphysical outlook (or explanation) as basically congenial and continuous with their experience of causation. In this sense the theoretical and metaphysical outlook (or explanation) of causality is concrete and directly open to experience, to the effect that empirical and observable experience seems to be a direct manifestation of the underlying reality of causality. Thus the Humean notion of causality as constant conjunction is to be explained by the objective nature of things, not by an appeal to the psychological propensity of man, as did Hume.

Insofar as the Chinese thinkers have provided a world picture in which the empirical notion of causality could apply, we may say that Chinese philosophy has its model of causality, and yet its model of causality is radically different from the Western model because the world picture or ontological background for the Chinese experience of causality is a different one. Perhaps, in reference to this ontological background, one may even suggest that the experience of causality, namely, causality in an empirical and observational sense, may even have a different meaning than what is suggested by the Humean definition, since Hume's definition of causality may inevitably carry an atomistic-mechanistic assumption about the objects in the world, while there is no such suggestion in the Chinese metaphysics.

Before I describe two important aspects of causality in the Chinese model, I will depict the two main traditions of Chinese philosophy which have evolved the metaphysical outlook underlying the Chinese model of causality. They are respectively Confucian and Taoist. Though there are many differences regarding these two schools in many important areas, they seem to concur on the main metaphysical understanding of the world. This is because they stem from the same source of ontological experience and insight.

The Confucianist World View

It is well known that the Confucianists have regarded Heaven (*t'ien*) as the origin of all things in the world. Heaven created everything, not in the way in which God created everything, but in the sense of generating all things through its internal, rich abundance of life. Heaven is the source of all forms of life. Heaven is also that order and pattern according to which things are created and conform to in their becoming. In this sense Confucianists speak of the Way of Heaven. In a way, Heaven is its Way of functioning, and in the development of this direction Confucianists approximate toward Taoists. There is of course another important aspect of Heaven as the Way: All things generated from Heaven have maintained a certain relation to Heaven and an interrelation with other things. In other words, the inner order of Heaven pervades all things and interrelates them so that all things have their place in the world when they derive their existence from Heaven. This inner order of things is explicitly referred to as the *li* (principle) of things by the Neo-Confucianists. Finally, Heaven continuously imparts its energy and life to things as it is the ultimate reality constantly looming in the background of all things. Heaven, therefore, is not only the initial source for all things but the ground and justification for the continuous existence of all things. In brief, Heaven is immanent in all things and constitutes the very nature of things. This is also true of human existence, for it is said in the *Chung Yung (The Doctrine of the Mean)*: "What is endowed in man by Heaven is nature.[6] In the *Ta-chuan (The Great Appendix)* of the *I Ching (The Book of Changes)*, it is said: "Heaven and Earth have interaction, and all things are thereby germinated, the male and the female have intercourse, and all things are thereby generated."[7]

This basic view regarding the origin of things from the single source of Heaven, and their interrelatedness can be called a *life-ontology*, for the whole world, its inner structure and all the processes of change are conceived after the *paradigm of life*, as man experienced in his own coming to be and becoming as well as in various life-processes in the world. Life is organized in both the time dimension and the space dimension of the universe. Life is not a single part of a whole, but a whole of parts; nor is it an isolated phenomenon which is externally related to external things. For life phenomenon or life experience, an item or part is always internally related to other parts in the whole as well as to the whole as a whole. To say that parts are internally related to one another and to the whole is to say that without relation the parts will not be parts and the whole will not be whole. In this sense, parts and whole are defined in the relationships in which they find themselves. A part is, therefore, unlike an atom which has its essence independently of relations with other things, nor is it like a member of a class, which is a result of abstraction in conceptualization and which is also independent of the existence of the class to which it belongs, as the latter could be granted existence as in Platoism.

The life paradigm is not only restricted to things individually, but extends to the whole world, as the whole world of things is conceived of as resulting from the same source of life, which is Heaven. The whole world under this conception is a great organic whole and unity with internal relational or interrelational structures in both time and space dimensions. For this reason the metaphysical outlook on reality is aptly and frequently referred to as organicism or the philosophy of organism.[8]

The philosophy of organism or life-ontology (or life-metaphysics) in Confucianism is best represented in the metaphysics of the *I Ching*. The original Confucian concept of Heaven gives place to the idea of change. But change is nothing but the continuous production and generation of life (*sheng-sheng*). The process of continuous generation of life is conceived in terms of the *yin-yang* metaphysics. *yin* and *yang* are universally observed and experienced as qualities of things and forces of happenings. They stand for two aspects, two sides, and two polarities of reality. Though *yin* and *yang* are two, they are dynamically one—that is, they pull toward each other and pull away from each other in different cases. In fact, they are not to be conceived of in separation from concrete things and processes. All individual things are composed of *yin* and *yang* forces, but their internal structure as well as their relations to other things are determined by the *yin-yang* distributions and their proportions therein. Both the intra-and interrelations of things are conducive to various forms or directions of change. The totality of things forms the context in which such change will take place.

It is regarding the determinants of change and their structure and relationship to the other things in the fold of all things that a thing finds its proper place in the world. Thus the *Ta-chuan* has explicitly identified this proper place of things as *li* (principles or order and patterns). Such a world is both an order and pattern and a process of change. We can see this combination in the first paragraph of the *Ta-chuan*:

The Heaven is high, the earth is low. Thus the creative and perceptive are determined. In correspondence with this difference between low and high, inferior and superior places are established. Movement and rest have their definite laws. According to these, firm and yielding lines are differentiated. Events follow definite trends, each according to its nature. Things are distinguished from one another in definite classes. In this way good fortune and misfortune come about. In the heavens phenomena take form; on earth shapes take form. In this way changes and transformations become manifest.[9]

From this passage it is clear that order is found in change and change manifests an order. This is the easy (*yi*) knowledge of the *yang* (the creative) and the *simple (ch'ien)* capacity of *yin* (the receptive). When one understands this, one will understand the ultimate rationale of the change of things. The *Ta-chuan* continues: "By means of the easy and the simple we grasp the *princples* under Heaven. When the laws under Heaven are grasped, therein lies its *proper placement* of the principle of things"[10] (italics mine). The so-called *principles* under Heaven and *proper placement* of things are precisely the order and change of things in the content of the interchange between *yin* and *yang*.

The Taoist World View

The Taoists, like the Confucianists, also strongly affirm the unity and singularity of the ultimate source from which all things arise. This ultimate source is called the *Tao* (the Way), which for Lao Tzu and Chuang Tzu cannot be identified with any conceivable or actual determinate being.[11] It is, therefore, referred to as the Void (*wu*) or that which exists above the great ultimate. Like the Confucian notion of Heaven it is continuously present and gives birth to a multitude of things. In *Tao Te Ching (The Book of the Way and the Power)* the statement that "*Tao* gives rise to one, one to two, two to three, and three to the ten thousand things"[12] underlies the fact that all things are derived from *Tao* and that there are a great multitude of things. *Tao*, in other words, is not a static identity but a concrete unity of life-generating processes. The uniformity of all things in activity is also suggested by the statement that "Man follows the ways of Earth, the Earth follows the ways of Heaven, Heaven follows the ways of *Tao*, *Tao* follows its own ways."[13]

In light of the generative power of Tao, one might say that Tao represents the ideal of the ultimate life-source contained in the idea of Heaven and combines with it the idea of order and pattern. It seems to be the natural extreme to which the Heaven idea can be extended. What specifically distinguishes *Tao* from Heaven, by way of accentuating the life-generating process of all things, is as follows:

1. *Tao* does not act and yet all things are created by its nonactivity. This means that *Tao* is the ultimate standard of spontaneity for the creativity of life. The possibility of the life-process and the generation of the multitude of things is explained by this nature of nonactivity. It is something which also unifies everything. This also leads to the idea that all things are self-transformations of the *Tao* which occur by *Tao* itself. This idea has very important consequences for the Chinese model of causality.

2. *Tao* is the source of all things and yet is not separable from things. To understand *Tao* is to understand the individual things themselves. The immanence and universality of Tao are specifically stressed by Chuang Tzu. This also leads to Chuang Tzu's thesis of the relativity of all distinctions that one can find in cosmic, social, perceptual, conceptual, and physical understandings. This, however, is not to deny that all distinctions are unreal because of this, but only means that one must not see distinctions as a hindrance to one's understanding of the conditions of them, that is, the *Tao*, in order to achieve ultimate freedom.

3. Taoists share with the *I Ching* thinkers the dialectical conception of the development of things in accordance with the *Tao*. The same *yin-yang* interchange principle is incorporated into the movement of *Tao* and thus underlies the movements of all things. But Taoists, especially Lao Tzu, tend to conceive of the dialectical movements between the two complementary polarities of *yin* and *yang* as a process of return and reversal. In other words, the return to the source of *Tao* is the motive force for the interchange of *yin* and *yang* and the reversal of a process is initially present in any process of change. On the other hand, the *I Ching* stressed simultaneously the reversal and developmental aspects of things. In Chuang Tzu, the *yin-yang* reversal is not stressed as much as in Lao Tzu. The dialectical movements of *Tao* are strictly the interpenetration of things as well as the mutual and spontaneous transformation of things without particular reference to the return to the source. All categories of happenings are interpreted as subsumed under the inner transformation of *Tao* in its most spontaneous creative moments.

4. Finally, for Lao Tzu, but not necessarily for Chuang Tzu, the movements of *Tao* are to be found in the soft and weak, simple, supple, lowly qualities of things. In fact, life itself is identified with the weak and soft. He says: "When a man is living, he is soft and supple. When he is dead, he becomes hard and rigid. When a plant is living, it is soft and tender. When it is dead, it becomes withered and dry.

Hence, the hard and rigid belong to the company of the dead, the soft and supple belong to the company of the living."[14] Combined with the principle of reversal, it is clear that the soft and weak are more powerful creative forces than the hard and the strong, and thus will lead to the defeat of the hard and the strong.

Chinese Model of Causality: Three Characterizing Principles

Given the earlier ontological and metaphysical description of Heaven and the *Tao*, one may now attempt to construct a picture or model of causality based on such metaphysical and ontological considerations as suggested by the Confucianists and Taoists. We may ask, in the first place, what fundamental principles inherent in the basic concepts and views of Confucian and Taoist metaphysical thought may be formulated for the purpose of constructing a concept of causality in the Chinese (Confucian and Taoist) perspective. Upon close scrutiny and an overall reflection, I think that we can derive the following three principles from the Confucian and Taoist metaphysics, which will lead to a characterization of causality in the Chinese perspective.

There is, in the first place, *a principle of holistic unity*. By this I mean that all things in the world are unified as a whole through their being continuously generated from the same source or origin. One may also say that all things are generatively unified. All things, therefore, are one under the image of *Tao* or Heaven. They all share the same nature and quality of reality. Besides, they are interrelated because they come from the same source, just as in a family. One may see them as belonging to a cosmic family, from a unity of the bipolar forces called Heaven and Earth. The oneness they share (*Tao*) both sustains and gives rise to the multitude of things.

Second, there is the *principle of internal life-movement*. By this I mean that all things in the world have an intrinsic life-force which moves them in a way in which motion is not imposed from other things or a God but is derived from the inexhaustible source of the energy of life, which is the Way. As the source is intrinsically related to an individual thing, the derivation of energy for movement is intrinsic, as in an organism, rather than extrinsic, as in a machine. Similarly, as all things are interrelated to form a network of interchange of processes, the transmission of moving force is conceived of as an exhibition of life activity, in the absence of which the individual things will cease to be defined. A no less important feature of this internal movement source is that the source of the life energy is infinite and inexhaustible, not in the sense that an individual can derive infinite energy from the source, but only in the sense that all things and their changes are ultimately initiated by the source and that there is no end to such a process of change and transformation. This principle of an internal-movement source can also be called the *principle of intrinsic life-growth*.

Finally, there is the *principle of organic balance*. By this I mean that all things and processes in the world are related in processes which proceed toward a balance and a harmony. This, of course, does not mean that when a balance or harmony is reached there will cease to be processes of change and transformation. That, in a certain sense, there is always harmony and balance in the world by the *principle of holistic unity* is not to be denied. Though everything has its proper placement in the whole scheme of things, all the movements, changes, and transformations in the world are activated for production of the same and for higher development. Because life is generated anew, the striving for balance and harmony on a larger plane continues. That we must understand balance and harmony in a dynamical and actual sense is crucial. The *yin-yang* polarities with their contrary and complementary qualities clearly illustrate the example of processes toward the balance and harmony of things.

Apparently, the principles just mentioned are metaphysical in nature. But I wish to point out that they should not be understood as just meta-physical principles, for they should be understood as principles of method-ology as well. In fact, to understand the metaphysics generated from these principles, one must simultaneously understand the way in which the meta-physical conclusions are guided and reached. In this sense they are inevita-bly normative principles of methodology.[15] As a methodological principle, the *principle of holistic unity* legislates that any individual thing must be understood in the whole context which forms its background, source, and network of inter-relations. One may, therefore, call this the *principle of wholeness*. Similarly, the *principle of internal life-movement* asks the thinker to focus always on the movements and changes in the world as natural and spontaneous happenings due to the internal life-force of reality, not to seek explanations in an external final cause. This principle can be method-ologically described as the *principle of internality*. Finally, the *principle of organic balance* in its methodological sense leads one to evaluate things and happenings by considering the negative and positive directions of change so that they may be seen to fit into a reality of balanced rela-tionship. One may therefore simply call this principle the *principle of organicity*. Altogether one may regard the three principles to be method-ological illustrations of a Chinese dialectic of thinking, in the sense that any thinking about things must simultaneously conform to these principles in order to correctly represent reality, as Confucian and Taoist metaphysics depict it.

Given these three principles governing the Confucian and Taoist method and content of metaphysical and cosmological thinking, I may now describe the Chinese model of causality in these terms.

Chinese Model of Causality: Correlative Thinking

It is clear that causality in terms of the three principles just mentioned is quite unlike causality in the Western model. If we may say that the Western model of causality is characterized by the atomistic, externalistic, and mechanistic principles, the Chinese counterpart is characterized by the holistic, internalistic, and organistic principles. These three metaphysical and methodological principles of Chinese philosophy may be said to formulate three basic aspects of Chinese causality.

Given any two things or events, A and B, which are causally related in the phenomenal causal sense, the explanation for this relationship is not that there is a general law which governs things of the types exemplified by A and B, but that A and B both belong to an order originating from the source of the totality of things. This order relating to A and B also relates all other things of different kinds. To understand this is not to understand a law specifically bearing upon A and B, but to understand an order of orders formed among things. It is to understand the *li* of things. The Chinese thinker generally regards an instance of a causal law (in the nineteenth-century scientific sense) as an occasion to advance to the total knowledge of the total world. Thus Chu Hsi(1130-1200) says:

Thus the initial teaching of the great *Great Learning* is to make sure that the learner will extend to the extreme all the known principles of things for all things in the world. When one has exercised oneself long enough in this way and becomes one day completely enlightened, then the inside and outside, the refined and the crude, of all things, will be understood and all the functions of my mind will become clear. Thus is called investigation of things. This is called the ultimate of our knowledge.[16]

From this one can see that the purpose of the investigation of things is not to seek laws governing individual relationships of things but to understand individual orders in regard to and in reference to the whole. The idea of law as something different from both individual things and individual orders as well as their totality finds no place in the holistic orientation of Chinese thinking. Because of this holistic consideration, causality is also subsumed under "correlative thinking," as formulated by Joseph Needham.[17] The essence of "correlative thinking" is to classify and coordinate different types of things into correlative orders and patterns, and thus to consider explanations of individual happenings as relating to these orders and patterns.[18] Both the philosophy of change and its symbolic system based on the *I Ching* and the theory of five powers (*wu-hsing*) provide a number of coordinate categories capable of correlating all processes in the world. All these categories represent some differentiation of the ultimate reality and are to be understood as ultimately intelligible in terms of this one reality—the *Tao*.

In the Han Dynasty, Tung Chung-shu (179-104 B.C.) advanced a highly elaborate system of correlation among colors, sounds, directions, places, political powers, historical stages, and other natural and human events and qualities. This is an extreme form of "correlative thinking" based on the *yin-yang* theory and the five powers theory. Its fundamental spirit of subsuming individual things and happenings into larger and clearer orders and patterns remains typical of Chinese thinking.

An important point about this "correlative thinking' which is not mentioned by Needham is that it not only cuts across both the natural and social worlds, but also cuts across the physical and mental worlds. This means that human emotional and mental states are also understood in terms of the same orders and patterns which explain natural social and historical events. This serves the purpose of the self-cultivation of the moral character and well-being of man, for one will achieve goodness only when one achieves order within oneself, which will correspond to the order under Heaven and in society. The very basis for this thinking, which is called "the coincidence of Heaven and man" (*t'ien-jên-ho-yi*) is again the holistic principle by which the objective and the subjective are not absolutely demarcated, but rather are considered intimately related, and the subject (man) is assumed to be able to participate in the creative works of the *Tao*.

If one can satisfy oneself by explaining causality in terms of correlative orders, one may still query how correlative orders are to be explained and how each order, which is exemplified in certain constant relations of things, is to be explained. In other words, one may wish to know what motivates the thought of the existence of orders as they are. The answer to these questions is to be found in the *principle of internality*. Needham has explained this principle of internality in its application to causality very lucidly. He says:

Things behave in particular ways not necessarily because of prior action or impulsions of other things, but because their position in the ever-moving cyclical universe was such that they were endowed with intrinsic natures which made that behavior inevitable for them. If they did not behave in those particular ways, they would lose their relational positions in the whole (which makes them what they are) and turn into something other than themselves. They were thus parts in existential dependence upon the whole world-organism. And they reacted upon one another not so much of mechanical impulsion or causation as by a kind of mysterious resonance.[19]

That things move and are related in movements is not due to the external forces applied to them in accordance with the laws of mechanisms or chemistry but is due to their intrinsic natures and their positions in the whole universe. The intrinsic natures of things have powers or forces to move things in relationships with one another, because the natures of things are founded on relationships among all things derived from the ultimate reality of things. This is as if everything has a life-vitality of its own and acts in concordance with each other thing to form a preestablished harmony. The preestablished harmony and concordance of the movements of things are not imposed from the outside but are a manifestation of the ultimate reality. It is something ultimate and given and yet not to be formulated in any determinate relationship. Thus not only each order and pattern, which relates two things in movements, is a spontaneous expression of the intrinsic nature of these two things, but all different orders and patterns of things are intrinsically related so that one order may be transformed into another on following an inner impulsion of life. This is exemplified in the mutual generating and destructive orders of the five powers.[20] Because of this internalistic consideration, all things are conceived to occur spontaneously and naturally and yet to conform to and exhibit harmonious patterns or orders as exemplified by the movements of the seasons and the alternation of day and night.

As nobody with the spirit of scientific causality would be willing to say that the spring causes the summer or the night causes the day, Chinese philosophers in the internalistic tradition would regard all cases of scientific causality on a par with the movement of the seasons and the succession of day and night. From the point of view of scientific causality, one may call this a "no-cause" theory. In fact, the very Taoist idea of "doing nothing" (*wu-wei*) strongly suggests the nonscientific "no-cause" theory in explaining the correlation of things in an order and a correlation of all orders and their mutual transformation. Nothing has externally moved things, because there is no external mover, be it the Aristotelian or Christian God, yet things are moved of their own accord.

Similarly, for Confucianists, Heaven cannot be an eternal movement. Confucius has said: "Four seasons proceed: what has Heaven to say?"[21] As for the Taoists, it is pointed out that it is simply because nothing is done that everything is done. This can be interpreted as meaning that because no external force has compelled things and ordered the orders, things move by themselves spontaneously. It is clear that the self-moving power is assumed to reside within each thing, and that when Tao is recognized to combine all things into oneness, the self-moving power things is nothing but the self-moving power of the *Tao*. Thus Wang Chung (1st century A.D.) concludes that "Things move because of their belonging to the natural kinds, not because of striving and purpose."[22] Wang Pi expresses the same idea in the same spirit: "We do not see Heaven command the four seasons, and yet they never swerve from their course."[23]

Things not only move by themselves, but move by themselves to exhibit the order and patterns in which they are related. Orders and patterns like relationships are powers. Even though these orders ad patterns should not be considered as causal necessities, they are necessities created by the things out of their internal nature. Thus one can speak of causal necessity without implying that one thing is caused by another. Nor should one draw the conclusion from this that the whole is static. On the contrary, the harmony exhibited in all orders of moving things is a creative state from which life is to be produced just as life is regenerated.

Chinese Model of Causality: Dialectical Laws

What is said above may lead us to think that there is no recognition of the general principle governing concrete things as comparable to the causal laws of Western mechanical science. In a sense this is true, for there are simply no precisely formulated causal laws as discovered by science, and there is no qualitative-experimental science to make such discoveries. But in another sense it is not true that there is no formulation of any general principle which explains the causation and mechanical interaction of things. I have already pointed out that there are two levels in which these principles can be formulated. On the strictly empirical level there are many empirical observations one can make regarding the conjunction and correlation of types of events in astronomy, medicine, biology, climatology or even such physical sciences as optics and mechanics.[24] They may not, however, possess lawlike forms of a theoretical nature. On the metaphysical level, one can see general principles or laws which are made on the basis of organic considerations. One may even suggest that all such principles are stated in light of the theory of organic balance and the principle of organicity, which recognizes the inevitability of coming and going as the ultimate reality of things and conceives the inner structure of such processes as conforming to a proportionate balance of power as provided by the *yin* and *yang* forces. Thus, all such general principles are simple (*ch'ien*) and easy (*yi*) in form. We may even suggest that all such principles *in toto* give an explication of the notion of causality in accordance with the principle of organicity.

As I have indicated, to think organically is to think dialectically. Chinese dialectics follows from the Confucian and Taoist metaphysical and methodological considerations of reality and man. The general principles governing changes are, therefore, basically dialectical. Whereas Western scientists make predictions and explanations on the basis of causal laws, the Chinese thinkers make predictions and explanations on the basis of dialectical laws. We may now refer to the *Tao Te Ching* for examples of such dialectical laws formulated on the basis of organicistic considerations.[25]

1. "While all things are stirring, I only contemplate the Return. For flourishing as they do, each of them will return to its root.
2. "Bend and you will be whole. Curl and you will be straight. Keep empty and you will be filled. Grow old and you will be renewed. Have little and you will gain. Have much and you will be confused.
3. "(For) a whirlwind does not last a whole morning. Nor does a sudden shower last a whole day.
4. "Wherever armies are stationed, thorn bushes grow. After a great war, bad years invariably follow.
5. "For to be overdeveloped is to hasten decay; and this is against *Tao*; and what is against *Tao* will soon cease to be.
6. "What is in the end to be shrunken, begins to be first stretched out. What is in the end to be weakened, begins by being first set on high. What is in the end to be despoiled, begins by being first richly endowed . . . The soft and weak overcome the hard and strong. The softest of all things overrides the hardest of all.
7. "All the myriad things carry the *yin* on their backs and hold the *yang* in their embrace, deriving their vital harmony from the proper blending of the two vital breaths.
8. "Restlessness overcomes old; but things calm overcome heat.
9. "Bad fortune is what good fortune leans on; good fortune is what bad fortune hides in.
10. "When a man is living, he is soft and supple, when he is dead, he becomes hard and rigid. When a plant is living, it is soft and tender; when it is dead, it becomes withered and dry. Hence, the hard and rigid belong to the company of the dead, the soft and supple belong to the company of the living. Therefore, a mighty army tends to fall by its own weight, just as dry wood is ready for the axe. The mighty and great will be laid low. The humble and weak will be exalted."[26]

Though no one will call what is listed above causal laws, no one can deny that most of the principles listed can be used as a basis for making predictions or even explanations of concrete events, either in the domain of human and historical affairs or in the domain of natural processes. Insofar as these principles satisfy some of the conditions which causality in the scientific-mechanical model satisfies, such as predictability, explanability and even controlability by human action, they perform the same function as scientific causality. One may consider them as illustrating the content of causality in the Chinese outlook. This content clearly presents a variety of dynamic laws for organic relationships, such as the law of complementariness, law of return, law of reversion, law of negative power, etc. Many similar principles can be adduced from other sources, such as the *I Ching, Lu Shih Chun Chiu*, and *Huai Nan Tzu*.

To conclude these three sections, the concept of causality in Chinese philosophy is so radically different from the Western scientific model of causality that one will not find any similarity between them. In fact we may suggest that the model of causality in Chinese philosophy is exactly contrary and converse to the mechanical-atomistic model of scientific Europe in the eighteenth and nineteenth centuries. Whereas the Western scientific concept of causality is atomistic, externalistic, and mechanistic, the Chinese model of causality is antiatomistic and therefore holistic, antiexternalistic and therefore internatistic, antimechanistic and therefore organistic. The very radical difference between them is not difficult to explain: It is the difference between the Image of Life and the Image of Machine. Insofar as life is a concrete experience of man and a machine is built from an abstract design and qualitative draft, one may also say that the Chinese model of causality is basically reflective of the concrete experience of life, history, and time, whereas the Western scientific model of causality is basically a reflection of abstract thinking and quantitative calculation. If one wonders why the Chinese model of causality is what it is from the scientific perspective, one must also keep in mind that it is equally valid and perhaps more appropriate to ask from the point of view of the Chinese model why the Western model of causality is developed at all. Before anyone seeks the reasons for these questions and judges the merits of these respective models, one must attempt to understand these models in their own right and on their own terms.

Notes

1. See *The Journal of Philosophy* 70, no. 17 (Oct., 1973):556-572
2. See D. Hume, *An Enquiry Concerning Human Understanding*, Section VII.
3. For example, Richard Taylor, in his article "Causation," has articulately challenged Hume's view. See *The Monist* 471, no. 2 (Winter, 1963): 287-313.
4. Taylor, "Causation," p. 303.
5. This is not to deny that cause and effect may not occur simultanenusly in time as, in fact, it always does. The point here is that before cause and effect are simultaneously called into existence through the act of causation (causality), there must be temporally prior conditions which are potentially sufficient and necessary for the causation. Even though Taylor rejects the temporal priority of cause, in view of the simultaneity of cause-effect relation, he does not seem to reject the temporal prior existence of potential causes. See Taylor, "Causation," p. 303.
6. This is the first sentence from the *Doctrine of the Mean*. Wing-tsit Chan translates it as "What Heaven (*t'ien*, nature) imparts to man is called human nature." See his *A Source Book in Chinese Philosophy*, (Princeton, N.J.: Princeton University Press, 1969), p. 98.
7. See Section 5 of the *Ta Chuan*, part II, in the *I Ching*; this part is not translated in Chan's *Source Book*.
8. The term "organicism" has been frequently used in literature in China to describe the philosophical world view of Chinese thinkers. One important and recent contribution to the use of this term and its enrichment is found in Joseph Needham's work *Science and Civilization in China*, 7 vols. (London: Cambridge University Press, 1962), 2:248, 281, 286, 91-92, etc.
9. Quoted, the *I Ching*, trans. Richard Wilhelm (Princeton, N.J.: Princeton University Press, 1972), 280.
10. Wilhelm, *I Ching*, p. 287, with modification.
11. In the essay called "The Great Master," Chuang Tsu says: *Tao* is real and truthful, (but) it is non-active and does nothing and has no form. It can be transmitted but cannot be possessed. It can be understood, but not seen. It is its own source and its own root. Before there is Heaven and Earth, it steadily exists from the ancient antiquity. It generates life-spirit pervading the future

and the past and gives birth to Heaven and Earth. It exists above the great ultimate and yet is not high. It exists below the six directions and is not deep. It exists before Heaven and Earth and is not long-living; it exists in high antiquity and is not old."

12. Quoted from *Tao Te Ching*, trans. John Wu (New York: St. John's University Press, 1961), section 42, 61.

13. Wu, *Tao Te Ching*, section 25, p. 35.

14. Wu, *Tao Te Ching*, section 76, p.109.

15. Perhaps any genuine metaphysical principle is unavoidably a principle of methodology. Kant has suggested this in formulating a transcendental justification of the rational ideas of metaphysics.

16. See Chu Hsi's commentary on the *Great Learning*.

17. The term "correlative thinking" is used by Joseph Needham in his work *Science and Civilization in China*, 2: 279 ff, to describe the thought system of correlating or coordinating different types of processes into simple interrelated orders of patterns, such as the theory of *yin-yang*, the symbolic system of the *I Ching* and the theory of the five powers. My explanation in this passage basically follows Needham.

18. Needham has taken this as the basis for calling Chinese thought organicistic. See Needham, *Science and Civilization in China*, 2:281.

19. From Needham, *Science and Civilization in China*, 2:281. Needham has quoted extensively from *Chun Chiu Fan Lu* of Tung Chung-shu to illustrate his point. Another passage from Needham (*Science and Civilization in China*, 2: 290) is also revealing. "The uncreated universal organism, whose every part, by a compulsion internal to itself and arising out of its own nature, willingly performed its functions in the cyclical recurrences of the whole, was mirrored in human society of a universal ideal of mutual good understanding, a supple refinement of interdependence and solidarities which could never be based on unconditional ordinances, in other words, on laws ... Thus the mechanical and the quantitative, the forces and the externally imposed were all absent. The notion of order excluded the notion of law."

20. Needham, *Science and Civilization in China*, 2: 253 ff.

21. See *Analects* 17.

22. See *Lun Heng* Ch. 19.

23. See Wang Pi's commentary on the *I Ching*, comments on 20th *Kua, Kuan*. Quoted from Needham, *Science and Civilization in China*, 2: 561.

24. I do not have enough space to discuss the scientific achievements of the Neo-Mohists in this article. See my review "On Chinese Science, A Review Essay," in *Journal of Chinese Philosophy* Vol. 4. No. 4, 395-407, 1977.

25. This is also a perfect piece of "correlative reasoning."

3. The Nature and Function of Skepticism in Chinese Philosophy

Two Senses of Skepticism and Their Exemplifications

What is skepticism? In answer to this question, two senses of skepticism, the negative and the positive, can be given. In a negative sense, skepticism is a philosophical position intended to negate or invalidate *all* knowledge and truth claims: if the totality (as indicated by the term "all') of knowledge and/or truth claims is unlimited, the skeptical position clearly cannot be adequately articulated, and the very nature of the skeptical position would then remain unanswered, unstated, unilluminated. Whether it should be called a philosophical position becomes a question. When Wittgenstein says that "Whereof one has nothing to say, one should be silent," he might refer to such a situation; whatever is true cannot be spoken and whatever is spoken is not true.

It appears clear that, if a skeptical position is to be without contradiction, it must be applied to a specific set of knowledge claims and/or truth claims which excludes at least the claim of the skeptical position itself. Given this restriction, the skeptical position still can be negative in the sense that the purport of the skeptic is to attack and destroy a given set of truth/knowledge claims. There is no specific effort to clarify or enlighten other positive points of the skeptical position. In the extreme case, the skeptic claims that if there is any truth at all, the truth is that there is no truth. But this truth has no positive content, for it is not even proved on a second-order level. The restricted skeptic in the negative sense simply produces agnostic arguments that, given any claim of truth or knowledge, there is no validity for that claim. He need only hold that his own claim is different and belongs to a metaphysical or metaphilosophical level, and therefore need not be included in the claims he negates.

The restricted skepticism in the positive sense, on the other hand, takes one forward step beyond the negative thesis of restricted skepticism. It argues positively for higher level truth and knowledge above and over the skeptically criticized knowledge and truth. The positivity of this skeptical position always tends to draw distinction between two levels or two realms of truth and knowledge: The affirmation of the higher level of truth and knowledge is based on the negation of the lower level of truth and knowledge and leads in some way to a reaffirmation of the lower level of truth and knowledge. When this dialectical process takes place, the negative skepticism transforms itself into the positive skepticism in which skeptical elements become integrated into a system of philosophical ideas concerning reality and nature in the world.

In light of a close examination of the tradition of skepticism in Western philosophy, we may suggest that skepticism in Western philosophy is sometimes negative in nature and sometimes positive in nature and thus serves a positive theoretical purpose. As an example of the restricted form of negative skepticism, we may cite the distrust of the law of contradiction underlying Aristotle's defense of that law. Aristotle knows that even the denial of the validity of the law of contradiction has to presuppose its validity if the denial is to make any sense at all. Thus, the skeptical view with regard to the law of contradiction is reduced to a state of nonarticulability. A second example of negative skepticism, perhaps less extreme than that of the Aristotelian critics, is that of Sextus Empiricus, who argues for the uncertainty and untrustworthiness of judgments, perceptions, and beliefs concerning the external world. He has produced various arguments against the validity of our knowledge of the world. He makes efforts to show how one may arrive at tranquility of mind by suspending judgments about the world. He even describes skepticism in the following terms:

Skepticism is an ability or mental attitude which opposes appearances to judgments in any way whatsoever, with the result that, owing to the equipollence of the objects and reasons thus opposed, we are brought directly first to a state of "'unperturbedness'" or quietude (*ataraxia*).[1]

From this description, it is clear that no judgments of knowledge can be considered valid against what is considered "appearance" and that, knowing the opposition between "appearances" and judgments, we shall naturally suspend our judgment and enjoy a state of tranquility. This skeptical position appears then to have a positive side. How do we account for this result? The answer is that the positive side of skepticism consists in a practical and supposedly beneficial situation which, however, bears on no higher level of illumination or understanding of truth. The simple point of the skeptic is that once all judgments are withdrawn we are not to be disturbed by uncertain expectation or vexation about the future, and thus we are able to enjoy the present. This is a position of agnosticism combined with determinism, aiming at achieving a happy state of well-being. Though Taoism (an example of the positive form of skepticism) in Chinese philosophy shares this practicality with Pyrrhonism, it goes beyond Pyrrhonism in trying to exhibit an ultimate metaphysical truth in terms of which petty or lower forms of truth become possible. Because of the lack of a metaphysical interest, and perhaps because of some implicit opposition to metaphysical thinking, the skeptical position in the West remains basically negative, even though sometimes practical-minded.

The antimetaphysical bent of negative skepticism is well illustrated in the works of Hume. With his psychology, Hume's philosophy goes beyond Pyrrhonism in extending skeptical doubt to not only knowledge of the external world but also to knowledge of the self and other minds. He has no scruples for rejecting metaphysical thinking on the basis of his skepticism. He has no reservation in urging us to lead a life of common sense and practicality. Thus, the negative skeptical theory does conduce to a positive practical life.[2] The negative side of Hume's skepticism is underscored by Kant, insofar as Kant tries to meet Hume's challenge by asserting and proving that we do have valid knowledge of the empirical world, even though we are unable to know reality in an ultimate metaphysical sense. Kant even attempts to show that, in the employment of practical reason, we may come to know certain truths of reality and thus transform the simplistic practicality of Pyrrhonism into a positive noumenon-certifying practical reason. It is indeed through Kant that the Western tradition of negative skepticism is transformed into a positive weapon against metaphysical thinking and an instrument for seeking positive truths in other areas.

In light of what we have said about negative skepticism, we may indeed define the skeptical position as a position satisfying the following conditions:

a. It is impossible for man to reach any knowledge of any truth or the real.
b. It is impossible for man to articulate any knowledge of any truth or the real in any coherent and systematic way.
c. There is no reason for man to believe that what we claim to know represents any truth or the real.

On the basis of these conditions, skeptics will draw the following conclusions:

a. Knowledge of the self is impossible.
b. Knowledge of the external world is impossible.
c. Knowledge of other minds is impossible.
d. Knowledge of the ultimate truth is impossible.

It is clear that this skeptical position can be applied to *a priori* knowledge as well as to empirical knowledge. A thoroughgoing and consistent skeptic who considers knowledge impossible in the fullest sense possible will have to remain silent and will turn out to be a mystic or a practicalist (like Hume) who accepts life and customs as they are without raising any questions of rational justification.

Before we turn to the question of how skepticism functions in Chinese philosophy, we must mention the distinction between the skeptical position and the skeptical method or the method of doubt. For a genuine skeptic, skeptical doubts destroy the validity of experiences and reason, and so he would not resort to other ways of knowing (including revelation, faith, intuition) as a way out of his skeptical doubt. He has no intention to retrieve or reconstruct what is destroyed by his skeptical doubt. But when the method of doubt is applied by Augustine or Descartes, there are positive reconstructive ends in view in their philosophy. Doubt sets the limit of reason and experience but introduces other positive ways of knowing or reaching truths—the same truth indeed which was destroyed by the doubt. In this regard, we can see that there is indeed a dialectical element in Cartesian or Augustinian skepticism. We may consider these along with Kant as examples of positive skepticism in the Western tradition.[3]

Dialectical Roles of Positive Skepticism in Chinese Philosophy

Though we cannot be certain that there never was any negative skepticism in Chinese philosophy, we are certain that what is referred to as positive skepticism is well exemplified in and, in fact, dominates the Chinese philosophical tradition. In light of the general consensus of the Chinese views on nature, life, and reality, it seems consistent to expect that all skeptical views in Chinese philosophy tend to be positive and highly constructive. I intend to explain this form of positive skepticism and its dialectical role in Chinese philosophy and then offer an explanation as to the grounds and reasons for positive skepticism in Chinese philosophy, as well as for the absence of negative skepticism.

The most typical form of positive skepticism, together with its transforming function, is philosophical Taoism or Taoist philosophy. In this chapter I will not give a full explication of Taoism, but shall confine the discussion to the explanation of how skeptical elements help to establish the Taoist position, or conversely, how the Taoist position helps to apply the skeptical method in a positive and constructive way. It suffices to say, in general, that Taoism represents a criticism of the commonsensical view of morality, life, and the world as embodied in early Confucianism. The Taoist criticism is based on and indeed provides a way toward a view and an experience of life, reality, and morality which are not skeptical. Skepticism is used in Taoism as a method of criticism for establishing an ultimate antiskeptical view of philosophy. In this sense, Taoism clearly is not a negative skeptical position; it is a constructive philosophy which contains skeptical elements for constructive purposes.

By concentrating on the logic and ontology of Taoism, we will understand why ultimate skepticism (the skeptical position) does not develop in Taoism; how the skeptical arguments used by Taoists to criticize morality and knowledge rely on antiskeptical metaphysical presuppositions; and finally how the very way in which the skeptical method was developed would necessarily lead to a nonskeptical or even an antiskeptical metaphysical view. The philosophical lesson we can draw from this is that skepticism cannot develop into an ultimate position in the Taoist metaphysical framework. Questions can be raised as to whether there is a metaphysical framework for developing skepticism of the extreme kind. One might even suggest that for a consistent skeptical position no articulatable metaphysics is possible or required, and that should such a metaphysics exist, it would coincide with an unutterable mysticism.

Taoism, in the writings of Lao Tzu (sixth or fourth centuries B.C.) and Chuang Tzu (399-295 B.C.) provides skeptical arguments or theses against the conventional and commonsensical, empirical and rational claims of knowledge, politics, and morality. Simultaneously, it also provides an antiskeptical metaphysical and yet ultimately practical view regarding nature, reality, and life. Now whether skeptical arguments come first or whether the metaphysics of *tao* comes first is an interesting question. Historically, it is possible to hold that skepticism regarding knowledge, politics, morality, and society comes before the development or the full development of the metaphysics of *tao*. Indeed, a few current scholars tend to hold this view.[4] The social and historical contexts in which Taoism arose lend a high degree of probability to the view that Taoism began as a reflection on the cause and nature of chaos, conflict, and unhappiness in the dynamic social and political processes of change, and gradually grew into a metaphysical position in terms of which the individual, as versus society and government, could nevertheless receive fulfillment in his deep contemplative experience of the *tao* or ultimate truth and reality. But, on the other hand, from a logical and phenomenological point of view, the rise of Taoist philosophy must have had its experiential basis, for pure social and political criticism is incapable of generating a metaphysics. Only metaphysical insight and contemplation of the truth as truth leads to a blooming of metaphysical thought. The experience of *tao* thus is not derived from social and political reaction alone but instead has roots in a deep-seated original understanding of life and nature. Because of these double aspects of Taoism, we may simply assume that the skeptical arguments and metaphysics of *tao* reinforce each other and form a dialectical process of establishing a theory of distinction between lower level (limited) truth and higher level (unlimited) truth, as communicated in *Chuang Tzu*.

Let us begin with the Taoist skeptical arguments against knowledge, morality, and value. The very basis of these skeptical arguments consists in recognizing the relativity, subjectivity, limitedness and ill effects of commonsensical knowledge; and, on the other hand, recognizing the transrelativity, universality, unlimitedness, as well as the good consequences of the metaphysical wisdom of the *tao* for the others.

In *Lao Tzu*, strong stress is laid on the relativity of perception, value, and knowledge, on the one hand, and the ill effects of them on the other. Regarding the relativity of perception, value, and knowledge, Lao Tzu has this to say:

If everyone knows why beauty is beauty, there is then the uncomeliness; [if everyone] knows what good is good, there is then the non-good; therefore being and nonbeing are mutually generative, the difficult and the easy are mutually completing, the long and the short are mutually forming, the high and the low are mutually leaning upon, the monotone and the rhythmic voice are mutually harmonizing; the fore and hind are mutually following.[5]

Values, existence, qualities, relations of space, time, and other relations are therefore distinguished in contexts where there is contrast. They are, therefore, individually identifiable relative to their correlative opposites. Their existence conditions and is conditioned by the existence of their opposites. What is relative is dependent on other conditions and does not exist independently of other conditions. Thus, to know what is relative does not yield any genuine knowledge of the total and ultimate truth or the *tao*. But to know is to recognize distinctions which are relatively conditioned. This knowledge, however, can not contribute to understanding of the truth (the *tao*). This is referred to by Lao Tzu as learning (*hsueh*) which is opposite to *tao*. Lao Tzu says:

To do learning is to accumulate daily: to do *tao* is to diminish daily. We diminish again and again so that we can arrive at nonactivity. When nothing is done, nothing will not be done.[6]

The contrast between *hsueh* and *tao* is one between relative knowledge and absolute knowledge. The former is conditioned, the latter unconditioned. Though Lao Tzu does not explicitly say that "doing learning (*hsueh*)" as versus "doing *tao*" does not yield true knowledge, but it is clear from the contrast between "doing learning" and "doing *tao*" that, in order to have true knowledge (namely, "doing *tao*"), we must abandon "doing learning." "If we abolish learning, we shall have *no worry*."[7] In learning, we tend to hold to one or the other side of relative distinctions which hide the truth, but in *tao* all distinctions are not taken seriously and, in fact, are to be ignored so that one would not hold one side of a relative distinction against the other. The state of nondistinction or the state where no relative distinction commands attention is described by Lao Tzu as that of *voidness (kung)* and/or the state of *tranquility (ching)*. It is a state where everything and all things are *allowed* to thrive and one can see a natural return of them to their origin—the *tao*. Thus Lao Tzu says:

To reach for the voidness to the ultimate to hold steadfast quietitude, ten thousand things will simultaneously thrive—and I shall see their return (*fu*)[8].

Thus the skeptical criticism with regard to the knowledge of things is clear. Knowledge of things depends on the recognition of existing relative distinctions, which block total truth from showing. Relativity of distinctions furthermore leads to the *one-sidedness* of one's view, which again blocks the total truth from showing itself.

The argument against knowledge and perception from the ill effects of them is straightforward in Lao Tzu. Lao Tzu simply points out:

Five colors make one's eyes blind; five sounds make one's ears deaf; five spices make one's mouth tasteless; riding on the horseback to do hunting makes one's mind mad; precious commodities make one's behavior secretive. Thus the sage only wishes to satisfy his stomach, but not to seek satisfaction of eyes. Thus he gets rid of the latter and takes former.[9]

Perception of the five senses and the knowledge based on them tend to produce the disturbing effect on one's mind and will, and leads one to a state of aroused emotions and desires. If one wants to avoid unhealthy or excessive emotions and desires, one would have to limit or diminish the use of one's senses or not let one's perception and knowledge become too complicated and involved. Thus Lao Tzu holds: "To have a simple appearance and to hold a simple mind, one should have less private feeling and less desires." Lao Tzu is insightful in linking knowledge to the volitional and appetitive nature of man. He appears to believe that the more knowledge one possesses, the more excessive his desires and needs are, and the more numerous the latter become the more the former will be generated. This is a vicious circle which will lead to the destruction of man as a wholesome entity. Thus, the skeptical criticism with regard to knowledge in Lao Tzu concerns not only its validity but its moral and metaphysical soundness.

In the writings of Chuang Tzu, the positive skeptical arguments based on the relativity and ill effects of knowledge, perception, and value are even more elaborated and developed than in Lao Tzu. The relativity of knowledge is developed into an ontological principle, to the effect that everything in the world, if well defined and distinctive, for its definition or distinction must depend on an opposite and, in fact, may be considered as derivable from an opposite. Thus, nothing is separate and separable from a relational context, and the relativity of a thing is precisely this relational dependence.

Nothing is not that; nothing is not this. From the point of view of 'that', one cannot see clearly 'this', but from the point of view of 'this' one can see oneself ('this') clearly. Thus it is said: "that is derived from this and this is dependent on that."[10]

Chuang Tzu furthermore points out:

This is that; that is this. That represents one sort of distinction between 'right and wrong.' (*Chi Wu Lun*)

Insofar as "that" and "this" represent different and opposite points of view or perspectives, they must generate different and opposite knowledge or perception which cannot be other than relative. No judgment of knowledge or perception is absolutely right or absolutely wrong, and therefore has no absolute validity.

Like Lao Tzu, Chuang Tzu points out that, behind the relative perspective of things, there is the absolute and unconditioned position of nonfixation and noncommitment to any specific position. It is the position where the opposition between "that" and "this" becomes irrelevant, nondetermining, and does not generate any specific knowledge or any attachment to such. It is the position of the *tao* or the axis of *tao* (*tao-shu*). He says:

Is there in reality a distinction between 'that' and 'this'? Is there in reality no distinction between 'that' and 'this'? When 'that' and 'this' are not opposed, the position will be called the axis of *tao* (*tao-shu*). When one holds the axis of *tao*, one is the center of the circle of things and can respond to infinite distinctions between right and wrong. [Since] there is an infinity of right, and since there is an infinity of wrong, so it is said that it is better to use the method of mutual illumination to reach truth than to rely on one distinction or another.

Thus for Chuang Tzu, and for Lao Tzu as well, truth or true knowledge comes from the denial of ordinary knowledge or perception which is based on a limited point of view and relative distinctions. The skeptical criticism against knowledge becomes an instrument for reaching a higher or deeper knowledge. In fact, the criticism is that one should not take ordinary knowledge at its face value, for if one does, one will not see truth; but, on the other hand, one should see the limitation and relativity of ordinary knowledge and thus reach the knowledge of the ultimate truth. Thus, what is skeptically denied or criticized serves the positive function of introducing a deeper knowledge. What is even more important to note is that, when the deeper knowledge is introduced and revealed by the skeptical criticism, what is thus skeptically criticized, namely, ordinary knowledge, can be reintroduced or reaffirmed without being eliminated. It will be accepted as far as it is useful and insofar as it constitutes a condition for recognizing the higher and total truth. This is the twofold dialectical role of doubt in Taoism: to reach the total truth and to reintroduce the limited relative truth or knowledge after the total truth is reached.

Chuang Tzu also agrees with Lao Tzu on the ill effects of knowledge and perception. The knowledge and perception which he rejects as introducing ill effects, and as useless or ineffectual, is primarily knowledge of skills and other know-how. In one of his essays called "Opening a Box," Chuang Tzu described how a masterful thief may carry away the box which a person has skillfully sealed in order to prevent the loss of its contents. Thus he asks:

With regard to what the world calls the most knowledgeable person, is he not storing something for a masterful thief?[11]

Thus Chuang Tzu recommends that:

Therefore only when sagehood is abolished and knowledge abandoned, will at thief cease to be.[12]

It is clear from this that Chuang Tzu considers knowledge as basically harmful. Even though the knowledge considered here may include simply know-how, it need not be so interpreted. From the preceding, Chuang Tzu could agree that partial knowledge and the knowledge of distinctions are what produce technology and induce emotion and as such, they are therefore morally and socially undesirable.

Chuang Tzu has many other arguments which are logically well-developed in criticism of knowledge, perception, and value judgments, beside those from their relativity and ill effects. The arguments from the relativity of standards of judgment strengthen the point that ordinary judgments presuppose some unexamined assumptions and depend on them as grounds for their validity. But there is no proof nor necessity for accepting these assumptions. Thus, he points out that although a feather of a bird in the autumn may appear to be small but can be judged to be large, it is very small when compared with much larger things. Similarly, with matters concerning duration in time, there is no absolute long or absolute short in time; and similarly with matters regarding the values of good or bad, and beauty or ugliness, there exist no absolute standards of judgment for them. Chuang Tzu's intent is to show that one should not be misled by knowledge and perception of things, for they are partially true at most, and only represent parts of things. Because of this, they need not be trusted or taken seriously.

Insofar as Chuang Tzu's argument is based on the subjectivity of knowledge and relativity of things, his position resembles Pyrrhonism. But Chuang Tzu, however, differs from the Pyrrhonist by drawing a positive conclusion from his own skeptical criticism. He urges a person to identify himself with Heaven and Earth and all the ten thousand things. He says:

Heaven and Earth co-live with me: ten thousand things identify with me.[13]

In doing this he comes to recognize subjective judgments as merely subjective, and to recognize the usefulness of the useless. He will free himself from the ordinary commitment to what is called reality and the ordinary doubt about dreams. The well-known parable of Chuang Tzu's dream of becoming a butterfly illustrates an ultimate *noncommittal position* toward reality, knowledge, and experience, which could encompass everything without anything being either affirmed or rejected. This is a non-Pyrrhonian position.

Finally, Chuang Tzu clearly makes the point that no judgment of right or wrong can be made in any dispute, and that no truth or falsity ever can be established. His argument for this is basically one from a third person. For, given two disputing persons, or given two opposite sides, no matter what a judge does, he can be equally questioned on a higher level, and another judge would have to settle the issue. But this leads to an infinite regress, so Chuang Tzu says:

Whom should I ask to judge? Do I make the judge the person who argues with my opponents? Surely he has agreed with my opponent, how could he judge? Do I make the judge the person who agrees with myself? Surely he has agreed with me, how could he judge? Do I make the judge the person who disagrees with both me and my opponent? But surely he already has disagreed with me and my opponent, how could he judge? Do I make the judge the person who agrees with both me and my opponent? Surely he has already agreed with me and my opponent, how could he judge? Thus I myself, my opponent, and a third person all could not know the true, and then whom do I want for knowing the true?[14]

What is interesting in this *reductio ad absurdum* is that a logical argument is used to show that argument does not logically settle any dispute about truth and knowledge. Chuang Tzu's recommendation is that one should treat the opposition between the two sides as if it is not an opposition, and thus "harmonize it with *natural relations (t'ien-ni)*. Let it go as freely as nature allows" (*Chi Wu Lun*). This means that one should not take the opposition seriously and should make no assertion whatsoever. This also amounts to accepting all sides of opposition in a comprehensive framework. This is indeed Chuang Tzu's true intention.

Skeptical tendencies are also found in the Ch'an Buddhistic philosophy. Ch'an Buddhism may be described as holding that no knowledge of the ultimate truth (truth in Enlightenment) is possible by way of language, speculation, or reasoning. But neither does the Ch'an Buddhist deny the relevance of the ordinary experiences of life, the ordinary use of language and the ordinary perception of the concrete situations of life. Ch'an Buddhism introduced an implicit metaphysical (ontological) perspective which makes skepticism a means for reaching Enlightenment, but is not a negative self-defeating methodology; that is, skepticism is employed not to establish any metaphysical view, but to positively reveal that none is relevant or necessary for the ultimate goal of enlightenment. A common Ch'an motto says:

[The Ch'an teaching is such that] the truth is transmitted outside the scriptures; there is no setting up of words and letters; point directly at a person's mind; one attains Buddhahood by seeing his self-nature.[15]

According to this motto, Ch'an Buddhists are found to be skeptical of all scriptural writings and, by extension, of all statements about truth in language. But the Ch'an skepticism, again, is not negative. for by rejecting all scriptural and linguistic approaches to truth, the Ch'an Buddhist simultaneously approaches truth. In fact, the very rejection of language and scripture is an occasion for reaching truth, in the sense that truth will be shown and one will see the truth. Because of this capacity for rejection, what is originally rejected can be reinstituted insofar as it is divested of the force of misguiding persons seeking truth. Thus, Ch'an skeptical doubt serves a positive twofold function: it reveals truth and in doing so neutralizes the value of scripture and language.

The Ch'an dialogue in the form of *koan* (public case, *kung-an*) is developed precisely for the purpose of achieving these double positive functions of skeptical doubt. To understand these two functions of skeptical doubt as embodied in koans is to understand the logic of *koan* hidden beneath the appearance of irrationality, irrelevancy, and sometimes even bizarreness. The use of such koans as "Show me your original face," "Show me the clap of a single hand," etc. is intended to push aside all conceptual presuppositions about truth, and is intended to induce truth to show itself or to give an opportunity for truth to show itself. Once the disciple sees this and grasps the truth, he can use language in the free and creative fashion which his enlightenment (seeing truth) brings, and can give an answer to a question without regard to relevancy and meaning. Truth is attained, the use of language is reinstituted, and the original skeptical doubt has performed a positive twofold function.[16]

Background Explanation of the Presence and Absence of Negative Skepticism

I have now explained the distinction and difference between the two kinds of skepticism, and their nature and function as respectively exemplified in the Western and the Chinese traditions. I hold that the Western tradition is characterized by the presence of the negative kind of skepticism, and the Chinese tradition is characterized by the absence of the negative kind of skepticism. Given this characteristic difference, it is both natural and desirable to seek the reasons why such a difference exists. To do so is to explain and give an account of what compelling circumstances have brought about or made possible this characteristic difference, or indeed, what compelling circumstances, if at all, brought about skepticism or skeptical doubt, whether negative or positive. It is obvious that no one can hope to historically trace and theoretically elaborate all the elements which contribute to the development of skepticism in such a short space. Without claiming historical or theoretical thoroughness, I wish to present a scheme for explanation in terms of which some major conditions for the development or lack of development of negative skepticism will be made clear.

In the first place, I wish to point out that skepticism in general is a result of certain restraining conditions man has introduced in his search for knowledge. It is not something rooted in human instinct or human reason. It is an outcome of the reflective experience over the frustration and disappointment in the zealous quest for knowledge. More specifically, it is a result of certain restraints man has formed and imposed in his quest for knowledge, regarding the method, concept, and model of knowledge. Thus, skepticism, as the negation of the quest for knowledge, is conditioned by the context of the quest for knowledge.

Two observations, however, must be made about this view of the origin of skepticism. First, though skepticism originates from the quest for knowledge, it is not necessary that all the forms of the quest for knowledge must result in skepticism. Skepticism exists only relative to certain *specific* restraining conditions one imposes on the quest for knowledge and on the concept of knowledge itself. This means that for certain other specific conditions there will be no skepticism and indeed that these other conditions will tend to prevent skepticism from arising. When we are clear about what conditions contribute to skeptical doubt, we shall then understand what other conditions will contribute to the elimination of skeptical doubt. For example, it can be shown that in the Confucian-Neo-Confucian philosophy, skepticism does not exist even though there is a nondogmatic philosophy of knowledge and an intense quest for knowledge.

Second, though skepticism is basically an epistemological position in the context of the quest for knowledge, it nevertheless has an ontological significance because it is based on some fundamental metaphysical or ontological vision or understanding of reality. Thus, I wish to hold that skepticism reflects not only an epistemological attitude, but that it also embodies an ontological stand. Consequently, one can consider the existence of skepticism and the nonexistence of skepticism as mirroring certain basic forms of the ontological apprehension of man in his relation to the world or reality.

In the West, several fundamental conditions on the quest for knowledge are laid down after the quest for knowledge is initiated. First, there are the requirements of the ultimacy and totality of knowledge. Second, there are the requirements of the unique precision and objectivity of knowledge. Third, there is the requirement of the certainty or certitude of knowledge. With regard to the first requirement, the ultimacy of knowledge is regarded as the absolute, unchanging validity of knowledge. Ultimate knowledge is held to be demonstratively clear, stable, and an exactly faithful image of the fixed forms of reality. Nothing less than ultimacy, namely, nothing

suggesting uncertainty, changeability, or inexactness, can satisfy this requirement for ultimacy. This is the Platonic and Aristotelian conception of knowledge, found or exemplified in logic and mathematics. It is continued up to
the present time in the the rationalists' view of demonstrative truth.

The requirement for totality is no less demanding. Knowledge must form
a total system, logically structured and ordered, free from inconsistency,
and complete in principle, if not in details. In fact, if knowledge is not total,
one may not suppose that one has reached the ultimate of knowledge.
Totality seems to be assimilated in the ultimate nature of knowledge. Potentiality for totality must be proved, if not actual totality. This explains how
shocking the Godel Incompleteness results may appear to be to those who
believe in the completeness of mathematical knowledge, as implied by the
formalism of Hilbert.

The other two requirements, that of exactness (or preciseness) and that
of objectivity, are no less restraining for a concept of knowledge. Though
exactness cannot be exactly defined, it is a methodological condition for
proving the clarity and distinctness of what we know. Perhaps it is because
of this requirement that complex matters and concepts are analyzed into
simple elements as basic constituents. In similar spirit, the requirement of
exactness leads to the development of reductionism and atomism in Western
epistemology. To have exact knowledge is to have knowledge definable in
exact and elementary units. This search for exactness coincides with the
search for simplicity, consistency, and definability and leads to such extreme
forms of reductionism as phenomenalism and logical atomism.

The requirement of objectivity must be understood in the context of an
implicitly introduced distinction and bifurcation between object and subject.
To require objectivity of knowledge is to require knowledge of the object
as detached and independent of the subject. Knowledge in this sense is a
mirror of external things and the laws governing them. It involves no value
judgments or anything to be explained in terms of the subjective experience of man. The primary model of an object is a physical object. Together
with the requirement for exactness, the requirement of objectivity tends to
reduce subjective existence of man or man's mind to physical entities. It
fosters deterministic thinking, and it conduces to modern philosophical
physicalism. It moreover leads to the development of the various sciences.

Lastly, but not leastly, there is the requirement for certitude or certainty
of knowledge. This requirement is one for securing security in knowledge,
and this can be aptly titled "epistemological security." What is required is
that which is known is known with certainty or certitude. Certitude or
certainty sometimes obtains when immediate knowledge obtains. But, at
other times, certitude or certainty only comes through a process of proof

or evidence-giving. Thus, in consequence of requiring certainty, various forms of proofs and proof procedures are developed in order to satisfy the requirement. This requirement becomes the very basis and motivating force for the development and advancement of logic and scientific methodology. Given the preceding requirements for knowledge, which we can term the rationalistic requirements for knowledge, I will lay down the following postulates which will explain the origins of skepticism in its negative form.

1. The more stringent these requirements are, the more difficult it is to satisfy them.
2. The more numerous these requirements are, the more difficult it is to satisfy them.
3. The more stringent the requirements for the ultimacy and totality of knowledge are, the more likely it is that skeptical doubts will develop.
4. The more stringent the requirements for exactness and objectivity are, the more likely it is that skeptical doubts will develop.
5. The more stringent the requirement for certitude is, the more likely it is skeptical doubts will develop.
6. The more likely it is the requirements for the ultimacy and totality of knowledge are to be satisfied, the less likely it is that the requirements for exactness and objectivity are to be satisfied and vice versa.
7. The more likely it is that the requirement for certitude is to be satisfied, the less likely it is that the requirements for ultimacy and totality and the requirement of exactness and objectivity are to be satisfied and vice versa.

These postulates are not as precisely formulated as one would like to see nor are they necessarily proved to be true. They are taken to be the background conditions necessary for a reasonable explanation of the origins of skepticism. When I say that they constitute necessary conditions for a reasonable explanation for the origins of skepticism, I do not intend that they must give rise to skepticism, because other necessary conditions might be pertinent. But it might turn out that these conditions are indeed sufficient, but not necessary. In fact, I am quite willing to take postulates 3, 4, 5 as stipulating stronger necessary conditions for the rise of skepticism. It is clear from these postulates that skepticism arose as a reaction and opposition to the stringency of the requirements for knowledge. The more stringent these requirements are, the stronger the reaction and opposition, thus the more likely it is for skepticism to arise. Similarly, the more numerous the requiremerits for knowledge are, the stronger the reaction and opposition. When the requirements for knowledge are both stringent and numerous, the reaction and opposition to them become strongest. This inverse relationship between skepticism and the requirements for knowledge seems to be both natural and intelligible. It seems to reflect the nature of reason and the psychology of the human mind. It is not therefore a simple psychological action but also a rational relation. As a rational relation, the inverse relation between skepticism and knowledge can be expressed by saying that, if no positive proof of a thesis is possible, then one would have to give a proof of the antithesis. Thus, if complete, ultimate, exact, objective, and certain knowledge is not possible, in the sense of being attainable or provable, then its impossibility must be proved. Skepticism is the effort and result of proving the converse of knowledge under the requirements for knowledge. Consequently, when all seven requirements for knowledge are stringently demanded for a model of knowledge, the rise of skepticism as the negation of all seven requirements and thus of the very model of knowledge satisfying these requirements is not surprising.

We may indeed present and illustrate the inverse relationships among the major rationalist requirements for knowledge, the impossibility of satisfying all of which leads to skepticism:

Diagram 1

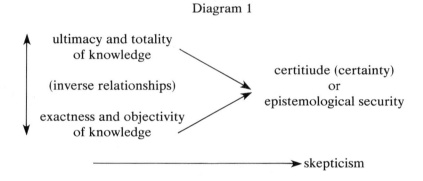

We may conclude that negative skepticism is the product of the demand for the satisfaction of all the requirements for knowledge. When all the requirements for knowledge are demanded, there is an inner tension and incompatability of all these requirements. Negative skepticism, therefore, can also be regarded as the outcome of the conflict and incompatability of the basic requirements for knowledge.

A deeper analysis of the ontological ground of the requirements for knowledge and the negation of such in skepticism shows parallel inverse relationships. Conflict and incompatability among requirements for ontological understanding could create ontological anxiety which negates and opposes the satisfaction of these requirements for understanding a model of reality. The ontological anxiety in the following diagram corresponds to skepticism in the epistemolological diagram.

Diagram 2

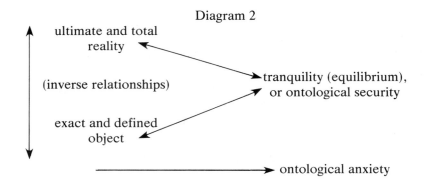

Although there is a parallel structure between these two structures, they do make a difference in regard to some skeptical positions in the Western tradition. Apparently, Pyrrhonism wishes to achieve tranquility of mind by suspending all judgments of knowledge. As with skepticism, Pyrrhonism arises from demands of satisfaction of all the requirements for knowledge in Diagram 1. As an ontological position it does not argue for ontological anxiety, but instead holds the need for tranquility by negating the search for exact understanding of the objective world in its ultimacy and totality. It is clear that a negative skeptic can be skeptical in an epistemological sense without being skeptical in an ontological sense. A negative skeptic thus can be defined in epistemological and/or ontological terms.

Regarding the two diagrams, we can also understand how positive skepticism, as exemplified in Chinese Taoism and Ch'an Buddhism, takes place. In order to eliminate imbalance and conflict of the requirements for knowledge, one has to relinquish *some* requirements for knowledge. The Taoists and Ch'an Buddhists generally can he said to relinquish the requirements for the exactness and objectivity of knowledge in order to preserve those for ultimacy, totality, and certitude. As we have pointed out, the Taoists and the Ch'an Buddhists are skeptical of objective knowledge of things, and they generally distrust conceptual definiteness, as this would block their vision of the ultimate and the total. Thus, the Taoist and Ch'an Buddhist position can he construed as rejecting the requirements for exactness and objectivity in order to attain the ultimacy, totality, and certitude of knowledge. In fact, for them this rejection is necessary and positively useful for attaining the ultimate totality and certitude of knowledge. Once the ultimate, total and certain knowledge is attained (called a state of enlightenment in Ch'an Buddhism), what is rejected can be accepted in the form of common sense and ordinary life. What is rejected is the need or urge to seek rational exactness and objectivity at the expense of the unity of the whole between object and subject or between the universal and the particular. This position is what I call positive skepticism. The ontological aspect of positive skepticism similarly consists in eliminating the notion of the exact object and the quest for the exact object in order to achieve the originally assumed unity and tranquility of mind. It is assumed that without the quest for the exact object, mind and reality in the ultimacy and totality are one. This is also the ultimate meaning of the ontological tranquility that man originally possesses.

It may be asked whether one could, in one's quest for knowledge, converse to Taoism and Ch'an Buddhism, relinquish the requirements for the totality and ultimacy of knowledge and concentrate on the exactness and objectivity of knowledge and its certitude. A positive reply to this is clearly in order. In fact, modern Western science from the seventeenth century on is precisely founded on the premises of this possibility. Science, as normally understood, does not have as its goal to present and achieve an ultimate and total knowledge of the world or reality which is the dream of rationalistic metaphysics. Instead, science is developed by confining its activity to a specific area of experience. What science stresses is the exactness and objectivity of knowledge in a specific area. Thus science is explicit about a distinction between the objective and the subjective, and the need for a quantitative mathematics for precision. Science also desires certitude and creditability. Though there is the inverse relation between degrees, science strives for certitude and credibility, as far as certitude and creditability allow, and simultaneously strives for exactness and objectivity, as far as exactness and objectivity allow. It may not achieve absolute certitude, and it generally settles on high probability. Science is even open-minded regarding the changeability of scientific knowledge. It allows revision and change of framework insofar as these basic standard requirements for knowledge are maintained at a reasonable level. In such an effort to achieve balance on a limited scale, science thus avoids skepticism. It seems evident that once science is pushed to generate total and ultimate knowledge, science loses its hold on certitude and tends to induce skeptical doubt and create ontological anxiety.

Science in its modern form, as in the preceding description, had not developed in China. Though there are many other factors which contribute to the lack of the development of science in China, a dominating reason seems to be that there is no stringent demand for an *exact* and *objective* knowledge and that there is no earnest need to avoid negative skepticism, because there is no negative skepticism. The reason for the lack of need for exact and objective knowledge is that there is no exact distinction and bifurcation between object and subject in reality. In the Chinese experience and in Chinese ontology, the first proposition is that man (subject) and Heaven and Earth (object) are one, and there is no bifurcation between the two. Chinese experience and Chinese metaphysics also hold that theory and practice, or knowledge and action, are inseparable, and that they are mutually constraining so that no external standard of exactness (such as theoretical mathematics and logic) is needed. As there is no stringent demand for an exact form of objective knowledge, tendencies toward science and skepticism are both lessened, even though the ontological need toward understanding a total and ultimate reality and toward achieving a state of equilibrium in man are sustained. In fact, not insisting on the requirements for the exactness and objectivity of knowledge, and the positive elaboration of the theory of the unity of man and Heaven and Earth, as well as the theory of the unity of theory and practice of Chinese philosophy, enables the total and ultimate knowledge of reality to be compatible with, and even be conducive to, the attainment of epistemological security or certitude. That this is indeed the case is illustrated in and explains why the main Chinese philosophical tradition of Confucian/Neo-Confucian philosophy does not develop any skeptical tendencies.

Confucian/Neo-Confucian philosophy is founded on the experience and the premise that man and nature form a primordial unity and whole, and this unity and whole of man and nature seems to provide a solution to the inner conflict and incompatibility among the requirements for knowledge, such as illustrated in Diagram 1. In the first place, the unity of man and nature enables one to seek the total and ultimate understanding of reality through a process of extension, beginning with man himself. To know the whole is to know oneself first and gradually reach an illumination of all, by the close and careful scrutiny of things. This is indicated in Chu Hsi's doctrine of the investigation of things. It is no less generally true of Lu Hsiang Shan's or Wang Yang-ming's doctrine of the mind.

Regarding the objectivity of knowledge, it has already been suggested that in the Confucian/Neo-Confucian tradition, as in Chinese philosophy in general, there is no bifurcation between object and subject, and this is possible precisely because of the unity of man and nature. Thus, truth and knowledge both have a subjective dimension and an objective dimension which are mutually supportive. The radical requirement for objectivity at the expense of subjectivity is stifled in the beginning of the formation of this model of knowledge.

Finally, the unity of man and nature as an experience of the totality and the whole of man and nature make it both natural and desirable to conceive theory and practiceor knowledge and action as a unity and whole. Knowledge is not valued or sought only for its own sake, and, thus, no theoretical exactness is regarded as essential for the comprehension of genuine knowledge. Practicality in life is sufficient to confirm a high degree of acceptance of knowledge. In this sense, even the knowledge of principles (*li*) in Neo-Confucianism does not exclude its application to ordinary life with all its practical purposefulness.

With this new approach to the requirements for knowledge in Chinese philosophy, the tension of conflicts and incompatibilities among them tend to vanish as they are absorbed into the metaphysics of the unity of man and nature. And indeed, the very compatibility and harmony and even unity of the reconstrued requirements for knowledge help to generate a sense of certitude or epistemological security, which is derived from an ontological sense of man's relevance to nature and is continuously reinforced by the ensuring sense of harmony and adjustment among the various possible requirements for knowledge.

The moral theory of Confucianism/Neo-Confucianism is embedded in the Confucian/Neo-Confucian metaphysical framework, in which morality becomes a part of the cosmological and ontological theory of the unity of man and nature. Again, the principle of the internal identification of man with the nature of Heaven, and the principle of the unity of theory and practice, plus the principle of the organic unity of the individual, society, and government make any skeptical doubt or argument against moral truth lose its relevance or force. Hence, unlike Taoism or Ch'an Buddhism, where in practical life in society and government is divorced from contemplation and meditation, the moral philosophy of Confucianism/Neo-Confucianism is free and immune from skeptical criticism; morality, like cosmology, becomes not only self-justifying, but self-fulfilling.[17]

In concluding, I assert that the very condition for sustaining skepticism is the same condition for developing science (and scientific methodology) and logic. The quest for certainty and absoluteness, as well as for specific or specified simplicity is what motivates both skepticism and logic. Skepticism is logic used to disprove logic or reason employed to defeat reason, and thus requires a very basic consciousness of logic and reason. Thus, skepticism goes hand in hand with reductionism and relativism, which either avoid skepticism or introduce skepticism at the recognition of the limitations of themselves.

Notes

1. See *Outlines of Pyrrhonism*, Bk.I, chapter 4, in Jason L. Saunders, ed., *Greek and Roman Philosophy After Aristotle*, (Glencoe, Ill.: The Free Press, 1966), p. 153.
2. A similar strain of thought was found in George Santayana's *Skepticism and Animal Faith*. But Santayana clearly differs from Hume in making an attempt to introduce a metaphysics of matter, essence, spirit and truth of his own.
3. But we must note a differentiating factor between these examples of positive skepticism and the positive skepticism which dominates Chinese philosophy: the knowledge reconstrued in Descartes is the same knowledge undermined previously by the method of doubt, whereas the knowledge criticized by doubt in Taoism, as we shall see, is affirmed along with the affirmation of a higher order of truth or knowledge.
4. For example, D. C. Lau in his translation of *Tao Te Ching*.
5. *Tao Te Ching*, No. 2.
6. *Tao Te Ching*, No. 48.
7. *Tao Te Ching*, No. 20.
8. *Tao Te Ching*, No. 16.
9. *Tao Te Ching*, No. 12.
10. *Chi Wu Lun*.
11. *Chu Hsia*.
12. *Chu Hsia*.
13. *Chi Wu Lun*.
14. *Chi Wu Lun*.
15. See *Chu Ting Shih Wan* and *Shih Men Cheng Tun*.
16. See my article "On Zen (Ch'an) Language and Zen Paradoxes," *Journal of Chinese Philosophy* Vol. I, No. 1, 78-102, December, 1973.
17. Moral skepticism only arises from *relativistic* and *atomistic* considerations of the individual, as well as from a bifurcation and a diversification between reason as a faculty of justification and experience as a faculty of application.

4. Conscience, Mind and the Individual in Chinese Philosophy

Methodological Considerations

In discussing matters of philosophical consequence, a contemporary analytical approach bas made it almost necessary for a philosopher participating in such discussions to be methodologically cautious. One main reason for this trait of analytical-mindedness is that one does not want to reach conclusions unwarranted by one's pre-refiected principles of validity. Another is that one wishes always to recognize one's limitations before serious objections are launched. Granted these virtues for methodological safeguards in philosophical discussions, one must, however, beware of the negative and contravening effects of methodological thinking when methodology itself is not methodologically scrutinized on a higher plane. In comparative studies in philosophy, anthropology and sociology, certain assumptions about methodology as one might find in contemporary analytical philosophy can prove extremely disturbing and restraining. This fact should prompt a conscientious investigator to question his methodology before defending his results on the basis of the methodology.

In light of what I have said above, I wish to mention two well-known theses in the analytical methodology of contemporary philosophy which may lead to ineffectual and perhaps restricting conclusions in comparative studies of philosophy or civilizations. I wish to mention these two theses, because what I will say in this chapter will not be said in conformity with these two theses, but rather significantly in accordance with the very converse of these two. One might say that it is the converse of these two methodological theses, not the theses themselves, which will vindicate and bring forth the most desirable understanding of this study.

There is in the first place the methodology resulting from the philosophical thesis of the indeterminacy of translation.[1] According to this thesis, there always exists an area of undetermined meaning for any term translated from one language to another. If this means that no meaning of a term in any language can be exhausted and defined in any interpretative system formulated in the same language or formulated in a different language, in such a way that it will not admit future modification, revision and re-interpretation, then this thesis will lead to a healthy encouragement of the creative employment of analysis and synthesis of human understanding toward theoretical and empirical findings. But on the other hand, if the advancement of the thesis entails the ultimate mandate that there will always be gaps in communication between two language systems or two cultural systems, then it must be subject to examination in the individual cases where gaps do exist, in order to decide whether these gaps are capable of being removed through the sharing of more experiences. As a normative principle, the postulation of the ultimate determinacy of meaning seems to be methodologically more helpful than the postulation of the indeterminacy of meaning in research work of a comparative nature, be it in language or in civilization. The very possibility of such comparative studies seems to presuppose the desirability or even the truth of this normative principle.

The second important methodological consideration in contemporary philosophy is that of semantic ascent.[2] The methodology of semantic ascent requires that we should always ask to what state of affairs does a given term apply or of what object is a term true, instead of seeking the seemingly direct referent of the term. Thus, for example, we should not look for entities called 'miles' in order to understand the meaning of 'miles', but instead examine under what circumstances and in what contexts the term 'miles' is used. This apparently will save us from positing (or hypothesizing), and hence, from multiplying, unnecessary abstract entities in our world. But again this useful device of analysis (which can be also called 'de-interpretation') could be pushed to the extreme and thus create a situation where important insights into reality based on genuine experiences of man can be denied. It is quite clear that there are many terms in one's philosophical language which must be interpreted in the context of the directly embodied experiences of a person, but which cannot be de-interpreted in a language which only admits sensory perception (or observation) as the ground of assertion of the individual things. It is also quite plausible that there are terms which refer to experiences which one cannot invoke if one does not have certain ontological understanding or practical experiences. Therefore, contrary to what semantic ascent requests for the revealing of the true nature of a term's meaning, perhaps this meaning has to be retrieved by cultivating the experiential conditions or even the experience itself, from which the term arises and acquires its initial meaningfulness. It is in this spirit of the converse of semantic ascent, which we may call *ontic descent*, that we should treat important terms from a different language or a different culture. We should determine the meanings of such terms in view of the experiential basis as well as the theoretical contexts of such terms. Specifically, before one can have solid ground for concluding that a certain term does not have an ontological referent, one must grant that such ontological reference is always possible and plausible on empirical or theoretical grounds.

To conclude my methodological reflections on comparative studies, I am asking for an open textual and proper (or natural) respect for claims in matters of experience and understanding (or judgments) in different languages or different philosophical systems. Experience may be limited, but it will always be the basis for theoretical generalization. To remove it from the consideration of ontological reference would be gross and unfair. On the other hand, I hope that we are sophisticated enough not to subject all terms of language to a merely contingently narrow scope of experience. We must also hold that comparative studies aim at making universal claims, and therefore communication between languages and civilizations is not only possible but contributes to the development of a universalized doctrine or theory.

Problematic and Scope of Inquiry

In this chapter my purpose is to describe as well as to analyze, to evaluate as well as to theorize about, the notions of conscience, mind and the individual in Chinese philosophy, with reference to the generally assumed common sense understanding or otherwise specified Western philosophical assumptions of these notions. One thing must be immediately made clear: our concern is not to tackle how Chinese philosophers think about the *essentially* defined problems of conscience, mind and the individual. This would assume, unwarrantedly, that Chinese philosophers have the same or similar ideas of conscience, mind and the individual as Western philosophers. On the contrary, we must point out that a Chinese philosopher's ideas of conscience, mind and the individual, as it were, are qualitatively and fundamentally different from any such notions in Western philosophy. Our concern here is therefore to describe and explicate certain Chinese philosophers' views in the area of philosophy of morality, social ethics and philosophy of mind which can be comparatively and fruitfully related to the Western problems of conscience, mind and the individual. This of course is not to deny that there are universal problems to be associated with the connotations of conscience, mind and the individual. In fact, in light of what we have said about the converse principle of the indeterminacy of translation, we should be able to ascertain the universal philosophical problems in a particular philosophical tradition. When problems of conscience, mind and the individual are understood in this universally determinable sense, there is even no objection to speak of the task of this chapter as that of tackling the Chinese philosopher's view on the problems of conscience, mind and the individual.

For the sake of brevity, let us understand the universally determinable problems of conscience,[3] mind and the individual as follows: If conscience is generally understood as the ability of an individual's mind to know and judge good and bad, right and wrong for the purpose of actual and potential conduct, then we wish to know what constitutes the *nature*, the *ground*, the *limit*, and the *function* of this ability in our moral life. We wish also to know how this ability is possible, how it is related to other abilities of the mind, and how it affects our view of the mind and individual and the individual's role and destiny in society, and perhaps how society itself, government and the universe should be conceived from a proper understanding of conscience. In this chapter I shall first discuss the Chinese theory of *liang-chih* (innate knowledge of goodness) as a theory of conscience which can be contrasted with theories of conscience in the West. I will then trace this notion of conscience to a theory of mind (*hsin*) in which the notion of conscience is embedded. After this we shall discuss how Chinese philosophers in the Confucian tradition conceive the status of the individual in society, as well as how they conceive the role that conscience plays in informing an ideal society and its application in actual society. Finally, I shall elucidate in separate sections the ontological and the sociological bases of the Chinese views of conscience, mind and the individual and their significances.

A Theory of Conscience — Conscience as *Liang-Chih* in Mencius (371-289 B.C.)

In the Confucian and Neo-Confucian tradition, *liang-chih* is the ability of the mind to know and judge good and bad, right and wrong, and is therefore the source of moral knowledge. In many aspects, if not all, *liang-chih* plays the same role as Western conscience in the area of moral decision and practical choice bearing on issues of right and wrong. It can therefore be called conscience in a Chinese sense. *Liang-chih* has usually been translated in current literature[4] as 'innate knowledge of goodness'. As I noted elsewhere,[5] this is not an exact and accurate rendering. The term *liang-chih* connotes the meanings both of 'knowing good' and 'knowing from goodness'. It also definitely suggests the presence of an inborn or inherent natural propensity of man's mind toward such knowledge and therefore presupposes the relevance of Mencius' doctrine that human nature in its primitive and primordial state is good. In the later development of this notion in the Neo-Confucian philosophy of Wang Yang-ming (1472-1528), *liang-chih* is clearly identified with the function of moral insights full of ontological import. It is even identified as the sole function of the mind, by which the true nature of the mind is ascertained and realized.

The nature of conscience as *liang-chih* can be glimpsed from the original context of Mencius in which the notion takes its shape:

> What a man is capable of doing without learning is his good ability (*liang-neng*). What a man knows without deliberation is his good knowledge (*liang-chih*). No child does not know love for his parents. When he grows up, no child does not know respect for his elder brothers. To love one's parents is benevolence (*jên*). To respect elders is righteousness (*yi*). They are principles which are universally present in all men under heaven.[6]

What a man is capable of doing and knowing without learning and without deliberation is from the inherent, given, inborn, innate and original nature of man. According to Mencius, man is considered as universally possessing this nature which is the defining quality of man. Though there are metaphysical reasons for making this suggestion, which I will make explicit later, Mencius urges this position basically on intuitive and yet empirical grounds. He asks us to imagine what a man will immediately *feel* when he *suddenly* sees a child about to fall into a well. The feeling that a man will immediately experience under such circumstances, according to Mencius, is the feeling of sympathy towards the child and thus an instinctive readiness to help the child. This is a demonstration of the truth regarding the goodness of human nature, because this instance of spontaneous response towards an endangered child is an instance of goodness, as goodness is always directed toward concrete life-situations. It is also basically a relation between two feeling human beings. Besides, goodness is socially desirable and intuitively identifiable. It is something no one can lose, and when deviated from under external influences, is always retrievable with proper restraint and discipline in life. Finally, it is believed that if human nature, when spontaneously responding, exhibits good in concrete feelings and concrete acts, it is up to the individual to retain, strengthen and heighten the consciousness of the state of mind at such moments. It is Mencius' belief that an individual can always become alert to the initial responsiveness of the mind in human situations and strive to derive clear principles from it so that they can be followed in similar situations without difficulty.

When such spontaneous inceptive insights of the moral mind (*liang-chih*) are rationally strengthened, cultivated and incorporated into one's character, they are called virtues (*te*), which have the potency to incline man towards good acts in life. It is the ideal of Confucianists, beginning with Confucius, to urge man to cultivate himself into a full virtuous character, which is finally described as sagehood (*sheng*). I shall discuss this notion of sagehood later.

It seems clear from Mencius' writing that *liang-chih* is definitively the faculty which constitutes the goodness of human nature. It may also be said that *liang-chih* is the goodness of human nature in operation. It is the unique condition for cognizing the goodness of human nature, which is the existential basis for the intuition of goodness. Thus, with *liang-chih* in oneself one can always tell good from bad, right from wrong, in a concrete situation. But this is not to say that *liang-chih*, the mind or the nature from which *liang-chih* derives itself contains fundamental axioms of good and right.[7] The classical Confucianists, including Mencius, did not say this. Mencius merely asserts that our nature or mind is good and *liang-chih* will intuitively respond in goodness. What one can infer from this is that *liang-chih* does not operate in isolation from life situations, and therefore it does not formulate knowledge of good and right independently of living contexts in which the mind responds with *liang-chih*. The knowledge of goodness is not a general principle to be separated from instances of its application. It is always located in instances of actual application. Another point in connection with this is that one will not discover all the principles of morality unless one has exposed oneself to all the particularities of life in which moral decisions and sentiments are elicited and aroused.[8] One might also draw the following conclusion: As the particularities in life and society are potentially unlimited, there are an unlimited number of instances of moral decisions and judgments.

As there is no problem of separating the knowledge of right and good from the application of such knowledge, there is no problem of applying moral principles to particular situations to form correct judgments; there is also no problem of identifying or verifying moral principles independently of their application. The only problem that one faces is bow to lay hold of the initial insight into good and right through the function of one's *liang-chih* and how to strengthen them and invoke the same or similar insights on other and perhaps all occasions. This problem is one of sharpening and enlarging the function of one's *liang-chih*. It is also the problem of the cultivation of one's mind or nature as formulated by Mencius. When we come to Wang Yang-ming, we see how he formulates the doctrine of fulfilling one's *liang-chih* (*chih-liang-chih*) as an answer to the problem of the cultivation of mind or nature as implicitly posed by Mencius. This doctrine elaborates more than ever on the nature and ground of *liang-chih* as first developed by Mencius.

One might make a distinction between a Platonic concept of moral knowledge and an Aristotelian concept of moral knowledge. The former will consider moral knowledge as separable from the experience of good and bad, right and wrong in living situations. The latter, however, does not consider it possible to separate moral knowledge from moral experience. It instead considers moral knowledge as arising from concrete moral experiences. With this distinction in mind, one can point out that the theory of *liang-chih* in Mencius is not a Platonic theory but an Aristotelian one in the above sense.

Dynamics of Conscience (*Liang-Chih*) in Action

Whereas Mencius does not specify whether the mind possesses moral principles of the knowledge of good and right in his theory of *liang-chih*, Wang Yang-ming explicitly develops a theory which will answer this question. His theory is thematically summarized in one proposition: "Mind is identical with principles" (*hsin-chi-li*). Wang Yang-ming says: "Mind is identical with principles. In the world, are there states of affairs or principles (of things) outside of mind?"[9] The purport of this question is not to reduce things and principles to mental entities in a subjective idealistic philosophy. What is intended is that mind, as an activity, defines and describes, creates and discovers the principles in terms of which things are to be understood and evaluated. This again implies the following two points: (1) Mind is creative, and, in a dynamic field of activity and experience, mind will evince whatever principles one might find among things; (2) Whatever principles mind evinces in its activities coincide necessarily with principles in the objective nature of things. These two points are the reasons why I say that mind, according to Wang Yang-ming, defines and describes, creates and discovers the principles at the same time. When this doctrine of "Mind is identical with principles" is specifically applied to moral situations which, for Wang Yang-ming, are the fundamental and original testing ground for his doctrine, it is apparent that Wang Yang-ming assumes that it is intuitively clear that moral principles and their knowledge are actualized when the mind applies itself to situations of moral significance.

When the mind is thus applied and when moral principles and their knowledge are actualized, we may call the mind the mind of *liang-chih* or we may say that the mind has truly applied itself. In this view, *liang-chih* is merely the genuine acts of the mind in its application to human situations. Wang Yang-ming calls this the "activation (*fa*) of mind."[10] He assumes that the mind can always be activated; it can be activated when one is alerted to a situation. This is the original Mencian point. But Wang Yang-ming further holds that the mind can be activated when one is to keep it free from the influence of selfish desires and prejudices. The moral problem of applying *liang-chih* is not to look for principles in things or to justify one's principles when found, but to apply and activate one's mind and let it creatively and intuitively judge good and bad, right or wrong in the most concrete sense. The ultimate faith is that one's good judgment is always forthcoming if one keeps one's mind free from selfish desires and prejudices. This faith is not totally blind, however, because one can justify it by constantly watching and cultivating the moral knowledge (*liang-chih*) of mind. The theory of the cultivation of *liang-chih*, therefore, becomes an integral part of the theory of *liang-chih*, because it is only through the cultivation of *liang-chih* that one can be assured of the full activity of *liang-chih* in different life situations.

As to whether one should not first seek principles of morality before applying them, we have the following dialogue between Wang's disciple and Wang:

[The disciple] asked: "In serving one's father with filial piety, in serving one's ruler with loyalty, and in treating one's friends with integrity, there are many principles in all these matters. It seems that one cannot discern them [principles]."[Wang] answered:"In serving one's father one does not seek the principles of filial piety in one's father; in serving one's ruler, one does not seek principles of loyalty in one's ruler; in making friends and governing people, one does not seek principles of integrity and benevolence. All [principles] come from this mind. Mind is principle. When this mind is not obstructed by selfish or private desires, it is heavenly principles (i.e., pure principles which is nothing other than the *liang-chih* itself); and nothing needs to be added from the outside. When one activates this mind of heavenly principles in serving one's father, it is filial piety; when one activates it in serving one's ruler, it is loyalty; when one activates it in making friends and governing people, it is integrity and benevolence. What one needs to do . i.e., to insure the activation of one's *liang-chih* and to arrive at a correct outcome is to eliminate one's desires and preserve one's heavenly principles [as inherent in one's mind].[11]

By strongly affirming the normal innate capacities of the mind in judging good and bad, right and wrong, and by indicating how these capacities can be assured of correct functioning, Wang Yang-ming is convinced that the mind itself can make right decisions and institute right acts toward good and right in any moral situation in life. Even though the situations which Wang Yang-ming indicates are *basic* simple life situations, there is no doubt for Wang Yang-ming that this holds true for *all* life situations no matter how complicated. This principle (or thesis), that the mind can arrive at right decisions and discover or define good in any human situation if the mind preserves its initial responsiveness in basic simple situations (a Mencian point), and if the mind is constantly strengthened or cultivated in such a way that it remains unobscured or unobstructed by selfish or private desires, can be called the *principle* (or *thesis*) *of moral creativity*. It is obvious that the principle (or thesis) of moral creativity makes both the search for moral principles prior to their application in concrete situations and the search for the justification of the application of one's moral principles in concrete situations unnecessary and otiose. The function of the principle of moral creativity lies in the cultivation of *liang-chih* as a constant and spontaneous device of moral insight and moral acts.[12]

In Wang Yang-ming, *liang-chih* can be analyzed into several important aspects.[13] (1) *Liang-chih* is not a passive or penultimate state of feeling born from goodness. It is an active perception (or experience) of goodness as the essence of one's nature. It is therefore described as a state of vacuity, intelligence, perceptiveness and sensitivity (*hsu-ling-ming-chueh*) and as a state of intelligent clarity and illuminating perception (*ling-chao-ming-chueh*). It is identified as the ultimate substance of mind. (2) The activity of the mind in terms of *liang-chih* not only generates all moral judgments (*chih-shan*) and moral acts in concrete situations, but is itself supremely good. In other words, *liang-chih* as the unobstructed and spontaneous activity of man is itself the standard of good and the source of good.[14] It is considered self-verifying and self-sustaining. It is not subject to external or any other forms of judgment. This means that it is like divinity discovering itself without any need to conform to any other standard. In this sense *liang-chih* is not only the ultimate reality of the mind, but that of the total reality. It is like God's will internalized and ingrained. (3) *Liang-chih* is further singled out from other movements in the mind as the constant natural light which will determine good and bad, right and wrong. It is recognized by Wang Yang-ming that mind may have many intentions activated, which may lead to courses of action. *Liang-chih* is considered the only special activation of mind which can immediately judge the morality of each and every activity of the mind. If this is not the case, it is because *liang-chih* is not properly cultivated. When *liang-chih* is properly cultivated, each and every activation of the mind (that is, each and every intention of the mind) will have received moral judgment from *liang-chih*. *Liang-chih* is what makes the mind a moral mind. It is, furthermore, that which makes self-knowledge of oneself possible, for one will know and affirm one's moral worth only when one is able to judge oneself (or one's intentions or thoughts) through the activity of *liang-chih*. (4) Finally, it must be noted that *liang-chih* is not merely a reflective form of the moral evaluative activity of the mind. It is also affirmed by Wang Yang-ming to be a form of active will[15] which will incline the mind towards the action which it sees as good. The reason for this affirmation is that *liang-chih* is an activation of the mind in the sense of willing and as such is always practically inclining. This aspect of *liang-chih* can be better explained in light of Wang Yang-ming's theory of the unity of knowledge and action (*chih-hsin-ho-yi*) expressed by Wang in the following words: "There is no knowledge which does not lead to action. If one knows but does not act, then one really does not know."[16]

Since I cannot fully explicate Wang's doctrine of *chih-hsin-ho-yi* in this space, I will indicate roughly some philosophical presuppositions and implications of this doctrine for Wang's theory of *liang-chih*. One of these philosophical presuppositions is that mind-activity is not to be serapated into exclusive acts of non-practical cognition and exclusive acts of non-cognitive valuation for inclination, but instead should be considered as always generating intentions (*yi*) having many dimensions. An intention is a cognition of something (inner or outer) as well as the evaluation of the object cognized. It is also an action potential which inclines one toward some course of action which embodies, exhibits or fulfills the evaluation in the intention. Given this holistic view of the activity of the mind, *liang-chih* is clearly very crucial for the direction of the mind toward action, for *liang-chih* will have the power resulting from its judgment of good and right to enforce that judgment in action, or to avoid its contrary in another action. In this sense, *liang-chih* must be understood not merely as the knowledge of innate good, but also as the *will* toward good. Thus, given a strongly cultivated and reinforced *liang-chih*, one will always desire to do or act out the good and right. On the other hand, if one loses sight of one's *liang-chih* or if one does not care to cultivate *liang-chih* into a strong watch-guard of one's mind, one may go astray and be misled by one's desires under the influence of intentions other than those of the natural light of *liang-chih*.

To see how to cultivate, reinforce and preserve one's *liang-chih*, we must now discuss in some detail Wang's doctrine of the *fulfillment of liang-chih (chih-liang-chih)*. The doctrine of *chih-liang-chih*, I presume, would seem esoteric in light of the history of the theory of conscience in the West. Apparently there is no suggestion made in the Western tradition that conscience must be cultivated and reinforced in some process of one's moral growth or self-realization. It appears that conscience in man is what is already given by God, which will tell us what is right and what is wrong; hence, there is no way for us to enlarge or strengthen it for better application. We can indeed use reason to verify or substantiate our conscious acts of mind. But on the other hand, there seems to be a strong tradition[17] suggesting that we can be totally and objectively wrong even if we have sincerely followed the judgments of conscience. Efforts to substantiate the judgments of conscience in light of reason, rational arguments and calculations (called moral casuistry) are generally agreed to be a worthy and relevant enterprise for achieving moral correctness and moral wisdom.

Now in the Wang Yang-ming tradition of *liang-chih*, such efforts, however, are regarded as unnecessary and irrelevant, for it is considered sufficient that *liang-chih* is always correct in its judgments and that *liang-chih* always applies itself. The central question for the Chinese Neo-Confucian philosopher is whether one follows one's *liang-chih* and develops it so that it can be followed when needed in life situations. It is of course understood that *liang-chih* is always needed in any life situation, whatever it is, since it is important that we do not let our intentions be activated without the confirmation of *liang-chih*. The doctrine of *chih-liang-chih* is unique in a theory of conscience, because it explains how *liang-chih* always applies itself in such a way that this process of application is ever regenerated. This kind of explanation mitigates the need to search for principles independently of moral decisions and justifications of the application of such principles.

There are several fundamental considerations in the doctrine of *chih-liang-chih* which guarantee that *liang-chih* will always correctly apply itself to the life situations of an individual. In the first place, it was suggested earlier that *liang-chih* intuitively tells good from bad, right from wrong in many concrete affairs of life. These affairs of life are basic and intimate relationships in which one is inevitably involved in one's family and social life. These are the relationships to one's parents and to one's brothers. It is natural for one to experience what *liang-chih* dictates as good in these relationships. One should always cherish these experiences and assimilate them into one's disposition and thus develop what Mencius calls the virtues of benevolence, righteousness, propriety and wisdom. The idea that one can start with *liang-chih* from some intimate relationship and then let *liang-chih* develop other relationships is also suggested by Confucius' theory of virtues; that is, that filial piety (*hsiao*) and brotherliness (*ti*) are the bases for the supreme virtue of benevolence (*jên*). Once one has established virtues in one's character, one can naturally respond to unfamiliar conditions and affairs through one's virtues which will be in accord with the operation of *liang-chih*. In this regard, to fulfill *liang-chih* is to cultivate one's character toward virtue, in the belief that virtue will always lead to good conduct which warrants the sanction of *liang-chih*. It is to be noted here that virtues need not lead to conscious decisions or judgments of good and right. Yet, insofar as virtue is conducive to good and right conduct and the ultimate good of *liang-chih* rests with action or the unity of practice and theory, virtue is at least important as a way for the satisfactory functioning (application) of *liang-chih*. Therefore, to develop virtue is to fulfill *liang-chih* in an important sense.

A second consideration regarding how *liang-chih* may provide correct principles of application in an unfamiliar situation bears upon Wang's assertion that when correct principles of application are required for achieving moral goodness, *liang-chih* can recognize a need and indeed constitutes the actual will to search for these principles. This is not to say that *liang-chih* embodies all correct principles of application or our knowledge of the objective world. This merely means that *liang-chih* motivates all the necessary investigations of things which will lead to the necessary extension of knowledge. Though Wang Yang-ming does not explicitly suggest that the investigation of things as motivated by the need of *liang-chih* must yield correct application or knowledge which it needs to fulfill good in a situation, still the unspoken assumption throughout his writings seems to underscore the fact that the sincere investigation of things will yield correct and relevant principles of application, as well as the knowledge necessary for the judgment of good and right by *liang-chih*. In answer to a query about whether one should look into the correct principles of application in serving one's parents, Wang Yang-ming says the following:

In wintertime one naturally thinks of one's parents being cold, thus one will seek principles of how to prevent cold; in summertime one naturally thinks of one's parents being hot, thus one will seek principles of how to prevent hotness. These are acts issuing from one's heart of sincerity and filial piety. One must always have this heart of sincerity and filial piety; then these acts will issue from them. Using a tree as an analogy, this heart of sincerity and filial piety is the root, and those acts of heart (to seek knowledge) are branches and leaves of the tree. A tree must first have roots, then it will have branches and leaves. One should not first seek branches and leaves, then plant the roots.[18]

The tree analogy clearly brings out Wang Yang-ming's point that *liang-chih* will naturally obtain its correct principles of application and knowledge, as well as his point that by tending to the basic affairs of life with *liang-chih*, one will be able to apply *liang-chih* to a variety of different affairs of life on the basis of one's virtue. Both points are crucial for understanding the moral force of this doctrine of *chih-liang-chih*.

Thirdly, a crucial aspect of the doctrine of *chih-liang-chih* also answers the question of how one can be assured that one's *liang-chih* will judge correctly in all life situations.[19] This answer lies in the admonition that one should discipline, watch and cultivate one's self in all the matters of life within the ordinary scope of living, small or large. Wang says: "Efforts (*kung-fu*) must penetrate through. How does one start a thought for doing what is right? A person needs to 'grind and temper' himself in all affairs of life and make his efforts (*kung-fu*) so that they will become beneficial to him."[20]

The idea of 'grind and temper' (*mou-lian*[20]) vividly suggests a process of keeping a watchful and serious (earnest) eye on all one's doings and being on guard for possible misdeeds or wrongdoings. It is to exercise one's moral sensibilities unceasingly so that one's moral decisions will come out naturally and spontaneously even when one is faced with difficult or unfamiliar situations. According to Wang Yang-ming, even when there is no particular affair for one to 'grind and temper' one's applicative ability of *liang-chih*, one must preserve the integrity and potential of one's *liang-chih* by 'nourishing and preserving it' (*ts'un-yang*). This is a form of cultivating *liang-chih* so that it remains clear and alert, ready to act on any occasion. "To reflect and inspect one's *liang-chih* is to preserve and nourish one's *liang-chih* when there are affairs for it to apply to; to preserve and nourish one's *liang-chih* is to inspect and reflect one's *liang-chih* when there are no affairs for it to apply to."[21] The very continuous activity of such a moral mind (*liang-chih*) is a guard against wrong judgments and forms the justification for (the validity of) the moral judgments or moral choices which one adopts on its basis. To explain the validity of this justification, one needs to go into the metaphysical framework in which the very idea of "*liang-chih*" is formulated. It is clear that this justification is not intended to demonstrate that one has exhibited sufficient virtue so that one's decisions and judgments should be warranted as a moral rule or norm.[22]

The ideal state of mind in which *liang-chih* is ready to apply and is capable of generating insights into moral situations is where mind is highly sensitive, lively and self-reflective. To fulfill *liang-chih* (*chih-liang-chih*) is to achieve this ideal state of mind. Wang Yang-ming has likened such a dynamic state of mind, in which conscience is always kept in activation, to the flow of water in a river.[23] It is, ontologically speaking, the highest creativity in life.

An important measure for enhancing, as well as for achieving the creative activity of *liang-chih*, i.e., for conducing to a state of mind where *liang-chih* can creatively apply without delay, doubt or difficulty, is the elimination of private and selfish desires. This brings us to the fourth and final aspect of the doctrine of *chih-liang-chih*. This fourth regard is that *chih-liang-chih* eliminates selfish desires (*ssu-yu*) and selfish intentions (*ssu-yi*). To understand this thesis, one must understand that for Wang Yang-ming, as for earlier Neo-Confucians in the Sung Dynasty, the mind (or heart) is made of vital nature (*ch'i*), which in substance is also the very stuff from which all things with forms and shapes are made. Consequently, Wang Yang-ming regards emotions and desires as part of the function of the mind or heart.

Although all Neo-Confucianists also assume that desires or emotions may occur in a natural fashion, they recognize, nevertheless, that desires or emotions may outdo themselves and create disorder and obstruction in one's mind, so that the mind as a whole may not function in accordance with one's nature of good. This is because desires and intentions are such that, while they are natural, they are apt to disturb and divert the growth of the total mind and its higher faculty of *liang-chih*. Thus, an important principle for the cultivation of one's mind toward truth and (potential action) is to control one's desires and emotions to the extent that they will not affect the natural movement of one's mind as an integral part of nature.[24] This suggests that the control and discipline of desires and emotions is a reflective means to vanguard the mind against its incapacitation and loss as an autonomous, active and creative organ.

In Wang Yang-ming's theoretical framework of *liang-chih* and *chih-liang-chih*, to eliminate selfish desires and intentions is to eliminate the desires and intentions which go against the dictates of *liang-chih*. A person can discern the inceptive deviation of desires and intentions through the constantly present *liang-chih*. If one has this discernment, one is able to eliminate selfish desires and intentions in their beginning state and thus permit the power of *liang-chih* to be more stabilized and strengthened. On the other hand, when *liang-chih* is constantly applied, and thus established as a regular disciplinary power within one's mind, then it is less likely for one to have selfish desires and intentions occurring in one's mind. Eventually, the reciprocal interaction of *liang-chih* with the control of desires and intentions will reinforce the potency of *liang-chih* and make it possible to apply itself successfully under any circumstances.

One must note that this does not mean that *liang-chih* runs counter to desires, emotions and intentions (movements of mind). This means only that when *liang-chih* is fulfilled, in the sense of eliminating selfish desires and intentions, all desires and intentions that conform to *liang-chih* will be recognized by it as good. To use Wang's words, "All seven feelings (joy, anger, sorrow, fear, love, hatred and desire) flow out of its nature and are the activities of *liang-chih*."[25] Under this consideration it is clear that Wang believes that *liang-chih* will function to correctly judge situations if it is free from the burden of what he calls selfish desires and intentions. The ability of *liang-chih* is such that what constitutes selfish desires and selfish intentions are self-evident to *liang-chih*. *Liang-chih* is thus able to certify for itself whether it operates without the obstruction of selfish desires and selfish intentions, or whether it operates at all.

One may now conclude that if Wang is correct, *liang-chih* can always arrive at correct moral judgments if it is free from the interference of habit-ual selfish desires and selfish intentions; conversely, whenever a judgment is incorrect, one must assume that one has acted under the influence of selfish desires and selfish intentions. This view of *liang-chih*'s functioning is, of course, highly intuitive and optimistic. But one can also see why the constant checking of one's mental attitude and thus, the constant cultivation of one's moral sensibilities is essential for the preservation of the strength of *liang-chih*.

From what we have said above, it is clear that the doctrine of *chih-liang-chih* is directly a theory of the cultivation of *liang-chih* and indirectly a theory of the application of *liang-chih* and justification of its application. I mean by the latter point that according to the doctrine of *chih-liang-chih*, the feasibility of *liang-chih* for its application in various situations is secured by a process of the cultivation of its strength, and that the trustworthiness of its judgments in all its applications is secured or justified again by appeal to its being constantly cultivated in the sense defined by the doctrine of *chih-liang-chih*. It is also clear from this that *liang-chih* does not involve itself in adducing prior valid principles for its application when it is applied, nor involves itself in justifying its application or judgment in its application. It is considered that there is no need for this. One might say that with the background of constant cultivation provided by the doctrine of *chi-liang-chih, liang-chih* will intuitively recognize valid principles or norms for justifying its judgments, which guarantee their perfect applicability in specific cases. In fact, these principles are concretized by the specific cases themselves when *liang-chih* applies itself. So, the only necessary condition for the correct judgments of liang-chih is to reinforce and cultivate *liang-chih* into a powerfully sensitive awareness and will in one's mind. From all these one can understand why rational casuistry for the purpose of justifying the application of conscience becomes totally dispensable in the Chinese *liang-chih* and *chih-liang-chih* theory of conscience. The ideas of casuistry and explicative justification do not even occur to the mind of the Chinese thinkers!

Two Types of Theories of Mind:
Conscience in Relation to Principles

Even though principles and their application play no role in the moral decisions and judgments of *liang-chih* in Wang Yang-ming's theory of *liang-chih* and *chih-liang-chih*, the ideas of principles (*li*) and their application are not totally missing from the discussions of *liang-chih* and the mind with which it is identified. In fact, Wang has to justify his dismissal of the relevance of principles and their application from the theory of *liang-chih* and *chih-liang-chih*. His justification takes two arguments: an ontological argument, and a methodological argument.

In his ontological argument, Wang asserts that the mind is principle (*hsin-chi-li*). As we have seen, this means that the activity and the substance of the mind forms what principles are. It is not that principles are deposited in the mind, but that they are creatively generated from the mind, as if it is a creative power. The mind defines itself and defines the universal and necessary principles by its nature, for again, as we have explained above, ontologically speaking, the mind shares with all other minds the ultimate reality (called the *Tao*) from which it derives itself. By the same token, the mind gives rise to the principles of application by defining them when principles of substances are generated for application in the contexts of life.

The methodological argument represents Wang's criticism of the doctrine of exhaustively investigating things (*ke-wu*) and knowing the principles of things (*chih-chih*), as held by Chu Hsi (1130-1200) in the twelfth century. Chu Hsi and his master Ch'eng Yi (1033-1107) assert that one must seek the knowledge of things and understand the principles (*li*) of things before one can realize the unity of mind in a rightous course. Without necessarily doing justice to this view of mind, Wang rejects this approach to the cultivation of the mind as being external and apt to lead to confusion and trivialities. He also sees this approach as leading to the loss of the original goodness of the mind, instead of exposing or increasing it. He says:

Some people do not know that the supreme good resides in my mind and thus seeks good from the outside, assuming that all things and affairs have definitive principles, and thus tries to look for supreme goodness in the middle of things and affairs. Consequently, they lose themselves in a confused state of unrelated information and broken ideas full of miscellany and disorder, and do not know a certain direction of the truth.[26]

What Wang Yang-ming objects to are the assumptions that the standard of goodness could be formed outside the evaluative-creative activities of the mind, that the mind should direct itself toward an outside world and that what the mind obtains from the outside can determine what the mind should feel, as if the mind is merely a passive information gatherer. For the present purpose, we need not worry whether this criticism of the principle-seeking efforts of the mind, presumably exemplified in the writings of Chu Hsi, is fair. However, it is clear from this that this criticism by Wang does apply to any potential interest in the performance of casuistic reasoning as the basis of moral decisions. For might it not appear that a theory of casuistic reasoning may lose itself in a labyrinth of unrelated bits of information and broken ideas, and lead to disorder and confusion and miscellany, which will totally defeat its original purpose of justification?

A reply to this criticism perhaps could be found in an accurate account of the mind and its relation to principles in the writings of Chu Hsi. According to Chu Hsi, mind cannot be so easily identified with *liang-chih* as Wang assumes, because by its nature, mind cannot be said to be a clear matter of principles. In other words, Chu Hsi holds that, whereas the nature (*hsing*) of man is principle, the mind is not simply nature and therefore cannot simply be principle. As nature is derived from the ultimate reality, it is potentially endowed with all the principles of things, but it takes some effort of the mind to discover them through a process of principle-seeking activities. Chu Hsi calls our attention to the fact that mind is made of vital nature (*ch'i*), which partakes of the rational nature (in the sense of reason and principle), but which also is bound to the vital activities of feelings and desires. He agrees with his masters Ch'eng Yi and Chang Tsai (1020-1077) in holding that "Mind synthesizes rational nature and (vital) feeling (*ching*)"[27] (*hsin-tung-hsing-ching*). Because of the ontological difference between the mind and nature, the mind must be exercised in a rational manner before it can reach a state of illumination of knowledge and insight into supreme goodness. Instead of holding that the mind, by its own power, could reveal its true identity, Chu Hsi, following the suggestion of Cheng Yi, holds that the true identity of the mind is only established in a process of the investigation of things and extension of the knowledge of the principles of things. In other words, he believes that the mind should look for principles in things, and what the mind gets from the outside will enable the mind to maintain and establish its truthfulness and avoid the traps of private and selfish desires and intentions. This implies that only after the mind has been clear about the principles of things, will the mind be able to issue sincere intentions conforming to the ultimate principle of nature.

On commenting on the doctrine of investigation of things (*ke-wu*) and the extension of knowledge (*chih-chih*) in the Confucian classic the *Great Learning*, which mentions *ke-wu* and *chih-chih* as the first two steps of the process of the cultivation of an individual and his mind toward supreme goodness, Chu Hsi says:

What the doctrine says in regard to the proposition that extension of knowledge comes from investigation of things, means that in order to attain any knowledge, I have to exhaust the principles of things in things. It is because the intelligence of the human mind is always capable of knowing, and all the things under Heaven are always with principles. It is only when the principles of things are not exhausted, the knowledge in the mind will not be complete. Thus the first teaching of the *Great Learning* is that a person of learning must further and exhaust the principles of all things under Heaven on the basis of principles that he already knows, so that he may arrive at the utmost (of the knowledge of principles of things). When the mind has been thus exercised long enough, and reached a state of sudden penetration and comprehensive understanding, then the insights into the inside and outside, the fine and crude nature of all things will be attained, and the great function of the total body of my mind will be completely revealed. This is called things investigated. This is called the arrival of knowledge.[28]

From this passage one can clearly see that Chu Hsi does not deny that the mind may have some knowledge of principle to start with, and that the ultimate goal of the mind's principle-seeking efforts is the total illumination of the mind by knowledge. Essentially what he envisions as the final characterization of the mind as an agent of moral judgment is not different from Wang Yang-ming's view in his doctrine of *liang-chih*. For Chu Hsi, the mind is *liang-chih* only when it possesses knowledge of the principles of things and there is no other thing than *liang-chih* in the mind. But, unlike Wang, Chu Hsi insists that the mind is to become *liang-chih* through a process of principle-seeking in terms of the investigation of things outside of the mind. There are three things to be said about this process of principle-seeking: First, the mind does not seek the principles of things only when something happens to the mind. The mind will make it a point to investigate things for knowledge of the principles independent of the moral promptings of the mind at any given moment. This suggests a detached research-oriented attitude of study which is rejected by Wang. Second, the mind will seek the principles of things in many empirical and practical areas of life. In many places Chu Hsi suggests a kind of scientific investigation into social events and natural phenomena. This clearly indicates the presence of an ethical-neutral attitude of study. Third, it is assumed that, by engaging in this sort of investigation of things in this large sense, the mind will suddenly become clear about the total and final principles of things and itself. This might be described as a step of induction and/or intuitive induction. This intuitive induction is possible because it is assumed that nature, from which the mind receives its rational ability, has contained all the ultimate truth of the world. With this mechanism of intuitive induction, it is clear that the mind is guarded against losing itself in a maze of unrelated bits of information and broken ideas, and thus the criticism of Wang becomes irrelevant.

Given the above understandings of Chu Hsi's theory of mind in relation to the principles of things, we might conclude that for Chu Hsi, *liang-chih* in Wang Yang-ming's sense needs principles for its function as a moral decision-making power. In so far as principles must be gathered or generated in a process of investigation and study, Chu Hsi seems not to rule out the need for casuistic reasoning, for one may regard casuistic reasoning as being identifiable with the use of principles on the basis of the investigation of things. One might even say that, whereas Wang dismisses the theoretical relevance of casuistic reasoning for *liang-chih*'s acts throughout his doctrine of *chih-liang-chih*, Chu Hsi admits its relevance on the basis of his doctrine of *ke-wu* and *chih-chih*. But on the other hand, lest the contrast be pushed too far beyond the limit, we must also be reminded that, for Chu Hsi as well as for Wang Yang-ming, there is not a single doubt that the mind will provide its own ground of justification for its moral judgments and moral decisions, even though these provisions are made possible in different processes, as recognized respectively by Wang and Chu. In the ultimate power of the mind as a moral forum, Chu Hsi and Wang are in total agreement. The two types of theories of mind which Wang and Chu respectively develop suggest two types of relationships of the mind to the principles or truths of the things as well as two types of processes of cultivation. They equally invest and confirm the total power of correct moral decisions in mind. Their difference, therefore, is not ontological, but merely methodological and epistemological.

Before we discuss the ontological basis of their agreement on the powers of the mind in moral practice and moral justification (reasoning), we must make a brief clarification of the notion of 'principles' (*li*) in our discussion of the relation between mind and principle in both philosophers. Principles (*li*), in these contexts, must be intentionally understood in a very broad and yet necessarily metaphysical sense. This notion of 'principle' suggests the ultimate reason and rationality of things, which not only explains why things are what they are, but why things are related to one other and to the ultimate reality in an orderly fashion. '*Li*' is a principle of unity as well as a principle of differentiation. It is ultimately a principle of unity in variety *par excellence*. Thus, the final understanding of principles is inevitably the understandings of one principle as illustrated by many principles. This ontological unification of all principles into oneness and one ultimate principle (called *Tao*) is what makes it metaphysically possible for the mind to make the intuitive-inductive jump into total understanding, which can be characterized as seeing different principles in different things and yet seeing them as belonging to one simple truth.

Another aspect of the notion of principle is that it is not completely an object of scientific and empirical investigation. It is something which one must experience, see and then embody in practice. Words like 'nourish' (*yang*), 'very acquainted with' (*shu*), 'deeply experience' (*ti-nien*), 'thoroughly understand' (*li-hui*), 'practise' (*ch'ien*), and 'embody and nourish' (*han-yang*), are used by Chu Hsi to describe the investigative process of studying *li*. In this sense, *li* is as interior and internal as Wang would make *liang-chih*. In both cases it is clear that the effects of the total application and justification of moral decisions are secured, for these decisions will ultimately be regarded as direct manifestations of *liang-chih* or the mind embodying *li*. Neo-Confucianists, including Chu Hsi and Wang Yang-ming, agree on the same ontological framework for the explanation of the operation of the mind and the justification of its operation. This includes the operation of *liang-chih*, as well as the vindication of the necessity of cultivation which is elaborated in the doctrine of *chih-liang-chih*. This conclusion hopefully demonstrates my earlier suggestion that though there is no proof procedures of *liang-chih*'s principles of application, the existence of the mind in the above sense does provide a reason for why these are unncessary and yet consistently intelligible on an ontological level.

Theory of Mind As The Ontological Ground of The Theories of *Liang-Chih* and *Chih-Liang-Chih*

From the very beginning of Confucianism, and perhaps from the very beginning of Chinese philosophy in the 9th millenium, there is a strong tendency to regard the mind of man as partaking of the ultimate reality[29], so that it is capable of comprehending it. At the same time, it is recognized that because of its vital nature, the mind may easily lose sight of its true identity, and become the slave of the lower functions of one's body. It is said in the *Book of Documents* in regard to the mind of man: "The mind of the Way is very small, the mind of man is very dangerous. One should concentrate on being alert and single willed so that one will always hold the mean."[30] The mind of the Way is the ultimate reality (the Way) revealing itself, whereas the mind of man is the activities of emotion and desires, by which individual man is individuated. To say that the mind of the Way is small is not to say that it is small in quality or in quantity, but to suggest that it is very subtle and very easily lost sight of. On the other hand, to say that the mind of man is dangerous is not to say that it is dangerous by itself, but that without proper understanding and restraint, one's desires and emotions may dominate oneself and subdue whatever one's perception of total truth is, which is beneficial for fulfilling the total potentiality of the mind.

Given this initial description of the mind, it is clear that one has to be very cautious in reviewing one's mind. It seems inevitable that one must attach great importance to a process of cultivation in which the mind of the

Way will become clearer and clearer and the mind of man will become more and more disciplined under the control and inspection of the mind. I have indicated one important goal of this process of cultivation in the doctrine of *chih-liang-chih*, i.e., it is to enable the mind to arrive at the correct judgment of right and good in any of its applications in life. I will now indicate another goal, perhaps sometimes regarded as a more important one for this process of cultivation of the mind. I will reserve the discussion of the very process of cultivation in attaining both goals for a later section. I will also reserve some brief discussion of the ontological basis of the constitution of the mind and its cultivation to a still later section.

The second important goal of the cultivation of the mind as seen against the background of the quotation from the *Book of Documents*, is to achieve unity and identity of one's mind, hence oneself, with the ultimate truth of the world. As the mind is the individuating principle of oneself, the Way is the ultimate reality embracing the multitude of all things, this goal of the cultivation of the mind is therefore one of identifying oneself as a person with all things in the world, in virtue of the highly cultivated state of one's mind and character. This state is referred to as benevolence (*jên*) most of the time. It is an attitude as well as an understanding of things that are recognized as belonging to a unity and yet creatively fulfilling a rich content of this unity unceasingly. Thus, the identification of oneself solely with all things, as the identification of one's mind with the Way, is therefore not a static merge into an 'undifferentiated continuum', as one may think at first glimpse. The Neo-Confucianist philosophy has specifically warned against this concept of identification, which they call tranquility (*ching*) or quietude (*chi*) which they attribute to the Buddhist or Taoist point of view. For the Neo-Confucianist philosophy, this state of identification is that of the dynamic interchange of life. It is to experience the creative impulse of the ultimate reality in its generation of life at a most pervasive and profound level. I will cite some sources in describing this dynamic state of identification of one's mind with the ultimate reality, as the final stage of one's cultivation of mind.[31]

In the *Chung Yung* (the *Doctrine of the Mean*) it is said that:

Only those who are utmostly sincere are capable of fulfilling their nature. Being capable of fulfilling one's nature, one is capable of fulfilling the nature of other men; being capable of fulfilling the nature of other men, one is capable of fulfilling the nature of things. Being capable of fulfilling the nature of things, one is able to assist Heaven and Earth in their creative productive-transformative functions (activities). Being able to assist Heaven and Earth in their creative productive-transformative activities, one will be able to form a unity of three with Heaven and Earth.[32]

The idea of utmost sincerity alludes to the experience of the ultimately real and whole of things in one's mind, without any intervention of selfish desires and emotion. It is a state of mind which is reached after persistent cultivation of one's mind, and, by implication (as in the following quotation from the same source), a state which is illuminated by knowledge and full of insights into the principles of things. The *Chung Yung* considers that one can gain knowledge of the truth and insights into the principles of things by cultivating "one's experience of reality in *mind*" (*ch'eng*). This is said to be due to the very nature of one's mind. It also affirms that by education and teaching one can arrive at the total experience of the reality of understanding. Finally, it asserts the dynamic equivalence between the experience of reality in mind and "the illuminated attainment of knowledge" (*ming*) in mind. It says:

From the *ch'eng* to *ming*, it is called nature; from *ming* to *ch'eng*, it is called teaching. If *ch'eng*, then*ming*. If *ming*, then *ch'eng*.[33]

One may indeed identify the *ch'eng* with *liang-chih* in the theory of *liang-chih*, and *ming* with the understanding of the principles of things in Chu Hsi's account of the mind. The dynamic equivalence between the two in the *Chung Yung* suggests that it would not consider Wang's theory to be superior to Chu Hsi's or vice versa. But in either case, the ontological principle of the unity of the mind and Heaven and Earth is upheld as being most important. For it is through this principle that one may reach the ultimate goal of the identification of mind and reality, in the sense given in the first quotation.

The second source which testifies to the capacity of the mind to identify with the ultimate reality and totality of things is Mencius. Mencius' theory of mind cannot be detailed here. But from our earlier discussion of *liang-chih*, it is clear that Mencius accepts the basic proposition that the human mind contains or is endowed with the ultimate reality called the Way. On this ground he is able to hold that human nature is good and to adduce empirical evidence to support that it is good. The evidence, as we have seen, comes from the feeling (response) of the mind.[34] This means that he does not consider the mind as separate from one's nature just as one's nature is not considered separate from the ultimate reality of all things. Apart from the fact that the feeling-response of the mind is the standard or basis for good judgment, Mencius also holds that the mind contains all truths. He remarks:

If one does not gain truth in one's mind, it is permissible to say that one should not apply one's mind to one's will and physical nature. If one does not gain truth through one's study and investigation of truth in the medium of language, however, it is not permissible to say that one need therefore not seek into one's mind.[35]

This clearly indicates that he regards the mind as containing all truths and, in fact, as the very source (fountainhead) from which truths originate. He goes further to affirm that "All things are complete within me,"[36] meaning that all principles are capable of being revealed in me. The supreme problem of moral living is one of how to reveal all the principles of things in one's mind. By affirming, finally, that he can cherish his vital nature (*ch'i*) with the vital nature of the ultimate reality (heaven and earth), he suggests not only that the mind is morally creative in initiating its own fulfillment, but that the mind is fulfilled when it can be said to dynamically identify itself with the ultimate reality through the identification of one's vital nature with the vital nature of the universe. It is from this ontological vital cultivation theory of the mind that Wang Yang-ming has derived his theory of *chih-liang-chih*.

The third source which testifies to the dynamic identification of the mind with the ultimate reality is the two Neo-Confucian philosophers Chang Tsai and Chu Hsi, who argue for the cultivation of *jên* (benevolence) as a virtue comprehending the whole universe as a unity of life. Chang Tsai says in his *Western Inscription*:

Heaven is my father and earth is my mother, and even such a small creature as I finds an intimate place in their midst. Therefore that which fills the universe I regard as my body and that which directs the universe I consider as my nature. All people are my brothers and sisters and all things are my companions.[37]

It takes a cultivation of one's mind to embody this feeling of the cosmic unity in one's mind. The very real possibility of this unity indicates the potentiality of the mind as an entity interpenetrating with the total reality itself.

Chu Hsi explains the origins of the mind and the qualities of the mind in terms of the ultimate nature of heaven and earth (the ultimate reality) and thus considers the highest virtue of the mind a man can reach to be the conscious unity of the mind of man and the mind of Heaven and Earth in *jên* from which all good deeds will arise. He says:

The mind of heaven and earth is to produce things. In the production of man and things, they receive the mind of heaven and earth as their mind. Therefore, with reference to the character of the mind, although it embraces and penetrates all and leaves nothing to be desired, nevertheless, one word will cover all of it, namely *jên* (humanity). The moral qualities of the mind of heaven and earth are four: origination, flourish, advantages, and firmness. And the principle of origination unites and controls them all. In their operation they constitute the course of the four seasons, and the vital force of spring permeates all. Therefore in the mind of man there are also four moral qualities—namely, *jên*, righteousness, propriety and wisdom—*jên* embraces them all. In their emanation and function, they constitute the feeling of love, respect, being right, and discrimination between right and wrong and the feeling of commiseration pervades them all.[38]

Finally, we might again quote from Wang Yang-ming to indicate that he, no less than the other earlier Confucianists, holds that the ultimate cultivation of oneself and one's mind is to reach a state of unity of man and heaven and earth. A person who is able to do so is referred to as the *Great Man* (*ta-jên*). He says in his essay 'Inquiry into the *Great Learning*':

The Great Man considers heaven, earth and the ten thousand things (totally of things) as one body. He regards all men under heaven as belonging to one family and all China as one person. If one person distinguishes 'you' from 'me' in considering the separation of different bodies and forms, he is a small man. That the Great Man is able to regard heaven, earth and the ten thousand things as one body, is not just to give an arbitrary opinion, it is because the *jên* of this mind is like this: He and the heaven, earth and the ten thousand things are one. Not only the mind of the Great Man, but even the mind of the small man is like this. The quality of the small man is that he makes himself into a small man.[39]

Wang then explains that the small man makes himself into a small man by following his desires and obscuring his mind with selfish intentions. He suggests that, if a person is intent on becoming a Great Man, he has only to remove his selfish desires so that he may realize his original nature of goodness, and thus restore the "original state of unity (of his mind) with the heaven, earth and the ten thousand things."

It is clear for Wang that when one has identified his mind with the ultimate reality, he is a Great Man. A Great Man, the same as a sage, is one who will do good things and could be said to perfect his *liang-chih* to the utmost degree, so that he will not make any errors whatsoever.

From the above discussions of the ultimate goal of the cultivation of the mind, we may conclude the following: (1) Mind is originally derived from the ultimate reality of *Tao*. It is not ontologically separable from the *Tao*. (2) In the existence of a person, where selfish desires and selfish intentions are not avoided, he may lose sight of this original identification of his mind with the *Tao*. Yet by a process of cultivation, which is initiated by the mind itself, the mind is ontologically integrable with the *Tao*, whereby all truth and principles will become clear to the mind. This process of cultivation can be regarded as a self-realization process of the mind in itself. (3) The identification of the mind with the ultimate reality will ontologically guarantee that the mind will correctly judge things. (4) The mind in its ontological sense is nothing but the *liang-chih* which Menclus and Wang Yang-ming talk about. Thus the ground of *liang-chih* and *chih-liang-chih* are provided by the ontological theory of mind in the Confucian tradition. (5) It is clear from the above quotations that generally all the major Confucianists and Neo-Confucianists subscribe to these basic views.

Understanding the Individual in the Theory of Mind

What is the status of the individual (*ch'i*) in light of the Confucian theories of mind and their common metaphysical foundation? To answer this question, one must first understand how the notion of the individual is conceived in the framework of the Confucian theory or theories of mind. The Confucianist, as well as other Chinese philosophers, generally conceives individual man in terms of a distinction and a relation between self and others. An individual is a self which is distinguished from others but is necessarily related to others in some way. It seems impossible to affirm the existence of the self without at the same time implicitly affirming the existence of others. Similarly, an individual is also conceived in terms of a distinction between concrete and general man. This distinction is founded on the idea that man has a universal nature which all individual men share and which is intrinsically good, but the concrete man could be such that his nature is influenced by the particularities of his temperament and vital desires. An individual can be an individual in virtue of the universal nature it has, or it can be an individual in virtue of the particularities of his temperament and his vital desires. In both cases of reference to an individual, the notion of the individual is relative, for there is no absolute essence which defines the individuality of an individual.

Not only do the Chinese philosophers conceive the individual as relatively determined, they also conceive it as something permitting change and transformation. To see this aspect of the Chinese notion of the individual, we have to refer to the Confucian theory (theories) of mind as a rationale. In fact, I believe that it is only through such theories of mind that we will obtain a deeper and clearer understanding of the general Chinese notion of the individual.

In the first place, we may assert that the mind is the individuating principle of the individual for the Chinese philosophers. An individual is a person who has a mind, as conceived by the two theories of mind. As we have seen above, the mind is not an abstract and general entity which is fixed once and for all. Nor is the mind only a faculty of reason as such. The peculiarities of the Chinese notion of mind is that it combines all the functions of mind and heart and instinct, and not just the logical rational abilities of an epistemological mind. We see that for both Wang Yang-ming and Chu Hsi, the mind is a concrete reality which can exhibit feelings, reasons and desires. The mind, therefore, may be described as a mind-heart, which can be compared to a microcosm of life. In fact, the constitutive element of mind is vital nature (*ch'i*), according to both theories of mind, and thus mind is made of the same material that all things in the world are made of. This brings us to another aspect of the mind as an individuating principle; the mind has an intimate relation to the body. It has an intimate relation to the basic material of which the body is made. The difference between body and mind is a matter of difference of crude and refined material (*ch'i*). One may say that ontologically there is no difference and that they form a unity and identity; the mind being heart, the body being mind-heart extended. It is generally assumed that there is an intimate interaction between mind and body. This intimate interaction, in fact, amounts to identification, for the bodily functions converge with the mental functions in equally contributing to the inner harmony and unity of the individual.

We may recall Mencius's view mentioned earlier, that a person can nourish and overflow a body with *ch'i* by gaining truth and insight into one's mind. This view is clearly founded on the understanding that the mind, in being *ch'i*, can directly arouse *ch'i* in the body. Man of course is not merely a matter of *ch'i*. He is also a matter of principle, for he can issue out principles (*li*) because he is endowed by the ultimate reality with the clear principles called nature (*hsing*). Every principle is a universal, and the fact that the mind as *ch'i* embodies them does not affect the particularizing forces of the mind. The mind can be particularized because of its feelings, desires and its identification with a body. The mind can be universalized because of its principles and its identification with the ultimate reality. An individual, therefore, can be individuated by his mind, insofar as his mind can exhibit particularizing emotions and desires and can be identified with the body. But on the other hand, in recognizing the mind as the individuating principle of the individual, we should not forget that, on two scores of metaphysical understanding, an individual is individuated from a universal source and shares with other individuals potentially the same qualities in virtue of the universal. First, there is the ultimate reality which reveals itself in principles. Second, there is the ultimate reality which is conceived as the material *chi* (vital force). Whereas Wang Yang-ming conceives *chi* and principle as identical, Chu Hsi thinks that they are not the same. But

whichever view one takes, it does not affect the fact that, for Chinese philosophers, the individual is not conceived as an irreducible entity, because
mind is not so conceived, insofar as mind is the principle of individuation
for the individual.

In Chinese philosophy, not only are the mind and the individual not
irreducible in the sense that they are not absolutely separate entities, but
they are also not irreducible in the sense that the state of the mind and the
state of the individual can be transformed through cultivation. The mind
and *liang-chi* can be cultivated, as we have seen. Thus, they may shed
selfish desires and prejudices and reach for a state where the ultimate reality will function creatively and where all things can be identified with the
mind. If this cultivational process of the mind is regarded as a potential
quality of the mind, one might think that an individual may lose its individuality through its cultivation of the mind. But this is not so. For an individual need not be individuated by selfish desires and feelings, but instead be
individuated by unselfish desires and feelings, or desires or feelings which
do not obstruct the advancement of the cultivation of the virtues of the
mind. As the description of the ultimate goal of the mind's self-cultivation
prescribes, the state where the mind is fully cultivated does not suggest loss
of individuality, but instead an exhibition of individuality through the creative activities of life, love, and participation in the universal. With this view
in mind, one might say that an individual becomes an ideal individual or is
to be ideally individuated by his efforts to cultivate his mind toward supreme
goodness. The very process of cultivation of the mind, not just the mind
itself, is the ultimate rationale and ground for the individuation of an individual. This process of cultivation coincides with the ontological or metaphysical ground of the natural individuation of the individual, which is the
creative activity of *ch'i*-material identifying with the principles, or *ch'i*-
material creating the principles in the concrete processes of the cosmic
generation of life.

We may call the principle that an individual in virtue of its mind can be
cultivated into an ideal state, the *principle of cultivability*. In describing
the Chinese Confucian theory of the individual, we have to appeal to another
principle apart from that of cultivability. This principle is the *principle of
relatability*, which, as we shall see, follows from the principle of cultivability as a necessary consequence.

In cultivating one's mind, an individual has to relate himself to other
individuals. This is regarded by the Confucianists as a self-evident and very
natural or spontaneous process. An individual is not given an essence which
is well-defined, but has to define himself in the process of relating to others, which serves the purpose of cultivating his mind. He has first to relate

himself to his parents in a most basic relationship. In both Confucius and Mencius, the cultivation of virtues relating to parents is regarded as the foundation for all the virtues of a superior man. In fact, the ultimate virtue of *jên*, which we have discussed earlier, is said to grow out of the filial piety toward one's parents and brotherly respect toward one's elder brothers. This growth is not merely a metaphysical way of describing the internal development of one's mind, but has literal reference to the enlargement of the scope of one's relationship to others. Apart from the child-parent relationship, there are four other relationships which an individual is expected to engage himself in: the relationship of younger and elder brothers, which I have already alluded to; the relationship of friend to friend; the relationship of wife to husband; and finally, the relationship of subject to ruler. Given the five relationships, an individual will define himself only when he enters himself into these relationships and develops the proper virtues regarding them. In other words, an individual will realize his potentiality for good only when he fulfills what is fitting and proper in these relationships. As Confucius suggests: "The individual should behave befitting a ruler when he is a ruler, should behave befitting a subject when he is a subject, should behave befitting a father when he is a father, and should behave befitting a son when he is a son."[40]

To generalize, an individual is to find his identity in a virtue (both act and mentality) befitting any relationship in which he relates himself. If he is able to relate himself in all relationships, finding a virtue befitting him in any context involving relationships, he is regarded to have defined his individuality and his mind can also be said to have been cultivated to an extreme degree. In the classical text of the *Great Learning*, it is suggested that there is an order to the steps of self-cultivation in the dimension of relatability:

In ancient times, the men who wished to realize the bright virtues under heaven first brought order to their states. Those who wished to bring order to their states first regulated their families. Those who wished to regulate their families first cultivated their own characters. Those who wished to cultivate their own characters first rectified their minds. Those who wished to rectify their minds first authenticated their intentions. Those who wished to authenticate their intentions first obtained knowledge. The attainment of knowledge consists in the investigation of things. When things are investigated, then knowledge will be attained; when intentions are authenticated, then knowledge will be attained; when intentions are authenticated, then the mind will be rectified; when the mind is rectified, then character will be cultivated; when the character is cultivated, the family will be regulated; when the family is regulated, the state will be well-ordered; when the state is well-ordered, the world will be pacified.[41]

The *Great Learning* has clearly stated the steps of a process of self-cultivation, going beyond internal rectification of the mind, it involves relationships to larger and larger groups of other individuals until it reaches the step where all men are related in a desirable order made possible by the individual. In this manner the individual enlarges himself and brings goodness to larger and larger groups of other individuals.

Three remarks should be made about the expansionable order of relatability. First, it is clear that Confucianists make no particular qualitative distinction between the ethical relations in a family and those in the society. Political and social relationships are equally treated as being deeply ethical, for they are all matters for the cultivation of oneself. Second, it is apparent that before relating oneself to others in a family, state and the world, it is essential that the individual should cultivate himself internally. But one must see this process of internal cultivation as being continuous with the process of externally relating, which will reinforce the goodness of the mind in its turn. The actuality and practice of relating oneself to others will thus stimulate broader and profounder ability of the mind, or the internal self of the individual. It can be compared to the way in which the *kung-fu* (efforts) made in bringing *liang-chih* to actual life situations will refine and sharpen the judging abilities of *liang-chih*. Third, it must be noted that the virtues which one develops in relating oneself to others are reciprocal virtues; by this the Confucianists mean that they are qualities which are universal and which one desires to be universalized. In this sense, all the qualities or virtues an individual develops in relating himself to others are not arbitrary, but have an objective status which is explained as deriving from the ultimate nature (the Way) of things. This amounts to saying that an individual has finally to define and identify himself in universal terms, as well as in a network of particular relationships to other particular individuals. The ability to relate oneself to others and to identify oneself in such relationships and their resulting virtues is an exclusive element in the cultivation of the individual as an individual.

I hope that the two fundamental principles of the cultivability of mind and relatability of the self demonstrate the fact that the Confucian notion of the individual rejects a substantial and absolute entity theory of the individual. Instead, the Confucianists have developed the view that an individual is to be defined in a natural process of the universal's penetrating into the particular, as well as in a cultivational process of the particular's penetrating into the universal, of which the relating of all individuals to one reality is a main and important dimension. Consequently, there is no immortal soul to save, but there is the ultimate dynamic identification with the ultimate reality (the *Tao*) to be achieved. One could, of course, query and worry that an individual in this view will lose itself in a network of social and political or ethical relationships. We might remind the critic, however, that, for the Confucianists, ethical, social and political relationships certainly do not exhaust the individual's individuality, for there is the final goal of the dynamic and ontological identification of the mind and self with heaven, earth, and their creative activities. It is in this identification and its consequent moral creativity, as shown in the doctrines of *liang-chih* and *chih-liang-chih* that an individual man finds his supreme form of expression. Of course, it is needless to say that the orthodox Confucianist would not allow this to take place until one had fulfilled all the orders of relatability as much as one can.

The Sociological Basis of the Confucian Conscience, Mind and Individual

Given a cogently formulated and widely propagated philosophical doctrine, it is always an interesting question to ask what sociological basis the doctrine may have. Modern philosophers seem not to be concerned with providing answers to questions of this kind, but modern sociologists and anthropologists may have developed a significant framework in which questions of this sort may be precisely formulated and may indeed receive significant answers. The Confucian and Neo-Confucian notions of conscience, mind and the individual are well-ingrained in the Chinese cultural tradition, as well as in the general social beliefs of the intellectual class, if not in all the social strata. It is therefore relevant to pose the problem of the sociological basis for these notions. Short of an exhaustive analysis of this problem, I will merely attempt to indicate some relevant aspects of Chinese society and Chinese culture which may shed light on the total answer to the problem posed.

I think that we must answer questions regarding the sociological basis of the Confucian notions of conscience, mind and the individual on two levels. On the first level, we must indicate from what social basis the Confucian and Neo-Confucian notions of conscience, mind and the individual arose. On the second level, we must indicate how these notions, after having been formulated under certain social circumstances, became influential and laid hold of the minds of people in the society. Finally, we must also indicate to what extent they have been received as valid and working standards for social behavior in the Chinese past and present.

Again, in the absence of a thorough investigation of the social and cultural roots of these Chinese philosophical concepts, I will simply make suggestions based on the circumstantial evidence of ancient history, literature and art designs regarding the social origins of the Confucian and Neo-Confucian notions of conscience, mind and the individual. It seems that they all are rooted in the social and cultural experiences of the unity of nature and man as a whole. In ancient China before the Chou time (12th-7th century B.C), there are ample indications in the oracle bones and archeological findings to show that man and heaven (nature) were experienced as homogeneously and harmoniously related. This may be called an experience of consanguinity. This experience can be assumed to be a most natural and spontaneous one, occurring between man and nature or heaven in the very beginnings of the experiences of the Chinese people, given the climate and geography of early China.

From this experience, the identification of man's ancestors with heaven and the conception of the birth of man as a natural process became common beliefs. The system of worship of one's ancestors also developed along with the worship of heaven as the generator of all the living things, as well as the ruler of man. In the moving course of history, heaven even lost its volitive and purposeful aspects, and thus became totally identified with a natural process of change and transformation of which man is part and parcel.

If the above description of the early Chinese experience is correct, it is easy to see why the Confucian notions of conscience, mind and the individual are such that they admit of no errors, are good, and are subject to cultivation and transformation.

A second social factor to mention, which bears upon the obtaining of the Confucian notion of *liang-chih* as a powerful basis for making correct moral judgments, is that Chinese society from the very earliest has beem centered on the family as the most fundamental and nuclear unit in society. Family feelings and relationships have been socially adopted as the standards and rationale for resolving differences and difficulties in varying contexts. In fact, even social organizations and political relationships tended to be modelled on family experiences. On this basis it is clear that insofar as *liang-chih* and the mind are called upon to deal with many new cases and render suitable judgments, they can easily do so by analogy with family model contexts, or by reducing different and difficult cases to family situations, with which *liang-chih* and the mind have had very deep experience. This point about family centralism is intended to suggest not only that the Confucian notions of conscience, mind and the individual may be rooted in family experience; but it is also intended to show why casuistic reasoning in support of the moral decisions of *liang-chih* was not developed, and would become dispensable even if developed. This is so because *liang-chih* and the mind can afford to deal intuitively with complex situations through their reduction to simple and familiar situations. Not only casuistic reasoning, but even logic in general, become superfluous.

It must be recognized, that from a very early time in Chinese history, theory and practice have reinforced each other. One must therefore assume that the types of social institutions and practices developed, back up these philosophical experiences and convictions, which, in turn, lead to further institutions sustaining such experiences and convictions. With this said, we can come to the momentous turning point in Chinese history at which the well-worked out Confucian views of conscience, mind and the individual were incorporated into the highest form of social consciousness, that is, political consciousness, as well as the political institutions. In 136 B.C. the Former Han Emperor Wu proclaimed the Confucian philosophy and learning as the state ideology for China, because he saw Confucianism as providing an ideological basis and social force which would stabilize and justify his political rule. From that time on, up to the very beginning of this century, Confucian thinking has been the orthodox foundation of government policy making, and thus has become entrenched in the consciousness of Chinese people for 2000 years. Keeping this fact in mind, it is again easy to see how the Confucian notions of conscience, mind and the individual may prevail in practice without invoking serious challenge and radical criticism. The theory and practice of these notions have been so persistently and consistently integrated in Chinese government, society and culture that a theoretical challenge almost becomes impossible in the given historical-social framework.

Today things have changed radically in China. But a careful scrutiny of the movements, characters and doctrines occurring on Chinese soil, divested of their apparent covering terminology, still leaves one wondering how much has been changed in violation of or in challenge to the Confucian/Neo Confucian notions of conscience, mind and the individual, when these can be said to apply to the present day life and society in China.

Concluding Remarks

In the above, I have successively dealt with the problems of conscience (*liang-chih*), the cultivation of conscience, theories of mind (*hsin*), the ontological basis for such a theory, the theory of the individual self (*ch'i*), and the sociological foundation of such a theory in the Confucian and Neo-Confucian philosophies, which are the dominating and representative views of Chinese philosophy and civilization. I will not summarize the theses and conclusions I have drawn, for they are too many to repeat here. I wish, however, to make two brief concluding remarks on this lengthy discussion.

First, the basic ideas and notions of conscience, mind and the individual must be seen to form a whole, organic unity. They support one another and therefore belong as a whole to the fabric of the total theory of Chinese metaphysics and ethics, as well as to the fundamental inventory of Chinese historical, cultural anJ social experiences. Second, if the doctrines of *liang-chih* and *chih-liang-chih* in Wang Yang-ming are to be accepted and practised, one can see that, to a large measure, philosophical argumentation and analysis can be dismissed or disposed of. For the goal of philosophy or philosophical thinking and reasoning would then be considered to be to reach a state of mind and a style of living in which one could always find right opinions and make correct judgments of value and goodness. The very attainment of this ability and the practical desirability of this attainment would make philosophical reasoning unnecessary. If it can be said that it is philosophical reasoning and the philosophical need for justification and proof that make disagreements possible, then, if the roots of disagreements are dispelled, the impulse to philosophical argument would have to be subjected to a style of living and a process of experience which would guarantee that attainment which man essentially and practically desires. The Confucian/Neo-Confucian notions of conscience, mind and the individual are all directed to the practical ends of social integration and individual realization. Their value and importance must therefore be judged by their internal consistency, experiential practicality and achievement of a better society, rather than by their pure theoretical completeness.

Notes

1. V.W. Quine first formulates this thesis in his modern classic, *Word and Object*, first published in 1960, Cambridge, Mass., 1967. See Chapter II.
2. The idea of 'semantic ascent' was first suggested and called the 'formal mode of speech' by Rudolf Carnap in his book *The Logical Syntax of Language*, New York, 1937. V.W. Quine gives the name 'semantic ascent' to this idea and generalizes it in the last section of his *Word and Object* (Cambridge: M.I.T., xvi-294 pp)
3. The word 'conscience' does not have a precise ordinary usage. Here I use it in the general sense of 'moral sense', without presupposing that it must have objective validity, for whether 'conscience' has objective validity depends on theory.
4. Primarily in the translations of Wing-tsit Chan, see his *A Source Book in Chinese Philosophy*, Princeton, N.J., 1963, and his *Instruction for Practical Living* by Wang Yang-ming, New York, 1963.
5. See my paper "Unity and Creativity in Wang Yang-ming's Philosophy of Mind," *Philosophy East and West* 23 (1973), 49-72.
6. See *Mencius* 7A-15 (*A Concordance to Meng Tzu*) by Harvard-Yenching Institute, January, 1941.
7. Perhaps, as we shall see, the Neo-Confucianist School of Chu Hsi (1130-1200) could form an exception to this statement.
8. The very process in which this discovery is made actual is regarded by Confucianists in general as a process of self-cultivation and self-realization.
9. See Wang Yang-ming's *Chuan Hsi Lu*, with commentaries by Yu Ching-yuan, Taipei, 1958, Part 1 #3. All translations of Wang are by myself unless otherwise indicated.
10. See Wang Yang-ming, *Ibid.*, Part I, #3.
11. See Wang Yang-ming, *Ibid.*, Part I, #3.
12. This means, of course, that *liang-chih* itself is creative.
13. See my paper, "Unity and Creativity in Wang Yang-ming's Philosophy of Mind."
14. We may call this assertion the *principle of moral unity*.
15. The 'active will' here is understood as the conscious, free, deciding faculty of the self, in the tradition of Kantian philosophy rather than as the blind force of impulsion, in the tradition of Schopenhauer and Nietzsche.

16. See Wang Yang-ming, *Chuan Hsi Lu*, Part I, #5. Cf. also my paper mentioned above.
17. See accounts of St. Augustine and Ockham in Frederic Copleston, S.J. *A History of Philosophy: Late Medieval and Renaissance Philosophy*, Vol. 3, Part I, New York, 1963, p. 62 f.
18. See Wang Yang-ming, *Chuan Hsi Lu,* Part I, #3.
19. It is apparent that this assurance is inductive rather than deductive.
20. See Wang Yang-ming, *Chuan Hsi Lu,* Part III, #3.
21. See Wang Yang-ming, *ibid.*, Part I, #35.
22. It is clear that the justification here is a self-correcting process, as in the case of induction. If the right judgments are forthcoming, then self-cultivation is the only way to obtain right judgments.
23. See Wang Yang-ming, *Chuan Hsi Lu*, Part III, middle part of record by Ch'ien Te-hung.
24. Mind, in its identification with principle, is a principle of casuistry which fulfills nature as well.
25. See Wang Yang-ming, *Chuan Hsi Lu*, Part IV, middle part of record by Ch'ien Te-hung.
26. See *Ta Hsueh Wen*, fourth paragraph.
27. See *Chin Ssu Lu*, ed. Chu Hsi and Lu Tsu-cien, chapter one. This book has been translated by Wang-tsit Chan and is titled *Reflections on Things at Hand*, New York, 1967.
28. My translation from Chu Hsi's *Commentary on the Great Learning (Ta Hsueh Chi Ch'u)*.
29. I use 'ultimate reality' in the sense of the ontologically real, which need not carry any suggestion of religious or theological reference.
30. See *Shang Shu (The Book of Documents)*, chapter on Hung Fan (The Great Norm) in *Shang Shu Shih Yi*, by Ch'u Wan-li, Taipei, 1956.
31. See my article "Reality and Understanding in the Confucian and Neo-Confucian Philosophy of Religion," in *International Quarterly of Philosophy 313* (1973), 33-61.
32. See *Chung Yung*, #22 in *A Concordance to Chung Yung and Ta Hsueh, Taipei, 1970.*
33. See *Chung-Yung*, #21.
34. A better term for the Mencian and perhaps for all Confucian notions of mind (*hsin*) is *heart-mind*, as mind acts not only in terms of perception and thinking but in terms of feelings, emotions and desires.
35. See *Mencius* 2A-2.
36. See *Mencius* 7A-4.
37. Quoted from Wing-tsit Chan, *A Source Book in Chinese Philosophy* Princeton, N.J., 1969, p. 497.

38. *Ibid.*, pp. 593-594.
39. See Chuan Hsi Lu, Appendix: *Ta Hsueh Wen* (*Inquiry into the Great Learning*), first paragraph.
40. See *Analects*, 12-11 in *A Concordance to the Analects*, by Harvard-Yenching Institute, Peiping, 1940.
41. See *Ta Hsueh*, first paragraph.

5. Chinese Philosophy and Symbolic Reference

Whitehead's Doctrine of Symbolic Reference

Whitehead's speculative philosophy does not exactly coincide or square with Chinese Philosophical systems in all regards or in all important respects. In fact there remains important differences, for example, between Whitehead's categories of creativity and Chinese categories of creativity. But one thing no one should deny is that Whitehead's speculative system provides many conceptual tools and methodological cues which can be used to illuminate and explore the content and implications of Chinese philosophy. One such conceptual tool and methodological cue is his doctrine of symbolic reference.

In the following, I shall briefly explain Whitehead's doctrine of symbolic reference and then apply this doctrine to explain and illuminate some important but often ignored features of thinking in the *I Ching* and the *Tao Te Ching*.

Symbolic reference for Whitehead is the way in which language or any system of symbolism works to clarify obscure meanings or ideas. The purpose of symbolic reference is threefold. Besides referring to objective facts and clarification of meanings and ideas of them, symbolic reference serves to bring into focus the present moment of subjective feelings and experiences associated with one's ideas and meanings or memories of objects and events. These appear to be common points for any theory of symbolic reference. But what should be noticed in Whitehead's account is the philosophical breadth and depth and importance which he attaches to this theory and the elaboration of its ground. He points out that what we refer to symbolically are objects and events we are aware of in some way and which affect our life in some way. Next, he points out what we use as symbols for reference to objects and things need not be arbitrary conventions but could be our own ideas, impressions, or experiences.

According to Whitehead, we perceive things in two different modes of perception. We perceive causal process or the relation of cause and effect

165

such as we perceive the lighting of a match by striking the match and by the eyestrain due to sudden lighting up in the dark. In this sense of perception we perceive in the sense of being affected and in the sense of experiencing the process of objective change. Whitehead calls this "perception in the mode of causal efficacy." On the other hand, as human beings we also perceive qualities of things as objects of our immediate consciousness. We see qualities such as colors, shapes, and sizes and so on, as if they are directly presented. According to Whitehead, perception in this sense is called "perception in the mode of presentational immediacy." Perceptions in the perceptual mode of causal efficacy are often indeterminate, indistinct, uncertain, temporally localized, whereas perceptions in the perceptual mode of presentational immediacy are clear, certain, determinate, distinct, and atemporal. Whitehead points out that perception in the mode of causal efficacy is more primitive and universal among living species than perception in the mode of presentational immediacy, the presence of which basically characterizes higher species including man. Now the most important point in Whitehead's doctrine of symbolic reference is that in symbolic reference we unify the two modes of perception by using percepta in the perceptual mode of presentational immediacy as symbols of percepta in the perceptual mode of causal efficacy.

Whitehead explains this process of symbolic reference as follows:

Symbolic reference between the two perceptive modes affords the main example of the principle which governs symbolism. The requisites for symbolism are that there be two species of percepta; and that a perceptum of one species has some 'ground' in common with a perceptum of another species, so that a correlation between the pairs of percepta is established.[1]

The requirement of a common ground in the process of symbolic reference is very important. For without a common ground there is no natural relevanceof one perceptual mode for the other. Of course I see no reason why Whitehead would deny that a common ground could be artificially instituted simply in virtue of acceptance of conventions. Then of course previously agreed on conventions could be common ground for symbolic reference. Whitehead did not specifically speak of symbolic reference of this sort. He is here involved with symbolic reference in perception and meaning in perception. His doctrine explains how we come to have objective knowledge of objects and events and their relations are based on our immediate perception. The common ground for the two perceptual modes mentioned is the specious present or presented locus of our perception in both modes as well as in the identical datum present in both perceptions. Whitehead says:

Thus symbolic reference, though in complex human experience it works both ways, is chiefly to be thought of as the elucidation of percepta in the mode of causal efficacy by the fluctuating interventions of percepta in the mode of presentational immediacy.[2]

   Clarification of perception and elucidation of one perception by another in the symbolic reference is made possible by the common ground they share as well as by the difference between the two. Symbolic reference therefore will precipitate the feelings and experiences associated with one perception on to another perception so that the latter becomes more intensified and more enriched. In Whitehead's words:

Thus there is 'symbolic reference' between the two species when the perception of a member of one species evokes as correlate the fusion of feelings, emotions, and derivative actions, which belong to either of the pairs of correlates, and which are also enhanced by this correlation.[3]

In other words, symbolic reference will induce a *unity of feeling* between the symbolizing perception and the symbolized perception. The fusion and unity of feeling clearly are not a one-way process just as the symbolic reference regarding the two modes of perception need not be considered a one-way process or one-direction process. Though normally because of natural tendencies toward simplicity we use data of immediate presentation to symbolize objects of causal efficacy, there is no reason the latter may not symbolize the former. This is clearly recognized by Whitehead:

There is no inherent distinction between the sort of percepta which are symbols, and the sort of percepta which are meanings. When two species are correlated by a 'ground' of relatedness, it depends upon the experiential process, constituting the percipient subject, as to which species is the group of symbols and which species is the group of meanings. Also it equally depends upon the percipient as to whether there is any symbolic reference at all.[4]

   Though the decision of the direction of symbolic reference lies with the percipient, there is no reason why the process of symbolic reference cannot be considered or stipulated as involving two-way direction. In a two-way symbolic reference, two systems of perception are symbolic referents of each other and mutually or reciprocally interact to form a unity of feeling which will illuminate and elucidate one another in regard to the meaning of each. In this two-way symbolic reference an organic unity (whole) is formed in terms of which symbols, and what is symbolized are mirrors to each other and contribute to our deeper understanding of each in the whole.

The ultimate significance of Whitehead's doctrine of symbolic reference derives from the underlying insight that man can form a correlation or unity of two systems of perception so that each system can be better understood in light of the other and the whole. The paradigms of generalized symbolic reference can be diagrammed as follows:

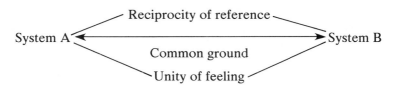

A and B are two systems of perception. The correlation of the two generates a focus of insight into meaning of the deeper reality, which cannot be seen by only one system alone.

Whitehead makes one final point about his doctrine of symbolic reference. How do we justify our symbolism? or how do we know which system of symbolic reference is correct? Whitehead's answer is simple. We can only justify our symbolism by considering how "fortunate" or how effective the consequence of observing or adopting it turns out to be in time. This is to say that whether our symbolism is correct or incorrect is determinable on the basis of pragmatic considerations. Whitehead uses the words "fortunate," and "unfortunate" to describe the consequences of adopting our symbolism. Fortunate consequence justifies our continuous trust in the symbolism. Unfortunate consequence, on the other hand, entitles us to drop the symbolism for our own good. This may take time to tell. But Whitehead also presents an alternative test. Good symbolism tends to generate a confluence and unity of feeling, whereas bad symbolism tends to generate conflict and depression of feelings between the symbols and the symbolized. For any symbolism we need therefore a comprehensive reflection to reach the final verdict on its value.

In the following I shall apply Whitehead's doctrine of symbolic reference to the explanation and elucidation of certain important features of Chinese philosophy embodied in the *I Ching* and *Tao Te Ching*. Specifically I shall interpret the two classical texts as presenting a system of mutual or reciprocal symbolic reference. I shall discuss these two texts with regard to the Principle of Common Ground, the Principle of Mutual Illumination and Unity of Feeling, as well as the Principle of Pragmatic Justification in the doctrine of symbolic reference.

I Ching As a System of Symbolic Reference

Even though the old texts of the *I Ching* do not contain any systematic interpretation of symbolism representing situation, form, and structure of changes, that the texts were developed for the double purposes of understanding reality and guiding human action is beyond any reasonable doubt. When the Commentaries on the *I Ching* were added in later times, the philosophical significance of the *I Ching* as a symbolic system becomes rather manifest. But still we lack a cogent explanation of the meaning and structure of experience embodied in the *I Ching*. Perhaps we should first affirm that the *I Ching* was founded on some primary experience of change and creativity of cosmos, which both the hexagramic symbolism and the philosophical Commentaries are intended to articulate and illuminate.

Considering the relation between the initial experiences of change and the symbolism, as well as the relation between the symbolism and the Commentaries, there exist apparently two major systems of symbolic reference in the present text of the *I Ching*. There is in the first place the system of symbolic reference in the hexagramic symbols to the primary experience of change. The hexagramic symbolism presents a clear image of the structure of change we experience in the mode of causal efficacy. What these hexagramic symbols represent are interlinking relations of transformation, influence, confrontation, dominance, harmonization, reconciliation, opposition, and so on in human affairs as well as in natural events. Human experiences of return, reversion, open-texturedness, fulfillment disorder, order, and so on, similarly receive a place in the representation of hexagramic systems and structure. The system of symbols with its cogent organic interrelatedness and hierarchal ordering brings to light a structure underlying our experiences and enhances our perception of various qualities of change and transformation. It seems quite clear that there is a common ground between the perception of symbols with their interrelatedness and the experience of change. The shapes, position, and directions of lines in hexagrams are indicative of a manifest manifold of our experience of change.

On the other hand, it is also clear that the background experiences that man has gone through illuminate the system of symbolism in the *I Ching*, for it brings out a host of possible orderly interpretations of the symbolic system. Thus, though the symbolism illuminates human experience of a certain time, our continual experiences also tend to enrich an understanding of the symbolism. The important thing to remember is that what is symbolized can be independently understood and could be used to interpret the symbolism already given. Thus both experience and symbolism become interdependable. One might say that they represent two processes in the texts of the *I Ching* which are mutually defining, mutually support-ive, and mutually illuminating. That this twofold process of symbolic refer-ence has been most fortunate or practically working makes it possible for us to attach great importance to the *I Ching* as a book of philosophi-cal insights.

Whereas the system of hexagrams as symbolism referring to our expe-rience of *i* (change)[5] clarifies and illuminates the structure of our experi-ence of *i*, there are two parallel subsystems of thought and perception in the *I Ching*, which are intended to articulate and illuminate the meanings of the system of symbolism as well as the meanings of the original experi-ence of *i*. One system of thought I shall refer to as philosophy of cosmos (or nature), and the other as philosophy of man (or human nature). These two systems of thought are equally important and are developed in the Com-mentaries of the *I Ching* (*Hsi Tzu Ta Chuan, Shuo Kua Chuan, Hsu Kua Chuan*) side by side. Unfortunately scholars and thinkers from the past to the present fail to notice this parallelism in the understanding of meanings of both the experience of *i* and the symbolism of *i*. It is, however, only natural to expect that, in light of Whitehead's doctrine of symbolic refer-ence, two or more systems of thought could develop with regard to one matrix of experience or one set of forms (images) of symbols of perception which constitute the common ground of reference and which make possi-ble their mutual relevance. That more than one system of thought develops is a blessing under certain circumstances, for it demonstrates the variety of manifestations of a reality of basic experience and leads to a rich end-result representation of that reality by way of Whiteheadian unification of feeling. The process no doubt will enrich our understanding of the origi-nal experience of *i*. This is what makes author of the *I Ching* (a) pro-found thinker(s).

The system of cosmos explains the cosmic experience in terms of the formation of heaven and earth, low and high, soft and hard, male and female. It describes the process of becoming in concrete naturalistic concepts and in the terms of principles of change. Thus it is said that

Heaven is high, the earth is low; thus the creative and the receptive are determined. In correspondence with this difference between low and high, inferior and superior places are established. Movement and rest have their definite laws: according to these, firm and yielding lines are differentiated. Events follow definite trends, each according to its nature. Things are distinguished from one another in definite classes. In this way good fortune and misfortune come about. In the heavens phenomena take form; on earth shapes take form. In this way change and transformation (*p'ien-hua*) become manifest.[6]

The system of cosmos also defines basic terms to be used to characterize the reality of change and its meaning:

One *yin* and one *yang* is called *tao* (the way). What we inherit from (the *tao*) is
good. What forms things in nature (*hsing*) . . . Being full of being is the great deed;
Being fresh and novel everyday is called luxiant virtue. To produce life is called
change. To form forms (*hsiang*) is called *ch'ien* (the creative principle). To follow
up [the *ch'ien*] is called *k'un* (the receptive principle). To exhaust numbers in order
to know the future is called derivation. To comprehend change is called conducting
an affair. The unpredictability of the changes (due to the interchange of *yin* and
yang) is called the divine.

Thus the closing the door is called *k'un*; opening the door is called *ch'ien*. One
closing and one opening is called change (*p'ien*); going and coming in an infinite
sequence is called penetration; to be seen is called form; to be formed is called an
utensil. To be instituted for use is called law; what is useful (to life) for going and
coming and people all use is called the divine. Thus *i* has the great ultimate, which
generates the two norms. Two norms generate four forms. Four forms generate
eight trigrams.[8]

From these it can be clearly seen that the philosophy of cosmos exists
relative to our experience of change and our understanding of the symbolism of change. The reference to the sequence of generation from the great
ultimate to the eight trigrams illustrates how a cosmological principle applies
equally to reality and to the symbolism of reality. Even the term *i* is logically capable of useful ambiguity. In light of the doctrine of symbolic reference, the cosmological principle of change (*i*) is embodied in both reality
and in the symbolism and texts, so that "*i*" refers to both symbolism and the
reality which by reciprocal reference form a "unity of feeling." This, of
course, is possible simplybecause both understanding of reality and understanding of texts share the same perception of change or principle of change,
which is their common ground of reference.

In *Shuo Kua* the unity of feeling for understanding the meaning of the
creative and the *receptive* and related attributes of the change as universal
principles extend over many areas of human experience. The creative is
strong. The receptive is yielding. The arousing is dangerous. The clinging
means dependence. Keeping still means standstill. The joyous means pleasure. The creative acts in the horse, the receptive acts in the cow, the arousing acts in the dragon, the gentle in the cock, the absymal in the pig, the
clinging in the pheasant, keeping still in the dog, the joyous in the sheep.
The creative manifests itself in the head, the receptive in the belly, the arous-

ing in the foot, the gentle in the thighs, the absymal in the ear, the clinging
(brightness) in the eye, keeping still in the hand, the joyous in the mouth.

The Creative is heaven. It is round, it is the prince, the father, jade, metal, cold, ice.
It is deep red, a good horse, an old horse, a lean horse, a wild horse, tree fruit. The
Receptive is the earth, the mother, it is cloth, a kettle, frugality, it is level, it is a cow
with a calf, a large wagon from the multitude, a shaft. Among the various kinds of
soil, it is the black.[9]

We do not have to speculate how these heterogenous things are unified
in central feelings toward cosmological categories of *ch'ien*, *k'un*, and related
experiences. It suffices to say that articulation of their consonance attests
to the existence of such a unity of feeling in Whitehead's scheme.
    In the *Hsu Kua* the meaning of the symbolism of *i* is indicated in terms
of transformations of situations, with these transformations dictated by the
intrinsic natural tendencies inherent in these situations. The philosophy of
cosmos fully justifies and indeed is responsible for conceiving hexagramic
situations as stages of changes which have the potential for organically
interacting between one another in the course of time. This no doubt introduces a dynamical dimension into the symbolism of *i* and leads to a powerful unity of enriched feeling not only among all units of the symbolism but
throughout our life experiences of change which lie behind the system of
the *i*-symbols. The following is an example of the *Hsu Kua* discourse:

When one has the trust of creatures: one sets them in motion; hence there follows
the hexagram of Preponderance of the Small. He who stands above things brings
them to completion. Hence there follows there hexagram of After Completion.
Things cannot exhaust themselves. Hence there follows, at the end, the hexagram
of Before Completion.[10]

We now come to the philosophy of man in the *I Ching*. Parallel to the
philosophy of the cosmos, the philosophy of man clearly assumes that man
can fully comprehend the world of change and through this understanding
can cultivate and transform himself into a perfection as well as contribute
to the actualization of perfection of other people and the world at large. In
this sense, man is considered to embody fundamental principles of change
and therefore possess the utmost capacity to participate in the creative
advance of life. In this regard the *Hsi Tzu* agrees with *Chung Yung* (the
Doctrine of the Mean) in considering man as forming a unity with heaven and
earth, as well as constituting a vehicle for the realization of the potential
values in the ultimate reality of heaven and earth. Thus it is said in *Hsi Tzu*:

Looking upward, we contemplate with its help to signs in the heaven; looking down-ward we examine the lines of the earth. Thus we come to know the circumstances of the dark and the light. Going back to the beginning of things and pursuing them to the end, we come to know the lessons of birth and of death. The unison of seed and power produces all things; the escape of the soul brings about change. Through this we can come to know the conditions of outgoing and returning spirits.

Since in this way man comes to resemble heaven and earth, he is not in conflict with them. His wisdom embraces all things and his *tao* brings order into the whole world; therefore he does not err. He is active everywhere but does not let himself be carried away. He rejoices in heaven and has knowledge of fate. Therefore he is free of care. He is content with his circumstances and genuine in his kindness, therefore he can practice love.[11]

Because man can penetrate into and participate in the creative activities of the *tao* and *i*, man can articulate the ultimate truth of change and make cor-rect judgments of action. The very creation of the symbolism of *i* and its prac-tice as presented in the ancient text is the outcome of the wisdom of the sages — the men who have perfected themselves. Thus the representation of universal truths of *i* in the *I Ching* already reflected the cosmic participation of heaven and earth. *Hsi Tzu* describes the formation of the *I Ching* in the following way:

Heaven and Earth determine the scene, and the changes take effect within it. The perfected nature of man, sustaining itself and enduring, is the category of the *tao* and of justice.[12]

The sages were able to survey all the confused diversities under heaven. They observed forms and phenomena and representations of things and their attributes. These are called images (symbolic images).[13]

The sages instituted the hexagram, so that phenomena might be perceived therein. They apprehended the judgments in order to indicate good for-tune and misfortune.[14]

Since the sagely wisdom of man concretizes in the *I Ching*, the *I Ching* is a mirror image of the truth of heaven and thus that of change itself. The *Book Of Change contains the measure of Heaven and Earth; therefore it enables us to comprehend the tao* of heaven and its order.[15]

In light of man making the symbol which symbolizes himself, the phi-losophy of man illustrates the meaning of the *i*—symbolism and brings to it a deep sense of ontological understanding and a deep feeling of truthful satisfaction.

In light of the nature of the philosophy of the cosmos and the nature of the philosophy of man in the *I Ching*, it is also clear that these two systems of thought are mutually illuminating and mutually supportive. They reciprocate with each other as two systems of symbolization, while they respectively receive and endow illumination of meanings from the hexagramic symbols. When two systems mutually support and illuminate, we have a case of reciprocity of symbolic reference. This is a new aspect of symbolic reference, which Whitehead has not pointed out but which is well-illustrated in the understanding of symbolism and experience of *i* in the two systems of *i* as explained earlier. The two systems of thought reciprocate in symbolic reference with each other and at the same time reciprocate in symbolic reference with the experience and symbolism of *i*. Thus an enriched unity of enriched feeling among the four is effectively realized.

We can represent what we have said about the philosophy of *i* and its structures of symbolic reference in the following summary diagram:

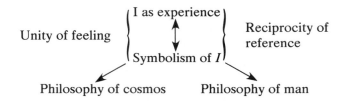

Tao Te Ching as a System of Symbolic Reference

We turn now to the *Tao Te Ching* of Lao Tzu as a system of symbolic reference. I shall be brief and merely indicate how the meaning of *tao* in Early Taoism becomes profoundly enriched when the structure of symbolic reference in the *Tao Te Ching* is made clear. *Tao Te Ching* speaks about the *tao* as the ultimate reality. What is the *tao*? *Tao Te Ching* says: "*Tao* can be spoken about, but it is not the ordinary *tao* (way). (Its) name can be spoken about, but it is not the ordinary name." Thus *tao* is not an ordinary concept and cannot be conceptually understood. Though the *Tao Te Ching* has many passages attempting to show and indicate what *tao* is, how it functions, how it is related to man and things as well as how it applies to government, the central burden of understanding *tao* falls on our experience and perception of *tao* in our ordinary life, which requires our intense concentration and subtle insight. Lao Tzu as the author of *Tao Te Ching* may be said to have acquired this concentration and insight, and moreover knew how to articulate and illuminate his experience and perception of *tao* in terms of concrete images and qualities of things. These concrete images and qualities of experience serve a twofold purpose: the purpose of identifying and showing the *tao* as universal, ultimate, and yet concrete and penetrating reality; and the purpose of inducing development of systems of thought which apply to various areas of human learning and interest on a common ground. This twofold purpose is important and necessary, for *tao* is intended as something unperceivable, indeterminate, and nondescribable in language.

Lao Tzu used the term *wu* (void) to refer to *tao*. He says of *tao*:

Its upper side is not bright, its under side not dim. Continual the unnameable moves on. Until it returns beyond the realm of things. We call it the formless form, the imageless image. We call it indefinable and unimaginable.[16]

Ten thousand things are generated from Being and Being is generated from the void.[17]

Wu of course need not be simply nothingness. It is something which is indeterminate and formless and yet gives rise to the formation and determination of things. It is something such that whereas it is empty of being, it is the inexhaustible source of being. It is also the becoming and transformation of things. For it is not simply tranquility nor immutability.

That *tao* is becoming and the source of becoming is clearly indicated by the statement: "*Tao* generates one, one generates two, two generates three, three generates the ten thousand things."[18] *Tao* is conceived not to involve any specific activity to perform any specific project, but it is nevertheless said to accomplish everything. In fact the whole universe is conceived to be a work of *tao* precisely because it does nothing. It is thus said : "The *tao* always does nothing, and yet nothing remains undone."[19] Among the many qualities of the *tao*, *tao* is strongly characterized not only as being the beginning of things but also as the end of things as well as the process of becoming of things. The becoming of things is a return to the origin after being originated and developed in the *tao*. "*Tao* therefore is the movement of reversion."[20] Thus one can observe the return or reversion of *tao* if one has grasped the emptiness and tranquility of *tao*. It is said:

Attain to utmost void, cling simple-heartedly to interior peace. While all things are stirring together, I only contemplate the return. For flourishing as they do, each of them will return to its root.[21]

Given all these characteristics of *tao*, how do we identify images of the *tao*? Specifically, how do we identify an image of *tao*, which is imageless? Namely, how does an image of *tao* represent the *tao* in terms of subtle power to change, move, and reverse things, not in reference to static configurations? Lao Tzu has indeed focused and developed a cluster of imageless and yet concrete images of *tao* in terms of which not only the nature of *tao* and our experience of it becomes perceptively clear, but paradigms and models for applying *tao* to life and society, method, and conception of reality become easy to define and develop with reference to these images of *tao*. These images of *tao* form an organic unity of structure and feeling and provide a ground for the differentiation and integration of parallel systems of thought based in them. These systems of thought, which can be called respectively aesthetics of *tao*, metaphysics of *tao*, dialectics of *tao*, and politics of *tao*, are parallel structures derived from the unity of feeling between the images of *tao* and the general experience of *tao*, which leads to achievement of a higher level of unity of feeling, by way of symbolic reference between these images and these systems of thought.

What are Lao Tzu's images of *tao*? The following images are developed in the *Tao Te Ching*, which warrants our notice, and on which I shall briefly comment in reference to their potentiality for illuminating the *tao* and articulating systems of thought and their use to life.

(1) Water as the image of *tao*. It is clear that water is soft, flexible in form, and embracing in scope, has extreme power for self-transformation and transformation of its resistant opponents. It reflects *tao* and presents an example for the goodness, beauty, and vast powerfulness of humility, softness, and submissiveness in attitude toward life and reality. Lao Tzu says:

The highest form of goodness is the water, water knows how to benefit all things without striving with them. It stays in places loathed by all men. Therefore it becomes near the *tao*.[22]

Nothing in the world is softer and meeker than water; But, for attacking the hard and the strong there is nothing like it. For nothing can take its place.[23]

Together with the image of *tao* as water, *tao* is likened to river, ocean. sea, and flood which are related to water. Thus Lao Tzu says:

The *tao* is to the world what a great river or ocean is to the streams and brooks.[24]

The great *tao* is universal like a flood . . . How can it be turned to the right or to the left? All creatures depend upon it, and it denies nothing to anyone. It does its work, but it makes no claim on itself.[25]

How does the sea become the king of all streams? Because it lies lower than they. Hence it is the king of all streams.[26]

(2) A child as the image of *tao*. A child, like water, is soft and nonoffensive. But a child more than water is full of potentiality of life and ability to learn, grow. and create. Because the child is pure, simple, and unpolluted by partial knowledge, bad habit, and evil thought, the child can do nothing and everything is possible for the child as he forms no block to the happening of things. He is therefore a seed of creativity and an occasion (or beginning) of novelty and a model of harmony. He is defenseless and therefore invites no harm and competition. Lao Tzu has this to say:

In keeping the spirit and the vital soul together, are you able to maintain their perfect harmony? In gathering your vital energy to attain suppleness, have you reached the state of a new born babe?[27]

One who is steeped in virtue is akin to the new-born babe. Wasps and poisonous serpents do not sting it, nor fierce beasts seize it. Nor birds or prey maul it. Its bones are tender, its sinew soft, but its grip is firm. It has not known the union of the male and the female, growing in its wholeness and keeping its vitality in its perfect integrity. It howls and screams all day long without getting hoarse, because it embodies perfect harmony.[28]

(3) The mother as the image of *tao*. The mother is the beginning of being. She is the source and reservoir of life. She provides nourishment and support for her children, and she is always ready to cherish and make things possible for her children. She is therefore not only the origin of life but the preserver of life. Since there is no natural obstacle between the mother and the children, to know the children leads us to know the mother; and to know the mother leads us to know the children.

The mother is self-effacing and unselfish toward her children. She is forever tender and soft and pays attention to minutest details of her family. She always understands and silently bears all the burdens of activities of life. Although Lao Tzu does not say too much about the virtue of the mother, it is clear that he intends that what we understand about a mother applies to the *tao* through a process of symbolic reference and a unification of feeling. He has these explicit statements to say about the mother.

There was something undefined and yet incomplete in itself, born before Heaven and Earth, silent and boundless, standing alone without change, yet pervading all without fail, it may be regarded as the mother of the world.[29]

All-under-Heaven have a common beginning. This beginning is the mother of the world. Having known the mother, we may proceed to know the children. Having known the children, we should go back and hold on to the mother. In so doing you will incur no risk even though your body be annihilated.[30]

The following statements contain an implicit reference to the mother image of Lao Tzu.

The spirit of the fountain dies not. It is called the mysterious feminine. The doorway of the mysterious feminine is called the root of heaven and earth. Lingering like a gossamer, it has only a hint of existence. And yet when you draw upon it, it is inexhaustible.[31]

A great country is like the lowland toward which all streams flow. It is the reservoir of all under heaven, the feminine of the world[32]

(4) The female as the image of *tao*. The last quoted statement from Lao Tzu already refers to the female in the primal sense of a mother. In that sense the female is the principle, not parallel nor complementary to the principle of the male. It is one, not one of the two. As one it gives rise to the two and everything. Now Lao Tzu also conceives the *tao* as possessing the virtues and qualities of the female and its function as opposite and a complement to the male. The female is again soft, quiet, flexible, gentle, and as such can conquer and assimulate the male (harsh, stubborn, offensive, and outstanding) to form a harmony and unity. Since without unity and harmony the actual world and life are not possible, the female can be said to make all actual processes in the world possible. It is hence the creative power for the realization and preservation of individual things. As a creative power it is inseparable from its potential for being a mother and its ability to rear a child. Being soft and yet capable of conquering the hard, it is similar to water. Thus the image of the female is always suggestive of the images of the mother and the child, and the water, and there cannot but exist a confluence of feelings associated with these three images. Lao Tzu has the following to say about the female in the ability to achieve unity, success, and primal innocence and creativity:

Know the masculine, keep the feminine, and be the brook of the world.[33]

The feminine always conquers the masculine by her quietness, by lowering herself through her quietness. Hence, if a great country can lower itself before a smaller country, it will win over the small country: and if a small country can lower itself beforeagreatcountry,itwillwinoverthegreatcountry;theonewinsbystooping; the other, by remaining low.[34]

In the opening and shifting of heaven's gate, are you able to play the feminine part?[35]

(5) The uncarved block is the image of *tao*. In the *Tao Te Ching* there are at least six references to the term *pu*, which means the uncarved block of wood. The term suggests simplicity of style and form and genuineness of quality and substance. Thus very often the term is used in these senses. This is a case where the meaning of a metaphor has been transformed into a literal concept and what it symbolizes becomes what is meant and intended. Clearly simplicity of life is difficult to define, but if we define it as the state of uncarved block of wood, we achieve a clearer vision of the quality of simplicity. Simplicity is not monotonousness nor crudeness. It is freshness full of fresh possibility. The nature of the uncarved block of wood is precisely an example of freshness with full potentiality for becoming different, useful, and interesting things. It is indeterminate, and yet because of its indeterminateness it can assume many shapes and patterns and can transform into determinate vessels. "When the uncarved block dispersed, it becomes useful vessel."[36]

What is valuable in *pu* is its usefulness and its potentiality to become and to achieve ideal goals, and in this regard it has very much the same nature of a child or mother or female or the water. But it is only in the image of the uncarved block the combination of qualities of stability, tranquility, and solidarity, indeterminate shape and unity stand out. Hence this image of *tao* seems to be a favorable one for Lao Tzu to refer to the *tao* and to ideal character of a man or a people. After denouncing the usefulness of wisdom, benevolence, and skill, Lao Tzu says:

These three are the criss-cross of *tao* and are not sufficient in themselves, therefore they should be subordinated to a higher principle. See the simple *su* and embrace [the quality] of the uncarved block (*pu*), diminish the self and curb the desires.[37]

For a person desiring to achieve true understanding of the *tao*, Lao Tzu offers the following admonition:

Know the glorious, keep the lowly, and be the valley of the world. To be the valley of the world is to live the abundant life of nature and to return again to the state of the uncarved block.[38]

Lao Tzu also explicitly likens *pu* to the *tao*, in virtue of the fact that *pu* is nameless like the *tao* and is indeterminate and nonoutstanding like the *tao*. "*Tao* is always nameless, small as it is in its state of uncarved block. It is inferior to nothing in the world." [39] When he refers to *tao as a method of settling stir and controlling desires of men, he uses the term pu*. He says:

It is time to keep them (things) in their place by the aid of the nameless uncarved block. The nameless uncarved block alone can curb the desires of men. When the desires of men are curbed, there will be peace and the world will 'settle down of its own accord. [40]

To return to the state of the uncarved block is a way to govern the state and to govern oneself. It is the way to achieve everything by doing nothing and a way to attain peace, harmony. and well-being without the disruptive inter-ference and domination of desires. [41] Apparently Lao Tzu regards the state of *pu* as the natural and original state of things in their beginning before knowledge and artifact are developed by men.

In the preceding we have discussed five main images of *tao* in the *Tao Te Ching*. Each of these images of *tao* serves as a symbol for the *tao* and leads to a unity of feeling between the symbol and the meaning of *tao*. All these main images of *tao* are also mutually supportive and mutually illumi-nating, and this fact of mutual symbolic reference leads to a still greater and stronger and deeper understanding of the *tao*. The concept of the *tao* as explained in terms of certain basic characteristics by Lao Tzu, on the other hand, calls forth these images rooted in our experience of the world and life. This shows not only that there exists a common ground between our perception of the *tao* and our perception of the images of *tao*, but that *tao* itself illuminates these images of *tao*, which illuminates *tao*. One may even suggest that these images embody the *tao* itself just as *tao* presents these images, so that *tao* and these images shine forth through each other. This is what we call *reciprocity of symbolic reference.*

Now we must remember that the images of *tao* which illuminates the *tao* do not just consist of these five. There are many explicit and implicit images of tao throughout Lao Tzu's work. For example, there is the bel-lows image referring to the emptiness and yet inexhaustibleness of life in the tao; there is the valley image having similar meaningfulness; there is the image of bending a bow referring to the balancing ability of the tao; there are images of the tao in terms of various qualities such as being bent, being curled, being low, being little, having few, having oneness, being utmost soft, being empty, being silent, being weak, and being nonconspicuous and so on.

When Lao Tzu says:

When a man is living he is soft and weak, when he is dead he becomes hard and rigid. When a plant is living, it is soft and tender, when it is dead, it becomes withered and dry. Hence the hard and rigid belong to the company of the dead, and the soft and supple belong to the company of the living.[42]

It is clear that he sees not only an analogy but an actual identification of qualities between softness, weakness, and life on the one hand, and between hardness, rigidity, and death on the other. The images of *tao* by the same token constitute not just an analogy but an actual identification of feelings and reality. *Tao* is one but has many manifestations of which the images of tao are natural tokens.

The whole book of the *Tao Te Ching* is represented by a cluster of images which function as a system of symbols referring to the ultimate reality of *tao*, and in doing so dynamically generate a unified field of concrete feelings, which endow effective meanings on the concept of tao. Given perceptive meanings for the concept of *tao* illuminated in the unity of feeling with images of tao, various systems of thought about the *tao* can be contextually constructed. In other words, one can explicate the concept of the *tao* regarding different disciplines of ideas, for the images of *tao* and the field of feelings and meanings generated thereby provide a fertile basis and fruitful source of developing these ideas. Specifically, we may mention the possibility of constructing a metaphysics of the *tao*, the dialectic of the *tao*, the ethics of the *tao*, the aesthetics of the *tao*, and the politics of the *tao*. To develop these conceptual systems, in light of the unity of feeling of the images of *tao*; requires a second article, and we have to satisfy ourselves now by simply pointing out that these systems can be considered or indeed shown to be separate but interrelated symbolisms, which reciprocate reference to one another and thus reflect and form a further mutually supportive network of unified and enriched feelings and meanings.

We may represent the structure of symbolic reference with its conceptual ramifications in the *Tao Te Ching* in the following diagram:

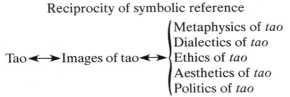

Reciprocity of symbolic reference

Tao ◄──► Images of tao ◄──► { Metaphysics of *tao* / Dialectics of *tao* / Ethics of *tao* / Aesthetics of *tao* / Politics of *tao* }

Unification of differentiated feelings

Concluding Remarks

I have explained some central ideas of the *I Ching* and the Tao Te Ching in the light of Whitehead's doctrine of symbolic reference. The explanation not only illustrates the fruitfulness of Whitehead's doctrine of symbolic reference, but at the same time extends the depth and scope of the doctrine by developing the principle of mutual or reciprocal symbolic reference. We have discussed many aspects of the *I Ching* and the *Tao Te Ching* as two structured symbolic systems. We have not particularly discussed the pragmatic justification of the two symbolic systems of the *I Ching* and the *Tao Te Ching*. Nevertheless, anyone who is familiar with the history of Chinese philosophy as well as various spheres of practical thinking and action can testify to the pragmatic efficacy or fortunateness (rightness) of these ideas from the *I Ching* and the *Tao Te Ching* in the best Whiteheadean sense of efficacy and rightness.

Notes

1. Alfred North Whitehead, *Process and Reality* (New York: The Macmillan Company, 1957), p.274.
2. Ibid., 271.
3. Ibid., 274.
4. Ibid., 276.
5. In traditional commentaries on the *I Ching, I* (change) has a threefold meaning attributed to it: change, no-change (patterns of nonchange) and ease of change.
6. See *Hsi Tzu Ta Chuan* (The Great Appendix) in the *I Ching,* trans. by Richard Wilhelm into German, and retranslated into English by Cary F. Baynes. First published in 1950, and reprinted in 1985.
7. Ibid., 297-301.
8. Ibid., 318.
9. Ibid., 275-276.
10. Ibid., 704, 709, 714.
11. Ibid., 294-295.
12. Ibid., 303.
13. Ibid., 304.
14. Ibid., 287.
15. Ibid., 293.
16. See the *Tao Te Ching* of Lao Tzu §14 (Ho-shang-kung version).
17. Ibid., §40.
18. Ibid., §42.
19. Ibid., §37.
20. Ibid., §40.
21. Ibid., §16.
22. Ibid., §8.
23. Ibid., §78.
24. Ibid., §32.
25. Ibid., §34.
26. Ibid., §66.
27. Ibid., §10.
28. Ibid., §55.

29. Ibid., §25.
30. Ibid., §52.
31. Ibid., §6.
32. Ibid., §61.
33. Ibid., §28.
34. Ibid., §61.
35. Ibid., §10.
36. Ibid., §28.
37. Ibid., §19.
38. Ibid., §28.
39. Ibid., §32.
40. Ibid., §37.
41. Ibid., §57, §15.
42. Ibid., §76.

6. Toward Constructing a Dialectics of Harmonization: Harmony and Conflict in Chinese Philosophy

Preliminary Remarks: Ambivalence of Themes and the Present Task

In recent Chinese studies, discussions and characterizations on various aspects of harmony and conflict pertaining to Chinese philosophy and Chinese thought have been developed, perhaps as a result of enthusiasm to understand the nature and evolution of Chinese philosophy as a whole.[1] Though many points have been suggested, no definite conclusions have been drawn nor have their potential importance and relevance for understanding Chinese society and its prospective transformation been reached. Three themes have been frequently touched upon and yet no clear and proper distinction among them has been made. There is in the first place the theme that there are harmony and conflict among the schools of thought in Chinese philosophy and that different forms of harmony and conflict are exemplified in the development of these schools; the second theme is that Chinese philosophy is rich with concepts of harmony and conflict and that concepts of harmony and conflict have been specifically elaborated in Chinese philosophy; thirdly there is the theme that many and indeed all important concepts in Chinese philosophy can be conceived and evaluated in a framework of harmony and conflict as two modes of thinking, or as two poles of orientation, or as two aspects of the changing reality.[2] Of course all these themes could be interrelated and intertwined for any single philosopher or any single philosophical writing in the history of Chinese philosophy.

In this chapter I shall confine myself to discussing the second and third themes with the objective of clarifying, constructing, analyzing and justifying types of harmony and conflict in major schools of Chinese philosophical thinking. My purpose is to pinpoint some underlying essential and unifying structure of all major Chinese philosophical views of harmony and

185

conflict in order to provide explanatory grounds for these views. I consider it crucial to understand first the model and method of philosophical thinking in Chinese philosophy which involves harmony and conflict as two mutually defining categories. In making an effort of this sort, I shall suggest a metaphysics of harmony and conflict and a consequent dialectics of harmonization in Chinese philosophical terms, according to which, one may even say that the concepts of harmony and conflict can be consistently defined and interpreted in the philosophical contexts of Chinese metaphysics and Chinese methodology. In other words, the intuitive meanings of harmony and conflict will be made clear in the articulated idioms of basic Chinese philosophy. Specifically, I shall bring out the intimate conceptual relationships between harmony and conflict as two modes of reality and experience in a metaphysical and dialectical framework, which has never been explicitly mentioned or discussed before.

After having clarified and elaborated the metaphysics of harmony and conflict and the dialectics of harmonization, I shall come to my second task: to relate and verify ideas bearing on harmony and conflict in the areas of Chinese moral, epistemological, social and political philosophies. It is in these areas that the metaphysics of harmony and conflict and the dialectics of harmonization will find their most significant application and will contribute to our general understanding of harmony and conflict in an individual as a moral person as well as in a society as a vehicle for personal development and fulfillment. Some comparisons with alternative views on ontology and methodology will be made. This will naturally lead to a reconsideration of a meaningful meeting between basic philosophical traditions in the East and the West by focussing on their methodological orientations. In terms of this reconsideration, historical experiences and the prospective transformation of man and society in line with some metaphysics and dialectics of harmony and conflict will be better explained and understood.

Metaphysics of Harmony and Conflict in Confucianism

Benjamin Schwartz, in his studies of some polarities in Neo-Confucianism, remarks[3] that the Neo-Confucianist thought must be understood both in the context of their times and in terms of the *problematik* inherent in the whole Confucian tradition. Schwartz is undoubtedly correct in stressing the importance of relating a school of thought to the set of problems which gives rise to the *school*, and thus relating its followers to its founder. This means that the development of thought is historically continuous and yet has an a-historical *problematik* which can be analytically studied. On this assumption I shall analyze the metaphysics and dialectics of harmony and conflict in Chinese philosophy as they are first formulated. An analytical understanding of them is useful for understanding other forms of thought in the historical development of Chinese philosophy.[4]

What are harmony and conflict in a Chinese metaphysical perspective? What methodological or dialectical principles are pertinent and inherent in a metaphysics of harmony and conflict? These two basic questions must be answered in light of two foundational schools of Chinese thought: Confucianism and Taoism. Nobody can deny that Confucianism and Taoism more than any other philosophical schools have shaped the mind of the intellectual *class* in China through the Classical Period up to the early 20th century. If we take a more speculative view, it can perhaps be argued that Confucianism and Taoism are themselves historically derived from the same fountainhead of Chinese cosmological experience and thus answer to the same *problematik* of Chinese thinking in the very beginning. I shall deal with the Confucian views primarily in terms of texts of the *I Ching (Book of Changes)* and Neo-Confucian writings[5] and shall deal with the Taoistic views as expressed in the well-known writings of Lao Tzu and Chuang Tzu.

I shall informally explain the notions of harmony and conflict for the purpose of our discussion. For an intuitive point of view, harmony means the following: For any two distinctive co-existing or succeeding forces, processes or entities, if there are mutual complementation and mutual support between the two, so that each depends on the other for strength, actuality, productiveness and value, then we can say that these two form a harmonious whole and an organic unity. In contrast, conflict means the absence of harmony between two distinctive, different or not different, forces, processes or entities, to the extent that each tends to cancel out the other, contradict the other, harm the other, or even perhaps destroy the other. As a consequence, there is no unity nor harmony underlying the conflicting elements. From this explanation of harmony and conflict, it may appear that we could have two different or two distinctive things which are not mutually conflicting and yet there is no harmony between the two. We then have a situation of indifference, irrelevance and non-relation, which is neutral to both harmony and conflict. But we must notice that in the course of human experience a situation of indifference, irrelevance and non-relation does not remain quite a neutral relationship, for such a situation is either more conducive to harmony or more conducive to conflict. Thus one might therefore talk of potential harmony and conflict as versus actualized harmony and conflict. It might be thus assumed that given any two different or two distinctive things, either these things tend to harmonize with each other or they tend to conflict with each other.

It should be pointed out that there are many types of harmony and conflict on different levels of nature and human existence. The qualitative and quantitative complexities of harmony and conflict are a natural reflection of multiple relationships in which a thing is to be defined and recognized. There is therefore no simple formula whereby all types of harmony and conflict can be uniformly characterized or described. Objectively and realistically speaking, we cannot even specify causes and conditions of harmony and conflict without specifying the contexts of relationships in which harmony or conflict arises. For our philosophical purpose, we might assume that a general metaphysical structure pervades all types of harmony and conflict and contributes to an understanding of the causes and conditions of harmony and conflict. We may also see that both harmony and conflict present certain values for man, and that as a rule both individual man and society at large, under normal circumstances, desire and prefer harmony as a greater value than conflict and thus are generally inclined to pursue the former rather than the latter. We may thus conceive the problem of harmony and conflict as the problem of explaining and justifying creation or pursuit of harmony and/or the problem of providing a resolution of conflict, potential or actual, in the interest of harmony.

For the Confucianist, harmony is the basic state and the underlying structure or reality whereas *conflict* does not have roots in reality, but rather represents an order of unnatural imbalance or a disorder of no lasting significance. The world, according to the Confucianist, is a process of change and development. Notwithstanding that there may appear variation, difference, divergence, tension, opposition, and antagonism in the world, the Confucianist insists that the overall tendency of the cosmic and social processes and individual life conduces to unity and harmony. As a powerful illustration, consider the essential principles of the *I Ching* of the following: (1) Reality (called the *Tao* or the way), which encompasses Heaven, Earth, man and the ten thousand things, is both a process of change and an ordered structure; (2) Creativity of life is the essence of change and the capacity of the *Tao* in producing life is unlimited;[6] (3) There are always two opposite and yet complementary forces or momenta in the process of change: they are referred to as the *yin* (the female principle-force-aspect) and the *yang* (the male principle-force-aspect; (4) The *Tao* is one and is the source and origin of all momenta of change and thus the fountainhead of all polarities. In this sense the *Tao* is referred to as the *t'ai-chi* (the Great Ultimate) of all things; (5) Difference and differentiation of things are manifestations of the interaction of the *yin* and the *yang* and are therefore identifiable with the *Tao*; (6) That all things come into being is due to the nature *(hsing)* of the *Tao*, and for any thing to be able to develop or follow the nature of the *Tao* there is goodness;[7] (7) Man can understand the dynamics of change and can conform to its principles in his conduct and achieve all-comprehensive goodness in the world (8) On achieving understanding of change man can also participate in the activity of change and realize the harmony between himself and the world; (9) Discord, misfortune and imperfection issue from man's failure to understand the reality of change and his consequent incapacity to harmonize with the world.

From this succinct characterization of the metaphysical scheme in the *I Ching*, several things bearing on the problem of harmony and conflict can be made clear.

First of all, the *I Ching* shows itself to be concerned with unification and generation of things as a basic element of harmony. This means that to the author[s] of the *I Ching* the world is a generative unity and the process of change is a natural harmonious orchestration of an abundance of things which has a beginning and an end: things begin with harmony and aim at harmony as their goal. Secondly, even though there exists temporal progression in things, temporal progression is unlimited creation of life. Accordingly, all things are generated in a process of change and life, and the ultimate goal of life can be achieved by means of man's conscious effort to unify himself with the *Tao*. Finally, the process of change is conceived as a generative unity of polarities which exist in opposition as well as in complementation, in terms of which not only change is explained but variety of things is also explained. What is noteworthy is that appearance of discrepancy, imperfection, conflict, contradiction or struggle in experience are regarded as misconceived and incomplete subprocesses of interaction of polarities. Insofar as polarities are ultimately identical with the *Tao*, polarities in the general sense of the *yin* and the *yang* as exemplified by cold and hot, hard and soft, rest and movement, high and low, do not exhibit any genuine opposition or antagonism — they are only opposite as far as they are complementary. They exist to make reality interesting, meaningful and complete. There is neither tension nor hostility between the *yin* and the *yang* if they are allowed to proceed in their inherent naturalness and simplicity. From this point of view, all forms of interaction of polarities of whatever degrees of complexity are symbolic of harmony, harmony in a dynamic sense, not in a static sense, that is, they are symbolic of existence of a state of holistic harmonization of things.

The real, the whole, the unified, and the natural are all defining qualities of harmony for the *I Ching*. The nature of man is such that he will realize this harmony both unconsciously and through his self-cultivation. The problem of man is how to harmonize himself at his maximal capacity with the course of nature, a given state of things or a process of change. It is believed that man is capable of achieving this harmonization between himself and nature through his self-cultivation. This is expressed by statements such as "The benevolent person naturally feels to form one body with [all] things" (*jen-che hui-jan yu wu tung-ti*)[8] and "The great man holds that Heaven, Earth and the ten thousand things form one body" (*ta-jen-che yi t'ien ti wan wu wei yi-ti*). Since the Han time this is referred to as the doctrine of unity of Heaven and man (*t'ien-jen ho-yi*) or the doctrine of the oneness of virtue between Heaven and man (*t'ien-jen ho-te*).[10] In the Great Appendix of the *I Ching* it is said that "Thus Heaven gives birth to divine things and the sage conforms to them; Heaven and Earth change and transform, and the sage follows them."[11] The very way for a man to become a sage and thus to harmonize himself with the world is to cultivate and develop himself toward a moral perfection. The cultivation and development of a man into a sage is described by the *I Ching* in the following lines:

[The sage] is like the Heaven and Earth and therefore does not deviate from the natural. His knowledge covers ten thousand things and his way saves the world. Therefore he does not go to the extreme. He comprehends all things and yet not indulge himself. He enjoys nature and knows the destiny. Therefore he does not have anxiety. He settles himself in the land and devotes himself to benevolence. Therefore he is capable of loving.

The above makes clear why the Confucianists have placed a strong stress on the moral cultivation and development of man. It is because they want man to be harmonized with the world and things in the world. This view is further indicated in the *Analects*, the *Doctrine of the Mean*, the *Great Learning*, and the *Mencius*, and even in the writings of Hsun Tzu. The moral cultivation and development of man involve many complex and polaristic considerations as we shall see. But the unfaltering belief for the Confucianist is that through the individual cultivation and development of a person goodness and harmony will ensue. When we come to Neo-Confucianism it is even more explicitly articulated that by cultivating oneself toward a moral perfection one will achieve a cosmological harmonization of all things which could eliminate conflict and tension.

If harmony is identified with goodness, and if conflict, as the opposite of harmony, is identified with evil or badness, conflict then requires harmonization. Two important points are noted about conflict in the *I Ching*: First, conflict is a matter of man's inability to conform to reality. Conflict is therefore essentially indicative of weakness of an individual or a community of individuals in his failure to appreciate intricacies of change and consequently to control or discipline himself for making conformity to nature possible. Second, conflict can always be avoided if one strives to conform with nature by cultivating one's understanding and adjusting one's action in a proper way with respect to a propitious time. It is against the background of these two propositions that admonitions and judgments of evil and misfortune in the *I Ching* must be understood. Hence, conflict in these judgments means essentially a lack of harmony between the individual and the situation or the time or the deeds of others, and as such ought to be harmonizable by intelligent efforts of the individual or a community of individuals.

Metaphysics of Harmony and Conflict in Taoism

We come to the metaphysics of harmony and conflict in Taoism. As in the *I Ching*, the *Tao Te Ching* affirms the oneness and all-comprehensiveness of the ultimate reality, namely the *Tao*. In the Taoistic cases, the ultimate reality of the *Tao* with its oneness, constancy, and all-comprehensiveness is now further characterized by its indeterminativeness, that is, voidness of any fixed and definite quality. In this sense the *Tao* is not only the ultimate reality, but the ultimatelessness.[12] *It is the voidness which is forever the boundless and the inexhaustible source of change and creativity of all things.* The polarization and interpenetration of the *yin* (again the female principle-force-aspect) and the *yang* (again the male principle-force-aspect) again exist as essential functions of the *Tao* in the Taoistic metaphysics of harmony and conflict. For example, in Lao Tzu, strength, nobility, brilliance and goodness of the *yang* are distinguished from the weak, the soft, the hidden, the negative, and the lowly, of the *yin* on the one hand, and yet are conceived as having derived and being derivable from these. It is clear that this notion of 'opposite-generating-opposite' is as equally conspicuously stressed in Lao Tzu as in the *I Ching*.

There is also another point of comparison. Whereas the *I Ching* has to a high degree of explicitness recognized the principle of return and reversion in terms of the pendulum swing of the triagrams and hexagrams, Lao Tzu has fully and explicitly formulated the principle of reversion (*fan*) or return (*fu*). He says of the *Tao*; "Weakness is the function of the *Tao*".[13] He also says, "The ten thousand things occur simultaneously and I thereby observe their return."[14] There is a subtle difference between reversion and return (recurrence): Reversion is the opposition of the opposite: it is the derivation of opposite from an overexerted position. Return on the other hand seems to suggest a return to the origin or source of change which is the *Tao* or voidness. Thus he says: "To return to the root is quietude."[15] Return could also mean reversion of reversion after reversion once occurs.

The whole process of change and transformation is to be thus characterized by the polar reversion and return of the *Tao*. Harmony in the Taoistic
sense clearly is no more than the natural unity of things and the natural
course of change according to the above-mentioned principles of polarization, interpenetration, reversion and reversion of reversion. It is also the
infinite creation of things in the manifold of the *Tao*. Lao Tzu no doubt has
accentuated this generative activity of nature and this constitutes an essential element of harmony of the *Tao*.

Lao Tzu suggests that values of good and bad, beauty and absence of
beauty, truth and absence of truth are mutually conditioned and thus mutually dependent for their existence and recognition. He generalizes this mutual
conditioning of values over all major categories of human experience. He says:

Therefore being and nonbeing mutually generate each other. The difficult and easy
mutually complete each other; the long and the short mutually define each other;
the high and the low mutually recline on each other; the simple and complex (sounds)
mutually harmonize each other; the before and the after mutually follow each.[16]

This is the inceptive formulation of the principle of relativity in Taoism
which is very much elaborated in the writings of Chuang Tzu.

According to Chuang Tzu, all things in the world are mutually dependent and mutually conditioned. Distinctions of values are our personal decisions which have no objective basis, whereas distinctions of facts are
equalizable but merely limited manifestations of the unlimited and indeterminate *Tao*. Chuang Tzu has this to say: "Nothing is not a That, nothing is
not a This. From the view-point of That, one does not see This, but from
This point of view, one can see This itself. Thus we say: That is derived
from This, and This is also dependent upon That."[17] In this sense all things
are parts of the one and there is no necessity nor sacredness nor absoluteness
in these distinctions. All distinctions and differences thus are nondistin-
guishable by themselves from the point of view of the *Tao* and make no
difference to the indeterminate reality of the oneness of the *Tao*. We may
call this a principle of ontological equalization or ontological relativization.
On the basis of this principle, it can be affirmed that there is no *conflict* nor
evil nor lack of relevancy in the difference and distinction of things and
values. It can be further inferred, as Chuang Tzu actually claims, that all
things are mutually transformable and all points of view are equally valid
and significant. Thus Chuang Tzu says:

... thus consider the example of a small piece of grass and a huge house beam or
the example of an extremely ugly woman and a beauty, from the point of view of

the Tao, they are all one and mutually consistent and compatible (mutually penetrating). When something perishes, something is created; and when something is created, something perishes. For all things, there is no perishing and no creation, all are mutually penetrating and form an oneness.[18]

This ontological equality of all things, big or small, is the ground for Chuang Tzu to disregard all distinctions and differences, yet at the same time accepting these distinctions and differences as relative entities in the phenomenal world.

Unlike Lao Tzu, Chuang Tzu does not stress the idea of return to the *Tao* as the source or origin. But Chuang Tzu reaches the same conclusion as Lao Tzu regarding *Tao*'s ultimacy and greatness by recognizing the inexhaustible richness in the *Tao*, whIch should pose no difficulty for *Tao*'s reality. For all things in the *Tao* are constituted by relativity and mutual transformability and thus are reducible to oneness and identity at the same time. Distinction and differences between things being ontologically transcendable, conflict, antagonism or hostility arising from distinction and difference are naturally ontologically transcended and absorbed into the *Tao*. Consequently there is no ontological status for conflict and antagonism in the enlightened eyes of the *Tao*. This amply explains why Chuang Tzu has treated many unhappy experiences of man as indicating an occasion to realize the absorbing power of the *Tao* and thus not to regard calamities as unhappy events. To do so is to understand the true meaning of being free and creative: free from bondage of attachment in value and free from prejudice conditioned by one perspective of view. He says:

Only those who understand (the *Tao*) understand the truth of mutual penetration and mutual identification of all things. Only those who can give up prejudices and transcend bounds of conditioning consider all things being realized in the constant course of nature.[19]

To be able to transcend and at the same time to embrace all things in the spirit of the *Tao*, a man will not encounter conflict and will eliminate conflict wherever and whenever conflict arises. For he will see conflict, antagonism, difference or distinction as simply complementary forms of harmony and identity and as resources for generating harmony and identity. This point is what Lao Tzu has initially suggested. Chuang Tzu has brought this point to its natural conclusion: That a man who realizes the identity and equality of all things will be most happy, and in this sense of happiness will reach the highest form of harmony, namely his equality and identification with the Way. Chuang Tzu thus has this insight to offer:

The constant course of nature is the usefulness (functioning) of the useless (the non-functioning). To know this usefulness is to comprehend all. To comprehend all is to be able to find joy and happiness under whatever circumstances of life. To be able to do so, one is close to the *Tao*.[20]

The Dialectics of Harmonization

In spite of the obvious difference of approaches and attitudes between Confucianists and Taoists in their metaphysical conceptions of the world and man's place in it, we must immediately note that the metaphysics of the *I Ching* and that of Taoism share the following in common: (1) They both recognize the world as a harmony or a harmonizing process in which all differences and conflicts among things have no ontological ultimacy but serve the purpose for completing a state of harmony of multitudinous life or for bringing forth a multitude of life in the creative momentum of the changing reality; (2) They both recognize that man can experience and encounter conflict and undesirable situations in life, but man can overcome them by developing his understanding and by accommodating his actions. In this sense conflict and antagonism are resolvable by human cultivation and human adjustment to nature which are within human power to achieve.

A metaphysics will determine a way of looking at things in the world as well as will present a way of resolving difficulties and conducting inquiry. A metaphysics will also provide a way for analyzing, evaluating and guiding affairs and problems of life. In this sense we may speak of the dialectics of harmony and conflict as based on the metaphysics of harmony and conflict. In light of the generality of the Confucian and Taoistic metaphysics of harmony and conflict given above, we may speak of a common dialectics for both Confucianists and Taoists as a means and a model method of conceiving, analyzing and treating the problem of harmony and conflict in the world and human life. This common dialectics, which we may refer to as the *dialectics of harmonization*,[21] can be formulated as follows:

1. All things come into existence by way of polarities (and relativities).
2. Polarities contain relativities, opposition, complementation, mutual generability at the same time.
3. All differences and distinctions of things are generated by (and explained by) polarities of principles, forces and aspects.
4. Polarities specifically produce the unlimited creativity of life (for *I Ching*), a process of return (for Lao Tzu) and mutual transformability of things (for Chuang Tzu), as well as reversion (for all three).

5. Conflict can be resolved by locating a relevant framework of polarities and their generative relationships in which the ultimate reality of oneness and the ontological equality of all things can be asserted.
6. Man can relate and discover ways of resolving conflict through understanding reality and himself.

If we regard the *tao* (reality) as harmonization of differences of things, and thus as unification of polarities underlying them, both differences and polarities being seeming sources and causes of conflict and antagonism, then we can apply the dialectics of harmonization to resolve conflict and antagonism in the following manner. First of all, we recognize that conflict and antagonism contain polarities and relativities and thus imply complementation and mutual generability. This will lead us to see that they thus contribute to and participate in a process of harmonization in reality. With this understanding we will see different sides of conflict and antagonism as ontologically equatable and dialectically identifiable in the infinite hold of the *tao*. Consequently we can project ourselves into a situation where conflict and antagonism will disappear through an overall process of adjustment of ourselves to the world. This process of adjustment can be called a process of harmonization.

In virtue of the inner dynamics of polarities and relativities, the presence of conflict and antagonism therefore demands a moral (practical) transformation of man together with an ontological (metaphysical) transformation of man's understanding (of the world) in accordance with the dialectics of harmonization.

Contrast with the Dialectics of Conflict

Insofar as we we can take the dialectics of harmonization as representing the traditional way of thinking through the wide-spread influences of Confucianism and Taoism, we can contrast it with other types of dialectics[22] as developed in other cultures and philosophies. Two prominent candidates for such alternative dialectics which carry profound philosophical and cultural significance immediately suggest themselves. One is the Hegelian-Marxist dialectics of uplifting progression which represents the modern West, and the Madhyamika dialectics of total negation and abandonment which represents the Buddhistic faith. The purpose of my comparison is to indicate that the dialectics of harmonization in Confucianism and Taoism is logically different from both the Hegelian-Marxist dialectics and the Madhyamika dialectics, and that it has to compete with them in the course of human history. It must be said from the beginning that as different types of dialectics all three have their different cultural backgrounds and correspond with different cultural experiences, needs and aspirations. In this sense there is no comparison in terms of their intrinsic merits and demerits. From a theoretical and speculative point of view, one might suggest that all three dialectics are complementary even though different and perhaps opposite. But if we take this view, we have already adopted the dialectics of harmonization on a higher level. There is no reason, however, why the other two dialectics could not recast the relationships among the three in their respective dialectical modes of thinking. It is up to human experience and human reason in their most comprehensive scope and with respect to their most comprehensive reflection that a final choice among the three is to be made with justification.

The Hegelian-Marxist dialectics consists in accepting the following propositions: (1) The world is (subjectively) given as oneness (thesis). (2) The world realizes itself in terms of opposition and conflict between the given and its negation (antithesis). (3) The world develops and realizes a higher level of existence by synthesizing conflicting elements in a more integrated configuration (synthesis). (4) The world will move on according to this sequence in an indefinite progression which will approximate to an ideal perfection. Though I sketch this dialectics in basic Hegelian terms, it can be easily embodied in a typical Marxist materialistic framework just as it can be rephrased in a typical Hegelian spiritualistic metaphysical framework. What is important is that there are three dominating characteristics of this type of dialectics which, it seems to me, are shared by the Hegelians as well as the Marxists.

First, this type of dialectics affirms that there is ontologically real objective conflict in reality or in the history of man, which takes the form of opposition between a given state and its negation or the form of opposition of one class against another class. This *sense* of conflict and negation implies antagonism, enmity and noncooperativeness. There is no implication of complementation and mutual dependence in this sense of conflict and negation, which is needed to form a complete whole: the whole on the other hand has to be realized as the limit of a dialectical progression. The existence of conflict therefore calls for struggle and strenuous striving in order to eliminate its implicit logical contradiction.

Secondly, the logically contradictory state of conflict is to be resolved by developing out of the conflict a synthetic integration of the two sides of the conflict on a higher plane. This sense of synthetic integration is suggested by the Hegelian term 'Aufheben' and the Marxist notion of social revolution. In the synthesis the earlier thesis and antithesis are totally transformed such that a novel entity comes into being.

Finally, the dialectical movement of reality is considered to be progressive evolution toward a higher and higher or more and more desirable state of being. There is a strong sense of progression which is linearly moving forward. The goal of such progression is highly idealistic whether in the Hegelian framework or in the Marxist framework. In fact it must be idealistic or utopian in the sense that it remains to be indefinitely approached. Now when we apply this type of dialectics to the problem of harmony and conflict, it is clear that conflict is considered a crucial objective element in reality, crucial in its role of advancing history to a higher stage of development. Whereas the dialectics of harmonization holds that conflict can be *resolved* or *avoided* by the individual who comes to understand the true nature of reality, the dialectics of conflict holds that conflict is a constituting ingredient of true nature of reality and thus cannot be resolved or avoided by the individual through understanding. In other words, the process of change for the dialectics of conflict is not essentially a harmony, but a process of disharmony. But disharmony, though objective, is not considered an evil or a disvalue but rather a necessity or even a tool for evolution and progression. As evolution and progression are indefinite, we cannot even really say that harmony is the goal of this dialectical change which centers around conflict and struggle. Struggle like harmony is equally instrumental in bringing higher and higher forms of integration which contains roots of real conflict in its existence. In contrast, though the dialectics of harmonization considers harmony as an essential nature of reality, however, it has yet to sacrifice a sharp sense of progression and moving forward which is articulated in the Hegelian-Marxist dialectics.

Contrast with the Dialectic of Transcendence

The Madhyamika dialectics is distinguished by negating all assertive propositions about reality as well as propositions about such propositions and so on and so forth. It is best expressed by the *tertralemma*[23] of the Mahayana Buddhist philosopher Nagarjuna (100-200 A.D.), who is known in Chinese Buddhism as Lung Shu. The *tetralemma* requires of any proposition that it is to be negated, its negation is to be negated, both itself and its negation are negated as well as both the negation of itself and the negation of its negation are to be negated. The essential idea is to achieve total and thorough detachment and transcendence from every truth claim about reality including detachment from an effort to do so. Such state of conjugated negations is called *nirvanna*, a state of true understanding (*prajna*) as well as true reality (*bodhi*) which are not to be described or committed to any definite speech or definite action. To put this in the dialectical terminology, this approach to reality is clearly characterized by the following ideas: (1) The world of reality is a result of assertion. (2) Any assertion involves an opposite which is negation of the assertion. (3) Though common sense recognizes the conflict between assertion and its negation, which underlies various forms of reality, yet in order to avoid any consequences (philosophical, logical and practical) of such conflict, and in order to reach the ultimate truth behind and above reality, one needs to abandon both in such a way that affirmation of neither is to be held. (4) True understanding of reality and emancipation of an individual from conflict and contradiction will be thus achieved and cherished.

I do not wish to discuss the practical-religious side of the negativistic Madhyamika dialectics as it is called. What is interesting is that, when it is applied to the problem of harmony and conflict, it wishes to resolve the problem by transcending the problem in a metaphysical framework of Nagarjuna who denies reality of causation. Harmony and conflict are recognized to pertain to a common sense level or for that matter, to an unreal and illusionary level. Though conflict is thereby recognized, it is to be transcended without affirming harmony and conflict on any level, because harmony itself is also abandoned as a goal. As a consequence, a person will become passive toward happenings in this world and will treat the world as a sequence of unrelated, nonsignificant and nonassertable appearances and processes. In contrast with the Hegelian-Marxist dialectics, there is in it no sense of progression or integration. In contrast with the Confucian-Taoistic dialectics there is in it no active harmonization which would encompass all differences in the world.

Our brief comparison of the three types of dialectics does not exhaust what we could say about these three types of dialectics and their comparative merits and demerits. However, in indicating their logical and philosophical differences we have successfully illustrated alternative ways of thinking and alternative approaches to the problem of harmony and conflict other than the indigenous Chinese views as expressed in the Confucian-Taoistic dialectics. But I have another purpose in making the comparison: Both the Madhyamika dialectics and the Hegelian-Marxist dialectics are potential competitors against the indigenous Chinese dialectics of harmonization from outside the Chinese milieu of culture and history. Historically speaking, there had been encounter and interaction in the development and growth of Chinese Buddhism during the 4th-9th centuries, between the Confucian-Taoistic dialectics of (harmonization and relativities) and the Madhyamika dialectics of transcendence and negation. We see that these encounters and interactions lead to a gradual integration of the Confucian-Taoistic dialectics into the Madhyamika dialectics. The doctrine of the three truths in T'ien T'ai, the free and creative acceptance of this world in Ch'an as well as the all-comprehensive doctrine of all-in-one and one-in-all in Hua Yen all testify to the introduction of elements of harmony and harmonization into the Madhyamika dialectics. The Confucian-Taoistic dialectics finally prevails over the Buddhistic themes in the revival of the Confucian School—the birth of Neo-Confucianism. On the other hand, even though the Confucian-Taoistic dialectics succeeds in overcoming the native Buddhistic dialectics of Madhyamika as a way of thinking, there is of course no denial that ingredients of the Buddhist dialectics and its associated metaphysics of man and the world may have also subtly entered the bloodstream of Neo-Confucianism.

In the present century we witness another encounter and an on-going process of interaction between the native Chinese dialectics of harmonization and the Western views of harmony and conflict as embodied in the Hegelian-Marxist dialectics of conflict. This encounter and interaction began as the Chinese civilization was forcibly precipitated into the brave new world of competing Western powers. The introduction of the Darwinian and Spencerian doctrine of evolution and the survival of the fittest in the beginning of this century,[24] the success of the 1949 Communist Revolution, and the subsequent propagandization of Marxist-Leninist-Maoist ideology in China all bear witness to the strength and influence of the Western dialectics of conflict in the development of Chinese society as well as to the temporal relative weakness of the Confucian China in meeting the trend of thought in the modern world. The modern fate of Confucian China, as Joseph Levenson argues,[25] is the failure of Confucianism to meet the challenges of the modern world and its problems. But this of course may be a contrived and presumptuous conclusion in light of a possible long-term competition of the two ideologies and their inherent dialectics in a process of stabilization and growth of modern China. The Marxist-Leninist-Maoist campaign in China during 1973-1975 against Confucius and Confucianism[26] seems to acutely suggest a battle of confrontation between the Confucian dialectics of harmonization and the Marxist dialectics of conflict, a battle which must be fought on many fronts. This was of course also reflected in the controversy over 'One divided into two' vs. 'Two combined into one' in early days of the Great Cultural Revolution.'[27] To define harmony as the ultimate goal and to accept all differences as an enrichment of reality and to look to no eternal evolution (as reflected in the doctrine of permanent revolution), *or* to utilize conflict as a means of moving ahead, to enforce uniformity as a driving force and to hold the progression as an eternal striving journey, is perhaps *still* an open and yet ultimate question which China encounters in all its cultural, political and economic activities.[28]

Dialectics of Harmonization in Chinese Ethical
Social and Political Philosophies

In light of what we have said about the Confucian-Taoistic dialectics of harmonization, we can come to an understanding of concepts of harmony and conflict and their roles in the ethical, social and political philosophies in traditional China. It is evident that the dialectics of harmonization has to an extensive extent applied itself to the ethical and social-political areas where problems of harmony and conflict take shape or take place. It must first be noticed that even though the dialectics of harmonization in terms of polarities and relativities involves relatively general polarities and relativities such as the *yin-yang* and the *this-that*, their application to other areas of human experience generates more complicated polarities of various types, some of which may not be obviously opposite, and some of which may not be obviously complementary. But whatever these polarities are, they are no doubt induced or inspired overall by the Confucian or/and Taoistic founder's dialectical visions of harmony and harmonization. In ethics, in socio-political philosophy, in scientific thinking, in medicine, in historiography and history as well as in art and literature, we always find a polaristic/relativistic description or prescription incorporating the basic ideas of the dialectics of harmonization either of the Confucian subtype or the Taoistic subtype or both.[29] Thus we might say that the Confucian-Taoistic dialectics of harmonization determines a multi-polaristic structure of the Chinese experience. This multi-polaristic structure is composed of a number of polaristic structures and their interrelations. How these structures and their interrelations are to be explained and explicated is a most difficult problem and we have so far made no thorough study of these. What I shall undertake in the rest of this chapter is to make some systematic analysis of these structures and their interrelationships in light of the dialectics of harmony and conflict.

As far as we can judge, the following major polaristic structures which pertain to ethical, socio-political areas of human experiences can be given.[30]

1. Inner and Outer (*nei* and *wai*)
2. Polish and Quality (*wen* and *chih*)
3. Self and Others (*chi* and *jên*)
4. Knowledge and Action (*chih* and *hsing*)
5. Righteousness and Utility (*yi* and *li*)
6. Benevolence and Righteousness (*jên* and *yi*)
7. Propriety and Righteousness (*li* and *yi*)
8. Law and Propriety (*fa* and *li*)

9. Nature and Learning (*hsing* and *hsüeh*)
10. Centrality and Harmony (*chung* and *ho*)
11. Heaven and Man (*t'ien* and *jên*)
12. Movement and Rest (*t'ung* and *ching*)
13. the Way and the Utensil (*tao* and *ch'i*)
14. the Metaphysical and the Physical (*hsing-erh-shang* and *hsing-erh-hsia*)
15. the Substance and the Function (*t'i* and *yung*)
16. Principle and Vital Force (*li* and *ch'i*)
17. Reason and Desires (*li* and *yu*)
18. Self-cultivation and Ordering of the world (*hsiu-shen* and *chih-kuo ping-t'ien-hsia*)

These polaristic structures involve polarities which are basically conceived as being opposite and yet complementary in accordance with the dialectics of harmonization. But we should observe that in the areas of ethical, social and political experiences of man, polarities are not simple relativities in the Taoistic sense, for, with a few exceptions, the two sides of a polarity are both desirable and both serve a positive human purpose. On the other hand, the correlative pair of a relativity need not be humanly desirable such as in the case of the relativity of war and peace or that of good and bad. One may further notice that polarities in the Confucianist sense may be relativistic but not all Taoistic relativities are polaristic in the Confucian sense of harmonization.

When we come to specify the exact meaning of harmonization for a polaristic structure (which is not necessarily a relativistic structure), we must also note that the polaristic structures in the ethical, social and political areas of human experiences are in one aspect different from the polaristic structure in the cosmological and ontological areas of human experiences. Whereas in the latter case there is a temporal or a logical sense of sequence involved so that we can speak of the alteration of the two states in a polarity, e.g. we can speak of temporal or logical alteration of the *yin* (the female principle) and the *yang* (the male principle) or that of *wu-chi* (the ultimateless) and *t'ai-chi* (the ultimate), in the former case the basic metaphor or paradigm of polarity is that of spatial coordination and conjunction in a certain finished state. In other words, it involves a spatial paradigm comparable to that of the high and the low, the left and the right or the outer and the inner which represents two simultaneously coexisting states which contrast and complement each other at the same time. Harmonization in this case is to be realized by a balanced and proportional correlation and interpenetration of the two sides of the polarity so that an organically functional whole is fulfilled.

With reference to the above clarification of the notion of a polaristic structure in the ethical, social and political areas, we can discuss and illustrate the application of the dialectics of harmonization to some typical polaristic structures in our listing. We shall focus on the polarities of the outer and the inner, knowledge and action, righteousness and utility, law and propriety, principle and vital force, as well as substance and function. We shall see that the first of these involves a number of others as exemplary or analogic subcases. We shall also note that the polarity of righteousness and utility and the polarity of law and propriety form the major and core themes or concerns of the classical Confucianism and thus form the basis for developing new theses or themes concerning them in later philosophical thinking, Confucianist or non-Confucianist. The polarity of principle and vital force represents primarily a Neo-Confucian concern, whereas the polarity of substance and function represents a modern Chinese Confucian approach at the end of the 19th century in face of the challenge from the West.

Polarity of the Outer and the Inner in the Dialectics of Harmonization

The idea of the polarity of the *outer* and the *inner* is expressed clearly in a passage from the *Doctrine of the Mean*: "To complete oneself is benevolence, to complete things is knowledge. [In doing both] one has achieved the virtue of nature: it is the way of unifying (*ho*) the *outer* and the *inner*. It is therefore always fit to practice it."[31] The *outer* refers to 'completion of things' and the *inner* refers to 'completion of self'. The distinction between the *outer* and the *inner* is a distinction between things outside oneself and nature in oneself. By extension we might say that the *outer* is the culture, objective order, environment, society, world and other people whereas the *inner* is the subjective self-existence, mind and various functions of human nature or human endowments. There is also this implication: the *outer* is given beyond my will and my cultivation, whereas the *inner*, as moral and spiritual potentialities of man, can be developed and cultivated at one's free will. Thus we can regard the *outer* and the *inner* as representing two orders of reality. The problem of harmony and conflict for the *outer* and the *inner* is that of producing a balanced and organic unity of reality in which the *outer* and the *inner* are polaristic, namely, opposite and complementary. Though Confucius seems to believe that the *outer* and the *inner* form an organic unity and harmonious whole on the ground that the *outer* can be ordered on the basis of the *ordering* of the *inner* in a self, there is no explicit mention that it must always be the case. This is further indicated in the Confucian polarities of the 'polish and quality' and the 'righteousness and propriety'.

For Confucius, an individual should polish and cultivate his personality according to *li*, which are social norms and rituals of behavior. But the individual must also at the same time pay attention to a sense of right which is internally embedded in one's nature of self-realization of nature. Thus the 'polish and quality' polarity leads to the 'righteousness and propriety' polarity. Apparently, it is possible that a man may have all the polish of propriety in his social behavior and yet lack a genuine sense of virtue and righteousness. Or he may have a sense of righteousness and yet fail to learn to behave in accordance with proprieties. Then it cannot be said that there is harmony in a person as there would be a discord and discrepancy between the *outer* and the *inner*. To resolve the discord and discrepancy is to achieve a correlation and correspondence between polish and quality and between propriety and righteousness at the same time. The very fact that one may fail to do so at one end or the other indicates the need of *harmonization*, and the very fact that to do well at one end may involve sacrifice at the other and *vice versa* indicates the existence of conflict. The Confucian ethics as advocated by Confucius were precisely developed to overcome this potential conflict and to enable one to achieve a maximum harmonization or harmony between the *outer* and the *inner* from which good is thought to issue.

Confucius does not prescribe how the harmony between the *outer* and the *inner* can be guaranteed to obtain. But he does have faith in that, if each person of a society and each ruler of a state are to cultivate their virtues which are inner, the outer order in terms of conformity to propriety will result. In view of this faith, his followers in the *Great Learning* and the *Doctrine of the Mean* and the *Mencius* have suggested in various degrees how and why the inner order is the basis for the outer order so that the outer order will follow from the inner one. Thus there is talk of 'root' (*pen*) and 'branch' (*mou*), end (*chung*) and beginning (*shih*) in the *Great Learning*.

According to the *Great Learning*, there is a continual growth and development from cultivating the inner realm as consisting in cultivating one's self, rectifying one's mind and making one's intentions sincere to the ordering of the outer realm as consisting in regulating one's family, governing well one's state and pacifying the whole world.

The *Doctrine of the Mean*, on the other hand, speaks of "Being sincere inside ourselves, one will be sincere outside."[33] Mencius similarly argues for the innate goodness (innate moral capacities) of man and for their realization, strengthening and extension. When these inner moral capacities are realized in life and extended to apply to others, then the society and state will be ordered. This amounts to saying that all good things in society and in the state are based upon and derivable from an inner self: Harmony is reached by developing the inner so that it can be manifested in the outer. According to this view, there is no conflict between the inner and the outer. All social conflicts are considered to result from either failure to conform to one's nature, or failure to cultivate one's innate goodness. Any conflict that one experiences in society is basically that between self-interest of the small man and good virtues of the superior man, the distinction between the two types of man having been drawn in the *Analects*. This conflict is avoidable if a ruler devotes himself to the cultivation of his inner virtues so that others will follow suit. The ultimate link between the inner and the outer is clearly assumed to exist in that the inner is inevitably manifested in the outer and inevitably deterrnines the outer. This means that one's intention will determine his action in the context of society as a whole. This also means that a man's behavior and action will inevitably influence others to emulate the same.

As Benjamin Schwartz points out,[34] there is bound to be tension between the outer and the inner as seen in the case of polarity between polish and quality or as seen in the case of polarity between propriety and righteousness. In the paradigm of the spatial relation of the outer to the inner, it seems also apparent that the outer as an entity coexisting with the inner may have its own problems, needs and qualities which are relatively independent of the inner. Even though there could be harmony (balance and unity) between the outer and the inner, the outer need not be harmonized with the inner on the basis of consideration of the inner. The very fact that society and state involve a multitude and an order other than an individual self may have appeared to many other philosophers to warrant different principles of ordering than those suggested by the inneristic views of the *Great Learning*, the *Doctrine of the Mean* and *Mencius*. Thus beginning with Kao Tzu there is the argument that even though benevolence (*jên*) is inner and based on one's nature, righteousness (*yi*) nevertheless is based on rational observation of outside facts and thus the outer order.[35] A natural extension of this view is that all *social virtues* must be rationally inculcated and learned, and in this sense social virtues have no inneristic meaning but only the outeristic meaning of correct behavior according to ritual and propriety. This is essentially Hsün Tzu's view. In this view outeristic considerations of society and state and their ordering and organization should determine and guide the inner growth of individual men. Thus an individual must be educated to be capable of subjecting himself to the system of rites of a society and regulations of a state as designed by the rational mind of sage rulers. Herewith we still have a sense of harmonization—harmonization of society and individual by ordering the society first and educating the individual therefrom. The conflict in society is primarily a result of discord between individual interests and social interests and is to be overcome by regulating the individuals according to the social order.

The outeristic considerations of ordering society and state finally take their radical form in the Legalistic philosophy whereby the ordering of society and state absolutely rules out the cultivation of the inner selves in individuals and is to be justified by the sole end and need for expanding the efficiency and control of state power and the increase of state wealth. Thus we reach a position which is dramatically opposed to the Mencian theory of self-cultivation as the basis and justification of state machinery and social order. The possibility of overcoming the tension between the outer and the inner by completely subjugating the one or the other end sharply point to the virtual conflict between the inner and the outer as symbolized by the historical conflict between the Legalistic school of law and the Mencian school of self-cultivation of virtue.[36]

Problem of Harmonization over Conflicts Between *Fa* and *Li*, *Yi* and *Li*

In connection with the conflict between the *outer* and the *inner*, we may introduce two more polarities which are full of potential conflict and which present a problem for the Confucian School. First, there is the conflict-ridden polarity between law *(fa)* and propriety *(li)*. It is well known that Confucius and his followers wished to diminish or even abolish the rule of law in favor of the ordering of state and society by propriety and virtue *(te)*. But the Confucianists nevertheless tacitly recognized that the majority of people, being self-interested small men, perhaps cannot be governed by *li* alone, and thus they recognized that tension will be always felt between reliance on governmental regulations and institutions on the one hand and reliance on virtuous persons and education on the other. This tension becomes even openly articulated in the Sung controversy between Wang An-shih's institutional approach and his critics' moralistic approach to the policies of government.[37] Perhaps this tension is rooted not just in a difference of means for achieving ordering of state and society, but also in a difference of goals for the ordering of state and society, which are not uniquely defined or uniformly agreed on by philosophers, even within the same school.

This brings us to the strong conflict which the orthodox Confucianists experience in the polarity between profit (*li*) and righteousness (*yi*). It must be noted that when I speak of the polarity of profit and righteousness I do not assume that the opposite and complementary relationship between the two has been worked out. I only assume that this relationship should be and is capable of being worked out in accordance with the Confucian dialectics of harmonization. From alternative dialectical points of view this relationship may never be worked out and even should not be worked out. But then from those points of view there need not exist polarity as such. For the Confucianists, however, this polarity exists, and Confucius himself had harmonized the demand of profit with demand of righteousness by subjecting the former to the judgment of the latter. If profit is not against righteousness, then one can pursue profit; if otherwise, profit should be avoided in order to achieve righteousness. It is also added that a superior man should always consider pursuit of righteousness his life goal, whereas a small man will do the contrary. This position of course is well-maintained by orthodox Confucianists such as Mencius and is well expressed by Tung Chung-shu's motto: "To pursue the righteousness without calculating its profit; to act correctly without thinking of successfulness."[38]

Profit *(li)* however in its nature is ambivalent: it can be the profit of a selfish individual or the profit and utility of a whole society and state. The enthusiasm of Mencius for righteousness even rules out consideration of profit for a state, even though one may have good faith that considerations of righteousness will lead to profitable consequences.[39] The Mohists and the Legalists in stressing the importance of wealth and/or power of state and society necessarily take a different view.[40] Thus the Mohist defines righteousness in terms of social utility or mutual profit, whereas the Legalist advocates the abolishment of considerations of *jên* and *yi* of Confucianism as if they are inhibiting the growth of state which must increase its power and wealth.

The various theoretical tensions and conflicts in goals and values as expressed in the polarity of *li* and *yi* and as experienced in the opposition between legalism and/or Mohism on the one hand, and the orthodox Confucianism on the other, lead to development of alternative forms of Confucianism in Sung, Ming and Ch'ing Periods. A study of the Utilitarian School in the Sung Period and the development of Practical Learning[41] *(shih-hsüeh)* in Ming and Ch'ing Eras bear ample witness of the fruitful dynamical tension between *li* and *yi* as a polarity. The very fact that the Confucianists can become self-critical and work out harmonization of the inner tension or conflict between *li* and *yi* is an indication that *li* and *yi* have gradually emerged as a fully actualized polaristic unity. Historically speaking, Confucianism, in confronting conflicts between its views and the views of the Legalism and Mohism, has had to apply its dialectics of harmonization for resolving these conflicts inherent in their encounters with other schools. To resolve these conflicts is to recognize and affirm and establish a true polarity. Our discussion of various forms of outer/inner polarities have shown how these forms are interrelated as well as what forms are faced and established by Confucianists early in their history and what tensions serve the purpose of stimulating the development of Confucianism in the direction of formulating or articulating polarities through its dialectics.

Polarity of *Chih and Hsing* and Their Harmonization

Now I shall indicate a similar drama and panorama of the development of another polarity, that of knowledge *(chih)* and action *(hsing)*. Confucius considers knowledge and learning as a guide to action. He says: "If one does not know propriety, one will not be able to establish oneself."[42] He also considers action as the goal of self-cultivation and social ordering. For him therefore the relation between *chih* and *hsing* is one of mutual support and complementation for developing a virtuous character and a good society. They are aspects of one unity, which need not even be opposite. Thus he says: "When one speaks, one needs to think of practice. When one acts, one needs to think of practice. Being a superior man, why can't a person quickly put this to practice?"[43] Speaking is related to knowing, for if one does not know right things, one will not be able to say right things. Though Confucius has maintained the basic unity of knowing and acting, he has not elaborated or exhausted all possible means, ends and ways of knowing, nor has he discussed the dynamics of action and the variety of action. Thus possible tensions and conflicts between *chih* and *hsing* remain to be explored and resolved. First of all, there is the question of what to know and how to organize our knowledge. Second, there is the question of how knowledge leads one to correct action.

For Confucius knowledge is either descriptive or normative, and is either of facts or of principles.[44] When we come to the Neo-Confucianism of the Sung Period, to know is to know primarily the principles of all things, and the objects of knowledge must include all principles *(li)* in the world. Generally speaking this is the position of Ch'eng I (1033-1107) and Chu Hsi (1130-1200). But these Neo-Confucianist principles primarily are ontological reasons constituting the existence of things and affairs of man and society. They need not articulate or include scientific knowledge or techniques in any modern sense. When we come to the 18th and 19th centuries, the horizon of knowledge becomes more and more identified with either scientific know-why or know-how or with ways of statecraft and policy-making to secure the world and benefit the nation *(chin-shih chih-yung)*. This is the view of the Practical Learning school such as Yen Yuan (1635-1704), Li Kung (1659-1735) and Kung Yang scholars of the 19th century such as Kung Chih-chen (1792-1841). When the content and scope of knowledge thus change, the relation of knowledge to action has to change as well and even the notion of action has to change and be enlarged. For Chu Hsi and his master Ch'eng I, to exhaust knowledge of principles is conducive to, and supportive of, fulfilling one's nature. Even though the very relation of influence and co-ordination between knowledge (as expressed in the concept of exhausting principles, *chiung-li*) and self-cultivation of nature (as expressed in the concept of residing in serious-mindedness, *chü-ching* is not exactly specified, he nevertheless considers both the former and the latter as individually necessary and collectively sufficient for a unified development of a virtuous and enlightened self. Perhaps he may not hold some metaphysical knowledge of *li* as a condition of social and political action, but he would definitely indicate how a man of profound knowledge of *li* may achieve a vision and a feeling attitude (or value) in reference to the humanity and whole universe as described in his essay on *jên* (benevolence).

The possibility that metaphysical and scholastic knowledge of *li* may impede general action of self-realization or may lack the impetus to do so was seized on by Wang Yang-ming (1472-1529) as a ground for criticizing the Chu Hsi approach and also as an excuse for stressing the direct and complete self-enlightening activities of good will or will of innate goodness[45] *(liang-chih)*. Wang's position was that action in the sense of self-fulfillment and in the sense of making judgment of good and bad by one's innate sense of goodness, so that correct action may result from it, is all important. Following Lu Hsiang-shan (1139-1193), Wang regarded scholastic knowledge (abstract-speculative or concrete-factual knowledge) as prohibiting the moral realization of man, and thus he regarded knowledge as just opposite but not complementary to action. Action is limited to moral action. In order to be harmonized with action in this sense, knowledge is to be redefined or redescribed. The potential tension and conflict between *chih* and *hsing* through the ambiguities of these two concepts are fully articulated in the debate between Chu Hsi and Lu Hsiang-shan[46] as well as in the continued controversy between schools of Chu Hsi and Wang Yang-ming. Even though individual Confucian philosophers such as Chu Hsi and Wang Yang-ming may have reached some subjective harmonization between knowledge and action, this harmonization is neither sufficiently explained nor comprehensive enough to allow the scope and content of action and knowledge to settle the questions of harmonization between the two. Thus their individual resolutions may not satisfy the dialectics of harmonization in its fullest application, and for this reason, may require further development in light of the requirement of this dialectics.

Schwartz is essentially right in pointing out the inherent irrelevance of Chu Hsi's intellectual works to daily life, and the consequence of potentially eliminating the outer realm in the transcendental individualism of the radicalist followers of Wang Yang-ming.[47] The very plausibility of criticism of both the Chu School and the Wang School by Ch'ing scholars such as Tai Chen (1723-1777) and Wang Fu-chih (1619-1692) and Yen Yuan powerfully testify to the insufficiency and unsatisfactoriness of the solution to the harmony and conflict problem between knowledge and action in the paradigms of knowledge and action defined by the Sung and Ch'ing masters. As knowledge and action continue to change in content, scope, quality and structure, the tension and conflict between the two remain highly disturbing for any society facing these changes in various directions and dimensions. It is no doubt especially the case with the Chinese situation today. The problem of harmonizing knowledge and action and overcoming their inherent tension and conflict according to the dialectics of harmonization still remains a basic and serious challenge for contemporary Confucian-oriented philosophers.[48]

Polarities of *Li-Ch'i*, *Li-Yu* and *T'i-Yung* and Their Harmonization Problems

I shall be brief on the last two polarities in the development of Chinese thinking. Regarding the polarity between principle *(li)* and vital force *(ch'i)*, I shall have very much to say and I have said very much elsewhere.[49] It is to be first noted that *li* and *ch'i* for the Neo-Confucianists form primarily a cosmic polarity which explains the process of change, formation and transformation of things and the nature of the ultimate reality. As a cosmic polarity, the polaristic structure of *li* and *ch'i* is explicitly described by Neo-Confucianist philosophers such as the Ch'eng Brothers and Chu Hsi. This constitutes a contribution to the development of the Neo-Confucian metaphysics. Even in the philosophical statements of Chou Tun-i (1017-1073) the unity of *li* and *ch'i* as opposite but complementary forms and forces of reality is implicitly assumed in his reference to the generative oneness of the *wu-chi* and *t'ai-chi*, and the *t'ai-chi* and *ying-yang*, as well as the *yin-yang* and *wu-hsing* (five powers). For Chu Hsi, this unity of *li* and *ch'i* is fully acknowledged and elaborated, even though he appears to take too seriously the seemingly paradoxical issue of deciding the priority between *li* and *ch'i*. In doing so, he falls into the trap of dualism.[50] On the other hand, there is no doubt that other philosophers of the Sung Neo-Confucianism may not have seen the polaristic structure as a dualistic structure in the existence of *li* and *ch'i*, and thus endeavored to solve the problem of possible tension and conflict between the two by reducing *li* to a *secondary* place and upholding *ch'i* to a primary place. Such is the *ch'i* monism of

Chang Tsai (1020-1077) in which *li* becomes the pattern of organization inherent in the substance of *ch'i*.[51]

With this cosmological-ontological background, the *li-ch'i* polaristic structure has been applied to explaining the problem of conflict and harmony of human reason, life-vitality, feelings and desires by the major Neo-Confucianists such as the Ch'eng Brothers, Chu Hsi and Chang Tsai. In this humanly relevant polaristic structure we find that most Neo-Confucianists recognized the harmonization of *li* and *ch'i* in the generation and growth of natural life. Except for a few later followers of the Wang Yang-ming School in the Ming Era,[52] it seems that there is no Neo-Confucianist who does not affirm the importance of *li* in the development and cultivation of human nature. But once the problem of cultivation of human nature is considered, immediately there arises the tension and conflict between the inclination of reason and that of desires[53] *(yu)*. Thus almost all major Sung-Ming Neo-Confucianists took this to be a major problem of ethics and social political philosophy and undertook to *harmonize* these two by advocating the control of desires and reducing or diminishing the number of desires.

As desires are often referred to as selfish desires *(ssu-yu)* and *li* as heavenly principle *(t'ien-li)*, the opposition of the two can also be described as that between public-mindedness or universal-mindedness and selfishness or self-interest. The resolution of this opposition which the Neo-Confucianists held was always the subjugation of the self-interest to the public-mindedness or mind which is identified with Heaven, earth and all human beings. This amounts to an opposition to individualism and utilitarianism in ethics and social and political philosophy, and to institutional decisions or policies favoring such. But to see this, of course, is to see that the potential tension and conflict between *li* and *yu* may lead to other positions than that adopted by the Neo-Confucianists. Thus for them, the problem of harmony and conflict has to be reconsidered under the dialectic of harmonization if one is to consistenlly hold to the Confucian position on a methodological level. It may be noted that Tai Chen, who criticized Chu Hsi and Wang Yang-ming for their opposition to desires and the vital nature of man, suggested the universalization principle as a test for preserving human desires of vital nature which are universal and as a test for rejecting human reason which is selfishly conceived and selfishly applied.[54] In this fashion he has suggested a new paradigm for realizing the polaristic structure of *li* and *yu*: both are instances of human goodness and both are mutually supportive of human life. This is no doubt a new approach to the harmonization of *li* and *yu* in human life.

Finally, the polaristic structure between substance *(t'i)* and function *(yung)* was focussed on by the Confucian statesman Chang Chih-tung (1837-

1909) in the late 19th century in search of harmony and harmonization to eliminate tension and conflict between the Western science and technology on the one hand and the Chinese culture and humanism on the other hand. The original *t'i-yung* paradigm formulated in the context of Neo-Confucianism,[55] however, applies to the everlasting and perennial way (the *tao*) and has a whole set of metaphysical or philosophical relationships worked out to indicate how harmony between substance of the *tao* and function of the *tao* is to be achieved where and when tension and conflict between the two occur. But when Chang Chih-tung applied this paradigm to the new situation of confrontation between the Western Learning and the Chinese Learning in order to harmonize their conflict,[56] no system of relationships for such harmony or harmonization had been worked out and thus the polaristic structure appeared to be sterile and uninspiring. This explains why this structure does not bring out an enduring and adequate policy and/or a course of action which would testify to the existence of the harmony. The harmony and harmonization in regard to this have yet to be worked out, perhaps in future days to come.

The very complicated situation of tension, conflict and unfriendly opposition of ideas, views and inferences, and values in the beginning of the 20th century and in the pre- as well as in the post-1911 Revolution days all point to the fact that not only the polarity between *t'i* and *yung* has yet to be substantiated, but perhaps new forms of polarity must be explored and constructed in order to apply the dialectics of harmonization fruitfully and successfully. After the Chinese Marxists rose to power in 1949, the very dialectic of harmonization was vehemently challenged and intentionally abandoned.

Concluding Remarks: Toward Development of Paradigms of Harmonization

In the above we have presented and constructed concepts and paradigms of harmony and conflict in major Chinese philosophical schools and have developed and generalized over a dialectical approach to the problem of harmony and conflict in Confucianism and Taoism. In reference to the Confucian system we have shown how the Confucian dialectics of harmonization produced a number of polaristic paradigms and structures in human experiences related to ethics, society and government. It may be said that the dialectics of harmonization as a way of thinking has implicitly and subconsciously guided Chinese thinkers to adopt all such paradigms and structures on the one hand, and these paradigms and structures in their turn help to organize the Chinese way of thinking in accordance with the dialectics of harmonization on the other. In either direction the typical Chinese thinker resolves to search for and to construct explicitly new polaristic structures in reference to old ones or in derivation from the raw experiences of life itself. This means that the dialectics of harmonization sufficiently and necessarily relates itself as the dominating image of understanding all major categories and methods of Chinese thinking in the social, ethical and political fields.

At this juncture it may be highly significant to ask to what extent paradigms of conflict, harmony and harmonization of conflicts under the dialectics of Confucianism and/or Taoism will continue in the present day to shape values, social behavior, social structure and historical development as well as the total future prospect in China. It is apparent that we cannot answer this question in this discussion. Still, to be able to raise this question is a valuable advance in understanding Chinese history and society and their relation to Chinese philosophy as their image and guiding light. What is certain of course is that Confucian and Taoist philosophers alike tend to see history and society in the image of their dialectics of harmonization and the conceptual polaristic paradigms and structures generated therefrom. In fact this dialectical view, as I have shown, is based on the reflection and experience of the ultimate reality as it is embodied in cosmos, history, society and life at large. Therefore in this sense an evaluation and understanding of human society, human history and human destiny can be said to be as naturalistic as it is humanistic, in full concordance with the Confucian and Taoistic dialectics of harmonization.

The above was not written with the intention of denying that Chinese history and Chinese society have not experienced upheavals of tension, conflict and antagonistic struggle. The point is that all these upheavals tend to be subsumed under the dialectics of harmonization from the Confucian view and/or the Taoistic view. With the introduction of Western thought, together with what they represent, into China in the late 19th century and early 20th century, the Chinese mind has been confronted with a seemingly chaotic and strange reality. This experience may be described as traumatic and the result might have been disastrous. But the dialectics of harmonization as worked out by the Confucianists and Taoists throughout past centuries seems to remain a viable means for the understanding, organization, and evaluation of the new reality with its new opposition and conflict. Again, there is no denial that this dialectics itself faces a real challenge, that the paradigms under the dialectics may have failed to yield realistic solutions of conflict and to achieve desirable results. In other words, there is no denial that, because of the failure of its paradigms from the past, this dialectics may face danger of elimination and replacement. The establishment of Chinese Marxism and its dialectics of conflict as a way of thinking and problem-resolving may indeed indicate the necessity of deep reflection on the value of the dialectics of harmonization. But we have no right to jump to premature conclusions without a thorough analysis of existing facts, nor without a patient observation of what is yet to happen.

One methodological precaution must be specifically mentioned. From a philosophical stance, that a paradigm may not work now does not imply that it will not work, nor does the failure of the dialectics of harmonization to construct a paradigm for resolving a given conflict into a polaristic structure imply the failure of the dialectics itself. Insofar as consistency and experiences are concerned, and in terms of the basic considerations of human need and human reason, the Confucian/Taoistic dialectics of harmonization is as strong and as sanguine as any worked-out dialectics and will therefore remain a staunch directive force and an effective model in competition with many others in the world.

Notes

1. E.g. see Derk Bodde, "Harmony and Conflict in Chinese Philosophy," in *Studies in Chinese Thought,* ed. Arthur F. Wright, (Chicago, 1953, 19-75); Benjamin Schwartz, "Some Polarities in Chinese Thought," in *Confucianism and Chinese Civilization,* ed. Arthur Wright (Atheneum, 1964), 3-15; Chung-ying Cheng, "Reason-Substance and Reason-Desire Relationships in 17th Century Neo-Confucianism," presented in Como Conference on 17th Century Neo-Confucianism, September 1969, included in *The Unfolding of Neo-Confucianism,* ed. Wm. Theodore de Bary, New York, 1975, 469-510. A few studies on the *I Ching* (the *Book of Changes*) tend to focus on the problem of resolving or explaining conflict in a harmony-orientated framework.

2. This third theme has not been clearly recognized by students of Chinese thought. One aim of the present analysis is to articulate this theme and its problems arising from it in various historical situations.

3. See Benjamin Schwarts' article mentioned in note 1.

4. These other forms of thought might be considered results of application of these fundamental metaphysics and dialectics.

5. By these I mean primarily philosophical writings of Chou Tun-i (1017-1073), Chang Tsai (1020-1077), Ch'eng Hao (1032-1085), Ch'eng I (1033-1107), Chu Hsi (1130-1200), and Wang Fu-chih (1619-1692).

6. This statement is basically an explanation and rendering of the Chinese statement *"Sheng-sheng-chih-wei-hsing"* in the Great Appendix of the *I Ching.*

7. Here 'nature' is intended to represent the Chinese term *hsing,* which in this context means genuine reality. The term 'nature' does not have the same connotation and denotation as *tzu-jan* (what exists naturally or what comes into being naturally) normally also translated as nature. This statement and the statement preceding it are based on the Chinese statements *"Yi-yin yi-yang chih-wei-tao, chi-chih-che shan-yeh, ch'eng-chih che-hsing-yeh"* in the Great Appenxix of the *I Ching.*

8. This is a statement made by Ch'eng Hao in his *Dialogues (Yu Lu).*

9. This is a statement made by Wang Yang-ming in an essay titled *Ta Hsueh Wen.*

10. In Han Confucianism, Tung Chung-shu (179-104 B.C.) implicitly held that Heaven and man are one in view of certain correspondence between Heaven and man;

214

in Sung Neo-Confucianism the emphasis is generally put on the thesis that man shares the same *virtue* and possesses the same potentiality as Heaven, and he is capable of achieving sagehood which embodies the greatness of Heaven. This thesis is specifically articulated by Chang Tsai in his *Hsi-min* (the Western Inscription) and Chu Hsi in his *Jên-shuo* (Essay on Jên). (For a translation of these two writings, see Win-tsit Chan's *A Source Book in Chinese Philosophy*, Princeton, N.J., 1963, 554 ff, 593 ff.) It seems clear that the Neo-Confucian doctrine of *t'ien-jên-ho-te* is more germane to the classical Confucian views in the *Doctrine of the Mean* and the *Mencius* than Tung Chung-shu's doctrine of *t'ien-jên-ho-yi*.

11. This translation and the next one were done by this author.

12. The ultimatelessness *(wu-chi)* indicates the boundlessness and indefiniteness of the ultimate reality *(t'ai-chi)*. The term *(wu-chi)* is first used in *Tao Te Ching*, whereas the term *ta'i-chi* is first used in the Great Appendix of the *I Ching*. It is Chou Tun-i in the Sung Period who combines the use of *wu-chi* and the use of *t'ai-chi* in his well-known statement *"wu-chi erh t'ai-chi"* (the Ultimateness and then the Great Ultimate).

13. See *Tao Te Ching*, #40.

14. See *Tao Te Ching*, #16.

15. See *Tao Te Ching*, #16.

16. See *Tao Te Ching*, #2.

17. See *Chuang Tzu*, chapter on *Chi Wu Lun* (on Making All Things Equal).

18. Ibid.

19. Ibid.

20. Ibid.

21. This type of dialectics is so called because it is directed toward establishing harmony between conflicting elements in the world or in the thinking. It is clear that both Confucianism and Taoism share this dialectical interest. But we must also note that Confucianism differs from Taoism in not so much stressing relativities of things and perspectives as Taoism. The primary dialectical interest of Confucianism is to reach harmony by comprehending the unity in variety without denying the individuality of things, whereas Taoism is primarily interested in the unity of things by pointing out relativities and limitations in individual existence. We may perhaps speak of Taoistic subtype of the dialectics of harmonization to be entitled the dialectics of relativities in distinction from the Confucianist subtype of the dialectics of harmonization to be entitled the dialectics of complementation.

22. I consider 'dialectics' to be a term used to describe the structure of a process toward reaching an understanding of reality. Dialectics therefore is basically a method of revealing what is real and valuable. In this broad sense of dialectics we can speak of various types of dialectics and we can also assign a common meaning to both the dialectics in Plato and the dialectics in Hegel.

23. For an explanation of the *tetralemma* (logic of four alternatives), see K. N. Jayatilleke, "The Logic of Four Alternatives," *Philosophy East and West 17, nos. 1-4 (1967),* 69-83. Cf. also *Richard S.Y. Chi, "Topics on Being and Logical Reasoning," Philosophy East and West* 24, no. 3 (1974): 293-300.

24. The Darwinian and Spencerian doctrine of evolution and the survival of the fittest was expounded by many intellectual writers in the first two decades of this century. The doctrine was first introduced by Yen Fu (1853-1921) and was endorsed by scholars such as Liang Chi-chao (1873-1929) and others. Cf. Benjamin Schwartz, *In Search of Wealth and Power, Yen Fu and the West* (Cambridge, 1964).

25. Cf. Joseph Levenson, *Confucian China and Its Modern Fate, A Trilogy,* Berkeley, Calif., 1965.

26. See the *Peking Review* in the period between 1973 and 1975.

27. See a sample of this controversy in *Chinese Studies of Philosophy, A Translation Journal,* Vol. VI, no. 1 (Fall 1974): 61 ff.

28. Apparently this question is to some extent explicitly discussed by major and lesser ideological and philosophical writers on mainland China. The aforesaid controversy over 'one divided into two' and 'two combined into one' is a good example. One might even venture to suggest that there is an underlying theoretical difference in the political struggle between Mao and Maoists on the one hand and the moderates on the other. This theoretical difference involves two sides or two approaches as described in this open question here.

29. See note 19.

30. The polaristic way of thinking pervasively and extensively characterizes the Chinese conception of problems, points of view and realities, which are not limited to Confucian/Neo-Confucian and Taoist writings. In *The Platform Sutra (Tan Ching)* of the well-known Sixth Patriarch of Ch'an (Zen) Buddhism Hui-neng (638-713), Hui-neng himself has formulated 36 polaristic parts *(tui)* in his lectures to disciples (see *The Platform Sutra of the Sixth Patriarch*, Philip B. Yampolsky, New York, 1967, 171 ff.). It is evident that there are far more recognizable pairs in the Confucianist/Neo-Confucianist, Taoistic, Buddhistic polaristic pairs than here identified.

31. Translation by this author.

32. The *Great Learning* says: "In ancient times those who desire to illuminate the illustrious virtue in the world must first govern well their states; those who desire to govern well their states must first regulate their families; those who desire to regulate their families must first cultivate their persons; those who desire to cultivate their persons must first rectify their minds; those who desire to rectify their minds must first make sincere their intentions; those who desire to make sincere their intentions must first extend their knowledge. The way for extending knowledge consists in investigation of things." The translation is mine.

The first two steps, the investigation of things and the extension of knowledge, seem to be subject to either an outeristic interpretation or an inneristic interpretation and thus remain ambivalent. This ambivalence becomes the source of divergence between the view of Chu Hsi who favors an outeristic interpretation and the view of Wang Yang-ming who favors an inneristic interpretation.

33. Translation by the author.
34. See Benjamin Schwartz, "Some Polarities in Chinese Thought."
35. See the *Book of Mencius*, Chapter 6.
36. This conflict is still discernible in modern and contemporary thinking under various forms and in various areas.
37. For an account of this controversy, see John Thomas Meskill (ed.), *Wang An-shih (1021-1086), Practical Reformer?* (Boston, 1963).
38. See Pan Ku, *Han Shu* (The History of Han), Biography of Tung Chung-shu. Cf. Tung Chung-Shu, *Chün Chiu Fan Lu* (Luxuriant Dews of the Spring and Autumn Annals) Chapter on *Tui-chiao-hsi-wang-yueh-ta-fu-pi-te-wei-jên*. Chu Hsi has quoted this motto in his *Dialogues (Yü Lü)* see *Shu Ching Ssu Lü*, edited by Chang Pei-hsing, Chapter 10.
39. See the famous reply Mencius made to the question of King Hui of Liang in the *Mencius*. Chapter 1.
40. It needs to be briefly pointed out that the Mohists and the Legalists stress importance of wealth and/or power of state and society for different reasons. A more accurate way of formulating the positions of the two seems to be: the Mohist would primarily stress the importance of the wealth of the society whereas the Legalist would primarily stress the importance of the power of the state.
41. Cf. my article 'Practical Learning in Yen Yuan, Chu Hsi and Wang Yang-ming', included as a chapter in Wm. Theodore de Bary and Irene Bloom, ed., *Principle and Practicality: Essays in Neo-Confucianism and Practical Learning,* New York, Columbia University, 1979, 37-67, now also a chapter in this book.
42. The *Analects* of Confucius, 20-3.
43. See the *Doctrine of the Mean*, #13, translation is mine.
44. Cf. my article "Theory and Practice in Confucianism," in *Journal of Chinese Philosophy*, 1, no. 2 (1974) 179-198.
45. Cf. my article "Unity and Creativity in Wang Yang-ming's Philosophy of Mind," in *Philosophy East and West* XXX, 114 (January and April, 1973):49-72.
46. Cf. Julian Ching, "The Goose Lake Monastery Debate (1175)," in *Journal of Chinese Philosophy* 1, no. 2 (1974): 161-179.
47. Cf. Benjamin Schwartz, "Some Polarities in Chinese Thought," for elaboration of this point.
48. Most of the contemporary Chinese thinker-scholars seem to be implicitly and unconsciously thinking along the line of the dialectics of harmonization but

none comes to a full consciousness of the explicit form of this problem or explicitly recognizes its importance in facing challenges from the Western views. By contemporary Chinese thinkers-scholars I refer to persons such as Hsiung Shih-li, Liang Shu-ming, T'ang Chun-yi and Mou Tsung-shan.

49. See my article, "Reason-Substance and Reason-Desire Relationships," in *The Unfolding of Neo-Confucianism*, ed. by Wm. Theodore De Barry et al. Columbia University Press, New York, 1975, p. 469ff.

50. Chu Hsi has been regarded as a dualist in regard to his metaphysics of *li* and *ch'i* and his moral philosophy of *li* and *yü*. But he need not be regarded as a metaphysical dualist if he simply takes the relation of *li* and *ch'i* to be like that of *t'ai-chi* and *wu-chi* in Chou Tun-i. Instead he wants to decide whether *li* or *chi* comes first and in what sense.

51. Cf. Chang Tsai develops his *ch'i*-monistic system in his major work *Cheng Meng* (Removing Ignorance) which has been commented on in good detail by Wang Fu-chih and was the inspiring source for Wang's own philosophy.

52. Some later followers of Wang Yang-ming School have developed a strong Ch'anist tendency and romantic individualism which became incompatible with the *li*-orthodoxy of Neo-Confucianism.

53. *Yü* is explained as the nature of temperament *(ch'i-chih-chih-hsing)* and *li* is explained as the nature of reason-righteousness *(yi-li chih-hsing)*.

54. Cf. my book, *Tai Chen's Inquiry into Goodness* (The East-West Center Press, 1971) Chapter 3.

55. This *t'i-yung* paradigm has appeared in Classical Confucian as well as Neo-Confucian texts.

56. See Chang Chih-tung (1837-1909), *Ch'üan Hsüeh P'ien* (Exhortations to Learning) (Wu Chang, 1895). Cf. Henry D. Bays, *"Chang Chih-tung and the Politics of Reform in China 1895-1905,"* University of Michigan Ph.D. dissertation, Ann Arbor, Microfilm, 1971.

Part II

Confucian Dimensions

7. Rectifying Names (*Cheng-Ming*) in Classical Confucianism

I

The concept of rectifying names (*cheng-ming*)[1] is a familiar one in the Confucian *Analects*. It occupies an important, if not a central, position in the political philosophy of Confucius. Since, according to Confucius, the rectification of names is the basis of the establishment of social harmony and political order, one might suspect that later political theories by Confucianists could be traced back to the Confucian doctrine of rectifying names. It need not be added that the theory of rectifying names, as developed by Hsün Tzu in the third century B.C., served the double purpose of strengthening his political doctrine of government, on the one hand, and repudiating doctrines of names, on the other.

In the writings of Mencius, the doctrine of rectifying names is no less important. He uses it as a proposal for describing facts in terms of their value in achieving or preserving social harmony and political order. In fact, by applying the doctrine of rectifying names he is able to maintain a cogency in his doctrines of benevolent government and the goodness of human nature.[2] However, here in this chapter I do not wish to discuss the complete development of the doctrine of rectifying names in the period from the fifth to the third century B.C. after it was proposed by Confucius. Instead, I wish to suggest some guidelines for interpreting Confucius's concept of rectifying names in relation to his theory of government and in regard to its methodological significance. I will further relate this doctrine of Confucius to a later work of the classical Confucian philosophy— *The Great Learning*[3] (*Ta Hsueh*)—in such a way that the latter will be shown to be its extension and exemplification.

II

The following two questions are likely to be asked in regard to Confucius's doctrine of rectifying names: What is the meaning of the doctrine of rectifying names? How can this doctrine be used to achieve social harmony and political order?

To answer the first question, one should explain what *names* signify to Confucius. Names for Confucius were not merely labels for things in nature, but also include labels for the relationships between individuals and the values inherent in those relationships. Thus, when Confucius said, in counting the advantages derived from the study of the *Book of Poetry*, that "We become largely acquainted with the names of the birds, beasts, and plants,"[4] he had in mind, of course, names as labels for things in nature. But when Confucius said of Tzu Ch'an, a great statesman in the province of Cheng, "He had four of the characteristics of a superior man—in his conduct of himself, he was humble; in serving his superior, he was respectful; in nourishing the people, he was kind; in ordering the people, he was just,"[5] he was not referring to things in nature, but to the various virtues of a man in relation to himself and other men. That, in the Confucian system, these virtuous characteristics are apparently not naturalistic qualities is due to the fact that an individual is not just a physical or biological entity, but an agent capable of having feelings, sentiments, thoughts, and ideals, which regulate and guide that person's life and conduct. Indeed, phenomenologically speaking, an individual is capable of having many more *intentional dispositions* to be described in terms of beliefs, knowledge, virtues, and temperaments. This is evident by the presence in our ordinary language of numerous terms that convey the moral, the social, the cultural, and other human qualities that apparently cannot be explained in naturalistic terms.

Without going into a detailed account of inherent human dispositions and capacities, we can focus, as Confucius does, on the relationships into which one can normally enter in one's social and ethical life, each such relationship normally suggesting a possible virtue. In these relationships one can be described as a parent, a child, a spouse, a sibling, a friend, and a loyal subject of the state. Thus it is clear that, for Confucius, labels denoting social positions and ethical relationships also are names. Names in this sense include specific terms indicating relationships between ruler and subject, parent and child, husband and wife, friend and friend, and younger and older siblings. These are later taken by Mencius and the *Doctrine of the Mean* (*Chung Yung*) as the five basic relationships among people.[6] These relationships suggest the possibilities of the virtues of loyalty and respect in the case of the ruler and the subject, kindness and filial piety in the case of the parent and child, mutual respect and performance of separate duties in the case of the husband and wife, truthfulness and trustworthiness in the case of the friends, and brotherly love and considerateness in the case of siblings.

Throughout the *Analects*, Confucius attempted to define and describe various virtues essential for maintaining good human relationships. Terms like benevolence (*jên*), righteousness (*yi*), propriety (*li*), intelligence (*chih*), courage (*yung*), and sincerity (*ch'eng*) are typical examples. These virtues represent capacities to achieve and preserve social harmony and political order because they are developed from human capacities.

After having explained what names are, it should be pointed out that names can be corrected. This is possible because our names may not accurately represent the realities we intend them to represent. Thus, in both the natural world and the human world, we might recognize things and facts incorrectly; that is, we might have a misguided and partial understanding of things and facts. Thus, to rectify names is to recognize certain truths about nature and humankind and avoid misrepresenting these truths.

Now if we confine rectifying names to questions of understanding truths about human nature and the human social and ethical capacities, the importance of rectifying names for achieving social harmony and political order will become obvious. Because one's understanding of individual and human relationships could be misguided and partial, it may be improved. This means, then, that the prejudices and false conceptions resulting from an inadequate understanding of such could be corrected or rectified. As one's practice of virtues depends upon one's understanding oneself and others, an improvement and rectification of one's understanding means an improvement and rectification of one's practice of virtue. This will inevitably contribute to the creation and maintenance of social harmony and political order.

III

Let us see how Confucius himself formulated his ideas regarding the doctrine of rectifying names. In one passage we have the following:

Duke Ching of Ch'i asked Confucius about government. Confucius replied, "*There is government*, when the prince is prince, and the minister is minister; when the father is father, and son is son." "Good!" said the duke; "if, indeed, the prince is not prince, the minister not minister, the father not father, and the son not son, although I have my revenue, can I enjoy it?"[7]

Here Confucius suggested that good government is possible only if a ruler behaves like a ruler, a minister behaves like a minister, a father behaves like a father, and a son behaves like a son. The terms *ruler, minister, father,* and *son* in the first use are names of social and biological relationships, but these same terms in the second use represent virtues that pertain to positions and relationships, suggesting significant possibilities of social well-being and individual, moral self-fulfillment. The statement that a ruler *is* a ruler, a minister *is* a minister, a father *is* a father, and a son *is* a son need not be tautological. For what Confucius said, in effect, is that the names *ruler*, *father*, and *son* can be correctly applied to individuals only when the individuals satisfy not only the conditions of occupying a position of authority or standing, but also satisfy conditions of possessing appropriate virtues, such as respect and loyalty in the relationship between ruler and minister, and kindness and filial piety in the relationship between father and son. If these conditions are fulfilled, then social harmony and political order will follow.

According to Confucius, social harmony and political order are represented by the orderly relationships between ruler and minister, father and son. In this way we see that rectifying names demands the correspondence of names to the natural facts as well as to the implementation of values. Thus, this doctrine does not just require definitional consistency, but implies a recognition of principles; that is, recognition of standards of action that can be used to judge what is true, good, and right, on the one hand, and what is false, bad, and wrong, on the other. To rectify names therefore is to establish standards of the true, the good, and the right. But because moral knowledge of right and wrong in a normal situation carries a command for doing right, to rectify names, therefore, is related to the program for carrying out the command for doing the appropriate thing in accordance with the proper situation. This is a reason why rectifying names has practical significance for human conduct and is not merely a matter of the correct use of language.

We must note, however, that in Confucianism rectifying names is regarded as a necessary condition, but not the only necessary condition, for achieving social harmony and political order. In a passage from the *Analects* in which explicit reference is made to the doctrine of rectifying names, we read:

Tzu-lu said, "The ruler of Wei has been waiting for you, in order to administer the government with you. What will you consider the first thing to be done?" The Master replied, "What is necessary is to rectify names." "So, indeed!" said Tzu-lu. "You are wide of the mark! Why must there be such a rectification?" The Master said, "How uncultivated you are, Yu! A superior man, in regard to what he does not know, shows a cautious reserve. If names be not correct, language is not in accordance with the truth of things. If language be not in accordance with the truth of things, affairs cannot be carried on to success. When affairs cannot be carried on to success, proprieties and music will not flourish. When proprieties and music do not flourish, punishments will not be properly awarded. When punishments are not properly awarded, the people do not know how to move hand or foot. Therefore a superior man considers it necessary that the names he uses may be spoken *appropriately*, and also that what he speaks may be carried out *appropriately*. What the superior man requires, is just that in his words there may be nothing incorrect."[8]

From this passage it is clear that rectifying names is considered the foremost and most basic requirement for administering a government. But that this requirement is not sufficient in itself is shown in the chain reasoning embodied in the passage. We may formulate this chain reasoning in the following manner:

names being not rectified	no coherent language
no coherent language	no successful affairs
no successful affairs	no flourishing of proprieties and music
no flourishing of proprieties and music	no punishments properly dispensed
no punishments properly dispensed	people do not know how to move hand or foot (that is, people do not know what to do)

This chain of reasoning implies that if names are not rectified, people do not know how to behave. By showing the consequences, we demonstrate the requirement that the correct behavior of people demands that names be rectified. This simply means that correct behavior implies rectifying names. In view of this, one might say that for Confucius other factors for achieving social harmony and political order are necessary, besides the rectification of names. Two such factors are those of effective education and the provision for favorable conditions of livelihood for the people.[9]

In the *Analects* we find two additional references to the doctrine of rectifying names:

The Master said, "When a prince's personal conduct is correct, his government is effective without the issuing of orders. If his personal conduct is not correct, he may issue orders, but they will not be followed.[10]

Chi K'ang asked Confucius about government. Confucius replied, "To govern means to rectify. If you lead the people with correctness, who will not dare not to be correct?"[11]

The first quotation indicates the importance of a ruler behaving as a model for his people to imitate. The correct comportment of a ruler consists in his conducting himself with benevolence; that is, in making efforts to benefit people. His conduct is correct only when he knows the standards of correct behavior for a ruler and acts in accordance with his knowledge. Then, he will be esteemed and followed by the people. This then, is the way to harmonize society and effectively govern people. The second passage explicitly defines government as a process of rectifying names and correcting behavior; namely, as a process of recognizing and following standards of good and right. Such recognition and practice will provide the sound basis for good society and good government.

IV

The doctrine of rectifying names is logically significant insofar as the principles of real definitions are concerned. Real definitions are definitions not based on arbitrary conventions, but on recognitions of the essential nature of things and relationships. We might say that these include definitions of physical objects in light of a recognition of the essential physical characteristics of things and moral virtues in light of a recognition of the inherent human capacities for achieving social harmony and political order. Because human beings have not only physical but also moral qualities, the definition of being human must take into account not only the physical but also the moral aspects of existence. Defining human beings in this way will necessarily involve reference to the possible fulfillment of human nature and orderly relationships with others. Thus, although Aristotle defined man as a rational animal, Confucius defined man as an animal capable of benevolence.[12]

To conclude, we might also note that to achieve an adequate definition of things, the following two basic semantic principles seem to be logically required by the doctrine of rectifying names. First, one type of thing may have many names. Second, no one name should apply to many different things. The problem of defining man is again a good illustration of both principles. A man can be defined as a physical being, but he can also be described as a social unit and a moral agent. He may receive, therefore, names such as *father, son, friend, brother,* etc., resulting from his various relationships to other people. On the other hand, the name *father* can apply to an individual who is biologically a father or who morally fulfills the virtues of being a father. But in a strict sense, it applies only to a man who is both biologically and morally a father. Making no distinctions between names applied to individual things will not only bring ambiguities to our language, but will also blur our understanding of the nature of things. This will block social communication and generate political chaos and disorder.

Thus, these two semantic principles that govern the rectification of names must be incorporated into the doctrine of rectifying names and, indeed, must be logically presupposed by it.

V

The doctrine of rectifying names underlies the relatively well-developed theory of government in the *Great Learning*. The author of the *Great Learning*[13] recognized a methodology that closely resembles that of rectifying names in spirit, the methodology of knowing the end of things. It says: "Things have their root and their branches. Affairs have their end and their beginning. To know what is first and what is last will lead near to what is taught in the *Great Learning*."[14] As pointed out, rectifying names consists in attaining a true knowledge of individuals and their relationships to others. In the *Great Learning*, to seek true knowledge is taken to be the same as "to illustrate illuminating virtue" (the so-called *ming-ming-te*), for the knowledge in question is the knowledge of virtue. This is a knowledge that unveils the nature of humankind and the human potentiality for achieving social harmony and political order. Hence, it is a moral knowledge, which provides individuals with wisdom and guidance for attaining well-being.

It is interesting to note that the beginning of the moral knowledge of an individual is considered, by the author of the *Great Learning*, to consist of taking the step of "investigating things" (*ko-wu*) and thereupon taking the step of "attaining knowledge" (*chih-chih*). The *Great Learning* does not provide its own interpretation of the so-called *ko-wu* and *chih-chih*, however, Chu Hsi's commentary reads:

The meaning of the expression, "The perfecting of knowledge depends on the investigation of things," is this: If we wish to carry our knowledge to the utmost, we must investigate the principles of all things we come into contact with, for the intelligent mind of man is certainly formed to know, and there is not a single thing in which its principles do not inhere. But so long as all principles are not investigated, man's knowledge is incomplete. On this account, the *Learning for Adults* [i.e., the *Great Learning*], at the outset of its lessons, instructs the learner, in regard to all things in the world, to proceed from what knowledge he has of their principles, and pursue his investigation of them, till he reaches the extreme point. After exerting himself in this way for a long time, he will suddenly find himself possessed of a wide and far-reaching penetration. Then, the qualities of all things, whether external or internal, the subtle or the coarse, will be apprehended, and the mind, in its entire substance and its relation to things, will be perfectly intelligent. This is called the investigation of things. This is called the perfection of knowledge.[15]

According to Chu Hsi's interpretation, the so-called investigation of things consists only in seeking the principles of things where things apparently are conceived as objects in the physical world. I believe that this is too narrow a conception. I must point out here that the investigation of things covers not only the natural world, but also human capacities and virtues as well. It is not simply a matter of observing the characteristics of things, but is a matter of defining and setting up a standard of the true and the right. In fact, a broad conception of this sort explains how investigating things and attaining knowledge make possible the achievement of social harmony and political order in the world on a solid basis.

To make the explanation in question clear, we remind ourselves that, according to the *Great Learning*, the process leading from investigating things and attaining knowledge to good government and social harmony also includes the following intermediate steps: making sincere intentions (*ch'eng-yi*), rectifying the mind (*cheng-hsin*), cultivating the person (*hsiu-shen*), and regulating the family (*ch'i-chia*). In fact, the *Great Learning* presented a syllogistic chain from the beginning of investigating things to the end of bringing order and peace to the world. It is intended by the *Great Learning* that there be a connection, more intimate than logical, between one step and another in this syllogistic chain. Such connections can be divided into two types: The first type is that of progressing from knowing what to do to doing what one knows. The second type is of *extending* the scope of one's moral action. The steps from investigating things to attaining knowledge, to making sincere intentions, to rectifying one's mind, and finally to cultivating a person, belong to the category of the first type of connections; whereas the steps from cultivating a person to regulating the family, to governing a state well (*chih-kuo*) to bringing peace to the world (*p'ing-t'ien-hsia*), belong to the category of the second type.

That the sincerity of intentions depends upon investigation and knowledge of things can be explained in more detail. The *Great Learning* has made an explicit statement about what is meant by making intentions sincere:"allowing no self-deception, as when we hate a bad smell and as when we love what is beautiful."[16] But how does a person come to hate a bad smell and love what is beautiful? The answer is that one comes to do so by directly feeling one's hate and one's love. The things one cannot feel directly one must judge in terms of right and wrong, true and false, by appealing to a standard of right or truth. One will have no standard without investigating things and obtaining true knowledge of them. The necessity of investigating things and obtaining true knowledge implies the necessity of seeking a standard of the right and the true, which coincides with the aims of rectifying names.

One who can judge right and wrong, true and false, according to a correct standard and does not deceive oneself may be said to be sincere in one's intentions in an important sense. That is, one's intentions no longer will be motivated or guided by individual prejudices and selfish interests. Only when one's intentions are made sincere in the light of the truth and the right, can one's mind be said to be rectified; that is, made to always follow the truth and the right. It is clear then that rectifying the mind presupposes the rectification of knowledge, the knowledge that guides a person's sincere intentions. One might say that this is so simply because human beings have the capacity to do what they know to be right and good. Perhaps, it is just in this sense that knowledge acquired from the investigation of things is called "knowing the fundamental" (*chih-pen*).

Now, to be able to justify one's likes and dislikes according to one's knowledge is what the *Great Learning* calls "cultivating a person." The *Great Learning* says that "there are few men in the world, who love and at the same time know the bad qualities of the object of their love, or who hate and yet know the excellences of the object of their hatred."[17] An individual who is cultivated as one who can do this will be a model for emulation. Thus, that person's family will be regulated in the sense that each person in the family will behave correctly according to his or her position, which is called the *regulation of the family*.

By extension, a person who has achieved the regulation of his or her family can be a virtuous example for people outside that family; for it can be assumed that by maintaining orderly relationships with others in society one will be able to cause all to do the same. This practice of virtue for a man in the position of ruling a state is called that of *governing a state well*. If a state is well governed, there is no doubt that the whole world could be ordered after the example of the well-governed state. Thus, we have seen how attainment of the true knowledge of things, which coincides with the aims of rectifying names, leads to social harmony and political order in the world.

If morality and political theory depend on rectifying names, then the knowledge of the fundamental, as proposed and explained in the *Great Learning*, must therefore be based upon this recognition. What I mean here is that this knowledge of the fundamental depends upon the true knowledge of things in correct definitions. True knowledge and correct definitions, plus the motivating power of moral knowledge for human behavior, necessarily entail the achievements of social harmony and political order. The principles of moral behavior from true knowledge make knowledge a practical wisdom. They bridge the gap between theory and practice and exhibit the intrinsic and organic relationships between them in the sense that knowing correct behavior should entail behaving correctly. This principle also allows one correct behavior to lead to more of the same. This again is what the *Great Learning* calls *self-cultivation of the individual person.*

To conclude, the *Great Learning* offers logical and practical observations on the necessity of generating social harmony and political order by the true knowledge acquired through a sequence of eight steps. An individual who has the true knowledge of things will strive to be good and fulfill his or her nature, and this will lead to moral order in society. The *Great Learning* thus exemplifies how knowledge guides practice and is completed by practice. In this sense, it proposes a theory of social harmony and political order on the basis of the doctrine of rectifying names.

Notes

1. The translation "rectifying names" for *cheng-ming* is taken from James Legge in his translations of the Confucian classics. See quotations from Legge in the paper contained in James Legge, *The Chinese Classics*, 3rd ed. (Hong Kong, 1960), 5 vols.

2. Mencius does not explicitly endorse the doctrine of rectifying names. But that he adopted this doctrine is evident from the fact that he frequently endeavored to define various human situations, virtues, acts of violating virtues, and types of virtuous personalities. For example, he said, "He who outrages the benevolence *proper to his nature*, is called a robber; he who outrages righteousness, is called a ruffian. The robber and the ruffian we call a mere fellow. I have heard of the cutting off of the fellow Chau, but I have not heard of the putting of a sovereign to death *in his case*." See *Mencius*, Book I, Part II, Chapter 8, trans. from Legge, II, 167. For each definition Mencius gave, he frequently drew moral judgments or judgments of value on the basis of the definition. In another example he argued that a benevolent king should not "entrap the people" (*wang-min*) because he defined such entrapment as incompatible with the benevolence (*jên*) of a benevolent king. See *Mencius*, Book I, Part I, 7. Finally, in his arguments for the goodness of human nature, Mencius seemed to consider human nature (*2hsing*) as definitionally equivalent to the beginnings of virtue as evidenced in feelings of commiseration, shame and dislike, reverence and respect, and approving or disapproving. This made it possible for him to defend his theory against all criticism. See Mencius, Book VI, Part I, particularly 1-6.

3. The dating of the *Ta Hsueh* has been a controversial problem in recent Chinese historical scholarship. I take the *Ta Hsueh* to have been committed to writing in the late Warring States period.

4. *Analects*, 17-9, trans. from Legge, I, 323.

5. Ibid., 5-15, Legge, I, 178.

6. Mencius, in referring to the beginnings of ethical relationships between people, clearly considers these as consisting in teaching "how, between father and son, there should be affection; between sovereign and minister, righteousness; between husband and wife, attention to their separate functions; between old

231

and young, a proper order; and between friends, fidelity." The *Mencius*, Book III, Part I, 4, trans. from Legge, II, 251-52. In the *Doctrine of the Mean*, 20, it is said that the principles governing between sovereign and minister, between father and son, between husband and wife, between elder brother and younger, and between friends, are five duties of universal obligation. See Legge, I, 406-07.

7. *Analects*, 12-11, trans. from Legge, I, 256.

8. *Analects*, 13-3, trans. from Legge, I, 263-264.

9. Confucius felt that people must be well provided for before they can be taught proprieties and virtues. See *Analects*, 13-9.

10. *Analects*, 13-6, trans. from Legge, I, 266.

11. *Analects*, 12-17, trans. from Legge, I, 258.

12. Confucius said: "Is any one able for one day to apply his strength to virtue? I have not seen the case in which his strength would be insufficient" (see *Analects*, 4-6, trans. Legge, I, 167). "Is virtue a thing remote? I wish to be virtuous, and lo! Virtue is at hand" (*Analects*, 7-29, trans. Legge,I, 204).

13. According to Chu Hsi, Confucius himself wrote the text (which consists of only six paragraphs) of the *Great Learning*, whereas Tseng Tzu, a disciple of Confucius, wrote the rest of the *Great Learning* as a commentary on the Confucian text. In the modern period, the traditional account of the authorship of the *Great Learning*, however, has been called into question. But the book, as a chapter of the *Record of Rites*, is generally dated back to the late Warring States period.

14. "Text of Confucius," the *Great Learning*, par. 3, trans. Legge, I, 357.

15. Chu Hsi, *Ta Hsueh Chang Chu*, trans. Legge, I, 365-66.

16. "Commentary of Tseng Tzu," the *Great Learning*, 6-7, trans. Legge, I, 366.

17. *Great Learning*, 8-7, trans. Legge, I, 369.

8. On *Yi* as a Universal Principle of Specific Application in Confucian Morality

Jên (benevolence) generally has been considered the most important concept in classical Confucianism. In the light of Confucius' own development of this concept and its numerous applications, the great importance of *jên* as a principle of human conduct as well as an ideal of human perfection can scarcely be overestimated. While granting this point, one who is concerned with the totality of the Confucian doctrine must hasten to add, first, that there are other important principles in Confucian morality, and *yi* is one of them which needs further explication; and second, that in the writings of Mencius, who succeeds Confucius as the leading proponent and promoter of Confucianism, *yi* is as important as *jên*.

Meaning and Function of *Yi* in Confucian Doctrine

We have to recognize the fact that unlike *jên*, in the Confucian *Analects*, *yi* has never received any manifest or explicit definition.[1] In fact it is curious that no disciple appears to raise the question of *yi*.[2] One explanation for this could be that Confucius and his disciples did not feel it necessary to clarify the notion of *yi* because it was insignificant. However, taking into consideration the fact that "*yi*" has been used in many crucial constructions dealing with normative judgments, a better explanation might be that Confucius and his disciples have taken the notion of *yi* for granted and that they assumed a universal and clear understanding of what constitutes *yi* and its roles in formulating and specifying norms and ends of human conduct. Therefore they had no need for clarification. The question then is what sort of understanding of *yi* has been presupposed in the constructions involving reference to *yi*. *Yi* is the very principle which should make a person's conduct morally acceptable to others and which should justify the morality of human action. In other words, it may be suggested that *yi* is the fundamental principle of morality that confers qualities of right and wrong on human actions and that produces a situation which intrinsically satisfies us as moral agents. This understanding should become clearer if we first examine the contexts in which *yi* occurs and then compare *yi* with the principle of *jên* in the Confucian doctrine.

In many instances Confucius takes *yi* to be the ultimate principle for the superior man. Thus he says that "the superior man holds *yi* to be the superior principle [of action]"[3] and that "the superior man compares [everything] to *yi*."[4] Thus *yi* is clearly a principle which relates to the character of a superior man and therefore relates to every virtue which relates to the character of a superior man.

Furthermore, *yi* is independent of material self-interest and is opposed to the lack of inclination toward the virtue of *jên*. That *yi* forms the necessary component of a virtuous life and restrains the inclinations toward material goods and desires of pleasure and comfort, thus formally qualifying good as good, can be shown as follows. First, with regard to material gains and all life activities, the lack of *yi* causes the meaninglessness of such gains.

Confucius says: "If not in accordance with *yi* I become rich and elevated, I regard [these gains] as floating clouds."[5] This implies that material gains are acceptable only when *yi* is present and the presence of *yi* is the criterion to judge the value of pursuing material gains. This also means that to pursue material gains is not intrinsically a worthwhile action, and its worthiness must be provided or sanctioned by the consideration of *yi*. *Yi* thus determines the total significance of one's life and activities. To substantiate this point, we give the following quotation: "As to how the superior man behaves with regard to others and in view of a situation, he has no particular preference, nor particular prohibition, but only has *yi* as its standard of evaluation."[8] From this, it is clear that *yi* is a universal and total principle which applies to every particular case of judging the worthiness or unworthiness of an action. It is that universality which, by justifying action according to a norm, justifies the moral superiority of a man. *Yi* is what makes justification according to a norm possible and constitutes the normativeness of an action so justified. Thus it represents a unity which penetrates into a variety of cases of action.

Yi not only makes material gains acceptable, should they be worthy of acceptance, it also makes virtues virtuous or worthy of acceptance as virtues. In other words, all general virtues in the Confucian system are subject to the qualification and sanctioning of *yi*: *yi* is the basis and foundation of all virtues, and, therefore, the necessary principle of virtue. It is the principle that makes virtues fit as virtue. This point is particularly clear when considering that a disposition of character will not be a virtue if it lacks the element of *yi*. Thus Confucius says, "if a superior man has courage but no *yi*, he will make trouble; if a small man has courage but no *yi*, he will become a bandit."[7]

According to a suggestion of Ch'en Ta-chi,[8] if one must learn anything, one must learn *yi* and learn to apply *yi*.

To like *jên*, yet not to like to learn, one will have the shortcoming of being a folly; to love knowledge, yet not to like to learn, one will have the shortcoming of being loose; to like honesty, yet not to like to learn, one will have the shortcoming of being sly; to like straightforwardness, yet not to like to learn, one will have the shortcoming of being tricky; to like courage, yet not to like to learn, one will have the shortcoming of being wild; to like being stern, yet not to like to learn, one will have the shortcoming of being undisciplined.[9]

Then the statement above would be clear evidence of the fact that basic virtues such as *jên*, knowledge, honesty, straightforwardness, courage, and sternness must be qualified by the principle of *yi* as well as justified as virtues within the restraints of *yi*. One must show, of course, how *yi* could qualify as well as justify every virtue as a virtue. It must be owing to the consideration that every virtue considered by itself could lead to an excess which violates other virtues and that all virtues must be applied in a particular situation with no loss of sight of the total good. *Yi* represents this ideal of totality as well as a decision-generating ability to apply a virtue properly and appropriately in a situation. Thus it is what makes a potential virtue a proper and appropriate actual virtue, for it has the power of realizing virtues in concrete situations. To learn this ability to relate the universal to the particular is precisely the secret of learning *yi*, the learning of which, of course, requires an understanding of the meaning of one's life and the meaning of the truth and goodness of unity and totality. In regard to the thesis that *yi* represents a perception of a unity and totality, one can see that Confucius has indeed suggested that "the superior man takes *yi* to his essence, and acts in accordance with *li*; expresses himself with modesty, and realizes himself by way of integrity."[10]

Confucius talks further about "fulfilling one's way by practising *yi*."[11] Thus *yi* can be considered the substratum of all virtues and as such the source from which other virtues possibly can be derived. It not only gives unity to all known virtues, it will be able to create more when needed.[12]

To summarize, *yi* is that principle which confers unity on virtues and creates a moral situation by its relevance both to moral considerations of the fitness of a virtue for a concrete situation and to the goodness of the totality. It further adjudicates among other established virtues to enable a moral agent to make a right decision to preserve the unity, order, and harmony of all virtues. As an ordering principle, *yi* clearly presents itself as relevant to particular situations by being able to generate decisions on right actions. On this basis, one can see the implicit relevance and justification of Confucius' statement, "In the case of a father stealing a sheep, or a son stealing a sheep, the father hides the fact for the son, and the son hides the fact for the father. In this, the virtue of frankness is found.[13] The point of this judgment is that more *yi* is exhibited in the action of hiding, considering the types of persons, principles, and offences involved. If we are permitted to take this as an example of a close application of *yi* to a particular situation used to generate a virtue of propriety and appropriateness, *yi* is established indeed as a principle of virtue generation and a principle of applicability in morality. A man of *yi*, therefore, must be a man of creative insights who is able to make appropriate moral judgments in particular situations, judgments which will preserve the totality of goodness and justice.

In the light of the preceding, perhaps we may analyze *yi* in terms of two components relevant to the process of moral decision-making, even though we have no explicit statement of what constitutes *yi* in the Confucian *Analects*. First, there is understanding or perception of an end on the part of the moral subject. This is the subjective self-knowledge of good truth (or the way). Second, there is a potential state or situation which needs a fitting action to make it a moral state or situation. There is an objective quality in a situation which one must correctly perceive in order to make an appropriate decision and to take a course of action. *Yi* as a principle of human conduct involves these two components or aspects and an understanding of them. The realization of *yi* is a matter of fitting the subjective standard or norm of worthiness to the objective situation. It is the very fitness of an action in a situation and the recognition of this fitness as well as the intrinsic satisfaction derived from the recognition, which constitute the complex principle of *yi* in application. In the light of this analysis, it is not surprising that in a later Confucian writing such as *Chung Yung* (*The Doctrine of the Mean*), *yi* is explicitly defined as appropriateness or fitness.[14] This definition brings to the surface the underlying meaning of the applicability of *yi*, an applicability which consists in fitting the universal to the particular as well as fitting the subjective to the objective. This applicability of *yi* naturally demands cultivation of the self in understanding these applications.

Perhaps it is on the basis of this universal-to-be-applied-to-the-particular character of *yi* that Confucius does not consider himself absolutely attached to a rigid principle for action. He recognizes the variety of actual life situations and recognizes furthermore that good must intrinsically grow out of a concrete situation. Thus, he does not cling to any generality that is independent of concrete reality. He has no absolute *yes* or absolute *no* (*wu-ko-wu-pu-ko*). But this does not mean that he cannot make a consistent decision for his action. On the contrary, simply because he is free from the bondage of human self-possession, he is free to apply the principle of *yi* which is embodied in his own person and which represents the unity of his existence. Thus he says, to repeat, "I have no preference, nor prohibitions, I only compare to *yi*." In this fashion he achieves a state of true freedom, a freedom which unbridles him of willfullness, necessity, stubbornness, and self-arrogance.[15] It is the same freedom which enables him to do whatever is right in doing what his heart dictates, because his doing is precisely his doing right.

To conclude, we may say that while *jên* gives substance to human virtue by way of extending oneself to others in terms of one's concern and love for others, *yi* gives meaning to human virtues by way of defining oneself in understanding one's end and the relation of oneself to the totality of all men. Similarly, while *li* (rite) actually exhibits virtues of human behavior and formulates rules by which human virtues can be stabilized and harmonized, *yi* confers on *li* the sanction of being relevant to the realization of *jên* and an awareness of self-realization and self-justification. As *yi* is the principle which mediates between the universal and the particular as well as between the understanding of the universal and the understanding of the particular, so also *yi* mediates between *jên* as the substance of virtue and *li* as the form of virtue. Thus, it may be considered the basis of a virtuous life, which guarantees the unity and concordance of substance and form in concrete situations.

Development of *Yi* in Mencius

In the writings of Mencius, *yi* becomes a dominating principle of virtue. Not only has the term "*yi*" been used more frequently in Mencius than in Confucius' *Analects*, but the meaning of *yi* as well as an understanding of its importance was given a depth nowhere achieved before. First, *yi* is given a position parallel to *jên* and is always referred to in conjunction with *jên*. This clearly shows that Mencius considers *yi* as important a virtue as *jên*, and yet recognizes some difference between the two. Mencius has contrasted *yi* with *li* (profit), and this fundamentally preserves the significance given to *yi* by Confucius: *Yi* is a principle of action independent of consideration of self-interest and material profit as well as that which preserves the autonomy of the self as an individual capable of fulfilling virtues. In this sense, *yi* is a universal of virtue which makes all virtues possible and therefore should be the foundation of all virtues. Second, apart from being the foundation of all virtues, *yi* is by itself an independent, separate virtue among four independent virtues, which Mencius enumerates as the pillars of morality and the good life. These four virtues are *jên, yi, li, and chih*. Even though Mencius did not formally define these virtues, he has suggested an explanation of these virtues, which is close to a definition. He alleges that: "The feeling of sympathy is the beginning of *jên*; the feeling of shame is the beginning of *yi*; the feeling of modesty is the beginning of *li*; and the feeling of right and wrong is the beginning of *chih*."[16] Mencius, furthermore, insists that these four feelings are the defining characteristics of a man and that they are internal and inherent in the nature of man, for without them a man is not man. In this sense *yi*, like other fundamental virtues, is a part of human nature, and, as Mencius strongly argues and urges, constitutes a reason why human nature is called good. At this point, we face three questions: (1) How do we understand *yi* in terms of the feeling of shame? (2) How is *yi* to be considered an inherent quality of man capable of development? (3) Do we still have any reason for suggesting *yi* as a fundamental principle of virtue in Mencius? Only after the third question is answered can we speak of the ontological significance of *yi*.

Yi is taken by Mencius as a type of feeling and sentiment in a man which motivates him toward actions preserving his dignity and consistency. It is as such the feeling and sentiment which will define and actualize one's individuality and one's freedom as an individual. That *yi* constitutes the inherent ontological principle of individuality will be explained later. Here we shall discuss *yi* as a feeling and sentiment inherent in human nature. In affirming that *yi* is a universal as well as a natural element, Mencius already implies that it is a natural part of human nature. Underlying the belief that *yi* and other virtures are matters of feeling and sentiment is the belief that human nature realizes itself in feeling and sentiment and that what is expressed there is the realization of human nature. Thus he says in a discussion of the goodness of human nature, "If one follows one's feelings, one can do good."[17] From this it is natural to expect that *yi*, like *jên*, is a natural manifestation of human nature. Though there is no passage which testifies to the immediate manifestation of *yi* in a man in a certain situation, it is only fair to suggest that *yi*, like *jên*, can be immediately realized under appropriate circumstances for all men and cannot really be lost, simply because *yi*, like *jên*, is a defining characteristic of human nature. Of course, this immediately realizable feeling of *yi* must be a fitting response to a situation and, therefore, can be explained as an ability to perceive what constitutes the fitting action relating to a situation. The action of *yi* can be similarly conceived of as the action of bringing about the quality of fitness in a situation.

That the feeling and sentiment of *yi* is a universal element of human nature has been already suggested. As a universal element of human nature, it is shared by all men. Thus Mencius says: "What is the principle that minds have shared in common? It is *li* and it is *yi*."[18] The feeling of shame which Mencius considers as the beginning of *yi*, we may say, is the feeling of not being able to do certain things (*yu-so-pu-wei*), just as the feeling of *jên* is the feeling of not being able to bear with certain things. This feeling of not being able to do certain things, of course, can be explained as owing to the intrinsic wrongness of certain things in a situation. Though Mencius does not give any explicit examples, the following remarks seem to me to illustrate the quality of *yi* in a concrete and vivid way.

1. "One bowl of rice and one bowl of soup, when had, will enable a (hungry) person to live, and when not had, will cause the death of a (hungry) person. But if one gives these with a distaining sound, a passerby will not want them; if one passes these with a kick, even a beggar will not want them. If ten thousand boxes of rice do not rightfully belong to me, and yet I receive them, what do these ten thousand boxes of rice do to me?"[19]
2. The wife and the concubine of a man from Ch'i feel ashamed when they find their husband begging for food from funeral sacrifices.

These two cases demonstrate how the feeling of not being able to do certain things is related to a situation and evokes certain responses. The feeling of shame may be regarded as one of such feelings which will preserve the dignity and individuality of a person. It is something which one also comes to know by nature. That is, in a certain situation a man can become aware of *yi*. This means that one becomes aware of certain distinctions and develops certain feelings toward them. In this regard all virtues and the feelings which founded them can be regarded as embodying the fundamental quality of *yi*—the self-knowledge and knowledge of the Way. In this sense, *yi* is not merely a feeling or sentiment, it is also an awareness of such a feeling as a representation of the value of individual independence. Therefore, it is what Mencius calls *liang-neng* and *liang-chih* or innate capacity of good as well as innate knowledge of good.[20]

The feeling and sentiment of shame or the feeling of not being able to do certain things, as the beginning of *yi*, must be cultivated in order to be firm and complete as well as consistent. In fact, *yi* as an actual form of virtue is distinct form, although rooted in, the feeling of shame. It implies, as we noted, an element of self-awareness and a conscious effort of choice. Thus Mencius says, "all men have something that they will not bear. If one applies to what he can bear with, it is *jên*. All men have something not to do. If one can apply this to what they actually do, it is *yi*."[21] That one can apply the feeling of not being able to do certain things to what one can do involves certainly a recognition that what one is able to do must be actions about which one will not be ashamed. In this fashion *yi* becomes a pervasive mode of living which gives meaning to every area of human conduct. It is also by means of cultivating one's sense of feeling of shame that one will be able to exhibit this sentiment and recognize its force in every human situation. A final important reason for cultivating one's feeling or sense of shame is to preserve the consistency of one's virtue therefore giving it strength. In fact, an action may not be genuinely *yi* if it does not preserve the consistency of the ideal of *yi*. The example of Ch'en Chung-tzu, which Mencius criticizes, amply illustrates how a man of *yi* without vision of *yi* as a whole ideal betrays himself, simply because he cannot consistently defend himself against charges of a lack of *yi* which are less obvious to him. As we shall see later, *yi*, when fully cultivated, should be as extensive as the whole universe and can be called the great flood of breath (*hao-jan-chih-ch'i*).[22]

Yi is considered rooted in the natural and spontaneous feelings of man. It is, metaphysically speaking, internal to and inherent in the nature of man, in which the potentiality of all feelings subsists. Nevertheless, *yi* is not totally subjective. When giving rise to actions, it maintains a quality which has both objectivity and normative force. *Yi* is what every moral man should follow with sincerity and perception. For as we have analyzed, *yi* is not simply a matter of a natural expression of a certain type of feeling but a perception of what is right action under some given circumstances. It is a perception enabling one to apply a universal principle to a specific situation to generate appropriate and fitting actions. Thus it involves an element of knowledge of norms. Because of this element of perception and knowledge of norms, *yi* also appears to be an objective principle as well as a quality in the nature of things perceived in relation to a moral agent in a situation. Thus, there arises the controversy over whether *yi* is indeed subjective and inherent in a person (or in the nature of a man), or is indeed external to a person as an objective quality of things. We can answer this question better if we examine the dispute of Mencius with Kan Tzu, a Taoist-inclined philosopher in Mencius' time. Kao Tzu says,

Food instinct and sexual instinct are matters of nature—*jên* is internal, not external. *Yi* is external, not internal. Mencius says: Why is it said that *jên* is internal, and *yi* is external. The answer is: If person is tall and I consider him tall, it is not because tallness is inherent in me. It is like the case where if something is and I consider it white, this is to recognize the whiteness from the external. Thus [I say] that *yi* is external.[23]

From Kao Tzu's point of view, *yi* is just a kind of response to the perception of a quality belonging to an object, such as the quality of tallness and the quality of whiteness. Therefore what makes *yi* possible is the objective situation, and the only subjective element is a simple recognition of a peculiar quality in the objective situation. This peculiar quality, though being objective like tallness and whiteness, is unlike them in being "nonnatural," in the sense used by G. E Moore. It is in this way very similar to the indefinable quality of goodness in Moore's *Ethica Principia*. The recognition of *yi* is similar to the recognition of goodness; both are a matter of intuition. As a subjective principle *yi* is no more than the intellectual capacity to intuit an unanalyzable and objective nonnatural quality of an action or a situation. In this sense Kao Tzu's position is very close to G. E. Moore's.

Mencius cannot accept the above position. For him, *yi* is not just an intellectual intuition of a certain quality; it is also a modification of the subjective state of a person and a projection of one's value, which governs one's action and conduct. For him, to objectify the values of *yi* into some quality, even called a nonnatural quality, is not appropriate for *yi* cannot be totally objectified and therefore universalized. Thus *yi* is not the same kind of quality as whiteness or tallness, even if it is nonnatural, for the natural quality of whiteness is common to both the white horse and the white person. But treating someone as older, considered as an instance of *yi*, is not the same as recognizing something as older or taller. One can recognize the age of a horse and consider it as old, for example, by giving an objective description of its age, but one cannot do this in regard to an old person. To treat an older person as older (*chang-jen-chih-chang*) depends upon an attitude of valuation and implies an attitude of respect and reverence, and therefore a projection of one's natural feelings toward a person in a situation. The objective quality of being older is not *yi* but to treat an older person as an older person with the feeling of reverence is *yi*. Thus Mencius says, "the whiteness of a white horse is not different from the whiteness of a white man. But can one not recognize treating an older horse as older as different from treating an older man as older? Do we say that the older man has the quality of *yi* or that the person who treats him as older [with the feeling of reverence] has the quality of *yi*?"[24]

Apparently Kao Tzu and Mencius disagree initially as to how to interpret *yi*, and this causes the difference between their views on the relation of *yi* to the nature of man. According to Kao Tzu, *jên* is a matter of the feeling of liking and cannot be forced upon a person by persuasion, because it has to come naturally. On the other hand, *yi* is not considered a matter of feeling from one's nature but a recognition of a given fact or quality. As a fact or quality is given externally, one's recognition of it must be considered external as well. Thus as Kao Tzu chooses not to recognize the subjective feeling of *yi* and treats *yi* as an intellectual principle, he can still draw the conclusion of the externality of *yi* in contrast to the internality of *jên*. Of course Kao Tzu is wrong to point out that the particular likes of various persons is a sufficient criterion to distinguish *jên* as internal from *yi* as external. For Mencius has rightly retorted that even one's particular likes do not vary with particular objects. This does not make the likes less internal and thus more external.[25] This same difficulty of mutual understanding applies to the determination of respect as a quality external or internal to the self. Respect for a person, of course, depends upon consideration of many external factors which give rise to the respectability of a person, but this does not mean that these external factors are *yi* or are capable of determining recognition of *yi*, just as common habits of eating and drinking are not *yi* or are not capable of determining recognition of *yi*. *Yi*, although universally and objectively intended, is an active part of one's nature, by means of which value-attitude is determined and recognition becomes really possible.[26]

Finally, we come to the ontological significance of *yi* as a principle of subjective self-determination. We have explained that such a principle will enable one to respond naturally to a situation and to choose an action to one's own satisfaction. But this principle in the form of *yi* also has its ontological import, which has been indicated by Mencius but which scarcely has been discussed in the literature. The ontological import of *yi* consists of this, that it gives autonomy and independence as well as self-sufficiency to an individual and makes an individual a creative agent in which everything in the universe becomes meaningful to him. In this sense *yi* is the power or force of the subjective, which completes as well as justifies the objective. Perhaps there are two tendencies in interpreting this ontological import of *yi*. First, *yi* and the development of *yi* to the utmost will enable the self to be united with the objective world, that is, to discover the ultimate significance of the world and self and to realize their oneness. Second, *yi* need not be considered as enabling the self to be united with the objective world, but can be considered as a principle which transforms the world into a world of self, a cultured world of value in which the self fulfills its goal of self-realization. Both views share the same concern with actual unification of the self with the world and the explicit fulfillment of consistency and sufficiency of individual life. In this regard they are indeed equivalent, The ultimate end of *yi* in life is perhaps that of achieving a state of perfection where the objective has assumed subjective significance and the subjective assumed objective (and therefore universal) validity. But what is important to recognize, of course, is that in the context of Mencius' discussion of *yi* as a natural feeling, *yi* is primarily a subjective principle and because of this the ontological significance of *yi* points to the subject-self as a creative source of action, value, self-understanding, as well as self-realization.

As an ontological principle that enables the self to grow into a universal reality, *yi* is closely related to *ch'i*. In fact it is in the context of dealing with the problem of how to achieve a state of "unperturbed mind" ("*pu-tung-hsin*") that Mencius introduces the idea of *ch'i* and of dealing with the problem of how to achieve a state of "great flood of *ch'i*" which makes this "*pu-tung-hsin*" possible that Mencius introduces the idea of *yi* as the self-determining principle of "*hao-jan-chih-ch'i*." To quote Mencius' statement relating *ch'i* to *yi*:

I know language. I am well at nourishing my great flood of *ch'i*. But what is the great flood of *ch'i*? [The answer is]: It is hard to define. As *ch'i* it is very great and very powerful. It needs to be nourished with straightforwardness and no harm should be done to it. Then it will fill, between heaven and earth. As *ch'i* it matches with *yi* and the Way (*tao*), and if one does not have this (*yi*), the man of [*ch'i*] will not be strong. [Thus] the *hao-jan-chih-ch'i* is born of collection of *yi*; it is what is gotten and taken by *yi*.[27]

Here Mencius clearly makes two points, both of which have ontological significance, First, an individual self can nourish itself into a state of being full of *ch'i* which relates to heaven and earth. This shows that one is not ontologically separated from the world. Second, the *hao-jan-chih-ch'i* which enables one to relate to the world has *yi* as its ontological source and foundation. In other words, when one discovers *yi* in oneself and becomes firm and constant in it, it will naturally lead to the ontological extension of oneself and will transform the world into a universe of significance internal to the individual self. But Mencius points out that *yi*, therefore, does not impose itself on *ch'i* and transform *ch'i* into *yi*, but instead causes the *ch'i* to be *hao-jan-chih-ch'i* in the very beginning. This explains the subjective nature of *ch'i* as a matter to be expressed in terms of one's feelings and to be realized in the context of.one's self-conscientious effort to bring one's internal feeling of self-consistency and integrity to the full.

Notes

1. For example, in characterizing *jên*, Confucius says in the *Analects*: "the man of *jên* always makes himself first to do difficult things, and makes himself last to consider gains. If a man can do this, he is indeed *jên*," (*Yung-yeh*); "to love man," (*Yen-yuan*); "if capable of doing five things (respect, kindness, integrity, acuteness, generosity) in the world, this is the *jên*," (*Yang-ho*); "solidarity, perserverance, truthfulness are close to *jên*," (*Yen-yuan*); "if the desires to make aggressions, and to desire to complain and covet are not available, then one can practise *jên*," (*Hsien-wen*); "to dwell in respect, and do things with reverence, and deal with friends in loyalty," (*Tzu-lu*); "the man of *jên* loves mountains," (*Yung-yeh*); "the man of *jên* does not feel worthy," (*Tzu-han*).
2. Many disciples have asked about *jên* (*wen-jên*), but none appears to ask about *yi* (*wen-yi*).
3. *Analects, Yang-ho.*
4. *Analects, Li-jên.*
5. *Analects, Shu-erh.*
6. *Analects, Li-jên.*
7. *Analects, Yang-ho.*
8. Chen, Tai-chi, *Collections of Studies on Confucius' Doctrine* (Taipei: Cheng Chung Book Co., 1961), p. 52.
9. *Analects, Yang-ho.*
10. *Analects, Wei-ling-kung.*
11. *Analects, Chi-shih.*
12. Even though Tseng Tzu has suggested that the principle of unity in Confucian doctrine is *chung-shu*—loyalty and kindness—it is clear that other interpretations are possible. Cf. Ta-chi Chen, *Collection of Studies on Confucius' Doctrine*, p. 55.
13. *Analects, Tzu-lu.*
14. See *Chung Yung*, chapter on *Ai-kung Asking about Government.*
15. *Analects, Tsu-kung.*
16. *Mencius*, 2A-6.
17. *Mencius*, 6A-6.
18. *Mencius*, 6A-7.

19. *Mencius*, 6A-10.
20. *Mencius*, 7A-15.
21. *Mencius*, 7B-31.
22. Cf. *Mencius*, 3B-10.
23. Mencius, 6A-4.
24. Ibid.
25. Cf. Mencius' statement: "Liking the barbecued food of the Chin people does not differ from liking the barbecued food of my people. Indeed the rules of regularity of things are sometimes like this, but still the liking of barbecued food quality is external to the self" (*Mencius*, 6A-4)
26. *Mencius*, 6A-5.
27. *Mencius*, 2A-2.

9. Some Aspects of the Confucian Notion of Mind

A Methodological Distinction

It seems important to recognize a methodological distinction in the study of Chinese ideas and values. In the first place, there is the historical approach which consists in relating ideas and values to historical events in order to focus on their social, cultural, and psychological backgrounds on the one hand, and on their influences of related kinds on the other.[1] It is in this way that the historical genesis of an idea can be explained, but not its meaning. For various dimensions of the meaning of an idea must be explained on the basis of philosophical analysis. This consists then in bringing out the logical implications and philosophical intents of an idea as well as in examining and evaluating its adequacy of conceptual relevance and its truthfulness to experience and understanding.

In the light of the above methodological distinction, it is here assumed that the philosophical analysis of the Confucian notion of mind will be basically independent of, even though generally related to, considerations of parallel causal developments of events in Chinese history. In other words, it is assumed that in one way or another Confucian thinkers have formulated their views on human mind and intended their views to be a philosophical account of the reality of man and nature.

Aside from my thesis that my analysis is not to be simply explained by a historical situation, it will also be maintained in this chapter that there is a basic unity and continuity in the development of the Confucian notion of mind in terms of which various Confucian thinkers can be related and interpreted. In this connection there is no denial, however, that there had been dynamic changes and marked differences regarding the notion of mind in various Confucian writings of various periods.[2] It is important to note

246

that these changes and differences have been developed within a single framework of concepts and problems. Specifically I will maintain that there are four fundamental characterizations of the concept of mind in the classical Confucianism of the pre-Chin period. These four characterizations define a conceptual framework in which Neo-Confucian elaborations of the notion of mind in the Sung-Ming period are possible. It is understood that this unity and continuity of the Confucian notion of mind from the classical period to the Sung-Ming period is compatible with historical discontinuity and separateness due to the rise of Neo-Taoists and Buddhists in between. It is also assumed that Neo-Taoism and Buddhism had exercised certain considerable and important influences on later Confucian thinkers. But these influences were by way of motivation, suggestiveness, and challenge, which need not necessarily entail conceptual similarity or identity. What I suggest here is that in regard to the Confucian notion of mind, it is far more convenient and fruitful to insist on the unity and continuity of the classical and Neo-Confucian schools than otherwise, for the very reason that the basic problems and the implicit solutions to these problems in understanding the mind are formulated in the classical writings of the Confucian school.

Four Basic Characterizations of the Classical Confucian Notion of Mind

In the pre-Chin period, from the sixth to the third century B.C., almost all Chinese philosophers have something to say about the human mind and the mind's relationship to knowledge, goodness, distinction between right and wrong, and to heaven and earth which represent total and ultimate reality. In the Confucian tradition, perhaps with the only exception of Confucius himself, all pre-Chin Confucianists have been explicitly concerned with the nature and function of the mind and its place in the cosmological process of formation and transformation, as well as the role of the mind in cultivating both the individual perfection of sagehood and the collective well-being of an ideal society — the world of great order and comprehensive peace. This fact is well testified to in the writings of the *Book of Mencius*, the *Ta Hsueh* (the *Great Learning*), the *Chung Yung* (the *Doctrine of the Mean*), the *Great Appendixes* of the *Book of Changes* (*I Ching), the various chapters of the Record of Rites*, as well as the writings of Hsun Tzu. Now on careful scrutiny of these basic writings of classical Confucianism, one can discern four fundamental and important Confucian characterizations of the mind. These four Confucian characterizations are fundamental and important in the sense that all problems regarding the notion of mind can be related to and given a formulation in terms of them.

Unity with Reality as the First Characterization of the Mind

The first characterization of the mind in classical Confucianism concerns the unity of mind with nature[3], that is, truth and reality at large, as indicated by the term *tao* (the Way). Given mind as a subjective entity on the one hand, and given nature as an objective existence on the other, since subjective mind is manifestly different from objective nature, one may naturally suggest, as in the case of Descartes, that mind and nature (including both body and matter) are essentially unrelated because they are different substances with different attributes. But in the Confucian tradition, it is strictly insisted upon from the very beginning that mind and nature, the subjective and the objective, are one and identical. This is because both the subjective and the objective are not conceived of as separate, static substances, but rather as processes and existences which exhibit the same reality and realize the same potentiality of reality. Ontologically one can say that the mind and nature are one and identical. This is because the mind contains nature in potentiality and is the consummation of nature, and nature contains the mind in actuality and is the foundation of the mind. The reality of the mind is the reality of nature or heaven and earth, and the activity of the mind is the activity of heaven and earth. Thus, the mind not only represents the Way, in fact it is *potentially* the Way. The reason that the mind can know the Way is precisely because the mind is the Way. Thus we may conclude that, according to the classical Confucian view, the mind is first characterized by the presence of an inherent ontic equilibrium of the Way and it shares the same potentiality of the Way.[4]

There is another reason why the mind is the Way. The Way forms human nature (*hsing*) and human nature is expressed in terms of activities of the mind. From this it can be seen that the mind and nature are not separate but one. Human nature is a natural and yet necessary completion of the Way, whereas the human mind is a self-realization and a self-recognition of the nature of man. In an ontological sense, human nature, the mind, and the Way are all one; therefore, one can say that the mind is nature and the Way because it manifests, completes, realizes, determines, fulfills, and consummates nature and the Way. On this basis one can, following Mencius, speak of the completion of the ten thousand things within me[5], and following the *Chung Yung*, speak of the fulfillment of the nature of things and other men and of participating in the creative activities of heaven and earth on the basis of fulfilling one's own nature[6]. One can further speak of the power of the formation and transformation of the sage as in the *Great Appendixes* of the *Book of Changes*.[7]

One important way of looking at this basic ontic unity and identify of the mind with the Way is to recognize that both the mind and the Way have the powers and attributes of formation and transformation (*hua*), both of which are creatively creative (*sheng-sheng*). The Way is actually creative and the mind is potentially so; this potentiality is also the potentiality of the Way, and thus the mind's fulfillment of this potentiality is also the self-fulfillment of the Way.

Now before we focus on the mind's realization and fulfillment of the potentiality of the Way, we want to identify this basic unity of the mind with the Way in terms of what the author of the *Chung Yung* calls *chung*, that is, the central equilibrium or unarousedness (*wei-fa*) of reality. The *chung* can be described as a state in which the mind and nature remain completely undifferentiated and a state where there is objective order and change, but where there is no subjective experiencing of order and change. We may indeed conceive the whole world as existing in a state of *chung*, or a state of balance, centrality, and equilibrium under the form of a cosmos full of harmony and goodness. We may indeed also conceive the mind in its original state as completely composed, tranquil, and devoid of the stimulation of knowledge, feelings, and desires.

One may even suggest that the state of *chung* can be experienced as the vanishing point of nondistinction between what is objective and what is subjective. It is asserted in the *Chung Yung* that the original mind is given in the state of *chung*.[8] This implies that the mind is primordially one with reality and one may also say that *chung* represents the ontological and objective foundation of the subjective mind and is as infinitely rich as the Way is.

Intrinsic Activity Toward the Realization of Harmony (*Ho*) as the Second Characterization of the Mind

In the light of the unity of the mind with the Way, the subjective capacity and nature of the mind can be conceived as derived from the ontic objectivity of the Way and heaven and earth. Since the objectivity of the Way consists of a perfect state of *chung*, or *wei-fa*, we can speak of the mind as representing a metaphysics of being. Now this metaphysics of being is to be complemented by a dynamics of becoming. The unity of the mind with the Way in the state of *chung* is to be similarly complemented by a creative process of self-development and self-completion. Cosmologically speaking, the Way presents itself in the process of the formation and transformation of ten thousand things according to the principles of the interaction and conjunction of *yin* and *yang*, the two aspects of the Way. This can be called the process of phenomenolization of the world. But speaking of the mind in individual men, the dynamics of becoming is a creative activity in terms of feelings and desires.[9]

The creative activity of the mind is manifested in the inception of responsiveness and sensibility of the mind toward phenomenal objects *external* to the mind. In fact, when the mind is conceived as an activity in terms of feelings and desires, the mind can be said to be subjective and internal in a proper sense and things in the world can be said to be objective and external in a proper sense. The activity of the mind is conceived in the *Chung Yung* as different from the original state of *chung* or *wei-fa* in which no feelings are aroused or stirred. Though the term *yi-fa* or aroused-ness is not actually used in the *Chung Yung* and has not been used at all until the time of Neo-Confucianism, it is clear from that text that the mind can pass from a state of unarousedness or *chung* to a state of arousedness or activity.

Mind as an activity is conceived in terms of basic feelings such as joy, anger, sorrow, and pleasure which are actually experienced by individual men. The activity of the mind also fulfills men's functions such as willing (*chih*), sensing (*kan*), perceiving (*chueh*), knowing (*chih*), and determining and controlling (*kuan*), and thinking (*ssu*). That the mind in action is many-faceted and involves many diverse functions, yet still remains one and unified is an important characteristic of the mind as an activity.

Furthermore, this activity of the mind as stressed above, already involved with the actuality of things, can be conceived as an *addressing* to actuality. It is the mind finding itself in a situation. It is indeed the active participation of the mind in the process of the formation and transformation of the Way, for the feelings expressing the mind are purposive and lead to concrete actions. That ideas and actions are related, that knowledge always leads to action, and that knowledge cannot be complete without subsequent or prior action and practice are essential doctrines in the Confucian classics, which pragmatically bear upon the notion of the mind as an activity of feelings and desires. That is, mind-activity, referring to the mind in the state of being aroused, is not purely contemplative but purposive and directed toward achieving the ability of formation and transformation of the Way in actual activity.

Now the basic question to ask in this connection is, what is it that mind-activity might achieve in terms of its feelings responding to things external to the mind? The answer related in the *Chung Yung* is that the mind can achieve harmony (*ho*) under the condition that mind-activity has hit the mark (*chung-chieh*)[10]. In fact, in this connection the *Chung Yung* formulates, along with the principle of *chung* which characterizes the ontological origin and potential basis of the mind as a state of equilibrium, the principle of harmony, which characterizes the actualization of mind-activity in a supreme state of the achievement of actuality.

One might say that the equilibrium or centrality of the mind is a state where actual feelings such as joy, anger, sorrow, and pleasure are still unstirred, unreleased, and unaroused; on the other hand, one might say that the harmony of the mind (*ho*) is a state of mind where feelings are stirred or released or aroused, and where, when stirred, the mind fulfills and realizes the potential ontic value inherent in its nature and therefore realizes the potential reality of the Way.

Before we consider what constitutes the basic condition of hitting the mark of the mind in terms of feelings, a question leading to a third characterization of the mind, we might dwell upon the notion of harmony (*ho*). The notion of harmony implies that different things exist in a perfect order of interrelationships. Thus, the notion of harmony contrasts with the relation of simple identity (*t'ung*), and this again implies that different, individual things are organically related in a whole which preserves the distinctions between and ordering among the individuals. *Ho* is therefore a state of variety in unity. Furthermore, *ho* is not a static state but a dynamic state of creative interchange between individual forces. It is a state of creative enjoyment and aesthetic appreciation. In this sense we might identify *ho* as a form of value, and indeed as the supreme form of value or goodness. As we shall see, the mind as an activity is a process of the realization of value, which can be characterized in such a way that creativity and harmony are directly experienced as the supreme embodiments of goodness.

Inward Recognition of the Will to Good for the Fulfillment of Good as the Third Characterization of the Mind

Now we come to consider the question of the achievement of mind-activity when mind-activity is said to hit the mark. We find no explicit clue to explain this notion of hitting the mark, but there are implicit indications in the *Chung Yung* that the mind can know the mark and the mark is nothing but the value or goodness inherent in a human situation or in a human relationship, such as is represented by a situation of performing a rite of reverence and a relationship between father and son. Finally, knowing the mark entails activity to fulfill a value which is the mark. Of course there is still the ambiguity between hitting the mark (or fulfilling a value) without knowing the mark, and hitting the mark as a consequence of knowing the mark. The *Chung Yung*, however, holds to the equivalence between the enlightenment or understanding (*ming*) of reality and the fulfillment or realization (*ch'eng*) of reality.[11] For, according to the *Chung Yung, ming* (enlightenment of the mind or the understanding of reality) leads to *ch'eng* (fulfillment of the potentiality of reality), and *ch'eng* leads to *ming*. In fact, the process of the fulfillment to understanding is in the nature (*hsing*) of man, and the process from understanding to fulfillment is in the nature of instruction (*chiao*), where *hsing* or nature is defined as what is endowed in man by heaven, *chiao* or instruction is defined as the cultivation of the Way, and the Way is activity in accordance with nature.[12]

In the light of the above one might conclude that hitting the mark (fulfilling value in reality) will naturally lead to knowing the mark (value in reality), and that knowing the mark will naturally lead to fulfilling value in reality. The previously suggested ambiguity now dissolves in the unity of knowing, activity, and self-fulfillment.

At this point I think that it would be useful to look into the *Mencius* for a definite characterization of the mind as an activity involving inward recognition of the will to good for fulfilling goodness in terms of feelings, which will manifest the activity of the mind in total goodness as well as in total awareness of its total goodness. It is well known that Mencius has argued for the inherent goodness of human nature. His argument shows that man naturally and spontaneously exhibits forms of feelings which we consider good. These forms of feelings are that of compassion or benevolence, that of modesty or reverence, that of shame, and finally that of the distinction between right and wrong. As the mind is conceived in terms of feelings, it is the mind in activity; and these four feelings are active actualizations of the mind in ontological unity with the Way.

Now what Mencius has stressed is that these feelings are naturally exhibited in the immediacy of a moment when a certain situation, such as the falling of a child into a well, confronts a man. It is clear that it is consistent to maintain that mind-activity can naturally *hit the mark* and fulfill a value and that, in the light of Mencius, in a certain situation every mind can be aroused. The arousing of the mind will first involve a recognition of a value and second, involve an act or effort to fulfill this value. The recognition of a value naturally and universally leads to action. This also implies that the intrinsic recognition of a value or good, intrinsically involves a value which indeed includes an effort and a determination to fulfill or concretize a value goodness.

The double movement of the mind in activity by way of determining and recognizing value or goodness and by way of determining and actually fulfilling goodness, constitutes what Mencius calls *liang-chih*, which has been translated as the "innate knowledge of goodness[13]." It should more accurately be rendered the "mind-knowing-itself-in-goodness," because the mind does know good and thereupon does not remain just a passive capacity, but becomes an activity of knowing, feeling, and doing toward the actual fulfillment of good.

That the mind does know goodness does not mean that there is an external good to be known. The good in question is indeed an intrinsic determination of value, and a purpose unqualified by any other conditions. In this sense good is absolutely determined and created by the mind. As such good is indefinable because it is unqualified and unconditional. Good is a unique quality of the mind, and as it belongs to the nature of the mind, it therefore constitutes the essence of the mind. Furthermore, good itself is both the self-knowledge of the mind and the self-fulfillment of the mind as an activity. Ontologically speaking, it is nothing less than the recognition of the primordial but dynamic unity of the mind with the Way. Good conceived as determined and created by the mind shows that the mind in activity recognizes itself as a will to good, which leads to the creation of good. This inward experience of the mind in activity has its necessity and universality which, according to Mencius, can be empirically demonstrated, given the immediacy and appropriateness of a human situation. Goodness thus demonstrated is embodied in concrete forms of feelings which carry with them a compulsion to action.

It is useful to compare Mencius with Kant at this juncture. The inward recognition of the will to good in the mind and the mind's self-determination for fulfilling good as an activity are not totally similar to Kant's good will as a self-legislatory agency, even though there is a certain similarity between the present interpretation of *liang-chih* and Kant's practical reason or good will. The similarity lies in the fact that both Mencius and Kant hold that good is dictated by the mind or reason and that good is an ontic manifestation of the mind in its act of self-determination and self-awareness. Good as thus determined naturally "governs" the mind, that is, the mind will act on considerations of good for its concrete fulfillment. Furthermore, Mencius and Kant will both agree on the lawlike character of good, namely the universal and necessary nature of good will and the morality of action on good will. There is an inward requirement for this universality and necessity. For Mencius this comes from the postulate of the unity of the mind with the Way. For Kant the good will exemplifies the rational for all rational beings, for it is definitive of rationality for any rational man. Finally, both Mencius and Kant will agree that good will has its ontological basis in the reality of freedom. Kant has specifically spoken of the presuppositions of laws of freedom as a notion explaining the self-legislating and self-governing agency of reason. On the other hand, Mencius conceives the mind as a natural consummation of the Way which can complete and perfect the potential reality of the Way. The freedom of the mind is also the freedom of the Way or ultimate reality. It is the source of the creative formation and transformation of the Way. As the mind can complete the Way, it is a freely determining agent which creates. Good is a creative recognition of freedom, whereas creativity is the mind's freedom in actualizing reality.

As to the dissimilarity between Mencius and Kant in regard to this third characterization of the mind, we wish merely to point out three important considerations. In the first place, the ontology of the mind in terms of heaven and the Way[14] is well-recognized by Mencius and is given meaning by other classical Confucian writings such as the *Chung Yung*. But in the case of Kant, the ontology of free will is basically an open question and is not open to understanding and knowledge. Yet, perhaps, the Confucian recognition of heaven and the Way is not understanding in Kant's sense, but deep experience and perception due to the basic unity of the mind with the Way, a postulate which is not present in Kant[15]. In the second place, Mencius and other classical Confucianists permit the good of the mind to be concretized in terms of human sentiments and feelings which can be directly experienced and empirically observed. That this is possible is due to the fact that the mind as a creator of good is also a source of feelings and sentiments, and, in fact, the beginnings of good are found in the beginnings of feelings and sentiments.

There is another reason for the identification of the beginnings of feelings and sentiments. Good is not an abstract form of universality of reason, but a deep experience of the reality of man. In this regard the classical Confucian view is much closer to Hume.[16], who insists on the sentiment of humanity as a basic source of moral values, than to Kant, who rejects the notion that inclinations have anything to do with morality, even as exemplifications of good will by an inward act of self-fulfillment of the mind.

Finally, we face another difference between Mencius and Kant. Whereas Kant finds it difficult to answer the question of how reason can be practical at all, or how reason itself can be good will that leads to moral action, the classical Confucian view, however, does not lead to this difficulty because it recognizes the practical dimension of any determination and recognition of good in mind-activity. For the knowing and comprehending of good entails the practice and fulfillment of good; and no good is absolutely good if it is merely contemplatively known but not totally fulfilled and concretized. To fulfill or concretize good is to go through a process of creative activity. Good itself therefore involves a potential and an effort (a will) to fulfill the potential in activity.

In connection with the last point, it may be stressed again that knowing in the classical Confucian writings can be interpreted both as an act of evaluation and as a determination to act. It is not pure cognition as such, nor is it passive and idle imagination. It is the beginning of an overt action and is directed toward action. The act of knowing good itself in the mind is as pragmatic as it is creative—to know in this sense is to freely create and achieve.

Possibility of Amissness and the Self-Correcting Capacity of Cultivation as the Fourth and Final Characterization of the Mind

We have seen that the mind has been characterized as a reality in unity with the Way, and as an activity which fulfills values in interactions with things and in terms of feelings. And finally the mind has been characterized as a self-determining good will, which creates good and recognizes the unconditional nature of good which leads universally and necessarily to the concrete fulfillment of values in human situations. Now we come to the final characterization of the mind as a self-correcting and self-disciplining process of cultivation. This aspect is to be recognized because of the possibility of amissness in mind-activity toward hitting the mark. We have seen that the mind naturally can recognize good and this recognition will naturally lead to consummation of good in actuality. But there is a possibility that the mind may not naturally perceive and determine good and there is also a possibility that the mind, after perceiving good in actuality, may not naturally strive for the consummation of good, because either the original unity of the mind with the Way is lost sight of or the creative activity of the mind is obtruded by exterior forces. That these possibilities exist are not denied by the classical Confucianists. A mind in activity, like a body in motion, cannot function properly simply because in the process of its activity toward a state of harmony it loses control of itself.

If we may permit this talk of the mind's departure from a state of original centrality and its possible loss of self-control, then we see that amissness and indeed badness are simply the absence and privation of good, and therefore, a lack of creativity and freedom in the mind. It is aptly described by Mencius as a loss, partial or complete, of the mind.[17]

This may not serve as an ultimate or adequate explanation of evil or badness in the world, but it as least indicates how evil or badness can be conceived, given the framework of the earlier characterizations of the Confucian notion of mind. As good is the ideal perfection and self-determination of mind-activity in its complete unity with the Way, the contrary of good involves a lack of this self-determination, a lack of this ideal perfection, and a lack of this complete unity. Perhaps Hsun Tzu's notion of obscuration (*pi*) explains how this imperfection, incompleteness, and lack of self-determination can take place. The mind can lose sight of its ideal form of good, thus losing its effort to fulfill good because it can be obsfurated by ignorance or dominated by desires or passions.[18] It can be limited by limitedness such as selfishness, because ignorance and selfishness are representations of partiality to the exclusion of the whole and total and therefore to the exclusion of the Way and its unity. These could take place because mind activity is a subtle process which is susceptible to influences under various conditions. When man is ignorant and selfish because his mind loses sight of the unity with the Way and ceases to be free and creative, his mind ceases to be good-producing and self-determining. In this sense we can see that badness, as the contrary of good, is a bondage which may fall upon man when he cannot maintain his freedom to create, perceive and fulfill good.

In order for one to preserve his intrinsic and inborn freedom and to hold fast to his capacity to determine good in actuality, classical Confucianists emphasize the importance of self-knowledge and the self-cultivation of the mind. This is an ideal which is most stressed in the *Great Learning*, the ideal of conscientiously disciplining one's intentions (or of making one's intentions sincere—*ch'eng-yi*) and rectifying one's mind (*chen-hsin*), based on a preliminary and enlightening action of *ke-wu* and *chih-chih*. Essentially this process of self-cultivation requires a conscious grasp and preservation of the initial or inceptive good-producing activity of the mind and thus requires a conscientious effort of the mind to follow a deeper understanding of the good-producing activity as a principle. This leads to the formation of virtuous character.

Virtues are the outcomes of such cultivation since they embody a disposition to act in such a way as dictated by the mind-knowing-itself-in-goodness (*liang-chih*). Virtues must also be constantly cultivated so that growth and the completion of mind activity as a value-determining activity can be made. The ideal of such completion is the achievement of sagehood (*sheng*), a state where complete harmonization of the inner feelings within oneself and the feelings of others is achieved. It is the achievement of constant freedom and creativity, a stage where equilibrium is harmony and harmony is equilibrium, knowing is acting and acting is knowing simultaneously and concordantly.[19]

Recapitulation of the Above

I have now completed my characterization of the Confucian notion of mind. To recapitulate, the mind accordingly finds its identity in its unity with nature and the Way; in this sense the mind is reality and we can speak of the mind as a reality. The mind is also an activity, which naturally transforms a state of centrality into a state of harmony and fulfills the potentiality of reality. In this sense, the mind is a creative agent and we can speak of the mind as an activity. The mind as an activity, furthermore, consists specifically in knowing and determining good and determining the effort to fulfill good and complete good in action. In this sense, the mind is good will and we can speak of the mind-knowing-itself-in-goodness (*liang-chih*). Finally, the mind is self-consciousness and the awareness of the distinction between what is good and right on the one side and what is bad and wrong on the other; it is the determination to preserve good and cultivate good as a constant principle of action. In this sense the mind is a creative and self-correcting process, and we can speak of the mind as a dynamic discipline involving various steps of cultivation and rectification.

Two Basic Related Questions

It might be noted that the above characterizations of the Confucian notion of mind are based on the so-called *Four Books*, and slight reference to Hsun Tzu as a classical Confucianist in the four characterizations has also been made. The question might be raised as to whether all these characterizations apply to Hsun Tzu. Without going into detail, my view is that Hsun Tzu can be shown to be in full agreement with this analysis of the Confucian notion of mind.[20] According to Hsun Tzu, the mind is one and identical with the Way in a state of voidness (*hsu*), tranquility (*ching*), and singleness (*yi*). The mind, therefore, can know the Way (*chih-tao*), and must be involved in actuality for fulfilling values. In fact the mind can know the Way and follow the Way (*hsin-chih-tao, jan-hou-ko-tao*). The mind is the self-guiding principle (*chih-chin-yeh, chih-shih-yeh, chih-to-yeh, chih-chu-yeh, chih-hsing-yeh, chih-tzu-yeh*) and is therefore a free and creative agency. It also recognizes the standard of good and reason which is basically inherent in the mind when the mind is completely enlightened and clarified (*ta-ching-ming*). Finally, the mind in its activity of knowing the Way could be amiss, misguided, and obscured by the partiality of sensations and desires. Therefore, discipline and learning are requisite for the cultivation of the mind as a source of values and as a basis for the will to act upon and fulfill values.

There is a second question to be answered for my clarification of the Confucian notion of mind: how is the Confucian notion of mind related to and different from other classical notions of the mind, if there are any? Here we might say that in the classical period there also existed Taoism, Mohism and Legalism, as well as Confucianism. But without going into a lengthy discussion of these three schools, each of which requires a separate treatment, I will merely confine myself to an imprecise differentiation of the Taoist view from the Confucian view. Apparently, the Taoist philosophers such as Lao Tzu and Chuang Tzu would agree with the first two Confucian characterizations of the mind. The mind is identical and in unity with the Way, and the mind is an activity that can wander easily and freely within the world of the Way. In this sense, the mind, furthermore, can achieve identity and equality with individual things as well as with the totality of things. The mind is freedom and creativity; yet, it does not have to involve self-recognition and self-determination which generate good, nor does it have to concentrate on, and direct itself to, specific action for fulfilling concrete goodness. Furthermore, there is no need to cultivate a principled and disciplined distinction between good and bad or right and wrong as a means of achieving self-fulfillment and the fulfillment of larger social values in terms of harmonization. Both good and the conscious knowledge of the distinction of good from the contrary of good are regarded as obstacles to freedom and the creativity of the mind. The pragmatic action of the mind is also regarded as an obstacle to the artistic vision of the totality of the mind and the Way. In the light of these basic Taoist ideas, it is clear that the last two characterizations form a watershed between Confucian philosophy and its Taoist counterpart.[21] These should also explain the Confucian character of the Neo-Confucianists' views in contradistinction to the Ch'an Buddhist views of the eleventh through sixteenth centuries in China.

Notes

1. This historical approach is exemplified by recent works of many sinologists and intellectual historians such as Joseph Levenson, William de Bary, Benjamin Schwartz, and Arthur Wright.
2. I distinguish between classical Confucianism in the Pre-Chin period, miscellaneous Confucianism in the Han period, Neo-Confucianism in the Sung-Ming period, and critical Neo-Confucianism in the Ching period and the modern era.
3. Here I use English term "nature" to indicate the reality of natural things and the ultimate reality of all things. It is intended as a neutral term for the Way introduced a little later in the text.
4. According to the *Chung Yung*, the primordial state of the Way is a state of equilibrium and centrality. This is brought out clearly in the writings of Wang Yang-ming in the sixteenth century.
5. The original statement in the *Mencius* is that "ten thousand things are complete with me."
6. The original statement in the *Chung Yung* is "If one is able to fulfill one's own nature, one will be able to fulfill the nature of other men; if one is able to fulfill the nature of other men, one will be able to fulfill the nature of all things; if one will be able to fulfill the nature of all things, one will be able to assist in the nourishing and transforming functions of heaven and earth and form a union with heaven and earth."
7. The original statement in the *Great Appendixes* of the *Book of Changes* is "[The sage is able] to exhaust the [potentiality of] the spirit, fulfill nature to the utmost, and know heaven."
8. The original statement in the *Chung Yung* is "The mind when unaroused (*wei-fa*) is *chung*."
9. Here the term "feeling" is used in a broad sense to include not just emotions but perceptions and insights.
10. The *Chung Yung* text runs: "Aroused and hitting the mark, [the mind activity] can be said to reach *ho*." For an explanation of *chung-chieh*, see the explanation in later paragraphs.
11. Both *ming* and *ch'eng* are potential qualities of reality and they become manifested in the full realization of the mind.

12. The three beginning statements of the *Chung Yung* are: "what is endowed by heaven is nature. Following nature is the Way, and cultivation of the Way is instruction."

13. This translation or the similar translation "innate knowledge" is suggested by Wing-tsit Chan in his *A Source Book in Chinese Philosophy*.

14. In the *Mencius*, heaven (*t'ien*) is the actuality of the Way and the Way is the activity of heaven. This is also the case with the Confucian *Analects*.

15. Even though Kant has somehow suggested that practical reason knows or reveals the noumenal in the principle of morality, it is not clear whether practical reason or reason in its practical employment is identical with the ultimate noumenon. Apparently it cannot be, from the critical point of view of Kant.

16. A very interesting and important historical conjecture I wish to put forward is that Hume and Shaftersburg had been influenced by the Confucian views represented in various European translations in the Age of Enlightenment, during which various European philosophers, including Leibniz, came to know Chinese Confucianism and admired it through correspondence with Jesuit missionaries in Ming China.

17. Mencius uses the term "*chih-pao*" which means self-violation and "*chih-ch'i*" which means self-abandonment, to describe one's loss of the original mind (*pen-hsin*). He also uses the terms "*fang*" and "*shih*," which respectively mean loosening and losing, to describe one's loss of the original mind.

18. The "*pi*" in Hsun Tzu suggests also the connotation of a lack of enlightenment and knowledge, not just the connotation of beclouding the mind. In the case of Mencius, as the original mind is considered full of knowledge (of good), ignorance is a result of the beclouding of the original mind. Domination by desires and passions causes loss of the mind.

19. This point is not fully brought out and explicitly stated until Wang Yang-ming in the sixteenth century.

20. For this we have to wait for a close, philosophical analysis of Hsun Tzu.

21. For this we have to wait for a close, philosophical analysis of Lao Tzu and Chuang Tzu.

10. Theory and Practice in Confucianism

Introduction

There are several basic methodological problems in a study of the relation between theory and practice in Confucianism. First, there is the problem of defining and identifying 'theory' and 'practice' in Confucianism. The intuitive concepts of theory and practice can correspond to a wide range of ideas in Confucian philosophy. A close look at Confucian writings will suggest the following correspondence: thinking (*ssu*), language (*yen*), principle (*li*), and knowledge (*chih*) correspond generally to the intuitive concept of theory, while learning (*hsueh*), practice or action (*hsing*), establishing (*li*), extending (*t'ui*), and applying one's thought (*yung*) correspond generally to the intuitive concept of practice. As these terms indicate different aspects of practical and theoretical activity, the problem of the exact relation between theory and practice must be a highly complicated one.

This leads to another observation on the topic of this chapter. The relation between theory and practice has been treated either as one of discrepancy or as one of unity in Chinese philosophy. Related questions are whether it is difficult to obtain knowledge and whether it is difficult to carry out practice. An answer to these questions has been given as early as the *Book of Documents*: "Knowing is not difficult: but practice is difficult."[1] Precisely how to understand this in the light of Confucianism can be an interesting question.

In the following, we shall first discuss the relation of theory to practice in Confucius and draw certain theoretical conclusions on the basis of our discussion. Then we shall relate Confucius' views to later Confucian works in the classical period, including the *Great Learning*, the *Doctrine of the Mean* and the *Mencius*. Finally, we shall reformulate the problem of the

261

relation between theory and practice in the context of Wang Yang-ming's philosophy. An analysis of Wang's position will lead to certain important observations on the concepts of theory and practice and their relationships in Chinese philosophy.

Theory and Practice in Confucius

The central concept in Confucianism is humanity (*jên*), which is conceived as a paradigm of virtue (*te*) and a principle of goodness. The concept of knowledge (*chih*) is secondary in importance in comparison with the concept of *jên*. After clarifying the significance of knowledge in Confucius, we can raise the question as to how *jên* can be related to *chih*. *Chih*, as employed by Confucius, seems to be basically ambivalent. There is the concept of *chih* in the sense of knowing facts and there is the concept of *chih* in the sense of knowing values and norms or knowing what one ought to do.

In referring to the first sense of knowledge, Confucius says "To see much and know many things, this is knowing in a secondary sense."[2] He also says, "It is possible to know things a hundred generations ago," and "One can know things to come after being told in the past."[3] It is clear that Confucius recognizes knowledge by experience and induction as being practically essential and important for a superior man. This importance is a practical one as we shall see a little later. Besides knowledge based on experience and induction, Confucius suggests knowledge by reflection and reasoning. He thus speaks of the unworthy case of "Knowing one corner of a thing without reflectively knowing the three corners of a thing."[4]

We have no conclusive evidence, however, to claim that Confucius holds a doctrine of innate knowledge.[5] From what we can tell from the *Analects*, Confucius is inclined to take the view that knowledge in the sense of knowing facts is the result of experience and induction, whereas knowledge of generalities about facts must be the upshot of both experience and intelligence as stimulated by experience. Man certainly does not know everything, and according to Confucius, man should recognize the limitation of his knowledge and be honest about what he does know and what he does not know. It is therefore assumed that man knows that he does not know everything at the same time as he knows that he knows something. This must be some kind of second order knowledge and thus a result of reflection and reasoning. To know that one does not know everything and thus to know in the second order sense what one does not know is a kind of knowledge, for it is a kind of knowledge reached by means of the reflective mind. This being a kind of knowledge means, furthermore, that one will not act on a proper basis without making a distinction between knowledge and ignorance, if he is to act at all.

Confucius stresses the fact that reflective knowledge must always be supported by experience and must be complemented with a process of continuous learning from experience. The term *'hsueh'* (learning) precisely captures the idea of continuous learning from experience. It is fundamental in Confucius's doctrine of virtues and the reason is not difficult to locate. Learning from experience is the only way to reach the knowledge corresponding to facts and is the only way to cultivate the desire for truth. It is assumed by Confucius that without learning from experience one will not be able to develop oneself in contact with reality or to apply oneself to the reality of human needs and human feelings. Learning from experience is not knowledge nor is it virtue. But learning from experience can be considered a source of the wisdom of life and the basis for developing one's potentiality in both knowing and acting.

Confucius says:

To like *jên*, yet not to like to learn, one will have the shortcoming of being a folly; to love knowledge, yet not to like to learn, one will have the shortcoming of being loose; to like honesty, yet not to like to learn, one will have the shortcoming of being sly; to like straightforwardness, yet not to like to learn, one will have the shortcoming of being tricky; to like courage, yet not to like to learn, one will have the shortcoming of being wild; to like being stern, yet not to like to learn, one will have the shortcoming of being undisciplined.[6]

From the above context one can see that learning from experience is for Confucius in general a process of rectification, cultivation and fulfillment or achievement. Without learning, no virtue and no accomplishment will last. Without learning, every form of good will degenerate and will become a deviation from the mean. In particular, we might say that without learning no virtue and no knowledge can guarantee correct practice and action. On this ground, learning from experience can be said to be a mediate step for obtaining knowledge from practice as well as one for incorporating knowledge in practice.

For Confucius, knowledge in the factual sense as well as in the reflective sense has no meaning separate from correct practice and action. They can be and are related by a process of learning from experience. One can regard action and practice as a part of the learning process. One can also regard knowing and thinking as a part of the learning process. The goal of learning by experience is to develop oneself and realize one's potentiality for goodness, to be a true and actualized man who is characterized by having the ultimate virtue of *jên*. In this sense, one may indeed regard *jên* as the motivating force for obtaining knowledge of any kind. One may also regard *jên* as a dynamic state of the unity of oneself in transforming knowledge into action and in assimilating action into knowledge. Learning from experience, therefore, can be regarded as an actual process of unfolding *jên* through the interaction between knowing and action. Confucius accentuates this idea by claiming that, "Thinking without learning is hazardous; learning without thinking is obscure."[7]

From the above, it is clear for Confucius that knowledge (in both the descriptive and the reflective sense) and practice are distinct and separated, yet can be related through a process of the realization of learning from experience. When thus related, they will contribute to the attainment of the ultimate virtue of *jên*. Now we must ask whether the knowledge of values and norms forms a different problem in relation to action.

Knowledge of values and norms for Confucius consists of knowing the meaning of life (*chih-sheng*), knowing oneself (*chih-chi*), knowing others (*chih-jên*), and knowing what is the right thing to do (*chih-yi*). What is knowing the meaning of life? Confucius says: "Not yet being able to serve man, how could I serve spirits?" He further says: "Not yet knowing life, how do I know death?"[8] To know life is to know the potentiality of life for fulfilling values in life. It is to know what one ought to do, and yet naturally will do in connection with other men and in connection with the world. It is to know what a man can do for achieving the harmony and well-being of men. It is to know what one really aspires to and what constitutes the nature and destiny of things. It is, finally, to know how to attain freedom and discipline at the same time. In other words, to know life and to know the meaning of life is to know oneself, know others, and know the will of heaven (*t'ien-ming*). All these are intimately related and in fact form a dynamic process and an organic unity of knowing and acting. Knowing in this normative sense gives rise to knowledge of the values of life and will motivate man toward attaining these values. To know in this sense is to know not only what to act toward, but to know the determination to act toward a goal.

Knowledge of values and norms is directive, restrictive and evaluative. It involves a natural inclination of practicality. It is therefore not a pure and simple cognitive process. It involves intellectual, volitional, emotional, and pragmatic components. The intellectual component is a cognition of a goal to which the volitional tendency for action can incline oneself. The volitional component is a determination of will toward the goal recognized by the intellect. The emotional component is a sense of urgency and a sentiment of the existential relevance for action toward the recognized value. It is that strength which supports, sustains, and preserves the determination of will. Finally, the pragmatic component of the knowledge of values is nothing other than the performance or fulfilment of knowing which creates a readiness for action. It is the element by virtue of which man can be said to be a doer, an agent.

Given the above analysis of the various components of the knowledge of values and norms and the process of knowing in the normative sense, we must keep in mind that for Confucius knowing in the normative sense (*chih-sheng, chih-chi, chih-jên, and chih-yi*) is a natural, rational and creative process. Several things can be said about this process of knowing in the normative sense. First, knowing in the normative sense is considered by Confucius the most fundamental knowing. It incorporates knowledge in the descriptive sense, but is more than just knowledge in the descriptive sense, because it consists in a knowledge which motivates and a motivation which generates intellectual cognition. It is an interaction of mind with world in the direction of actualizing a value recognized by mind. It is an activity of nature (*hsing*), not just an impression of mind (*hsin*). As the knowledge of values presents a natural tendency toward action, there are doubtless the directiveness and purposiveness of this tendency toward action. It therefore involves a state of mentality in which there is freedom from hesitancy and arbitrariness. Thus Confucius says: "The one who knows has no doubts (*huo*)."[9] The implication of this proposition is that a person without a knowledge of values will not be able to act with a clear goal in view nor with a determination of will. He will be simply unmotivated and cannot be said to be able to act at all. This means that having a knowledge of values is having a readiness to act and having a consistency and coherence in acting.

Second, the knowledge of values is to be understood against a background of action and can not be accomplished until actions are actually involved. This means that the very concept of the knowledge of values (in the case of knowing oneself, others, life and righteousness) logically involves the concept of action as a presupposition, not only as a consequence. In this sense a knowledge of values is considered a virtue in conjunction with the other two virtues of benevolence and courage. Like the virtue of benevolence, we must not simply know what the values are or that values are values, but know how to act on the knowledge of values. In other words, one must have acted in accordance with the knowledge of values, for a disposition to act can only be identified on the basis of an accomplished action. This can easily be understood in the case of benevolence. A man is benevolent not simply because he knows what benevolence is by definition, but because he can identify it in action and because he can and indeed has performed the action of benevolence so that his identification can be said to be reliable.

All virtues involve an initial transformation of the person who knows the virtues, because he can not know the virtues until he has already participated in their formation. This is also true of the knowledge of values. That the knowledge of values presupposes an accomplished practice in accordance with the knowledge can be understood as simply the following: Knowledge of values presupposes a process of learning from experience. It is essentially a natural product of human experience.

Third, the knowledge of values involves a practical flexibility in realizing values as recognized by a person. This practical flexibility consists in being able to apply a principle to a variety of particular cases without doing injustice to both the principle and the particular cases. This is the so-called knowing righteousness or 'concentrating on righteousness of people' (*wu-min-chih-yi*). Righteousness is a value which is unique and relative to every unique situation. To have a knowledge of values is to be able to see a fitting action for a situation and act accordingly. It involves a practical perceptiveness and a flexible management. It is thus highly creative and represents the primordial insights into ideal and good action.

Finally, Confucius' doctrine of the knowledge of values simply indicates the important fact that virtues as forms of good are good relative to a set of conditions and not ready-made as a mode of intuition. In fact, good practice or good action can not be said to be good without a rational element of knowing. Consciousness of good in knowledge of values is, however, merely a necessary condition for the knowledge of values. It is necessary for any form of goodness that an element of perception of good must be present. Good cannot even be defined without involving a knowledge or consciousness of good or of what good is. Good action, thus, by its very nature involves an element of the consciousness of good. This answers to the Socratic dictum: Knowledge is virtue. But we must keep in mind that this knowledge in question is primarily knowledge of values and thus already forms a unity of theory and practice. Good is partially theoretical and partially practical. Good obtains when there is an element of self-effort.

Theory and Practice in the *Great Learning*, the *Doctrine of the Mean*, and the *Mencius*

As we have seen, Confucius has presented two fundamental concepts of knowledge in the *Analects*. In later Confucian writings, such as the *Great Learning*, the *Doctrine of the Mean* and the *Mencius*, the main concern is apparently the knowledge of values and norms, or knowledge in the normative sense. The practical, the volitional and the emotional elements of this knowledge are explicitly given attention. Thus in the *Great Learning*, the following is initially stated:

The way of the Great Learning consists in *illuminating* the illustrious virtue, in loving people and in resting in supreme goodness. When one *knows* where to rest, one will then have concentration; when one has concentration, one will then have tranquility; when one has tranquility, one will then be composed; when one is composed, one will be able to deliberate; when one deliberates, one will then gain something. Things have their fundamentals and their non-fundamentals. Affairs have endings and beginnings. If one knows which comes before and which comes after, one will be close to the way.[10]

The illuminating and knowing referred to in this quotation are not simply knowing what to do and how to do a certain thing, but knowing what is right to do and knowing what one is capable of doing, and thus knowing the readiness to act and the actual performance of action worthy of knowing. This indicates, therefore, a practical attitude and a state of mind, the accomplishment of which already presupposes and symbolizes the attainment of a disposition and capability for practice.

The *Great Learning* goes further to specify steps of the development of knowing in this normative sense. These steps involve many commitments to action and many achievements of practical attitudes, and thus present a coherent sequence of cultivation in both a mental and a behavioral sense. It is said in the *Great Learning*:

In the ancient times, when one wishes to illuminate the illustrious virtue in the world, one will first of all govern well his state; when one wishes to govern well one's state, one will first of all regulate one's family; when one wishes to regulate one's family, one will first of all cultivate one's person; when one wishes to cultivate one's person, one will first of all rectify one's mind; when one wishes to rectify one's mind, one will first of all make sincere one's intentions; when one wishes to make sincere one's intentions, one will first of all extend one's knowledge. Extending of knowledge consists in investigating things.[11]

Like the concept of knowing, the concepts of governing well, regulating, cultivating, rectifying, and making sincere, can be said to be both a practical disposition and an actual performance, aside from being an intellectual recognition and an affirmation of values and goals. Thus they are knowledge of values and norms in our sense. What is significant in this connection is that all these terms combine to indicate an organic interrelatedness among the practical dispositions and actual performances involved.

No disposition toward an action and no performance of an action are isolated matters, but instead an action and a disposition will lead to other actions and other dispositions in an order of development and presupposition. The sequence of steps in the above presents an order of presupposition. But in the same context, an order of development is also presented:

When one has investigated things, one will have extended one's knowledge; when one has extended one's knowledge, one will have made his intentions sincere; when one has made his intentions sincere, one will have rectified one's mind; when one has rectified one's mind, one will have cultivated one's person; when one has cultivated one's person, one will have regulated one's family; when one has regulated one's family, one will have governed well one's state; when one has governed well one's state, one will have pacified the whole world.[12]

If we look into the individual explanations in the *Great Learning* of making sincere one's intentions, rectifying one's mind, cultivating one's person, regulating one's family, governing well one's state, and pacifying the world or illuminating the illustrious virtue in the world, it is clear that these steps all are explicitly and intimately related to certain modes of mental disposition and patterns of behavior. Thus, for example, making sincere one's intentions involves a determination to be honest with one's likes and dislikes; rectifying one's mind involves a state of mind free from undesirable emotions such as anger and fear; regulating one's family involves the attitude of love and dislike toward those worthy of love and those deserving aversion and therefore involves a tendency to act in accordance with the attitudes of love and dislike. Governing a state well involves the practice of virtues such as brotherhood, filial piety and kindness. All these must be exhibited in actual relationships among men. Finally, to pacify the world one must follow the principle of reciprocity in every action and in every relationship. It is said in the *Great Learning*:

What one dislikes from the above, one will not apply to the below; what one dislikes from the below, one will not serve the above; what one dislikes from the front, one will not apply to the behind; what one dislikes from the behind, one will not apply to the front; what one dislikes from the right, one will not apply to the left; what one dislikes from the left, one will not apply to the right.[13]

Thus the ruler must make himself a paradigm of virtue in his dealing with people before his people can actually follow him.

We may conclude our discussion on the *Great Learning* with two remarks. First, it is clear that these steps in developing oneself are intimately related not only in a sequence of presupposition, but in an order of development. They are, furthermore, intimately related in an order of growing from within to without. The steps of making sincere one's intentions, rectifying one's mind, and cultivating one's person point to an attainment within oneself. They are more or less predominantly a dispositional trait with relatively little reference to overt behavior. On the other hand, the steps of regulating a family, governing a state well, and pacifying the world point to an exterior attainment with regard to other people. They are predominantly dispositions based on the performance of virtues and thus involve action in one's dealing with the world and other men. The relation between attainment within and achievement without forms a unity and a dynamic whole — the attainment within will lead to achievement without and achievement without will lead to a more solidified attainment within. The growing process of one's practical personality is a result of the interaction between attainment within and achievement without.

Second, we have intentionally ignored the practical significance of the steps called 'extending knowledge' and 'investigating things'. The interpretation of these two steps constitutes a controversial point for later Confucianists and Neo-Confucianists of the Sung-Ming period. Apparently we can identify the knowledge in question with either descriptive knowledge or the knowledge of values and norms. In Neo-Confucianism, Ch'eng I and Chu Hsi are inclined to interpret them in terms of descriptive knowledge, whereas Lu Hsiang-shan and Wang Yang-ming exclusively interpret them in terms of normative and evaluative knowledge. In the full context of the *Great Learning*, extending knowledge by way of investigating things certainly is not merely descriptive knowledge as such, nor simply normative and evaluative knowledge as such. It necessarily involves descriptive knowledge, because it refers to things outside one's mind, and because in the tradition of the Confucian teaching, knowing things descriptively can bear upon one's action by making correct judgment possible. But it is more than descriptive knowledge, for it must entail the cultivation of one's intentions and the rectification of mind, both being practical achievement. Thus it must involve a practical dimension of commitment to values and goals and so forms a normative knowledge. To be fair to the rich ambiguity of the concept of knowledge in this context, our suggestion is that it represents a kind of synthesis of descriptive knowledge and normative knowledge, such that the former will serve to solidify and support the latter. It is a kind of achievement of the fundamental nature of man — an intellectual-practical complex of self-conscious dispositions in balance with the affairs of the world. Even when Ch'eng I and Chu Hsi come to interpret this knowledge in terms of fully understanding *li* (principles) (*chiung-li*), they are not exempted from a practical concern. That this is clear is evidenced by their conceiving of the understanding of *li* as a foundation of one's cultivation of oneself toward being a better person.

In the *Doctrine of the Mean*, the knowledge of values and norms still is the main concern. Man is clearly conceived as forming a unity with the ultimate reality called heaven (*t'ien*), and is furthermore conceived as being able to actualize his potentiality of goodness in concrete situations which bear on things in the world and on other men. To follow nature so that man will naturally realize his potential goodness is called the Way. To consciously and conscientiously cultivate the natural process of the realization of this potential goodness is called teaching and education. These fundamental ideas no doubt point to a natural and inborn ability of man to pursue good toward perfection. Perhaps by making clear the meaning of good in man, we shall be in a better position to determine the significance of normative knowledge in the *Doctrine of the Mean*.

In an ontological sense good is nothing other than the heavenly-endowed nature and the naturally pursued way of realization of the heavenly-endowed nature. More specifically, the *Doctrine of the Mean* conceives goodness a a state of equilibrium (*chung*), as well as a state of harmonization (*ho*). It says:

When joy, anger, sorrow, and mirth are not released [from mind], [the nature] is called a state of equilibrium; when these are released and respond correctly to their targets, [the nature] is called a state of harmony. Equilibrium is the great root of the world; harmonization is the attained way of the world. In being able to fulfil equilibrium and harmonization, heaven and earth will be well-positioned and ten thousand things well-nourished.[14]

The state of equilibrium is a state of relative rest in which all emotions are unaroused. If there is any knowledge related to this state of equilibrium, it must be a natural sense of equilibrium given by nature. The state of harmonization is a state of relative motion in which emotions are aroused and yet fulfilled, in the sense that the aroused emotions satisfy the good purposes of the growth of life. The arousing of emotions can be simply regarded as a necessary step in developing oneself in relation with others. The satisfaction of these emotions can be regarded as the achievement of values in the concrete situations of life. These values are all characterized by the attainment of harmony in actuality. The attainment of harmony in question is indicated by a well-ordered relationship among things and by a natural tendency to act and grow among all things. Thus harmonization is a higher form of goodness than equilibrium, and indeed is the goal for a state of equilibrium to attain. From this point of view, the potential goodness in man begins with equilibrium and aims at harmonization as the goal of its actualization. In fact, the relative relationship between equilibrium and harmonization can be further explained as a constant interchange.

Equilibrium is equilibrium relative to a state of motion and response, and it can be regarded as a form of achieved harmonization as well, simply because harmonization is harmonization only relative to a state of rest and tranquility. It can be regarded as a form of settling equilibrium and therefore a beginning state for a higher form of harmonization. Thus, the potential good in man can be conceived as the consistency of the dimension of equilibrium with the dimension of harmonization, in a dynamic continuous process of development, reorganization, reordering, growth, and creation. The ultimate goal of this development is clearly indicated in the *Doctrine of the Mean*.

Only the most sincere in the world can fulfil one's nature. Having fulfilled one's nature, he is capable of doing all things. He is capable of participating in the creative and nourishing activities of heaven and earth and forms a trinity with heaven and earth.[15]

The most sincere in the world is one who can maintain his equilibrium as a starting point for the harmonization of all things. The ideas of the fulfillment of one's nature, the nature of others, and of all things in the world can be understood as a gradual achievement of equilibrium and harmonization *within* oneself, of equilibrium and harmonization *between* oneself and others, and finally, of equilibrium and harmonization *among* all things. The ultimate goal is a reasserted unity of oneself with the total reality in the conscious creative activity of perfection and realization.

Now if we regard the above depicted process as a process of knowing in the normative sense, we can immediately see that in this sense, action and the consciousness of action not only form two dimensions of man in his normative knowing, but form a process of interaction between the two, which leads the knower to a greater state of being and achievement. In knowing values and norms one is engaged in becoming them and in creating them. Knowing in this sense has great ontological and cosmological significance. This is clearly stated in the *Doctrine of the Mean* in the following terms: "Being true and good, one becomes enlightened in understanding; Being enlightened in understanding; one becomes true and good."[16] "Being true and good" is the root of the creative action of a man, which is bound to lead to an understanding of truth and good. But a genuine understanding of truth and good will naturally reinforce the inclination to embody truth and good, to seek truth and good and even to create truth and good.

The process of knowing in the normative sense, in other words, has the power of transforming oneself, others and the world in accordance with the values envisioned by the mind. Furthermore, it has the power of generating values in natural unison with the reality of the world. This is the very secret of knowing in the normative sense, as revealed by the *Doctrine of the Mean* where it says:

To accomplish oneself is a matter of benevolence (*jên*); to accomplish all things is a matter of knowledge (*chih*). These are virtues of the nature. These represent the unification of the way within and the way without. These preserve the propriety of time and situation.[17]

The knowledge referred to in this quotation is precisely knowing in the normative sense, which we have discussed in light of the interchange between preserving the potential (equilibrium) and fulfilling the potential (harmonization) in a unity of understanding and existential performance.

As we come to Mencius, the problem of the relationship between knowledge and action assumes a new perspective. It becomes the problem of how one should preserve the natural and inborn sense of right and good and extend it to cover every phase of one's living and activity. The knowledge in question is again no more than knowledge in the normative sense, and the action in question is no more than the action of fulfilling the potentiality of man. Though Mencius does recognize the relevance of the knowledge of facts for making correct judgments, he has laid exclusive emphasis on the knowledge of norms and values as a matter of the inborn nature of man. He explicitly formulates the foundation of normative and evaluative knowledge in terms of the inborn nature of man. He does this in two steps First, he argues that human nature is inherently good. The inherent goodness of man consists in man's potentiality for achieving harmony within oneself and a unity of consciousness with things in the world. Second, he argues that man has an inborn knowledge of goodness.

The goodness of the nature of man is evinced by the natural feelings and sentiments of the various virtues. There are four such fundamental feelings and sentiments, which are the feelings and sentiments of compassion, shame, modesty or reverence, and the distinction between right and wrong. These feelings and sentiments are natural and can be immediately experienced under the proper circumstances. In fact, according to Mencius, these feelings and sentiments are so natural and universal that nobody can escape from them. They are the beginnings of virtues such as benevolence, righteousness, propriety and wisdom. These virtues are the contents of human goodness, the fulfilment of which ensures a state of harmonization and a state of the well-being of all things in the world, including men. In experiencing these fundamental feelings and sentiments, one will naturally come to know what the values and norms of action are and will naturally feel inclined to act accordingly. This shows that the knowledge of values and norms is rooted in the pre-existence (or endowment) of values and norms in the nature of man, and that the practicality of such knowledge is derived from the fact that by nature man desires to fulfill his feelings and sentiments in a process of interacting with other men.

The second important point in Mencius, in regard to the foundation and nature of normative and evaluative knowledge, is that man not only naturally comes to exhibit the basic feelings and sentiments of virtue, but also comes naturally to know what is good and bad and hold to the good through this knowing. Mencius calls this knowledge the inborn knowledge of goodness (*liang-chih*). It is a natural reflection on what one can correctly do, which carries with it a power and inclination to determine the goal of development. The difference between this inborn ability of knowing and the ability of exhibiting basic feelings and sentiments is that the latter is an existential state involving behavior which leads to the achievement of a certain understanding, knowledge and perception. On the other hand, the former is considered by Mencius as the ontological foundation of virtues, in that it gives unity to the feelings and sentiments of virtue, and in that it makes all feelings and sentiments possible. Furthermore, it entails proper action and preserves proper practice.

Mencius speaks of *liang-chih* as that knowing or knowledge which is free from deliberation. This of course shows the intuitive character of *liang-chih*. This seems to correspond to the concept of enlightenment in understanding (*ming*) in the *Doctrine of the Mean*. But it is more than *ming* as referred to in the *Doctrine of the Mean*, for it incorporates all virtuous responses in life situations and reveals an effort to hold to these responses so that they can be extended into firm virtues. This is the true source of the practicality of the knowledge of values and norms.

In concluding, for Mencius the ultimate goal of life is to maintain one's mind or *liang-chih* for the development of the whole man and the whole of mankind in accordance with *liang-chih*. He speaks of acquiring 'the great flood of breath' (*hao-jan-chih-ch'i*) in a person as an idea of such perfection. It can be seen that knowledge for Mencius has practical power because it is based on the practical power of life.

Wang Yang-ming and the Unity of Theory and Action

In the tradition of Confucianism, Wang Yang-ming, the leading Neo-Confucianist of the Ming dynasty, has concentrated on the issue of the relationship between knowledge and action. He is opposed to Ch'eng I and Chu Hsi in their assumed separating of knowledge from moral practice. This opposition in fact goes deeper than the apparent separation of intellectual knowledge from moral practice. It is an opposition to their assumed separating of the objective perspective of understanding from the subjective perspective of commitment to value and action. We shall not have space to deal with the topic of the Neo-Confucianist controversy over the relationship between knowledge and action with regard to Ch'eng I, Chu Hsi and Wang Yang-ming. We shall only investigate how Wang Yang-ming contributes to an understanding of the relationship between knowledge and action in the Confucian philosophy.

In the first place, Wang holds the thesis of the unity of knowledge and practice. There are two meanings to this thesis. The first meaning is that knowledge without action can not lead to the real understanding of the principles of things and can not be considered an achievement of the mind. In this interpretation, the so-called knowledge is taken in the general sense, which therefore includes both descriptive knowledge and evaluative knowledge. Knowledge in general is closely related to action, because knowledge must be based on a process of learning (*hsueh*) and no process of learning is separate from action. This clearly is a classical point taken from Confucius, which Wang simply elaborates. Wang gives the examples of learning filial piety and of learning archery. In learning filial piety, the learner must actually serve the parents in order to know what filial piety means. In learning archery, one must learn how to pull the bow and aim at the target in order to learn how to do archery. In both cases, practice is involved before knowledge can be claimed. Wang then generalizes to every case of knowledge and learning, and advances his thesis of the unity of knowing and acting by coordinating both in the process of learning. Clearly Wang is correct in doing this if he can prove that all cases of knowing are of knowing how. But he did not make a distinction between knowing *that*, knowing *what* and knowing *how*. It may be assumed that in general he conceives knowing *that* and knowing *what* as initially and eventually involving knowing *how*. His point is a strong one in light of the fact that we have to learn to know *that* and to know *what* by knowing *how*. The key word 'learning' provides a context for relating knowing *that* and knowing *what* to knowing *how*, and therefore to acting and practicing of some kind. Learning, in his use, specifically consists of the steps of inquiring, thinking, distinguishing and confirming. All these are bound to bear upon action of one kind or the other.[18]

The deeper sense of unity between knowledge and action for Wang Yang-ming consists in identifying the act of knowing with the act of practice, as well as in identifying the act of practice with the act of knowing. He says: "Where one knows in the most authentic and real sense, there is acting; where one acts in the most perceptive and discerning way, there is knowing. The cultivation of knowing and acting can not originally be separated."[19] From this statement, Wang seems to believe that knowing and acting are mutually inclusive in an ontological sense and each will immediately involve the other. The question is how to understand this. Several things suggest themselves. First, for Wang, the very concept of acting depends on the concept of knowing correct understanding. One can not be said to act if there is no knowledge involved in the actor and if the actor does not know the significance or value of his acting. On the other hand, one will not understand knowing without having the disposition to act or without in fact acting. For Wang conceives knowing as a matter of deep experience and commitment and not as a simple matter of conceptualization. Indeed, he conceives knowing as a matter of the orientation of life. From this point of view, knowledge clearly presupposes an act of some kind which will give rise to action, and indeed will not be vividly realized apart from the process of practice. This leads to a second observation.

In the intimate sense of commitment to value and action, knowledge in Wang's use is clearly knowledge of values and norms and can not be simply knowledge of facts. Knowledge of values and norms is more explicitly and powerfully presented in Wang than in any earlier writers. In fact, classical Confucianists, including Confucius, merely implicitly assume a distinction between the knowledge of facts and knowledge of values. It is Wang who first insists on the primary and exclusive importance of the knowledge of values and norms in comparison with that of facts. It is also Wang who first takes unity with action as a dominating characteristic of this knowledge. Thus, it is on this basis that our third observation concerns why Wang formulates his doctrine of the fullfllment of the inborn knowledge of goodness (*chih-liang-chih*). Wang inherits Mencius's view on the natural and necessary realization of the knowledge of good and right and expounds it to give substance to his doctrine of the unity of knowledge and action.

As the knowledge of values and norms must have an origin and a potential for development, Wang identifies this origin with the inborn sense of the distinction between good and bad, and right and wrong in Mencius' sense. But he goes a step further than Mencius in holding that this inborn sense of the distinction between good and bad, and right and wrong is the substance of the mind in which all principles and truths are virtually presented. Thus, to develop and actualize this inborn sense of good and right is to fulfill the natural potentiality of the mind. This means that the mind is by nature practically directed toward values which the natural perception of the mind discerns. This perception can be strengthened by action, which again will strengthen the perception of values and the commitment to them. Unity of knowledge and action thus becomes ultimately a matter of the unity between the objective world and the subjective discerning mind.

Finally, Wang's thesis on the unity between knowledge and action involves the *Chung Yung* thesis on the equilibrium and harmonization of the mind as two dimensions of the mean. Wang holds in general that there is no alienation and no separation between the equilibrium and harmonization of the mind, as there is no separation between knowledge and action. Equilibrium represents the initial perception of good and the potential commitment to good, whereas harmonization represents the consequential realization and actual fulfilment of good in the interaction between the tendency toward equilibrium and the tendency toward harmonization in the mind. The unity of knowledge and action therefore becomes a natural phase of the activity of the nature of man.

We must point out that Wang fails to stress or perhaps fails to see the dialectical relation between knowing and acting, as he fails to stress and see the dialectical relationship between the equilibrium and harmonization of nature. Our suggestion is as follows: The state of equilibrium naturally leads to a state of harmonization, which again can be considered a state of harmonization of a higher form of fulfilment and thus a beginning stage for further harmonization and fulfilment of values. Similarly, knowing, in the very beginning, involves practicality, which can be regarded as giving rise to a higher form of knowing with a larger scope of practicality, and will continue into a higher form of practical knowing again. This dynamic and dialectical process of growth will constitute the creative process of self-fulfillment and self-cultivation into sageliness, as conceived by the classical Confucian philosophers.

Concluding Remarks

In the above we have discussed various views in Confucianism on the relationship between knowledge and action. We have specifically distinguished between two senses of knowledge in the *Analects*: Knowledge in the descriptive sense and knowledge in the normative and evaluative sense. We have seen that for Confucius knowledge in both senses is related to action, but knowledge in the normative and evaluative sense, i.e. knowledge of values and norms, is most fundamental in developing and fulfilling the potential nature of man. Furthermore, even in Confucius knowledge in the normative and evaluative sense has to be understood in a context of action and the actual doings of man in relation to or in regard to other men. It naturally leads to a moral practice, which in turn enriches the knowledge of values and norms. In the later developments of Confucianism, we have seen that this normative and evaluative knowledge has been greatly elaborated and has been considered the ultimate end to be attained in life.

We have pointed out that knowledge itself is conceived as a dynamic process of the self-realization and self-fulfilment of one's nature. It combines a perception of life, an ideal of reality, a determination of will, and an actual efficiency to concentrate on sharpening the perception, fulfilling the ideal and preserving the determination. In the terminology of the *Chung Yung*, the dialectical relationships between enlightenment and being true and good, and that between equilibrium and harmonization, have been discussed by us and have been used to elucidate the dynamic and dialectical relationship between moral knowing and moral doing. It is on this basis that we have further examined Wang Yang-ming's doctrine of the unity between knowledge and action. We have found that even though it is somewhat inadequate, this doctrine is useful and meaningful for explaining the relationship between knowing and doing in terms of personal experience.

To conclude and sum up, there are four important contributions of Confucianism to the understanding of the relation between knowledge and action. First, practical knowledge or knowledge in the normative and evaluative sense is knowledge because it involves an understanding of one's own nature and the nature of things in general. It is practical because it is prompted by certain natural realizations of the potentiality of life in action and is directed toward attaining a goal of perfection, as recognized by the mind in its self-understanding. Practical knowledge, therefore, is both ontological and practical, both a perception of value and a rule of action. It must be understood against a background theory of human nature and its relation to ultimate reality.

Second, practical knowledge is naturally obtained in the realization of human nature. It can be refined and cultivated by self-reflection, realization, the understanding of reality and an effort to achieve equilibrium and harmonization both within and without. Confucianists maintain the primary importance of developing the natural need for practical knowledge and the ultimate importance of its full consummation, which consists of a state of freedom and creativity. Confucianists further claim that it is in this development and accomplishment of practical knowledge that man will be happy and well-preserved, while everything else will be secondary in relation to the attainment of practical knowledge; i.e., the attainment of other things can be justified with reference to the attainment and perfection of practical knowledge, and practical knowledge alone is capable of transforming a man from a lesser state to a greater state of perfection. Thus, descriptive knowledge, on the basis of which scientific and theoretic knowledge develops, is always held to be secondary and subject to the consideration of its uses for practical knowledge. In other words, descriptive knowledge must be reaffirmed in a system of values and norms and therefore given a normative and evaluative content. In this fashion, descriptive knowledge can be related to moral and practical action in life, against a background of achieved and projected values and rules of action.

Third, descriptive knowledge in Confucius and perhaps in some Neo-Confucianists can still be interpreted as being of practical concern in a different manner, for it can be related to action in a process of learning. Learning means empirical inquiry involving various performances such as actual observation, checking and correcting, and applying these to concrete cases, etc. Thus, even descriptive knowledge has its neutral pragmatic significance.

Finally, the Confucianist position on the primacy and ultimacy of practical knowledge brings up the difficult problem of how to relate practical knowledge to theoretical knowledge in modern science. While Confucianists may not necessarily dispense with theoretical knowledge in science in favor of practical knowledge, they will naturally regard the latter as most worthy of our attention and the former as only an outgrowth of intellectual interest, which is not sufficient for attaining the goal of a total life. Confucianists will not accept the Kantian position of dividing the former and the latter into two different domains of activity which are unrelated to each other. They will nevertheless agree with Kant in regarding practical knowledge as being ontological and pertaining to the *noumenon* of man, but they will not regard intellectual understanding as a self-sufficient activity. On the contrary, the latter must always be subservient to the practical interests of man through the affirmation of the primacy and ultimacy of the natural practicality of man as a whole.

We might therefore suggest that the modern problem of relating knowledge to action in light of our study of Confucianism entails three fundamental considerations. First, it entails consideration as to how to coordinate and relate knowledge to action in a given system or process of action or in a given system of knowledge or a process of knowing. Second, it entails consideration as to how to define, describe and justify the best system of knowledge and the best system of action in which knowledge in different senses can be related to action in different senses. Finally and specifically, it entails consideration as to how to relate morality and activity in art to the developed scientific corpus in any given system of knowledge and action.

Notes

1. See *Shu Ching* (the *Book of Documents*) in Ch'u wan-li's *Shang Shu Shih Yi*, Shuoming (2), Taipei, 1956.
2. See *Lün Yu* (the *Analects*) in *Concordance to the Analects*, 7/28, Harvard-Yenching Institute Series, 1940.
3. Ibid., 1/15.
4. Ibid., 7/8.
5. Confucius says: "I was not born with knowledge. I earnestly seek knowledge because of my love of antiquity." Ibid., 7/20. He also says: "Those who were born with knowledge are of the highest grade. Those who know by learning are of the next grade. Those who learn when encountering difficulty are of an even lower grade. Those who do not learn when encountering difficulty are of the lowest grade." Ibid., 16/9. As a whole, Confucius seems to consider those born with knowledge a rarity.
6. Ibid., 17/7.
7. Ibid., 2/15.
8. Ibid., 11/12.
9. Ibid., 9/29.
10. See *Chung Yung* (the *Doctrine of the Mean*), §1, in *Hsueh Yung Chang Chu Yin Te* (*Concordance to the Great Learning* and the *Doctrine of the Mean*), Taipei, 1970.
11. Ibid.,§1.
12. Ibid.,§1.
13. Ibid.,§11.
14. See *Ta Hsueh* (the *Great Learning*), §1.
15. Ibid., 22.
16. See *Chung Yung*, §21. Here I translate the term *ch'eng* (being sincere) as 'being true and good', in order to bring out the metaphysical connotation of the term.
17. Ibid., §25.
18. See *Chuan Hsi Lu (Instructions for a Practical Learning)*, edition with notes by Yu Chin-yuan, Taipei, 1958. Wang's Letter to Ku Tung-chiao in Part II.
19. Ibid., Wang's letter to Ku Tung-chiao in Part II.

11. Dialectic of Confucian Morality and Metaphysics of Man: A Philosophical Analysis

Three Stages of The Development of Confucian Morality

The moral philosophy of classical Confucianism can be understood as having three stages of development. The first stage is that of background suppositions. This involves considerations of the pre-Confucian conceptual background which provides an ontological basis for the development of the Confucian view of man and the development of moral consciousness of self in terms of subject-nature (*hsing* versus *ming*). We can analyze the subject-nature of the self as the actuality and potentiality of living as this is experienced by the self, as the capacity of relating oneself to others and to the universal, and finally as a dynamic sense of agency and freedom over *ming*, the necessity and determination of the objective. Against this ontological background, we can see that we are in a better position to understand the Confucian morality and its religious significance. We are able to see how the Confucian morality presupposes an ontological understanding of the human condition, the ideal of perfection and transcendence, and the source of delivery for achieving the ideal, as these terms are used by Professor John E. Smith.[1] This ontological understanding of the human condition, the ideal of perfection and transcendence, and the source of delivery provides a unifying ground for the existence of man and his transformation.[2] Thus the pre-Confucian concepts *t'ien-ti, tao-te, sheng-hsing, ling-ming* and their dynamic developments as well as their intrinsic interrelationships must be regarded as more than simply a historical basis for the development of the Confucian moral philosophy: they must be regarded as an ontological ground and antecedent of the formulation of the Confucian moral philosophy as guided by a moral consciousness of man and his place in the world.

The second stage of development of the Confucian moral philosophy involves considerations of the content and nature of moral consciousness and its incorporation in a moral life as a process of the realization of the subject-nature of man. This is amply illustrated by the great contributions of Confucius. Under the perspective of this stage of development, a stage of moral self-understanding, a moral transformation of the background ontological concepts such as *t'ien, te, and hsing* takes place. The individual self is no longer conceived as an object in the world, but rather as a subject capable of achieving an ideal of perfection independent of the contingencies and limitations of the empirical world. This results from a recognition of the intrinsic independence of subject-nature (*hsing*) from object-nature (*ming*) as well as a consciousness of the inner freedom and power of the self for realizing a complete freedom. This subjectivization of self from the point of view of *jên* and *hsing* in the second stage of development, as we may call it, can be contrasted with objectifying individuals from the point of view of *t'ien* and *ming* in the first stage of development. In the light of an understanding of the content of the Confucian morality, this development can be called universal autonomization of individual moral consciousness and moral life.

The third stage of development of the classical Confucian morality involves considerations of an explicit ontological reference of moral consciousness and moral life and their ultimate justification. The ontological reference and justification of the moral consciousness and moral life of the self consists in exhibiting explicitly the ontological ground of man's existence and its fundamental ability to reform and transform the self and the world constructively. The self under this stage of development is regarded not only as autonomous and free from the necessary limitations and objective determinations imposed by the reality of *t'ien* and *ming*, but as a determining force which acts on reality and transforms limitations and determinations of reality into a manifestation of inner freedom and power of the moral self. This forms an ontological justification of morality, because it exhibits an ontological import of morality in the ground of human existence. This stage of development of the Confucian view can be called that of ontological self-realization of subject-nature. It is also one of an individual embodiment of the universal. This stage of development is seen in the post-Confucian works *Mencius, Chung Yung* and *Ta Chuan* of the *Book of Changes (I Ching)*.

Three Stages of Development as Three Dimensions of a Theory

We may now point out that the above-mentioned stages of development of the classical Confucian morality can be regarded as three dimensions of the Confucian moral theory. The first represents the base of speculation, the second the content of speculation, and the third the justification of speculation. They necessarily provide therefore, a general timeless framework in which a morality, with its ontological presuppositions and consequences, can be understood. We assert that unless these stages of development are understood as dimensions of a theory, we shall not be able to appreciate the logic and problematic of a living morality. On the other hand, we are aware that unless these three stages of development are grasped as intimate unfoldings of a single process, we shall not be able to appreciate the dynamics and dialectic of a moral life. Thus it is only by considering Confucian morality both as a process of dynamic development and as a theoretical structure that we shall achieve a full understanding of Confucian morality and its importance for moral philosophy and for the metaphysical foundations of morality in general.

From a dynamic and dialectical point of view, what do we learn from an understanding of Confucian moral philosophy? The answer to this question is to be found in the light of the three stages of development of the Confucian view. These three stages present a chain of discoveries involving the self: the discovery of the particularity of individual selves, the discovery of the universal in the individual, and finally the discovery of the individual in the universal. The first discovery is a recognition of self as a given in the world. The second is a recognition of self as a potentiality for realizing values pertaining to the universal (the total humanity). Therefore it involves a recognition of a universal rule. Finally, the third is a recognition of freedom and power of self-determination and self-transformation. From realizing self as a datum to realizing self as a process of universal relating there is a self-transcendence in the sense that the self is no longer considered to be bounded by itself, because it can be related to others and the world. From universal relating in terms of universal rules for achieving freedom, there is a further transcendence of the self, a transcendence which is characterized by a return to what is being transcended and a transformation or remaking of the given self. This dialectic of moral consciousness and moral life is clearly illustrated by the movement of the morality of *t'ien* and *ming* in pre-Confucian sources (*pu-tzu, ching-wen, Book of Poetry* [*Shih Ching*], *Book of Documents*) [*Shu Ching*] to that of *hsing, ch'eng* and *hua* in *Mencius, Chung Yung*, and *Ta Chuan* (*Book of Changes*).

Thus from the Confucian standpoint we can generalize that a morality must have at least three levels: the datum of self, the potential of self to realize the universal, and the actualized self in freedom. To be moral in this framework is to preserve the self, to discipline the self in realizing the universal and following the rule, and to fulfill the self as a manifestation of freedom. As these moves are intimately related in the dialectical development of the Confucian morality, they provide a model of self-realization for the moral consciousness and moral life of man. This moral dialectic will testify to how an individual discovers his need, his subject-nature, and his capacity to fulfill himself to the utmost in the face of objective determinations and the necessary limitations of reality. One may even suggest that it is due to the recognition of the existence of objective determinations and necessary limitations by the empirical self that the self may be awakened to its spiritual potentiality of freedom and lead a life in accordance with a self-defined process of realizing the potentiality of freedom.

From a logical and structural point of view, we may again ask what we can learn from the Confucian moral philosophy. The answer is that the logic and structure of the Confucian morality provide a general model for understanding the logic and structure of basic moral consciousness and the moral life of man. We have seen that the second stage of development of the Confucian morality presents a rich source of moral insights and moral self-understanding. We have seen that this moral consciousness is not ungrounded or unjustified. On the contrary, it presupposes an ontological understanding of man in the first stage of development and it gives rise to an ontological justification of morality in the third stage of development. Of course it is possible that one may only admit the second stage of development of the Confucian morality as being in fact proper to the Confucian morality and argue for moral autonomy in the Confucian system. In other words, one may not consider morality in the Confucian system as an ontological manifestation or as in need of an ontological justification. Furthermore, it is also possible that one may even provide radically different interpretations of the base or presuppositions and justification of morality in the Confucian system. These are possible because the Confucian morality is expressed, like any system of morality, in terms of a set of norms of behavior. Of course the Confucian morality, again like any system of morality, must depend for its meaningfulness on an inner life of moral agents who make moral decisions and formulate moral reasons. Still, one need not consider the ontological framework of the morality or its ontological justification for the validity of moral reasons and the relevancy of moral decisions.

On this basis, one may even suggest that a given system of morality is quite possibly compatible with a set of meta-moral or ontological interpretations, which interpretations may not be compatible with one another. In the light of the possibility of various ways of interpreting a morality, we may certainly distinguish between a surface structure of morality and a depth structure of morality. A surface structure of morality may be universal, whereas the depth structure of morality may not. That is, it is logically possible that the surface structure of different moralities is the same, while different moralities have different depth structures. What this brings out is, first, that there are many important logical problems of justification involved in the study of moral consciousness as indicated in the study of the Confucian system, and, second, that one may still have to find the meta-moral meaning of a morality in terms of its ontological presupposition and ontological justification in order to understand it completely. As the Confucian case shows, one must understand the need of morality and the meaning of moral principles in an overall understanding of man and reality. The Confucian moral philosophy provides a paradigm of the continuous interplay between the moral and the ontological in the formation and trans-formation of morality itself.

Confucian Morality as a Manifestation of Religious Consciousness

It is important not only to see Confucian morality as a self-sufficient moral system with an ontological justification, but to see it and its ontologi-cal justification as presenting a structure of religious consciousness. In my use the term "religious consciousness" indicates an ultimate concern with an ultimate reality that defines a goal for the transformation of man. There-fore any religious consciousness must involve an awareness of the need and possibility of the transformation of man, a recognition of the end and ideal of such a transformation, and finally the affirmation of a means and a goal-directed process of transformation. To return to Professor John Smith's terminology, a religious consciousness involves in its structure a recogni-tion of the *need*, the *ideal* and the *deliverer*. The recognition of the need presupposes that of the present condition of man. In other words, it must provide an existential understanding of the human condition which reveals the need for transformation. This implies that the religious consciousness is derived in part from recognizing an element of the negative in the human condition which generates all human problems that we have experienced. Furthermore, the religious consciousness must recognize an ideal of per-fection from its experience of negativity in the human condition. It must define the ideal as the goal of all existence and in particular as the goal of human existence. The ontological ground of the ideal must also be recog-nized. The recognition of the ideal of perfection should naturally lead to a recognition of a way of delivering man from his predicament into the ideal state of perfection or the state of freedom from imperfection.

It is true that there are different forms of recognition of what consti-tutes the human condition, what constitutes the ideal of transformation, and what constitutes an effective means of transformation. As there are such different recognitions, there are different forms of religious consciousness. What is most important to realize is that a religious consciousness has in itself a dynamic unity: this unity is expressed in the fact that the recognition of the need of transformation in the human condition necessarily gives rise to recognition of the ideal of transformation and this latter again necessarily gives rise to the recognition of the way of transformation. This dynamic unity of religious consciousness poses the question as to whether it presupposes some form of ontological unity, namely, whether the need, the ideal, and the way of delivery all have the same ontological ground.

In the foregoing analysis we can see that there are four basic questions to be asked about a religious consciousness in any attempt to determine its structure and content: the question of the need of transformation, the question of the ideal of transformation, the question of the way or means of transformation, and the question of the ontological ground of the need, the ideal, and the means of transformation, and their relationships. Against a background of understanding a religious consciousness in terms of these four questions, we may now discuss briefly the nature and structure of the religious consciousness of the Confucian morality and compare it with that of the Christian tradition.

In the first place, although it is not stressed in the literature, Confucianism does present a picture of the human condition which, as we have seen, emerges from the analysis of the notion of *ming*. The Confucian philosopher clearly recognizes man as limited and determined in many ways by external conditions. This is the object-nature of man. As an object, man suffers from the inevitability of death, the historicity and temporality of human existence, and the burden of the passivity of passion and irrationality. In his life he also suffers misgivings, doubts, fears, and conflicts. These negative elements in the human character and human existence can be considered as characterizing the object-nature of man, and they are brought out explicitly and clearly in the reflections of Neo-Confucianists such as Ch'eng Yi and Chu Hsi in the twelfth and thirteenth centuries. But they are nevertheless recognized clearly by Confucius, Mencius, and the authors of *Chung Yung, Ta Hsueh* and *Ta Chuan*.

At the same time, when the negative elements in human character and human existence are recognized, the positive elements of human character and human existence are also affirmed by the Confucianists. They recognize the existence of an active subject-nature of man, that is, they recognize man as a subject capable of controlling, disciplining, and perfecting himself. This insight into the subject-nature of man is naturally obtained in the self-consciousness of man and in an understanding of his ontological ground, but it is to be maintained and to become a source of freedom and power only through constant efforts to reflect on oneself and one's ontological identity in the actual transactions of oneself with others and the world. One may even argue that we are aware of the power of our subject-nature only when we directly encounter the necessary objective limitations and determinations of life and human existence. The world is a condition for realizing the inner roots of freedom and the power of self-determination.

In the light of this understanding we may see how the ideal of transformation and the way of transformation of the human condition are simultaneously defined. The ideal of transformation is the full actualization of the subject-nature intrinsic to an individual, as explained above. This full actualization of subject-nature has three meanings which define the nature of the ideal of transformation. The first meaning is that it is a genuine realization of the ontological ground of human existence in the ultimate reality and therefore an achievement of being, insofar as being itself can be so achieved. In other words, the actualization of subject-nature is a development and consummation of reality, and the possibility of this actualization indicates the dynamic and creative nature of reality itself, of which man is a part and an agency for its perfecting. The second meaning is that the full actualization of subject-nature is a realization of freedom inherent in human existence, a freedom which consists in perceiving and giving meaning to the actuality and development of the potentiality of man. Finally, the third meaning is that by the process of actualizing one's subject-nature one will transcend the limitations and objective determinations imposed by the world and therefore will transform the negative elements of life into something positive, for it is in the process of actualizing the subject-nature of self that the negative and the evil become a condition for the positive and the good.

From this description of the ideal of transformation, one can see that the means of transformation is derived only from a recognition of the ideal transformation as ontologically continuous with the existence of man. The force delivering man from his present condition consists in the self-awareness and self-mastery of his own subject-nature. From the Confucian perspective, even though the deliverer is no more than the person who feels the need and seeks delivery, the delivery is not a matter of simple self-reliance, for the self involved is already a self understood in relation to a vast reality which is its source of freedom and power of transformation. Indeed, the subject-nature is that which comes from an affirmation of the affinity or identity of oneself with a source of freedom and power. Therefore the self, in delivering itself from its actuality of limitations, becomes a dynamic self which can be considered as an enlargement of the given self. He is in fact already co-working with the sources of power and freedom—*t'ien-ti*. When he has brought the subject-nature to its full actualization, he also becomes a full manifestation of the creative function of reality. The distinction between self and the source, of course, then, becomes a matter of unity in variety which exhibits the characteristics of dynamic harmonization (*wei*), universal productiveness (*yü*), and creative transformability (*hua*), as recognized in the *Mencius, Chung Yung*, and *Ta Chuan*. By realizing the unity of self with reality in this full sense, all limitations of the life and existence of man are removed. Then the erstwhile limitations can be regarded instead as constituting apparent forms of expression of freedom of the enlarged individual.

Perhaps it is in regard to experience and the assumption of the basic identity of the self (in its subject-nature) with an ultimate reality as the source of freedom and power of transformation that Confucianism as a philosophy of religion differs from Christianity. From the orthodox Christian point of view, the deliverer of man and man himself do not share the same ontological ground. This discrepancy therefore naturally explains man's degraded state and the human predicament. Furthermore, it explains how God as the deliverer of man may indeed deliver man from his imperfect state. A candid comparison between the Confucian view and the orthodox Christian view indicates that the Confucian process of achieving an inner transformation of one's nature prior to the outward actualization of one's potentiality in social and personal life (in morality) seems to be the very converse of the Christian process of recognizing another source of delivery for the purpose of, and therefore prior to, finding meaning in the existence of man. In my opinion the difference is one of ontological identification and justification: whereas the Confucianist recognizes an ontological unity between the need, the ideal, and the deliverer, the orthodox Christian disclaims the existence of such a unity. Thus, to resolve the difference between the Confucian and Christian religious consciousnesses is to resolve the opposition between the unity and the disunity of the need, the ideal, and the deliverer of man. There is no reason why Confucianism and Christianity may not approach each other in a framework of philosophy of religion which admits a rich dialectic of development of religious consciousnesses and which takes full account of the question of unity in variety and the question of the ontological ground of man. Furthermore, it is significant that both Confucian and Christian religious consciousnesses, despite their fundamental difference in regard to questions of ontological grounds, can be said to be equivalent in preserving a sort of moral autonomy in the sense that the moral philosophy of each tradition can be interpreted as a means of fulfilling universal values in individual life. This then brings us back to a consideration of the Confucian morality and its philosophy of man in comparison with that of Kant and Hume, two major founders of the modern philosophy of morality in the Western tradition. My remarks here will be brief and only suggestive.

Comparison with the Kantian Morality

I wish first to stress the points of difference between Confucian morality and the moral philosophy of Kant. From our analysis of the Confucian notion of morality and its metaphysical foundations, we see that the Confucian morality is not a matter of conformity to the dictates of reason as required by Kant. From the Confucian point of view, morality is a matter of directly and consciously manifesting and discovering ones subject-nature and of making self-determined efforts to actualize this subject-nature. Because of this fact, elements of sentiment or feelings of inclination which are rooted in the subject-nature of self enter into morality and indeed create or shape both an understanding of good and a will to fulfill good. One may suggest indeed that the subject-nature of man is a totality which exhibits itself in a will to goodness as well as in feelings of love of good and natural inclinations to do good. This is explicitly stressed in Mencius' doctrine of the innate goodness of man. The goodness innate in man is a totality which involves a deep awareness of reality as a source of freedom and power, on the one hand, and on the other, a natural and spontaneous expressiveness for actualization of the self in the world. One might say that in Confucian morality the rational is not held in differentiation from the natural in the practicality of moral performance. The fusion of elements of will, feeling, and reason (as involved in an awareness of the integrity of reality) is clearly exemplified in the doctrine of *jên* as the basis for all other virtues such as *yi, li,* and *chih.* Even though Mencius at times gives the impression of positioning *yi* in coordination with the primordial Confucian virtue of *jên*, his emphasis on *yi* (in contradistinction from Confucius' emphasis on *jên*) can be interpreted as pinpointing an element of will for following a universal rule (or duty) in the totality of virtues (*te*) which has as its authentic manifestation the Confucian *jên*. That this stress on the unity of divergent virtues in terms of *jên* is an important feature of the Confucian morality is testified to in the later Neo-Confucian systems of Chang Tsai, Chu Hsi, Lu Hsiang-shan, and Tai Chen. It is indeed already implicitly present in the Confucian-Mencian view of *hsing* or subject-nature, as we have previously noted.

Because Confucian morality stresses the intrinsic unity of reason, will, and feeling, it has a kind of moral flexibility, a flexibility expressed by Confucius' virtue of timeliness (*shih*) and asserted in Mencius' view of moral decision according to circumstances (*ch'uan*) which intimately and directly bind the universality of morality to the individuality of a person. In view of this flexibility, morality is not merely a matter of observing moral principles, but of *creating* moral principles in the light of one's self-understanding and understanding of the meaning of the total reality in given situations. If observation of moral principles as dictated by reason is the predominant consideration of Kant, then cultivation of the person as a creator of moral principles is the predominant consideration of the Confucian theory. Thus for the Confucian philosophers, morality is to be embedded in an ontological theory of man and his transformation.

Three more points of comparison can be suggested between the Confucian view and the Kantian view: (1) From the Confucian standpoint, the Kantian categorical imperative defines quite well a self-contained moral consciousness of man and justifies the autonomy of morality, yet it is not clear how the universal principle of morality pertains to particular situations and how a person may apply it to make concrete moral decisions. In other words, from the Confucian perspective, the Kantian theory lacks a serious appreciation of the question of applicability and therefore lacks a principle of concrete practicality for relating principles of morality to the reality of the total man. Kant claims that his moral principle is synthetic *a priori*, which means that it will naturally apply to the moral experience of man. Yet unlike the pure employment of reason in science, which demonstrably guarantees the possibility of experience, the practical employment of reason does not seem to guarantee the possibility of moral experience in general. One may push the analogy with the pure employment of reason in science a little farther. Whereas transcendental categories provide a set of conditions for the possibility of scientific experience, the actual construction of a scientific theory depends on the actual investigation into experience and facts. Similarly, granted that moral principles prescribe a priori conditions of moral experience, it takes an actual understanding of the reality of man and his life situations to realize moral actions and moral freedom. This is of course a general criticism of the Kantian view, and need not be considered as having been derived from the Confucian view. Yet the Confucian view does seem to present a case where a principle of application to concrete situations such as *yi* is formulated, and where the concrete meaning of practice in moral life is very much stressed.

(2) The first point has made clear that universality of rational command in the Kantian theory is a component of the moral consciousness of man. In the case of the Confucian morality, universality of moral consciousness is rooted in individual feelings and experiences which, as we have pointed out, need not be a matter of strict rationality. The moral feelings and experiences of man acquire universality, however, in the light of an

understanding of an ontology of man. Thus there is a basic difference between Kant and Confucius, the difference between conceiving the universality of morality as a condition of morality or as a consequence of morality. In other words, whereas rationalized universality appears to be a basis of morality for Kant, the experience of individuality of subject-nature is the basis for morality for the Confucianists. In the light of this difference, one can say that the Confucian theory should be less susceptible to criticism by, and less vulnerable to the revolt of, contemporary existentialists such as Sartre.

(3) Of course one may defend Kant against Sartre's criticism about the incompatibility of rational moral principles with human freedom by developing Kant's concept of freedom of will to the effect that Sartre's criticism will lose its force. But as it stands, the ontology of will and freedom is not quite explicitly and clearly worked out, as it is in the case of the Confucian conception of subject-nature (*hsing*) as a transforming power of the objective *ming*. Perhaps Confucianists and Kantians will indeed agree that morality must presuppose an ontology of man which justifies the possibility of man's transformation. But again there seem to exist more dialectical considerations of this relationship between the morality and ontology of man and his transformation in the Confucian view than in the Kantian view.

Comparison with the Humean Morality

Hume's theory, as presented in his *Treatise of Human Nature* and *An Enquiry Concerning the Principles of Morals*, can be said to share with the Confucian view a concern with the empirical facts of morality. As the historical and dialectical development of the Confucian morality shows, morality in the Confucian tradition is based on and considered as necessarily based on the actual moral experiences of man. There is no reason why Confucius or his followers may not agree with Hume that one has to look into the empirical conditions of morality before one can speculate about their significance for an understanding of man. But it is clear that Hume appears to hold his moral theory on the basis of an empirical theory of man, and this theory therefore lacks a dialectical structure in revealing the metaphysical foundation of the transcendental conditions of morality. The Confucian view, as we have seen, carefully presents morality in a framework of an ontology of man, explicitly relates it to an understanding of reality and its relation to man, and culminates in a high level of religious consciousness.

We must point out, however, that there is a fundamental area of similarity between the Confucian and the Humean views. As a humanist and a utilitarian of a subtle kind, Hume does share with Confucianists the same

practicality and the same moral realism. Morality, for him as for Confucianists, is not a system of lofty principles, but instead is organized around an
important class of qualities of man as revealed in the encounter of the
individual with others and the world. Furthermore, these qualities are not
matters of rational dictates, but are instead feelings and sentiments rooted
in human nature. Hume's notion of the sentiment of benevolence or humanity is very close to the Confucian *jên* in the *Analects*, and could be very
much a result of the influence of Confucianism in eighteenth century
England and Europe.

In the light of the foregoing discussion, it is clear that Hume's view
does not have the shortcomings of that of Kant. But it is also clear that
Hume does not have the strength of Kant either. This is so because, let us
stress again, he does not go deep enough in presenting a metaphysical foundation of morality and relate morality to fundamental questions of reality,
as we find in the Kantian and in the Confucian views.[3]

There is one final comparison to be made between the Confucian view
and the Humean view. This is in regard to the conception of good. In the
Confucian morality we have seen that good (*shan* and its embodiments in
various virtues such as *jên* and *yi*, etc.) satisfies the following conditions:
(1) good involves a self-consciousness of the subject-nature; (2) it involves a
sense of community in view of the fact that virtues are ways of relating
oneself to others; (3) it implies a universality of application and a reference
to the particularity of individual persons; and, finally, (4) it involves a reference to a reality as a source and as a goal, that is, good is conceived as a
direct presentation and manifestation of the reality of man as well as of the
ultimate and the unlimited. It is clear that the Humean notion of good
would satisfy the Confucian conditions (1), (2), and (3), but not (4), because
it lacks a dialectical understanding of an ontology of man and his nature.

Retort to Sartre's Criticism

In contemporary existential philosophy, Sartre has raised doubts and
objections to the traditional notion of human nature. He is critical of any
fixed concept of human nature, for in his view such a concept will prevent
man from realizing that freedom which is existentially given in man's self-
understanding. It is not clear how this criticism affects the Confucian morality, as the latter is based on an ontological view of the nature of man. It is
clear, however, that if we regard human nature as an absolute and objective
universal, man may not realize his freedom, but assumes responsibility for
his actions by realizing this universal human nature. At this point the
Confucian moral philosopher would take sides with Kant and reject Sartre,

insisting that to recognize the universal in the individual man is precisely the way of realizing one's freedom, because it is the way of transcending one's limitations in particularity and assuming responsibility on the strength of reason and will.

Yet this may miss Sartre's real point. One may say that what Sartre wishes to question is related to the ontological justification of morality: he questions whether man should be conceived as an object to be defined in terms of objective features instead of being conceived as a pure subject. Our dialectical analysis of the Confucian morality and its metaphysical foundations has provided an answer to this question. From the Confucian point of view, it is certainly to be admitted that there is a dialectical tension between the objective and the subjective and between the universal and the individual, in the very existence of man and his own self-experience. Yet the Confucianist recognizes that there is also a dialectical equilibrium and unity between the objective and the subjective and between the universal and the individual in the very self-consciousness of this tension. The problem involved here is how one may regard this self-consciousness as a starting point for a process of transforming the objective into the subjective and the universal into the individual, as well as for a process of giving meaning to the subjective in terms of the objective and to the individual in terms of the universal. This process of transformation is to characterize the very phenomenon of human existence, and it has an intrinsic meaningfulness for the individual in his actual encounter with others and the world.

From the perspective of the Confucian standpoint the objective of human existence is the unlimited and the indeterminate; the subjective of human existence is the actualizing power and the liberating agency. We have seen that in the dialectic of Confucian morality, the subjectivity of human existence is called *hsing* or subject-nature, whereas the objectivity of human existence is called *ming* or object-nature. For the Confucian moral philosopher, the problem of how to transform *ming* into *hsing* is intrinsic to the dynamics of human nature. Consequently, the problem of morality is not the existence of a human nature, but that of a right understanding of human nature and its inner dynamics. If man does not have a nature, apart from the apparent paradox of having freedom given as his very nature, he will have to discover the whole alienated world as his nature and has tragically to confront this world-nature in an irreversible battle of self-emancipation. For the Confucian morality the world is my nature, as my nature is rooted in the reality of the very world, and is regarded as a potential process of fulfilling the meaningfulness of the world. Man's freedom is a result of his self-transformation and dynamic creativeness.

Notes

1. See his *Experience and God* (New York: Oxford University Press, 1968), Chap. 6.
2. Here one may suggest that the ontological ground constitutes another important component of an understanding of the structure of a morality or a religion beside those of the human condition, the ideal, and deliverer, as discussed in Professor John Smith's book mentioned above.
3. Regarding the question of the power of practical reason, one may suggest that there is a definite difference between Kant and Hume: whereas Kant considers reason as capable of practical authority because reason is a will to good, Hume separates the will to good from intelligence and therefore finds the practical use of reason in the decisions of moral sense.

12. Confucian Methodology and Understanding the Human Person

I

Chinese Philosophy may be characterized as concretely rationalistic, organically naturalistic, intrinsically humanistic and morality-oriented pragmatistic.[1] Although these features characterize Chinese philosophy in general, they characterize the Confucian philosophy in specific particularity *par excellence*. With a strong emphasis on the holistic integrity and unity of the human person and with a concentration on the human person as a vehicle for fulfilling the ultimate value in the world, the Confucian philosophy is unquestionably intrinsically humanistic and is staunchly opposed to a bifurcation of human existence by either contrasting and confronting it with an external divinity to be submitted to, or doing so with an external material world to be controlled and exploited. The Confucian philosophy is no doubt concretely rationalistic, specifically because of its dedication to the human use of human reason for solving human problems and for formulating criteria for the solution of human problems in concrete reference to an understanding of human potentiality and perfectibility.

The metaphysical and cosmological picture of reality in the Confucian philosophy is based on a close observation and experience of the rhythmic changes in nature in correlation with close observation of changes in human affairs in the individual, society, and history. On this basis it is easy to see that the metaphysical and cosmological tenets of the Confucian philosophy extols the importance of doing things with a morally cultivated personality and cultivating the moral growth of one's personality by day to day practice and conduct of human affairs. It stresses the intellectual interdependence and interpenetration between knowing and moral growth, which are re-flected in the Confucian doctrine of the unity of theory and practice.

In light of this salient characterization of Confucian philosophy, one might wonder what makes it so outstanding and perhaps so different from all other philosophies. Regarding the latter point, it may be remarked that although one can draw similarities in one area or another between Confucian philosophy and other unrelated philosophies in the West, the general and fundamental differences between Confucian philosophy and any Western philosophy nevertheless are conspicuous. It is certainly important to recog-nize these differences, which we can indeed formulate in reference to the above salient characterization of Confucian philosophy:

1. Confucian philosophy is intrinsically humanistic: Western philoso-phy is extrinsically humanistic.
2. Confucian philosophy is concretely rationalistic: Western philoso-phy is abstractly rationalistic.
3. Confucian philosophy is organically naturalistic: Western philoso-phy is nonorganically naturalistic if naturalistic at all.
4. Confucian philosophy is axiologically pragmatistic and morality-oriented: Western philosophy is utility-oriented and epistemologically pragmatistic.

II

Without going into detail regarding these differences and their justifi-cation, we may address one important question to Confucian Philosophy: What is the methodology which endows Confucian Philosophy with its out-standing characteristics? Can we clarify this methodology which underlies Confucian philosophical views and perspectives? In order to answer these questions, we should in my view focus on the implicit orientation underly-ing and sustaining Confucian philosophy as it is known to us. The Confucian methodology will emerge consequently as a result of such examination. This methodology is first alluded to and can perhaps even be said to be suggested by Confucius in the *Analects*; and it becomes gradually more and more pronounced and enriched in the later writings of Confucian phi-losophy. In fact, in the *Doctrine of the Mean* and in the *Great Learning* this methodology becomes so explicitly formulated that the central tenets of Confucian philosophy are most illuminated. This methodology also received explication in Hsun Tzu, Mencius, and the *Great Appendix* of the *I Ching* so that its importance can never be understated. The Sung-Ming Philoso-phy of Neo-Confucianism may be said to introduce a systematic specula-

tion surrounding this methodology as this methodology indeed defines the
Confucian philosophical point of view.

We may say that the Confucian methodology begins with Confucius'
vision that the human person can achieve a state of perfection which not
only satisfies his needs as a human person but will enable him to relate
himself to other men, and by developing this potentiality in relating, this
state of perfection will be one where order and harmony in both individual
and society are totally realized. This very vision may also be said to lead to
an ever creative rethinking of the human person's ultimate destiny and
ultimate aspirations, hence producing a sequence of efforts made to understand the inner dynamics of man's existence and the outer form of his activities and intentionality in light of this vision. This methodology may be said
to consist of guidance by a vision and an ever-deepening understanding of
the human person based on close observation and experience of him, in the
context of human relationships and in the context of principles governing
human relationships. The Confucian vision guides the actual understanding of the human person; and the actual observation of man refines and
strengthens the vision. One may indeed assume that Confucius has achieved
a dynamical understanding or awareness which enables him to determine
and see the meaningfulness of his own being and destiny. This understanding may be said to have three significances for Confucius himself.

1. It exhibits an image of human powers in his observation of human
   affairs.
2. It exhibits an image of human perfection in his own enthusiasm to
   learn from the human person.
3. It exhibits an image of the way to apply human powers for human's
   perfection in his effort to perfect human person.

In light of this understanding we may say that the Confucian methodology therefore is both a procedure and a product of a procedure, an outcome of reflection as well as a product of observation, an act of integration
as well as an item of actually acting out or carrying out a human vision. It is
therefore a methodology of demonstrating creativity in the human person
in teaching, learning, defining, as well as explaining and evaluating human
activities and all things related to them or containing them. It can be therefore called a dialectics of understanding through self-cultivation, as well as
a dialectic of self-cultivation through understanding. This also means that
this methodology has an ontological aspect, an axiological aspect as well as
a transformational aspect. For it is used to relate, to know and to transform.

III

We may now choose three basic statements from Confucius to illustrate the Confucian vision of the human person and the consequent understanding of the human person in terms of human creative potentiality. I shall apply a hermeneutical analysis to these three fundamental and important Confucian propositions for revealing the Confucian understanding of the human person, and thus for making explicit the Confucian methodology of thinking in general. The first statement is the Confucian observation: "It is the human person who can fulfill the way, not the way the human person."[2] This means that human person has a special function and capacity in the world and is born to be equal to such a function and capacity, namely those of fulfilling and way (*tao*). Here an understanding of the way is in order. The way is the way to benefit the world, and to create the well-being of oneself and others. It is also the way to understand the truth and good which satisfies the deep moral needs of the human person. One may quote the *Great Learning* by saying that the way is the way of "Realizing the bright virtue, loving the people and reaching and resting in the ultimate good." The bright virtue is to be found in oneself—in one's nature—in what a person ought to be and a person can be if he exercises his will to seek good. The bright virtue is that which will define the value and worth of a person. It is the creative essence and power of a human person which enables him to fulfill the values of his life and the values of the life of others. In the *Doctrine of the Mean* it is said that "It is the utmost sincere person who is capable of fulfilling his nature, and doing this, thus is capable of fulfilling the nature of others, and doing this, thus is capable of fulfilling the nature of all things in the world and thus form a trinity with heaven and earth."

Without explaining for the time being the significance of sincerity and ultimate sincerity, it is clear that in the Confucian view the way is very closely related to the nature of the human person. The nature of the human person, which indeed is a central idea in the whole Confucian philosophical heritage, is not simply to be known or experienced, but is to be fulfilled by learning, thinking, distinguishing and diligent practice. In other words, the nature of the human person, though having a structure and tendency of its own, is not to be fully grasped by abstract discussion, but is to be fulfilled in actual process of the human person's interacting with himself and others. In this sense, one might regard the nature of the human person both as creative and intentional: it is creative because it is not determined and it has a free power of its own—a moral agency which determines one's mode of being and being worthwhile. It is intentional because it receives its being and direction of development from the self-awareness of the human mind—a natural extension of the nature of the human person, for the mind manifests the nature of the human person.

What we have said so far not only illustrates what the way is which the human person can fulfill—it also illustrates how the way relates to the human person and how this relation determines the manner of fulfilling the way as well as giving meaning to such fulfillment.

The second statement relevant for the Confucian understanding of the human person again indicates the creativity of the human person and at the same time brings out the ideal state of humanity the human person can achieve and should aspire to: "If I desire *jên, jên* is right here."[3] Although there are a few explanations and illustrations of *jên* both in the *Analects* and in other classical writings as well as in various later commentaries, *jên* remains a fascinating term requiring to be understood afresh each time. *Jên* is the beginning and the end of a full process of humanizing a human person or, for that matter, a process of human perfecting. *Jên* is also such a process of continuing achievement and effort toward the end of humanization and perfection. *Jên* thus has both a will element and an ideal element— it is a unity of knowing (in a sense to be further elaborated) and of acting out human potentiality for attaining a higher level of existence. The point Confucius wishes to make is indeed philosophically very profound. *Jên* is a twofold knowledge the human person can have: it is a knowledge that the human person is limited and imperfect; it is a knowledge that the human person can reach perfection and transcend his limitation by disciplining himself and extending himself to others. But *jên* as knowledge may be said to be inborn knowledge, for one comes to know it from the very beginning of one's being able to relate to other people. In this sense *jên* is rooted in one's very nature and being. Thus when Confucius says that if one desires *jên*, it is reached outright, he is not referring to some slight of hand, but to the very basic fact that human nature has in itself the deep need to reach for others and for all people. It is a need to transcend oneself to a higher level of universality and spirituality and to a larger extension of the human interrelationship in well-being and unity at the same time. *Jên*-transcendence is always accompanied by *jên*-extension. In this fashion there is no need to develop absolute individualism as in the West under the influence of the Christian theology. Nor is there a need to produce a popular evangelism as in the other direction of development of Christian religion.

To have *jên* is to relate to people in the reasonable and natural context of living. It is to construct means and ways for realizing interpersonal harmony in accordance with the principle of fairness and righteousness *yi*, another virtue rooted in the nature of man. Indeed *jên* commands the use of reason for the service of humanity. It thus leads to the development of other virtues such as *yi* and *li* (propriety, ritual) for the proper realization, expression and communication of *jên*. For *yi* we may say that it results from the human use of reason for human affairs: it is to do things in a proper way with proportion, balance and fairness so that things and affairs will fall into shape and that people can rest assured of an order productive of vitality, stability and wellbeing.

Li in a sense is simply *yi* externalized in rules of conduct and decorum which reflect the human use of reason for sweetness and light, i.e., for both an enjoyable and a natural course of instituting *yi*, and consequently *jên* in a human society. We can thus say that *li* is the way to make human intercourse and human transaction natural and smooth so that the means becomes equally valuable and satisfying as the end of fulfilling *jên*. *Li* is to naturalize and humanize the rational as applied to human behavior, the latter being so often incorporated in the form of *fa* (law).

When one understands now how *li* relates to *yi* and how *yi* relates to *jên* (recall that Confucius says: "To control oneself and fulfil *li* is *jên*") and *li* both and when one realizes that reason (not explicitly stated, but only implicitly assumed) plays the role of making such relations intrinsically possible, there is no mystical sense of magic to be attached to the powerful operation of *li* in interpersonal relationships. For the very power and significance of *li* comes from the bottom of human nature and thus proves to be ultimately most satisfying, if human nature is attuned to the best of its receptance and sensitivity through education and self-cultivation. In Mencius it becomes clear that *yi* and *li*, like *jên*, are rooted in human nature and partake of both the creativity and intentionality of human nature. Thus the broader and deeper meaning of *li* and yi are to be sought in their creative and intentional aspects which make it difficult to fully subject them to explicit rational delineation and definition.

The main thrust of this discussion is to show that Confucius in particular and Confucianists in general have recognized the creative depth stratum of human existence—which can be called "human nature" (*hsing*); and this human nature is to be understood as both self-creative and capable of uplifting one to a level of perfection. It can therefore be called the *jên*-nature of the human person. It is the key to creating a better individual, a better society, a better government and a better world as later Confucianists argue and show (in the *Great Learning*, the *Doctrine of the Mean* and the *Mencius*). It is indeed to stir and nurture the root of humanity which gives a function to human reason, dictating that it should be humanly used for human ends. In other words, *jên*-nature guides and adjusts, mediates, prompts, inspires and disciplines reason and intellect just as a sense of value and goal guides our knowledge and scientific inquiries. To desire for *jên* is to return to the root, to the basis of human being. When one returns to the root, then there will be truth and goodness—the way will present itself. Thus Confucius says, "The superior man seeks the roots. When roots are established, then there comes the way."[4]

In this connection we may bring out another point of *jên* as the root of the nature of the human person. *Jên* may manifest itself in different ways and different contexts, but it always manifests itself in a natural order. In this light we can see how Confucius comes to suggest filial piety (*hsiao*) and brotherly love (*ti*) as the root of *jên*. For to be filially pious is to be naturally good in one's relation to one's parents, and to be brotherly is to be naturally good in one's relations to one's siblings. As parents and siblings are naturally close to us and known to us, to have a *natural* feeling for loving and benefitting them is a naturel manifestation of the nature of the human person, and thus a natural manifestation of *jên*. On the basis of filial piety and brotherly love, and becoming aware of their significance, one can exercise *jên* in an ever enlarging circle of humanity and in an ever refined way in various human situations until one fulfills the potentiality of *jên* in the human person and thus the potentiality of the nature of the human person. Then we could reach what Confucius calls *sagehood* (*sheng*)—a state of the perfection of humanity.

The third Confucian statement which is relevant for formulating and substantiating the Confucian methodology of understanding the human person is as follows: "A person can/should devote himself to the way (*tao*), and persist on virtues (*te*): do not divert from benevolence (*jên*), but learn the arts."[5] This may appear to be a normative statement about what a person can and should do in order to achieve the ideal state of sagehood. But in deeper analysis this statement reveals an understanding of the ultimate orientation which the human person needs to take and to find both peace and strength in his conduct of life, for this orientation of life has a perennial significance for anyone who is able to reflect on what he really wants to do in his life. This orientation suggests a larger framework in terms of which life becomes motivated and meaningful and assumes a position that can be the basis for self-fulfillment and the fulfillment of others. This is what Mencius calls "establishing the great, so that the small cannot take over."[6] But in order to do this, one has to have insight into the nature of things and arrive at a correct understanding of the the *tao*, the *te* (virtues), the *jên* and the arts. We have explained the notion of *tao* and that of *jên*. For the *tao*, perhaps we should also mention that the *tao* mentioned in the quoted passage is fundamentally the *tao* of heaven and derivatively the *tao* of the human person, the *tao* of government. The *tao* is the reality, the principle of which reveals itself in nature, in the human person and in society and government.

To understand this reality independent of particularity, one has to look closely into things and see their meaning. Seeing the brook flowing by, Confucius remarks "Flowing so fast like this."[7] Despite its simple appearance, the remark reveals the profound feeling and observation that change is of the essence of all things and change as prompted by an inner source of power reveals creativity which makes the reality ever present and ever new. Let us combine this statement with the following remark: "What does heaven speak? The four seasons evolve. What does heaven speak? The ten thousand things are produced."[8] The creativity of heaven itself becomes the ultimate secret of reality. This metaphysical aspect of the *tao* which Confucius seldom touches explicitly in the *Analects* nevertheless is the source of energy and enthusiasm for a man to devote himself to realize the ultimate truth in himself and the ultimate good in things and in society. The *tao* in its presentation is an objective order and ideal norm by which things are judged. This objective order and ideal norm in fact constitute the essence of what things really are as well as what they should be (what things should be is what they really are); and this is the *te* or the true nature of things. It is what makes things what they are. It is therefore inherent in each thing. In this sense, *tao* is universal whereas *te* is individual. *Tao* reveals itself in all times, whereas *te* is the hidden source of *power* of individual growth, fulfillment and attainment. This applies to all things, and it specifically applies to man.

In the case of the human peron the *te* is the nature of the human person which reveals itself in the form of the sentiment of *jên*, and can become diversified in all other sentiments and principles of conduct which are referred to as virtues. Yet no matter how virtues are diversified, their source and goal are one and the same: the *jên* or the true identity of the human person, the innermost reality of the human person, which in the flowing reality of change ultimately makes the human person the human person. That is why Confucius says: "My way is threaded with oneness."[9] This oneness evidently refers to the inner reality of the human person which finds its expression in *jên* and other virtues. Given the way as the order of things, and given the nature (*te*) as the true identity of things, *jên* provides the power to realize and actualize the true nature of the human person and the desirable order of the human person which is the society of individuals all governed by their true nature and virtues. But in order that the desirable order of the human person becomes desirable, the human person has to cultivate his abilities and capabilities as well and thus he has to learn things.

Learning (*hsueh*) is thus most exalted by Confucius as the basic ground of the self-cultivation of a person. Even the way has to be learned. To learn is to learn from history, culture and well-paved patterns of experience. It is to open oneself to modifications of reality so that one can comprehend more, integrate more and indeed grow and realize one's potentiality and achieve larger scope and higher level of intra- and inter-personal unity and harmony.

There are two passages in the *Analects* which indicate the importance of learning and thus the importance of what is learned as arts. In one passage Confucius remarks to his son: "If one does not learn poetry, one does not know how to speak." "If one does not learn Rites, one does not know how to establish oneself in society."[10] In another passage Confucius remarks to his disciple:

If a person likes *jên*, but does not like learning, he will be encumbered by silliness; if a person likes knowledge, but does not like learning, he will be encumbered by lack of restraints; if a person likes truthfulness, but does not like learning, he will be encumbered by narrow mindedness; if a person likes candidness but does not like to learn, he will be encumbered by hastiness; if a person likes bravery, but does not like learning, he will be encumbered by disorder; if a person likes strength, but does not like learning, he would be encumbered by instability.[11]

From these two passages, one can see that learning is indeed different from all the virtues and yet is required by all virtues for their smooth and correct application. In this sense learning is in fact learning from reality and from things outside us: it is to recognize things as things and to assess their meaningfulness so that one can correctly relate to them and one can correctly act toward them. To learn, in other words, is to integrate, to order, and remain true to reality with an ultimate direct sense of reality as the *tao*, the ever changing and ever present creativity itself. It is indeed the basis with which man can achieve unity of himself with others and realize the state of harmony and well-being for all. With this understanding of learning, human arts can be understood as well-trodden ways of learning as well as the well-recognized achievements of what is learned by man, namely archery, charioteering, history, numbers, rites, music (poetry). These arts provide recognized ways for realizing humanity in the individual and in the society. They are ways in which to realize the true virtue of the human person and hence all the true nature of the human person.

To sum up the significant points of the Confucian statement, we may say that the value and worth of a person come from his ability to relate to ultimate reality and to reflect upon his true virtue, to actively engage in realizing his nature in relation to other men in order to form a large community of mutual love, and to seek ways for making all these possible. In making his points, Confucius has recognized again as in the first and second statements the creative power in the human person which not only reaches to the truth and reality of things, but which enables him to relate to and integrate all these to form a world of cultivated harmony in which the true nature of the human person is exhibited—for his nature is exhibited in his achievements, in which reality is fully realized—for reality itself becomes manifest and illuminated in the human person. The world of ultimate reality and the world of the nature of the human person become ultimately one. This is the intrinsic authentication of the human person as it is the intrinsic humanization of reality. In this sense Confucian humanism is the true essence of Confucian philosophy and this humanism is indeed found in the process and ability of the human person to transform humanity into ultimate value and to transform reality into ultimate humanity. This methodology for understanding the human person can be called the dialectics of humanization.

IV

At this juncture one may still ask what constitutes the explicit principles of the Confucian methodology in light of the above analysis of three Confucian statements. The answer to that query is that in so far as our analysis of the three Confucian statements reveals the principles of understanding the human person, the principles of the Confucian methodology *are* these principles. In fact, one might even say that understanding the human person in his natural tendency for seeking truth, for recognizing reality and for fulfilling life and achieving order in society and government constitutes the Confucian methodology. But understanding the human person is a most difficult thing, for it is different from understanding things or physical objects. It is different also from understanding a specific art or technique. To understand the human person is to understand an ever-changing and ever-present whole individual with a depth of meaning and projection of value in a whole and yet everchanging and ever-present context of actions and intentionalities. It is, therefore, to understand man in a holistic and utterly synthetic way.

What is required for such a way of understanding is that this understanding should detect all subtle relationships, interrelationships, formations and beginnings of formations, processes and transformations of processes without losing sight of the whole, the unity and the simplicity of reality of the human person in singular and plural configuration. When such rich details of human reality are preserved, one might lose sight of the whole singularity of the human individual. On the other hand, when one concentrates on the singular unity and simplicity of the human person, one may render the human reality an impoverished abstraction and may also effect a reduction of the emerging web of human effects and intentionalities to epithets of simple entities such as Freudian or modern psychological or psychoanalytic theory tends to do.

The Confucian understanding of the human person is both rich and ordered, preserving simplicity without becoming reductionistic. The key notion for such a non-reductionistic view of the human person which yet preserves simplicity is ultimately the Confucian vision of the unity the human person shares with nature and the creativity in the nature of the human person. In Confucius it is identified as the *te* and the *tao* which reveal themselves in *jên* and other virtues. In Mencius it is explicitly stated as *shan* (*goodness*) which derives from the way of heaven and which can reveal itself in four basic cardinal virtues: *Jên, yi, li, chih*. In the *Doctrine of the Mean*, it is the self-fulfilling nature of the creativity of the human person which is called *ch'eng* or sincerity which metaphysically corresponds to the creative assertion or manifestation of reality. With the affirmation of the nature of the human person rooted in reality and with the recognition of reality as ever creative and present as the world demonstrates, humanity has its way too—the human way is that of humanization of reality beginning with a self-consciousness of one's nature and undergoing a process of self-cultivation in *jên* and other virtues to reach a goal where what should be becomes what is, since what is in the nature of things is what should be. The resulting picture of the human person is one of organic unity, a unity of the variety of interpenetrating relationships and interdependencies, a unity of individual acts, and intentions in a single peron, and a unity of harmonious interactions in a community of human persons as well as in a unity of organized and yet well-adjusted processes of rule and admnistration, and finally in a unity of the human person in a cosmos with the cosmos as understood by the human person and humanized by the human person. These unities here are achieved by the integrating creative power of the human person which is his nature. Thus to understand the human person is to understand this integrative creative power for achieving order, harmony and value without the brutality of reductionism, without the scatteredness of phenomenological descriptivism, as well as without the dogmatism of a religion-oriented normative ethics.

One may ask how the Confucian understanding of the human person is possible, to use the Kantian approach. It is possible because the Confucians insist on using the whole human person as the root metaphor for understanding the human person. The proper study of mankind is the human person, so the proper model and methodology for understanding humankind is the human person: the human person is the model and methodology for understanding—not something less nor something more than the human person. To achieve this precision of understanding without exceeding and without diminishing is precisely the wisdom and the insight of Confucius which are demonstrated and shown in the lines of the *Analects* and in the web of views and paradigms in the Confucian writings. To see this requires insight and wisdom too. But insight and wisdom can come from close observation and careful reflection on the human person. Here is how one may even understand Confucius and his understanding of the human person. To say this is not to say that one can understand the human person by self-knowledge as in Socrates or by observing human behavior as in the modern behavioral empirical sciences. The Confucian methodology does not suggest a beginning as such: indeed, it combines both without reducing one to the other. Yet this combination is done in a larger framework which one must come to see through learning, history, language and civilization. This is the framework of knowing or learning of the *tao*, cultivating the *te*, extending the *jên* and the virtues and continually seeking truth by experience, questioning, comparing, distinguishing, and practicing as the *Doctrine of the Mean* admonishes.

V

To summarize, we may suggest that for understanding the human person it is required that the following forms of understanding, no matter how small, take place at the same time without each presupposing the other:

1. knowing and authenticating the self-individual;
2. knowing and establishing a sympathetic bond with others;
3. knowing and establishing a rational and reasonable norm governing the relationships and actions of the human person;
4. knowing the arts as a means of grasping the larger framework of value and reality.

1. can be said to be knowing by authentication which is represented by the virtue *ch'eng*. 2. can be said to be knowing by extending the self and reciprocating oneself with others, which is represented by the virtue *jên*. 3. can be said to be knowing by applying reason which is represented by the virtue *yi*. 4. can be said to be knowing by seeing and observing at large and at the root the value of truth and reality which is represented by the virtue *chih*. When all these knowings take place, they reinforce one another, correct one another and complement each other until a more detailed and

more refined picture of the human person emerges. This picture of the human person will include the individual the human person in a web of relationships and forms which both guide and reflect a realization of the human person. The understanding of the human person occurs when such a picture emerges.

One may suggest that this understanding therefore derives from a *hermeneutical* circle of understanding because it assumes a circle of understanding parts in terms of whole and vice versa. This understanding is further non-reductionistic as it includes hermeneutical circles which always enlarge the scope of comprehension of human experiences and strivings and ideal attainments. As we also remarked earlier, this understanding is basically oneness-oriented and thus non-dualistic, for it centers on the nature of the human person and its creative activities for its fulfllment. Finally, this understanding is no doubt pragmatically inclusive in the sense that understanding is not simply achieved by pure reasoning and speculation, but instead includes practical learning and practice as integral parts, for knowing according to Confucius is always related to practice and is complemented by practice. This also indicates that this understanding is integrative, in so far as one has to see that every experience of knowing contributes to a more integrated understanding and a fuller picture of the human person. In the web of knowing and learning one can see the interdependence of all knowing, learning and practical doings. Again, this is best illustrated by the Confucian statement: "If one does not know the mandate of heaven, one cannot be the superior man; if one does not know *li*, one cannot establish oneself in society; if one does not know the right and the wrong of one's language, one cannot know the wrong and the right of others."[12]

To be more thorough in our description of the Confucian understanding of the human person, we may also say that this understanding is organic and dialectical in so far as it relies on an ability to organize and to relate all experience into a harmonious and yet meaningful whole and manages this organization in an ordered, yet dynamic and open process of change and shift in which the dialectical creativity towards ordering and structuring must be affirmed.

The above-discussed understanding of the human person is no doubt achieved by the Confucian methodology of understanding. We may now represent this understanding as an organic integration of human learning in a hermeneutical process of dialectical complementation, contrast, opposition and unification. If we follow the Confucian distinction between the inner cultivation and the outer activities of a person, if we contrast the human person with heaven—the manifestation of the larger and original ultimate reality—and if we identify the individual human person as the self-authenticating (*chih-ch'eng*) power and nature of the human self, then we can see that a coordinate system of above and below, right and left, would indicate directions of integration and frameworking. An ever-enlarging circle will indicate the dialectical movement of integration for the understanding of the human person, beginning with the centering of self (*chung*) and moving toward a state of integrated order and harmony (*ho*). A diagram thus representing the picture of the understanding of human nature can be established as in Figure 1.

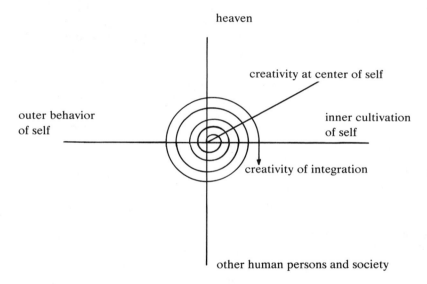

Fig. 1. Wholeness and harmony to be realized in human person.

To further illuminate this diagrammatic framework, we may indeed formulate two aspects of the Confucian methodology for understanding the human person, namely the dialectic of centralization and the dialectics of harmonization. These two dialectics are mutually complementary as they form two essential movements for understanding the whole person. In fact these two dialectics are briefly stated in the *Doctrine of the Mean*. It says:

When the feelings of joy, anger, sorrow and happiness are not yet activated, the state of mind is called equilibrium; when they are activated and fit the right measure, this state is called harmony. Equilibrium is the great foundation of the world; harmony is the perfect way of the world. To have reached the state of equilibrium (when not activated) and the state of harmony (when activated), Heaven and Earth will be well positioned and the ten thousand things will be well nurtured and grow.

The state of *chung* and the state of *ho* clearly are two aspects of the same reality, whether the reality refers to the mind or to cosmological-ontological Nature. The human mind, and for that matter, the human person and cosmological-ontological Nature, must be in either of the states, and it cannot simply remain in one state. For otherwise it will contradict the ever-changing and ever-present creative nature of things. Thus the two states of *chung* and *ho* form a process of interchange, and therefore a process of creative transformation, formation and growth. This is precisely the way in which the individual human person learns to relate to the world and integrate himself and harmonize with others in society and community. It is also precisely how nature renews its life-circle and manifests its creative vitality. In this sense, these two aspects of the same process also become two movements of growth and development, each characterized by its peculiar mode and attainment.

In the movement toward preserving the *chung* in the human person, all feelings and emotions must be kept in stability and potential rest. The ability to maintain such discipline is due to the power of understanding the nature of the human person as rooted in the ultimate reality of boundless creativity which at bottom makes no movement and yet is ready to creatively assume any formation or transformation. Thus the dialectics of centralization consists in experiencing the ultimate reality of the nature of the human person by maintaining the *chung*—or the *chung*-movement—of preserving the original nature at the root of creativity. When this dialectics applies to nature, it means also seeking the root-source of the natural changes.

On the other hand, the dialectics of harmonization consists in creatively seeking to realize and fulfill the root-nature of the human person in correlation with other people and things in the world, and the purpose of such movement is to create a large harmony which achieves the integration of the self with the community and world, and thus realize the nature of the human person and the nature of the world.

The two dialecticses together present a methodology for understanding the human person as an entity as well as a process which can and also must realize its nature in realizing the nature of all things, so that it can be defined at the same time when the world is defined. Both dialectics therefore constitute an essential procedure for understanding the human person and the essential components of the Confucian methodology for such an understanding.

VI

This chapter does not pretend to do justice to a full discussion of the Confucian methodology which is essentially a methodology for understanding the human person. In the *Analects* as well as in other later writings of the Confucianists and also in the Confucian commentaries on the *I Ching*, one will see many paradigms and norms and principles for understanding the human person or illustrating such an understanding. We may see for example the principle of rectifying names in the *Analects*, the principles of unity of theory and practice, the paradigms of self-cultivation, and interdependent norms of knowing and evaluation, willing and knowing, individual and society, extension and uplifting, the arguments for innate goodness of the nature of the human person in the *Mencius*, etc. All seem to present or guide one to an understanding of the human person. They need the methodology discussed here for integrating and simplifying in order to preserve a whole unity of the understanding. If modern philosophies are to learn anything from the Confucian methodology for understanding the human person, the most important thing to learn from such a methodology and its fruits is that the human person must be constantly examined, cultivated and organized in such way that the more integrative and more open the framework for understanding is, the more intimate and the more intense our understanding of the human person will be, for the human person always needs to be integrated in a larger framework in order that his being and existence can be more defined and more developed.

Notes

1. Cf. my article, "Chinese Philosophy: A Characterization," which first appeared in *Inquiry*, No. 14, April 1971, 95-119. [Chapter 1 in this book.]
2. See the *Analects*, 15:29.
3. Ibid, 7:30.
4. Ibid, 1:2.
5. Ibid, 7:6.
6. See The Mencius, 6A:15.
7. See the *Analects*, 9:17.
8. Ibid, 17:17.
9. Ibid, 4:15.
10. Ibid, 16:13.
11. Ibid, 17:9.
12. Ibid, 20:3.

13. Legalism versus Confucianism: A Philosophical Appraisal

Issues and Problems

In 1974, a campaign against Confucianism and Confucius was launched on the Chinese mainland.[1] This campaign was shot through and through with the political ideology of Marxism and Maoism and was obviously intended to serve a political end. Confucius and Confucianism are castigated for their restorationism and historical backwardness, as well as for their so-called class background. Placing them within their historical contexts, this critique of Confucianism and Confucius is combined with praise and promotion of the Legalists of the classical period. In fact, Legalism has been used as the basis for criticizing and repudiating Confucianism. The antagonism between Confucianism and Legalism is described as a class struggle from the Marxist economic historical dialectical perspective. Thus, the whole campaign presupposes the validity of the Marxist-Maoist theory of Chinese traditional history, which depicts the development from a slave-owning society to a feudalist society which was dominated by the landlord class.[2] However, such presuppositions of the Marxist-Maoist ideological method of analysis are shrouded in obscurity and no effort is made to secure objective understanding of the development of Confucianism and Legalism, or to secure an objective understanding of how human history advances in Chinese society.

Apart from political ideological considerations, there are a number of basic issues surrounding the true nature of the opposition between Legalism and Confucianism. There is first of all the problem of the ambiguity of the term "*fa* (law) in classical Chinese philosophy: In what way, we may ask, does the Legalist conceive "*fa*"? To what end does "*fa*" subserve? How does Confucianism conceive *fa*? Does it denounce it or accept it on differ-

311

ent grounds and for different purposes other than the Legalists? The clarification of these questions will, on the one hand, exhibit the true nature of
Legalism and its social and political objectives, and on the other hand,
explain the Legalist burden imposed on the term "*fa*" in modern contexts
of its use. In order to correctly understand Legalism, we shall describe how
it arises, what its program of political and social control essentially involves,
and how the Legalists justify their programs. With this background at hand,
we shall then be able to understand why Legalists in their historical contexts criticize Confucianism and whether their criticisms are valid.

I hold that there is a genuine antagonism between Legalism and
Confuciamsm, in virtue of their basic orientations and philosophical convictions. I also hold that, although Legalism was instrumental in effecting
the unification of China under the Ch'in state, the underlying Chinese culture, value and life-style could not develop under the Legalistic regime,
which consequently succumbed. In this sense, Confucianism not only theoretically avenges itself, but historically demonstrates a power far beyond
what Legalism envisions. Thus, a genuine grasp of the true spirit of
Confucianism is both necessary and sufficient for the preservation of basic
values recognized as rooted in the authentic nature of man and for waging
a long-range battle against the process of dehumanization and social regimentation symbolically embodied in Legalism. Awareness of this implies
that Confucianism is not just historically relevant, but is relevant for the
reconstruction of a correct understanding of man and society. In this connection, we can see that Confucian humanism, though opposed to Legalism, is compatible with rule of law, and indeed could absorb the rule of law
on a humanistic basis. When this is done, a Confucian democracy in light
of the Confucian humanism will become the best weapon against the spectre
of a Legalistic tyranny.

Objections to the Marxist Historical Reduction of Philosophy

The nature of society, and how society evolves in history are complicated questions. They require thorough-going objective scientific research
and study in order to form adequate answers to them. As societies differ
from one place to another, it is difficult to design a formula of explanation
which will precisely fit all societies. It is certainly naive to consider that all
societies linearly move from one stage to another stage according to a
certain schedule. Yet, Marx's theory of the historical development of societies, seems to give such a formula of explanation. When the Chinese Marxists
apply such a formula to Chinese history, it generates a forced political
picture of ancient China. Clearly, there is no reason why a non-Marxist

theory of Chinese society and history based upon anthropology, archeology, and social science will not give a better and more coherent description and explanation of ancient Chinese society. The Marxist approach politicizes every aspect of human cultural activity and then reduces it to an economic level of productive force and productive relations. Nonetheless, a culture or a society constitutes an organic whole. When it has grown to having a certain complicated structure, all its parts become interdependent, and there is no ready formula to reduce an organic portion to another without destroying the organic totality.

In light of the above remarks, it is quite obvious that no one can really reduce philosophical thinking nor the visions of man and society to political and economic expressions and advocations of some narrowly defined class interests, even if it can be granted that certain economic and political conditions may induce or stimulate certain philosophical thoughts, and certain other philosophical thoughts may evolve certain social-political visions which reflect man's commitment to values under certain social, political or economic conditions. To politicize philosophical thought is not to recognize what philosophy genuinely is: Philosophy is as much a product of reason and moral conscience as a product of society and culture. Though it develops from a historical context, it can achieve autonomy and transcendence by establishing the ideal goal for man to strive for and by defining paradigm norms for man to follow and emulate. In this sense, philosophy by nature is truly ideal and idealistic in its search for absolute values and universal truths.

There are two fundamental aspects of philosophical thought which should underscore the independence and autonomy of philosophy from politics and economics: (1) Philosophical thought embodies a vision of values which emerges from social and cultural consciousness, but which also defines and enriches it. It becomes autonomous once it is extended for necessary and universal application to humanity; (2) Philosophical thought demonstrates the freedom of the human spirit and the self-awakening of humanity. It is not only regulative-perscriptive, but also constitutive, of human experience, which cannot be said to be totally determined by social and political economy.

By reflecting on human reason and conscience we recognize that human beings are essentially free, and they can express their freedom through philosophy, art and religion. As human beings are not predetermined, consequently they cannot be reduced to social and economic forces. It is through the failure to see this that Confucianism is depicted as an expression of class interests instead of being viewed as expressing the vision of an ideal society of ideal men, as well as expressing faith in man's potentiality to reach and fulfill the ideal of humanity on both individual and societal levels. Philosophy, though independent of politics and economics, still can serve as a guiding principle for politics and economics providing their foundations. It is not a handmaid to politics or economics, as it is not a handmaid to religion. The historical materialism of Marxism tends to reduce philosophy to servility under party control, just as the theology of the medieval period tended to reduce philosophy to servility under church control. In both cases, the reduction of philosophy is a reduction of man and his autonomy and freedom. We must oppose this reduction on behalf of man's freedom and autonomy. The opposition between Confucianism and Legalism therefore acquires special significance in light of our understanding of man and his aspirations.[3]

The Ambiguity of the Terms "Law" (*fa*) and "Legalism" (*fa-chia*)

We must ask what the terms "*fa*" and "*fa-chia*" mean when we consider the opposition and antagonism between Legalism and Confucianism. We might be misled by interpreting "*fa*" as meaning the legislated laws in a modern civil democratic society. We may also think that Confucianism is against the rule of law, in the best sense of the word, from the impression that Confucianism is anti-legalistic. In fact, the Chinese word "*fa*" is an ancient word with many connotations. It stood for many things throughout the antiquity of the early Chou period (or perhaps early Shang) to the time of the *fa-chia*. What defines the *fa* of *fa-chia* is not the form or even the content of the *fa*, but the presupposed motive or intent and the planned objective and goal in the Legalist sense. It is only with reference to the Legalist intent and objective that *fa* acquires a Legalist meaning and perhaps a specific content relative to the Legalist intent and objective. Yet, we must see *fa* in a relatively independent sense which can in principle lend itself to other functions and determinations relative to different goals and to different intents in particular frameworks other than the Legalist one.

If we investigate the use and meaning of the term *fa*, written in its archaic form as 灋 , we find that it has two primary meanings and uses in ancient literature, such as the *Five Classics*, the *Four Books*, and other historical and philosophical writings in the period of the late Chou. In one primary sense, *fa* is no more than the "method" or "model" for doing something, and therefore exists for persons to learn if they want to do something adequately. One finds *fa* in this sense in the *Book of Documents* and Mo Tzu's work.[4] In this regard, *fa* can be used as a verb, as *fa* is to emulate or follow some model. In this regard we could speak of *fa-tu* (institutional measures), *fa-yi* (norms), *fa-chi* (constitutional regulations), or even *fa-shu* (technique or method). We could also speak of *fa* in the sense of connection with various predetermined norms; thus we can speak of *li-fa* (norms of propriety), *ch'an-fa* (method of war), and *ping-chun-chih-fa* (norms for measurement). The best definition of *fa* in this sense is given by the "Great Appendix" of the *Book of Changes*: "To institute something so that we can use it is called (*fa*)".[5] In this sense, *fa* is merely an objective structure or form for achieving a value. It is part of any institutional structure and part of any administrative process. We shall see that in this sense Confucians do not disparage against *fa* at all. In fact, *fa* in this sense of norms and measures is an ancient idea and an ancient practice. Confucianism, like other schools of thought, may not elaborate on this tradition, though it does not abandon it and indeed to a large extent embraces it as an essential element in the administration of government.

Equally ancient, but much more narrow in meaning and reference, is *fa* in the sense of code and terms of punishment. In this sense of a code of punishment, *fa* is derived from the ancient character 灋 , which according to Hsu Shen in *Shuo Wen Chieh Chih* means *hsing* (terms of punishment).[6] The character 灋 is a combination of two characters, water and an instrument for straightening crooked wood. Thus, in the sense of *hsing,* *fa* (simplified later to 法) is considered as an instrument for straightening the non-straight by force. In the *Chou Shu* and the *Chou Li*, we see reference to *wu-hsing-chih-fa* or the "laws of punishment." H. G. Creel thought that the term *fa* appeared very late and was not found in the *I Ching* and the *Shih Ching*. He was mistaken, for he did not recognize that the meaning of *fa* is embodied in such characters as *tien* (典), *tse* (則), and even *hsing* (型).All these words appear in the most ancient writings he has not mentioned. It is to be noted that this narrow sense of *fa* as a code of punishment also can be regarded as a method of punishment (*hsing-fa* 刑法). But when a method of punishment is codified, specifically in particular rules, it becomes a method of *fa* in the Legalist sense. Thus we reach a definite meaning for *fa* in the Legalist sense: *fa* is specifically a term for a code of punishment or codified norm of punishment. We shall see that this code of punishment encloses a very large area of application for the Legalists and is used to achieve a certain goal which is not traditionally considered in ancient Chinese history to be achieved by the use of *fa* in the sense of punishment.

Our distinction of *fa* into these two senses is highly important, not only for avoiding confusion about the meanings of *fa*, but also for recognizing the true nature of the meanings as employed in Legalism, and for understanding the true spirit of Confucianism in reference to the use of *fa*.

The Rise and Basic Program of Legalism

Most scholars discuss the rise and origin of a school of thought in terms of its historical background and the influence it has made. But a school of thought represents a point of view, an effort to establish a new set of values, and/or a new method to implement the set of values it advocates. Although historical background and historical influence from preceding views show how a school of thought originates, it does not necessarily illuminate the essential starting point of the school, which consists in adopting and formulating a distinctive point of view, we may ask what is the set of values from a distinctive point of view? Further, we may ask what is its method for implementing this set of values. I shall now answer these questions.[7]

The point of view of Legalism is one of an absolute ruler who wants to control and dominate his state so that it will achieve power and wealth. The ruler wants absolute power over his people and thus has to establish strict and tight control. He wants to make all decisions and wants these decisions to be obeyed and carried out by his subjects., The power he has satisfies him because he can use it for its further expansion. Thus the power he has serves a purpose, the purpose of becoming a leader among his peers, and perhaps the purpose of eliminating all forces competing with him so that he will subject all other powers to his own dominion. In this sense, the Legalist point of view is that of unifying all divided powers under one power to establish a centralized powerful state under the ruling authority of one person.

In order to establish this central authority and to wield power, the ruler has to set up an administration which can carry out the directives of the ruler in systematic and efficient ways. Thus the ruler has to devise and design a government, as well as to adopt an attitude and technique or method, which will contribute to the accumulating and maintaining of the power of the ruler and the efficiency of the administration. One may call the Legalist point of view an administrative or governmental point of view. This Legalist point of view is inevitably utilitarian. It is directed not only toward the concentration of the power of control in the person of the ruler and the efficient and unopposed wielding of this power with art and technique, but also toward accumulating material wealth and military strength in the state. As the creation of a powerful and rich state is the Legalist goal, the Legalist ruler or minister has to formulate every policy and measure in accord with the utilitarian goal. If we ask what would be the reason and the goal behind the effort to create a rich and powerful state, the answer would be: When a state becomes rich and powerful, it can conquer all states and unify the world. Thus the goal for becoming a rich and powerful state is to become more powerful and more rich. It is said in the *Book of Lord Shang*: "The strong state engages in wars of conquest, the weaker state concentrates on defense."[8] It is also said that, "How does a man obtain a title of respect and possess a vast land and become ruler? It is because he has won the war. How does a man lose his title and territory and become vanquished? It is because he was defeated in the war. There is no case where a man becomes a ruler without a war of conquest, nor a man loses his state without a war of defeat."[9]

At the time of Lord Shang (359-338 B.C.), there already existed the problem of how to unify China. There is no denying that Lord Shang had a strong desire to make the Ch'in state, which he served as the Prime Minister, a unifier of China and sought to achieve a state of political unity under the ruler of Ch'in. Thus he advocated the doctrine of strengthening military power and acquiring material wealth for the state, so that the state may undertake the war of conquest and for that matter, a war of unification. The policy, in accordance with this utilitarian goal of military strengthening the state and increasing the national income, is clearly formulated by Lord Shang in terms of enlisting all men in the state as soldiers and promoting agricultural production. This has been referred to as the policy of stressing war and stressing husbandry. Regarding enlistment of all people as soldiers and stressing the importance of winning war, Lord Shang has this to say:

If people are brave, the war will be won;
If people are not brave, the war will be lost.
If one can unify people through training for war, people will be brave;
If one cannot unify people through training for war, people will not be brave. The sage ruler sees that rule comes from the war, therefore he commands all people (enlist as soldiers) for war."[10]

Regarding the policy of stressing husbandry, Lord Shang had this to say:

A state can become prosperous, because (of the policy of) stressing husbandry and war; all those who govern a state worry about the scattering of people and their lack of consolidation. Thus the sage designs (a way of) unifying the people by consolidating them in doing husbandry."[11]

The way in which the sage governs a state is to command all people to do husbandry when they are in the state, and to do warfare when they are out of the state . . . (in this way) the goal of wealth and power can be easily achieved."[12]

What Shang Yang sets forth is in fact a policy which combines husbandry (production) with military preparedness (warring ability), so that people can produce in peace and can fight war. This policy of regimentation amounts to putting the life of people at the disposal of the state to the extent that all human efforts of society are aimed at achieving national strength and wealth, as desired and controlled by the ruler. Power and wealth define the guiding principles and values of the legalistic, utilitarian point of view.

Finally, in order to achieve the goal of power and wealth, and in order to facilitate this achievement through the agency of the ruler's own administration, control, and manipulation, the Legalists introduced the *fa* as an instrument (understood in the sense of a code of punishment and reward). Although it cannot be denied that the Legalists, such as Lord Shang and Han Fei Tzu, recognized *fa* (in the broad sense) to be the administrative method and technique for control (as suggested by the term *shu*) which is an essential element for maintaining control and power, they do appeal more to *fa* in the narrow sense of a penal code and award system which serves as a basic element in the enforcement of the Legalist policies and programs. Lord Shang, as a practitioner of Legalism, relies on the use of a penal code and award system as a means for achieving his goal of concentration of power in the ruler, strengthening the military power of the state and increasing its wealth. The peculiarities of the Legalist notions of *fa* in this narrow sense consist in: (a) making *fa* universally applicable to all people, disregarding their status or situation; (b) applying *fa* basically to major areas of people's lives; and (c) making the terms of punishment as heavy as possible. In light of (a), the Legalist *fa* has the effect of abolishing the privileges of the aristocracy and establishing the equality of all people in the state before the *fa*. In light of (b), *fa* succeeds in regimenting and terrifying society and people for the purpose of the state's objectives, and extensively limits individual freedom and individual rights, such as the right to pursue one's education and one's well-being. The rights of individuals are sacrificed for the good of the state. In light of (c), *fa* becomes a most effective tool for enforcing the policies of the ruler. The ruler coerces people into submission to his will by instilling fear of punishment and promoting desire for award. The *fa* of Legalism is to be publicly promulgated so that people are made to know it, and thus it creates a state of control through the efforts of the people to obey the law.

The Legalists justify their use of the positive *fa* in terms of their understanding of the psychology and nature of man. Thus, Han Fei Tzu says:

In order to govern the world we must follow human feelings. Human feelings have likings and dislikings. Thus, award and punishment have a use. When award and punishment have a use, then order and prohibitions can be established, and the way of good government will ensue.[13]

Han Fei Tzu also summarizes the essence of the Legalist's *fa* in the following way:

In awarding, nothing is better than to make the award large and reliable, thus to make people who would receive it, profit from it; in punishing, nothing is better than to make the punishment heavy and necessary, and thus to make people fear it. Law is no better than being one and firm so that people will know it.[14]

In the above I have given a description and analysis of the essential ideas of the Legalists in terms of the major writings of Lord Shang and Han Fei Tzu. We must recognize that although the *fa-chia* has a tradition going back to Kuang Tzu (fl. 685-645 B.C.), and although Legalism has been attributed to other classical thinkers, such as Shen Pu Hai and Shen Tao, the ideas and political programs of Lord Shang and Han Fei Tzu need not be shared completely by Kuang Tzu or Shen Pu Hai. In the case of Kuang Tzu, it has been noted that although he also aims at achieving strength and wealth as goals of the government and promoting husbandry for this purpose, he does not suppress merchants and commerce, as did Lord Shang and Han Fei Tzu. Nor does he oppose the use of *li* and *yi* as principles of education and social behavior, again another point contrary to Lord Shang and Han Fei Tzu. In the case of Shen Pu Hai, what is emphasized is the art of the governmental technique of administration, not a positive code of punishment, nor is there any obsession with the power of the ruler.[15]

At this point we may query how the Legalist program and doctrine, as we have described them, were to be implemented, and what historical, social and political circumstances prompted their development and practice. One should also question how much contribution the Legalist program and doctrine has made to the history and society of China, and in what aspects Legalism has influenced later practice and ideas in Chinese history. It is not the purpose of this chapter to give answers to these questions. It suffices to say that Legalism arose because of the urgency of the time and because of the social, political and economic situation in the late Chou period, and that it has made great impact on the course of Chinese history, society, and government. But are we to conclude that Legalism is superior and more influential in value than other doctrines? Are we to say that other doctrines are mistaken or false because they did not prevail at that time? We have to respond to such questions of value in light of our understanding of humanity and its inspirations, both on an individual and a

320 Part II: Confucian Dimensions

social level. We have to see what forms the natural choice for man regarding his self-image and his outlook on values. Therefore, we have to judge Legalism not just on historical grounds, but also on comprehensive philosophical grounds, so that we will see both its utilitarian successfulness and its anti-humanistic weaknesses and limitations. We have to reveal the implications of Legalism for human society as well as the presuppositions underlying the program and doctrine of Legalism. In this way, we can give a fair and more accurate evaluation of the antagonism between Legalism and Confucianism. We shall therefore examine the Confucian philosophy, government and administration and see why Confucianism was advocated in Chinese history and how it is believed to be superior to Legalism, and how Legalism was eventually abrogated and Confucianism accepted as the general teaching.

The Political Philosophy of Confucius and Mencius and Its Grounding

The period referred to as Spring and Autumn (722-481 B.C.) can be said to be a period of Great Transformation. It is characterized by the erosion of the Chou central authority, the power struggle among all feudal states, the quick collapse of the older ethical economic order, and the wide-open search for values. It was a period when continuity was confronted with discontinuity, memory of the past with dreams of the future, ideal with reality, faith with knowledge, will with rationality, and self-interest with public mindedness. It is in this era that we see the opposition and antagonism between Confucianists and Legalists. Before we tackle the true nature of the relationship between the Legalists and the Confucianists and their antagonism, we must recognize that Confucianists developed their philosophy based on a perception and diagnosis of the society and its problems at a time which would be obviously different from that of the Legalists. The only way we can understand the Confucian philosophy with greater clarity is by carefully analyzing and considering the writings and views of Confucius and Mencius by themselves, without introducing any doctrinal presuppositions about their so-called class background or their political aims.[16]

In contrast to the Legalists, who proposed reform programs purely from the point of view of the state and ruler (a ruler-centric or state-centric point of view), Confucius wishes to reform the state and society from the humanistic point of view. By the humanistic point of view, I mean the point of view stressing the importance of individuals and the values of humanity over government and the interests of the state or its ruler. Nowhere does Confucius deny the significance of the role of the ruler. The message of his humanism is that the ruler is to be one who can see the importance of individual people and the values of society. Therefore he can make the effort and is in a position to carry out the government in accordance with the spirit of humanity. Thus it can be said that Confucius sees the government and state as a tool for realizing universal humanity, and that on this basis, the government can be said to be worth its existence and become acceptable by the people. Confucius calls for a government and a ruler who have the interest of the people as a whole in mind and the realization of the values of humanity as their goal; hence, a government and ruler of benevolence (*jên*). The doctrine of *jên*, as the doctrine of humanity (the inner and universal values of men as men), is the true foundation of government and society. It is by this that true order and harmony will ensue.

What is *jên*? According to Confucius, *jên* is to love people (*ai-jên*).[17] To love people presupposes recognizing individuality of self and other people. That individual men interacted and formed associations through their common humanity is a historical fact for Confucius. To love people is to treat man as an end, not as a means. It is to recognize universal humanity as a value and to realize and fulfill oneself in the process of loving other people. The following dialogue will make the Confucian doctrine of *jên* amply clear.

Tzu Kung asks: If someone can widely benefit people and can render help to the populace, how is this? Can he be called *jên*? The Master answers: he is not merely *jên*. He is already a sage. Even Yao and Shun are short of this. A person of *jên* is one who is wishing to establish oneself, makes effort to establish others and who is wishing to perfect himself and makes an effort to perfect others.[18]

It is clear that *jên* is to cultivate oneself and then extend cultivation to others, but to cultivate *jên* is to extend *jên* to others. *Jên* can be said then to consist in discovering the universal value in oneself and in recognizing universal humanity in others. It is to abolish selfishness, egocentricity, and eccentricity of the self. It is therefore a process of self-perfection and self-realization. It is formulated as the principle of not doing to others what one does not wish others to do to oneself. In combining the positive and negative formulations of the *jên* principle, we may call it the Principle of Reciprocity or as *Ta Hsueh* (The Great Learning) has called it, the Way of Measuring and Squaring (the *tao* of *chieh-chu*). That man can see relations as reciprocally related and can relate himself to others through reciprocity is not something distant to seek. It is inherent in man's nature: It takes mere reflection and attention to ascertain this. Thus Confucius says, "If I wish *jên*, *jên* is close at hand."[19]

Although Confucius considers *jên* as being basically rooted in the nature of individuals and as constituting the very basis for individual morality, *jên* is nevertheless for Confucius the starting point for good government and society. That *jên* is the foundation for good government and good society can be understood in at least three important ways: (1) If everyone in society practises *jên*, society naturally falls into order and government would be naturally well-maintained; (2) When the ruler practises *jên* he will care for all the people in the society, and he will make efforts to induce all people to practise *jên* and achieve a good government and society; (3) The practice of *jên* on the part of the ruler will produce and induce emulation of *jên* from all others. Thus in reply to Chi Kang Tzu's question on government, Confucius says: "If one wants to do good, people will be good. The virtue of the superior man is like the wind. The virtue of the small man is like the grass. The wind on the grass will bend the grass."[20] Thus to cultivate oneself, with respect to *jên*, is the beginning of good government. When Confucius speaks of cultivating oneself (*hsiu-chi*), he refers to cultivating oneself for developing and extending *jên*. One needs nothing but a sense of earnestness (*ching*) and sincerity (*ch'eng*) in order to cultivate oneself and discover one's *jên*. On the basis of self-cultivation, one would naturally lead or tread a path toward a good society and good government. Thus he advocates that the way of becoming a superior man (*chun-tzu*) is that of "cultivating oneself with the sense of reverence", followed by "cultivating oneself in order to pacify others" and "cultivating oneself in order to pacify all the people." To sum up, *jên* is the nature of what can be cultivated in oneself, and the process of self-cultivation is the basis for both ethical and political practice.[21]

On the basis of what we describe as the humanistic point of view of Confucius' conception of government, we can understand how all his suggestions for political reform and for social reintegration are different from the Legalists, in so far as Confucius believes that good government begins with the good individual and a good individual has the power and ability to be good.

The Confucian *jên*-oriented point of view is opposed to the Legalist ruler-centric point of view, which relies on power and control and which negates the worth of the individual man. We may say that the Confucian point of view is interioristic and the Legalist view is exterioristic. In so far as Confucianists believe that the individual man can achieve good government through his self-cultivation and extension of virtue to others, their view is inevitably opposed to the Legalists, who believe that the state and the ruler come in importance before individuals, and that it is necessary for the state to reform the individuals, but not necessary for the individuals to reform the state. We may call the Confucian view a realizational one and the Legalist view an impositional one. Finally, the Confucianists hold that universal humanism is the standard behavior and this can be discovered, extended and realized among all men. Also the Confucianist is opposed to the Legalist view that there is no universal objective value standard, but all values come from laws enacted after the will and the power interest of the ruler. This contrast, we may say, is that of natural law *versus* positive law. The Confucianist holds that human regulations must conform to and be based upon the natural laws of human nature and human reason and must be individually alterable and universally applicable, whereas the Legalist denies this and holds that human nature does not have a positive value content and human reason cannot make intrinsic distinction between good and bad, or between right and wrong.[22]

In order to bring out the full contrast between Confucianism and Legalism, we might point out that Confucius is not blind to the need for rules governing human behavior in society. However, these rules he would call *li* (rules of propriety), instead of *fa* (laws of punishment and reward). Although the existence of *li* has its historical and societal significances, we still would give a universal significance to the Confucian notion of the rule of *li* or the rule by *li*, independent of historical and societal contexts. *Li* may generally be described as an objectified principle, norm, or rule of human behavior resulting from consideration of *jên*. *Li* is rooted in *jên* and is a vehicle for fulfilling *jên* on a societal and governmental level. Thus *li* is also understood to be rooted in one's natural sense of reverence, and in one's natural consideration for order, harmony, and the peaceful and happy interrelationships of men in fulfilling their functions. *Li* is organizational and normative. It embodies the universal sentiments of humanity, but is intended to preserve the proper place of an individual person in society. In its ultimate sense, it may be identified with respect for the dignity of man in his intercourse with other men. Thus *li* is again interioristic, realizational, and humanistic. Of course, *li* can be particularistic, instead of universalistic, like the *fa* (law). This is because *li* pays more attention to the individuality of socialized humanity than simply to an individual independent of social context. In this sense, it should be said to be concretely universalistic, rather than abstractly universalistic like *fa*. With *li*, the ruler need not impose his will upon the people. With *li*, people will have become self-governing and self-confining, and thus form an interpersonal harmony. Hence, the effect of *li* on government is one of harmony coming of itself, rather than order imposed from outside. Yu Tzu says: "The use of *li* is such that harmony is valued in *li*. The way of ancient kings is thus elegant: All things small and large follow it."[23]

In this connection, it might be suggested that Confucius looks backward to history for examples of good government and appeals to traditional systems of values and practices for establishing a good government. Is he therefore backward-looking? Does he recognize the needs of the changing society of his time? The answer to both these questions is that although Confucius is conservative in his political ideal of reform, he is at the same time highly innovative. He is aware of social changes, but for him change does not mean giving up the universal and constant value underlying all human efforts. He considers the social change of his time as an occasion for discovering and affirming the universal value and constant truth of humanity. Thus he succeeds in giving a universal meaning to terms like *jên*, *te*, and so on. He may also be said to give a new and universal meaning to the concept of *li*. He recognizes that *li* has a cause and is subject to change and revision according to different times and needs. But he would insist that *li* has its universal content and significance and should not vary in that respect: *li* is the norm and value which guides society and expresses humanity. In this sense, even his conservatism can be said to be innovative. He wishes to stress cultural continuity in the course of social changes and alert his contemporaries to the danger that should cultural continuity be totally eliminated, there would be no "individual sense of identity." One good example showing Confucius' innovative thinking is that he recognizes Kuan Chung as a person of great *jên*, even though Kuan Chung acts in a way which is not exactly like a sage: Kuan Chung helps his ruler to achieve a state of supremacy of power in disregard of the central Chou Kingdom. However, he did this to forstall the oncoming political disorder and foreign invasion, and this is where his merit lies.[24]

When we come to Mencius, we can see that the humanism of Confucius and the Confucian political philosophy become even more definitely formulated and sharply defined. Mencius provides an explicit metaphysical-axiological foundation for the discovery, affirmation, cultivation, extension and practice of *jên*. As is well known, he holds that the innate nature of man is good, and he has attempted to show how this thesis can be established. Thus to Mencius, the goodness of man is not a mere desirable ideal but a plain fact of human existence. On this basis, he argues that good government strictly follows from a good ruler. A good ruler is one who rules by good example and uses goodness to edify people.

Mencius is even more explicit about the achievement of good government in the following respects: (1) He strictly and emphatically distinguishes between *yi* (righteousness) and *li* (profit), and rejects considerations of the latter as relevant for good government. In fact, he sees disorder as originating from considerations of profit, to the exclusion of considerations of *yi*.

Without going into detail on this very important point, we might say that Mencius regards *li* as representing the point of view of the interests of the ruler and *yi* as representing the point of view of the interest of people as a whole. Thus the distinction between *li* and *yi* is in fact a distinction between the ruler-centric stand and the people- or societal-centric stand. To be righteous (*yi*), a ruler will have to see things from the point of view of the likes and dislikes of the people, and in this sense *yi* is no doubt rooted in the sense of *jên* as Confucius advocated. Mencius singles out *yi* as a principle specifically related to actions affecting the welfare of others and the whole people. (2) Mencius is very explicit and emphatic about the Confucian need for education. Education is considered the basis for good government. It is needed not for control and manipulation on the part of government or the ruler, but for self-control and self-refinement on the part of the people. If a government does not educate its people, the government could not be said to provide adequately for the people. This shows the individual-humanistic essence of Mencius' political philosophy. (3) Although Mencius emphasizes *yi* as opposed to *li*, and education as opposed to control, he is not blind to social and economic programs which provide actual benefits and comforts to the people for stabilizing their life and enabling them to pursue higher goals in life. His famous dictum that "If there is no fixed property, there would be no fixed heart," reflects his vital concern with the economic basis of life. He even suggested a program of material sustenance and community care for the people. Thus he is pragmatic without being utilitarianan. This demonstrates a thorough humanistic and humanitarian spirit in his approaches to government. This also shows how Confucianism may embody institutional programs aside from the advocation of the observance of *li*.

Mencius may also appear conservative in upholding institutions of the past. But this must be understood in an idealistic sense. He appeals to them as examples or models rather than as absolute policies. Indeed, he is as innovative as Confucius in his humanistic view of government. Even more explicitly than Confucius, he holds that people are the most important things in a society, the next most important things are the institutions and rules of society and government, and finally the least important thing is the ruler. This point of view no doubt manifests clearly once and for all the humanistic-democratic concerns of Confucius' view of government, as opposed to the anti-humanistic and anti-democratic doctrine of the Legalists.[25]

Is Hsun Tzu a Confucianist?

In recent literature published on the Chinese mainland, Hsin Tzu has been described and titled a Legalist philosopher.[26] He is thus grouped with

Shang Yang and Han Fei Tzu in representing the Legalist tradition in contrast to the Confucianist tradition. Since Hsun Tzu was always known as a Confucianist (*ju*), and since he also regarded himself as such,[27] to label him and describe him as a Legalist, or attribute Legalist views to him on the grounds of his extant works, seems to be both unfair and misleading. There is no doubt about the fact that Hsun Tzu had taught both Han Fei and Li Ssu, the prime minister of the Chin State under the first Emperor; yet this is no reason why Hsun Tzu should be called Legalistic. On the contrary, it would be proper and natural to expect that Han Fei and Li Ssu had been under the influence of Hsun Tzu as a Confucianist. It is also true that Hsun Tzu holds the view that human nature is bad—a view which both Han Fei and Li Ssu accepted as a basis for their Legalistic theory of government and their proposal for social control. But this should hardly make Hzun Tzu a Legalist. His view of human nature only leads to stressing the importance of education, self-cultivation, and the adequate institution of moral encouragement and moral refinement in terms of *li* (properties). Thus we should ask: Do we really have a good reason to say that Hsun Tzu is a Legalist instead of a Confucianist? Does Hsun Tzu's idea of *li* suggest the meaning of *fa* of the Legalist? Did Hsun Tzu stress or argue for the Legalist *fa* at all in his writings? In the following I shall briefly discuss these questions and show that Hsun Tzu is beyond any question a Confucianist, and that consequently it is both a distortion and a mistake to call Hsu Tzu a Legalist. I shall appeal to the criteria I have established above for judging Confucianism as opposed to Legalism.

In the first place, Hsun Tzu advocates the importance of education and learning for individual persons in society. In his well-known essay, "Admonitions to Learning" (Chuan Hsueh) he suggests that education begins with reading the Confucian Classics, *The Book of Poetry*, *The Book of Documents*, and the *Record of Rites*. He wanted to see individual persons trained and refined as virtuous men attaining sagehood, again a Confucianist ideal. His doctrine that human nature is bad is an empirical doctrine based on his observations, like many other doctrines. This doctrine has been traditionally branded as anti-Confucianist because it is the opposite of Mencius' doctrine of the innate goodness of human nature, which was accepted as Confucianist. Whether a doctrine is Confucianistic or non-Confucianistic depends on both its motivation and logically drawn conclusion. For Hsun Tzu, his doctrine of human nature warrants him to advocate the importance of education and the cultivation of *li*. Both theses are Confucianistic in essence. Confucianists have good faith in man's perfectibility and Hsun Tzu never fails to show this good faith through his program for education and the cultivation of the self. He has even written a whole essay discussing the meaning and process of self-cultivation (*hsiu-sheng*), in which the Confucian method of self-reflection (*chih-shen*) *is well incorporated.*[28] Besides, Hsun Tzu believes in the social rectification of one's character and in man's innate capacity for understanding and reasoning. In both regards he sees man as capable of achieving a refined personal individuality and a well-ordered sense of social integration. His doctrine of human nature is also frequently misunderstood as a doctrine condemning man to a state of helplessness and total dependency on conditions external to him. This appears Legalistic and is comparable to Han Fei and Li Ssu's views regarding the fate of man. Actually, Hsün Tzu's doctrine amounts to no more than the statement that man's nature, if not guided and disciplined, will lead to actions which will be considered morally undesirable or socially unacceptable (namely, anti-social), from a societal point of view. This doctrine assumes that we need social norms and that we should develop and use them to shape the characters of men so that they will fit with social norms.

In the second place, Hsün Tzu's conception of *li* is not the Legalist conception of *fa*. In his essay on *li* he describes how *li* originates and on what basis it is founded.[29] He points out that *li* is intended to distinguish and separate what we can desire and seek from what we should not desire and seek, for the purpose of avoiding competition and war for what we desire and seek. Thus he describes *li* as an institution of social rules which serves to "nourish man's desires" and "satisfies man's demands," and thus to "enable desires not to exhaust things and things not to be bent by desires."[30] He simply calls the practice of *li* the art of nourishment (*yang*), and the institution of *li* the art of division (*feng*). We may say that *li*, for Hsun Tzu, are rules and rites, unified and introduced in society to regulate and coordinate human desires, in order to realize harmonious human relationships, better comforts and elegant order. *Li* is therefore to him vitally essential for the maintenance of order in society, as it is vitally essential for the survival of man as a whole. In this sense, *li* for Hsün Tzu is based on the consideration of life itself, an observation of the natural fact of heaven and earth, and a reverential attitude toward the ancestoral past and the teachings of sagely rulers, who initially devised *li* for social purposes.

In light of this understanding of *li*, Hsün Tzu is able to give a rational account of the rise of *li* as known to himself. In this regard, he is not opposed to seeking what is best in the ancient tradition, like Confucius and Mencius did. He further regards *li* as a means of self-cultivation and stresses the importance of *li* in the process of education. He says that "*li* is for rectifying one's person, the teacher is for rectifying the *li*."[31] (Hsiu Shen) He frequently uses *li* in conjunction with *yi* (righteousness) and *fa* (norm), such as *li-yi* and *li-fa*. The first use, of course, suggests his Confucian attitude. But does the second use suggest a Legalist connotation? The answer again is no. *Li-fa* is not law in the form of *li* or *li* in the form of *fa*. It is simply codes or norms of *li* since, for Hsun Tzu, *li* is not simply an internal sentiment and individual custom. It does have an objective status understood as fully regulative and normative dictum for interpersonal behavior. It is not *fa* in the same sense of codes of punishment and reward, as imposed on society from a self-righteous ruler. It is introduced through education inculcated through cultivation and reinforced through reasoning. It serves the purpose of refining the society and government through refining the individuals. Thus regarding the motivation, goals and conceived effects of *li*, *li* cannot be the same as the Legalist *fa*, since it suggests nothing in common with the Legalist *fa*.

Although Hsün Tzu has used the term "*fa*" throughout his writings, the dominant meaning of, and reference to, *fa* is codes of *li*, norms of behavior, or measures, methods and principles for governmental organization and institutions. *Fa* therefore is closely tied to the term measures (*tu*) and institutions (*chih*). Briefly speaking, *fa* is a system of *li* and principles which administer distributive justice and institutionalized norms for orderly social transactions. It may also be pointed out that *fa* is derived from *li* in its sense of reason. It is not an embodiment of the will of the ruler. Thus Hsün Tzu has this to say: "Regarding all things and actions, if they benefit reason (*li*), establish them; if they do not benefit reason, abolish them. This is called fitting with things."[32] In his celebrated essay on institutions of government, Hsun Tzu considered *li* and *yi* as two major values for organizing government.[33] However, he does propose that bureaucratic institution and administration are a matter of following norms called *fa*. He speaks of the "institution by the king" (*wang-che-chih-chih*) and the "law of the king" (*wang-che-chih-fa*).[34] But what he means by this has only to do with preserving old customs on the color of clothing, palace construction, funerals, utensils, music, the grading of taxation, the regulation of commerce etc. They belong to what we have referred as *fa* in the original primary sense, but not in the secondary sense as codes of punishment and reward, which was made primary by the Legalist, as I have already noted.

Hsün Tzu did use the word *hsing* (punishment) to refer to codes of punishment. He refered to *hsing* in the spirit of the Confucian understanding of *hsing*. He says: "The great divide of conducting government is to those who behave good, we treat with *li* and to those who do not behave good, we apply *hsing*."[35] He does not advocate the use of codes of punishment and reward in the place of *li* and *yi* but he does assign a proper place to the *hsing* in the institution of government (*cheng*). This is not only compatible with Confucianism, but is in fact a continuation of the ancient system with which Confucianism has shown affinity.

Finally, we must note that Hsun Tzu is not a utilitarian from the point of view of the state ruler, as a Legalist must be. On the contrary, he follows the Confucian distinction between *li* (profit) and *yi* (righteousness), and advocates the priority of the consideration of *yi* and *jên* over the consideration of *li*. He says that "The superior man is very short on seeking profit," and advises that one should act "When profit is little and righteousness is much."[36] To him, a superior man is precisely a person who can overcome his selfish interest and self-interest by thoughts of public good (*kung-yi*).[37] Thus a superior man will only follow *jên* and *yi*.[38] But regarding the state and society as a whole, Hsun Tzu shows a great interest in making the state and people rich. He thinks that the ruler should establish institutions in accordance with principles of *li* and *yi* and seek to increase the wealth of the people by not levying too heavy a tax, by controlling governmental expenses, and by not interfering with farming time. Though he cannot be said to enlarge on developing trade and commerce, he is for efficient flow of commodities and grains so that the people may have their needs met.[40] Although he talks of reducing the number of merchants,[41] he does not propose to suppress the merchant class like the Legalists did. His economic views and his endorsement of the policy for preserving the interests of peasants and the people at large is compatible with the Confucian and pre-Confucian theory and ideal of good government.

In the above, we have discussed major aspects of Hsun Tzu's philosophy of government. We find that there is very little one can identify as representing a Legalist position. What is important to notice is that the above analysis has demonstrated that the fundamental Confucian point of view is consistently presented and argued for in Hsun Tzu. Hsun Tzu's philosophy is humanistic, anti-utilitarian and represents the standpoint of the whole society of individuals, as opposed to that of the state and the ruler which seek their own interests and good. Hsun Tzu has shown good faith that society will be good when individuals are well-cultivated and educated, since society cannot be dictated to be good by the government. He does not deny ancient systems and denigrate ancient sage-kings. Although he agrees that we can adopt the measures of later kings and be inventive ourselves, he never intends to ignore the experiences and meritorious standards and practices of the ancient kings. His emphasis on *li* and *yi* reflects precisely such an attitude. That he is an internalist and or cultivationist (free-willist) with regard to the perfectibility of man goes beyond doubt. All these point to the obvious conclusion that Hsun Tzu is a great Confucian, and that he holds a view that is no less Confucianist than Mencius. It is simply a mistake to title Hsun Tzu a Legalist.

The True Nature of the Antagonism Between Legalism and Confucianism

It is not to be denied that Confucianism and Legalism are opposed to each other in both spirit and substance. They can even be said to be contradictory to each other. They both cannot be held to be true. With regard to the objectives of government, they both cannot be held to be false. Given this strong theoretical antagonism between them, and given the historical rivalry and hostility between the Confucianists and Legalists since the time of Confucius, we must recognize and understand why this antagonism, hostility and rivalry exist and how one comes to power at the expense of the other, as well as what variable circumstances enable one to defeat the other at different times.

If we look into the theoretical content of Legalism and Confucianism, we see that they embrace opposite points of view. The Confucianists are democracy-oriented, society-oriented, internalistic, individually-inclined, educationalistic, realizational, and developmental; whereas the Legalists are deterministic, dictatorship-orientated, ruler-oriented, manipulational, state-dominated, and externalistic. Their goals and objectives, based respectively on Confucianism and Legalism, would be totally different. They would have produced two totally different types of government, two types of society and two types of individual persons. They thus require two types of rulership. Therefore, we may regard these two systems of thoughts as two different models for the construction of government, society and the individual. There could be, of course, other models for government and society. For example, there could be the Taoistic and Mohistic models. We can order such models in a spectrum according to criteria of humanism (in the sense that the individual dignity of man and his development are respected as ultimate values) and humanitarianism (in the sense that the efforts of the government benefit the whole society *versus* some other external abstract entity). We can easily decide that the Confucian model of government is a thoroughly humanistic and thoroughly humanitarian model, whereas the Legalist model is a thoroughly anti-humanistic and thoroughly non-humanitarian model. They occupy two antipodes of the spectrum. We can, in fact, explain all the major differences between the Confucianist and the Legalist in terms of their assertion and denial of humanism and humanitarianism; that is the assertion and denial of humanity, individual self-fulfillment, and an internally harmonized society as ultimate values. Confucianism wishes to see man developed as a morally self-governed autonomous entity in society, to see society as an order based on mutual help and mutual respect among morally autonomous men, and to see the state ruler as a sagely man who devotes himself to the development of individual and society. The Legalist, on the contrary, wants the state ruler to adjudicate over individual and social values and subject them to a non-personal system of control for the purpose of satisfying an external objective, according to which both individual and society would evaluate values.

Now we face the question concerning on what ground the model of government and society is to be chosen. We want to know why one should choose the Confucianistic model instead of the Legalistic one, or vice-versa. The answer to this question begins with our opening our eyes to the facts of reason, then seeing what model best fits with our nature and potentiality as human beings. As human beings, we can reflect on our own experience and all the historical experiences of mankind in order to determine which model of government is of the most value and is most true to our nature. It seems obvious that Confucianism has provided a model which is based on universal humanity and appeals to both our mind and heart. It also seems obvious that as human beings we cannot deny that we hope for a government which is both humanistic and humanitarian; which recognizes individual potentialities for self-fulfillment, freedom and equality for such development; and which provides and guarantees the opportunity for the achievement of such values. If we recognize the Confucian model as a humanistic and humanitarian model, we must no doubt recognize Confucianism as the desirable and truthful basis for conducting a society and organizing a government. We must for the same reason reject Legalism as undesirable and untruthful to the long range goals of humanity, as it poses dangers for the humanistic and humanitarian causes of man.

It is true that human history has shown that sometimes the Legalist method of government succeeds in dominating a given society, whereas the Confucian model of government was defeated and even laid aside and castigated so that people would not learn of its existence. The temporary successfulness of a Legalist model is due to the exigencies of history, in which humanity has been lost sight of and individual men are subject to catastrophic disorder, extremities and chaos, such as constant war and poverty for which they are not prepared, and they have no time to develop a strength for reintegration and reorganization. This is precisely the case with the successfulness of the Ch'in, which unified China in 221 B.C. under the guidance of the Legalistic philosophy. The First Emperor thus founded the first Legalistic government on an anti-humanist and non-humanitarian basis. The Ch'in had successfully unified China and achieved many things of significant consequence for later history. But this does not exonerate Legalism from being a government which is harmful to humanity and the development of a humane society. That it did not last long shows that its existence is exigent, and merely fulfills a historical task without fulfilling the intrinsic and universal ends of humanity and society. It not only would not last when the exigent circumstances of history change, but also its legitimacy would be called into question in the face of the re-awakened awareness of humanity and the needs of society. History has spoken for itself. The quick transition from the Ch'in to the Han was a historical inevitability. In a very short period, the values of Confucianism as a guiding light for motivating government and directing governmental objectives were recognized and the Confucian philosophy and its model for government and society were adopted as official ideology.

It is interesting to note that when the Legalist criticizes the Confucianist, his criticisms are all based on exigency and thus lack universal validity. Thus in the *Book of Lord Shang*, we see criticisms of Confucianism to the effect that if the government permits the study of *li, yueh, shih* and *shu*, (the cultivation of goodness, filial piety and brotherly love, sincerity, truthfulness, personal integrity, benevolence, righteousness, anti-militarism, and non-agressionism), the government will be very much weakened in both wealth and the ability to fight a war. Shang Yang's criticisms are apparently based on his policy of promoting production inside and engaging in war outside. It is based on what is recognized as a particular need of his time. Yet this criticism fails to recognize the universal aspect of Confucian values and their usefulness and necessity for the survival of the human race and the development of humanity. Similarly, Han Fei makes the same type of arguments against Confucianism. These arguments are either question-begging or blind to the values of humanity and social development on a universalistic basis. On the other hand, when we turn around to see how the Confucianist criticizes the Legalist program or how he retorts to the Legalist arguments, we find that the Confucianist presents a view from a universalistic basis: a basis rooted in the recognition of the values of humanity and social development, independent of the exigencies of history and the specific needs of the time. Thus, Confucius criticized the Legalistic program as one which would make people escape from punishment, yet without the sense of shame.[42] Confucius suggests that if we guide people with virtue and govern them with propriety, people will have a sense of shame and will seek to arrive at good. Similarly, Mencius says of the Legalists: "They merely try to persuade people by force, it is not persuasion in heart."[43] Both the Confucian and Mencian point is revealing. The Legalist government may succeed in ordering society, but the consequent social order is imposed from outside, not ingrown within, and therefore will not last and will in fact collapse because it is against the inner wishes of the people. Hsun Tzu has also advanced a pertinent criticism of the Legalists. He says: "Shen Tzu (Shen Tao) is obsessed with law but does not know the usefulness of the sagely. Shen Tzu (Shen Pu Hai) is obsessed with power but does not know harmony."[44] This means that the Legalists are partial-minded and fail to see the totality of things.

On the whole, the Confucianists have a total view of history and society and see government under the universal form of humanity. They may be said to be idealistic, but it is a fact that we need idealistic visions and idealism; it is an integral part of humanity. To deny idealism is to deny an important part of humanity. The examination of the mutual criticisms between Confucianism and Legalism shows that the real antagonism between the two models of government is one between particularism and universalism, between the idealistic vision of the totality of man, nature and values, and the technique of mechanical control for a partial objective. To recapitulate, it is the antagonism between humanist and anti-humanist (nihilism), between humanitarianism and anti-humanitarianism. The Marxist explanation of this antagonism, based on class struggles, seems to obscure, distort, and prejudice the true nature of Confucianism.

Conclusion: Can Confucianistic Humanism Combine Science and the Rule of Law in the Modern World?

Since Confucianism has projected an ideal moral order in ancient times, and looks at innovations in present times with reservations, the question has been raised as to whether Confucianism may be compatible with a modern world in which scientific and technological inventions compete for acceptance, and novelty and progress are the catchwords. In view of what we have described as the essential doctrines of the Confucianist, there is no difficulty to give a reply. Confucianistic humanism is totally compatible with science and technology, and the Confucianists are in a good position to make the best use of science and technology. The important point about Confucianism is that it provides a point of view for reaching, and formulating a standard of evaluation, and a scale of priority for judging values relevant to man, society and government. This Confucian point of view is also one which harmorizes the objectivity of science and technology with the subjectivity of man. According to this view, science is for the betterment of man and society, and is to be developed for that purpose. Government is the agency which evaluates and sees to it that the humanistic ends of science and technology are always attained. Instead of letting science and technology deprive man of his humanity or endangering his potentiality for self-fulfillment, thus making man an object for scientific and technological exploitation, science and technology should be humanized for humanist and humanitarian uses. Science and technology are to create and release energy for man's use, not to subject man to its control and manipulation. The Confucian viewpoint guarantees a proper place for the development of scientific knowledge in the community of man.

It has been pointed out earlier that the Confucian model for government is society-oriented and inclines toward individual self-fulfillment. It takes the point of view of both individual and society, and recognizes that they are interdependent for their mutual development and perfection. Furthermore, it recognizes that the government and the ruler should make this mutual development their main goal. Is this point of view democratic or is it congenial with a democratic system as we understand it in the modern world? Again, the answer is positive. Although Confucianism has not evolved the specific mechanism for modern democratic government, it nevertheless would readily recognize democratic government as the most suitable form of government for optimal satisfaction of the humanistic and humanitarian ends of man. Even in the Confucian *Record of Rites*, the ideal of the Great Unity of the World (*shih-chieh-ta-t'ung*) is proclaimed as the ultimate goal of man. That this is possible is based on the very recognition that the government under heaven belongs to all men (*t'ien-hsia-wei-kung*).[45]

In light of the Confucian universalistic doctrine of human nature and the general principles of Confucian humanism and humanitarianism, we do not see any theoretical difficulty for introducing and embedding democratic institutions and apparatus into practice under a Confucian framework of human values. Similarly, we do not see any theoretical difficulty for introducing and embedding science and technology into the Confucian system of values, with its standards of evaluation.

In conclusion, one may ask whether the rule of law is compatible and congenial with Confucian ethics, and the humanistic faith and natural law background. To answer this question, we must keep in mind the distinction between *fa* (law) in the positive sense of codes of punishment and reward, and *fa* in the general sense of institutionalization of norms for social behavior and government. We see that Confucianists never question the importance of *fa* in the general sense. A government will not be organized and function without its structure of rules or organization. Similarly, a society will not be in order if there is no normative sanction and prohibition. But the Confucianist would insist that for introducing any organization in government and norm in society, one must understand that such an organization and norm will serve the general humanistic and humanitarian purposes. It should preserve man as a self-fulfilling individual and society as a network for preserving and fulfilling humanity. That is to say, fundamental human values must guide the legislation of norms and institutions or organizations. Ideally, these rules for structuring society and public behavior are self-regulated and internalized in the individuals in society through learning and education. In this sense they are called *li*. But insofar as the larger and basic human values are concerned, there is no difficulty for Confucianism to embrace the legislation of laws from a democratic and social point of view. If the rule of law in democracy is relevant to Confucian ends, laws can be seen as formalized *li* and a most generalized *li* in the traditional sense. The important questions to ask are whether the rule of law can live up to the humanistic and humanitarian ends of the government, and whether as a means for ordering society for humanistic and humanitarian ends, it is really humanistic and humanitarian. To answer these questions, a humanistic and humanitarian critique of the *law* and *government* must be constantly monitored.

To reinforce this positive posture of Confucianism, what needs to be pointed out are the following: (1) Confucianism is not without a law-like tradition. It recognizes the need for codes of criminal punishment; it opposes unjustified enlargement to regiment human behavior and deprive man of freedom and moral autonomy. That is why Confucianism is opposite and opposed to Legalism. It seeks to put law into proper use and within a humanistic framework. This has been shown in the long history of Chinese law since the Han dynasty, when the Confucianization of law was a process for humanizing law.[46] (2) The Confucian philosophy of government only deals with ultimate values and general principles. It does not intend to provide a system of technique or rigid legislation for the organization of government and society. It gives freedom to individual rulers to adopt flexible measures consistent with different circumstances. Although the Confucianist recognizes the relevance of flexible measures under specific circumstances (*chuan*), he nevertheless insists on the absolute, abiding by the general principles of humanity and justice. This means that according to the Confucian view, positive laws can be enacted, but they must be based on considerations of the natural laws of human nature. Recent discussions on the differences and integration between positive and natural law in jurisprudence make the Confucian view specifically relevant.[47] It can even be suggested that the Confucian view can provide the basis for such synthesis, as it can provide a basis of interacting rules of law with the morality of human values. (3) The Confucian view holds that good men and good laws (*fa*) are equally important, and the former is more important than the latter, for without the former, good law might be discarded and abused, while with the former, the latter will be introduced and made good use of. This point is highly instructive, for it reminds us that law in the positive sense is created by man for the purpose of serving man, and that man can always create law. This does not imply that man needs no law. In fact, this holds that a good man would create good law. What is good can no doubt be introduced and sanctioned by society. Not only are science and technology to be humanized, but law and legislation must also be humanized. Confucian humanism and humanitarianism provide a context and framework for such humanization, through which human values and the rule of law will remain not only compatible, but also will be integrated to achieve the ideal unity of the individual and society.

Notes

1. For reference materials of the Anti-Confucian campaign, see *Chinese Studies in Philosophy*, Vol. IV, Nos. 1-2, 1972-73; Vol. V, No. 3, 1974; Vol. IX, Nos. 3-4, 1978.
2. For elaboration of this view see Kuo mo-jo, *Chung-kuo-Ku-tai she-hui yen-chiu* (The Study of Ancient Chinese Society), Peking, 1964; and Lu Cheng-yu, *Yin-Chou Shin-tai te Chung-Kuo she-hui* (Chinese Society in the Yin-Chou Period), Peking, 1962.
3. All philosophical schools are historical in one sense and a-historical in another; in the a-historical sense they can be regulated as paradigms and models *for* the formation of human society and individual human consciousness. The study of the opposition of Confucianism and Legalism can be seen as a study of social models opposite to each other.
4. See discussion by H. G. Creel in his *Shen Pu Hai*, 1974, Chicago, 144 ff. For the concept of *fa* in Mohist logic, see my article, "On Implication (*tse*) and Inference (*ku*) in Chinese Grammar and Chinese Logic," *Journal of Chinese Philosophy*, 2, 1975, pp. 225-244.
5. See Hsi Tzu Shang, Chapter 11, *The Book of Changes* (translation by Richard Wilhelm, Princeton University Press, 1950), cf. p. 318.
6. See Hsu Shen, *Shuo wen chieh chih*, Peking 1963, p.202.
7. We shall answer these questions from a hermeneutical point of view, based on a synthetic interpretation of the basic texts of legalism such as *Han Fei Tzu* and *Shang Chun Shu*. A philosophical-textual analysis and study of these and other works of Legalism inclusive of Shen Tao and Shen Pu Hai, however, will reveal many different strains of thought under the general rubric of Legalism.
8. See *Shang Chun Shu (Book of Lord Shang)*, Kai Sei chapter.
9. Ibid., Shu Tse chapter.
10. Ibid., Hua Tse chapter.
11. Ibid., Nung Ch'an chapter.
12. Ibid., Shuan Ti chapter.
13. See *Han Fei Tzu*, Pa Ching chapter.
14. Ibid., Wu Tu chapter.

15. This has been made amply clear by H. G. Creel's work on *Shen Pu Hai*, University of Chicago, ibid., 135 ff.
16. The basic texts of Confucianism consists of the *Four Books*, the *Analects*, the *Mencius*, the *Great Learning* and the *Doctrine of the Mean*.
17. See the *Analects*, Chapter 12, Section 22.
18. Ibid., 6-30.
19. Ibid., 7-30.
20. Ibid., 12-19.
21. See on page 19.
22. This distinction is important for understanding the difference of grounding in Confucianism and Legalism.
23. See the *Analects*, 1-12.
24. Ibid., 14-17.
25. For more detailed study of Mencius, see my article "Warring States Confucianism and the Thought of Mencius," in *Chinese Studies in Philosophy*, Spring 1977, Vol. 8, No. 3, 4-66.
26. See, for example, T'ang Hsiao-wen, "Why is Hsun Tzu Called a Legalist?" in *Chinese Studies in Philosophy*, Fall 1976, Vol. 8, No. 1, 21-35.
27. For example, see the writings of Hsun Tzu, Tsu Hsiao chapter.
28. Cf. Antonio Cua's recent article, "Dimensions of *Li* (propriety): Reflections on an Aspect of Hsun Tzu's Ethics," *Philosophy East and West*, 29, No. 4, 1979.
29. See Ibid., Li-Lun.
30. Ibid., Li-Lun.
31. Ibid., Hsiu-shen essay.
32. Ibid., Ju Hsiao essay.
33. Ibid., Wang Chih essay.
34. Ibid., Wang Chih essay.
35. Ibid., Wang Chih essay.
36. Ibid., Hsiu Shen essay.
37. Ibid., Hsiu Shen essay.
38. Ibid., Pu Kou essay.
39. Ibid., Pu Kou essay.
40. Ibid., Wang Chih essay.
41. Ibid., Pu Kou essay.
42. See the *Analects*, 2-3.
43. See the *Mencius*, First Kung Sun Ch'ou chapter.
44. See *Hsun Tzu*, Chieh Pi chapter.
45. See *Li Chi*, Ta-Tung chapter and the chapter on the Great Learning.
46. Cf. Herbert Ma, "Law and Morality in Chinese Theory and Practice" and my commentary on Ma's paper, in *Philosophy East and West*, Vol. 21, No. 4, 1971.
47. See Ibid.

14. Confucius, Heidegger, and the Philosophy of the *I Ching*: On Mutual Interpretations of Ontologies

From Confucian *T'ien/Hsing* to Heideggerian *Sein/Dasein*

In the classical Confucian writings two important concepts have evolved in the understanding of the nature of humankind and its grounding. These two concepts, *hsing* (human nature) and *t'ien* (heaven), are not simply developed for understanding human nature and its grounding: they embody the understanding that *emerges* and is *concretized* in one's encounter with oneself and the world. Thus, they are not merely concepts but profound experiences of life that reveal and illuminate themselves. The opening statement of the *Chung Yung* (*The Doctrine of the Mean*), "What Heaven [*t'ien*] ordains [*ming*] is nature [*hsing*]," is particularly significant in this regard. The human nature is derived from Heaven, because heaven necessitates *being* human, and it is in the nature of Heaven that the nature of humans is necessitated, and hence the emergence and existence of human beings. Similarly, with the necessitation of the human nature, the nature of Heaven is also affirmed in necessity. One may note three important meanings here: (1) Although *hsing* is ordained (in the sense of necessitation and endowing) by Heaven, the coming into being of *hsing* is a natural flow from the inner nature of Heaven and therefore is a natural realization of Heaven that reveals the *nature* of Heaven. (2) *Hsing* and *t'ien*, being ontogenetically identical, are at the same time phenomenologically different in the sense of being differentially enriched and displayed. There is identity in difference and difference in identity. (3) The *ming* (ordaining/endowment) signifies both human activities and transhuman processes: both objectivity and subjectivity of being. In fact, it is through the subjective that the objective (as determinate world) reveals itself and through the objective that the subjective (as commanding agency) reveals itself. This mutuality between the objective and the subjective is an experience of interpenetration that also provides a basis for the understanding of the interpenetration between the transcendent and the immanent, and the outer (*wai*) and the inner (*nei*).¹

With the above understanding of *hsing* and *t'ien*, we have provided a context for understanding Heidegger's philosophy of *Dasein* (human being) and *Sein* (Being) and the theory of Being and Time implicit in this philosophy. At the end of *Being and Time*, Heidegger wrote:

Something like 'Being' has been disclosed in the understanding of Being which belongs to existent *Dasein* as a way in which it understands. Being has been disclosed in a preliminary way, though non-conceptually; and this makes it possible for *Dasein* as existent Being-in-the-world to comport itself towards entities—towards those which it encounters within-the-world as well as towards itself as existent. *How is this disclosive* understanding of Being at all possible for *Dasein*? Can this question be answered by going back to the primordial constitution of Being of the *Dasein* by which Being is understood?²

In this exceptionally suggestive passage, Heidegger establishes a relationship between Being and *Dasein* by way of *Dasein's* understanding of Being. The way *Dasein* understands Being is through *Dasein's* own natural experience and internal realization of itself, not through objective and external comprehension by reason. This is how non-conceptual disclosing of Being can be understood: Understanding is a matter of disclosing Being and disclosing of Being is a matter of Being itself. Therefore, understanding of Being by *Dasein* belongs to what Heidegger called *fundamental ontology* and not to epistemology. This disclosing of Being in *Dasein's* understanding of Being may be said to situate or orient *Dasein* in a world of beings or entities that are themselves not self-conscious *Dasein*. It reveals *Dasein* to the world and enables *Dasein* to be related to the beings in the world; this internal structure of *Dasein* shows the internal structure of Being as a totality related to *Dasein*.

All these Heideggerian points, perhaps, can be understood better in reference to the two Confucian concepts of *hsing* and *t'ien* and their relationships. If we see Being as basically identical to *t'ien* with all its hidden virtues and powers, and if we see *Dasein* as identical to the *hsing* (nature), which makes human existence possible, then the *relationship* between Being and *Dasein* should be the relationship between *t'ien* and *hsing*. This relationship is clearly demonstrated in the statement of the *Chung Yung*: "What *t'ien* ordains is *hsing*." This is an ontological understanding of the being of *t'ien* by the being of *hsing*, which truly implies a self-understanding of *hsing* itself. In Heidegger's terms: *Dasein* as *hsing* discloses Being as *t'ien* in understanding the ordering or necessitating of *hsing* by *t'ien*. This understanding, which is a form of the self-understanding of *Dasein*, provides a ground for the existence of *hsing* in the being of *t'ien* by disclosing both *t'ien* and its activity of giving or ordering. All these points have ontological significance because they bear upon the disclosure of Being in the sense of the ultimate reality. They also mutually imply each other, for the being of one leads to the being of the other. The mutual ontological implication between *t'ien* and *hsing* is obvious.[3] A logical consequence of this mutual implication is that what is revealed and experienced in *Dasein* bears on the experience of Being and vice versa. That is, *hsing* bespeaks *t'ien* just as *t'ien* bespeaks *hsing*, as is made quite clear in the writings of the *Chung Yung* and the *Mencius*.

Before we make use of the above *t'ien-hsing* relationship as a paradigm for understanding the relationship between Being and *Dasein* and between Being and time in terms of the philosophy of the *I Ching*, we can make the following two observations for the purpose of clarifying the methodology of interpretation presupposed in our interpretation of Heidegger in light of the Confucian writings. First, although we treat *t'ien* in Confucianism as equivalent to Being in Heidegger, we do not assume that they are identical in semantic meaning. What justifies our equation is their intended meaning of the fundamental reality and the ultimate ground that makes all statements possible and meaningful. In terms of this intended meaning, *t'ien* in its primordial Confucian context discloses the same "thing" as the term *Being* in its Heideggerian context.[4] One should also beware that there is a dialectical development and unfolding of the intended meaning of the *t'ien* in the history of Chinese philosophy. As I have noted elsewhere,[5] the ancient concept *t'ien* is further enriched and complemented with other philosophical concepts such as *tao* (the Way) in Taoist philosophy, *t'ai-chi* (the Great Ultimate) in the *I Ching*, and *li* (principle) or *ch'i* (vital energy) in Neo-Confucian philosophy. The dialectical evolution of these concepts is such that each reinterprets and redefines the other, and thus assimilates the other as part-meanings of a whole-meaning. This meaning-absorption process of dialectical evolution is an everdeepening and everwidening process for understanding Being, because it relates more deeply and widely to experience of Being.[6] During this process the intended meaning of Being in the fundamental and ultimate sense remains not only unchanged but reaffirmed. Thus in the same spirit in which we speak of Being in terms of the *t'ien*, we can speak of Being in terms of the *tao*, the *t'ai-chi*, and the *li*. Because these expressions do not exclude each other, we can see them as possible ways of revealing and disclosing Being.[7]

Second, Heidegger characterizes humanity as *Dasein*, [8] as an entity that "[I]n its very Being, that Being is an issue for it."[9] This suggests that humankind is unique in being ontologically related to Being in such a unique way that one discloses Being in understanding Being. Although one has an understanding of Being, it does not mean that humankind has *fully* understood itself in Being. As Heidegger says, "*Dasein* always understands itself in terms of its existence—in terms of a possibility of itself: to be itself or not itself."[10] Only the particular individual can decide his or her existence and no matter what is decided, that existence shows the state of Being constituting its existence.[11] That one faces death—the end of being, that one cares and has anxiety (*Angst*) about it, that one's existence is essentially futural, are some important determining features of *Dasein*.

In Confucian philosophy, human existentiality is perceived as a matter of self-affirmation and self-cultivation on behalf of the individual: One has to recognize one's own unique being, which is expressed by affirmation of the value and worth one is capable of achieving and aspires to achieve. Thus, Mencius says: "How little does man differ from birds and beasts! Common people remove the difference, but the superior man preserves it!"[12] He also says: "Man cannot be without a sense of shame. If one is shamed by having no sense of shame, he is truly shameless."[13] He further says: "All things are complete in me. If I reflect upon this self and be truly myself, there is no greater joy than that."[14] That one individual is existentially different from other things is evident from these passages. Although the Confucians do not explicitly speak of existentiality, they are no doubt very much concerned with marking out the individual existentially, if we see existentiality as a matter of self-understanding, understanding of self in relation to other things and the ultimate reality such as Heaven and the *tao*. The existential basis for one's unique being is one's ability to see and understand oneself as different from all other things and one's ability to decide and insist on this difference in his thinking and action.

The Difference between Heidegger and Confucius: The Existentiality of *Hsing-Ming*

At this juncture we may point out a fundamental difference between the approaches to human existentiality of Heidegger and the Confucians. Whereas Heidegger wishes to stress the existential tension of human existence in terms of anxiety in the face of death, nothingness and the finitude of being, the Confucianists wishes to call attention to the human potentiality for self-cultivation (not only self-understanding) into a sagely being. This stems from Confucius's view that one can desire virtues such as *jên* and that whenever and wherever one desires so will one attain it. Mencius expounds an even stronger claim of goodness in human nature (*hsing*) that, when cultivated and acted upon, will lead the person to a state of perfection of virtues (*jên, yi, li, chih, hsing*). For both Confucius and Mencius the perfection of virtues is an existential state of perfection of Being or a state of Being where the perfection of Being is disclosed. Virtues are simply means to insist on a state of Being and to reach a perfect state of Being. For expressing this essential nature and capacity of man, the expression *hsing* is firmly established. *Hsing* therefore is the essence of human existence that gives rise to one's existentiality and possibilities of one's self-cultivation and self-transformation. For this reason we see *hsing* as capturing the same intended meaning of *Dasein* in identifying human existence, even though the extensional reference in characterizing *Dasein* is different. The term *hsing* becomes thoroughly entrenched and developed in classical Confucianism through the *Four Books*, the *Li Chih* and the *Hsun Tzu*.

Although we remarked on the difference of approach between Heidegger and the Confucians, there is still no reason to differentiate between the two in view of a total consideration of their intended references. The being of *Dasein* is not simply revealed in existential tensions of *Dasein*, but also experienced as Being of Being, that is, as in one's effort to perfect oneself and in one's reflection on the ground of Being. As we shall see, even the temporality of the future experienced by *Dasein*, which gives ontological meaning to care, is not simply a revelation of the being of *Dasein* but defines the being of the underlying and comprehensive Being and, in this sense, gives rise to time. In his later works, Heidegger seems to move from the concern of temporality within the self to a display of the relationship of time and Being that absorb and appropriate each other, and that both absorb and appropriate *Dasein* and therefore ontologically reconstitute *Dasein*. This is a very positive grounding of *Dasein* in Being. Heidegger wrote (*Identity and Difference*, 1957):

[But] man's distinctive feature lies in this, that he, as the being who thinks, is open to Being, and so answers to it. Man is essentially this relationship of responding to Being, and he is only this. This 'only' does not mean a limitation, but rather an excess. A belonging to Being prevails within man, a belonging which listens to Being because it is appropriated to Being.[15]

That man *(Dasein)* and Being are appropriated to each other and belong to each other corresponds to what Confucian philosophy affirms and realizes.

In Confucian philosophy human existence (*jên-sheng*) is not only a matter of nature (*hsing*); there is also the consideration of *ming* (determination). If we regard *hsing* as a definition of human existence in its active aspect, we can regard *ming* as a definition of human existence in its passive aspect. *Ming* is the natural yet determined or determinate development of things that are not willed nor controllable or changeable by an individual person: something the person alone can do nothing about. In contrast, *hsing* is something that the person can do something about, can develop and cultivate according to his or her will and effort. Thus Mencius said of *hsing* that one must nourish one's *hsing*: "If one can fulfill one's mind, then he knows his nature *(hsing)*. Once knowing one's nature one knows Heaven. Preserve one's mind and nourish one's nature; this is the way to serve Heaven."[16] *Hsing* is natural to and inherent in human existence, and one can know it and develop it by fulfilling one's mind, which is considered a matter of self-mastery and self-discipline. Mencius also considered *hsing* good: To know and develop one's nature is to develop and fulfill goodness in oneself and thus open oneself to Heaven. If we identify Heaven with Being as suggested earlier, then it is clear that nature is the natural avenue for *Dasein* to reach Being. A Being-reaching life is authentic, which means that a Being-cultivated life that defines what the good life is is the essence of authentic life. To be good is the Mencian paradigm for being authentic, and is possible only through the presence of *hsing* in human existence. On the other hand, *ming* therefore is not necessarily bad, as it is also natural and indigenous to human existence. It is that part of human existence that is not subject to self-fulfillment *(chin)* or explicit knowing *(chih)*. It is exhibited in the limitations and finitude that one suffers in life.

As *ming* is something inherently natural to human existence, it is inevitable and necessitating. Thus Mencius says: "What one cannot reach and yet arrives at [despite oneself] is *ming*."[17] Yet *ming* shares with *t'ien* the same uncontrollability: "What one cannot achieve and yet becomes achieved is Heaven."[18] The difference between *ming* and *t'ien* is that *ming* limits the individual being, whereas *t'ien* generates and cherishes the individual being. From a fundamental ontological point of view, *ming* is *t'ien* and *t'ien* is *ming*: They belong to each other. Therefore, we can speak of the Mandate of Heaven *(t'ien-ming)*. *T'ien* also exhibits its power through *ming* even in generating and ordering things. Thus we have the *Chung Yung* statement, "What Heaven ordains (or mandates) is nature." This also means that what Heaven mandates in terms of value and its specification is nature. But as *ming* also belongs to *t'ien*, both what comes naturally and what is mandated are also *ming* in terms of limitation and receptivity of Being. This means that there is *ming* in *hsing* and there is *hsing* in *ming*, depending on what and how one sees and evaluates an individual as Mencius has already recognized.[19] The relationship between *t'ien* and *ming*, on the one hand,

and the relationship between *ming* and *hsing*, on the other, therefore can be expressed thus: *T'ien* gives rise to both *ming* and *hsing*, which both define an individual being. Both *ming* and *hsing* interpenetrate in the individual Being, represent and fulfill different functions of being human: *Hsing* is able to fulfill the individual in terms of reaching the identification with *t'ien*, whereas *ming* is able to fulfill the individual in terms of interaction with other individual things. The former represents a vertical dimension (or movement) of the Being of the individual, whereas the latter represents a horizontal dimension. The former transcends time; the latter is determined by time.

$$t'ien \left\{ \begin{array}{c} hsing \\ \\ ming \end{array} \right\} \quad j\hat{e}n \ (Dasein) \quad \left\{ \begin{array}{l} hsing\text{: Being (identification)} \\ \\ ming\text{: time (determination)} \end{array} \right.$$

The *ming*-dimension in human existence is also well illustrated in Confucius' *Analects*: "There is *ming* in the life and death of a person."[20] In reference to the early death of his disciple, Yen Hui, Confucius laments that this is a matter of *ming* and exhibits a sense of regret and yet a recognition of the inevitability of the event.[21] Because *ming* is an aspect of the being of a person, one should acknowledge its presence and be prepared for its impact. Thus, Confucius said: "If a person does not know *ming*, he cannot be a superior man."[22] As this *ming* is originally derived from *t'ien*, he marks out the maturity of being fifty as consisting in knowing *t'ien-ming*.[23] As to how to orient or position oneself toward *ming* once it is recognized and acknowledged, Confucius counseled: "[give] oneself to *ming* and *jên* (the virtue of benevolence)."[24] To give "oneself to *ming*" of course is not simply following *ming*, but whenever confronting events beyond one's control to take them in stride and not lose heart, nor stop pursuing the fulfillment of one's virtue. *Ming* is not a deterrent to one's virtue, but sometimes is even an occasion for fulfilling one's nature, because *ming* is the *ming* of life, and thus life itself seen as given is *ming*. Life is *ming* from the *ming* point of view. Life is *hsing* from the *hsing* point of view. Thus, Confucius considered "offering one's life at the critical moment of danger" as one of the three conditions for being an accomplished man (*ch'eng-jên*).[25] Whereas Confucius spoke of "being in danger and offering one's life,"[26] Mencius spoke of "establishing one's *ming*" (*li-ming*) in the sense of making oneself ready for accepting what takes place uncontrollably without a sense of loss. Thus he said: "To have a short life or a long life does not make one doubt about one's duty to cultivate one's nature. One should cultivate oneself to wait for whatever will happen. This is whereby one establishes one's *ming*.[27] To establish one's *ming*, one has to do one's best to avoid what is undesirable and fulfill what is desirable. One who succeeds in doing this is also said to "follow the *ming* in the right way" (*cheng-ming*) or to "smoothly receive the *ming* in the right way" (*shun-shou-ch'i-cheng*). Thus Mencius said: "Nothing in life is not *ming*, but one needs to receive it and receive it in the right way. Thus those who know the *ming* do not stand beneath a dangerous cliff-wall. Those who died with their way fulfilled can be said to follow *ming* in the right way. Those who died in chains are not following *ming* in the right way."[28] From this one can also see how *ming* itself is related to a positive and active attitude of life, which would be an exhibition of the nature of a person.

A Confucian Interpretation of *Dasein*

With Confucian observations on the *hsing* and *ming* of individual human beings in mind, we can now see how *Dasein* can be analyzed in terms of them. When *Dasein* is said to belong to and disclose Being, *Dasein* is the being of *hsing* and therefore can be identified with *hsing*, as we have done. But when Heidegger described *Dasein*'s Being as care and as distinctively disclosed in the state of anxiety,[29] he pointed out a certain state of mind a person experiences when facing the limitation of one's being; that is, one's *ming*. In this sense the existential analysis of *Dasein* in terms of anxiety, care and the certain possibility of death corresponds to our Confucian analysis of *ming*. What distinguishes Heidegger from the Confucian view of *ming* is that the former yields both a subjective-internal-existential representation of *ming* and an objective-external-existential characterization of *ming*: anxiety and care represent the subjective-internal-existential aspect of *ming* as experienced by a person, whereas the certain possibility of death (i.e., "the possibility of the impossibility of existence"[30]) obviously reveals the objective-external-existential aspect of *ming* that the Confucianists also recognized. Confucianists, however, did not lose sight of the existential-internal-subjective experience of a person, which involves the consideration of mind. In Mencius, a warning against a *lapse* from the right mind into the wrong *mind* through losing one's *mind* (*fung-hsin*), of course, corresponds to Heidegger's idea of *falling* (*verfallen*).[31] *Falling* makes the individual existence inauthentic. Hence, we can allow *ming* to be more structured in terms of Heidegger's analysis of care, falling, and thrownness. Heidegger himself said: "The Being of that disclosedness is constituted by states of mind, understanding and discourse";[32] we therefore can interpret *Dasein*'s being in terms of the Confucian *ming*. Thus, strictly speaking, *Dasein* should be the being of *ming-hsing* in combination, not *hsing* alone.

Given this above interpretation of the *Dasein-Sein* relation in terms of Confucian philosophy, we are able to see one most important consequence. The being of a human person embodies the Being of the ultimate reality to the fullest extent. When a person is able to do this—of course, it is ontologically within one's power to do so—and as far as one is capable of sustaining this vision and effort, one is an authentic person and leads an authentic life: All one experiences reveals and discloses the Being of the ultimate reality. Ontologically we have to see that, with the authenticity of a human person sustained, the human person realizes Being. What the human person has intimately and deeply experienced in his or her subjectivity has manifested objective significance. This subjectivity is a vehicle for realizing the objective in the sense that whatever one naturally and truthfully experiences bears upon and manifests a universal necessary aspect of Being, the value and significance of which is bestowed by Being just as whatever reality the human person possesses is bestowed by Being.

Authentic *Dasein* in Heidegger is the ontological-existential state of Being of *Dasein* that sustains its self-identity, ends-in-view, uniqueness, subject-nature and potentiality for development (potentiality-for-Being-in-the-world) without falling into the commonplace order of things and objects that are instrumental and tool-like (things *ready-to-hand, das Zuhandene*) or things or objects that are made subject to investigation and manipulation of science and technology (things *present-at-hand, das Vorhandene*). In other words, authenticity should lead to an everfresh realization and disclosure of Being and not to its hiding and covering up. In this sense, authenticity is much the same as the *ch'eng* (sincerity or authenticity) in the *Chung Yung*:

The "substance of *ch'eng* (*ch'eng-che*) is the Way of Heaven. To realize and substantiate the Way of Heaven (*ch'eng-chih-che*) is the Way of Man. The substance of *ch'eng* is such that equilibrium of Being is reached and maintained without effort and without thinking. A person who can accord with the Way without effort and thinking is the Sage. To realize the Way consists in choosing the good and persisting in following the good.

It is apparent that the "substance of *ch'eng*" (*ch'eng-che*) is Being in its full realization; it is the ideal for *Dasein* to realize. *Dasein* has the potentiality for this realization and therefore is *ch'eng-chih-che*; that is, one can authenticate one's being and keep authenticating one's being if one chooses to do so. To do this is to do good. Good is to realize Being (the Way of Heaven) without being led astray. One also has to exercise one's will and persist in the realization of Being. This means that one will have to face tension and temptation. This state of facing the tension and temptation is best described as the state of *care*. It is interesting to note that for Heidegger the Being of *Dasein* in its assertion of its self against falling and being objectified in things ready-to-hand and/or present-to-hand is founded upon care: Care is in this sense the essence of *Dasein*'s being. Heidegger said: "The entire stock of what lies therein may be counted up formally and recorded: anxiousness as a state of mind is a way of being-in-the-world."[33]

The *Chung Yung* makes it clear that when one makes an effort to authenticate (*ch'eng*) oneself, one is able to realize the Way of Heaven to its fullest extent.

Only the authentic person is capable of realizing his nature, he is able to realize the nature of others; once realizing the nature of others, he is able to realize the nature of things; once realizing the nature of things, he is able to support the function and process of transformation and growth of Heaven and Earth. Once being able to support the function and process of transformation and growth of Heaven and Earth, he is able to participate in the creative works of Heaven and Earth together with Heaven and Earth.

If we translate this view into Heideggerian language, we can see that *Dasein* is able to disclose and realize the being of all people and things, and finally fulfill and disclose Being itself. From this we see the importance of the dialectical link from understanding of Being and reality to understanding the being of *Dasein* and vice versa.

In the final paragraph of *Being and Time*, after saying that Being has been disclosed in the understanding of Being in *Dasein*, Heidegger posed the following questions: "*How is this disclosive understanding of Being at all possible for Dasein?* Can this question be answered by going back to the *primordial constitution-of-Being* of that *Dasein* by which Being is understood?"[34] It is clear from the preceding interpretation of the Heideggerian notion of *Dasein* in a Confucian hermeneutic that *Dasein* as human person discloses Being, which is that person's ground and source, by coming to understanding oneself, and at the same time understanding its ontological reality by disclosing this very ontological reality.

To disclose one's ontological reality is to realize one's own authentic being. Heidegger is correct in suggesting that we go back to the primordial constitution of Being of *Dasein* for such ontological understanding. The doctrine of *hsing* in relation to *t'ien* and the doctrine of *ch'eng* in relation to *hsing* make this amply clear. However, we can go a step further in the understanding and disclosing of Being in developing a deeper insight into *Dasein*. Heidegger has provided such deeper insight through his existential-ontological analysis of *Dasein* in terms of care and temporality, whereas the Confucian philosophy of the *I Ching* provides a deeper insight into the nature of Being in terms of creativity (*sheng*) and transformation (*hua*), which constitute the fundamental meaning of change (*i*).

The preceding discussion has established the principle that whatever is revealed and realized in the nature of a person reveals and realizes the nature of Being, and thus the principle that the subjectivity of the self dialectically fulfills the objectivity of the world through the fulfillment of the primordial unity of the two by way of the *ch'eng*-realization of the human person. Therefore, it is both natural and logical to see that the analysis of *Dasein* in terms of care and temporality discloses primordial modes of Being in terms of creativity and transformation. An integration of the Heideggerian philosophy of *Dasein* and the Confucian philosophy of the human person makes this result possible. Or we put this in a reverse way: This result makes the integration of the Heideggerian philosophy of *Dasein* and the Confucian philosophy of human person possible. This illustrates what elsewhere I have called an *ontohermeneutical circle of understanding.*[35]

As noted earlier, Heidegger described *Dasein* as an "entity for which, in its being, that being is an issue."[36] By this he means that *Dasein* understands (or realizes its own being in understanding) itself as "self-projective being towards its own most potentiality-for-Being.[37] This suggests that *Dasein* is *oriented* toward realizing its potential nature and is living or thinking in a mode that goes beyond its present existential state of Being.[38] Heidegger focused on this "beyond-itself-ness" and called it *Dasein's* "Being-ahead-of-itself," which, in close analysis, means "ahead-of-itself-in-already-being-in-a-world."[39] This is significant because *Dasein* is found in a situation of dual nature: It is already in the world and yet it inclines itself to go beyond this state of being-in-the-world.[40]

Being in the world as a state of thrownness (*Geworfenheit*) into existence (into the "there") already suggests the falling of *Dasein*, on the one hand, and the necessity to deal with things and objects in the world, on the other: This is the reason why *Dasein* is concerned with dealing with things ready-to-hand within the world (called by Heidegger *being-alongside*). Falling also means falling into inauthentic living or amongst things ready-to-hand or present-to-hand. Care suggests concern, anxiety, and solicitude; but basically care is *Dasein's* attitude toward itself within the world because of the facticity of falling and because of the possibility of further falling by losing the authenticity of being. Therefore, care is an ontological expression for both *Dasein's* desire to realize itself and its desire to avoid losing itself by falling. The ontological structure of care in this sense is indeed "ahead-of-itself-in-already-being-in-the-world."

By comparison, Confucian thinking also exhibits this aspect of Being (*sein*) in the thinking and living of a human person. Confucius said: "The superior man cares about (*yu*) the realization of the *tao*, but does not care about (*yu*) the happening of poverty."[41] I translate the Chinese word *yu* as care instead of worry or anxiety because I want to stress the existential-ontological significance of *yu*. To care about the realization of the *tao* is precisely to care about realizing the potentiality-of-being in a world of objects and utility. It is care about one's nature and one's efforts in realizing its fundamental being. Of course, Confucian philosophy does not treat the being of a human person as a falling or thrownness (*Geworfenheit*). As made clear in the very beginning, human nature is *t'ien*-endowed, and thus is a fulfillment of Being instead of a falling from Being. Furthermore, a human person can further fulfill himself or herself by developing and realizing Being. This is the aspect of creativity latent in Heidegger's philosophy, but made explicit in Confucius and the *I Ching*. Confucius said: "Man can enlarge the Way, not the Way enlarging man."[42]

By upholding and expanding his doctrine of *jên* that reveals the purity and authenticity of *hsing* and its being-toward-potentiality-of-being, Confucius furthermore is able to alleviate and remove *yu* in one's *Being*. Thus, he said: "The man of *jên* does not have care."[43] In fact all virtues are ways for maintaining the authenticity of Being and uplifting the self from temptations of the world of things and objects. The superior man therefore is not a "thing ready-to-hand" nor a "thing present-to-hand."[44] *Yu* in the sense of care is a highly creative force within the being of the human person. It is a disclosure of the creative force in *Dasein* in its ability to drive the human person moving *forward* and *upward* to realize the Being of Heaven or the Way.

Care or *Yu-huan* and Temporality or Time

In the Confucian *Great Appendix (Hsi Tzu)* of the *I Ching*, it is said that "The rise of the *I*-thinking, does it take place in the middle ancient time? The author of the *I*-thinking, does he have misgivings (*yu-huan*)?"[45] Here the term *yu-huan* is used to indicate the profound care the author of the *I*[46] experienced about the disintegration of humanity and the social-political order. The *middle ancient time* refers to the latter period of the Hsia-Shang Dynasties, where disorder, violence, and cruelty to humanity reigned (a state indeed representing a fall, according to Chu Hsi). Therefore, the *yu-huan* (the profound care) the authors of the *I Ching* experienced centered on the meaning and purpose of Being of *Dasein* for both the individual and the human community. It carried an ontological-existential significance. With *yu-huan* thus explained, the creative function of *yu-huan* as care is also clear.

Because of this *yu-huan*, the authors of the *I Ching* could reflect on the deep meaning of Being and human existence and therefore construct the system of the *I*, which, under this interpretation, is a natural disclosure and revelation of the Ways of Being. The very existence of *yu-huan* as care also gives us insight into the development of the *I Ching* as fundamentally ontological and existential. The popular conception of the *I Ching* as only a book of divination mispresents its true nature as a disclosure of Being in the Heideggerian sense. In fact, it took Confucius and his school of the sixth to fifth century B.C. to discover and reveal the *yu-huan* basis of the formation of the *I Ching*. They were able to do so precisely because they experienced the same profound *yu-huan*. However, to stress the ontological-existential nature of the *I*-system is not to deny or diminish its usefulness. It is simply to point out that the ontological disclosure of Being in the *I Ching* should not be hidden by the practical usefulness of the book. To realize the *aletheia* of the ontological Being of the *I Ching*, we have to see the *I Ching* as derived from and based on the *yu-huan* experience of *Dasein*'s being-in-the-world, which reveals not only the self of the human person in terms of care, but, even more profoundly, the essence of care in terms of temporality and time. This leads us to Heidegger's existential analytic of *Dasein* again.

It is significant to note that for Heidegger time comes from temporality and temporality comes from the authentic existence of *Dasein*. This means that the authentic existence of *Dasein* has a rich structure that makes temporal experience possible. But the basis of this temporal experience by *Dasein* is *Dasein* itself. It is the same basis for care and for what Heidegger called the self-constancy and totality of *Dasein*. In a certain sense, to understand *Dasein* is to understand this basis of *Dasein*. As we will note later, this basis of *Dasein* is Being *(Sein)* in the fundamental ontological sense. Hence, to understand time and temporality is to understand *Dasein* in its fundamental structure, which discloses Being, and therefore to understand Being itself. Yet the thesis that temporality comes from *Dasein* is still significant because it underlines the fact that time in its most intimate sense is the temporality of the human self: Time is not an abstract entity independent of existence of events and things.[47] The most subtle and elaborate being among all things concerns human existence, and therefore human existence reveals the most vivid and most subtle elements of time. Heidegger's use of the term *temporality* seems to suggest this point: There is no time without temporality and no temporality without *Dasein*. Time therefore is temporality revealed in the structure of Dasein.

In *Being and Time* Heidegger treated *time* as resulting from the falling and consequent the inauthenticity of *Dasein* and, therefore, with reference to everyday things and objects. However, I will use time in its fundamental ontological sense, which denotes the basis of temporality of *Dasein* as revealed by the structure of *Dasein*. This ontological sense of time became evident to Heidegger himself in his later work, *On Time and Being*.[48]

In the following text, I wish to show that Heidegger's analysis of temporality as the ontological meaning of care bespeaks an important theme in the philosophy of the *I Ching*—understanding change and temporality is the deepest concern of the authentic ideal man referred to as the Sage. Whereas the *I Ching* focuses on the change (*I*) as the fundamental-ontological reality in a universal and totalistic sense, Heidegger provided an insight into this reality under the form of self and subjectivity. The *I Ching* does not directly address the subjective care in temporality, yet in its concern with practical states of well-being or ill-being the care element is also presented. Similarly, in *Being and Time* the fundamental being of time is not directly addressed. Yet, as the last paragraph of that work shows, there already is an awakening to the fundamental ontology of time as the horizon of Being, which is discussed in the later book, *On Time and Being*. In this sense the *I Ching* philosophy of time as change and transformation greatly anticipates the later Heidegger's understanding of time and Being and their relationships, and thus provides a forum for the further development of Heidegger's philosophy of time and Being in the contemporary West. This, of course, is not to say that Heidegger's analysis of temporality as the care of *Dasein*'s mode of experience serves no useful purpose. It sheds great light on the reason and ontological meaning of practicality in one's concern with divination in the philosophy of the *I Ching*.

The subjective structure of *Dasein* lies in the care of *Dasein* that results from sustaining the authenticity of its disclosing Being in confronting the possibility of falling into inauthenticity that is a "lower" level of Being. *Dasein* has the "potentiality-for-being-a-whole," yet it may lose its presently attained state of authenticity if it cannot develop its potentiality. But these possibilities of falling, sustaining, and developing already presuppose a sense of time deeply, and maybe also unintentionally, experienced within the inner structure of *Dasein*, which makes possible the falling, sustaining, and development of *Dasein*'s potentiality.

Unity of the Future and Unity of Time

Heidegger refers to the inner experience of time as "anticipatory resoluteness" (*vorlaufende Entschlossenheit*).[49] However, Heidegger explains "anticipatory resoluteness" as "Being towards one's own most distinctive potentiality-for-being."[50] He says, "This sort of thing is possible only in that *Dasein can, indeed*, come towards itself in its own most possibility, and that it can put up with this possibility as a possibility in thus letting itself come towards itself—in other words, that it exists.[51]

If we interpret the coming as having an ontological significance of moving and the potentiality of *Dasein* as having an ontological significance of being-in-becoming, then what Heidegger says is that *Dasein* is capable of transforming itself in virtue of as well as in accordance with Being in a potential form. When he further defines the future (*Zu-kunft*) as the primordial phenomenon of coming-towards (*zu-kommen*),[52] he reveals how the future remains essentially a movement with a center and a direction. The future is a movement toward the center of *Dasein*. If we understand the center of *Dasein* as Being, the future is nothing but the movement of Being toward Being: It is the self-transformation of Being. Yet this self-transformation of Being from Being to Being is not meaningless. It continuously realizes the potentiality of Being, and therefore unfolds the horizon of Being. For the philosophy of the *I Ching*, change is always creative and transformative. The creativity and transformativity of change seems to fulfill the potentiality of Being and time in the Heideggerian sense of future. We will discuss this point later.

Heidegger seems to recognize that, although the futural relies on the sense of anticipation of *Dasein*, anticipation is made possible by the coming toward itself of *Dasein* as Being. Thus the future basically still reveals itself as a movement of *Dasein* in virtue of Being. He says, "Anticipation makes *Dasein* authentically futural, and in such a way that the anticipation itself is possible only in so far as *Dasein*, as *being*, is always coming towards itself—that is to say, in so far as it is futural in its being in general."[53]

Another important implication of the understanding of the futural as a coming toward is that there is "the having-been" of *Dasein*. *Dasein* must have been so that it may come toward itself. The having-been-ness of *Dasein* therefore is presupposed in the movement toward itself. This also means that coming toward itself is a *return* to itself and a coming back. Thus, Heidegger says, "[O]nly in so far as *Dasein* is an 'I am-as-having-been,' can Dasein come towards itself futurally in such a way that it comes back. As authentically futural, *Dasein* is authentically as 'having-been.'"[54] He emphasizes that "only so far as it is futural, can *Dasein* be authentically as having been. The character of 'having been' arises, in a certain way, from the future."[55] The futural in this sense is a condition of the past, but we say this only with reference to the sense of futural anticipation as a primordial mode of existence of *Dasein*. From the point of view of the potentiality of the being of *Dasein* within universal Being, the being of having-been must be a ground for the futural so that Being has an end-in-view for its coming back. In this sense, the having-been of the past also is a condition of the futural. To take into account the total structure of the self-movement of Being underlying *Dasein*, past and future as two modes of existence mutually condition each other and therefore can be said to coarise at the same time, with time here understood as the primordial self-disclosure of Being. When Heidegger later spoke of time as "horizon of Being," he seems to have intended this understanding.

The coming back of *Dasein* to itself as potentiality of Being of course can be understood better in reference to Lao Tzu's statements: "All the ten thousand things coarise, I thereby see them return *(fu)*." "*To reverse (fan)* is the movement of the *tao*." [56] This underscores the ontological-cosmological fact that all movements of the *tao* and within the *tao* are return and reversion. If we see *Dasein* as an essential disclosure of Being, the inner structure of human consciousness naturally embodies a dimension of being in the sense of anticipating the future together with a sense of the having-been, and both would occur within a sense of *Dasein* identifiable with the total Being that is the *tao*. The Taoist model of understanding provides a useful interpretation of Heidegger's analysis of temporality.

Temporality in the full sense means not only the coarising of the future and past, it also means the copresence of the present. Heidegger explains this possibility and actual occurrence by pointing out that *Dasein* has to encounter things ready-to-hand in its being and action.[57] This again can be traced to the nature of *Dasein* as Being-in-the-world along with other things that form the world. In this sense the present also is conditional on the futural, because it is due to the futural's coming back that the movement of *Dasein* must realize the present. The present is the movement of the future with reference to the world in which *Dasein* finds itself. Again, we also might suggest that ontologically speaking the present makes possible the movement of the future. Therefore, we come to realize the unity and mutual interdependence of the three states or modes (called *ecstases*) of time and temporality[58]—the past, the present, and the future. This unity and mutual interdependence of the three modes of time is essentially what Heidegger calls *temporality*.

As Heidegger derived the future from his consideration of the inner experience of care of *Dasein*, he is justified in referring to the unity of time as the unity of the future, because the central experience of care is the deepest concern with the future—to anticipate what is coming to itself. This consideration enables Heidegger to describe the unity of future as that "which makes present in the process of having been,"[59] and assert that "Temporality reveals itself as the meaning of authentic care."[60] If one defines *Dasein* in terms of primordial disclosure of itself, temporality as "unity of the future" further defines *Dasein* in terms of an existential analytical mode of the being of *Dasein*. In light of this existential-analytical definition, human existence clearly is seen to possess temporality as its essence and must disclose and realize itself in the mode of care understood here as primordial unity of the futural. Ontologically speaking, this means that human existence discloses and realizes itself in the unity of time through the self-movement of Being. In the first sense, we see that Heidegger correctly notes: *Dasein's* totality of Being as care means: Ahead-of-itself-already-being-in(a world) as Being alongside (entities encountered within-the-world).[61] But, in the second sense, we see that human existence indeed is an event of the movement of Being with time or temporality revealed as a feature of the movement. We may refer to this event of the movement of Being as a process of becoming or a process of transformation, which is the explicit theme of the philosophy of the *I Ching*.

In Heidegger's analysis of temporality as the ontological meaning of care, it is important that one recognize a primordial sense of time in the unity with the future or in the phenomenon of temporality, which is deeply rooted in the realization of human existence. Human existence is existence as a being of time and this being of time reveals what Being in the universal sense really is. Time is the essence of Being that makes Being and consequently the being of *Dasein* possible. To see temporality as deeply human is to also see human existence as deeply temporal. This is to see both as essentially characteristic of universal Being. Therefore, the unity of the future is not merely subjectively human, but ontologically universal. It is revealed primordially in human experience, and one may see that human existence is the primordial way in which it can be revealed. Through an analysis of this unity of the future, we also see that time in the primordial ontological sense is a unity of movement and a unity of mutual dependence and interpenetration. It is a mode of the primordial and authentic existence of Being. To separate time into past, present, and future is to fall into a level of less authentic being and therefore a cover-up of the authentic primordial reality of Being. This means that we cannot find the meaning of time in the time of things and objects and should always work into the care mode of human existence for grasping time. In this sense, we also can see the primary meaning of human existence (existentiality) as consisting in the future, which means the unity of the future.

The Possibility of Primordial Time or Temporality: From Heidegger to the *I Ching*

In an ontological sense we have to ask how primordial time comes about, or equivalently, how the self-movement of Being within *Dasein* takes place. This is the ultimate question of the possibility of temporality and time. We see that with regard to this question, the Heidegger of *Being and Time* had to jump to a new understanding of time and Being in a new mode. In *Being and Time* Heidegger suggested that "Temporality temporalizes" as an answer. He says, "Temporality temporalizes, and indeed it temporalizes possible ways of itself. These make possible the multiplicity of *Dasein*'s modes of Being, and especially the basic possibility of authentic or inauthentic existence."[62] But this statement would be hardly intelligible if we did not see temporality as the temporality of Being. Hence, to say that "Temporality temporalizes" is to say that Being temporalizes. The unity of the future is an inner feature of *Dasein*, and the unity of time is an inner feature of Being. Hence, we come to the recognition that time (in the primordial sense of temporality) essentially defines both Being and *Dasein*. Time is the mode of both disclosing and realizing *Dasein* (in the form of care) and Being (in the form of the self-movement of Being). With this understanding, one important consequence follows: Even if human beings recognize their very being as human beings as finite in the course of time, human beings need not confine their being to this temporal finitude, as the unity of future in the ontological sense is the unity of time, and therefore no limit to the time of this unity can be set.

Heidegger makes the point of seeing *Dasein*'s care as Being-toward death, which is authentic Being toward the possibility of the impossibility of *Dasein*'s existence. He is correct in pointing out that, in the anticipatory self-movement of *Dasein*, the future of *Dasein* reveals itself as finite. But again this is to see *Dasein* as *Dasein* only in the context of Being-in-the-world and in the mode of care, so that it derives its finitude of being from the finitude of the future.[63] Heidegger concludes that the primordial coming toward oneself is the meaning of existing in "one's ownmost nullity."[64] This means that anticipation of the future gives rise to an awareness of the finitude of being that further leads to an understanding of the void as the basis of one's own being. Yet Heidegger fails to see that in regarding temporality as the self-movement of Being that reveals itself in *Dasein*, *Dasein* need not experience the closing of the future for its potentiality of Being, but instead goes beyond the finitude of its being by realizing the authentic infinitude of its potential Being through its identification with Being. Furthermore, he would not come to see the void or nullity as an end of its Being without realizing the ontological meaning of the world and the end of its being. The void can be seen as a form of Being that makes possible the self-movement of Being, whereas the end of *Dasein*'s Being may be regarded as the occasion for the experience of Being as the very ground of one's being, which engenders a new sense of the self-identity of *Dasein*'s being that transcends its finitude and historicity.

All these issues have been made clear in the philosophy of the *I Ching* and also seem to be realized in the later works of Heidegger himself. The hint of this understanding is already obvious from the last part of the last paragraph of *Being and Time*, in which the question of the primordial constitution of being of *Dasein* is raised.

The existential-ontological constitution of *Dasein*'s being is grounded in temporality. Hence the ecstatical projection of Being must be made possible by some primary way in which ecstatical temporality temporalizes. How is this mode of the temporalizing of temporality to be interpreted? Is there a way which leads from primordial time to the Being of *Being*? Does *time* itself manifest itself as the horizon of Being?[65]

In the following text, I shall concentrate briefly on the philosophy of the *I Ching* to answer Heidegger's questions and therefore demonstrate that the implications of Heidegger's analysis of *Dasein* and temporality can be worked out in the philosophy of the *I Ching*, which ontologically-existentially complements the existential analytic of *Dasein*. We have already explored the common ground of care-anxiety between Heidegger's explanation of *Dasein* and the *I Ching*'s explanation of a human person's realization of "transformation (*I*)". Following this clue of "care" I shall explore temporality, transformation, and creativity in the framework of the philosophy of the *I Ching*. In particular, I will relate transformation and creativity as themes that could transform the Heideggerian analysis of time and Being and create a new understanding of time and Being with reference to Heidegger's philosophy.

In my earlier discussion, I pointed out the anxiety and care aspect of the origination of the philosophy of the *I Ching*. Because of the profound anxiety and care of the *I Ching* authors for sustaining the authenticity of living and upholding the way of harmonious order in human society, things in the world are investigated closely and the human self is deeply reflected upon, consequently this investigation and reflection discloses the way of transformation (*I*) among all things, including human beings and their timely harmonization. As I pointed out elsewhere, [66] the philosophy of the *I Ching* is revealed and developed only through a profound understanding of Being and Becoming in both human existence and the universe. In fact, Confucianism has particularly stressed that human existence carries the profound secret of Being and Becoming. Hence, it is important to understand oneself, to cultivate oneself, to transform oneself in order to embody the universal Way and consequently to realize the self-willing necessity of Heaven. It is assumed that human existence is ontologically interpenetrated with universal Being, and therefore one cannot know oneself without knowing the world nor know the world without knowing the inner stirrings of the individual self.

Anxiety, care, and misgivings of oneself are concerned with correct knowledge and correct action in the world. They reflect the desire of human beings to pursue the total good of the self and world in the sense of pursuing and enriching the inner harmony of the self and the outer harmony of the world. The philosophy of the *I Ching* is developed from this motivation in anxiety and care. This explains both the practicality it contains and the usefulness it inspires. For the practicality it contains, we may simply note that the symbolism of the *I Ching*'s *kua* has attached judgments and decisions on the good fortune or misfortune of whatever the symbolism reveals. These judgments and decisions indicate whether a given situation is blameworthy, propitious, or difficult and in what aspect and with regard to what actions. This shows that the individual person must be concerned with his or her orientation, situation, and action in the world, which provides personal significance. Hence, these reveal the roots and content of existential care in the real life of a person. Furthermore, the divinatory practice is able to make the judgments and decisions relevant to a particular situation and makes the understanding of time applicable and meaningfully useful. The ontological disclosure of Being and the meaning of Being must be systematic, self-consistent, and abundantly rich for this particularistic practicality and applicability. However, it is often the case that people only remember the practicality without seeing its underlying ontological significance. It is important therefore to retrieve and disclose the ontological significance of the practicality of the *I Ching* through the existential analysis of the roots of care and anxiety in the origination of the philosophical insights of the *I Ching*.

Time as Timing and as Timeliness

Concerning the theme of temporality as the unity of time, there is apparently no explicit discussion in the *I Ching*. Nevertheless when we take into consideration the meaning of time and temporality and the contexts of the time-reference in the *I Ching*, temporality as the unity of time and temporality as revealing both the internal reality of an individual and the external concrescence of events and happenings become clear. In the presentation of the symbolic form (the *kua*), the movement of time intimately depends on the positioning of the *forces* that altogether form an organic whole of situational transformation. Time is required as an inner structure of the successful formation and transformation of an event. Thus, "Understanding extensively the beginning and ending of the way of creativity, the six positions (in the *kua*) accomplish themselves because of right time" (*Tuan* commentary on the *ch'ien*). Right timing or timeliness (*shih, shih-chung*) is the prerequisite for the convergence and congregation of all forces that bring out desirable order and harmony. In this sense, the *I Ching* speaks of *shih-ch'eng* (accomplished because of time), *chi-shih* (making the right time), "riding with time" (*yu-shih-chieh-hsing*), "become alert because of time" (*yin-ch'i-shih-erh-t'i*), and "reaching the ultimate with time" (*yu-shih-chieh-chi*).[67] In this sense time is not experienced as a coming-back of *Dasein* in the Heideggerian sense of temporality, but an intrinsic movement of the fundamental Being that not only reveals Being, but creates an intrinsic order of Being. In this sense, we may say that time is understood as the basis for the development, cultivation and realization of human beings and all other beings. We may call time in this sense "time as timing," and we can speak of "Time times" a la Heidegger as a way of indicating the intrinsic harmonizing and transforming process of time as the essence of Being or reality.

There is of course, no inconsistency between Heideggerian temporality and the primary ontological "time as timing" in the *I Ching*. Heideggerian temporality reflects the movement of time inside the Being of *Dasein*, which in a primary ontological perspective reveals the fundamental time as timing. Or to use a later Heideggerian expression, temporality reveals time as a feature of fundamental Being, hence transcending the finitude of *Dasein*, enclosing both *Dasein* and the void as parts of the comprehensive movement. This aspect of time is called *transformation* (*hua*) in the *I Ching* and *appropriation* (*Ereignis*) in the later Heidegger.

Heidegger's explanation of this event of Appropriation is as follows: "What determines both time and Being in their own, that is, in their belonging together, we shall call *Ereignis*, the event of Appropriation. *Ereignis* will be translated as Appropriation or event of Appropriation. One should bear in mind, however, that 'event,' is not simply an occurrence, but that which makes any occurrence possible.[68] Heidegger stresses the belonging-together of time and Being, which amounts to defining Being and time in a dialectical way. Being is time giving rise to Being, and time is Being giving rise to time. The relation of the free and indeterminate relation of mutual appropriation of time-giving and Being-giving brings forth time and Being. This means that from a totalistic point of view a dialectical self-movement of transformation and creativity of the ultimate reality is both time and Being. This ultimate reality is recognized as the Great Ultimate (*t'ai-chi*) in the *I Ching*. Joan Stambaugh puts this later Heideggerian primary ontological insight on time into focus, when she says: "Appropriation (Being) and time clearly coalesce in this analysis without, however, simply collapsing into an indifferent sameness. Time is the way in which Appropriation appropriates. As for Appropriation, we can neither say that it *is* nor that it is given (*es gibt*)."[69] Appropriation, indeed, is not nor is it given, because it is the source of giving and being given, which combines both being for giving and nonbeing (void) for being given, as the *I Ching* notion of the Great Ultimate indicates.

With regard to the aspect of time, things take place and the world is identical with a self-generating process. Hence, Being becomes an event of Appropriation (making one's own) that reveals the reality as well as the Being of *Dasein*. Time as "the truth of Being"[70] is precisely the movement of transformation of Being itself and the very event of Appropriation that defines Being. This view on time goes beyond temporality in *Being and Time*, and in a sense reaches the perspective of the notion of "time as timing" in the *I Ching*. Of course, for Heidegger, the fundamental ontology of *time* from which alone all other ontologies can take their rise still must be sought in the existential analytic of *Dasein*. The "time as timing" in the *I Ching* therefore represents a fundamental ontological view on time, which grows out of an understanding of temporality in the human sense.

On one level, the primary ontology of time as the timing of Being is well-presented in the *I Ching* text. On another level, the temporality of *Dasein* also is fully implicated therein. In fact, with a close scrutiny, one can see that in referring to the "meaning of time" (*shih-yi*), *Tuan* commentaries on judgments of many symbolic *kua* contain an understanding of temporality as the unity of time or of future. Take for example the *Sui* (Following) *kua* ☲☳ (joy above and arousing below). It indicates a situation of movements oriented relative to each other. But this situation represents the inner reality of a human individual, for whom it is lively and uniquely meaningful. The inner situation (world) of the individual is that there are movements oriented relative to each other bringing out an anticipation of the futural in a meaning-giving process of going through the having-been. Each line in the *kua* indicates a future that determines the meaning of the earlier line that becomes present from having-been. The having-been can be identified with an earlier *kua*-situation presupposed in the presence of this given *kua*. Hence the first line starts with the meaning given by the meaning of other lines of the future to form the meaning of the total *kua*—hence, the mutual interdetermination of lines, reflecting indetermination of past, present, and future. In this regard we look at the unity of time rather than simply at the unity of the future. But this unity of time nevertheless includes the unity of the future.

To be specific, *Sui* is a *kua* of propitiousness, with the following lines of movement: The first line is propitious because of the propitious position that a *yang* power occupies relative to future lines, which, in turn, in light of the basic meanings of the *yin-yang* primary ontology and the text, reveals the propitiousness of the situation as an integral experience of the individual. Yet there is anticipation and anxiety to face. The second and third lines indicate a situation of danger or misfortune. In the fourth line position misfortune not only threatens but actually materializes. But by the fifth position goodness results in light of both the past and the future. The sixth line represents a situation of relaxation, which emerges from its position and its inner virtue. All these movements are moments of inner time or the temporality of *Dasein*, particularly in light of the *Da*-nature (thereness) of the being of individuals. A human being realizes oneself through the change and transformation of situation, which both necessitates and is necessitated by the change and transformation of the situation, and hence leads to different states of care and anxiety in the individual's anticipatory experience. This is how the *Tuan Chuan* of *Sui* speaks of the meaning of temporality (*shih-yi*) of the *Sui*. Similarly, we have many other *kua*s whose *shih-yi* (temporality) are discussed and presented.[71]

Because the *I Ching* philosophy of time stresses the creative participation and transformation of the individual person in a situation, temporality is not merely a matter of futurity and the unity of the future and time, but a matter of using temporality for creative transformation to reach harmonization. Hence, *shih-yi* has its usefulness and function in transforming the person toward a better state. It therefore realizes a useful "function of time" (*shih-yung*) and leads to the primary ontological use of temporality, which we now can refer to as *timeliness*. Thus, *time* is not merely temporality, but timeliness. It is from the notion of timeliness that we can easily see the development of the notion of "time as *timing*." In the primary ontological sense, the process for this development is this: When one comes reflectively to review the movements or moments of movement in a symbolic form of the situation, one sees time as the constituent of reality from which humankind arises. The disclosure of Being as time and time as Being is made when one examines oneself and one's existential situation in totality. Hence we understand the time of Being in the primary ontological sense. Therefore one can still say that the time of Being arises from the temporality of *Dasein*.

One important consequence also follows from this understanding. One can relate one's existence and situation to the primary ontological time and make existential adjustment accordingly. This is because time in the primary ontological sense is transformation itself and one can transform oneself by participating in and appropriating the transformation of the primary ontological time. Hence we derive the practicality of time by applying primary ontological time as timing to temporality to yield the *timeliness* in the transformation of an individual. This aspect of the practical transformation of *Dasein*, however, is never touched upon by Heidegger even in his later writings and remains exclusively a unique contribution of the *I Ching* philosophy and the Confucian metaphysics of humanity.

We may represent the development and derivation of time in Figure 1.

Figure 1. Ontologies of time and their dialectical relationships

Time as Temporality	*Time as Timing*	*Time as Timeliness*
Phenomenological Ontology of *Dasein*-Time (*Being and Time*)	Primary Ontology of *Sein* (Being) (*I Ching, On Time and Being*)	Practical Ontology of Participatory Transformation (*I Ching*)

If we consider the time revealed in these three processes as three dimensions of the primary ontological time, which remain basically undefinable, emerge only when language and thought are able to grasp them conceptually, then we may introduce the overall notion of *time as timeless* that contains the three dimensions of time and yet transcends them in such a way that one is not confined to any such dimension, but reaches for a relationship of identity of difference among them. In this final notion of *time as timeless*, one also comes to realize the horizon of Being (reality) as a totality of *time*.[72]

The Theme of Transformation in the *I Ching*

The philosophy of the *I Ching* contains the themes of care, transformation (*pien/hua*), and creativity (*sheng-sheng*), the first two of which are to some extent discussed in later Heidegger, but nevertheless not integrated or fully spelled out. Some brief exploration into these two important themes therefore is necessary.[73]

Concerning the theme of transformation, the very notion of *I* (change or transformation) suggests that the book of *I* (the *I Ching*) is a book about transformation. *I* is traditionally assigned three meanings: change (*pien-i*), nonchange (*pu-i*), and simple facility (*ch'ien-i*). To inquire into the philosophical understanding of these meanings, one has to realize that change is nothing other than the transformation that is making things different from time to time. As we understand time as timing intrinsic to Being, change is a process of the timing of the happening of things from reality. Relative to transformation, there is the unchanged principle of change to be followed and embodied in all processes of change. As to simplicity, it is recognized that all changes begin with simple beginnings and simplicity is a natural course of development of all things from the ultimate reality. In light of this explanation, transformation is simply the simple and natural change embodying the unchanged principle of change.

Now the crucial question is, How does change or transformation occur as a metaphysical or ontological fact? The philosophy of the *I Ching* provides the following answer. On the one hand, transformation is considered to have no substance and no scope. It is universal and pervasive Being, or we may say that Being becomes realized through the very activity and process of transformation. In this sense, transformation (*I*) is the Becoming of Being as well as the Being of Becoming. Thus, the *Hsi Tzu* says: "The spirit has no location and the transformation (*I*) has no substance/form." But, on the other hand, the *Hsi Tzu* says: "Transformation (*I*) has the Great Ultimate (*t'ai-chi*) whereby norms (of *yin* and *yang*) are produced. The two norms produced four forms, and four forms produced eight trigrams (*kua*)." However, there is no contradiction between the two observations, because the Great Ultimate is not substance but the source itself that transforms according to the unchanged principle of transformation. The generative process from the Great Ultimate to the eight trigrams explains the nature of transformation in a cosmological sense. The world of things and men has been formed on the basis of the natural polarization of the Great Ultimate. This cosmological form of transformation also reveals the general principle of transformation within and among all things. "It is the exchange of one *yin* and one *yang* which is called the Way (*tao*).[74]

The so-called *yin-yang* represents two moments or two aspects of the process of transformation or change, which are to be understood in an extensive context of contrastive and correlative understandings of qualities and movements of things and their relationships—qualities and movements such as feminine and masculine, dark and bright, closed and open, coming and going. To generalize over these qualities and movements we reach the *yin-yang* polarity of transformation that could be said to be both the moving process and the resulting phase of transformation in things. The *I Ching* refers to this *yin-yang* polarity as *ch'ien/k'un*, meaning a polarity of creativity (*ch'ien*) and receptivity (*k'un*), respectively symbolized as ☰ and ☷. We may regard this generalized principle of transformation as present in all movement in the world and therefore producing both the integration and differentiation of concrete things. The *I Ching* has relied on this principle to explain the rise of heaven and earth, seasons, man and woman and all other things. The *Hsi Tzu* explains: "Therefore 'closing gate' (*ho*) is called *k'un*, 'opening gate' (*pi*) is called *ch'ien*. One closing and one opening is called change (*pien*). The going and coming which are infinite are called penetration[75] (*t'ung*)." *Closing gate* and *opening gate* refer to the movements of the creativity and receptivity of transformation, but they can be also seen as moments and phases revealing or disclosing reality or hiding or concealing reality. All forms of reality can be explained as phenomena or the results of such an alternation of disclosing and concealing, which are creative movements of the ultimate reality.

In this connection we can point out that in Heidegger some understanding of Being as transformation by closing and opening is suggested. It is apparent that "closing gate" is a matter of concealment and "opening gate" is a matter of unhiddenness or unconcealment (*aletheia*). Thus, Heidegger says,

Being means presencing, Thought with regard to what presences, presencing shows itself as letting-presence. But now we must try to think this letting-presence explicitly in so far as presencing is admitted. Letting shows its character in bringing into unconcealment. To let-presence means: to unconceal to bring to openness. In unconcealing prevails a giving, the giving that gives presencing, that is, Being in letting-presence.[76]

What Heidegger says seems to provide a metaphysical description of the principle of *ch'ien* (creativity). When Heidegger proceeds to say the following,

Along the way, we have already thought more about it, although it was not explicitly said, namely, that to giving as sending these belongs keeping back—such that the denial of the present and the withholding of the present, play within the giving of what has been and what will be. What we have mentioned just now—keeping back, denial, withholding—shows something like a self-withdrawing, something we might call for short: withdrawal.[77]

he seems to refer to the working of the metaphysical principle of *k'un* (receptivity). For in contrast to *ch'ien* as letting-presence, *k'un* clearly is holding back or withdrawal and consequently concealment. Heidegger intends his statements to explain the relation of Being to time in their mutual determination from which the formation and transformation of all beings are supposed to be understood. Heidegger has termed what determines time and Being in their belonging together the *event of Appropriation*. The event of Appropriation is precisely the creative moment of transformation by the *ch'ien* principle of the Great Ultimate, because the event reveals and extends time. But when Heidegger says that "Appropriation expropriates itself of itself[78]," it can be understood as a receptive moment of transformation by the *k'un* principle of the Great Ultimate. Through both Appropriation and Expropriation, the Great Ultimate (Being) makes both Being and time possible and possible in their togetherness.

If we see the event of Appropriation as uniquely combining the opening and concealing of time, then it can be seen as just a different expression for the *I Ching* concept of the *t'ai-chi*.[79] Being belongs to Appropriation because Being is transformation, and transformation is "the extending of true time which opens and conceals"—a restatement of the "closing gate" and "opening gate" of the Way in the philosophy of the *I Ching*.

The Theme of Creativity in the *I Ching*

What we need particularly to bring to our attention about the theme of creativity in the philosophy of the *I Ching*, apart from what has been said earlier, is that creativity (*sheng-sheng*) is a manifold happening that results in the formation of the world and things. As creativity is essential to the transformation of things, transformation also is essential to creativity. At this point we can make explicit a distinction implicit in the Chinese terms *pien-hua* generally referring to change or transformation. The distinction is the distinction between *pien* and *hua*: *pien* is simply change or the transformation of a given state or thing without referring to the emergence or birth of a new thing. However, *hua* refers to a change or transformation of a given state where a new thing emerges. Hence, *pien* precedes *hua* and *hua* follows *pien*. *Pien* is the removing of the given and *hua* is the creation of the new. With this understanding it can be seen that creativity in change consists basically of *pien* and *hua*. The *Hsi Tzu* (Section 1) says that "When natural objects are formed in sky and natural forms formed on earth,then *pien-hua* (change-from and change-to) becomes conspicuous." Section 12 of the *Hsi Tzu* also says: "To change-to (*hua*), and then to regulate it comes from change-from (*pien*)." The *Hsi Tzu* often refers to change-movement (*pien-tung*) (Section 8) and change-penetration (*pien-t'ung*). The first describes the movement of change, the second the successful completion of the change and bringing out of new light for a new phase. Hence, we may consider the transformation that gives rise to creativity as consisting of three phases: *pien-tung* (change-movement), (*pien-t'ung*) change-penetration, and *pien-hua* (change-emergence).

A sage is assumed to be able to penetrate into the movements of change in these three phases, and the symbolic *kuas* and their interrelationships are supposed to reveal the possibilities of Being for Being, and reveal possibilities of situation for a person through their relationships of change and transformation.

The *Hsi Tzu* (Section 5) says: "To be creative of creativity (*sheng-sheng*) is called *I* (change or transformation), to form natural objects is called *ch'ien* (creativity) and to follow the way of the creative is called *k'un* (receptivity)." By this description of creativity, the transformation of Being is capable of producing heaven, earth, humankind, and all the ten thousand things. This understanding of creativity has been well-presented in the Neo-Confucian essay "Discourse on the Diagram of the Great Ultimate," by Chou Tun-i (1017-1073).

The important point about creativity in the *I Ching* is twofold. It produces the world of things; and it also produces different relationships of beings and different forms of becoming as symbolized by the trigrams and hexagrams of the *I Ching* text. In light of the Appropriation between time and Being that makes time and Being two aspects of the same thing, all the symbolic forms of the *I Ching* can be said to be disclosures of Being, transformed creatively from the time-Being Appropriation.

In Heidegger's paper on 'The Thing" of 1950,[80] he comes to a position on creativity that corresponds to the philosophy of the *I Ching*. Heidegger speculates on the "outpouring" of world (or what he calls "worlding" of the world) from Being in the following terms:

In the gift of the outpouring that is drink, mortals stay in their own way. In the gift of the outpouring that is a libation, the divinities stay in their own way, they who receive back the gift of giving as the gift of the donation. In the gift of the outpouring, mortal and divinities each dwell in their different ways. Earth and sky dwell in the gift of the outpouring. In the gift of the outpouring earth and sky, divinities and mortals dwell *together all at once*. These four, at one because of what they themselves are, belong together. Preceding everything that is present, they are enfolded into a single fourfold.[81]

The "gift of outpouring" is the creative movement of the giving of Being (the *tao* or the *t'ai-chi*), and the receiving of the "gift of outpouring" is the world of earth, sky, divinities and mortals. This world-making cosmology no doubt can be rephrased as the formation of heaven, earth, mortals, and spirits in the philosophy of the *I Ching* by way of the creative movements of transformation of the *t'ai-chi* and *yin-yang*. This reveals once again how Heidegger comes close to the philosophy of the *I Ching* in terms of which his philosophy of Time and Being receives a new dimension of meaning.

Concluding Remarks

Earlier I discussed the Confucian philosophy of heaven (*t'ien*) and nature (*hsing*) and their relationship for the purpose of interpreting the Heideggerian philosophy of *Dasein* so that we may illuminate the meaning of *Dasein* in relationship to *Sein*. I advanced to Heidegger's existential analysis of "care" and "temporality" and related them to the notions of anxiety or care and time in the philosophy of the *I Ching*. We can see that the philosophy of the *I Ching* illuminates both time and Being and their relationship, which gives meaning to Heidegger's philosophy of time and Being. Yet, Heidegger also becomes instrumental in illuminating the Confucian philosophy of heaven and humanity and the *I Ching* philosophy of time and Being. An integrative philosophy of humanity, heaven, time, and Being therefore is developed from mutual interpretation and conceptual interpenetration of Confucius, Heidegger and the philosophy of the *I Ching*. An important methodological lesson also manifests itself: Ontological understanding of truth and reality will develop only in a process of mutual interpretation and illumination of given ontologies of different traditions. This lesson is well illustrated in the history of Chinese philosophy.

Notes

1. Two types of transcendence are to be distinguished: transcendence of the transcendent totally unrelated or unlinked to the transcended, and transcendence of the transcendent still fundamentally related and linked to the transcended. The former can be referred to as the transcendent transcendent, the latter the immanent transcendent. The former is exemplified by the God of the Christian orthodoxy, the latter by the relation of inner (*nei*) to outer (*wai*) in Confucian and Taoist philosophy.
2. See *Being and Time*, trans. John Macquarrie and Edward Robinson, New York, 1962, H. 437, p. 488.
3. In the spirit of the ontology of understanding in Heidegger, I can even point out that conceptual or logical implication discloses Being and hence belongs to ontology.
4. See *Being and Time*, Introduction, section 3, pp 28-31.
5. See my Chinese article, "*Chung-kuo- che-hsueh fan-ch'ou ch'u-t'an*" (Preliminary Inquiries into the Categories of Chinese Philosophy) *Han Hsueh Yen Chiu* (Sinological Studies Bulletin), Taipei, 1985.
6. Historicity is an existential realization of Being, so to speak.
7. Heidegger himself tried to understand the *tao* in terms of Being or vice versa in his later years.
8. *Being and Time*, Introduction, Sec. 4, H. 12, p. 32.
9. Ibid., p. 32.
10. Ibid., P. 33.
11. This is called by Heidegger *existentiality* of the existence of an entity (H. 13, p. 33).
12. See the *Mencius*, 4B-19.
13. Ibid., 7A-6.
14. Ibid., B-4.
15. Trans. Joan Stambaugh, New York, 1969, p. 31.
16. *Mencius*, 7A-1.
17. Ibid., 5A-6.
18. Ibid.
19. *Mencius*, 7A-24.

20. *Analects*, 12-5.

21. Ibid., 6-3, 11-7.

22. Ibid., 20-1.

23. Ibid., 2-4.

24. Ibid., 9-2.

25. Ibid., 14-12; see also 19-1.

26. Ibid., 19-1.

27. See *Mencius*, 7A-1.

28. See ibid., 7A-2.

29. Cf. *Being and Time*, VI, §40, §44.

30. I.e., "the possibility of impossibility of existence, H. 250, 262, 265, 306.

31. Ibid., V, §38.

32. See ibid., part V, Being-in as Such, §38.

33. See ibid., H. 191, p. 235.

34. See ibid., H. 437, p. 488.

35. The ideal goal of comparative philosophy is to produce an integration of two traditions of philosophy or two philosophies under comparison by inducing a mutual penetration between the two. This interpenetration of the two traditions of philosophy or two philosophies will necessarily produce the onto-hermeneutical circle of understanding.

36. See *Being and Time*, H. 191, p. 236.

37. Ibid.

38. Heidegger also uses the term *beyond itself* (*über sich hinaus*) in referring to *Dasein*'s Being toward the potentiality-for-Being. Ibid., H. 192, p. 236.

39. Ibid.

40. *Dasein*'s Being is codetermined by both Being and the world and therefore *Dasein* is always Being-in-the-world. Heidegger explicitly said: "If by this 'something' we understand an entity *within-the-world*, then it tacitly implies that the *world* has been presupposed; and this phenomenon of the world co-determines the state of Being of the I, if indeed it is to be possible for the 'I' to be something like an 'I think something': In saying 'I', I have in view the intity which in each case I am as an 'I-am-in-a-world' " (Ibid., H. 321, p. 368).

41. See the *Analects*, 12-4.

42. Ibid., 15-29.

43. Ibid., 9-29, 14-28.

44. Confucius said, "*Chun-tzu pu-ch'i*" (2-12), to explain *ch'i* (tool or utensil) in terms of the Heideggerian concepts of things ready-to-hand and things present-to-hand is most appropriate as the Heideggerian concepts of tool and object express what Confucius intended in his use of the term *chi*.

45. See the *I Ching*, §7 of the *Hsi Tzu*, part II.

46. Here the term *I* refers to the *I Ching* symbolic system and the judgments attached to the individual *kua* (images or forms).

47. In my paper "On the Hierarchal Theory of Time: With Reference to Chinese Philosophy of Time," I discussed time on different levels, including the level of human mind. See *Journal of Chinese Philosophy* 10, no. 4 (Dec, 1873): pp 351-384.

48. Perhaps I can describe three senses of time in an understanding of time: time as the temporality of Dasein; time as the everyday objective time of things, events, and objects; time as the fundamental-ontological time of original Being. The metalanguage use of *time* in all these three senses is possible precisely because the fundamental-ontological time is revealed and disclosed on different levels and in different contexts. Later this chapter I also introduce a fourth sense of time, time as timeliness. Time as timeliness (*shih-chung*) is the creative application of oneself in action to achieve harmony of events and development (fulfillment) of oneself.

49. *Being and Time*, H. 324, p. 370.

50. Ibid., H. 325, p. 372.

51. Ibid.

52. Ibid.

53. Ibid., H. 325, p. 373.

54. Ibid., H. 325, p. 373.

55. Ibid.

56. See the *Tao Te Ching*, §16, §40.

57. See *Being and Time*, H. 326, p. 374.

58. Ibid., H. 328, p. 377.

59. Ibid., H. 326, p. 374.

60. Ibid.

61. See ibid., H. 327, p. 375.

62. See ibid., H. 328, p. 377.

63. Note that Heidegger treated finitude of future and hence finitude of being as primary, and treated the in-finite time as derived from the inauthentic way of temporalizing among all things. See ibid., H. 330, p. 379.

64. Ibid, H. 330, p. 379.

65. See ibid., p. 488, p. 437.

66. See my paper "On Timeliness (*shih-chung*) in the *Analects* and the *I Ching*: An Inquiry into the Philosophical Relationship between Confucius and the *I Ching*," in *Proceedings of International Sinological Conference*, Academia Sinica, Taipei, Taiwan, October 1981, pp. 177-338.

67. All these expressions occur in the *Tuan Chuan* and *Hsiang Chuan* of the first two *kuas*, *ch'ien* and *k'un*, of the *I Ching*. These express the natural harmonization and accomplished order among things and human beings.

68. See *On Time and Being*, trans. Jean Stambaugh, 1972, p. 19.

69. Ibid., in her introduction to *On Time and Being*, p. xi.
70. See ibid., p. 28.
71. We have the *Yü (Joy)* ䷏, *Yi* (Jaw) ䷚, *Ta-Kou* (Great Excess) ䷛, *Hsi-K'an* (Abyss)䷜ , *Tun* (Retreat)䷠ , and other *kua*s, whose *shih-yi* are explicitly mentioned. But actually, all sixty-four *kua*s reveal *shih-yi* or temporalities of their own.
72. Paul Tillich, in *Systematic Theology* in three volumes, published in 1951-1963, Chicago, differentiates between time as *chronos* (the quantitative clock time) and time as *kairos* (the qualitative right time in which something can be done). Awareness of *kairos* requires vision. See Tillich, *Systematic Theology*, pp. 369-72. Also see Paul Tillich's other works. I am grateful to Professor Bill Paul for calling my attention to this important reference that jibes with the idea of timeliness in the *I Ching*.
73. The theme of practicality can be also developed from the philosophy of the *I Ching*, the discussion of which, however, will be reserved for another occasion.
74. *I Ching*.
75. Ibid., § 11.
76. *On Time and Being*, p. 5.
77. Ibid., p. 22.
78. Ibid., pp. 22-23.
79. Ibid., p. 21.
80. See Martin Heidegger, *Poetry, Language and Thought*, trans. Albert Hofstadter, New York, 1971, pp. 163-186.
81. Ibid., p. 173.

Part III

Neo-Confucian Dimensions

15. Method, Knowledge and Truth in Chu Hsi

Introductory Remarks

Although most recent writings on Chu Hsi (1130—1200) discusses his views on method (*fang-fa*), knowledge (*hsueh-chih*), and truth (*hsing-li*), very few seem to be able to show how Chu Hsi's views on these are related and how they are justified.[1] None indeed seem to be able to bring these views to bear upon the fundamental problems of validity and knowledge and the correct relationship of method to knowledge and knowledge to truth. When we examine Chu Hsi's writings, particularly the *Recorded Sayings* (*Yü Lei*)[2], we shall find that there are three levels and three dimensions of understanding his basic concepts of *li* and *hsing*: the ontological, the epistemological, and the axiological. The difficulty stems not only from failure to see the collation of meanings that should be differentiated according to these three levels and these three dimensions, but failure to see how they form a unity in an overarching methodology, integrating the ontology, epistemology, and axiology of *hsing-li*.

If *hsing-li* can be considered the objective content and reference of human knowledge and human understanding, *knowing* would be both a process of seeking revelation and fulfillment of *li* and *hsing* and the end product of such a process. The gap between the knowing mind and the object of knowledge must be bridged by a methodology capable of integrating mind and the world, knowledge and truth. In this sense, this methodology is both a procedure for fulfilling and developing the human mind toward truth and a procedure for determining truth in the interest of mind; and as such, this methodology acquires both an ontological and an epistemological significance. A correct understanding of this methodology will reveal a basic unity between the knowing mind and the reality that is to be known and consequently a basic insight into this unity. The nature of this unity and the nature of this insight need critical explication so that we can understand Chu Hsi's philosophy better.

In the following discussion we shall examine the meaning of knowledge and truth in Chu Hsi and how his methodology is derived and justified. Whereas methodology illuminates epistemology and ontology, the latter also illuminates the former. Thus we shall determine how the *tao*, the *hsing* (nature), and the *chih* (knowing) are related. Insofar as there are two functions of mind, and consequently two methods of understanding (namely, *ching-hsueh* and *han-yang*) in Chu Hsi, we may recognize a unity of two functions and two methods as integrated in the nature of humankind and as revealed in the full use of the human mind. For this reason we will be able to see Chu Hsi's unique and fruitful contributions to a methodology of understanding.

Telos of Learning and Understanding

Knowing and knowledge in the Chinese philosophical context, whether Confucianist or Taoist, lack the implication of theoretical understanding or conceptual understanding; namely, to know is not to see things intellectually or to have one's intellectual interests or curiosities satisfied. In a genuine Chinese philosophical perspective, knowing and knowledge are to be tied to a deep sense of understanding that has practical and axiological significance. To know is to know for a certain purpose or to know in relation to values or self-fulfillment, social adjustment, or to lead to the total truth and understanding of oneself and reality. The Confucianist tradition perhaps is responsible for bringing knowledge into focus with values of humanity and self-fulfillment. It succeeded in doing this by creating an axiological framework or reference system of values of life, society, and reality in which knowing and knowledge are to be located, placed, or embedded. As to how one comes to know this framework and its ultimate values, the assumption is that by nature one can come to know them if one knows what one's nature is. This kind of knowledge *perhaps* is what Mencius called "innate knowledge of goodness" (*liang-chih*) or what Confucius called "knowing *jên* (*chih-jên*)" and "knowing *te*" (*chih-te*). We may also call this knowledge *primary knowledge*.

Primary knowledge of nature is twofold in essence: On the one hand, it involves the dimension of knowing one's nature; on the other, it involves the dimension of knowing what is good for the cultivation and full development of one's nature. We may resort to Confucius for illustration. Although Confucius did not suggest that one knows one's nature, all his statements about what one can do and achieve imply a pre-theoretical understanding of the nature of being human. Thus, when he said: "If I wish to have *jên* (benevolence), *jên* comes within the reach of me,"[3] he implied that one can determine virtuous conduct because one already has virtue within one's nature: Nature in the individual means simply the capacity to achieve goodness and the free power to fulfill that capacity. This implication is reflected in another saying in the *Analects*: "Man can enlarge the way (the *tao*). It is not the *tao* that can enlarge man."[4] This also suggests that, although the *tao* comprehends all goodness, it is not the *tao*, but the man who is endowed ontologically with the special power for fulfilling the *tao*. When we look into the *Analects* we will find that all statements about virtue imply this double meaning of human nature: Virtue is the virtual content of nature and nature has the receptive power to fulfill and make explicit and illuminate the virtue. One not only has goodness in one's nature and the power to fulfill it, one also has the impulse to do it if one follows one's nature.

We may now conclude that the reason for one to seek knowledge is to fulfill one's mind and, through this, fulfill one's nature and reach the ultimate unity with the *tao* or with heaven and earth. Because the ideal state (called *sagehood*) of fulfillment of one's nature and forming unity with heaven and earth is a goal for seeking knowledge and cultivating oneself, there is inevitably the question of the methodology for achieving this goal. At this juncture we may immediately recognize the importance of Chu Hsi's program of methodologizing about learning and knowing, this program being to develop a person into sagehood. The teleological or axiological framework must be kept in mind for understanding and evaluating his methodology.

Knowledge and Truth in Fulfillment of Nature

To help understand Chu Hsi's methodology, I begin with Chu Hsi's introduction of the concepts of *chih* (knowing) and *li* (principle) into the interpretation of the fulfillment of one's nature. In commenting on the Chung Yung passage on "fulfilling one's nature," Chu Hsi said:

In fulfilling one's nature, no virtue is not substantiated. Therefore there is no self-interest of human desired in me and what is mandated by heaven in me will be discerned and followed. No matter how big or small, how refined or crude, there is nothing left not to be fulfilled. The natures of other men and things are also my nature. They differ only insofar as they assume different forms and are endowed with different *ch'i* (vitality). *In speaking of being capable of fulfilling them, it is meant that what one knows is not unclear and what one does is not improper.*[5] (italics mine)

Thus, we can see that to fulfill (*ching*) one's nature is to *know* in clarity and *act* in propriety in reference to all aspects of one's nature. Although at this point Chu Hsi did not bring out the concepts of *li*, *li* is precisely what can be regarded as principles regulating things big and small, refined and crude, that can be discerned to one's being.

When Chu Hsi came to comment on Mencius' doctrine of fulfilling the mind (*ching-hsin*), the concept of *li* emerged as a constituting element in the *mind* and thus made *knowing* (*chih*) basically directed toward *li*; in this we have the paradigm of "exhausting *li*" or "exhausting *t'ien-li*."

Chu Hsi interpreted mind as "spirit of illumination" (*shen-ming*) of man which is "endowed with ten thousand *li*" (*chu-wan-li*) and "responds to ten thousand affairs" (*yin-wan-shih*). He also pointed out that the *li* in the mind is derived from the *li* of heaven. He said: "The mind of man is nothing but a *totality* of *li* (*ch'üan-li*). If one does not exhaust *li* [meaning: knowing the *li*], there is obscuration in one's mind, and one will not fulfill the content of the mind. Therefore one who can recognize the totality of one's mind and does nothing not to fulfill it must be one who is capable of exhausting *t'ien-li* and there is nothing he does not know. To know the *li* (in mind), one will know where it comes from."[6] In light of what he says about the *ke-wu* (investigation of things), Chu Hsi suggested that "knowing nature" (*chih-hsing*) is *ke-wu*, and *ching-hsin* consequently is the utmost of knowing the *li* that is the *ke-wu*.

Following the same line of thought, Chu Hsi also interpreted the "to fulfill one's form" (*ch'ien-hsing*) as "exhausting the *li* associated with one's form." "The crowd has this form and yet cannot fulfill its *li*. Thus they cannot fulfill their forms, only the sage has this form and yet can fulfill its *li*. Then we can speak of fulfilling his form without regret."[7] It is clear that Chu Hsi would interpret all fulfillment and exhaustion paradigms as basically a matter of knowing *li* or knowing *li* universally and throughout time.

This position again is strongly indicated in Chu Hsi's interpretation of the doctrine of *ke-wu* (investigation of things) in the *Ta Hsueh*. This he does by supplementing what he considered a missing commentary in the original *Ta Hsueh*:

"Extension of knowledge (*chih-chih*) resides in investigation of things (*ke-wu*)" means that if I desire to extend my knowledge we must exhaust the *li* of the things) right in things. The subtleties of human mind always have knowledge and things under heaven always have principles (*li*). It is because the *li* has not been exhausted, so the knowledge is not completed. Thus the *Ta Hsueh*, in teaching the beginners, asks the student to look further into the *li* already known of things under heaven so that he can reach the ultimate. After one has made sufficient effort sufficiently long, one may have a thorough understanding all at sudden, then [one will see] the inside and outside, the fine and the crude of all things and thus the total great function of my mind will not be unilluminated. This is things investigated; this is the ultimate of knowledge.[8]

Several points can be made explicit from this important passage. First, the human mind has the ability to know and an inclination to know, whereas things can be known in virtue of their *li*: This *knowing* is basically a knowing of *li* in things. But insofar as one's mind can have a "thorough and penetrating understanding," one may say that mind can see the ultimate *li* of things, and one may naturally suggest that the ultimate *li* is innate in the mind itself. Second, Chu Hsi reached the position that the great function of mind is to know the ultimate *li*, the *li* that corresponds to the "thorough and penetrating understanding" of things by mind. This ultimate *li* is what Chu Hsi in other contexts called "the substance of the *tao* (*tao-t'i*)" or "the original substance" (*pen-t'i*). The so-called utmost of knowing is knowledge of the *tao-t'i* or *pen-t'i*, and this is what Chu Hsi took to be the essence of the doctrine of *ke-wu chih-chih*. Third, "to exhaust *li*" (*ch'iung-li*) and consequently "to fulfill mind" (*ching-hsin*) or "know nature" (*chih-hsing*) are different ways of saying the same thing; that is, to reach the ultimate of *li*, namely, the *tao-t'i* or *pen-t'i*, which is also referred to as the *t'ai-chi* (the great ultimate).

Fourth, the idiom "to exhaust *li* right in things presented" (*chi-wu erh ch'iung-li*) simply means to seek *li* of the things so that it may contribute to one's "thorough and penetrating understanding" and one's knowledge of the ultimate *li*. This is possible only if one sees the *li* of things as related to the same *li* in other things and as derived from the ultimate *li*. Thus, the *li* to be exhausted is basically relational and forms a structure and hierarchy of its own. In particular, these *li* have to be understood in relation or in association with other *li*. Thus, "exhaust *li*" (*ch'iung-li*) is both inductive and deductive and forms a process that leads to the emergence of an organic total vista of reality under which things will be better understood and one can better adjust to things. Wang Yang-Ming had a profound misunderstanding of Chu Hsi's doctrine of *ch'iung-li*, and thus after falling sick on "exhausting the *li* of bamboos," he rejected the doctrine and interpreted *ke-wu* not as *ch'iung-li*, but as "rectifying things" (*cheng-shih*).

At this point, it can be pointed out that to understand *li* is to understand something metaphysically significant. Chu Hsi developed a theory of *li* on the basis of his predecessors Chou Tun-i and the Ch'eng Brothers, in which the *t'ai-chi* as *li*, the *li* as *t'ai-chi*, and the relationships of *li* to *ch'i* and *hsing* are all well-developed. This is where Chu Hsi's philosophical system-building lies. But the most important thing to note is that he came to the metaphysics of *li* from the need to justify understanding, on the one hand, and from the need to universalize and unify knowledge of things so that a higher order can be achieved, on the other. In reaching *li* he also recognized the deeper and the greater function of the mind: the mind as potentially having all *li* as it is given by nature (*hsing*), hence making *hsing* the underlying substance for the *mind* and the ultimate ground for the knowledge of *li*.

Two Dimensions of Knowing

Hsing as the very context and matrix for knowing reality validates knowledge and produces the "comprehensive and penetrating understanding" needed for seeing the unity of *li* or the *t'ai-chi*. This implies that to know *li* is not a simple matter. It involves two dimensions of knowing: knowing the things so that we know the *li* and their interrelationships; and knowing the nature that provides the context of unity of *li* and the transcendence of knowing things for knowing *li* and for knowing the unity and ultimacy of *li*—the *t'ai-chi*. We may call the former knowing learning or studying (*hsüeh*), and we may call the latter knowing "nourishing" or "self-experiencing" (*hanyang*). We shall see that both these are necessary for a complete realization of *human nature*. A correct understanding of these two forms of knowing in Chu Hsi is essential for evaluating his theory against the Lu-Wang theory, which puts emphasis on the second form of knowing at the expense of the first. This understanding will also explain why Chu Hsi, following Ch'eng I, argued for the equal importance of learning and studying things, on the one hand, and the nourishing of oneself, on the other hand. We shall see how the balance of the two are to be achieved and what rationale can be used for evaluation and explanation.

If we recall our earlier concern with the problem of telos of knowledge, we also may observe that no matter how knowledge is conceived, knowledge must produce the moral and ontological effects of fulfillment of nature as discussed; namely, knowledge must produce freedom of action, self-attainment, and a sense, a power in transforming reality—centrality of organization and harmonization with all things. Insofar as knowledge is basically knowledge of *li*, knowledge of *li* must produce all these effects, or should satisfy these goals. This may be said to be the metaphysical or *moral* justification of knowledge of *li*.

As to how knowledge of *li* may satisfy these goals, it might be regarded as a basic postulate in Chu Hsi's philosophy that *li* must be defined or conceived in such a way that to know *li* gives rise to all the moral and metaphysical values. In this sense knowledge of *li* is not merely empirical and objective knowledge, but transempirical or metaphysical knowledge (or knowledge of *pen-t'i*); and not merely transempirical or metaphysical knowledge, but knowledge that transforms, moves, organizes as well as ontologically enriches the individual self. Knowledge of *li*, in other words, for Chu Hsi, creatively *fulfills* the individual nature in the sense of fulfillment just explained. In this sense, to know *li* is to develop a self-transformation of oneself that demonstrates itself in the realization of moral values and a power of transforming reality (other persons and things) that are intrinsically significant and form a perfection of nature. This *self-transforming* knowledge thus is different from conceptual or scientific knowledge, for the latter lacks, whereas the former possesses, the agency of self-transformation and moral creation and consummation of values.

In volume 9 on learning of *Chu Tzu Lu Lei*, Chu Hsi said:

The efforts of a student consist only of "residing in serious-mindedness" (*chü-ching*) and "exhausting principles" (*ch'iung-li*). These two things are mutually reinforcing. When exhausting principle, the efforts of *chü-ching* become daily progressive, and when residing in serious-mindedness, the efforts of *ch'iung-li* become daily improved. This is like a person walking with two feet: when the left foot moves, then the right foot stops; when the right foot moves, then the left foot stops. It is also like one thing hanging in the air, if depressed on the right side, it will rise on the right side. Actually this is one thing.[9]

Among all statements made by Chu Hsi regarding how learning is conducted, this statement seems to give the clearest statement of Chu Hsi's methodology for learning. It is evident that what Chu Hsi holds here is that there are two requirements for learning the way or the *tao-t'i*, as we have seen. One is to learn so that one acquires knowledge which, as we have seen, amounts to understanding thoroughly the *li* of things. The second requirement has to do with the preservation of the original nature of the mind, so that one can approach the *pen-t'i* and organize and utilize knowledge for understanding the *tao*. The full methodology of learning the way or *pen-t'i* then has two dimensions: the dimension of exhausting *li* and the dimension of applying *ching*. The two become substantiated in terms of practice (*li-hsing*). We may represent the "learning-the-way-methodology" in terms of the following structure:

The *tao-t'i* not only is the justification of learning, but the standard as well as the goal of learning and knowing for by the *tao-t'i* learning is evaluated and judged for its adequacy. But the *tao-t'i* also is the source of learn-

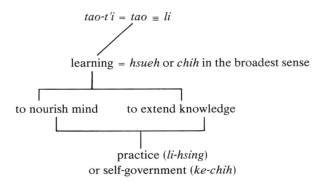

ing as well as the source of the zeal and desire for learning. Hence, the *tao-t'i* is the starting point as well as the ending point of learning. The whole process of learning consequently can be regarded as a self-fulfillment process for the *tao-t'i* itself.

Chü-ching as a Constitutive Requirement of Learning

Why is *chü-ching* important in the process of learning? The answer is to be found in the recognition that learning is learning of the ultimate reality and this ultimate reality is potentially present in human mind. Based on this recognition we may interpret this requirement of *chü-ching* as one of making efforts *to preserve the whole mind so that one can experience the ultimate reality*. It also may be interpreted as the requirement to hold and refine mind's capacity to know reality as a whole so that one will not lose one's bearing on the *tao*—the ultimate reality. In this connection we may consider how *chü-ching* is essential for *han-yang* (nourishing mind). The term *han-yang* has the meaning both of "immersion" (*han*) and "nurturing" (*yang*). This suggests that *han-yang* means to immerse in one's mind so as to nurture the understanding of the way as well as to nurture the mind for understanding the way. Ontologically speaking, *han-yang* means to apply one's mind to reflect on one's mind and to hold to one's integrity. With this understanding of *han-yang*, we can see why Chu Hsi, following Ch'eng Hao, should treat *chü-ching* as the primary dimension of learning. The proposition than *han-yang* consists of *chü-ching* suggests then that there is a specific *procedure* for maintaining *han-yang*. Namely, *chü-ching* is what makes *han-yang* possible and what increases the quality and quantity of *han-yang*.

What is then this special procedure called *chü-ching*? What are its paradigms? How do we understand it? In the *Chin Ssu Lu*, *chü-ching* is referred as *yung-ching* (to apply *ching*) or even sometimes as *chih-ching* (to hold *ching*) by Ch'eng Hao and Ch'eng I. In explaining this notion of *chü-ching* both Ch'eng Hao and Ch'eng I referred to a paradigm in the *Wen Yen* commentary on *Kün 6-2* in the *I Ching*, where it is said "Straighten corrections, square rightness. The superior man uses *ching* to straighten the inner, uses righteousness (*yi*) to square the outer. When *ching* and *yi* are established, the virtuous will not be left alone." Ch'eng I explained this:

The superior man "*holds* the *ching* (*ch'ih-ching*) in order to straighten its inner; and abide by the righteousness" (*sou-yi*) in order to square its outer. Once *ching* is established, the inner will be straightened; once righteousness is manifested, the outer is square. But to say that righteousness is manifested is not to say that righteousness is outside. Once *ching* and *yi* are established, the virtue of the superior man becomes great!

Ch'eng Hao also agreed with this and said, "*Ching* and *yi* mutually reinforce each other and move up the way to reach the virtue of heaven" (ibid., p. 51). Ch'eng Hao even regarded *ching* and *yi* as the way of the *k'un* (the receptive) to contrast with the way of the *ch'ien* (the creative) in cultivating one's outer behavior (ibid., p. 54). From this Ch'eng Hao concluded the paradigm formulating the two dimensions and two requirements of "learning the way": *Han-yang* must depend upon *yung-ching*; to advance to learning (*hsüeh*) must consist in extension of knowledge (*chih-chih*).

From this, one can see that *chü-ching* is a matter of holding steadfast to one's mind for reaching the virtue of the heaven: It is an internal attitude or posture of mind that we may describe as "whole-mindedness or "right-mindedness," insofar as it enables one to control one's mind in wholeness and to achieve the right attitude for manifesting virtue.

Chü-ching therefore can be said to be the virtue of straightness inside and righteousness outside. Insofar as the inside and outside cannot separate, straightness and righteousness cannot separate. *Ching* therefore is the natural virtue of mind as manifestation of nature (*hsing*), which needs the mind's effort to exercise its manifestation and steadfastness. Thus Ch'eng Hao further explains: *Ching* is a matter of *han-yang* and must involve applying to things and therefore must depend on "collecting righteousness" (insofar as "collecting righteousness" means to direct one's mind to things). If one does not collect righteousness, there would be nothing for the mind to apply[11]. This means that *ching* would then be an empty virtue, equivalent to *ching* (quietude) devoid of life activity.

The difference between *ching* and *yi* is further explained by Ch'eng I as follows: "*Ching* is only the way to comfort oneself (*ch'ih-chi*) and by *yi* one knows the distinction of right and wrong. To act in following *li* (principle) is righteousness"[12]. Ch'eng I even gave an example to illustrate this. If a person wishes to follow filial piety, it is not enough to have the mind of filial piety, it is also necessary to know how to *act* filial piety. From this it is clear that *ching* is not only no quietude, it further requires application in terms of knowing *how*. It may be described as a readiness to apply to things. Insofar as *ching* is the mental attention required for reaching the virtue of heaven, on the one hand, and insofar as it is directed toward application to things, on the other, it is basically a state of centrality of mind and thus can be explained as two-directional force inherent in the mind and constitutes a basis for all virtues. In this sense it can be called the previrtue virtue of mind: This justifies furthermore the description of *ching* as wholemindedness or right-mindedness.

Ch'eng I developed a more metaphysically significant interpretation of the concept of *ching*. According to Ch'eng I, if we wish our mind to rid itself of thoughts without at the same time reducing the mind to voidness and quietude, we must have mastery of our mind. But how does one have mastery of one's mind? Ch'eng I suggested the method of *ching*. In this light he explained *ching* as follows: "The so-called *ching* is such that to have mastery and oneness [of one's mind] is called *ching*. [Note that *chü-yi* here is translated as having mastery and oneness (of one's mind), but it can be also translated as mastering oneness (of one's mind).] The so-called *yi* (oneness) is such that having no accommodation (*wu-shih*) is called *yi*."[13] Ch'eng I pointed out that if one does not hold steadfast to oneness, then one's mind would be dissipated into confusion and divergence and lose mastery completely. From this understanding of *ching*, *ching* can be interpreted as self-control and one-mindedness. Being one-minded, one will not be overwhelmed by external things and yet will not be fixated in quietude. The mind would then be able to exercise movement and rest at its will and according to proper circumstances. In this sense, *ching* becomes an ontological state of mind.

This state of mind described in terms of *ching* (one-mindedness) is significant for the moral development of a person. In fact, according to Ch'eng I, by maintaining the mind in the ontological state of *ching*, a person will naturally achieve "centrality" (*chung*) of unactivated emotions of joy, anger, sorrow, and happiness and consequently will be able to move from "centrality" to "harmony" (*ho*) when emotions of joy, anger, sorrow, and happiness are activated. This means that one will be able to meet propriety in demonstrating or realizing one's emotions when the mind is guided by *ching*—one-mindedness. Thus Ch'eng I said:"If one speaks of preserving and nourishing one's mind prior to the release of joy, anger, sorrow, and happiness, that is permissible. But if one speaks of seeking centrality amidst joy, anger, sorrow, and happiness, that is not permissible"[14]. To preserve and nourish one's mind is to develop mind into the ontological state of oneness and self-mastery. *Ching* can induce harmony of activated emotions because *ching* transforms the mind into a state of self-mastery that has the potential and ability to respond to things in proper measure—a true application of the *chung*. Hence, *ching* can be said to be identifiable with *chung*. In this sense, *ching* cannot be quietude (*ching*) in the Taoist sense, but contains virtual force of movement within bounds of propriety.

In light of this clarification of *ching*, we can understand why *chü-ching* and *ch'iung-li* are said by Chu Hsi to refer to one substance, even though they are two items or two concepts[15]; for they both refer to the mind and *are* to function for the investigation of things leading to *ch'iung-li* or preserving the oneness and wholeness of the mind, leading to a metaphysical self-reflection of mind. As Chu Hsi pointed out, both functions of mind are essential for developing the human person into sagehood. They also are complementary to each other, for one is in a condition to promote and assist the other. Chu Hsi said, thus: "Holding *ching* is the basis of *ch'iung-li*, when the *li* is made clear, this becomes the help for nourishing the mind."[16]

Now one may still question the rationale and theoretical basis for the complementation of *chü-ching* and *ch'iung-li*. Throughout Chu Hsi's writings, this rationale was never clearly formulated nor the question quite explicitly posed. However, there is one very suggestive passage in the *Chu Tzu Yü Lei*: "*Chü-ching* is one way and one principle of contraction and holding-steadfast whereas *ch'iung-li* is one way and one principle of extending and finding ultimate reasons."[17] Chu Hsi also said that "These two are like each other and are not obstructive of each other."[18] But this in fact is not quite correct. *Chü-ching* and *ch'iung-li* are two things not obstructive of each other, yet they appear to have different functions and represent different modes of movement—contraction and extension. This means that they belong to different principles of reality and reality-formation and -transformation. These different principles are those of *yang* and *yin*. In this light, the holistic paradigm of *yin-yang* opposition and complementation in the diagram of the Great Ultimate applies to the mind and its functions. The holistic paradigm of *yin-yang* relation illuminates and illustrates the relation of *chü-ching* and *ch'iung-li*. In this light, the relation between *chü-ching* and *ch'iung-li* becomes *understandable* and *explainable*. Not only the difference and opposition between the two are understandable and explainable, their complementation, unity, and mutual stimulation also are understandable and explainable. Thus, when Chu Hsi said that these two things mutually reinforce and stimulate, he made a good point, even though he did not explain why.

In fact, the *yin-yang* paradigm of the great ultimate not only provides a logical explanation of *chü-ching* and *ch'iung-li*, it provides a metaphysical explanation of the functions of the mind. Namely, mind is a great ultimate with *chü-ching* and *ch'iung-li* representing the *yin* and *yang* activities of the mind substance of the great ultimate. This point should coincide with Chu Hsi's remark on another occasion:"The principle of mind is the great ultimate. The movement and rest of mind is *yin* and *yang*."[19] This also means that *chü-ching* and *ch'iung-li* are equally necessary and natural in a metaphysical sense for maintaining the substance-status of the mind.

Insofar as *ching* comprehends the roots of movement and rest, *ching* can be described as *potential creativity*, which is a mode of the substance of mind, so to speak. In such a state *ching* also may be said to hold the self-nature of mind before it is activated in knowing and acting. It can be described as *root-mindedness*—a mind finding its root-nature. To contrast with knowing, insofar as *knowing* (in the sense of investigating things and extending knowledge) is activation of the mind—a manifestation of the *yang* principle, the *ching* is the preservation of the mind—a manifestation of the *yin* principle. As the mind is open to knowing, *ching* is the force and principle to make mind start to know possible and thus *ching* plays the role of *yin* as the root for movement, namely the root for the principle of *yang*. But once the mind has knowledge, then *ching* will order and preserve (*sou*) the *knowledge*. In this the sense, *ching* becomes the penetrating principle linking the beginning and ending of *minding* as a way of self-fulfillment. *Ching* can be described as metaphysical self-reflection of mind or *self-minding* of the *mind*. This leads to a most important point suggested by Mencius.

Mencius said: "The way of learning is merely to seek the wandering mind" (6A-11). This beautiful expression indicates the essence of *ching* in the sense of "self-minding" of mind. The wandering mind (*wang-hsin*) Mencius spoke of is the mind losing its self-mastery and incapable of minding itself. When the mind wanders, it loses its sense of direction and learning, and there can be no focus for learning and knowing. Thus, to seek the lost or wandering mind is the way of the *ching. Ching* is both the ability to seek and the ability to restore the wandering mind. It is also the outcome of such a search—the state of self-minding and self-concentration.

Mencius also spoke of two basic principles for learning that can be said to further explicate the concept of *ching*. The first principle is that of "not to forget" (*wu-wang*) and the second principle is that of "not to help to grow" (*wu-ch'u-chang*).[20] Mencius formulated these two principles in discussing how to know *yi* (righteousness) for "nourishing the great flood of *ch'i* (vitality)." The mind is a matter of *ch'i* embodying *li* according to most of the Neo-Confucianists including Chu Hsi. Then the *mind* can naturally develop its *ch'i* in concert with the *li* (called the *tao* and *yi* by Mencius). For Mencius, this process is not a contriving and artificial one, but one based on righteousness.

We may suggest that *ching* is the natural *process* of mind-development which one must not forget, nor must one push it or force it to grow. One can reach *ching* therefore if one can relate to one's original mind (*pen-hsin*) or "the mind of innocent child" (*ch'ih-tzu-chih-hsin*). In a deeper ontological sense, *ching* is the original mind or the mind of the innocent child—the mind that gives authenticity to one's existence, instills integrity to one's action, and provides impetus for seeking knowledge and learning without losing self-control and moral guidance. *Ching* thus becomes the ultimate guiding principle for learning and knowing.

Throughout the *Yü Lei*, Chu Hsi referred directly and indirectly to *ching* numerous times, particularly from *ch'üan* 8 to *ch'üan* 12. He speaks of *chü-ching*, *han-hang*, *tzun-yang* (of the mind). He has covered the three major senses of the *ching* and principles of abiding by *ching* in these. His concept of *ching* or *chü-ching* derived essentially from the Ch'eng Brothers. We need not quote from Chu Hsi here. But the unique contribution Chu Hsi made concerns how the *chü-ching* relates to *ch'iung-li*. He insightfully asserted that both *chü-ching and ch'iung-li* mutually complement, reciprocate, reinforce, and form a unity with each other, and they derive from one body. However, there is one problem that Chu Hsi did not settle to satisfaction. When queried which comes first, extending knowledge or preserving the mind, Chu Hsi said:"One must first extend knowledge and then preserve the mind."[21] When queried how Ch'eng I could say that there is no extension of knowledge not residing in the *ching*, Chu Hsi said: "This is only to speak in outline. When one desires to exhaust *li*, one must have the intention. Without the intention, how one can understand clearly" (ibid.). But apparently Chu Hsi did not make clear his justification for the priority of *chih-chih* over *chü-ching*. It appears that if such a justification could be made, it would not bear on the ultimate notion of the *ching*. In this ultimate notion of *ching*, *ching* already is the original mind: It is the beginning and potential for extending knowledge and learning. But, of course, in a secondary sense, the *chü-ching* becomes meaningful and active only after there is knowledge to relate to the original mind. The relationship between extension of knowledge and *chü-ching* (*han-hang*) in light of our explanation earlier can be perhaps diagrammed as follows:

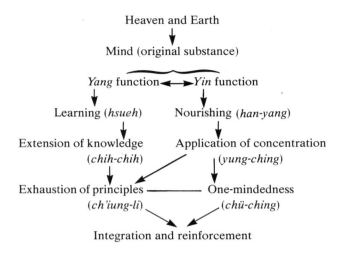

Heaven and Earth

Mind (original substance)

Yang function ←→ *Yin* function

Learning (*hsueh*)   Nourishing (*han-yang*)

Extension of knowledge   Application of concentration
(*chih-chih*)   (*yung-ching*)

Exhaustion of principles ———— One-mindedness
(*ch'iung-li*)   (*chü-ching*)

Integration and reinforcement

This diagram indicates how the mind, as derived from heaven and earth, has two inherent functions, *yin* and *yang*, that ground and originate its ability to learn and extend knowledge, on the one hand, and its ability to preserve *mind* in its wholeness and oneness, on the other. Both abilities are necessary to each other and complement and reinforce each other just like the *yin* and *yang* are necessary to each other and complement and reinforce each other.

Methodological Structure in Chu Hsi

In light of our analysis of the methodology of learning of Chu Hsi, we find that the two categorical principles of his methodology—"nourishing one's mind and advancing one's learning"—are interrelated and form a unity, and that they have to be understood correctly in relation to the nature of mind and the relation of mind to heaven and earth. In fact, the methodological unity of nourishing and learning, and the consequential epistemological unity of "applying *ching*" and "fulfilling *li*," must be understood in light of the *t'ai-chi* principle of *yin-yang* unity on an ontological level. The methodological emphasis on "nourishing" and "applying *ching*" acquires epistemological significance specifically because of the role it plays in generating a total and profound knowledge of principles from the mind. This means that the methodology of nourishing one's mind by "applying *ching*" becomes epistemologically important because of the ontological basis and background from which it also derives its justification.

"Nourishing the mind by way of applying *ching*" is a function of the *yin* just as "advancing the learning by way of reaching knowledge of the principles" is a function of the *yang*. The unity of *yin* and *yang* functions provides the unity of the "nourishing the mind" and "advancing the learning" and their reciprocal complementarity and mutual creative stimulation. This leads to the conception of the total fulfillment of the great function of mind in a process of learning. This total fulfillment of the great function of mind thus has an ontological significance. It shows the great function of heaven and earth in creativity. Thus we have the bridge from the doctrine of the *Great Learning* on learning to the *Doctrine of the Mean* on creative participation in activities of heaven and earth. To generalize, we may say that, for Chu Hsi, the methodology of learning embodies and thus reflects and presupposes his epistemology of principles (*li*); and the latter, by the same token, embodies and thus reflects and presupposes his ontology of *t'ai-chi* and *yin-yang*. One could not understand his methodology of learning unless one sees his epistemology of *li* and his ontology of *t'ai-chi* and *yin-yang*. When one comes to the levels of epistemology and ontology, one comes to have a full appreciation of his methodology of learning and understanding, their why and how, as far as their two dimensions or two requirements are concerned.

Another important aspect of Chu Hsi's methodology consists in the application of this methodology to life and practice. We can see from the arrangements of topics in the *Chin Ssu Lu* (edited by Chu Hsi and Lü Tzu-ch'ien) not only that the understanding of the *tao-t'i* comes before learning (*wei-hsueh*), reaching for knowledge (*chih-chih*), and preserving and nourishing one's mind (*tsun-yang*), but that *wei-hsueh*, *chih-chin*, and *tsun-yang* are followed by governing one's self (*ke-chih*), under which title cultivation, discipline, and fulfillment of the whole self are discussed. The same order of topics also is observed in the *Yü Lei*. In the *Yü Lei*, the idea of *ke-chih* is represented by the idea of earnest practice (*li-hsing*) just as the idea of *tsun-yang* is represented by the idea of "holding and abiding" (*ch'ih-sou*). This order of topics suggests an ordering of principles for Chu Hsi's methodology of learning. To learn is to seek the *tao-t'i* and to apply to life and practice what one has learned. The categorical principles of "nourishing" and "studying" thus fulfill a double function: They are ways to reach the ultimate total truth, they also are ways to guide, order, and perfect one's actual life. One may even suggest that the scope of application of the knowledge of principles to practice and life can grow larger and larger as one learns more and more about the *li*. Thus, we can understand the process from the self-cultivation to regulating family to governing well one's state and to pacifying the world as a natural extension of one's practice and application of the learning of the *tao-t'i*. In this fashion we can see how Chu

Hsi's methodology of learning provides and articulates a clear model for understanding the Confucian statement: "To learn from below and to reach for the above" (*hsia-hsüeh-erh-shang-ta*).[22]

In light of the above, we may represent Chu Hsi's methodology of learning as follows:

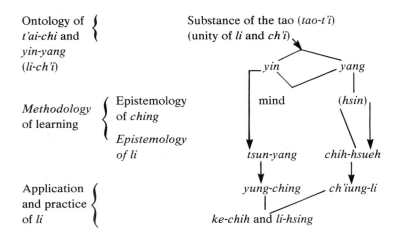

Ontology of ⎰
t'ai-chi and ⎱
yin-yang
(*li-ch'i*)

Methodology ⎰ Epistemology
of learning ⎱ of *ching*
  Epistemology
  of *li*

Application ⎰
and practice ⎨
of *li* ⎱

Substance of the tao (*tao-t'i*)
(unity of *li* and *ch'i*)

yin   yang

mind   (*hsin*)

tsun-yang   chih-hsueh

yung-ching   ch'iung-li
ke-chih and li-hsing

Contemporary Analytic Relevancies

How do Chu Hsi's views on method, knowledge, and truth stand in light of contemporary Western philosophy? Specifically, how can his views be understood in light of the analytical approach in contemporary Western philosophy? If we look into literature in contemporary studies in epistemology, we will find that some basic ideas in contemporary studies on knowledge and truth elucidate Chu Hsi's view. This also could mean that Chu Hsi's views on method, knowledge, and truth approach certain basic views in contemporary epistemology, and suggest a profound contemporary significance. Here, I shall merely discuss briefly three aspects of Chu Hsi's methodology in light of contemporary works of Roderick Chisholm, a distinguished and influential philosopher on knowledge and truth.

First, in his *Theory of Knowledge*[23] Chisholm argued, following the example of A. Meinong, that there are "self-presenting states of affairs" that constitute a proper starting place for knowing, on the one hand, and provide a basis and justification of all knowledge, on the other. According to Chisholm's definition of *self-presentation* of states of affairs, states of affairs that are self-presenting for a person are those that occur at certain times and, when they occur, necessarily are directly evident for that person. An alternative way of explaining this is this: h is self-presenting for S at t if h is true at t; and necessarily, if h is true at t, then h is evident for S at t.[24]

For a proposition to be directly evident for one person, of course, means that the person will accept the proposition as true. For a state of affairs to be directly evident for one person means that the person will accept the state of affairs as naturally given and representing reality or truth. The idea of self-presentation of truth or fact therefore implies (1) the fact or truth when presented gives rise to genuine knowledge; (2) presentation of the fact or truth is a presentation to the mind; (3) the mind, when presented with the fact or truth, immediately recognizes it as fact or truth, which means that the mind has a truth-recognizing and truth-preserving capacity and an ontological import derived from such capacity.

With this understanding of self-presentation of reality and truth, we may see that Chu Hsi and indeed his predecessors, the Ch'eng Brothers, all believe in self-presentation of reality and truth. One may say that Chu Hsi together with Ch'eng Brothers founded their philosophy of *ti'en-li* on the basis of the self-presenting virtue of *t'ien-li* as well as the self-presentation-cognitive power of the mind. All *t'ien-li* or *li* eventually are self-presenting to a person if a person engages in learning. In fact, Chu Hsi's theory of *ch'iung-li* suggests that *li* already is presented in things and inherent in one's mind; it just takes the effort of learning to make *li* presented in mind. *Li* will naturally present itself when the mind is unobscured by desires and bias and when learning persists. Learning therefore is simply a way to achieve the self-presentation of *li*. When *li* is self-presented, one has knowledge; if not, one does not have knowledge. Knowledge of *li* comes naturally and spontaneously, because it is in the nature of self-presentation that *li* becomes knowledge of *li*. This also reflects the receptive power of mind called *ling-chüeh* (subtle perception), which obtains when one devotes oneself to learning.

Although the notion of self-presentation of reality and truth elucidates Chu Hsi's epistemology of *li*, it must be recognized that Chu Hsi's view on *li* goes beyond the scope of self-presenting truth granted by Chisholm or Meinong. For Chu Hsi, all *li* and ultimate *li* are known through their self-presentation and mind-cultivation, but for Chisholm self-presentation as a source of knowledge applies only to sense perception and inner consciousness of one's thoughts and feelings, leaving external things, other minds, ethics, and metaphysics to the category of the indirectly evident and inference by logic, induction, or criteria.[25] In other words, for Chu Hsi self-presentation is a mode of knowing for all inclusive truth, including truth through reading, truth of external things, other persons, ethics, and metaphysics, perhaps specifically truth of metaphysics, which is the foundation of all truth and learning for Chu Hsi.

This leads to the second point about Chu Hsi's methodology of learning in light of Chisholm. Because of the gap between knowledge by indirect evidence and truth, Chisholm has to acknowledge that one may have knowledge (in the indirectly evidential sense) that could be false. He said: "Hence, if we are not to be skeptics, and if we are not to restrict the evident to what is directly evident, we must face the possibility that a belief may be a belief in what is evident, or a belief for which we have adequate evidence and at the same time, be a belief in what is false."[26] This is certainly an undesirable conclusion, a conclusion testifying to the problem of the discrepancy between knowledge and truth.

To resolve this discrepancy, one can define truth in terms of knowledge. But this merely divorces truth from reality, and the problem of knowing reality still persists. The only solution therefore seems to consist in requiring that: (1) All truth must be directly evident to the mind; and (2) all indirectly evident propositions must be considered only as hypotheses. This seems to be precisely Chu Hsi's position. For him truth (*li*) must be fully evident to the person; otherwise, one cannot be said to have understood the truth. The idea of *tao-t'i* is the idea of total truth. As soon as one reaches the *tao-t'i*, one comes to have full knowledge. This is clearly evidenced in Chu Hsi's statement on the totality of the great function of mind. When one reaches the point of "sudden inner penetration" (*hou-jan-kuan-t'ung*), one cannot be said to have knowledge of truth.

Truth for Chu Hsi is totalistic and the evidence for such totalistic understanding is the fulfillment of the total function of mind by way of the process of learning. The experience of "sudden interpenetration" in the mind is an index and criterion for grasping the whole truth and thus for having full knowledge. In other words, as suggested earlier, for Chu Hsi, there can be no truth apart from total truth and no knowledge apart from full knowledge. Consequently, the method of learning can be said to provide a context for full knowledge of the total truth. The method of knowing in this light therefore has to be one of self-presentation and direct evidencing, and there is no other way of knowing that can resolve the problem of discrepancy between knowledge and truth.

Chisholm in a way recognizes the significance of this view, but he raises the following question: "But how are to assure ourselves that a belief that is evident to *us* is one that would also be evident to a being for whom all truth are evident?"[27] Chisholm's answer is that "We will now be asked to assume not only that there is such a being, a being for whom all truths are evident, but also that each of us is identical with that being, and therefore with each other."[28] This conclusion Chisholm calls the *coherence theory of truth* belonging to the idealistic tradition.[29] He was not ready to embrace this conclusion, for it seemed to him to assume too much. In light of Chu Hsi's metaphysics and methodology, however, we need not be so pessimistic. For ontologically there is no need to separate one individual mind from that of another. Chu Hsi's philosophy of mind permits that, in achieving ultimate understanding of *li*, one's mind is the same as the mind of sages and, for that matter, the same as the mind of heaven and earth. In other words, all minds share the same *t'ai-chi*, and the purpose of learning is precisely to enable the individual person's mind to identify with the mind of heaven and earth or the mind of sages as discussed. This also is best evidenced by Lu Hsiang-shan's statement "Everyone has this same mind and every mind has this same principle."[30]

As to whether there is such a being to which all truth is evident, the answer is that the mind of heaven and earth is precisely such a being. But, here, evidence should mean self-presentation. As we have seen, the mind of heaven and earth is understood precisely as the total self-presentation of total truth (*tao-t'i*) in nature and world. Are these statements merely assumptions, given our explanation of the self-presenting nature of truth (*li*) and the totalistic characteristic of *li*? The answer is that what may appear to be assumptions to Chisholm may be said to be self-evident truth pertaining to the total self-presentation of total truth for a mind in a persistent process of learning. This is indeed the ultimate justification of Chu Hsi's methodology of learning. In this methodology, the concept of method also becomes self-presenting and there is consistency of method, knowledge, and truth in Chu Hsi's philosophy.[31] This is the third point about Chu Hsi's methodology in light of Chisholm.

Notes

1. See the *Journal of Chinese Philosophy* Vol. 5, No. 2, June 1978, also Chang Chung-yuan's article, *Kant's Aesthetics and the East*, JCP Vol 3. Sept. 1976, #4 p. 399.
2. *Yü Lei* is an authentic record of Chu Hsi's sayings on all important topics in Chinese Philosophy as well as reflections and comments on Confucian Classics. It is a primary source for study of Chu Hsi.
3. See the *Analects* 7-30.
4. See the *Analects* 15-29.
5. See Chu Hsi's *Shih Shu Chi Ch'u*.
6. See *Meng Tzu Chi Ch'u* on *Ching-hsin*.
7. Ibid., on *Mencius* 38.
8. See Ta Hsueh P'u Chuan.
9. Chu Tzu Lu Lei, 445.
10. See *Chin Ssu Lu*, Chapter 2, 40.
11. Ibid., 62.
12. Ibid., 63.
13. Ibid., 150.
14. Ibid., 153.
15. Ibid., 446.
16. Ibid., 446.
17. Ibid., 446.
18. Ibid., 446.
19. Ibid., 314.
20. See the *Mencius*, 2A-2.
21. See *Chu Tzu Lu Lei*, 449.
22. See the *Analects*, 14-35.
23. Robert Chisholm, *Theory of Knowledge*, Englewood Cliffs, N.J., 1977.
24. See Chisolm's *Theory of Knowledge*, 22.
25. See Chislom, op. cit., Chapters 4 and 7.
26. Ibid., 99.
27. Ibid., 100.
28. Ibid., 100.

29. Ibid., 100.
30. It is a statement from *The Complete Works of Lu Hsiang-shan.*
31. Under such a consistency, however, nothing suggests that Chu Hsi's philosophy or methodology must be regarded as idealistic. One may also suspect that Chu Hsi's methodology may not yield the scientific knowledge required by the modern physical sciences. To comment on this, it suffices to point out that clearly Chu Hsi's methodology does not yield all the scientific knowledge required by the modern sciences nor is this the goal of his pursuit, but it is not clear whether Chu Hsi's methodology of learning may not yield the method of science that yields scientific knowledge if we allow a relatively independent development of *chih-chih* on the practical and applied level and a delayed integration of scientific knowledge with axiological values of self-cultivation, moral practice, and self-fulfillment.

16. Unity and Creativity in Wang Yang-ming's Philosophy of Mind

General Remarks on Wang Yang-ming's Philosophy of Mind

When discussing Wang Yang-ming, one cannot avoid questioning his philosophy of mind. What is his philosophy of mind? The proper answer to this question is that Wang's philosophy of mind is his total philosophy, which consists of a special *philosophy* of mind and a philosophy of *mind*, in a special sense. It is indeed in this twofold sense of philosophy of mind that the Chinese term *hsin hsüeh* (or the study of mind) is to be understood. It is typical of Wang Yang-ming that his philosophy of mind consists of a theory of experience and a theory of method, the former referring to a phenomenological account of whatever the mind experiences and the latter referring to a transcendental critique of how ideal values of the experiencing mind might be fully realized and developed. Indeed, the *philosophy* of mind is based on actual observations of the functioning of the mind and is developed for the purpose of achieving an adequate understanding of the mind in relation to various levels of reality. On the other hand, the philosophy of *mind* is based on a metaphysical view of *mind*, and is developed for the purpose of applying this view to the actual functionings of the mind in order that *mind* can reach a state of ultimate value (called goodness) and reality.

I believe that the substantial view and the methodological view, the descriptive-phenomenological elements and the normative-practical elements, are well blended in all Neo-Confucian philosophers and are conspicuously illustrated by Wang Yang-ming. Thus one can see that the doctrine of "mind-is-principle" (*hsin-chi-li*) is basically a descriptive-phenomenological view or a substantial view of elements, though not without methodological as well as normative-practical significance. The doctrine of "unity of knowing and acting" (*chih-hsing-ho-yi*), as the third well-formed doctrine in Yang-ming's philosophy, represents a balanced combination of a substantial component and a methodological component, and therefore seems to form, as it were, a natural bridge and connection between the first doctrine and the last doctrine.

From these general meta-philosophical reflections of Yang-ming's philosophy of mind as a whole, it is not difficult to see that his philosophy of mind is indeed one of unity, a unity of experience and method, a unity of description and prescription, and a unity of cognition and performance. All these unities are only to be explained by the creative insights of Yang-ming into mind and reality, and are to be conceived of as a creative agency, which leads to many important philosophical theses, which cannot be otherwise understood, as well as to fruitful answers to many philosophical problems which cannot be otherwise formulated.

In this chapter I shall not give a detailed formulation of Yang-ming's philosophy of mind but will instead deal with the essential features and kinds of unity and creativity in his philosophy of mind in the twofold sense as indicated earlier. I shall hold that the best spirit of Wang's philosophy of mind is found in his understanding the unity and creativity of an ultimate reality, which understanding ultimately accrues to his notion of *mind*.

Nonsubstantial Substance (Original Reality) of Mind

As a concept, *mind* (*hsin*) in Wang Yang-ming must be understood in different senses. In a metaphysical sense *mind* is the same as *t'ien* (heaven) or the ultimate reality and its way of operating, and thus is as comprehensive and as powerful as *t'ien*. On a more restricted level—the level of the existence of man—mind is the same as *hsing* (nature), which is the universal and potential reality for all men. It is the source of all of man's activities, motivations, feelings, and perceptions. It is in fact a unity which does not exclude the physical existence of man. In the narrowest sense, *mind* is the commanding and controlling agency of the physical body of a man or function of the nature of man. It is rooted in nature but manifests itself in a distinctive mode of existence, which must be independently characterized. The dominating feature of the mind in this mode of existence is the combined *unity* and *creativity* as indicated earlier, by which the potential of the universals *t'ien* and *nature*, their unity and creativity, can be fully realized.

The realization of unity and creativity on different levels by the mind should result in different concrete virtues. On the level of *t'ien*, the realization of the potential of *t'ien* by the mind leads to a rich exhibition of *t'ien-li* (principles of heaven). On the level of *hsing* (nature), the realization of the potential of *hsing* by the mind leads to a rich exhibition of such *p'iao-te* (manifest virtues) as *jên* (benevolence), *yi* (righteousness), *li* (propriety), and *chih* (wisdom), which are the basis for bringing unity, harmony, and goodness to humanity as a whole. The actual consequence of fulfilling the potential of the mind itself is the concrete and universal application of the principles of unity and creativity to produce more unity and creativity on every level of existence and in every area of life-experience. Thus, realization of the mind itself is self-justifying and self-sustained. All these in a metaphysical sense comprise Yang-ming's doctrines of "unity of knowing and acting" and "fulfilling the mind's knowledge of goodness."[1]

Several points can be made about this metaphysical view of the mind which will bear upon a well-known philosophical thesis of Wang Yang-ming:

1. The mind, which is identified with *t'ien*, *t'i*, *hsing*, and *ming*, is the same mind in different concrete manifestations. The increasing comprehension of mind does not diminish its constant concreteness. For *t'ien*, *ming*, *t'i*, and *hsing* in both their classical and their Sung Neo-Confucian contexts are concrete terms indicating concrete processes and realities, not mere abstractions detached from reality. In this sense *mind* in its most comprehensive aspect is to be given meaning by the experiencing of actual phenomena and events in the world. The important point about mind in this view is that the mind must be understood as the ultimate reality with its unity and creativity. It is due to the unity in this ultimate reality[2] that the mind can and should be identified with realities of different scopes; and it is due to the creativity in this ultimate reality that the mind can be understood in terms of and considered enfolded in realities of different scopes.

   It is in this sense that the *mind* of a person is not merely his mind but, originally, the *mind* of the total universe.[3] And the reality of things in the universe is not merely part of the universe, but part of the *mind* which experiences and contributes to the understanding of reality as reality.

2. If we ask about the metaphysical constituent of what the mind is made of, a simple answer is *ch'i* (vapor, vital force). Yang-ming speaks about *ch'i* in many contexts, and all indicate the unity and a creative agency, it must be the concrete activity of *ch'i* itself. The main function of the mind in its narrowest application is *liang-chih* (knowledge of innate goodness). The *liang-chih* of the mind, as the defining substance of mind (*pen-t'i*), is called *ch'i* in its actual operation.[4] In other passages, Yang-ming explicitly says that "*ch'i* is nature, and nature is *ch'i*" in giving a proper meaning to K'ao Tzu's assertion that living is called nature.[5] As the mind is not different from *hsing*,

mind is not different from *ch'i*. The reason *mind* should be meta-physically identified with *ch'i* rather than with *li*—both *li* and *ch'i* being two fundamental principles of Chu Hsi's philosophy—is that *ch'i* is not confined to one form, but is formless and most active. It is considered the source of all forms and all distinctions, these being explained on the creativity of *ch'i*.[6]

We may now represent the mind in Wang Yang-ming's philosophy in its two dimensions of unity and creativity. In one dimension the mind achieves its unity with *t'ien* and *ming*, *t'i* and *hsing*, and *sheng* (the physical body). Its creativity is seen in the existence of the mind as consisting of reality of different scopes. In another dimension, the unity and creativity of the mind is demonstrated by closely examining Yang-ming's basic doctrines of *chih-hsing-ho-yi* and *chih-liang-chih*; both relate the mind to practice and every actual aspect of life. As we shall see, the doctrine of *chih-liang-chih* together with the doctrine of *chih-hsing-ho-yi* is not merely ethical in its application but is important for ontologically fulfilling the unity of the mind, principles, and their creative differentiation.[7] It thus represents the ultimate development of Wang Yang-ming's philosophy of the unity and creativity of the mind par excellence. A representation of these two dimensions of unity and the creativity according to Wang Yang-ming is given as follows:

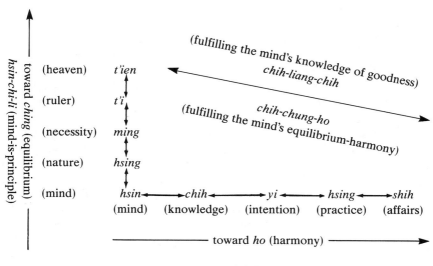

chih-hsing-ho-yi
(unity of knowing and acting)

Original Reality of the Mind as Manifested in *liang-chih*

The mind, as a centralized reality (*t'i*) of creative powers, but not as a mere mirrorlike consciousness, is capable of many functions. The activation of these functions is both natural and a matter of cultivation. It is natural because the mind by its metaphysical nature will manifest itself in different forms of activity. On the other hand, the activation of functions and capabilities of the mind is a result of moral effort, a process of self-correction and self-guidance, which is understood only in moral and metaphysical terms.

In a process of realizing its functions (*yung*), the substance (*t'i*) of the mind is naturally always in a state of vacuity, intelligence, perceptiveness, and sensitivity (*hsu-ling-ming-chüeh*) or a state of intelligent clarity and illuminating perception (*ling-chao-ming-chüeh*). The terms *hsu-ling-ming-chüeh* or *ling-chao-ming-chüeh* are metaphysical and must be understood in terms of the unity and creativity of the mind.[8] For what makes the mind *ling-chao-ming-chüeh* or *hsu-ling-ming-chüeh* is nothing but the intrinsic qualities of the mind in interaction with things in the world. To conceive of the mind in this fashion is to conceive of the mind as a creative agency of various functions, which nevertheless forms a unity of ultimateness and primariness.

We have seen that insofar as the mind is understood as original reality (*pen-t'i*) in a metaphysical sense, the mind is also called the *liang-chih-pen-t'i*. But what is this *liang-chih-pen-t'i*? In the classical Mencian sense it is an ability that is not a result of learning or thinking but that both knows and determines the value of good or bad in a thing. I think it is in this primary, Mencian sense that Yang-ming speaks of *liang-chih*. Thus he says: "*Liang-chih* is what Mencius called the feeling of right and wrong which is possessed by all men. The feeling of right and wrong is known without thinking and made possible without learning. It is because of this it is called *liang-chih*."[9]

I think that there are at least four aspects of this primary sense of *liang-chih* which have not been explicitly spelled out, but which are important to clarify.

First, *liang-chih* is a perception of right and wrong in the *mind* and an ability to judge good and bad. It is a perceptive grasp and understanding which will direct oneself to goodness and will enable oneself to realize one's nature. It is the perceptive grasp and understanding of the ultimate goodness of nature. This perception of the ultimate goodness of nature is to be explained in two directions. (1) To experience ultimate goodness is to perceive the innateness of reality of one's nature in the total reality and thus to perceive the unity of oneself with the ultimate reality: there is no demarcation between oneself and the ultimate reality. It is, furthermore, the creative power which fulfills the nature of oneself and everything else. It is the same power which gives life to the whole reality and preserves the totality as a living reality. (2) To grasp the ultimate goodness of one's nature or mind is to see it as a standard from which one is to derive judgments of good and bad for courses of action: for a course of action will be worthy only when it contributes to the manifestation or the understanding of this ultimate goodness. These two aspects of perceiving goodness are well integrated in the idea of *liang-chih-chih*, which also explains why this perception itself is good and practically creative. The perception of goodness and the goodness of perception are two phases of the same reality and process, which is dictated by the *pen-t'i* conception of *liang-chih* or conception of *liang-chih* as *pen-t'i*.[10]

Second, the existence of *liang-chih* as a perception and as a judging ability regarding good and bad must be understood as supremely and ultimately good, and good beyond comparison. For it is by conformity with the nature of *liang-chih* that good and bad in application must be decided. The ultimate good of *liang-chih* is thus ontological good or good as a standard: It is good simply by its existence in virtue of its giveness and existence. It must be thus existentially understood.[11]

Third, *liang-chih* is self-knowledge or self-reflective knowledge. Wang Yang-ming has stressed this point. The self-knowledge in *liang-chih* is the knowledge of good and bad when *liang-chih* is activated in relation to individual affairs of life. In this sense *liang-chih* is making an evaluative judgment of one's intentions. The self-knowledge becomes a basis for action and choice. Whether one chooses the good or bad and develops it or not is not a matter of self-knowledge but a matter of *chih-liang-chih* (fulfilling one's innate knowledge of goodness). Yang-ming says: "In all cases when intentions are activated, the *liang-chih* of my mind by no means does not know itself in this. Is it good? The *liang-chih* of my mind naturally knows. Is it not good? It is also the *liang-chih* of my mind which will naturally know."[12] He also says: "The *liang-chih* naturally knows itself. It is, of course, easy. But if one cannot fulfill one's *liang-chih*, then one has a case of 'knowing being not difficult, but practicing being difficult.' "[13] I shall discuss later the nature and significance of *chih-liang-chih*.

By virtue of what we said earlier, *liang-chih* as *pen-t'i* is naturally the ruling power (*ch'u-che*) of one's existence. It is the ruling principle because, again, it is the most fundamental, and because it is the source of unity and creativity in all man's activities and in his position in the world.

Finally, *liang-chih* is *pen-t'i* or *hsin-t'i-pen-t'i* (the original reality of mind) as such it is identified with heaven, nature, *ming*, and *t'ien-li*. It is the ultimate unity and source of creativity in a metaphysical sense. It is basically a power or will (*yi*) that is practical and creative. It is thus conceived of as the foundation of action (*hsing*), and thus it always provides both guidance and momentum for action.

Given the above explanation of the mind as *liang-chih*, it is clear that the mind, on the one hand, is a perceptive state[14] which embodies the substance of goodness; but, on the other hand, is a sensitive process of response, growth, and development. This creative and active process-nature aspect of *liang-chih-pen-t'i* or the mind is brought out very clearly in the following passage: "Someone asked: 'The early Confucianists say that like the flying of birds and jumping of fish the engagement of the mind in specific effort and activity (*pi-yu-shih-yen*) is vitally lively as well.' (Yang-ming) answers: '(What is presented) as vitally active in the heaven and earth is nothing but this principle; and this is but the unceasing activities of my *liang-chih*'."[15]

On *yi* as Activation of the Mind and as a Form of Creativity

The result of actual creativity of the mind as a process of response is called *yi* (intentions) by Yang-ming. It occurs where the mind has activated itself (*hsin-chih-fa-tung-chu*). But when the mind activates itself, the mind remains perceptive, and therefore can know (*chih*) where it has activated itself. The object of such activation is called *wu* (thing) and more often called *shih* (a state of affairs or situation). Thus activation of the mind, in response to the world in a situation and as a form of interaction with the world, is a complex relation and forms a unity which is made possible by the mind. It is by the creativity of the mind that an individual relation in such a situation and in situations involving such a relation is created.

The mind is not only unified with *yi* and *chih* and *wu* in a concrete situation, it is identified with the actual senses of the body, for the very sensibility of senses is conceived as a function of the mind. The concreteness of such a situation involving *yi* is located in the specific reference to things. In other words, *yi* is initiated or arises only in reference to and in response to concrete things.[16]

As directed toward a thing and involved in a situation, *yi* may be thus considered a motivating force for action and realization of a value in a situation. It can be identified with what is willed and wanted in a situation. In this sense *yi* is the beginning of action and an occasion for acquiring direct experience or knowledge of the value of a situation.[17]

What is clearly brought out here is that *yi* is the practicality for action and the occasion of an experience, which the mind can tell to be desirable (good) or undesirable (bad), and thus a basis for decision-making or choice-making. *Yi* therefore can be regarded as the creative agency of the mind, for it is through *yi* that the mind becomes related to the world in a specific relation that leads to action. *Yi* is the motivating force for knowledge. And not only is *yi* the motivating force for knowledge and the direction for action, it is where things become meaningful to us. In this sense *yi* gives meaning to things, and thus Yang-ming speaks of *wu* (things) as *shih* (affairs). Affairs are things becoming related or being related to us. Without *yi* things are unrelated to us and are not understood in such relation. Thus *wu* is in this sense conditioned and constituted by *yi*.[18]

All the actual examples of *wu* clearly indicate that they are *shih* in the sense of states of affairs. Thus Yang-ming speaks of employing *yi* when serving one's parents, governing people, studying, or when hearing a litigation. All these affairs are *wu* and thus *shih* for Yang-ming. To employ *yi* at these affairs is to relate these affairs to oneself and to experience them to determine the values which one needs to fulfill in relation to them. Thus we may indeed regard the creative employment of *yi* as the basis for fulfilling *chih-hsing-ho-yi* and *chih-liang-chih*, which are ways of realizing the unity and creativity of mind and man.

Unity and Creativity of the Mind in Its Activation: *Chih-Hsing-Ho-Yi*

If we look carefully into passages of Wang Yang-ming's writings dealing with the unity of knowledge and practice (*chih-hsing-ho-yi*), we can easily see that this unity of knowledge and practice is itself a demonstration of the unity and creativity of the mind. The basis for this unity is *yi*, which is, on the one hand, the creative response of mind to things through mind's knowledge, and, on the other hand, the directive force and purpose for action. *Yi* itself has shown its unity and creativity of mind, and therefore the unity of knowledge and action will lie in *yi*. Two implicit principles underlie this unity and creativity of mind in its activation in the form of *yi*.

First, in the light of our metaphysical understanding of the mind, the mind is the ultimate reality and thus the principle of heaven (*t'ien-li*), which is thus good in its ultimate form.[19] It is not merely an objectified static state but an active and creative agency, which is described by our term "creativity": it is creativity with insight, understanding, and enlightenment (*ming*). Perhaps it can be called enlightened creativity. It is a unity, not because it is one principle, but because from it all principles will reveal themselves in the concrete creative application of the mind to things, and to it all principles will converge for meaningfulness and fulfillment. Thus, the activity of the mind is both creative and spontaneous: it is always enlightened or in accordance with supreme goodness and its understanding.

Second, *yi* can be conceived of as an individualized mind-activity, which is to realize reason (*li*) in concrete situations. It is a form of self-realization. It is thus practical from the very beginning. In fact, one may take "practical action" as a means or a way by which the mind activates or responds spontaneously, if there is no obstruction. What I am not suggesting is that *chih* (knowledge) and *hsing* (action) are not separate and separable, in an ontological sense, at the very beginning: It is not as though we know first, then act accordingly. Instead, it is that one simultaneously knows of good and acts according to knowledge of good, where good is individualized and spontaneous activation or response of mind in the form of *yi*.[20]

In a state of complete goodness and genuine reality, the mind will recognize the need of a situation and for that matter will recognize the nature of the situation. The mind will respond naturally to the need of the situation it recognizes: this is what is referred to as *fa* (arousing). What results from this response is always good and is called virtue. Thus filial piety, loyalty, integrity, and benevolence are concrete creative results of mind's responses or activities: they are examples of good. But as such and as virtues, they are not merely knowledge but actions: they are involved in doing certain things. This is clearly illustrated in Mencius' example of showing the innate goodness of man's nature by pointing to the natural response of a man to the sight of an endangered child by the side of a well. In this well-known example, a man recognizes a situation (namely, the child about to fall into a well), and will naturally feel for the child and rush to help the child in spite of danger to himself. It is an act of empathy and a great virtue of love or benevolence. This act is purposeful, for it has the goal of saving the child. To achieve this goal, one will naturally involve oneself in an action or a series of actions.

It is quite clear that Wang Yang-ming would see this as a good example of unity of knowledge and action. From this example we can also see that knowledge is purposefully oriented and evaluation-involved. The recognition of a factual situation carries with it a judgment of what is needed and a judgment of what is to be done or ought to be done for fulfilling the need, and thus a recognition of the goal for one's action and of the means to attaining the goal. All these are intimately related as natural functions of the mind and together compel the person to act according to the judgment of the mind. The resulting action and its achievement cannot fail to be good and to be a virtue.

In more complex situations one may have to be certain of the correct recognition of a situation, or of what is needed in a situation, or of what needs to be done as well as of how it can be done. In making these efforts, knowledge is required and efforts for acquiring knowledge must be initiated. But this is not, according to Wang Yang-ming, to acquire knowledge apart from consideration of the judgment of purpose and evaluation of good and bad by the mind. Instead they serve the mind's judgment of purpose and its evaluation of good and bad and must, therefore, be considered as resulting from the creative intentions of the mind. They are subsumed under them so that they will lead to concrete life-activities and valuable actions (virtuous acts). In this sense the mind's evaluation and purposeful judgments give both unity and creative momentum to the search for knowledge, and resulting actions complete and achieve this unity and creativity in concrete forms (virtues). Thus, when asked by his disciple Hsü Ai whether one should consider studying or learning various rites or information about natural ways of securing warmth or coolness in serving one's parents, Yang-ming's answer is penetrating.

In wintertime, one naturally thinks about the coldness of the parents, and thus will seek to understand the principles of how to make them warm. In summertime, one will naturally think about the hotness of the parents, and thus will seek to understand the principles of how to make them cool. These are the consequences derived from (or issuing from) the mind of sincerity and filial piety. Only when there is such a mind of sincerity and filial piety, will there be such consequences.[21]

From this it is clear that Yang-ming does not deny or denounce searching for knowledge and information of a certain kind. But any such search, according to him, must be rooted in or prompted by a desire or will to bring about a certain value in a spontaneously elicited action. What he stresses amounts to: (1) any search for knowledge and information must be motivated by the will-desire type of response of the mind, as a whole, which is justified by its intrinsic goodness; (2) such a search is further directed toward an end as determined and perceived by the mind in such responsive activity; and (3) any knowledge and information must be gathered in such a framework and with such a rooting as to be meaningful and significant. It is in this sense, as determined by (1), (2), and (3), that Yang-ming speaks of the mind of sincerity and filial piety as roots and leaves of a tree and the search for principles of cold and hotness as branches of the tree. He holds that one must have the roots of a tree to have the branches and leaves of the tree, and that one does not first seek the branches and leaves and then plant the roots.

It can be seen than Yang-ming believes that any search for knowledge and information must be purposeful and motivated by values felt in the mind, and in this sense it depends on two conditions: (1) the genuine responsiveness (*yi*) of the mind, and (2) the goal-serving actions it will generate. The unity of knowledge and action is, therefore, nothing but the unity of the mind as ultimate reality in its creative fulfillment of its potential values (individual felt goodness in situations), and it is to be understood as a continuum of knowledge and action in a dynamic context of whole, where the initial response leads to action requiring knowledge and information which, in turn, will serve and satisfy the goal of action. From this point of view, it is easy to see that the doctrine of the unity of knowledge and action will inevitably lead to the doctrine of *chih-liang-chih*.

More Philosophical Points about *chih-hsing-ho-yi*

First, because the activation of the mind in the form of *yi* is basically practical and action-oriented, the search for knowledge to satisfy the goal and purpose of action as embodied in *yi* is not to be understood apart from the existence of *yi*. It would appear that searching for knowledge and knowledge resulting from this search must always be instrumental for the performance of an action or a type of action which is characterized as virtuous. It is motivated by a desire to act and is directed toward fulfilling the desire to act. To understand such actions as virtues one must understand that *yi* as the activation (*fa*) of the mind is not only a desire to act but is a simultaneous recognition of the act as good. To recognize something as good is to desire acting for the good recognized or to fulfill the good in terms of concrete action. Thus Yang-ming says: "There is no knowledge which does not lead to action. If one knows but does not act, then one really does not know."[22]

In this sense, knowledge is clearly the knowledge of good in the activation of the mind or in the occurrence of *yi*. This knowledge is a response to a situation in which one finds oneself. This point is identical with the Socratic motto: No one voluntarily commits a wrong which one knows to be wrong. In other words, one's wrong is always committed in ignorance. To have knowledge is to always act with righteousness thus leading to virtue. From this Socrates draws the conclusion that knowledge is virtue, where knowledge, of course, must be understood as moral knowledge or knowledge involving evaluation of right or wrong and a desire to act according to what is right.

It is in this sense that knowledge and action are potentially and originally one; it is in the nature of the activation of the mind that it will determine the potential of an act which will be recognized by the mind as good or bad. The good will lead to good action and the bad will lead to bad action, for the good naturally will be liked and acted upon, whereas the bad, if not recognized as bad or if the mind is obscured, can be liked also and acted upon, otherwise it will be avoided. Thus Yang-ming points to the situation where one naturally likes good looks and naturally dislikes a bad smell as an example of how the mind makes a choice that embodies the potential unity of knowledge and action. For, to see good looks as good looks is knowledge, and to like it is action. This means that to like a thing could lead to some action, such as decorating and protecting the object of one's likes. Similarly, if one does not like something, one will act to get rid of the object of one's dislike.

What Yang-ming wishes to maintain is that seeing something good is to like it and smelling something bad is to dislike it. But to see something good or to smell something bad is not simply to see a good thing or to smell a bad thing, but rather to see something as good or to smell something as bad: it involves a judgment of good and bad. This, according to Yang-ming, is natural according to the activation of the mind, the mind of innate good-ness (*liang-chih*). The judgment of something as good or bad is already a potential unity of knowledge and action. That this unity is possible and that the mind activates in this way is due to the creativity of the mind—mind naturally and always responds and manifests its activities according to what its nature is. *Yi*, in its ability to motivate, and *liang-chih*, in its ability to judge good or bad, are creative aspects of the mind.

From this view of the potential unity of knowledge and action, it is true that knowledge is the beginning of action and action is the comple-tion of knowledge.[23] It is no less true that action is the beginning of knowl-edge, and knowledge is the completion of action. For knowledge in ques-tion is always *liang-chih*, which inevitably involves action, and action in the sense of *yi* can always move the mind to seek knowledge for the sake of action. Because knowledge and action are potentially two aspects of the activation of the mind, in the actual course of realizing this unity, knowledge and action must mutually entail and condition one another to make a creative development of the mind. Thus, more action leads to more knowledge and more knowledge leads to more action. This could lead to an enlargement of the scope of knowledge and to more effective action. Somehow, Yang-ming does not see this creative potential in the unity of action and knowledge. He sees only that knowledge must lead to action but fails to see that action provides the situation and occasion for the search for knowledge. However, he does see that knowledge is activation of the mind and therefore is purposeful and thus related to *yi*. It is *yi* which is a natural exemplification and a creative manifestation of the mind. Knowl-edge cannot be otherwise understood according to Yang-ming. This becomes his reason for objecting to taking knowledge as merely a reflection of things.

There is another creative aspect of the unity of knowledge and action, that is, what is recognized as good and thereby motivates one to act is the recognition of the *ought* in a situation. To recognize the *ought* is to seek to fulfill it. But in order to fulfill it, one has to acquire the knowledge of how; thus, the *ought* should lead to natural searching for knowledge. *Ought* in this sense could imply *can*, if one knows adequately. *Ought* entails doing something which is naturally activated by the mind in some natural situation. The unity here, between what is and what ought to be and what can be, is therefore achieved through the interplay of knowledge and action. What is in the mind naturally gives use to what ought to be which, in its turn, gives rise to what is in action. The puzzle of the relation between *ought* and *is* in Western ethics is resolved in a metaphysical understanding of the mind and its activation in Yang-ming's philosophy of mind.

From the above, it becomes clear that the unity of knowledge and action must be understood in terms of the original unity of the mind and its creative response to situations. The creative response of the mind is *yi*, which is the driving force for action and which should naturally conform to the perception of goodness (*liang-chih*) of the mind in normal cases. *Yi* itself is the basis for the unity of actual action and search for knowledge for fulfillment of action in a goal-achieving process. In this process, knowledge is not ignored but developed as a result of *yi*.

Furthermore, the creativity of the mind, which reveals itself in the potential unity of knowledge and action, is revealed also in the fact that the mind can respond to different situations with different evaluations of good and desires for different forms of action. To retain these different goals, there could be different ways of searching for knowledge and different results of such searchings.

This is how Yang-ming explains that at different times there can be different intellectual works which bear upon knowledge. Thus, according to Yang-ming, Duke Chou devised *li* (system of rights) and *yüeh* (system of temple music) to civilize the world. And this is done in spite of the fact that Yao and Shun (two sage kings), as sage kings, were capable of doing these before Duke Chou. Similarly, Confucius edited the *Six Classics* in order to edify the people, and this was done in spite of the fact that Duke Chou, as a sage, could do it before Confucius. Yang-ming regards these intellectual activities as resulting from the natural responses of a sagely mind at different times. At different times a sagely mind can respond adequately to the intellectual needs of the times. There is no point to making exterior efforts to obtain intellectual information or to doing intellectual investigations independently of the felt need of a sagely mind. The important thing is to keep the mind as clear and as sensitive and as lively as possible.

According to what has been explained as the true and original reality of the mind, the mind can respond to a situation, and in the case where it is kept clear and sensitive, the mind's creative response will always be good, as it is purely guided by its own activity, which naturally leads to desirable actions or the search for intellectual knowledge for desirable actions. Thus the important thing, according to Yang-ming, is to maintain the clarity of the mind which will be needed to unify knowledge and action in conformity to ultimate goodness (reality). He says: "Thus I know that (when) a sage meets his time (situation), there will be such a thing. One should be concerned with whether the mirror (mind) is clear or not. He should not be worried with whether things will be seen (or reflected) by the mind. Thus scholars should take to task whether one's mind is being illuminated, but not take to task whether one can fully investigate all things and events."[24] He suggests: "The mind of a sage is like a clear mirror. If it is only a clarity, then it will respond naturally and nothing will not be illuminated."[25] Though this passage inevitably suggests some Ch'anist conceptions of the mind, the natural and unlimited possible ways of responses of the mind are creative impulses to be related to human affairs and to a course of perfecting humanity, and in this regard, Yang-ming is then unmistakably Confucianist.

To summarize the philosophical points of Wang Yang-ming's doctrine of *chih-hsing-ho-yi*: He emphasizes the practical and creative impulses of the mind and goal-oriented behaviors as a form of fulfillment and development. He is against the view that one can detach one's self from consideration of the real need of a situation, which a creative mind senses, and the real desire or need of the mind, which is inevitably practical and motivating in pursuing the principles of things. He is further against the view that one must exhaust all principles of things to reach goodness. Goodness to him is always intrinsic or a dynamic unity and a source for creative responses in a variety of circumstances. One must be sensitive to what one genuinely feels in a relationship and situation and respond to it in the form of *yi*, with judgment of the good and bad of the mind (in this regard, *liang-chih*). Then virtue and good deeds will result.[26] It is impossible for one to seek goodness merely in things and affairs. Goodness is intrinsic and must be intimately experienced by the mind and determined by the mind. Then, when applied to things, concrete forms of action will ensue and guarantee the bringing about of goodness.[27]

If Chu Hsi is to be identified with the view that one should detach oneself from evaluating activities of the mind in pursuing principles of things and that one can thereby attain the virtues of the mind, then Wang Yang-ming is definitely opposed to Chu Hsi. As it were, Yang-ming is opposed to this Chu Hsi-type of doctrine of *k'e-wu* (investigation of things). It can be argued that the *should* in "one should detach oneself from evaluative activities of mind in pursuing principles of things" is in fact an evaluative perception of mind (*liang-chih*).

Unity and Creativity of the Mind in Consummation: *chih-liang-chih*

To insure the natural responses of the mind to be both good and motivated by goodness, Yang-ming must develop his doctrine of *chih-liang-chih*. One may say that this later doctrine is a natural consequence of reflection on the *pen-t'i* nature of the mind in the interplay of knowledge and action. It is developed, however, as a practical measure for attaining good in concrete life and as a dynamic link between the ontological ground of *chih-hsing-ho-yi*, namely, *hsin-chi-li*, and the actual performance of *chih-hsin-ho-yi*. It brings the ontological unity of the creativity of the mind to every concrete form of action and refers every form of concrete action to the ultimate ground of the creative unity of the mind.

We have explained *liang-chih* as the creative substance of the mind and its function as manifesting what is good and what is perceived or recognized as good. That *liang-chih* is the standard of good itself is due to the recognition that the mind itself is a supreme good (a supreme good in the *pen-t'i* sense of mind).[28] It is the disposition of the mind to recognize and grasp good, and, therefore, the power to judge good or bad as a course of action. It is naturally the essential character inherent in the mind.

At times, Yang-ming seems to waver between two views regarding the power of *liang-chih*. In his early period, *liang-chih* is held to be not merely a perception of good, which may not deny the motivating power for action, but in fact to be equivalent to the creative response of the mind (*yi*).[29]

In this sense *liang-chih* will lead to good action by its intrinsic power of motivation from a creative mind. This may be considered an ideal case of the natural unity of knowing and acting, because *liang-chih* is given full play in its manifestation or activation (*fa*) of the mind. However, in the latter part of Yang-ming's writings, it is clear that *liang-chih* may not function with the natural motivating force it intrinsically has, because there could be selfish desires which motivate one's actions without the guidance of *liang-chih*. That there could be obstruction or domination of selfish desires or selfish intentions (*ssu-yü-ch'ang-ai* or *ssu-yi-ch'ang-ai*)[30] is a natural fact affirmed by Yang-ming. Like other Sung Confucianists, Yang-ming does not seem to devise any metaphysical theory for explaining the origin and source of selfish desires or intentions. It is recognized that man in his actual concrete behavior may become excessive or deficient in his doing something or may react to a situation with undesirable feelings. Feelings like anger and pleasure can be often issued at the spur of the moment without real justification. Man can be ignorant or misguided by wrong information or conceptions and act on them—for example, one can overeat without knowing what is properly needed for nutrition.[31]

To detect one's desire for goodness or badness in the mind and to eliminate all possible obstructions of bad desires so that only good will prevail, and will prevail under any circumstance, is the main purport of the doctrine of *chih-liang-chih*. It might be suggested that as selfish desires do often arise in the conduct of one's life, the effort to forestall these desires before they arise or to prevent them from being acted upon is the effort of *chih-liang-chih*. It is an effort interpreted by Yang-ming as *chih-chih*[32] and *ch'eng-yi*. That this effort is possible reveals another creative function of the mind. Yang-ming says:

In the case of the ordinary man, there could not be any obstruction of selfish intentions. Therefore one should make an effort to extend knowledge and investigate things, (which consist in) overcoming the selfish desires and restoring the principles (*li*). Thus the *liang-chih* of one's mind will have no obstruction and will prevail and flow. This is to extend the knowledge. Once knowledge is extended, then the desires (or intentions, *yi*) will be sincere.[33]

What is significant here is that *chih-chih* in the *Book of Great Learning* is understood as *chih-liang-chih*, which is to bring out the good in each concrete situation of life. Whether this identification of *chih-chih* with *chih-liang-chih* is justified from an objective point of view is another question. But from the internal point of view of Yang-ming's doctrine of *hsin-chi-li* and *chih-hsing-ho-yi*, *chih-chih* cannot be but understood as *chih-liang-chih*, for the *chih* in question is no more than a perception of good as a ground of action. And thus to obtain *chih* is to obtain a ground for action which, in the light of our analysis of *hsin-[chih]-pen-ti*, is the creative and unlearned power of creative unity, which coincides with Mencius' notion of *liang-chih*.

Note that the proposition that if one's knowledge is extended then the intentions will be sincere implies two things: (1) the *liang-chih* in action (concrete perception of good) does entail genuine intentions or desires to act in the absence of selfish desires; (2) such desires or intentions will bring out goodness.

Sincere intentions (*ch'eng-yi*) are understood as intentions that always lead to good actions. *Ch'eng-yi* is to make *yi* conform to the reality of goodness or perception of good in *liang-chih*, which naturally will entail *yi* conforming to it in the absence of selfish desires.[34] *Ch'eng-yi* is to follow the good recognized in *liang-chih* and to avoid or eliminate badness as recognized in *liang-chih*. What *liang-chih* reveals is always good, but as *yi* may not initially occur according to *liang-chih*, but instead according to selfish intentions, *ch'eng-yi* is to bring *liang-chih* to see the evil of the selfish intentions and forbid it with new intentions to do good.

Not only does the doctrine of *chih-liang-chih* unify the concepts of *chih-chih* and *ch'eng-yi*, it also unifies the concepts of *cheng-hsin*, *chin-hsing*, *k'e-wu*, *ming-ming-t'e*, and *ch'iung-li*; and all these refer to the same process of making the *pen-t'i* of the mind unobstructed by desires and function creatively as bases or grounds of intentions and actions thereof. That is, all are regarded as different descriptions of the creative ability of the mind to preserve its original authenticity, unity, and creative responsiveness. Thus Yang-ming says: "The efforts for illuminating the illustrious virtues in the great searching is only *ch'eng-yi*. The efforts for *ch'eng-yi* is only *k'e-wu*."[35] He also suggests:

K'e-wu is like the *k'e* in Mencius' statement "the great man is able to rectify (*k'e*) the mind of the ruler." It is to remove the non-uprightness of one's mind and to complete the uprightness of a person. Where one's intentions and thoughts dwell, one should attempt to remove the non-uprightness therein in order to complete its uprightness. This is to exhaust the principles (*li*), if not being engaged in preserving the *li* of heaven, everywhere and everywhen. The *li* of heaven is the bright virtue (*ming-t'e*). To exhaust the principle is to illuminate the bright virtues.[36]

Within these contexts, it is clear that these basic concepts, *ch'eng-yi*, *ching-hsing*, *cheng-hsin*, *k'e-wu*, *ch'iung-li*, *ming-ming-t'e*, are all equivalents. In fact, given our understanding of Yang-ming's basic terms of *hsin*, *hsing*, *wu*, *yi*, *li*, and *ming-t'e*, these equivalents also follow as a consequence. They can all be regarded as ontologically the same, for they have the same ultimate *pen-t'i*, and they merely represent different aspects of the unity of the *pen-t'i* referred to as the mind of *pen-t'i* or *pen-t'i-chih-hsin*. Similarly, the various activities of *ch'eng* (to rectify), *ch'eng* (to make sincere), *ching* (to exhaust), *k'e* (to rectify), *ch'iung* (to exhaust), *ming* (to brighten or illuminate), all refer to different aspects of the creativity of the *pen-t'i*: They are all directed to the concrete perception of good and its realization in life. All these efforts are made to prevent the mind from being misled and dominated by selfish desires and to enable the mind to effectively embody, perceive, and fulfill good in concrete situations of life. They are the creative functions (*yung*) of the *pen-t'i-[chih]-hsin*. Thus Yang-ming says: "Now I speak of the unity of knowing and acting. This is to enable one to understand whenever an intention takes place, it is already an action. If activation of the mind has no goodness, one must overthrow this no-good intention, and do this exhaustively so that an intention which is not good will not hide in one's bosom. This is the purpose of (speaking about unity of knowing and acting)."[37] *Chih-liang-chih* is to effectively bring the unity of knowing and acting into actuality in accordance with potential goodness of one's true nature.

The above should give a clear indication as to how Wang Yang-ming actually argued for the unity of the mind (or ultimate reality). For without this ultimate reality of the unity of the mind, the relationship of all these conceptions would be difficult to establish. The creativity of the mind is shown in the actual activities of the mind in terms of all these concepts. But the creativity of the mind, which underlies all these activities and the activities of *liang-chih*, is also explicitly indicated and stressed by Yang-ming. As the mind is in unity with heaven as ultimate reality, the unceasing activity of heaven as ultimate reality must imply the unceasing activity of the mind. Thus Yang-ming says:

The transformation of vital forces (*ch'i-chi*) in heaven and earth is fundamentally unceasing. Yet it has a controlling agent (which is the constant *tao*). Thus neither going forward nor moving backward, neither going too fast nor moving too slowly, in spite of thousands of changes and transformations, the controlling agent is always stable. Man is born endowed with this (and because of this).[38]

Yang-ming further regards the mind as being constantly in a state of responsiveness in the absence of selfish desires.[39] Thus *chih-liang-chih* itself must be considered a constant unceasing activity of life. He says: "One should always make efforts for fulfilling the *liang-chih*, then one can be lively and active, like the flowing water of a river. If this is discontinued for a single moment, it will not be like the process of heaven and earth. This is the utmost of the learning. The sage is nothing but this."[40] He also stresses: "*Liang-chih* is the principle of change (*yi*). Its ways are always moving and changing and never staying at one place, and it circulates all the six positions of the *yi*-trigrams."[41]

When *liang-chih* or the mind is cultivated in the above sense to the utmost, it naturally becomes the source of good and good actions. It will naturally activate and realize goodness. Not only will there be no selfish desires to detain oneself, all good will come out naturally from the natural activation of the mind. At this point, the mind of an individual is indeed identified with the ultimate reality of heaven and earth and becomes realized and revealed as a comprehensive and unlimited creative unity. Yang-ming describes this state of creative activity of the mind as follows: "The sage only conforms to the activation (*fa*) and application (*yung*) of his *liang-chih*, so that heaven and earth and ten thousand things are all within the range of the activation and application of my *liang-chih*. Where is anything going beyond my *liang-chih and acting as obstructions?*"[42]

As *liang-chih* is the mind in its full employment, and as the mind is ultimate reality, it is therefore not difficult to see why Yang-ming ultimately identifies *liang-chih* with heaven (*t'ien*). He says: "A priori the existence of *liang-chih* does not run counter to heaven, heaven is *liang-chih*. A posteriori the existence of *liang-chih* follows the timely course of heaven, *liang-chih* therefore is heaven."[43] Thus to fulfill (*chih*) *liang-chih*, therefore, is to fulfill the originally given potential reality of heaven and earth. This is a state which the *Chung-yung* (the *Doctrine of the Mean*) has described as "participating in the creative activities of heaven and earth."

Chih-liang-chih and Unity and Creativity of the Mind in *Chung-ho*

The ultimate state of the mind as *pen-t'i* as revealed in the creative application of *liang-chih* is referred to frequently as *chung-ho* (*equilibrium-harmony*). The terms *chung* (equilibrium) and *ho* (harmony), as derived from the *Doctrine of the Mean*, are combined to indicate a unity which is creatively active. Even though *chung* is explicitly defined as the state of mind of nonactivation or preactivation (*wei-fa*), and *ho* is explicitly defined as the state of mind in activation (*fa*) which meets the mean, these two states cannot be actually separated, for they share the same reality and represent the same reality in its creative fulfillment of the potentiality of heaven. *Wei-fa* or *chung* is for the purpose of *fa* and *ho*. *Fa* and *ho* are to lead to a state of further creative potency.

In this regard they are very much like the knowing and acting in a creative unity as inspired by the mind. In fact *ho*, as achieved by the mind, is the action which conforms to good. The means or standard that the mind must meet is the creative recognition of good and a course of action for concretely fulfilling this good. Thus the notion of *chung* and the notion of *ho* are the same notion of a universal reality. They characterize the existence of the mind as a creative agency in its best state. Thus, Yang-ming always refers to the *pen-t'i* (fundamental reality) as *chung-ho*,[44] or the *pen-t'i* of the mind.[45] When the mind is given the strength to free itself from the influence of selfish desires, the mind will naturally repose (*wei-fa*), and yet can naturally respond in an appropriate way (*chung-chieh*), according to which, all things will find their proper places in a comprehensive harmony (*ho*).[46]

Chung-ho, the unity in creativity and creativity in unity, is the ultimate good and is inherent in every man.[47] When the mind is only identified with ultimate reality, it is *chung*. When it naturally responds according to *liang-chih* and goodness, it is *ho*. The unity of *chung-ho* has made quite clear the creative function of the mind.[48]

Because, according to Yang-ming, *chung* and *ho* cannot be separated and instead should be regarded as a whole of creative unity, he does not think that the problem of experiencing the state of *chung* as discussed by Ch'eng Yi-chuan (Ch'eng Yi), Li Yen-ping, and Chu Hsi is very much of a problem. It is a problem only when one separates the *chung* from the *ho*; for then, one cannot seek *chung* in any state of activation of feelings, and seeking itself as a state of activation (*yi-fa*) makes this impossible. To resolve this difficulty, Yang-ming suggests that one can seek *chung* in terms of one's experience of one's mind as a whole as well as in the process of realizing or experiencing one's *liang-chih*.[49]

In answering the question about the distinction between *yi-fa* (activation of the mind) and *wei-fa* (nonactivation of the mind or *chung*), Yang-ming affirms that there is indeed no true distinction between *yi-fa* and *wei-fa*. He also says that if one really sees the nondistinction between *yi-fa* and *wei-fa*, one can, of course, speak of the distinction for the purpose of education.[50] Then in answer to the suggestion that "in the state of *wei-fa*, it is not that there is no *ho*, and in the state of *yi-fa*, it is not that there is no *chung*. It is like the chiming of a bell: before the bell is struck one cannot say that there is no chiming; and after it is struck one cannot say that there is chiming. But there is after all a striking and a non-striking."[51] This is only to be understood as indicating that, in the original unity of the mind, there is a potential creative responsiveness, and in its creative responsiveness the unity is never lost. This is the unity and creativity of the ultimate reality. To understand the mind and its powers for *chung-ho* is to understand this creativity of unity and unity of creativity. It is to understand it in a metaphysical framework as described above.

With this understanding of the ontological nature of the mind and in terms of *chung-ho*, one can see that there is little difficulty in understanding the import and true purpose of Yang-ming's so-called "four-sentence teaching" (*shih-chu-ch'ao*). The four-sentence teaching goes as follows: "Without good and without bad is the substance (*ti*) of the mind. With good and bad is the movement of intentions (*yi*). To know good and bad is (the function of) *liang-chih*. To act on the good and remove the bad is (the effort of) *k'e-wu* (rectifying things)."

It has been suggested that this "four-sentence teaching" of Yang-ming represents some non-Confucian thinking and, in fact, embodies the Ch'anist view on the original reality of the mind. For there is clearly a suggestion regarding the original reality of the mind as being without good and bad. Even Yang-ming's own interpretation of what he means is not wholly satisfactory. He told his disciples that those with wisdom can penetrate (wu) into the original reality and realize that it is neither good nor bad, but those who have descended into activations of intentions have to concentrate on acting on good and removing bad.[52] There is no clarification of the first sentence, nor any clear picture of how to reconcile the state of reality or substance of the mind and activation of the mind. I suspect that, because of this ambiguity of Yang-ming's explanation, later issues regarding hsin-[chih]-pen-t'i (the original substance of the mind) arise within its own disciples, which finally lead to many divergent schools.

Indeed given this incomplete and unsatisfactory answer from Yang-ming, a Ch'anist view of the reality or substance of the mind is always possible. But in spite of all these historical developments, we may suggest that, in light of our analysis of the unity and creativity of the mind in Yang-ming's metaphysical philosophy, we may find a clear and satisfactory answer to the interpretation of the "four-sentence teaching."

We affirm that the lack of good and bad in the substance of the mind is to be understood as a state of supreme goodness as explained earlier. In this state of supreme goodness, good is good by its existence and as a standard. This view is indeed held by Yang-ming. He says: "What is without good and bad is the tranquillity of li (principles), and what is good or bad is the movement of vital force (ch'i). If not moved by (or in) vital force, (then the mind) is without good and bad, and is called supreme goodness."[53] But to say this is to say that the mind is not yet aroused or activated in dealing with concrete affairs. The term wu-shan-wu-o (without good and without bad) then simply means "not yet become yi or involved with intentions." But this does not mean that the mind should not or naturally can stay in a state of freedom from activation of intentions and in separation from concrete things of life. Thus the second point for a correct understanding of the "four-sentence teaching" is that the substance of the mind is capable of acting on things and must indeed act on things. That is, the substance of the mind must respond to the world and lead to the creation of good and the creative fulfillment of itself. This is so understood because it is precisely the nature of the mind as indicated by Yang-ming's doctrines of chih-hsin-ho-yi, chih-liang-chih, and chung-ho unity.

In view of what we have said about these doctrines, it is clear that even the mind-substance in the "four-sentence teaching" must express itself in creative involvement with the world so that good will always issue.[54] That the mind-substance must be so creatively involved and still remain fundamentally a unity is vividly and clearly indicated by Yang-ming's two analogical examples showing the growth of learning and a learning mind. The first example is the growth of the child. The child before birth has no learning and knowledge. But after birth, he will cry and laugh, and then begin to recognize his parents and brothers, and then become capable of standing and walking, holding, and shouldering, and finally will be able to do all things in the world. The second example is the planting of a tree from seed. In the beginning, there is only a seed and budding but no trunk. Then it has a trunk but no branches. With branches it comes to have leaves and then flowers and fruits as well.[55]

With these two examples, Yang-ming suggests that the ability and knowledge of a sage derive from actual cultivation of the state of nonactivation (*wei-fa*) and equilibrium (*chung*). He strongly urges cultivation of this state for its proper and full growth and development into an actuality of rich existence and concrete good. Thus the mind-substance of the "four-sentence teaching" must therefore, in its proper growth and development, involve the creative distinction of good from bad, and the creative fulfillment of good in action as advocated in Yang-ming's doctrines of *chih-hsing-ho-yi* and *chih-liang-chih*. It is in this creativity of unity that Yang-ming of the "four-sentence teaching" can be said to be essentially Confucianist (but not Ch'anist) in the best spirit of the *Book of Changes*, the *Analects*, the *Mencius* and the *Doctrine of the Mean*.[56]

Notes

1. The following passage from Wang Yang-ming serves to illustrate this view of the mind: "The other day Cheng asked, 'The sentiments of sympathy, shamefulness, modesty and moral distinction, are they the manifest virtues of nature?' (Wang Yang-ming) answered, '*Jên, yi, li, chih*, are also manifest virtues (of nature). The nature underlying them is only one. Regarding its shapes and substance, (this unifying nature) is called *t'ien* (heaven). Regarding its commanding and directing power, it is called *t'i* (ruler). Regarding its way of flow and operation, it is called *ming* (determination). Regarding its endowment in man, it is called *hsing* (nature). Regarding its dominating and commanding agency in a person, it is called *ming*. In the activation of the mind, when the mind meets a relationship toward father, it (will be realized) as filial piety; when it meets a relationship toward the ruler, it will be realized as loyalty. From this on, the names (of the virtues) can multiply infinitely, but the nature remains the only one. It is like a man who is a son to a father and a father to a son. From this, (the names) may multiply infinitely, but the person remains only one. If a man only concentrates on developing (cultivating) his nature, and sees his nature clearly, then the ten thousand principles of things will become brightly exhibited' " (*Ch'uan-hsi-lu*, Part I, no. 39; hereafter cited as *CHL*).

   All the translations in this article from Wang Yang-ming's original writings in Chinese are done by myself. The reader should nevertheless consult Wing-tsit Chan's well-documented translation of Wang Yang-ming's works—*Instructions for Practical Living and Other Neo-Confucian Writings* (New York, 1964).
2. This should be called *t'ai-chi*, which is not actually so addressed by Wang Yang-ming, but which is addressed instead in terms of *chung-ho*, as we shall see.
3. Wang Yang-ming says: "Man is the mind of heaven and earth. Heaven, earth and the ten thousand things form originally a unity with me" (*CHL*, Part II, Answer to Nieh Wen-wei). In affirming that man is the mind of heaven and earth and that the mind is only a perceptive intelligence (*ling-ming*), Yang-ming says: "One thus knows that filling heaven and earth and between them is only this *ling-ming*. Man is only separated from heaven and earth by his body. My *ling-ming* is the ruling authority of heaven and earth and all spirits. If heaven does not have my *ling-ming*, who is to look up to its height? If earth does not

have my *ling-ming*, who is to look into its depth? If spirits do not have my *ling-ming*, who is to discriminate between fortune and misfortune (on the basis of) them? If heaven and earth and spirits and the ten thousand things separate themselves from my *ling-ming*, there will be no heaven, earth, and spirits, and the ten thousand things there also will not be my *ling-ming*. Thus, one may say that (all these and my *ling-ming* or mind) are penetrated with one vital force (*ch'i*). How could we separate one from the other?" (*CHL*, Part IV, Recorded by Huang Yi-fang). From these passages it could be apparent that Yang-ming embraces a subjective idealistic position. But if we take seriously his assertion that if my mind is separated from heaven and earth and other things then there will be no my mind, it becomes evident that he is arguing for a position of organic naturalism in which things exist in a whole and the mind is both a manifestation of the whole and an agency contributing to the forming of the whole. This would be the correct meaning of the statement that man is the mind of heaven and earth, and all other things in the universe.

4. *CHL*, Part II, Answer to the Letter of Lu Yüan-ching.

5. *CHL*, Part III, Recorded by Huang Hsiu-i.

6. Though Wang does not elaborate on his view of mind as *ch'i*, my explanation suggested above should be amply useful for explaining differences between Chu Hsi and Wang Yang-ming. Chu speaks of *li* as one which is scattered in a variety of things. There is the intended unity of principles. But how to guarantee the unity and how to differentiate this unity into a manifold of things depends upon a dynamic principle which is not explicitly provided by Chu Hsi. Though Chu Hsi defines *mind* as the quintessence of *ch'i*, he conceives the mind as being vacuous, perceptive and unobstructed (*hsu-ling-p'u-mei*). Though these characterizations would meet acceptance by Yang-ming, Chu Hsi would still differentiate the mind from the nature to which *li* belongs and would thus hold that the mind achieves goodness by conforming to the principles of nature.

7. It is clear that Yang-ming agrees with Chu Hsi in speaking of the *hsin-[chih]-pen-t'i* or *hsin-t'i* as referring to the existence of the mind. For Yang-ming, the *hsin-t'i* is the same thing as the original reality of heaven, world-process, the ruling unity and nature. It is referred to also as *liang-chih-pen-t'i* (the original reality of knowledge of what goodness is) (*CHL*, Part III, Record by Huang Yi-fang), *t'ien-li-pen-t'i* (the original reality of the principle of heaven) (*CHL*, Part I, no. 44), or *jên-ti-pen-t'i* (the original reality of man) (*CHL*, Part III, Record by Huang Yi-fang), or *chen-chi* (true self) (*CHL*, Part I, No. 7), or *ch'eng* (sincerity) (*CHL*, Part I, no. 6).

8. See *CHL*, Part II, Answer to the Letter of Ku Tung-chao; *To-hsüeh wen*.

9. *Ta-hsüeh wen*.

10. In this connection, it becomes clear that the English translation currently used for *liang-chih*, namely, innate knowledge of goodness, is not sufficiently com-

prehensive for all the important meanings and references of the Chinese term. At least the significance of *liang-chih* as *pen-t'i*, which is considered the ultimate model for goodness, is not represented. Of course with this recognition one can still use this term with the metaphysical import explained above.

11. One may elaborate on this point by specifying two levels on which an existentialism of goodness can be understood. On the general level man is conceived of as inevitably sharing the goodness of nature for it shares the nature of heaven. In this sense his ideals and values must conform to this potential or the implicit existence of nature in man, for they must implicitly and potentially be thus defined and determined. On a more specific level, man is conceived of as inevitably applying this *liang-chih* (or innate goodness) to the affairs of life for determining actions. In such applications he can be misled or be overwhelmed by selfish desires or anything which is external to his nature, and he must make efforts to avoid any deviation by keeping his *liang-chih* clear and by correcting any deviations by strengthening his abilities of application. On both these levels, unity and creativity are required, for they are actual values and processes for maintaining pure and active *liang-chih* and for making the results of applying *liang-chih* to life conform to the genuine and authentic existence of *liang-chih*.

12. *Ta-hsüeh wen.*

13. *CHL*, Part III, Record by Huang Yi-fang.

14. Though it can be a potential one, for as Yang-ming pointed out in a query to a disciple, in sleep though the mind is not active, it can become active when awake. The mind or *liang-chih* apparently is also conceived of as a disposition. In sleep *liang-chih* merely reposes (*sou-chien-liang-hi*). (Cf. *CHL*, Part III, Record by Chien T'e-hung.)

15. *CHL*, Part III, Record by Hung Yi-fang.

16. Thus Yang-ming says: "Ears, eyes, mouth, nose, and four limbs are the body. But without the mind, how could they see, hear, speak, and move. If the mind desires to see, hear, speak, and move without ears, eyes, mouth, nose, and four limbs, this is also impossible. Thus without mind there cannot be body, and without body there cannot be mind. The substantial aspect (of this whole) is the body; the ruling aspect of (this whole unity) is the mind. Where the activating forces rest is *yi*: the intelligence and perceptiveness of this *yi* is *chih* (knowing). Where the *yi* refers to and attaches to is the thing. All these are one thing. The *yi* is never suspended in the air but must be attached to things and situations." (*CHL*, Part III, Record by Chen Chiu-chuan.)

17. Thus Yang-ming says: "Man must have the mind of desiring to eat, then one can come to know food. The desire to eat food is *yi* and is the beginning of action or practice. The good taste or bad taste of eating food must be known after food enters the mouth. How could there be knowledge of good or bad taste of eating food before food enters one's mouth? One must have the mind of desir-

ing to walk, then one will come to know the road. The mind of desiring to walk is *yi* and is the beginning of action. The danger and ease of a road must be known after one has personally gone through the road. How could there be knowledge of danger and ease of a road before one has personally experienced the walking? Thus one comes to know the soup and then drinks it, and comes to know clothing and then dresses oneself. With these examples, the application of this principle (*chih-hsing-ho-yi*) is beyond doubt." (*CHL*, Part II, Answer to Letter of Ku Tung-chao.)

18. Thus Yang-ming says: "The *liang-chih* of the *hsu-ming-ling-chueh*, in its response and interaction (*k'un*), stirs and is called *yi*. One must have *chih* (knowledge), then there is *yi*. If there is no *chih*, there is no *yi*. Is *chih* not the substance of *yi*? Where *yi* employs itself must involve a thing (*wu*) and a thing is affairs (*shih*). In all cases where *yi* employs itself, there is no case without *wu*. If there is this *yi*, where is this *wu*? If there is no such *yi*, there is no such *wu*. Is *wu* not the employment of *yi*?" (*CHL*, Part II, Answer to the Letter of Ku Tung-chao.)

19. Yang-ming says: "Supreme good is the *pen-t'i* of the mind, if one has reached understanding of virtues to the degree of utmost refinedness and unity, one will reach such an understanding" (*CHL*, Part I, no. 2).

20. This is not to say that *yi* is always good; if the mind is obscured by selfish desires, the response of the mind can be deviated from good. Thus to guarantee the goodness of one's response and action, one has to keep one's mind as unobstructed and as pure as possible so that what it naturally activates or responds to can always be good by its original nature. Thus Yang-ming says: "When the mind has no obstructions from selfish desires, it is *t'ien-li*; nothing needs to be added from the outside. With this mind completely of *t'ien-li*, when one responds [to the need of] serving one's father, there will be filial piety; when one responds [to the need of] serving one's ruler, there will be loyalty; when one responds to the need of making friends and governing people, there will be integrity and benevolence. If one makes an effort in removing selfish desires of man from one's mind and preserve one's *t'ien-li*, one will have all these" (*CHL*, Part I, no. 3).

21. *CHL*, Part I, no. 3.

22. *CHL*, Part I, no. 5.

23. *CHL*, Part I, no. 5. Wang Yang-ming also says: "Knowledge is the guiding principle of action and action is the actual performance of knowledge" (*CHL*, Part I, no. 5). In this context knowledge is clearly *yi* in general, or knowledge of good embodies a desire for action.

24. *CHL*, Part I, no. 20.

25. Ibid.

26. *CHL*, Part I, no. 3.

27. In this sense Yang-ming is strongly opposed to K'ao Tzu's view on the extrinsic character of righteousness (*yi*), and holds together with Mencius that *yi*

(righteousness) is inherent in the mind as a creative determination of the mind in relation to or in response to external things.

28. *CHL*, Part III, Recorded by Huang Chih.

29. Thus Yang-ming says: "Knowing is the *pen-t'i* of the mind. The mind naturally comes to know. Seeing one's father, one naturally knows filial piety. Seeing one's brother, one naturally comes to know one's brother. Seeing a child about to fall into a well, one naturally knows to feel sympathy. This is what *liang-chih* is. It does not depend on the outside for (its occurrence)" (*CHL*, Part I, no. 9).

30. *CHL*, Part III, Record by Huang Chih.

31. *CHL*, Part III, Record by Chen Chiu-chuan.

32. By Chu Hsi's interpretation *chih-chih* is to obtain knowledge of principles by investigating things (*k'e-wu*). But Yang-ming interprets *k'e-wu* here as rectifying (*cheng*) affairs, and thus *chih-chih* as illuminating affairs with evaluation of the mind.

33. *CHL*, Part I, no. 9.

34. This point is clearly made in *Ta-hsüeh wen* in discussing *ch'eng-yi*.

35. *CHL*, Part I, no. 6.

36. *CHL*, Part I, no. 7.

37. *CHL*, Part I, Record by Huang Chih.

38. *CHL*, Part III, no. 98.

39. *CHL*, Part III, Record by Huang Yi-fang.

40. *CHL*, Part III, Record by Chien T'e-hung.

41. *CHL*, Part III, Record by Huang Yi-fang.

42. *CHL*, Part III, Record by Chien T'e-hung.

43. Ibid.

44. *CHL*, Part I, no. 56.

45. Ibid., no. 68.

46. Ibid.

47. Ibid., no. 71.

48. One may also identify *chung* as the *t'i* (substance) and *ho* as the *yung* (function). But here Yang-ming wishes to say that *t'i* and *yung* are not separable and share the same reality. He explicitly says: "Mind cannot take tranquillity and movement as its *t'i* and *yung*" (*CHL*, no. 101). Cf. also No. 119 where he says *chung-ho* is the restoration of the *pen-t'i* of nature.

49. Ibid., no. 70. He says: "If one knows the extreme and the deficient (and seeks to avoid it), that is *chung-ho*" (*CHL*, Part III, Record by Chien T'e-hung).

50. *CHL*, Part III, Record by Chien T'e-hung.

51. Yang-ming says: "Before striking, the bell-chiming is originally world-stirring; after striking, the bell is completely quiet" (ibid.).

52. *CHL*, Part III, Record by Chien T'e-hung.

53. *CHL*, Part I, no. 95.

54. Yang-ming has explained the difference between his view of *wu-shan-wu-o* and the Buddhists' one by stressing that the Buddhists merely cling to the principle of *wu-shan-wu-o* and disregard everything and thus cannot rule the world, whereas the sage will act in accordance with the *t'ien-li* (the principle of heaven) for dealing with the world, but he will not let himself be guided by the movement of vital forces (*tung-chi*) (cf. *CHL*, Part I, no. 45). This implies a view that badness (*o*) arises from movement of *ch'i*, which is very much similar to the views of Chu Hsi and Ch'en Yi. Perhaps a better view is that whereas *ch'i* can be regarded as the constitution of all things, badness comes from lack of attention to what one's substance-mind naturally responds to independently of selfish desires.

55. For examples, see *CHL*, Part I, no. 30.

56. It is not denied that Wang Yang-ming has been influenced by both Taoism and Ch'an Buddhism in his use of idioms and ways of thinking in his formulation of the Confucian philosophy. But these influences can be best construed or regarded as contributing to his unique insights into Confucian metaphysics and its practicality. For a good discussion of the influence of Taoism on Wang Yang-ming, see Liu Ts'un-jan's "Wang Yang-ming yu Tao-chiao" [Wang Yang-ming and Taoism], in the *Journal of the Institute of Chinese Studies of the Chinese University of Hong Kong*, 3, no. 2 (1970): 489-509. For a good discussion of the question of the Ch'anist or Buddhist influence on Wang Yang-ming, see Wing-tsit Chan's "How Buddhistic Is Wang Yang-ming?" in *Philosophy East and West*, 12 (1962): 203-216. Also confer with Wu Yi's "*Chung-yung chih ch'eng ko-yi ch'en p'ien Fu-hsueh ssu-hsiang ti kung-shu*" [*Ch'eng* of *Chung-yung* Can Cure the Buddhist Thought of Its Emptiness], in *Wen-yi-fu-hsing Monthly* [Renaissance Monthly], no. 18 (June, 1971): 5-11.

17. Practical Learning in Yen Yuan, Chu Hsi, and Wang Yang-ming

Ambivalence of Practicality in Confucianism

Confucianism as a philosophy is practically motivated. It is *intended* to apply to practical life and to achieve moral transformation of individuals and society. It therefore is practical as opposed to theoretical; namely as contrasted to being concerned merely with impractical speculation and theoretical knowing. But, when one questions whether traditional Confucianism is utilitarian or whether it led to a pursuit of modern practical scientific knowledge of use in social and economical (or technological) advancement, the answer seems to be inevitably negative. It is understandable, of course, that Confucianism, despite its doctrines of the investigation of things (*ke-wu*) and the extension of knowledge (*chih-chih*) in the *Ta Hsueh* (*Great Learning*) and Neo-Confucianism in the Sung-Ming period, did not lend itself to the development of modern science, whether practical or theoretical. The well-known Japanese Sinologist Hattori Unokichi flatly stated that Confucianism is not utilitarian or positivistic.[1] He maintained that classical Confucianists and Neo-Confucianists in general justify righteous action by virtuous motivation rather than by results of utility. These remarks seem to pinpoint an apparent ambivalence of "practicality" in Confucian philosophy: Confucian philosophy is practical in the sense of being concerned with morality, social interactions, and political activities, but is not practical in the sense of being concerned with economy and technology. If we may call practicality in the former sense *moral practicality* and practicality in the latter sense *utilitarian practicality*, we can say that Confucian philosophy in general is a philosophy of moral practicality, but not of utilitarian practicality.

Against this distinction between the two types of practicalities in Confucian philosophy, we may first explain the use of "practical learning" (*shih hsüeh*) as a phase in the development of Confucian thought and investigate to what extent *shih hsüeh* endorses utilitarian practicality and criticizes moral practicality and how it relates to or reconciles both. In this article, I wish to consider these problems in light of the writings and systems of Chu Hsi (1130-1200) and Wang Yang-ming (1472-1527), who, as a matter of historical irony, simultaneously are the very target of attack by *shih-hsüeh* and the very source of *shih hsüeh* in the later eighteenth and early nineteenth centuries. Yet, it is noticeable in the course of its development that there were Confucianists who conscientiously sought to promote utilitarian practicality at the expense of moral practicality. Hence, we have an ambivalence of practicality in Confucian thought.

What is *Shih-Hsüeh* (Practical Learning)?

"Practical learning" (*shih hsüeh*) developed from a genuine critique of the main currents of Sung-Ming Neo-Confucianism. Although Chu Hsi and Wang Yang-ming belonged to different and opposite schools of thought, they are grouped together as one antipode of practical learning. To understand what practical learning is and how it developed, it would be best to concentrate on the doctrine of practical learning in Yen Yuan (1635-1704) and Kung Chih-ch'ien (1792-1841), for Yen Yuan is well known as a strong critic of Sung-Ming Neo-Confucianism and Kung Chih-ch'en was an advocate of enlightened economical philosophy in late Ching Confucianism.

Throughout Yen Yuan's philosophical writings the idea of *shih* is central and predominant. *Shih* is not only a matter of moral *practice* or a matter of achieving *actual* deeds, but a very fundamental principle of the universe, a principle of reality to be witnessed in the activities of all things. He traced this philosophy of *shih* to pre-Confucian sage-rulers and related what they said and did to their contributions of *shih* to the universe as well as to society. He said:

Before Confucius and Mencius all those to whom Heaven and Earth gave birth in order to direct the course of events are engaged in practical thinking (language) and practiced doing (*shih-wen shih-hsing*) and devoted to developing things of substance and real use (*shih-t'i shih-yung*). They are thus able to create actual deeds (*shih-chi*) for Heaven and Earth so that people are peacefully settled and production abounds.[2]

This reference to *shih* in thinking (language), doing, substance, and use gives a very rich meaning to the term. *Shih* is to be exhibited in all spheres of life; *shih* leads to visible benefits in society; *shih* is derived from heaven and earth and is intended to be the path of truth and righteousness. In these contexts of *shih*, we can define *shih-hsüeh*. *Shih-hsüeh* (practical learning) is the learning of thinking (speaking) and doing, both internally with regard to the principle (substance) and externally with regard to application of the principle (use) for benefitting people and producing results beneficial to society at large. Though Yen Yuan himself nowhere suggested this explanation of *shih-hsüeh*, that this represents his essential view is beyond any doubt.

In most cases Yen referred to *shih-hsüeh* as a verb phrase, rather than as a noun phrase. *Shih-hsüeh* is not "practical learning" but to learn vigorously through practice and for the purpose of practice. In this sense of *shih*, Yen Yuan also spoke of *shih-chiao* or to teach vigorously through actual deeds for the purpose of practice.[3] What one learns or what one teaches is something that satisfies the needs of people and society, as just explained. Yen Yuan, in fact, concretely pinpointed what he considered to be the content of *shih-hsüeh* (as a verb phrase). These are what he frequently referred to as the three matters (*san-shih*) and six functions (*lü-fu*) of Yao and Shün and the six virtues (*lü-te*), six doings (*lü-hsing*), and six arts (*lü-yi*) of Duke Chou and Confucius. An examination will reveal these to be as follows. The three matters refer to rectification of virtues (*cheng-te*), strong protection of life (*hou-shen*), and development of ability (*li-yung*) mentioned in the *Shang Shu* (the *Book of Documents*). The six functions (of government) are functions pertaining to offices of warfare, agriculture, economy, storage, fire and water control, as well as of general works mentioned in the *Chou Li* (the *Rites of Chou*). The six virtues apparently refer to those of benevolence (*jên*), righteousness (*yi*), wisdom (*chih*), propriety (*li*), loyalty (*chung*), and integrity (*hsin*). The six doings apparently refer to language (*wen*), action (*hsing*), loyalty (*chung*), integrity (*hsin*), filial piety (*hsiao*), and respect toward elder brothers (*li*). Finally, the six arts refer to the learning of rites (*li*), the learning of music (*yüeh*), the learning of archery (*hsieh*), the learning of charioteering (*yü*), the learning of history (*shu*), and the learning of numbers (*shu*).

Though all these subjects have had their historical contents, when Yen Yuan mentioned them he clearly had only their respective fields in mind. The three matters of the *Book of Documents* are the guiding principles for his *shih-hsüeh*; the six arts are applications of these principles in the education of a person; and performance of the six functions, of course, is to be expected from a government and its functionaries.[4] But these delineate the areas for a Confucian scholar. The six virtues and six doings are matters of moral practicality, which are as important as the utilitarian practicality of the six arts and six functions. They are all important in "actually ordering Heaven and Earth (*shih-wei-t'ien-ti*)" and "actually nourishing the ten thousand things" (*shih-yu-wan-wu*)."[5] Borrowing the frequently used categories of "inner" and "outer" in Confucian philosophy, we may describe the six arts and six functions as pertaining to an outer activity of a person whereas the six virtues and six doings pertain to an inner cultivation of a person. We may further suggest that what we call *utilitarian practicality* pertains to the outer requirements of learning and what we call *moral practicality*, on the other hand, pertains to inner requirements of learning. Understood in these terms, we may clearly see that Yen Yuan vividly and efficiently sketched and established the program of *shih-hsüeh* as well as set the guidelines for a course in *hsüeh* (learning) for the purpose of *shih* and toward the goal of *shih*. This is precisely his reason and thesis in writing his essay "On Preserving Learning" (*Tseng Hsueh Pien*).

[I] authored the essay on preserving learning, to illuminate the Way of the three matters, six functions, six virtues, six doings, and six arts of Yao, Shun, Chou, and Confucius. My main purpose is to point out that the Way (truth) does not lie in merely understanding and awakening from reading but that one should follow the Confucian School, in acquiring wide knowledge and yet in practicing simple rites so that one can *substantially learn* (*shih-hsüeh*) [what one learns] and actually practice what one learns, without idleness throughout one's life.

With *shih-hsüeh* thus defined and described, Yen Yuan acquired a solid ground in launching his criticism of Buddhism, Taoism, and the Neo-Confucian teachings of Chu Hsi, Wang Yang-ming, and their followers. He attacked them for their doctrine of emptiness (*kung*) and their attempt to "cut all practical learning (*shih-hsüeh*)" (*tuan-ching shih-hsüeh*).

Yen Yuan contrasted *shih-hsüeh* with the "learning of letters" (*wen*), on the one hand, and with the "absence of learning" (*yeh*), on the other hand. "Learning of letters" is the learning of conventional, empty, and soulless texts and dogmas or the learning of commentary, meditation manuals, and compositions to meet civil examinations. The content of such learning is considered by Yen Yuan to be dominated by the canonized teachings of Sung-Ming Neo-Confucianism and to contain the Ch'anist literature of Wang Yang-ming, Taoists, and Buddhists. These things are branded as being against *shih* because, in Yen's eyes, they are very different from what sage-kings and Confucius and Mencius practiced and thus are irrelevant to the needs of life and society. On the other hand, the "absence of learning" is a state where learning and civilization are abolished and violence toward learning and the learned is allowed. Contrasted against this background, "practical learning" stands out as a logically necessary and substantially sound state of inquiry and investigation." It is not confined to the superficial recitation of dogmas for the purposes of pleasing authorities or seeking an appointment in government. It is not useless, body-weakening and mind-emaciating word-exercises, or empty metaphysical talk, or quiet sitting with no contribution to the reform of affairs of state and society. It is the seeking of knowledge of the things one can apply to life and society for the advancement of the social good or, at least, for the strengthening one's spirit and body. It involves a study of the fundamental principles of the cosmos and history in the original texts of Confucian heritage as well as of the original spirit of the sage-kings and Confucius.

In describing the need for an assertion of practical learning, Yen Yuan also showed a historical perspective. He thought that if there were too much learning of letters in a society, the people of that society might rebel against it and thus overreact by way of violent suppression of the thinking, education, and culture associated with *wen*. Therefore, *shih-hsüeh* is required to prevent the irrational overthrow of culture due to the overconcern with *wen*. Before this reaction sets in, practical learning must be developed to stall a historical crisis. From this perspective, practical learning not only represents the genuine medium between too much learning of letters and the complete abandonment of civilization, but by being timely developed would meet the needs of society and history.[8] This seems to suggest a characterization of the two domains of *shih-hsüeh*. *Shih-hsüeh* is the learning of *shih*. *Shih* is not *hsu* (empty) and therefore does not include matters of study and meditation on words and texts. *Shih-hsüeh* concerns matters of things (*wu*) and affairs (*shih*) and therefore the knowledge and knowhow (*yi*) concerning things. It is also learning to practice and work for the good of society.

Yen Yuan, as he himself testified, had worked on the doctrines of the Ch'eng brothers and Chu Hsi when he was thirty. But five years later, he was awakened to the truth of the doctrine of the goodness of nature in Mencius after his grandparents passed away; he decided that the teachings of Chu Hsi and Ch'eng brothers were not genuinely Confucian. This is when he started to formulate his doctrine of *shih-hsüeh*. Although he frequently referred to the Neo-Confucian dialogues of Ch'eng-Chu-Lu-Wang, he chose to explicitly criticize and comment on the views of Ch'eng and Chu Hsi in his *Tseng Hsueh* and *Tseng Hsing* essays. Generally, Yen gave his approval to Chu Hsi's criticism of Buddhists, Taoists, and the school of Lu (and thus by implication the school of Wang). But he insisted that Chu and Ch'eng themselves were not exempt from the charges of the emptiness, triviality, speculativeness, arrogance, and impracticality they found in the Lu school.[9] The following quotation is an example of such criticism by Chu Hsi:

If we compare both the theory and practice of Chu Hsi with those of the classical Confucianist, we see that they are radically different. It may appear that Chu Hsi is much too strong on *chih* (knowledge of theory) and weak on practice. But in point of fact [Chu Hsi] is weak not only on practice (*shih-hsing*), but also in theory. . . . We must deplore (his doctrine of) quiet sitting (*ching-tso*) and mental concentration (*chü-chin*) as it leads to quietude and uselessness (*chi-so wu-yung*).[10]

To accentuate his teaching of *shih-hsüeh*, Yen corrected the well-known motto of the Han Confucianist Tung Chung-shu, "Follow righteousness without pursuing the utility; illuminate the way without calculating the success" into "Follow righteousness in order to pursue the utility; illuminate the way in order to calculate the success."[11] Evidently what Yen referred to as *utility* (*li*) and *actual results* (*kung*) are what bear on the actual improvements and advancements of social welfare in terms of the functioning of government and the contributions of individuals. They form the very subject matter of Yen Yuan's utilitarian practicality or *shih-hsüeh*.

To give a more contemporary meaning to what Yen Yuan called *shih-hsüeh*, one may look at this list of important subjects of study in the curriculum of an educational academy.[12] There are four categories of subjects of study: (1) subjects of humanity—writing, music (arts), history, arithmetic, astronomy, geography, etc.; (2) subjects of martial arts—strategies of the Yellow Emperor, Chiang T'ai-kung, and Sun Wu, defense and attack tactics, warfare on water and land, archery and charioteering, shooting and boxing, etc.; (3) subjects of the classics and history—the thirteen classics, dynastic histories, edicts, memorials, poetry and (Confucian) prose, etc.; (4) subjects of knowhow and science—the studies of water, fire, engineering, geometry, etc. Hou Wai-lu suggested that (1) corresponds to pure science, (2) corresponds to military science, (3) corresponds to social science, and (4) corresponds to technical science.[13] That these explicitly exclude metaphysical subjects such as the study of *li* (principle) is strikingly remarkable. Lest we become misled by this description of "practical learning," which excludes metaphysical studies, we must be reminded that in practice Yen Yuan did not ignore philosophical or even metaphysical thinking. He developed a metaphysics[14] of practical learning, which he intended to use to encourage and justify the concern and promotion of practical learning.

About fifty years later, Kung Chih-chen (1792-1841) seems to have succeeded Yen Yuan in promoting the development of practical learning as a cure for the social and political evils of his time. Kung was more violent and more direct in attacking the political and social practices of his time, because his time had seen more problems due to administrative callousness and social stagnation. Although he did not single out the Neo-Confucianism of the Sung period as a target of attack, he strongly attacked what that doctrine stands for (for instance, the examination system [*ko-chu*]) on the grounds that it stifles talent and leads to nothing but plagiarism and empty talk.[15] Kung, more than Yen, focused his attention on matters of economic and social reform for bettering the well-being of the people. He thus advanced a strong utilitarian philosophy to meet the challenge of his time, a philosophy that leads to thoughts of enriching the nation and strengthening the army (*fu-kuo-chiang-ping*) as held by Yen Fu (1893-1921) at the end of nineteenth century. On the point of enriching the people, he promoted land reform, antimonopoly commerce, and lower taxes.[16] On the point of strengthening the army, he suggested the establishment of a provincial administration for the western regions (*hsi-yu*) of China and promoted migration from inland areas to the western regions.[17]

In Kung, one can see that practical learning, if not in name at least in fact, had made the following two important developments: (1) The term *practical learning* had not been much used, but with the waning of the "Chu learning" (*Chu-hsueh*), practical learning is tied up with the development of the "learning of Kung Yang" (*Kung-yang-hsueh*) in the New Text School (*Ching-wen hsueh-pai*). Though we cannot elaborate on the history of the struggle between the New Text School and the Old Text School (*ku-wen hsueh-pai*), it is apparent that from the end of the seventeenth century until the end of eighteenth century the search for universal and deep meanings in the Confucian classics lent itself to the search for applications of the classics to political and economical problems of the time, and thus to the rejection of the historical and textual philological research (*shün-ku-hsueh*) endorsed by *ku-wen hsueh-pai*. Kung distinguished three stages of the history of Confucian learning: The first stage he calls the stage of order; the second, the stage of disorder; and the third, the stage of disintegration. With regard to the stage of order, he said:

[T]his way of harmony and happiness between the ruler and its ministers and the people, this study of sage-kings' and Confucian writings in order to bring out truth, and this actual establishment of social and political order are indeed one.[18]

His distinction of these stages of Confucian learning leads to K'ang Yu-wei's (1858-1927) theory of "three periods," again based on the *Kung-yang hsueh*. This means that practical learning still was embedded in as well as justified on the grounds of classical Confucian writings. (2) A study of Kung's time and the subsequent history of China shows that the economic, social, and political conditions in China and the aggressive pressures of the Western powers on China combined to create a crisis that led to the overgrowing criticism and abandonment of Sung-Ming Neo-Confucianism, on the one hand, and to the ever-increasing need for practical learning as a means of national and cultural survival on the other.

To summarize briefly, practical learning is not a simply entity but has its own development and combines many factors. It is both against the Neo-Confucian philosophy and related to it in complex ways. It also is a product of the crisis of eighteenth-century China. It therefore has both a theoretical significance and a historical significance. Any study of the practical learning must therefore explicitly specify in which respect it is to be understood.

Can One Deduce *Shih-Hsüeh* from *Li-Hsüeh?*

Even though *shih-hsüeh* results from a strong criticism of and reaction against Sun-Ming Neo-Confucian philosophy, it is nevertheless not clear in what fundamental way that *shih-hsüeh* is incompatible with Neo-Confucian philosophy and in what way the two still can be considered compatible. In the following text, I wish to show that *shih-hsüeh* is not theoretically incompatible with the philosophies of Chu Hsi and Wang Yang-ming, and that, given appropriate conditions, *shih-hsüeh* can be generated from their philosophies. But this is not to say that the Chu school or the Wang school has seen the possibility of this generation, or that this generation could take place in the absence of stimuli from historic and social conditions or independent of a criticism of inhibitory tendencies in the doctrines of Chu and Wang, which could contribute to the development of *shih-hsüeh*. Thus we can understand *shih-hsüeh* as basically originating from a historic or social source, but having made no radical change of a theoretical nature in the metaphysics or ethics of Neo-Confucianism.

In spite of Chu Hsi's metaphysical speculations on *li* (principle) and *ch'i* (vital force or vital nature), in spite of his philosophizing about how to investigate things in terms of knowing *li*, and furthermore, in spite of his leaning toward bookish knowledge without sufficiently stressing practical applications in life and society, it can be shown that the essentials of practical learning are basically present in his views and, in this sense, are generable from his philosophy. By displaying this generation, it will be clear that the attack on Chu Hsi's Neo-Confucian philosophy (*Chu-hsüeh*) from the practical learning school cannot be philosophically valid, if Chu Hsi's own philosophy is intended by *Chu-hsüeh*. It also will be clear that it requires a special vision to develop *shih-hsüeh* from *Chu-hsüeh*, and that *shih-hsüeh* failed historically to develop from *Chu-hsüeh* precisely because of a lack of such special vision on the part of the Sung-Ming Neo-Confucianists. As mentioned earlier, *shih-hsüeh* presupposes an understanding of *shih*, a concern with problems of *shih*, as well as a responsiveness to social needs of the time. The social and political change in the eighteenth century has provided a context for such understanding, such concern, and such responsiveness. These are what underlie the special vision required for conscientiously developing *shih-hsüeh* from *Chu-hsüeh*.

To appreciate how *shih-hsüeh* is potentially present in the works of Chu Hsi, we shall first of all focus on the similarity between *shih-hsüeh* and *Chu-hsüeh*. In the first place, contrary to what the practical learning advocates say, *shih* and Chu Hsi's philosophy share a rather close similarity in their common criticism of impractical, irrelevant, and empty subjects of learning and study. As we have seen, *shih-hsüeh* has regarded textual criticism and the study of letters and prose for the purpose of civil examination as a waste of time and as weakening the will of mind. Similarly, Chu Hsi endorsed the view that the study of prose and textual criticism for the purpose of civil examination is of no value for attaining the truth. Thus, he said:

The so-called learning starts with being an intellectual (*shih*) and continues to learn to become a sage. Yi Chuan (Ch'eng Yi) says one can learn three ways: Learn the prose, learn the textual criticism and learn the doctrine of Confucius. If one wishes to understand truth (*tao*), there is no other way but learning the doctrine of Confucius.[19]

Chu Hsi deplored the bad and degrading effects of learning for passing the civil examination (*ko-chü*), which deprives men of a high purpose in life and the concentration of mind in search of principles and righteousness. Chu Hsi even sharply pointed out that the learning of prose for civil examinations demoralizes and disintegrates the innate sense of righteousness in a person and leads to selfishness and profit making as the goal of life. He said:

Thus in regard to learning of the ancient and present things, and in regard to matters or right and profit, one will fail to make a distinction and will fail to see what is proper and what should be done. Thus even though a person may be well read and expert in literary composition, this will merely serve to harm his mind. One must reverse this. Then one can talk about the right method of learning.[20]

Chu Hsi was similarly opposed to empty talk and empty thinking, which do not focus on actual and useful matters of life. By this he meant far-reaching thinking without application to life and practice or incapable of being applied to life and society. On this ground and on the ground of the failure to give up attachment to self-interest, Chu Hsi opposed Buddhism and Taoism and strongly defended Confucianism as the most just and balanced doctrine. He said:

In learning one should not become far-reaching and high-sounding. One need only pay attention to one's words and conduct (practice) so that one will be substantial. Nowadays scholars talk of truth (*tao*); only talks of principles (*li*), but do not talk of things (*shih*); only talk of mind, but do not talk of body. The talk is profound, but there is no evidence for its truth. It elapses into emptiness and heterodoxy.[21]

In saying this, Chu Hsi, of course, did not mean to denounce *li* as an improper subject of study. What he suggested is that, when one studies *li*, one should study it in connection with concrete affairs or things. This is what he calls *shih*. The "profundity" of thinking divorced from concrete affairs or things and separated from practice is nothing but what Chu Hsi calls *high illusion* (*kao-huan*).[22] It is evident that practical learning is precisely opposed to such high illusions.

A positive account of Chu Hsi's theory of learning and knowing will bring out even more affinity between *Chu-hsüeh* and practical learning. A first principle par excellence for Chu Hsi's theory of learning is that learning must embody references to actual reality and must incorporate and command practice. In other words, learning is not separated from the intimate concerns of one's nature, or from things that one may find useful in developing one's nature or in realizing the principle of things. Chu Hsi was opposed to mere practice without the learning of principle just as he was opposed to learning mere principle without practice. Thus, he said:

If one has understanding but does not practice what one understands, then one's understanding has no use. It is empty understanding only. If one merely does things without understanding, then doing things will have no goal, it is only blind activity.[23]

Knowing and practice are mutually dependent; like eyes without feet cannot walk, feet without eyes cannot see. On the question of priority, knowing should be first. On the question of importance, practice should be more important.[24]

Given this basic view of learning, learning clearly was conceived by Chu Hsi as having the objective of being applicable to life and concrete reality and entailing useful results for society or one's self-realization. In these perspectives Chu Hsi felt learning should be practical and concrete (*shih*) just as Yen Yuan felt it should.

Specifically, Chu Hsi defined learning as "[that process] in which one seeks knowledge and knowhow in what one does not know or does not know how [to do]."[25] If one has known something or acquired a certain ability to do something, one can put one's knowledge and one's ability to practice. This was called by Chu Hsi as "review of one's learning (hsi)."[26] Both the learning and review of learning are comprehensive and unlimited in scope and thus do not exclude anything that practical learning *admits* or promotes from its scope. Thus, Chu Hsi said:

> It is vitally important for learning to frequently review what one learns. It should be always uppermost in one's mind and thinking. Nothing one should not learn, at no time one should not learn, and in nowhere one should not learn.[27]

Perhaps one difficulty with this approach to learning is that it is too broad and too diluted, lacking a point of focus and thus a sense of urgency. This issue, therefore, appears to be not that it does not include the subjects of practical learning, but rather that it does not single out the subjects of practical learning for special attention.

Another difficulty for this approach to learning is in connection with Chu Hsi's constant references to the study of ideas and writings of sages from the past. In this sense learning is more retrospective than prospective. It is in practice, though not in principle, very much confined to the Confucian subjects of learning how to develop one's nature and learning how to pacify the world and serve a ruler in a correct and upright way. If this is the practical usefulness intended by Chu Hsi, then there is a contrast between the goals and the methods of Chu Hsi's learning and those of the practical learning represented by Yen Yuan and Kuang Chih-chen. Whereas Chu Hsi wished to see learning aim at self-cultivation and the making of a sage, practical learning as a whole is intended for strengthening the state at its paramount end. It therefore is a delimitation of the Confucian theory of learning through self-cultivation as promoted in Chu Hsi's philosophy. Chu Hsi has characterized his theory of learning in the framework of the *Great Learning*.

> To read and to exhaustively investigate principles, to broadly study the prescribed teachings of sages and worthies in the past and in the present, the learning will be practically useful.[28]

> Learning is not identical with reading. But if not reading, then one could not know the way of learning. The sages only teach men to make one's intention, rectify one's mind, cultivate one's person, regulate one's family, govern well one's state, and pacify the world. The so-called learning is to learn this. If not reading, one does not know how to cultivate one's person, nor how to regulate one's family or govern one's state.[29]

Because learning is conceived to be guided by the principles of the *Great Learning*, it is apparent that learning can be extended freely as was originally intended by Chu Hsi. Combined with Chu Hsi's theory of *li* and his integrated theory of *ke-wu* (investigation of things) and *chih-chih* (extension of knowledge) in the *Great Learning*, learning ultimately becomes a matter of seeking an understanding of *li*, not a practice of a life of useful results as Chu Hsi appears to claim. Chu Hsi's stress on learning to understand *li* cannot be understated, and this I believe constitutes an obstacle that practical learning rejects and criticizes severely. Consider the following statements of Chu Hsi:

It is through learning that one encounters *li* in one's life. If not learning, then one won't be able to see *li* in its perfection, in its large scope, and in its accurate detail.[30]

If one's mind becomes familiar with learning, then one naturally will see wherein *li* lies. If one's mind becomes familiar with learning, then one's mind will be delicate and perceptive. If one's mind does not see *li*, it is because one's mind is still crude.[31]

Once Chu Hsi introduces this theory of *li*, it appears that his general doctrine of learning becomes removed from the originally intended idea of practical applicability to life and society. This is because *li* is considered basically inherent in one's mind. *Li* is the nature that a person's mind becomes aware of in the process of his learning. Learning, therefore, ultimately serves the purpose of achieving self-awakening in a person, which defines an important aspect of sagehood but which, nevertheless, could lead to possible Buddhistic interpretations.

Learning is not what grows outside, but is originally innate in oneself. Yao and Shun derive it from their nature, and *li* is not lost. Tang and Wu return to it, though losing it somewhat but succeeding in restoring to one's good nature. Learning is only restoring *li* to one's old nature (*fu-chi-chiu-hsing*).[32]

If learning is only "restoring *li* to one's old nature," then learning really cannot be directed outside but remains metaphysical as well as moralistic. Thus, learning has its main effect in transforming one's temperament (*ch'i-chih*) so that one can enter the truth (*tao*). Chu Hsi said:

In the beginning of one's learning with great effort, one should inquire and think and practice; then one can transform one's temperament and enter the *tao*.[33]

Learning then becomes inward and a matter of cultivation of one's character, not outward and a matter of transforming the society into an economically better one.

"Practice" (*hsing*), according to Chu Hsi, is a matter of close observation of *li* in life, not a devotion to seeking solutions to the social problems of the time. It therefore is not genuine, "practical" (*shih*) practice nor the practice of *shih* in its social and economic sense. Despite some difficulties that prevent Chu Hsi's doctrine of learning from actually developing into practical learning, and despite the fact that these difficulties may have created serious misunderstandings and misled Chu Hsi's followers or commentators to advocate a doctrine or adopt a practice that the advocates of practical learning criticize, we must nevertheless do justice to Chu Hsi's theory of learning by recognizing its original intent and its flexible scope, which are highly compatible with the theory and practice of practical learning. We must reiterate that under suitable social stimulation it is conceivable that Chu Hsi's theory of learning would conduce to the development of practical learning. As a clue to the last assertion we again quote Chu Hsi to testify to his understanding that learning includes practical and useful studies and incorporates precisely the subjects that practical learning earnestly seeks to promote.

In talking about learning and study for governing oneself and others, there are many things to learn. As to astronomy, geography, principles of rites and music, military science, penal codes, all are subjects of study characterized by practical usefulness. The study of them is not outside what one should do. In ancient time men are taught the six arts (*lü-yi*), in order to develop their minds. They are taught just for this purpose. In comparison with empty word-play and document compiling, the great merit of the former and the great demerit of the latter cannot be measured.[34]

In this passage, of particular interest is Chu Hsi's mention of the six arts as subjects of teaching and learning. No one will doubt that these words could just as easily have been written by a staunch advocate of practical learning such as Yen Yuan or Kung Chih-chen.

Though Chu Hsi used the word *shih* in many contexts and on many occasions, such as "sincerity is *shih*" (*ch'eng-shih-shih*) and "sincerity is the *li* of actuality" (*ch'eng-shih-li-yeh*),[35] he generally meant by *shih* the truthful principle or the real principle of things. *Shih* in this sense clearly is tied up with his doctrine of *li*. But to my knowledge, on at least two occasions, Chu Hsi talked of *shih-hsüeh*, which does not appear to have to do with the study of *li*, but instead suggests a connotation of *shih-hsüeh* in the sense of social and political application. He said, in a memorial to the throne when he was sixty-seven years old, in connection with his proposal to compile and edit the ancient documents or rites (*li*) and *Yi Li*: "By compiling and editing these, we may expect to preserve what is deserved so that it may last forever, and so that students of the future may know *shih-hsüeh* and sometime it may serve as an aid to the putting up of institutions for the society and state."[36] On another occasion Chu Hsi said:

If one takes passing a civil examination as a means for supporting one's parents and undertakes no learning for one's cultivation, it shows that one lacks good ideals. If one considers passing the examination as hindering *shih-hsüeh*, why does he consider that as hindering eating and drinking water? This merely shows one's lack of ideas.[37]

Shih-hsüeh clearly is intended to bear on the ordering of society and the governing of the state and therefore acquires a sense that is not remote from the *shih-hsüeh* in Yen Yuan's philosophy.

In this connection it is interesting to note that Chu Hsi is by all means the first major Neo-Confucianist to apply the significant and suggestive term *shih-hsüeh*.[38]

A special note must be added concerning the relation between *Chu-hsüeh* and the Che-tung schools (Yüng K'ang school and Yung Chia school), to clarify the meaning of *shih-hsüeh* in Chu's usage. Ch'en Liang (1143-1194) of the Yüng K'ang school urged adoption of political and economic measures for strengthening the state and procuring power in the spirit of Han and T'ang. This clearly is a utilitarian doctrine that Chu Hsi criticized as lacking righteous motivation as well as lacking sagely cultivation of oneself. Yeh Shih (1150-1223) of the Yung Chia school was more moderate in his advocation of utility, as he based this advocation on the ground of social institutions conforming to the Neo-Confucian doctrines, but he still regarded Chu Hsi's principle, "Follow righteousness without pursuing the utility, illuminate the way without calculating the success" (in the words of Tung Chung-shu, c.179-104 B.C.), as too impractical and unrealistic.[39] The contrast between Chu Hsi's idea of *shih-hsüeh* and that of the Che-tung schools brings out the nonutilitarian, if not antiutilitarian, character of Chu's concern with practical affairs in his learning and philosophy.

How Practical-Minded Was Chu Hsi in His Political Life?

Chu Hsi had a long and eventful political career of forty-seven years, but it appears that he had not wielded any significant influence over national affairs. On the contrary, he had frequently become the target of abuse and persecution by those who opposed his teachings or his orthodox Confucian approach, characterized by a sense of righteousness, candor, and public-

Part III: Neo-Confucian Dimensions

mindedness.[40] Two important facts in Chu Hsi's political career are worthy of special mention and explanation.

1. Chu Hsi in general had been very much concerned with establishing schools for higher learning. During his administration of Nan Kang (1179-1180), Chu Hsi undertook to restore the White Deer Grotto Academy and caused it to flourish. He also was known for the relief work done under his direction, including the establishment of a commune loan granary for relieving famine. This shows Chu Hsi to be an able and competent administrator who always had the economic and moral welfare of people in mind.

2. Chu Hsi was not slow to petition the throne for political reform on matters he regarded as being of national importance. In his memorial he was very candid and voiced his views on many areas of affairs in the interests of government and people. His attempt to rectify the weaknesses of the emperor is well known in his Wu Shen Feng Shih petition of 1187. He had acted as a teacher and guide to the throne, but chose to retire when his advice went unheeded.

In view of these facts in Chu Hsi's political career, it is clear that Chu Hsi generally put into practice what he believed in good faith, and that he truly acted as a conscientious Confucian statesman both in relation to his ruler and in relation to the people under his care. To say this is to say that he was practical-minded and not a mere speculative philosopher. One may also conclude that his learning and philosophy of *li* did not prevent him from taking a practical attitude toward the concrete affairs of society in the sense of the utilitarian practicality of *shih-hsüeh*.

To determine whether Chu Hsi's philosophy contains the utilitarian practicality of *shih-hsüeh*, one should inquire into Chu Hsi's thoughts about methods of government and his considerations regarding the managing of government. If by the utilitarian practicality of *shih-hsüeh* we ultimately mean ordering the state, stabilizing a society, and benefitting peoples' economic welfare and educational guides, then what constitutes Chu Hsi's political thinking should determine, to a large extent, whether his learning and philosophy shared this practicality.

It is true that Chu Hsi's attitude toward practice was not a utilitarian one. He subscribed to Tung Chung-shu's maximum:"Follow righteousness without pursuing the utility; illuminate the Way without calculating the success." In this view, to follow (do) righteousness is part of knowing righteousness, which does not require procuring actual benefits; to illuminate the Way is part of understanding the Way, which does not require demonstration in social, political, or economic successes. He said:

One should carry out one's plans in a fair and upright way; whether they succeed or not is decided by Heaven. Some men in the past succeeded not because they had intelligence, but because there is coincidence. All unnecessary devices and efforts and intricate calculations are not to help, and are all in vain.[41]

This attitude toward doing things, of course, does not mean that Chu Hsi was completely indifferent to consequences. But it does mean that one should do one's best and let no possible failure hamper one from doing one's best. It also implies that one should employ only righteous methods for arriving at righteous goals. No one should consider these two principles as negating or denying that once motivation and actual practice objectives are rectified, objectives and consequences are not relevant for judging the value of teaching or of a doctrine.

Chu Hsi takes the governing of a state as a serious matter. He seems to suggest three basic measures for achieving good government.

1. He urged that ministers "invite the able and sagely, reject the vicious and the crooked, and open one's mind to all men under heaven for securing order under Heaven."[42]
2. He urged that the ruler be unselfish and public-minded and rectify his mind to listen and get close to the righteous and detach from the small man.
3. He also believed that "Learning and clarifying true meanings and principles of things will enlighten the minds of people and enable more people to know principles, and thus one need not worry about failure in government."[43]

Chu Hsi truly followed Confucius when he asserted that, to govern well, one has to start with rectifying one's mind and making sincere one's intentions.[44] But when he held that one should investigate things and extend knowledge by clarifying principles, he not only advanced the thesis of the *Great Learning*, but forwarded his own thesis of learning *li*. As a whole, Chu Hsi concluded that government depends on the existence of good persons and that a good system is not sufficient.[45] In this regard he was not conservative and does not look backward for what is good, but defended what is good on its own merits. Thus, he did not defend the well-field system (*ching-t'ien-chih*) when questioned about it, nor the system of feudal establishment (*feng-chien*).

In his own philosophical remarks, Chu Hsi showed great concern with concrete matters for administering government. Here I will merely give a few illustrations from his sayings.

If one takes the job of a county magistrate, it is proper for one to administer lega-
tional justice, eliminate robbery and theft, encourage farming, and suppress inde-
cent activities.[46]

In the second place, Chu Hsi showed great sensitivity to what was needed
in public measure to benefit the state and society. Thus, in regard to the
economic burden of the people in his time, he said:

Today people are poor, because the substance of the army costs the financial burden [of people]. [The government should] adopt the policy of settling the soldiers
to cultivate land in order to lighten the burden of the people.[47]

He also urged adoption of some other economic measures for improving
the economy of the people:

Today [the people are] poor. [In order to mend the situation], the government
should correctly check the land ownership so that taxes are correctly levied. [When
the government] knows the correct income of the taxes, it can plan its budget on
the basis of the revenue and eliminate waste as well as wipe out taxes of incorrect
title. This will save the people from poverty. If the government does not recognize
the people as belonging to the government as one's ownself, this is lack of kindness
[toward the people.][48]

In regard to famine due to drought, he said: "To set up relief is no wonder
solution; one needs to plan irrigation. [Without irrigation] relief is not a
solution."[49] In regard to the current military situation, Chu Hsi held and
urged that the ruler should rectify himself and make an effort to lead the
soldiers in strengthening the military power against foreign invaders.[50]

Finally, as already noted, Chu Hsi paid attention to and laid great stress
on educational matters, and urged establishment of schools for transformation of social mores as the basis of good government.

Is Wang Yang-ming's *Hsin-Hsüeh* Incompatible with *Shih-Hsüeh?*

Even though advocates of practical learning in the seventeenth and
eighteenth centuries criticized the Wang-ming school as empty and Ch'an-
dominated, scarcely any explanation was given as to how Wang Yang-ming
and his learning should be evaluated from the point of view of *shih-hsüeh*.
Again, the problem of understanding what constitutes practically (*shih*)
may have more than one answer. Apparently *shih* cannot mean utility and
profit for Wang Yang-ming. In fact, he rejected *shih-hsüeh* in this sense.

Neither does *shih* mean the application or use of principles to things, for
Wang neither recognized nor separated the existence of principles from the
concrete use of them. Nor does *shih* simply mean concern with affairs of
society and the state as is the case with Chu Hsi, for Wang Yang-ming
aimed at something more fundamental than simple or mere concern with
affairs of society and the state. In the following text, I shall explain what
Wang Yang-ming explicitly rejected as not practical (*shih*) and what he
accepted as practical (*shih*). I argue that his philosophy of the unity of
knowledge, action, the fulfillment of the innate knowledge of goodness
forms an essential dimension of practicality. I also indicate that the practical learning concept of the seventeenth century should be considered a
spiritual heir of Wang's philosophy of practicality, even though no acknowl-
edgement to Wang was ever made by the *shih-hsüeh* advocates.

First of all, Wang Yang-ming contrasted *shih* with *ming* (name), and
thus pinpointed the dominating meaning of *shih* as actual or real and as
what actually has been done. He said: "In learning, the great weakness is
love of name . . . . Name contrasts with actuality (*shih*). The more one is
concerned with actuality, the less one is concerned with name."[51] This concept of *shih* is related to the concept of revealing or realizing the innate
knowledge of goodness in one's life, as we shall see. It is something inside
oneself and yet universal among people. It does not entail success in one's
political career or in one's intellectual enterprise, but it leads one to be a
sagely person, one who truly realizes one's nature and the nature of others.
Conversely, the 'name' signifies something on the surface that has no root
in one's true self and thus is limited to external successes or achievements
of no use to one's self-cultivation. Clearly, Wang Yang-ming rejects not only
name in the sense of renown, but in the sense of knowledge, education,
literary ability, or scholarship. For all these may serve the purpose of seeking utility and self-interest and therefore become obstacles for attaining
goodness. He said:

> The wide scope of one's erudition will only make [one] proud; the great amount of
> one's knowledge will cause [one] to practice evil; the large expanse of one's under-
> standing will only help [one] to increase disputes; the richness of prose will enable
> [one] to disguise one's deception.[52]

Yang-ming specifically rejected the study of textual criticism and flowery
prose, and in this respect he was in agreement with the advocates of *shih-
hsüeh*. But it is noteworthy that Wang Yang-ming went one step further
than practical learning, in that, whereas practical learning sees great importance in the knowledge of things, Wang suspected that seeking knowledge

of things and learning principles would never preserve one's true insight into the goodness of one's nature. For this reason Wang rejected Chu Hsi's doctrine of seeking principles. Wang Yang-ming called his own learning the "learning of sagehood" (*sheng-hsüeh*) and also sometimes even spoke of *hsin-hsüeh* (the learning of the mind). The question now is how this learning of sagehood, or *hsin-hsüeh*, can be regarded as containing or presenting a dimension of practicality.

The essence of Wang's philosophy is that one should endeavor to become a sage, who regards heaven and earth and all people and things as a unity of close relationships and thus deserving of his care and love. In more specific terms, the goal of one's education is to reach harmony and achieve the well-being of all people so that the goodness of the universe will be realized in these through one. This requires a person to be thoroughly unselfish and thoroughly enlightened concerning his or her true nature and the nature of others and the world. One must be thoroughly unselfish, one must restore and retain the mind of universal sympathy toward other people, and must be motivated to act in accordance with equity and fairness. One also must be thoroughly enlightened because one must arrive at right perceptions and judgments about what should be and could be done.

According to Wang, the beginning point of being unselfish also is the beginning point of being enlightened, so that being unselfish and being enlightened are mutually interdependent and simultaneously derived from the same root nature and capacity of humankind. This capacity he emphatically referred to as *liang-chih* (the innate knowledge of goodness), following Mencius. *Liang-chih* is innate in everyone and therefore is both universal among people and particular and proper to each individual. It also is the ultimate quality of humankind issuing from Heaven and Earth and can be aptly identified with the illustrious virtue (*ming-te*) in the *Great Learning* and sincerity (*ch'eng*) in the *Doctrine of the Mean*. Although *liang-chih* is universal among people and proper to a particular person, it needs great effort and attention to preserve the activity and awareness of *liang-chih* in a person, and it will take even greater effort and attention to bring *liang-chih* to bear upon every affair of life. However, with the constant and continuous cultivation of *liang-chih*, one will be able to achieve a mentality of unselfishness and an enlightened vision in one's judgments and actions. In this way, a person can be said to be learning to be a sage or applying one's mind correctly. This is what Wang called the doctrine of fulfilling *liang-chih* (*chih-liang-chih*). It is a doctrine of learning to maintain one's uprighteousness and clarity, and one's rationality and goodness even under the most adverse conditions.

Wang Yang-ming clearly saw the learning of sagehood, in this sense, as a most practical undertaking, and no one can deny that this learning, given its philosophical presuppositions, is indeed practical, in the sense involving considerations of achieving goodness for people and society.[53]

The learning of sagehood, by way of retaining and developing *liang-chih*, is not only practical in the sense of realizing goodness in oneself and society, but also practical in another sense as defined by Wang's doctrine of the unity of knowledge and action (*chih-hsing-ho-yi*). Wang held that knowledge and action must not be regarded as two separate things but instead should be conceived as ultimately unified in their generation and completion. This was a great insight into the nature of knowledge and the nature of practice. As Wang pointed out: "Knowledge is the plan (*chü-yi*) of action, action is the effort (*kung-fu*) of knowledge; knowledge is the beginning of action and action is the completion of knowledge."[54] This view underlines the intentionality of knowing (*chih*) and practicing (*hsing*) and their dynamic and dialectical relationship, which are most obvious in political, social, and moral activities. By his assertion of the unity of knowledge and action he brought to light a fundamental dimension of the mind; namely, the practicality (in the sense of an act or action) of the mind. According to Wang,

Whenever one genuinely knows, there is action; whenever one acts perceptively, there is knowledge. Efforts of knowledge and action are really not separable. It is only because in later days scholars give separate attention to them and thus lose the sight of the original substance of knowledge and action, that there is the view on combining both and advancing both. True knowledge is for the sake of action; and to have no action, knowledge cannot be called knowledge.[55]

The important point about Wang's thesis on the unity of *chih* and *hsing* is that *chih* and *hsing* originally were one and never intended to be separated. One who looks into the metaphysical ground of this original unity of knowledge and action can clearly see that this metaphysical ground is found in the existence of *liang-chih* that everyone inherits from heaven. *Liang-chih* not only is the defining quality of a morally good mind and nature, but also is the source of the practicality of perspective and cognitive activities. This is to say that the mind promises every perceptive and cognitive act with an act of volition and desire so that knowledge inevitably points to action, which is also the satisfaction or completion of the whole act of the mind. That the mind is as described is an essential part of Wang's doctrine of the mind and *liang-chih*. In conjunction with Wang's theory of *chih-liang-chih*, this doctrine also underscores Wang's idea of learning as learning to become a sage who will fulfill or bring about goodness in individuals and society.[56]

In the above I have analyzed and pinpointed the notion of practicality in Wang's philosophy and theory. We can see that this morally and metaphysically significant notion of practicality is not the same practicality that the philosophers of *shih-hsüeh* advocate, for in their view the doctrine of mind and *chih-liang-chih* will lead only to empty talk and idle thinking and therefore controverts the practicality of *shih-hsüeh*. They justified their valuation by pointing to the Ch'anist followers of the Wang school. But for Wang Yang-ming, however, there is a sense of practicality as defined by his doctrine of the mind and *chih-liang-chih*, which is more fundamental than the practicality of *shih-hsüeh*, yet not incompatible with it. Practicality (an act or action of the mind) in this sense, is the source of all practicalities and unifies as well as evaluates all other practicalities. Thus, on the basis of this fundamental practicality of the mind, Wang objects to ignoring more practicality in advancing utilitarian practicality and to not developing an attitude of moral practicality before developing that of utilitarian practicality. Once moral practicality is developed, Wang seemed ready to accept utilitarian practicality as a means for promoting an orderly and materially well-provided for society. For example, Wang said in regard to the function of schools:

In school one should regard cherishment of virtue as the objectives of education. But in [developing] diverse abilities in the areas of arts and music, or in the areas of government and education, or in the areas of irrigation, geography, and husbandry, one can refine these abilities in school on the basis of one's already accomplished virtues.[57]

One might therefore conclude that, whenever we take the essentials of Wang's philosophy into consideration, it is revealed that *shih-hsüeh* could have a proper place in Wang's philosophy and that even though *shih-hsüeh* is not directly derivable from Wang's philosophy, it is highly relevant for understanding Wang's philosophy.

Practicality in the Political Career of Wang Yang-ming

In personality and in practice Wang Yang-ming was a highly motivated and active person. Even though he was versatile in his abilities and had attempted many subjects of studies, he sought study and learning as a way to fulfill his deep aspiration to reach for truth and existential-intellectual satisfaction. In fact, a close examination of his biography shows that the knowledge and learning he acquired were direct results of his efforts to reach for truth and existential-intellectual satisfaction. His philosophy of mind and *chih-liang-chih* therefore is a crystalization of intellectual inquiry as well as a reflection on wisdom borne of his life experience in adversity and hardship. Though he studied many "impractical" subjects such as Taoism and Buddhism in his early career, which may in some way have continued to influence his Confucianist thinking in the later period of his life, for twenty-nine years Wang had concentrated more or less on the practical affairs and practical learning of his time. For the practical affairs that commanded his concern, none is more noteworthy than his preoccupation with military studies. At the age of twenty-six, he was alarmed about border fights and started closely studying the classics of the military arts. His interest in participating in current politics, for the purpose of improving government and strengthening the state, also became dominant in this period. After obtaining a *chin-shih* degree at the age of twenty-eight, Wang, for the next twenty-nine years until his death in 1529, proved himself to be a tough-minded veteran in politics, though often forced to be so. Wang also had achieved much military success for the government. For himself, he had succeeded in advancing his doctrine and thinking in a most energetic manner and taught many disciples in the school of thought he established.

Here we are unable to give a thorough account of Wang's political career to testify to the rich but not uncharacteristic practicality of his career. Our purpose in mentioning his career is merely to focus on the fact that Wang's teaching of practicality is borne out by his practice of what he taught and is, in fact, to a large measure inspired by his experiences in political life. We also are interested in pointing out that in his practice Wang cannot be regarded as objecting to the practical learning of several centuries later, but had indirectly contributed to the need for developing *shih-hsüeh* at the later time. However, one should not forget that, although practical in his military and political activities, Wang never gave up moral practicality as the basis and guiding principle of his career and activities. This should explain why his political and military practice often led to personal disaster in spite of his achievements.

Three things can be said about Wang's political career that reflect his moral practicality and his relevant analysis of practical affairs in his time. In the first place, he had written a memorial on border affairs (*Pien Wu Shu*) at the age of twenty-eight. This memorial shows his close concern with national security and his sincere wish to improve on affairs of the military. His proposal on seeking talent, organizing the army, extending cultivating of the land, and adopting the code of discipline are all sound measures and show a practical but correct mind at work.

In the second place, Wang was good at the administration of local government. In his term as magistrate of Lu Ling county at the age of thirty-nine, he brought real peace and order to the locality and won fame as a capable administrator. His organizational and governmental ability also was demonstrated in his military pacifying movement in Southern Chiang Hsi and Kuanghsi Ssu T'ien. His relief and reform policies on local government had introduced a solid foundation to those troubled areas. This is reflected in his drafting of the "Covenant for Governing the South Chiang Hsi Area" (*Nan Kan Hsiang Yuen*) and "Memorial on Pacifying Locality in Order to Secure Lasting Peace" (*Chu-chih ping-fu t'i-feng yi tu chiu-an su*).[58]

Finally, Wang Yang-ming showed great dexterousness and tactical acumen in leading military campaigns and expeditions. He was assigned to three different military operations against rebels and bandits, and in short periods successfully and effectively accomplished his assignments. At the age of forty-five, in 1517-1518, he pacified the unrest in the southern Chiang Hsi area. At the age of forty-eight, in 1520, he routed the Shen Hou rebellion. At age of fifty-six, in 1528, one year before his death, he pacified the unrest of the Kuanghsi border regions. These three events in Wang's political career suffice to show that Wang, as a Neo-Confucianist, did not hesitate to deal with practical affairs in a practical way as guided by his practical philosophy of moral cultivation. In this regard, Wang is strongly comparable to Chu Hsi, yet he had engaged himself in many more practical activities than Chu Hsi did.

Concluding Remarks

I have shown, in my examination and analysis of practicality (*shih*) in the philosophy of Yen Yuan, that there can be many meanings to practicality. *Shih-hsüeh*, in its most relevant sense as a seventeenth- and eighteenth-century movement in China, is the learning of things in response to the social needs of the time. We have also shown that, theoretically, practical learning (*shih-hsüeh*) can be traced to the theory and practice of Chu Hsi and Wang Yang-ming. Even though in appearance *shih-hsüeh* is promoted and developed at the expense of *Chu-hsüeh* (the school of Chu Hsi) and *Wang-hsüeh* (the school of Wang Yang-ming), in reality both Chu Hsi's and Wang Yang-ming's doctrines and careers initiated a deep concern with meeting the social problems of the time and contain nothing incompatible with *shih-hsüeh*. A strong case, in fact, can be made for the view that, through the acceptance of moral practicality in Chu Hsi's and Wang's doctrines, the utilitarian practicality of *shih-hsüeh* receives the philosophical and moral justification and sanction for being articulated and promoted. This is simply borne out by the fact that most of the advocates of *shih-hsüeh* unambiguously subscribe to the fundamental Confucian tenet that good government must concentrate on bringing well-being to people. Yen Yuan clearly was a paradigm of this Confucian commitment. Kung Chih-chen in his advocation of Kung Yang learning was no less exemplary of the Confucian political belief. I also have shown that Chu Hsi's philosophy can be conceived as providing a basis for *shih-hsüeh* and that Wang Yang-ming's theory of the unity of knowledge and action constitutes an important pillar for the incorporation of *shih-hsüeh* in government and society. The political careers of Chu and Wang, furthermore, testify to the vigor and ability of a Confucianist in applying that doctrine to reality, which constantly inspired many practitioners of *shih-hsüeh* in eighteenth and nineteenth century China.

As a final remark, in saying that Chu Hsi and Wang Yang-ming both in theory and practice could be conceived to have given rise to *shih-hsüeh*, I am not denying that in history it was due to the impractical developments of the Chu Hsi and Wang Yang-ming schools, their outward postures, their insensibilities toward social demands, and their failures to answer the urgent problems of the time that *shih-hsüeh* has been vigorously formulated to replace them.

Notes

1. Hattori Unakichi, *Confucianism and Contemporary Thought*, Taipei, 1964, p. 1955.
2. See Yen Yuan, *Tseng Hsueh Pien* (*On Preserving Learning*), Shanghai, 1937. "Shang Tai-ch'ang Lü Fu-ting hsien-sheng shu" (Letter to Mr. Lü Fu-ting of Tai Chang).
3. See ibid., "Ming-ching."
4. See *Lien Wang pien* as mentioned in Hou Wai-lu's *Chung-kuo chao-chi chi-mu ssu-hsiang shih* (*History of Early Enlightenment Thought of China*), Peking, 1958, p. 381.
5. See Yen Yuan, *Tseng Hsueh Pien*, ibid., p. 9.
6. Ibid., p. 9.
7. Ibid., "Hsueh Pien," I, p. 12.
8. Yen Yuan once speaks of *shih-yueh* in the following terms: "If heaven does not abandon me, I will enrich the world with seven words; reclaim land, equalize landownership, [and] conduct water irrigation. I will strengthen the world with six words; make people soldiers, make officials generals. I will pacify the world with nine words; select talent [for] government, rectify laws [and] norms, [and] promote rites [and] music." See the *Yen Hsi-tsai hsien-shen nien-pu* (*Bibliography of Mr. Yen Hsi-tsai*).
9. See Yen Yuan, *Tseng Hsueh Pien*, III, p. 37.
10. Ibid., p. 49.
11. See Yen Yuan, *Ssu Shu Cheng Wu* (*Corrections on Interpretations of the Four Books*), part I.
12. See *Hsi-tsai Chi Yu* (*Record of Peripheral Writings of Hsi-tsai*), in Book II, "Chang-nan shu yuan chi."
13. See Hou Wai-lu, *Chung-kuo Chao-chi chi-ming Esu-hsiang Shih* (*History of Chinese Early Enlightenment Thought*), Peking, 1958, 33 ff.
14. See my article, "*Li-Ch'i* and *Li-Yu* Relationships in Seventeenth-Century Neo-Confucian Philosophy," Chapter 20 in this book.
15. See *Ting Yueh Wen Chi* (Collected Essays of Ting-Yüen), book two.
16. See ibid., Book 2, and first part.
17. See ibid., second part.

18. See ibid., first part. "*Yi-ping chih chi Tso-yi*, number 6" (*Essays in the Year of Yi-ping*), #6).
19. Quoted from Chang Pei-hsing's *Shu Ching-ssu lu* (*Sequent to Reflections on Things in Hang.*), (a collection of Chu Hsi's writings and sayings), Book II, p. 361.
20. Quoted in ibid., Book II, pp. 56-57.
21. Quoted in ibid., p. 35.
22. Ibid., p. 41.
23. Ibid., p. 37.
24. Ibid., p. 38.
25. Ibid., p. 37.
26. Ibid., p. 37.
27. Ibid., p. 36.
28. Ibid., p. 37.
29. Ibid., p. 39.
30. Ibid., p. 45.
31. Ibid., p. 44.
32. Ibid., p. 45.
33. Ibid., p. 43.
34. Ibid., p. 47.
35. See *Chu Tzu Yu-lei* (*Conversations of Chu Hsi*), sections 6 and 23.
36. See Wang Meng-hung, *Chu Tsu Nien Pu* (*Bibliography of Chu Hsi*), Taipei, 1971, p. 221.
37. From *Shu Ching Ssu-lu*, p. 133.
38. In a special note communicated to me, Wing-tsit Chan pointed out that Lu Hsiang-shang, a contemporary of Chu Hsi, also used the term *shih-hsüeh* in a sentence that suggests *shih-hsüeh* as a verb phrase. "[one should] single-mindedly concentrate in genuine learning, and [should] not spend time in empty talk." *"yi-yi shih-hsueh, pu-shih kung-yen,"* in *Collected Works of Hsiang-shan*, pp. 19-49. Chan also pointed out that this usage of *shih-hsüeh* is dated still later than Chu Hsi's usage.
39. Cf. Chu Hsi's saying in ibid., p. 175.
40. Cf. the informative article by Contard M. Schirokauer, "Chu Hsi's Political Career: A Study in Ambivalence," in *Confucian Personalities*, ed. Arthur F. Wright and Denis Twitchett, Stanford, Calif., 1962, pp. 162-188. Cf. also Wang Meng-hung, *Chu Tzu Nien Pu* (*The Bibliography of Chu Tzu*), Taipei, 1971.
41. *Shu Ching Ssu Lü*, p. 175.
42. Ibid., p. 177.
43. Ibid., p. 181.
44. Cf. ibid., p. 154.
45. Cf. ibid., p. 162. Chu Hsi said, "Institutions are easy to talk about, but all depends on whether there are good people to carry out good institutions."

46. *Shu Ching Ssu Lü*, p. 151.
47. Ibid., p. 164.
48. Ibid., p. 193.
49. Ibid., p. 189.
50. See the text of Wu Shen Feng Shih petition, in Fan Shou-Kang, *Chu Tzu Chi Chi che-hsueh* (*Chu Tzu and His Philosophy*), Taipei, 1964, pp. 282-291.
51. *Chuan Hsi Lu* (*Instinctions for a Practical Living*), ed. Yu Ching-Yuan, Taipei, 1958. Cf. also Wing-tsit Chan's translated edition *Instinctions for Practical Living*, New York, 1963.
52. Quoted from his essay *Pa-p'en She-yuan lun* (*Uproot the Seen and Stop the Source*), in Chang Hsi-chih, *Yang-ming Hsueh Chüan* (*The Record of Learning of Yang-ming*), Taipei, 1961, pp. 173 ff.
53. See his essay *Ta Hsueh Wen* (*Inquiry into the Great Learning*), in the part discussing realization of one's virtue by loving and getting close to people.
54. *Chuan Hsi Lü*, Part I.
55. Ibid., Part I.
56. Cf. Wang's essay, *Ta Hsueh Wen*, and part II of *Chuan Hsi Lu*.
57. Quoted from his essay *Pa-p'en She-yuan lun* in *Ch'uan-hsi lu*, part 2.
58. Cf. *Wang Wen-ch'eng Kung Shu* (*The Completed Works of Duke Wang-ch'eng* [Wang Yang-ming]), Book 6, pp. 77 ff; and Book 7, pp. 93 ff.

18. Religious Reality and Religious Understanding in Confucianism and Neo-Confucianism

In order to present a more adequate and precise characterization of Confucianism and Neo-Confucianism as a form of religious thought than has previously been done, we shall first propose a broad and yet relevant notion of religion and distinguish four fundamental types of religious thought. We shall then analyze Confucianism and Neo-Confucianism against this theoretical backdrop and attempt to identify it with one of these four types.

The Notion of Religion and the Four Main Types of Religious Thought

Even though in contemporary philosophical writings there exist many different views regarding the nature of religion and its significance for the human person and the individual self, it has been in general agreed that religion plays a fundamental role in the development of man and the fulfilment of his life.

We may for our purpose here conceive religion as being basically concerned in a most intimate and direct way with problems of fundamental significance to the human person and their life. To be more specific, we may take religion to be an activity involved with the problems of relating to the *ultimate* and the *total* for the individual and relating the individual to the ultimate and the total.[1] In other words, religion can be conceived as a form of involvement of the self and individual with the ultimate and the total. To explain the significance of this form of involvement with the ultimate and the total reality would be the main concern of religious thought— whether this be described as theology, religious philosophy, or otherwise is not to the point here.

Given the above understanding of religion, we may suggest four basic types of religious thinking in the light of a general understanding of the human experience in religion.

1) The first type is directed toward the existentially experienced presence of the ultimate and the total reality as another person. This other person has been traditionally called God. This tradition we shall take to be exemplified in one type of orthodox Christianity, which is to be identified specifically with Augustine and Aquinas.[2] The key feature of this tradition consists in the existential experience of the power of God in the form of faith; for faith itself, as stressed by Augustine and Aquinas, is a form of the intimate experience of the identity of the human person as revealed by God, who is an external source and a transcendent other.[3] What is interesting and intriguing in this experience is that, on the one hand, the experience of the identity of the human person and the power of God is conceived to be most subjective, whereas, on the other, the source and object of this experience is conceived to be most objective. It is because of this absolute objectivity of God that the absolute subjectivity of experience of faith is reached. The religious experience of an individual is therefore in a sense preconditioned by an absolute existential and ontic bifurcation. We may perhaps call this type of religious experience "*individual existential projection of the ultimate and the total*." Philosophical reflection based on the understanding of this existential projection of the ultimate and the total would conceive God as an object of existential projection.

2) The second type of religious thinking is directed toward the existentially experienced presence of the ultimate and the total reality as a larger or internal identity of the self or the individual. The major difference between this type of religious experience and the first type is that here the ultimate and the total reality is not experienced in terms of intimate personal identification as an object that is other, or another person in particular. Because of the non-differentiation of the experiencing self from the reality of the experience, the object of the experience is felt to be part of the experiencing subject as a whole. Because of this part-whole relationship, not only is the ultimate and the total not conceived as a person, but the experiencing self is conceived to be even dissolved as a person. The source of such experience is the subject himself, a self which, in a dialectical and dynamic course of self-exercise, comes to recognize intimately the value of the ultimate and the total. In this sense, the reality of the ultimate and the total can be said to *infuse* itself, but not *project* itself, into the individual existence. The infusion in question is a matter of re-development and re-making of the self. We may take the Buddhist experience of enlightenment and the Vedantic experience of self-fulfilment as typical exemplifications of this type of religious experience. The Buddhist and the Vedantic philosophies are therefore naturally and obviously related to philosophical reflection on this type of religious experience. In brief, this type of reli-

gious experience is one of "*existential infusion of the ultimate and the total.*" A philosophical reflection based on this type of experience would conceive of the ultimate and the total as presence by existential infusion.

3) The third type of religious thinking can be said to be concerned with "deducing" religion; that is, deducing a set of fundamental beliefs about certain characteristics of the ultimate and the total from rational premises, or establishing them on a rational ground or in conformity with the requirements of reason. From this perspective, religion is "within the limits of reason," as Kant puts it.[4] But religion also becomes a postulate to be called into the picture because there is a rational need for its presence. Thus when Kant justifies religion and the need for postulating the existence of an infinite God and the immortality of soul in his attempt to prove the rationality of religion on the basis of a rational morality, he appears at least to have given religion an objective and rational basis, and has succeeded in making religion dependent on morality, but not in substantiating religion on its own terms.

What characterizes this perspective is a reliance on reason as the guiding principle for the establishment of a rational religion. It is important to note that this type of philosophical thinking about religion treats religious concern as a rational need that is to be rationally guaranteed. It further regards the object of religious consciousness as an object of rational perception and rational demand. Such an object is only hypothetical and constructional in nature, designed to satisfy the emotional and practical needs of the moral fulfilment of the human person. The essence of this type of philosophy of religion may be considered to lie in making religion a matter of rational argumentation. The religious properties of the ultimate and the total are entities posited by such rational argumentation. These aspects are amply borne out by Kant's view of religion.

4) Finally, we come to the last type of religious thinking, which combines elements of the rationality of the third type with elements of the existential fulfilment of the second type. Instead of positing the ultimate and the total as a needed rational construction to satisfy practical and moral demands, as in Kant's system, it presents it as the existential fulfilment of the rational through a process of embodying the practical and the moral. In fact, this combination can also be regarded as a rational exhibition or manifestation of the existential fulfilment of morality and the human person. For the existential fulfilment of the moral human person is not projected into an absolutely transcending object which is the ultimate and the total, but is understood as immanent within the human person, to be experienced as the ultimate and the total and, at the same time, given the form of rationality, so that it obtains a place in the exigencies of reason. What is most significant here is, of course, that this equivalence between the existential

fulfilment of the rational and the rational display of the existential fulfilment makes the life of an individual a dynamic process of inner growth and
spiritual involution. It is therefore to be understood in a metaphysical
scheme of the unity of the transcendent and the immanent, the subjective
and the objective, life and reason. In other places, I have pointed out that
Confucianism represents this type of religious thinking, in which the moral
consciousness of the human person becomes a specific manifestation of
the human person's consciousness of the ultimate and the total, and the
consciousness of the ultimate and the total in the human person becomes
also a specific moral fulfilment of the human person's nature and its ultimate
goodness.[5] Furthermore, morality is where the relation of the individual to
the ultimate and the total and its significance are realized simultaneously.

Application to Confucianism and Neo-Confucianism

It is the purpose of this chapter to discuss and analyze the Confucian
and Neo-Confucian philosophical tradition as a form of religious thinking
against the background of the four types theoretically delineated above.
Perhaps it is because we do not generally take a sufficiently theoretical
perspective on problems of religion and develop a grasp of possible alternatives to already established perspectives that we fail to appreciate the
religious consciousness of Confucianism and Neo-Confucianism, it can be
readily seen that Confucianism and Neo-Confucianism, as most people
understand them, cannot fit into the first type of religious thinking, for the
notion of an absolute transcendent God as an object of existential awe and
worship is foreign to this tradition.[6] Nor does the second type characterize
the main trend of the total tradition of Confucianism and Neo-Confucianism.[7] The non-rational mystical experience of an individual as such has no
real place in the scheme of interrelated things in which moral value and
rational order are realized at the same time.

As to the third type of religious thinking, it was only developed out of
a well-defined background of scientific and logical rationalism. Since there
is no such explicit self-critical and formal rationality in Chinese thought,
there is no significant suggestion of a rationally argued need for religion as
a practical and moral presupposition in the Confucian and Neo-Confucian
tradition. Thus, the only possibility remaining open is the fourth type of
religious thinking, of which Confucianism and Neo-Confucianism may be
said to provide a most rich and suggestive example.

For the sake of discussing the various issues and characteristics proper
to the Confucian and Neo-Confucian religious philosophy, we shall first try
to make clear the nature of the consciousness of the ultimate and the total

reality as found in the Confucian and Neo-Confucian tradition; then we shall deal with the mode of grasping the ultimate and the total reality in this tradition. We shall call the first problem that of *religious reality*, the second that of *religious understanding*. We shall see that the problem of religious reality is not separable from the problem of religious understanding in Confucianism and Neo-Confucianism, because understanding as a way of experiencing reality and reality as a source of understanding the ultimate and the total are not separable. We shall further see that this non-separation is in effect based on an ontological unity between self and *Heaven* (or the ultimate and the total), as well as a dynamic identification between the understanding-of-the-ultimate-and-the-total and the ultimate-and-the-total-of-the-understanding as a form of rational expression of the ultimate and the total.

The Consciousness of Religious Reality in Confucianism

In Confucianism, the consciousness of the ultimate and the total has undergone a dialectical development[8] from the pre-Confucian sources to the philosophy of human nature of Mencius and the *Doctrine of the Mean*. It is obvious and evident that the pre-Confucian *t'ien* (Heaven) represents the ultimate source and authority of things in the world. *T'ien* in the first place gives life to living things and order to all things in the world. It is the constant generative power for all motion in the cosmos. This is considered the ultimate virtue of Heaven. What is significant to note in connection with this creative function of Heaven is that Heaven is related to the human person in a direct relation of begetting and consanguinity, because Heaven has been identified with the ancestorship of the human person. This is evident in the combined notion of Heaven-Lord (*t'ien-ti*) in the *Book of Poetry:* Heaven-Lord is the supreme power over the world and the human person is identified with one of the ancestor kings in the distant past. In this sense, the existence of Heaven as a source of life is clearly a mark of humanity in general. This mere fact of consanguinity underscores a highly significant point: there is no ontological nor any other type of separation or alienation between the human person and Heaven. Thus, unlike the Christian God as conceived in the first type of religious thinking indicated above, Heaven and the human person originally and primordially form a unity and whole, and there is a oneness of *being* for both. This has significant consequences in the consciousness of the ultimate and the total in the human person as exhibited by both Confucianism and Taoism. Two such consequences need to be mentioned. These constitute two primary features of religious reality in Chinese philosophy, beside that of creativity, consanguinity, and unity of being between Heaven and the human person.

The first such consequence from the consanguinity and unity of being between the human person and the reality of Heaven is the worldliness of the religious reality of Heaven. This is nowhere better indicated than in the direct attribution of concern to Heaven with mundane affairs of political rule. Heaven is always assumed to be seriously concerned with the well-being of people as a whole, and the ruler of a people is therefore by the very possession and exercise of the power to rule charged with the serious duty of caring for the well-being of the people as a community of men. This political care and concern of Heaven with the well-being of people in this world *via* the actual political rule of people contrasts very vividly with the need for redemption from this world and deliverance into another of the souls of individual men in Western types of religion.[9]

This difference is not merely a superficial one, for it pinpoints some fundamental issues and perspectives of Chinese religious thinking. The lack of a substantive notion of individual soul, the lack of the negative evaluation of the world, the lack of the essential limitedness of the human person's self-fulfilling potentiality and of the view of the human person as fallen, in the Confucian and Taoist traditions, are to be accounted for by the total theoretical self-sufficiency of such philosophies. Each in its own distinct but similar way sees no such requirements as necessary, and thus presents a religious outlook in which the postulation of such needs are, on the contrary, considered precisely a matter to be accounted for.[10] In other words, this worldliness needs no external explanation in Confucianism and Taoism and can be regarded as a form of the manifestation of the consciousness of the ultimate and the total which satisfies the primary needs of the human person as seen by Confucianism and Taoism.

In the case of Confucianism, the human person is seen to be interwoven into a community of men and thus becomes refined and developed only in the development of the social order of men. Political rule is thus seen to be no more than the extension and application of the moral principle of the self-cultivation of the human person toward the state of perfection. This characteristic worldliness of the ultimate and the total in the Confucian consciousness is therefore intrinsically and organically related to the Confucian view of the human person as a dynamic entity in which Heaven has found its isomorphic counterpart and has revealed itself. This explains the internality of Heaven as a part of human nature and the innateness of the goodness of the human person, as we shall explain a little later. It further explains why the assumption of an indestructibly closed entity called a soul becomes superficial and unnecessary.[11]

A further consequence of the unity and consanguinity of Heaven with the human person is the internality of Heaven as part of the human person and the innateness of the goodness of the human person as suggested earlier. In the *Great Learning*, it has been forcefully asserted that "What is ordained by Heaven is nature"; what is ordained (*ming*) by Heaven is what is constituted by Heaven, for the ordainment (*ming*) is nothing other than the actual participation of Heaven under the form of necessity and regularity. In the "Great Appendix" of the *Book of Changes* we find the view that what follows from nature is what derives from Heaven and the following is no more than the participation of Heaven under the form of spontaneity. The necessity and regularity of the interaction of the way of the masculine and the way of the feminine bring out the nature of everything, including the human person. This is one aspect of the internality of Heaven as part of human nature.

A more remarkable part of human nature consists in the fact that human nature as given by Heaven can be cultivated into a comprehensive state of perfection and thus fulfills the spiritual potentiality of Heaven itself as the ultimate and the total reality. This is indicated by the view that an authentic and sincere human person can fulfill both his nature and that of all things to the utmost and participate in the co-creative activities of Heaven and earth and thus form a trinity with Heaven and earth.[12] In the "Great Appendix" of the *Book of Changes* it is asserted that the power of the nature of the human person can accomplish the great works of the Way and can penetrate into the ultimate and supreme state of divine illumination (*shen-ming*) and subtle transformation (*pien-hua*). In the light of this, the internality of Heaven in human nature flows precisely from the potentiality and the motivating force for fulfilment of this potentiality in the nature of the human person. Not only has the human person all his potentiality from Heaven; he has the motor energy within him for the actualization of his potentiality. This is an important aspect of the consciousness of the ultimate and the total in the experience of Heaven in Confucianism. Such a consciousness carries with it a consciousness of the intrinsic affinity between the human person's nature and the reality of Heaven. It carries with it also a consciousness of the dynamic urge for realization, as well as the confidence in his ability to realize the reality of Heaven in *the human person*. This point contrasts strongly with the ultimate reliance on God for the redemption of the human person in the Christian tradition.

The innate goodness of the human person follows from the internality of Heaven in the human person. The whole reality of Heaven and its incessant activity of creative movement and transformation of what is potential into what is actual are intrinsically good and in the nature of things.[13]

There are two other fundamental characteristics of the classical Chinese consciousness of the ultimate and the total which need explicit statement. First, there is the idea of the self-consciousness of religious reality as a morally and intelligently realized being.[14] In the pre-Confucian sources and in the Confucian writings, Heaven, for example, is addressed as if it is a fully living person whose perception and judgment penetrate to the roots of good and bad for the human person. This is not surprising in light of the fact that Heaven has been identified as the ancestor of the human person. He begets as well as politically rules the human person.[15] But as we shall see, the identification of the ultimate and the total as a person has been changed in later writings to a considerable extent. To Mencius,[16] Heaven is no more than *nature* cultivatable toward goodness, or *natura naturans*, while in Han Tzu[17] it becomes no more than the *natura naturata*, or nature to be studied for the possible external good of the human person. This depersonalization of Heaven, as we may call it, in the third century B.C. is perhaps the result of the rational, naturalistic, as well as metaphysical criticism of *t'ien* as a living person by naturalistic thinkers associated with Taoism.[18] *T'ien* is subsumed under the Way (*tao*), the spontaneous and yet necessary activity of a comprehensive reality with its regularity. Thus, *t'ien* gradually loses its personalistic traits. But granted this change toward depersonalization, the consciousness of *t'ien* as a vast presence still carries with it a dimension of self-consciousness in the intelligence of *t'ien* as a result of internal reflection.

It might be said that in the full activation of the consciousness of Heaven as the ultimate and the total source of life and value, the human person's self-consciousness should be naturally a matter of necessity. This element of self-consciousness is clearly indicated in the *Chung Yung*, as testified to by the injunction that the superior the human person should be cautious about his solitude in the light of the fact that what is hidden is most obvious, what is obscure is most manifest. But this perceptive and illuminating ability and consciousness of the ultimate and the total is more evidently exhibited as the internal self-consciousness of goodness and authenticity of the nature of the human person. Such goodness and authenticity are also those of the primary creative being of Heaven. This is called "innate knowing (of the good)" (*liang-chih*) in Mencius, "the ultimately sincere feeling" (*chih-ch'eng*) in the *Chung Yung*, and the "virtue of feeling penetration" (*kan-t'ung*) in the *Book of Changes*.[19] It seems to be identified with the love (benevolence, *jên*) implicit in the *Analects* of Confucius.

The internal perception of the ultimate and the total in the human person's consciousness of the human person, though it can be regarded as a factor which must lead to a personalistic conception of the religious reality, need not be so regarded. The significant fact, as has been indicated, is that in the latter development of classical Confucianism, religious reality, as the object of religious consciousness, is more non-personalistic than personalistic. This could be regarded as a natural result of the heightened consciousness of the internality of Heaven as part of nature. But is this incompatible with the attribution of perceptiveness to the religious reality? Clearly there need not be such incompatibility, for in the ultimate and the total the ideal development of the human person's nature is fulfilled and there is no reason why the ultimate and the total cannot be regarded as a fully perceptive human-like entity. But before such consummation, the consciousness of good is a property of the human person in the process of fulfilment and is a property of the effort toward such fulfillment. In other words, the Confucian development of *t'ien* indicates that we should regard the ultimate and the total as the interaction between the process of the human person's effort toward achieving the impersonal potential ideal represented by the notion of the ultimate and the total and the process of realizing this in the cultivation of the human person and his consciousness. The divine or supreme illumination (*shen-ming*) is a matter to be achieved. It is inherent in nature, but it is to be fulfilled by every individual the human person in his effort for self-realization.

The ultimate and the total in this perception can be said to be neither absolutely personalistic nor absolutely impersonalistic, because it can be both. The internality of Heaven in nature makes this possible. That it cannot be confined to the personalistic view is because Heaven is the potential for the human person's development. That Heaven can be addressed as a person is because the individual has reached an ideal of identification of himself with the ultimate and the total. This is an immanent point of view of Heaven as a person, not a transcendent point of view of God as a person. In the latter, God is another person ontologically distinct from my being and existence, but in the former case, Heaven is not another person, but an ideal extension of my being and existence or an internal creative source of my energy and my perception of the internal good.

In the above, we have presented a description and characterization of the consciousness of the ultimate and the total in classical Confucian philosophy. Such a consciousness, we may summarize, involves a total of six characteristics: consciousness of a creative power, consciousness of consanguinity with the human person, consciousness of this-worldliness, consciousness of internality, consciousness of innate goodness, and identification of the personal with the non-personal. We may now make a similar inquiry into Neo-Confucianism in order to determine whether these characteristics of the consciousness of the ultimate and the total can be said to be continued in the Neo-Confucian tradition.

The Consciousness of Religious Reality in Neo-Confucianism

It is apparent in both the early Neo-Confucianists such as Chou Tun-yi, Chang Tsai, and the Ch'eng Brothers and the later Neo-Confucianists such as Chu Hsi, Lu Hsiang-shan, and Wang Yang-ming, that the consciousness of the reality of the ultimate and the total has been explicitly maintained and certainly even more highly developed and cultivated. Significantly, Chu Hsi has chosen a general term to refer to the ultimate and the total as the Substance of the Way (*tao-t'i*).[20] This represents a generalized consciousness of the ultimate and the total which explains dialectically how all things come into being. Even though the Taoist notion of the ultimate (*wu-chi*) is involved in this notion, the purpose of this involvement, as correctly observed by Chu Hsi, is to bring out the immensity and unlimitedness of the ultimate and the total.[21] In Chang Tsai, we find a similar metaphysics of the ultimate and the total in *ch'i* (the vital force); the human person as a creation of the way is in the middle of the way and can be an agent for creation as he partakes of the creative energy and potential of the way.[22]

In the light of these Neo-Confucian perspectives, we can now see that the ultimate and the total reality which is of fundamental significance to the human person has been given an explicit rational structure in a more or less systematic form of metaphysical reasoning. This, however, is not derived from a mere postulation of reason, but is, as clearly shown by the lives of the Neo-Confucian masters, a result of the deep and serious experience of the individual. One may even suggest that it is through the profound experience of these masters that a rational reflection on such experience becomes possible. This emphasis on experience and the cultivation of the ultimate and the total in Neo-Confucianism clearly provides a background for the grasp and understanding of the ultimate and the total. As we shall see, the reality of the ultimate and the total and the understanding of the reality of the ultimate and the total mutually penetrate each other and constitute two sides of the dynamic process of realizing the reality of the ultimate and the total in the human person in both Confucianism and Neo-Confucianism. What we wish to stress is that this is explicitly developed and preserved in the Neo-Confucian view; the metaphysics of *tao-t'i* and the theory of cultivation are not separate and are not separable.

Because of the development of systematic metaphysics in Neo-Confucianism, there is clearly little personalism in the Neo-Confucian consciousness of the ultimate and the total. The internal nature of the human person has also been given an extensive metaphysical structure in the evolution of the concept of *li* (principle of being).[23] The introduction of *li* is clearly premised on the reflection that anything in the nature of things can be fitted into a rationally explicit system of understanding; nature is to be understood rather than merely experienced, or, in other words, what is to be experienced must be understood as a matter of the intelligent and perceptive mind.

Though there could be many divergent metaphysical interpretations of *li*, as often found among Neo-Confucianists, it is clear that all Neo-Confucianists could agree that the understanding of *li* would satisfy our desire to understand both the world and ourselves. It is therefore a function of reason and knowledge invested with ontological significance. *Li* is further identified, in some cases, with the objectively conceived ultimate itself (e.g. as in Chu Hsi).[24] A whole spectrum of identification between the metaphysical reality of the ultimate and the total and the intuitively experienced or intellectually manifested reason or mind is possible in the framework of Neo-Confucianism in general. What concerns us here is the fact that *li* serves as a link between the rational consciousness of the ultimate and the total and the ultimate and the total of such consciousness. *Li* embraces and explicitly unifies both the world of things and the world of mind (self).[26] Without going into a detailed critique of *li*, what is clear is that *li* pertains to a new aspect of the ultimate and the total. This new aspect is that of rationality.[26] In the light of the evolution of the consciousness of this characteristic of the ultimate and the total, we could add other characteristics and elements in the existential and concrete fulfilment of *li*; for one may speak of unity, creativity, and a personalistic identification of *li*. On the other hand, of course, we may speak of the Neo-Confucian philosophy of *li* as a rational display of the existential fulfilment of the ultimate and the total as revealed in the classical Confucian experience and consciousness of such.

There are two more points to be made with regard to the Neo-Confucian contribution toward the Confucian consciousness of the ultimate and the total. First, as we have observed above, the development of the notion of *li* (we may call it "the theory of objectivity") in Neo-Confucianism involves at the same time a development of the theory of subjectivity (namely, a theory of mind or *hsin*). Though mind had been frequently discussed in the classical philosophies, the subtle potentiality of mind for embodying the objective *li* and fulfilling the Way had not been seriously entertained until the Neo-Confucianists. Beginning with Chang Tsai, the doctrine of "*hsin-t'ung hsing-chin*" (unity of nature and feeling in mind) played an important role in understanding in both the Ch'eng Brothers' and Chu Hsi's philosophy of the ultimate and the total reality and their philosophy of the understanding of the same.[27] Even though there are vast differences between these two approaches, for our purpose here we merely wish to concentrate on their agreement. Mind is both an activity and a state of the highest manifestation. It is the source of self-activation and virtue. It is also, therefore, creative as the source of all things. It is indeed the source of goodness and manifest goodness, so that a conscientious effort can be made to develop goodness to the utmost. In short, this notion of mind indicates a full grasp of the internality of the ultimate and the total, and makes the attainment of the ultimate and the total a matter of the intimate and direct achievement of oneself.

The second point about Neo-Confucian novelty in regard to consciousness of the ultimate and the total is the explicit and full realization of the ontological import of morality and the moral import of ontological understanding. In Ch'eng Hao and Chu Hsi, for example, the Confucian virtues of *jên* (benevolence), *yi* (righteousness), *li* (propriety), and *ch'ih* (wisdom) are explicitly identified with *li* and thus are provided with a rational-metaphysical basis.[29] *Jên*, in particular, is conceived as a source of cosmic creation and therefore as a virtue of heaven and earth, the concrete representation of the ultimate and the total.[30] From this it is clear that the morality of *jên*, *yi*, *li* and *chih* can be said, on the one hand, to be a manifestation of the ultimate and the total as initially rooted in the human person and, on the other, to be an actual application of the ontological understanding of *li*, such as the mind of the human person is primordially capable of having. We find similar basic views in other Neo-Confucianists beside Chu Hsi. It is in this respect that we see that Neo-Confucianism constitutes a condition for interpreting the Confucian experience and consciousness of the ultimate and the total as a moral (existential) fulfillment of the rational and the metaphysical, and that it provides a natural basis for interpreting *li* as a rational understanding of the existential and moral experience of the ultimate and the total. This fits perfectly with what we have explained above with respect to the fourth type of religious thought in contrast to the other three types.

Religious Understanding in Confucianism

In pre-Confucian sources, such as the *Book of Documents* and the *Book of Poetry*, to know and to understand the Will of Heaven (*t'ien-ming*) as the guide of human decision and conduct is to cultivate a sense of awe toward Heaven and a practice of following what is identified with the Will of Heaven. The Will of Heaven is not arbitrarily determined, but is rather determined as a form of supreme good for the large mass of people in the world. This means that to understand the heavenly reality is to comprehend the rise and fall of dynastic kings and the intrinsic reasons for their rise and fall in terms of commitment to values. This understanding, therefore, necessarily involves, on the one hand, a knowledge of what is good and, on the other, how good can be practiced and preserved, both knowledges involving actual exemplifications in the community and in history. It is an understanding not achieved by an individual at an individual time, as this cannot be so easily achieved, but an understanding continually accumulated, confirmed, and refined from generation to generation. It is an understanding which will be continuously improved time and again in light of new experience. It is an understanding in the making. It is an understanding which will be deeply ingrained in the minds of the individuals of the community and genuinely reflect the religious reality as perceived and defined by the community. It is furthermore an understanding which inevitably leads to a creative practice of life and contributes to the ultimate formation of the consciousness of the religious reality.

The Confucian view on understanding the ultimate and the total clearly follows the pattern elucidated above. It is a path to be slowly cultivated and relies upon each human person for rectification and enlargement. The *Doctrine of the Mean* thus says that "To cultivate the way is the teaching." There cannot be genuine understanding of Heaven and its will without a program of cultivation. This cultivation in the light of the above must apparently involve two basic lines: (1) to perceive and carefully evaluate the historical evolution of the community in which the Will of Heaven has been implicitly written, and (2) to go through or experience the dynamic process of developing one's nature and fulfilling one's potentiality as much as one can in accordance with the norm of the good for all. Both these aspects of cultivation are exemplified in the case of Confucius. Confucius speaks of learning from practice and history. He says that he was not born with knowledge, but liked to study antiquity and was quick to seek what is true.[31] He even asserts that he does not originate ideas but only relates them from the past. This means that he discovered what is valuable from understanding the historical experience of the human person.[32] On the other hand, Confucius is not limited to the study of historical lessons; he is concerned with establishing and fulfilling the objective values of righteousness and truth. He says, "If one concentrates on the righteousness of people and keeps oneself at a distance from the ghosts and spirits, one can be said to have knowledge."[33] He also points out that a superior human person worries over and seeks the fulfillment of the Way, not the gratification of food and the avoidance of poverty.[34] The Way is the order and harmony among men. It is also clear that this devotion and commitment to the way does not make one spend time on the conventional practice of worshipping local ghosts and spirits. It is in fact, a transcending beyond this practice and is directed toward a rational understanding of what the human person desires and is capable of achieving.

Finally, in Confucius there is an understanding of the religious reality as a result of a long process of self-cultivation and internal self-discipline. Thus, Confucius enumerates the steps of the process of his disciplining of his character and shaping his spirit. He speaks of "knowing the Will of Heaven (*t'ien-ming*) at fifty," as following from "achieving a feeling of no temptation at forty," "establishing himself at thirty," and "devoting himself to study at fifteen."[35] Apparently the starting point for achieving an understanding of the ultimate and the total and establishing its significance for practical life is to study the actual experience accumulated by the human person. Even though this is not sufficient, it has to be considered a basis for the realization of virtues (righteousness and benevolence, for example) in one's life. This latter is represented by establishing oneself at thirty, and seeing no temptation at forty. Thus, when at fifty the understanding of the Will of Heaven is achieved, this understanding is thoroughly an ingraining and revelation of the ultimate purpose of life—the achievement of spiritual growth toward freedom and solidarity. The Will of Heaven must be regarded as the consolidated meaningfulness of the whole and the ultimate for one's life and the consolidated meaningfulness of the individual for the whole and the ultimate. It is a source of courage, benevolence, and wisdom—all the virtues which present life in a form of harmonization.

From the above Confucian point of view, to know the Will of Heaven is to provide moral life with a metaphysical holistic basis and thus to strengthen its cultivation and development in order to make it a source of constant creativity. Consequently, to know *t'ien-ming* in this sense is not a mere end in itself; it is also directed toward the achievement of total freedom in practical life. Thus Confucius speaks of achieving comprehensive understanding at sixty and attaining a state of doing what one's heart pleases without straying from the right path. The goal of religious understanding can be described as the life of moral practice accompanied by moral consciousness. It is a life in which the knowledge and practice of one's life support each other and together form a source of ultimate freedom—an expression of self without restraint, and yet in strict conformity to duty and goodness.[36] Taken more intrinsically, this achievement of freedom and understanding is an achievement of creating duty and order. It is therefore identified with the creative performance and capacity of the ultimate Way.

Though Confucius has not explicitly stated that the basis for attaining an understanding of the ultimate and the total is in one's nature, his actual attainment of such understanding and the nature of his understanding the same leave no doubt that there is an original unity of the nature of the human person and the nature of Heaven, and that in cultivating oneself by learning and practice one will naturally come to appreciate the reality of the ultimate and the total and derive the significance of one's life from such an appreciation. In *Mencius*, it is explicitly pointed out that by nature the human person is in a state of existence tending toward realizing what is genuine and proper to the human person, i.e., what is identified as good and fulfilled as virtues. This state of existence is called in general "feeling-mind" (*hsin*), or "mind-feelings."[37] From these feelings, virtues express themselves and grow. It is on this basis that human nature is called good. Not only is the human person conceived as having this mind of feelings which directly exemplify virtue, but he is also conceived as endowed specifically with a nature of moral knowing (called *liang-chih*), by which the human person naturally sees and clings to a principle of action in accordance with the good. Because of this, the human person is spontaneously in a state of mental awareness of discrimination between right and wrong (*shih-fei-chih-hsin*), which is the root of knowledge or wisdom (*chih*).[38] It is clear that Mencius considers the moral knowing of intrinsic values to be rooted in a state of natural feeling and therefore a state of the existence of the human person. In other words, moral awareness is moral existence and moral existence is moral awareness. Since the nature of the human person is basically homogeneous with that of the ultimate and the total, the moral knowledge and moral awareness of a the human person must be cultivated and preserved as the basis for fulfilling the complete understanding of the ultimate and the total—a state indicated by Mencius as one wherein all things are complete within oneself.[39] This state of awareness is also a totality of feelings, which is indicated by Mencius' notion of the *hao-jan-chih-ch'i* (the great flood of vital nature).[40] This extended sense of substantive living in reference to both Heaven and earth (the ultimate and the total) is both the source of and the insight into the righteousness of one's actions.

It is in the *Chung Yung* that the nature of religious understanding attains a new height of development. The key concept involved is sincerity (*ch'eng*). *Ch'eng* is not a simple quality of the human person which enables one to participate in the creative activities of the ultimate and the total as identified with Heaven and earth. It is a quality which reveals to the human person the ultimate Way and its power from the very nature of the human person. In this regard, *ch'eng* is the reality-demonstrating quality of the reality of the ultimate and the total. It therefore truly belongs to the reality of the ultimate and the total as well as to the human person who comprehends reality. It is hence the original nature of the human person which forms a unity with the reality of the ultimate and the total. It is, furthermore, the potent power in the human person to initially sense reality, and subsequently under due conditions to illuminate the real and to enrich it by enriching himself through the practice of "fulfilling natures" (*chin-hsing*).

This is the reason why the activity and power to fulfill the real is called the "way of the human person" in *Chung Yung*. This implies, of course, the infinite creativity of the nature of the real. Perhaps we may summarize our description of the power of *ch'eng* as a way of understanding the ultimate and the total as mainly consisting of abilities to realize the ultimate unity between the objective (world) and the subjective (mind) and to realize the creative potential of an individual in concordance with the ultimate and the total, and thus the ability to bring to full achievement the value of an individual. Because of this realization, there is no need to state a Cartesian doubt nor is there any occasion for the rise of skepticism and solipsism. The lack of both is amply testified to by the large corpus of writings in the Confucian tradition.[41]

What needs to be finally remarked on is that in the light of *Chung Yung*, the sense of the genuineness and authenticity of reality and the power of realizing the nature of things have two aspects, as indicated by the proposition that *ch'eng* will lead to understanding (*ming*) and *ming* will lead to *ch'eng*. *Ming* is a mental illumination of reality which will lead to a more powerful grasp of reality in *ch'eng*, whereas *ch'eng* is a state of being which has an inner glow and light for seeking the way of the ultimate and the total. I shall discuss this dynamic identifying relation a little later.

In this connection, we must mention another important contribution of the cultivation of the understanding of the ultimate and the total in the work of the *Great Learning*. The *Great Learning* holds that, "The way of great learning consists in illuminating the illustrious virtue in the world (*ming-ming-te*) and in renovating (and loving) the people and finally in reaching and resting in the supreme goodness."[42] The *Great Learning*, in explaining "the illumination of illustrious virtue in the world," introduces the well-known eight steps of cultivation, beginning with the requirement of investigating things in the world (*ke-wu*) and extending knowledge of things (*chih-chih*), and ending with governing well a state and pacifying the world at large. Without going into detail about these steps, it is clear that the *Great Learning* establishes a chain of necessary steps which involves perception and practice, thinking and observation about things in the world, and exercising oneself and others in social living in the community.

This means that the ultimate goal of "illustrating the illustrious virtue in the world" presupposes a course of active participation in worldly affairs for its ordering and harmonization. If we may identify *ming-te* with the reality-demonstrating quality, and thus the *ch'eng* of the ultimate and the total, and *ming-ming-te* with realizing the reality-demonstrating quality, then the *Great Learning* makes it quite clear that one cannot know the reality of the ultimate and the total without participating in worldly affairs. To fully project oneself in an ethical and political life is a prerequisite for coming to see the ultimate and the total. This conforms very well with the *Chung Yung* view of working toward *ming* (understanding) from *ch'eng* (participation). On the other hand, to start with investigating things as the initial step toward *ch'eng* agrees perfectly with the *Chung Yung*'s prescription of working toward *ch'eng* from *ming*.

In the *Great Learning*, there is no explication of the next two steps after the stage of *ming-ming-te*; that is, the stage of loving and renovating people (*ch'in-min*) and the stage of seeking and resting in the supreme good (*chih-yü-chih-shan*) have not been assigned a place in the philosophy of cultivating the understanding of the ultimate and the total. In the light of our discussion here, we may conceive *ch'in-min* simply as a matter of fulfilling the natures of people and things and *chih-yü-chih-shan* as a matter of attaining and preserving the power of the ultimate *ch'eng* (*chih-ch'eng*), i.e. the power of transformation and creation, and therefore the power of participating in the works and activities of the ultimate and the total. The methodology of the *Great Learning* thus provides a basis for linking knowledge and practice in ethical and political life to the ultimate understanding and realization of the ultimate and the total. This last state is called *divine* intelligence (*shen-ming*) in the *Book of Changes*.[43] A human person can achieve this state because he can communicate (*kan-t'ung*) with the ultimate and the total.[44] This *kan-t'ung* is evidently a function of the *ch'eng* and *ming* of the nature of the human person in accordance with the true nature of the ultimate and the total.

Religious Understanding in Neo-Confucianism

In Neo-Confucianism, the clear understanding the ultimate and the total is explicitly taken to be the main concern of the human person. In the tradition of Chou Tun-yi, Chang Tsai, Chu Hsi, and others, it is clear that a comprehension of the *tao-t'i* (the Substance of the Way, thus the ultimate and the total) is the basis for applying oneself to the practical affairs of the human person. Therefore there is an even more systematic emphasis on cultivating the understanding of the ultimate and the total. In the metaphysical writings of Chou Tun-yi and Chang Tsai, to preserve and experience the quality of *ch'eng* in the human person is the most important step toward achieving an understanding of the ultimate and the total, be it called the great ultimate (*t'ai-chi*) or the great harmony (*t'ai-ho*).[45] In fact, Chou Tun-yi explicitly takes *ch'eng* to be the basis for becoming a sage, for according to him, all the creative and ordering activities of the great ultimate reality are functions of *ch'eng*.[46] *Ch'eng* can be identified with the *t'ai-chi* itself and therefore the ultimate source of action and change. This quality is again

asserted to be experienced by the human person as the human person originates from this quality of the great ultimate and is capable of pursuing the
ultimate reality by way of distinguishing virtues from non-virtues.

In Chang Tsai, the perceptive aspect of *ch'eng* is brought to the fore.
Ch'eng and *ming* are related together and are called the innate knowledge
of heavenly virtue (*ch'eng-ming-so-chih nai t'ien-te-so-chih*).[47] It is a direct
manifestation of reality and therefore constitutes the original nature of
the human person. Perhaps it is on this basis that Chang Tsai draws the
conclusion that human persons should love other human persons and participate in the course of events of the world. For what is in one's nature
according to the "revelation" of *ch'eng* is open and universalizable and
should be realized in realizing the openness and universality of nature experienced as *ch'eng*. This leads to a view of experience of *jên* (love) as a
significant factor in the ultimate understanding of reality. Experience of *jên*
is an experience of the affinity and organic unity among all things. To understand the ultimate and the total is to understand the *jên* activity of it; this
means to understand an open, creative and genuine reality. That one can
feel *jên* in terms of the activity of heaven and earth and can see the activity
of heaven and earth in terms of an attitude and state of feeling is the only
way to understand the ultimate and the total. In this sense, experience of
jên as derived from a sense of genuine reality germane to one's nature is
precisely a way of understanding the reality of the ultimate and the total.
Thus, both Chang Tsai and Chu Hsi come to assert the metaphysical significance of Confucian virtues such as *jên* and righteousness.[48] *Jên* is considered a comprehensive creative activity and even creativity itself, and
righteousness the rational ordering of things in the world. Thus the question as to how to cultivate an understanding of the ultimate and the total is
to be answered by seeing moral virtues as representing the metaphysical
activities of the ultimate and the total. To succeed in this is to be aware of
the metaphysical foundation and ontological significance of moral life.

The Ch'eng Brothers specifically suggest some relevant philosophical
points in regard to how to attain such a metaphysical understanding of
morality. In the first place, Ch'eng Hao admonishes one to "see the phenomena of the creation of life in and by Heaven and earth."[49] This seeing is not
merely a matter of observation, but a matter of deep experience. In fact,
the "phenomena of the creation of life" (*sheng-wu-ch'i-hsiang*) cannot be
simply observed, but must be felt and experienced. This primary ability in
the human person to make such a "seeing" possible bespeaks the innateness
of the heavenly nature within the human person. Thus it is not surprising
that the creative power of the ultimate and the total as found in Heaven
and earth can be regarded as leading to a confirmation of *jên* (feelings of

love and sympathy) as inherent in the human person. The very "seeing" (*kuan*) itself represents a natural and close interaction between the human person and Heaven and earth; the purpose of religious understanding is to enlarge and strengthen as well as to develop this initial tie between the human person and the ultimate and the total. One cannot get religious sentiment from understanding devoid of religious significance. Understanding is a form of cultivating the already given power of the comprehension of the ultimate and the total in the form of "seeing" the phenomena of creative life in the cosmos. One can be reminded of Confucius' testimony to this experience of "seeing" creative life in his own statements. "It [the water] goes so fast like this," and "Four seasons rotate and what has Heaven said? Ten thousand things are generated and what has Heaven said?"[50]

Perhaps following the suggestions made by Chou Tun-yi and Chang Tsai concerning *ch'eng*, both Ch'eng Brothers came to advance a doctrine of self-cultivation which can be said to clearly bear upon what we call religious understanding of the ultimate and the total. This is the doctrine of "residing in a state of serious-concentration (*chü-ching*) and exhausting the principles of things (*ch'iung-li*)."[51] What are *chü-ching* and *ch'iung-li* and how are they related to the process of understanding the ultimate and the total? In the light of the above discussion, *ching* is clearly a state of mind which is directed toward the ultimate and the total as the goal and source of the individual life. It is therefore a mental awareness as well as an existential persistence which is not dominated by individual and selfish interests and desires. It is a feeling and mood from which virtues such as *jên* can be derived. In this sense, *ching* can be explained as the same thing as the creative life in its original undividedness and the beginning of full religious understanding. Indeed, it has been described and defined by the younger Ch'eng, Ch'eng I (Yi-chuan) as a state of concentratedness and undeviatedness or undominatedness (*chü-yi* and *wu-shih*).[52] It is therefore a state of existential singularity and the original unity of nature. It is a state of mind as it is rooted in an awareness of the original and primordial infinite creativeness of Heaven and earth; it is a state of nature as it is the original and primordial creativeness realized in the human person. To discover and preserve *ching* is to discover and preserve the primordial nature of Heaven and the awareness of this at the same time. It is called the achievement of preserving and maintaining one's virtue (*han-yang*).[53] It is a way to recognize and understand the ultimate and the total.

It must be pointed out that the Ch'eng Brothers do not take *chü-ching* as the exclusive method of understanding the Way. They also advocate the importance of applying oneself to the investigation of individual things (*ke-wu*).[54] This is regarded as equally important as *chü-ching*, for by investigating individual things and gaining knowledge a human person can make himself useful and thereby can engage himself in the practical affairs of life. *Ke-wu* is achieved specifically by penetrating fully the principles of things and this requires devotion to learning and studying. There is here no indication of the development of the notion of scientific inquiry. For whereas scientific inquiry is intended to lead to the objective truth of facts as such, which does not presuppose a unity between the human person and the total nature, the investigation of things by means of getting to the bottom of the principles of things is intended to enable us to know the particulars firstly with reference to the ultimate and the total, and secondly, with reference to practice and practical life. Thus the principles (*li*) of things are not scientific laws, nor merely patterns of things, but the significances of these with regard to the ultimate and the total as revealed and experienced by the human person of *ching*. Indeed it is through this attitude of undivided concentration that we can relate the individual to the ultimate and the total, as *ching* is a state where one experiences the ultimate and the total. It is also through *ching* that one is able to relate one's knowledge to practice and action and one can acquire knowledge applicable to practical life, for *ching* is also a state where action in accordance with the Way can flow out most naturally. Because of this, the investigation of things by means of penetrating to *li* will always lead to certain concrete principles of righteousness (*yi*) or principles of application to actual life, which preserve the consistency and balance of life. This cultivation, permitting the continuation and refinement of *ching* is therefore an understanding of the ultimate and the total.

As we may now see, for Neo-Confucianists like the Ch'eng Brothers and their systematic follower Chu Hsi, the understanding of the ultimate and the total takes two directions, which are related as if in a circle. There is the direction toward preserving the original mind and nature of creativity experienced by oneself, which is the basis for the correct investigation of things and the penetration to *li*. There is the other direction toward discovering and refining particular principles of practical living, which will provide a firmer basis for consistently enlarging and holding to the consciousness and intensified experience of the ultimate and the total in the cultivation of *ching*. Thus *ching*, like *ch'eng*, is both the starting point and the end for understanding the Way. This methodology of understanding the ultimate and the total as developed by the Ch'eng Brothers and Chu Hsi clearly indicates both a continuation and a systematization of the classical Confucian tradition. The twofold directionality of understanding is the high mark of the achievement of them. It enables one to see more clearly the true nature and the true function of religious understanding in Confucianism and Neo-Confucianism. This Confucian and Neo-Confucian understanding may be called an "organic and integrated understanding of life," which is clearly illustrated by the doctrines of *chü-ching* and *ch'iung-li* of the Ch'eng Brothers and Chu Hsi.

In Lu Chiu-yuan and Wang Yang-ming, this methodology of "organic and integrated understanding" is also implicitly developed. In regard to the human person's original and primordial ability to comprehend and realize the Way, I find little disagreement between Ch'eng-Chu's doctrine of the *chü-ching* and Lu's doctrine of seeking one's original mind (*pen-hsin*) and Wang's doctrine of fulfilling one's innate knowledge of goodness (*chih-liang-chih*).[55] For in close analysis, the existential as well as the practical dimensions of *chih-liang-chih* are exactly similar in intention, if not in extension, to those of *chü-ching*. We will not go into the details of these for lack of space. We may merely point out that while more strongly stressing than Ch'eng Yi and Chu Hsi the potentiality of *chih-liang-chih* for attaining a sage's wisdom of comprehending and embodying the Way (the ultimate and the total), Lu and Wang are lacking in providing a direction toward fulfilling individual cases of the practical significance of life that is to be derived only from the controlled and disciplined virtue of studying and learning as developed by Ch'eng-Chu.

Conclusion I: The Dynamic Unity of Religious Reality and Religious Understanding in Confucianism and Neo-Confucianism

In the above, we have developed the notions of religious reality and of religious understanding in Confucian and Neo-Confucian philosophy as a basis for speaking of Confucian and Neo-Confucian religious thought. We have seen that there is a proper context for developing the Confucian and Neo-Confucian notions of religious reality and the religious understanding of the ultimate and the total, together with the Confucian and Neo-Confucian doctrines of the cultivation of religious understanding. What is understood as being religious in Confucian and Neo-Confucian philosophy is therefore defined and characterized by the Confucian and Neo-Confucian conception of the ultimate and the total and the human person's relation to the ultimate and the total. We have seen that the human person by his nature and mind can naturally know and experience unity with the ultimate and the total and that this experienced unity gives rise to a significant and genuine desire and will in the human person to pursue a full understanding and full grasp of the ultimate and the total. In light of Confucius' practical application of this essential experience of the unity of the human person with the Way, and in light of the "organic and integrated understanding" of the ultimate reality in Neo-Confucian philosophy, it is also clear that this unity between the human person and the Way is to be fully displayed and realized as a natural process of fulfilling an individual life in the full engagement of the individual in ethical and political activities. Moral practice and moral reflection on the practice of the human person, as prerequisites for maintaining the integrity of the human person in contact with and in relation to other human persons, are a natural process resulting from the effort to cultivate the experience and understanding of the unity between the human person and the Way. But they are also an essential aspect of cultivating the experience and embodiment of the Way, as more or less explicitly recognized by Ch'eng-Chu.

It can also be understood that a full realization of the moral life in the genuine Confucian sense, with the commitment to practice *jên* and *yi* or even *li*, will result in a natural manifestation and revelation of the consciousness of the ultimate and the total. In other words, the religious, or the consciousness of the ultimate and the total, will be a natural extension and integration of the moral life, since moral life reveals a reality which is perceived, embraced, and activated as the source and goal of life itself, including as its aspects life's self-realization and self-manifestation. We may even say that the religious is the understanding of the ultimate and the total as an intrinsic source and ontological justification of moral life. In this fashion, moral life and moral sentiments are enriched by the affirmation and consciousness of the ultimate and the total: moral and ethical life becomes a constant motor force for carrying on the infinitely creative process of the realization of reality. On the other hand, the consciousness of the Way will constantly stimulate practical life and moral practice. One can indeed speak of moral autonomy as in Kant, but one need not postulate a set of religious postulates for morality to make morality meaningful; for morality is intrinsically meaningful and yet is at the same time a full realization of the religious as a consciousness, as well as a state of existence, of the ultimate and the total in the human person.

If we take practical life and moral practice as an ordered and well-balanced way of fulfilling all the potentiality of life, and if we take this again as an achievement of the concrete organic rationality of life, then it is clear that the religious is precisely a full manifestation or an explicit exhibition of the rational and the reasonable. The religious consciousness is not separate from the rational and the reasonable, but is continuous and integrated in full measure with the rational and the reasonable. Thus religion in the Confucian sense of the term is not reasoned out as a postulate, but is instead rationally presented in the concrete self-fulfilling process and achievement of moral life and moral living. Thus religion in this sense is not contrasted with the objectivity of reason and nature, as in the case of Western religion, but is a unity of the subjective and the objective, as it is a *consummation* of the lived unity between the objective and the subjective. For the natural and the moral are seen as both the means and the end of religion in this sense.

We may further suggest that in the Confucian and Neo-Confucian context religious reality is in effect identifiable with religious understanding. In other words, religious understanding can be regarded as a manifestation of religious reality and religious reality can be regarded as a creation of religious understanding. In fact, the organic and integrated nature of religious understanding precisely reflects the nature and characteristics of religious reality. Religious reality as the ultimate and the total is only found in an understanding and cultivation of mind, which shows forth and is not merely aware of religious reality as a goal and source of creative life and moral living. To be aware of religious reality is to be aware religiously, for it is to let the inner core of one's nature show forth in its most genuine and authentic totality and fullness.

In order to make more clear and more systematic the relation of religious reality and religious understanding, we may distinguish the following aspects of what may be called the organic unity and dynamic identification of religious reality and religious understanding in Confucianism and Neo-Confucianism:

1) The organic and integrative understanding of the ultimate and the total clearly indicates a unity of religious reality with the religious understanding of religious reality, for it is on the basis of the creativity of religious reality that religious understanding becomes possible, whereas religious understanding once cultivated will add to the vividness and intensity of the realization of religious reality both objectively and within the consciousness and nature of the human person. This mutual relationship between the self-demonstrative creativity of religious reality and religious understanding in the human person is quite clearly indicated in the *Chung Yung* statement on the interpenetration (in the human person and in things) between *ch'eng* and *ming*, as discussed earlier.

2) There is dynamic or creative identification of religious reality and religious understanding in terms of the dynamic and creative identification of knowledge in terms of the dynamic and creative identification of knowledge and action or practice. It is clear that religious reality in Confucianism and Neo-Confucianism is itself nothing but the actual universal process of ceaseless creativity, and this is basically a form of action and practice. On the other hand, religious understanding begins and goes through individual instances of knowing, studying, learning, and inquiring as seen in the Neo-Confucian doctrine of the investigation of things. Thus the relation between religious reality and religious understanding can be regarded as one between knowledge and action in general.

Now it can be shown that knowledge and action are unifiable in many ways. Among these ways, one is to regard knowing as a form of action and as derivable only from action, whereas action in its subtlest form also carries a realization of self-awareness or knowledge of self. Seen in this light, both religious reality and religious understanding must intimately involve each other in the human person, as do the theory and action of any art. Yi-chuan once said, "If one knows it, one must love it; if one loves it, one must seek it; if one seeks it, one must get it."[56] Knowledge and religious understanding must lead to a grasp (existential experience) of religious reality, and conversely a grasp (existential experience) of religious reality must lead to a perceptive seeing and knowing of religious reality in one's mind. Practice and virtue must be reinforced and continued with knowledge of the same, which reinforces and makes their own continuity possible.

3) Finally, one may say that objectively and ontologically, both religious reality and religious understanding are aspects of the same thing or are different exemplifications of the same thing. Thus one may say that religious understanding is a form of religious reality in the human person, and religious reality, as the human person is aware of it, is religious understanding of the most complete and comprehensive kind. It is an accomplished self-understanding of the human person in his ultimate fulfilment of himself. Ch'eng I says, referring to the religious reality of the ultimate and the total, "in Heaven it is called necessity (*ming*), in righteousness it is called the principle (*li*), in the human person it is called nature (*hsing*); when controlling the body of a person, it is called mind (*hsin*); these are in fact one."[57] The unity of *ming*, *li*, and *hsing* which is asserted here does not prevent them from dynamically exhibiting themselves in a diversity of realizations; so, similarly, their dynamical diversity should not prevent their dynamically converging to and coming from the same unity and totality of source and goal. Thus, in an ontological sense, the religious understanding of the human person and religious reality as a self-demonstrating process are genuinely one. They are also dynamically one through the creative function and potentiality of each: they inevitably become one.

Conclusion II: A New Notion of the Numinous

Rudolph Otto, in his book, *The Idea of the Holy*, has presented an analysis of a distinctively religious quality in religion which he calls the quality of the *numinous*.[58] Apparently, the numinous is the object of a unique psychological aspect of religious experience. The interesting contribution of Otto is in his listing of a number of distinctive elements in the psychological experience of the numinous or the holy in religion. These elements are as follows: (1) an element of supreme dignity and magnanimity; (2) an element of holy tremor (or dread or awefulness); (3) an element of overpoweringness; (4) an element of plenitude of being; (5) an element of "energy" or urgency of a personal will; (6) an element of creature-consciousness; (7) an element of fascination.[59]

Now, assuming a correct background understanding of Otto's listing of elements in the analysis of the religious or the numinous, one can readily see that any religious experience and religious sentiment within the framework of Confucian and Neo-Confucian religious thought, as we have developed it, must be significantly different from those identified by Otto, (even though there would be similarity in many aspects between the numinous as understood from a Western Christian and from a Confucian-Neo-Confucian viewpoint). It can be clearly recognized that religious understanding as a mental attitude and feeling in Confucian-Neo-Confucian philosophy readily admits of an element of supreme dignity (or magnanimity) and an element of plenitude of being (or power). The supreme dignity of Heaven and the Way is often referred to as divine illumination (*shen-ming*), or simply divine (*shen*), in the classical Confucian writings. The feeling of the plenitude of being (or power) is clearly present in the Confucian remarks on the silence of Heaven and the universal creative power of Heaven in the Ch'eng Brothers. In a sense, even the element of overpoweringness and the element of the urgency of a personal will are conspicuously present in the Confucian consciousness of the religious whole. The reference to the completion of one's nature and the overflooding of *ch'i* (vital force) in Mencius is indeed a case of such overpoweringness, if we construe this sense of overpoweringness as an enlargement of the individual self, but not as derived from a force from the outside. The urgency or energy of a personal God would apply if no reference to personal goal were mentioned. This urgency, however, is not important as a stabilizing force of the mind's grasp of the great ultimate, but the moral discipline for achieving profundity will certainly bring forth a feeling of energy and urgency in the Confucian and Neo-Confucian devotion to the cultivation of the Way.

Apart from these, the other elements as listed above seem to be conspicuously missing and essentially unnecessary. For example, there cannot be found any holy tremor or dread in Confucianism and Neo-Confucianism; instead of awe, there is calm and clarity. There is, furthermore, no element of creature-consciousness, nor any element of the wholly Other. The Confucianist and the Neo-Confucianist never feel an ontological separation and alienation between the ultimate and the total as a creator, on the one hand, and the human person as a mere creature, on the other. The human person is not felt to be a trivializable entity, but is instead understood and treated as a creator or co-creator who can partake of the works which exemplify the genuine character of the creativity of the ultimate reality. Thus, instead of having creature-consciousness, the human person has creator-consciousness. Instead of the consciousness of the wholly Other, there is the consciousness of the wholly homogeneous, for the ultimate way is never separated from the human person in whom the way exhibits itself and through whom the way can be fulfilled in concrete terms. Because of the lack of these two elements, there is no apparent need for the element of the love of God or for the element of fascination, which taken by itself is the mystical element. In Christianity the love for God is a love directed toward something transcendent and is demanded as the first duty of the human person. But in Confucianism, love applies primarily to Heaven's love for the human peson, not the human person's love for Heaven (or God), for love (*jên*) is seen as an essential property of Heaven which makes life and living, creation and improving, possible. For the Confucianists and the Neo-Confucianists, the element of fascination is not a proper reaction to religious reality for the human person, though the human person can by this element of fascination hold to the pursuit of good. A rational calm, which must be cultivated for a useful and intelligent life and understanding of the Way, is both a Confucian and Neo-Confucian rule of life. Perhaps this is so because there is no personal God and thus there are no personal feelings toward a personal God.

To supplement and complement what is missing in describing the numinous in Confucianism and Neo-Confucianism, we may suggest a new notion of the numinous, which in theory excludes those missing elements, but which introduces new elements which are not seen by Otto in his own notion. These new elements which would define a new notion of the numinous on Confucian and Neo-Confucian grounds are the following: (1) the element of the potential completeness in the human person's nature, (2) the element of the organic unity of all distinct life processes, (3) the element of the universal presence of principles and virtues in things, (4) the element of infinite creative love in Heaven and earth, which can be referred to as the element of the universal *jên*. An explanation of these can be easily provided in light of our discussion above. Without further development, we simply present this new notion of the numinous which will incorporate what has been listed above to supplement and complement what is lost from Otto's angle.

We may say, then, that here we have developed a new notion of the numinous in the light of our critique of Otto's concept. We may call it the Confucian and Neo-Confucian notion of the numinous, and we suggest that it is precisely this notion that constitutes the religious significance of Confucianism and Neo-Confucianism.

Notes

1. Paul Tillich has considered religion to be the search for Ultimate Reality and therefore as the human person's concern with the ultimate. See his *Biblical Religion and the Search for Ultimate Reality* (Chicago, 1955). Here I introduce the notion of the total as part of what religion is concerned with because the ultimate and fundamental concern of the human person must be directed toward a totality which goes beyond the individual, the incomplete, the imperfect, as well as the conditioned.

2. Even though there are basic differences between the theology of Augustine and that of Aquinas, both would take faith in God as a gift from God and thus fundamentally different from the natural reason of the human person. Aquinas' Aristotelianism does not prevent him from attaching unique importance to faith in distinction from reason.

3. That God is a totally other person who transcends this world is strongly stressed by orthodox theologians of Christianity as well as by more recent Christian theologians of different kinds.

4. See Kant's book *Religion Within the Limits of Reason Alone*, trans. Theodore M. Greene and Hoyt M. Hudson (New York, 1960).

5. See my article "Dialectic of Confucian Morality and the Metaphysics of Man," *Philosophy East & West* (April, 1971).

6. Many early Christian missionaries, such as James Legge, attempted to identify the Confucian *t'ien* (Heaven) with the Christian God, but that cannot be done, as can be seen from our analysis of the notion of *t'ien* in this article.

7. Though some strain of transcendental mysticism might be identified in the later Neo-Confucianism of the 17th century, the overall and main tradition of Confucianism and Neo-Confucianism is characterized by as conscientious effort to eliminate mystical elements in the theory and cultivation of Confucian *jên* (benevolence) and *yi* (righteousness), and Neo-Confucian *li* (principles of being), *hsing* (nature), and *hsin* (mind).

8. By the term "dialectical development" I mean a development based on the synthesis and unification of divergent, heterogeneous and perhaps conflicting factors in the course of the development. The study of the development of

477

Confucianism and Neo-Confucianism from this point of view has been initiated in my previously cited article (note 5).

9. The political concern of Heaven with the human person's earthly well-being is evidenced by the underlying conception of *Heaven* or Lord on High in the *Book of Documents*.

10. Any fundamental perspective on the human person's relation to the world and the ultimate and the total carries with it many metaphysical and psychological presuppositions. It is not to be understood alone and independently of these presuppositions. A detailed study of such interrelated presuppositions for any fundamental perspective on the human person's relation to the world and the ultimate and the total is as essential as understanding the fundamental perspective itself.

11. The assumption of soul becomes superficial and unneeded in Confucianism because the self of a human person can be transformed, developed, and cultivated into a state of being co-extensive with Heaven.

12. See the *Doctrine of the Mean* (*Chung Yung*).

13. Mencius said, "What is desirable is good." See *Mencius*, 7B-25. In the *Great Appendix* of the *Book of Changes* it is said, "The interchange of *Yin* and *Yang* is called the Way. What succeeds this is good and what accomplishes this is nature."

14. This is clear from the addressing of Heaven or the Lord on High (*ti*) as a person in the *Book of Documents* and the *Book of Poetry*.

15. See *Book of Documents* and the *Book of Poetry*.

16. Mencius said, "To fulfill one's mind to the utmost is to know the nature (of a man); to know the nature (of a man) is to know Heaven. To preserve one's mind and cultivate one's nature is the way to serve Heaven." See *Mencius* 7B-1.

17. See Hsun Tzu's essay on Heaven, *T'ien Lun*.

18. This view has been suggested by Kuo mo-jo. See his paper, "The Development of the Concept of *T'ien-tao* in the Pre-Chin Period," *Ch'ing Tung Shih Tai*, Science Publishing Co., 1962.

19. Mencius said, "What a man can do without learning is the innate capacity; what a man knows without deliberation is innate knowing (of the good)" (*Mencius*, 7A-15). The *Chung Yung* said, "Only those who are ultimately sincere in the world can fulfill their nature to the utmost." The "Great Appendix" of the *Book of Changes* said, "[The wisdom of] *Book of Changes* is not bound by thoughts and actions. It is quiet and motionless. By virtue of direct feeling (*kan*) all the principles of the world will be comprehended (*t'ung*)."

20. Chu Hsi applies the term "*tao-ti*" to the first chapter of his *Chin Ssu Lu* "Reflections on Things at Hand," which deals with the fundamental principles of the ultimate and the total in the writings of Chou Tun-yi, Chang Tsai, the Ch'eng Brothers: Ch'eng Hao (Ming-tao) and Ch'eng I (Yi-chuan).

21. Cf. Chu Hsi's letter in answer to Lu Tzu-chin (Lu Hsiang-shan) in *Complete Works of Chou Tzu*, Book 1, on *Discourse on the Diagram of the Great Ultimate*.

22. Cf. Chang Tsai, *On Rectifying Youthful Ignorance*, Chapter 1.
23. *Li* in the Neo-Confucian philosophy receives its close formulation and elaboration in the Ch'eng Brothers and Chu Hsi. It is both principles of being and intimate knowledge of such. It is, in fact, a rich concept embodying a continuum of concepts referring to reality as well as to the significance of reality, in Heaven as well as in a human person. There are many types of theorizing on *li* in Neo-Confucianism as variously exemplified in the writings of Chang Tsai, the Ch'eng Brothers, Chu Hsi, Lu Hsiang-shan, Wang Yang-ming, and others.
24. Chu Hsi says, "The *t'ai-chi* [the great ultimate] is not something else; it is *yin-yang* and is in *yin-yang*; it is five powers and is in five powers; it is ten thousand things and is in ten thousand things. All these are merely one *li*." He also says "nature is *li*." See *Chu Tzu Yü Lei*. (Records of Sayings of Chu Hsi.)
25. Wang Yang-ming takes the task of investigating things and exhausting the principles of things as essentially a matter of fulfilling one's innate knowledge of goodness. He says, "The innate knowledge of goodness in my mind is the so-called heavenly principles of existence (*t'ien-li*)." On this basis he advocates unification of *li* with *hsin* (mind). See his *Ch'uan Hsi Lu* (Instructions for Practical Living), Book 2.
26. Perhaps we should describe this aspect of rationality as organic rationality, for it builds an organic relationship between the nature and mind of a human person and the principles of the existence of all things in the world, to the effect that there is an interpenetrating unity between the two sides in both metaphysical and epistemological senses.
27. See *Chin Ssu Lu*, Chapter I. Cf. also *Chu Tzu Yü lei*, 98-8a.
28. Mind is conceived in both Lu Hsiang-shan and Wang Yang-ming as the ultimate reality as well as the source of goodness.
29. Cf. Cheng Hao, *Ho-nan Ch'eng Ssu Yi Shu*, 2; Chu Hsi, *Chu Wen Kang Wen Chi*, 67.
30. Cf. Chu Hsi's essay on *jên* referred to in note 29.
31. The *Analects, shu-erh*.
32. Ibid., *shu-erh*.
33. Ibid., *yung-yeh*.
34. Ibid., *wei-ling-kung*.
35. Ibid., *wei-ch'eng*.
36. Cf. my paper, "Theory and Practice in Confucianism," in *Proceedings of Seminar in World Philosophy*, at Center for Advanced Study in Philosophy, University of Madras, India, December 7-17, 1970.
37. It is in this sense of mind-feeling or feeling in mind that Mencius speaks of the beginnings of the four cardinal virtues—*jên* (benevolence), *yi* (righteousness), *li* (propriety), and *chih* (wisdom). See *Mencius*, 2A-6. One may say that mind-feeling or feeling-mind is a feeling and perception in one which has the power of inclining or motivating one to act in a certain way.

38. The awareness of discrimination between right and wrong is the guide for the right path to the cultivation of one's nature, and thus the source of wisdom which characterizes the ideal state of the full realization of nature in a sage (*sheng*).

39. *Mencius*, 7A-4.

40. Ibid., 2A-2.

41. This is a very important trait of Confucian philosophy in particular and Chinese philosophy in general, which accounts for the lack of logical theories and theoretical sciences in Chinese history.

42. In this passage there is the controversy between Chu Hsi and Wang Yang-ming over whether the people are to be renovated or loved. Chu Hsi thinks that the people should be renovated and Wang Yang-ming thinks that the people should be loved. The question has never been asked how renovation of the people can be achieved and what end can be served by loving the people. My answer is that renovation of the people can be achieved by loving the people, whereas loving the people serves the end of renovating the people. Hence, the rapprochement between Chu Hsi and Wang Yang-ming. It is also the reason for incorporating the notion of renovating the people and the notion of loving the people in my translation here.

43. See the "Great Appendix" of the *Book of Changes*.

44. Ibid.

45. See Chou Tun-yi's *Discourse on the Diagram of the Great Ultimate* for the notion of *t'ai-chi* and see Chang Tsai's *Rectifying Youthful Ignorance* (Chapter 1) for the notion of *t'ai-ho*.

46. See Chou Tun-yi's *Commentary on the Book of Changes* (*T'ung shu*).

47. See Chang Tsai's *Rectifying Youthful Ignorance*, Chapter 6.

48. See Chang Tsai's *Western Inscription* and Chu Hsi's *Essay on Jên*.

49. See *Chin Ssu Lu*, Chapter 1. Here I take the key word of the passage to be *sheng* as a verb. If we take *sheng* as an adjective, then we get a less vivid sentence: "See the phenomena of living things in heaven and earth," which is not adopted here.

50. See the *Analects*.

51. See *Ho Nan Ch'eng Shih Yi Shu*, Chapters 2-18.

52. See *Chin Ssu Lu*, Chapter 2.

53. Ibid.

54. Ibid.

55. Cf. *Complete Works of Lu Hsiang-shan, Books 1, pp. 34-35; Wang Yang-ming's Ch'uan Hsi Lu*, Book 2.

56. See *Chin Ssu Lu*, Chapter 2.

57. See ibid., Chapter 1.

58. Translated by J. W. Harvey (New York, 1936).

59. Cf. ibid., Chapters 2-6.

19. The Consistency and Meaning of the Four-Sentence Teaching in *Ming Ju Hsüeh An*

Classical Background of Sung-Ming Neo-Confucianism

A common assumption for the philosophy of Ch'eng I and Chu Hsi is that man must genuinely understand or deeply experience the *li* (principle) or *t'ien-li* (heavenly principle) in things. This understanding or experience, no matter how we describe it, has both ontological and moral significance. It has ontological significance because it involves the complete self-realization of the nature of man which involves the simultaneous achievement of man's ultimate identity in relation to heaven and earth and all things in the world. It has moral significance because it provides man with a ground on the basis of which to act with confidence and righteousness and which frees man from doubts and uncertainties as to what is right and wrong.[1] That man wants to find his true place in the world and that man wants to act in accordance with righteousness and to produce goodness through his act, can be said to present two main goals for human understanding. To understand genuinely or to experience deeply *li* or *t'ien-li* can be considered an answer to both aspirations. The Sung philosophy of Ch'eng I and Chu Hsi seem to concentrate on defining these two goals and on explaining how they can be attained. In Ming philosophy, Wang Yang-ming searches for a new way to satisfy these two goals. He does not want to concentrate on an objective order of *li* as a key. Instead he attempts to settle upon just the mind's own self-understanding as the fundamental starting point for the realization of one's place in the world and its value, as well as considering it as providing the ultimate basis for right decisions on conduct. In this sense Wang Yang-ming has demarcated a new course for Confucianism and yet, at the same time, has plunged Confucianism into new interpretations. He has led his disciples on a new course verging on Ch'an Buddhism which accordingly led to criticism from orthodox Confucians.

481

The most basic idioms and ideals for the realization of humanity and the achievement of righteous conduct in life were already defined in the classical writings of Confucianism. In the Appendices of the *I Ching* we see that there are idioms of *ch'iung-li* (exhaustively investigating principles), *chin-hsing* (fulfilling nature completely), and *chih-ming* (reaching ultimate destiny).[2] In the *Analects* we see Confucius' concern with *chih-t'ien* (knowing heaven), and *chih-jên* (knowing man), *chih-yen* (knowing speech), and *ch'eng-jên* (achieving humanity). In *Mencius* we see discussions of *chin-hsin* (completely fulfilling mind), *chih-hsing* (knowing nature), and *li-ming* (establishing ultimate destiny). In the following passage Mencius seems to paraphrase the statement on *ch'iung-li*, *chin-hsing*, and *chih-ming* in the *I Ching*:

In fulfilling one's mind, one knows the nature; knowing one's nature, one knows heaven. To preserve the mind and nourish the nature is the way to serve heaven. To live a short life or to have longevity is not to be altered. One will cultivate one's person to await [what is determined], and this is the way to establish one's ultimate destiny (*Book of Mencius*, Chapter 7).

But Mencius also speaks of *ch'ien-hsing* (fulfilling form), *yang-ch'i* (nourishing the vital force), *chi-yi (assembling the righteousness), and *chü-yi* (choosing righteousness). In the *Ta Hsüeh* we find new idioms such as *ch'eng-yi* (making sincere the intentions), *ke-wu* (investigating things), *chih-chih* (extending knowledge), and *ch'eng-hsin* (rectifying mind). In the *Chung Yung* we find idioms such as *chih-chung-ho* (reaching equilibrium and harmony) and *chih-ch'u* (reaching subtleties). There are nominal idioms such as *chih-ch'eng* (perfect sincerity), *chih-shan* (perfect good), *liang-chih* (capacity for moral knowledge), and *liang-neng* (capacity for moral practice). All these idioms and others, together with the basic propositions and the contexts which involve them, can be seen as forming the basis for a burgeoning moral psychology and a burgeoning moral metaphysics of man—a moral psychology which both describes how it is indeed possible for man to reach an ultimate state of fulfillment and goodness and also prescribes the path toward that state. They provide a moral metaphysics which indicates the nature of man, the nature of an ontological reality and man's relation to that ontological reality. They both depict the place for man in the ultimate scheme of things and indicate his moral worth in a humanly satisfying way. Both of these—a moral psychology and a moral metaphysics—provide a basis for understanding what man should do in his personal life and in his social intercourse with others in the network of social and political relationships. They thus also provide a basis for a pragmatic ethics of practical morality. If we take practical morality as the central and ultimate concern of man's activity, and as involving the total unfolding of man as man, then practical morality can find its justification in both psychology and metaphysics, just as the latter two have their roots in practical morality.

The main issue in Sung-Ming Neo-Confucianism seems to be one of relating the latter-day concept of *li* to classical idioms of moral psychology, moral metaphysics and morality, not only for the purpose of unravelling the deeper meanings of *li* as a concept, but for the purpose of retrieving and developing the logical implications of classical idioms in a new light. From a methodological point of view it might be said that Neo-Confucianists of the Sung-Ming periods were awakened to the rich and deep meaningfulness of the classical Confucian idioms in moral psychology, metaphysics and morality.[3] They wanted to achieve a synthesis and development of these idioms in terms of new concepts such as *li*, *ch'i* (vital force), *hsing* (nature) and *hsin* (mind). They also wanted to develop a systematic organization and theory for all the concepts around a center of nuclear concepts.

With these two points in view, one can clearly understand where the values and contributions of Sung-Ming Neo-Confucianists lie and how they can be understood and should be evaluated. As it has been generally understood, the central thesis of Chu Hsi and Ch'eng I is that *hsing* (nature) is *li*. This thesis represents, no doubt, a theoretical synthesis and forms a new center of thinking. But this thesis cannot be understood unless seen against the whole background of the classical idioms in moral psychology, moral metaphysics, and moral theory. Similarly when we come to see Wang Yang-ming's contributions to Confucian philosophy, what do we see? The answer is clear: Wang Yang-ming has made a creative synthesis of *li* with *hsin* (mind). Although following the steps of Lu Hsiang-shan, Wang Yang-ming has outgrown Lu by injecting new life and new meaning into the motto, "*hsin-chi-li*" (mind is principle) *via* a new understanding of *chih-chih* and *ke-wu*. It was through a process of intense growth amidst most difficult and pressing conditions that Wang initially made his discovery of reality and the criterion of the real—to be self-contained in one's self. This is his discovery of new meaning for the Mencian *liang-chih*. In Wang Yang-ming's thought, *liang-chih* not only provides a criterion of the right, it also provides a criterion of the good and the criterion of the real. This is to affirm that one's mind is capable of determining and grasping the real, the right, and the good without seeking them from outside.

Wang Yang-ming considers his discovery as not just a moral discovery but an ontological discovery—a discovery of the nature of reality. This is a new center of thought from which other thoughts develop as explanations and elaborations. From this perspective we can see that the formation of his doctrines of the unity of *chih* (knowledge), *hsing* (action), and *chih-liang-chih* (fulfilling the capacity of moral knowledge) actually represent his efforts to reach and perfect his understanding of the ontological substance (*pen-t'i*) of *liang-chih* and bring it to bear on all aspects of human life. So *liang-chih* and *chih-liang-chih* are nuclear concepts in Wang Yang-ming which form the center of his teaching and the center of the learning for his disciples.

The Four-Sentence Teaching as the Total Theory of *chih-liang-chih* (Fulfilling the Ability to Know Goodness) in Wang Yang-Ming: Issues and Interpretations

The intellectual career of Wang Yang-ming is a journey involving not only the attempt to define more and more closely the meanings of his doctrines and drawing implications from them but also the attempt to organize a total and coherent theory about the doctrine of *chih-liang-chih* which embraces the ontological, the epistemological, the moral as well as the pragmatic elements of classical Confucianism. In this regard we may note that Wang Yang-ming's formulation of the paradoxical Four-Sentence Teaching (*shih-chü-chiao*) just two years before his death (1529) is an effort to introduce a capping stone for his theory of *chih-liang-chih*. This shows that this theory was made full-fledged and that Wang Yang-ming achieved a full awareness of various philosophical issues. The Four-Sentence Teaching not only gives an organized unity to Wang's philosophy, it also sets the basic tone for the development of ideas in his followers and provides a clue to our thorough understanding of Wang's school of Confucianism.

Wang Yang-ming's Four-Sentence Teaching, dated 1527 in the records of his disciples Ch'ien Hsu-shan and Wang Chi, comprises the following statements:

1. Devoid of good and evil is the substance of mind (*hsin-chih-t'i*).
2. Involved with good and evil is the movement of intention (*yi-chih-tung* or *yi* activity).
3. Knowing good and evil as [the function of] good-knowing (*liang-chih*).
4. To do good and to remove evil is the act of rectifying affairs (*ke-wu*).

The controversy around his teaching involves such questions as: (1) whether the "substance of mind" (*hsin-chih-t'i*, hitherto referred to as *pen-t'i* or the original substance) is indeed devoid of good and evil; (2) what the "substance of mind" is; (3) how good and evil arise at all; and (4) whether good therefore has an ontological foundation. Since there are so many questions, and since it is difficult to answer them all, many later scholars have come to doubt the place and validity of the Four-Sentence Teaching in Wang Yang-ming's philosophy.

Huang Tsung-hsi specifically has expressed his doubt about the validity of the Four-Sentence Teaching, which he attributed to the report of

Wang Chi, and thus concluded that the Four-Sentence Teaching is the unde-
cided teaching of the master and therefore was not recorded in his writings.[4]
Now it is true that Wang Yang-ming did not record this Four-Sentence Teaching in his own writings, yet there is no historical ground for attributing its
existence to the invention of Wang Chi. For in the extant writings of both of
Wang Yang-ming's two major disciples, Wang Chi[5] and Ch'ien Te-hung,[6] we
find the Four-Sentence Teaching. From this we can conclude that apparently
it was taught orally to his disciples. Nevertheless, it is to be granted that this
teaching is an abstruse one, open to different interpretations. In fact, it
could be said to confuse and perhaps to confound the Confucian principle
of activity with the Buddhist principle of passivity. However, there is no
reason to suspect that Wang Yang-ming did not or could not seriously hold
this view, and that this view may not receive a relevant interpretation which
not only preserves but also extends and systematizes Wang's doctrine of
chih-liang-chih. In fact, as we shall see, Wang himself is aware of the apparent difficulty of this doctrine, which is why he cautions both Wang Chi and
Ch'ien Te-hung as to its correct understanding.

The main problem in understanding the Four-Sentence Teaching involves
how to preserve the consistency of the teaching and give it a deep meaning
to the teaching which preserves Wang's Confucian inclinations. In the interest of consistency, Wang Chi holds that, if the "substance of mind" is devoid
of good and evil, then *yi* (intention) would be devoid of good and evil. This,
of course, presupposes that for Wang Chi, *wu* will depend on *chih*, *chih* will
depend on *yi*, and *yi* will depend on the "substance of mind." Thus it is
consistent to hold the doctrine of the absence of good and evil in the "substance of mind," *yi*, *chih*, and *wu*. Conversely, if we could speak of the good
or evil of *yi*, then we would have to speak of the good or evil of the mind-
substance, contrary to Wang's teaching.

Ch'ien's interpretation of the Four-Sentence Teaching is different. He
holds that the mind-substance does not have goodness or evil as its characteristics, yet man has intentions due to his habits and therefore has desires
which can be said to be good and evil. It is because of the good and evil of
intentions that we can exercise the discipline of self-cultivation to get rid of
evil and preserve good. Thus, according to Ch'ien, the meaningfulness of
self-cultivation depends on the existence of good and evil in intentions.
Apparently, Ch'ien just assumes that the ontological absence of good and
evil is compatible with the epistemological presence of good and evil in
intention, though he fails to explain or demonstrate how they are compatible.

Wang's own interpretation consists of uniting the two interpretations
into one and holds that each interpretation has its usefulness in educating
and enlightening people. Wang Chi's interpretation is for enlightening the

gifted mind, and Ch'ien's interpretation is for enlightening average minds. Wang says (according to Ch'ien):

The gifted person will achieve enlightenment through the original source. The mind of men is originally clear and unobstructed, and is originally the equilibrium (*chung*) of the unactivated (*wei-fa*). The gifted one, once understands the original substance, will understand that the original substance is precisely the effort (*kung-fu*). What exists inside and outside of a man can all be altogether understood?[7]

This passage indicates that Wang does not deny that one should forget *kung-fu* (the effort) once one understands the *pen-t'i* (the original substance).[8] As *kung-fu* involves the endeavors to preserve good and to remove evil, we may say it involves applying the *pen-t'i* to generate *kung-fu*. This passage provides a procedure for understanding *pen-t'i* by understanding *kung-fu*.

On the other hand, Wang's comment on Ch'ien's interpretation is this:

Man may still have the mind of habit, and so the *pen-t'i* could be observed. There-fore I teach that one must do good and remove evil in concrete terms of intentions and desires after one's *kung-fu* (in preserving good and removing evil) becomes mature, and all residues of habit are thoroughly removed, one will have a full and clear understanding of the *pen-t'i* (mind).[9]

Apparently, the message here is to reach for the *pen-t'i* through *kung-fu*. It seems clear that the first understanding is for the gifted and the second for the average mind, for the *pen-t'i* of mind is more difficult to grasp as a whole than to pay attention to individual acts and intentions. Wang Yang-ming, according to Ch'ien, seems to suggest that: (1) the teaching for the gifted is so difficult to grasp that very few people can realize it, and (2) if we do not teach most people to strive to preserve good and remove evil, but only teach them to concentrate on the *pen-t'i*, we will have led them into emptiness and quietness—a state of Buddhist detachment and transcen-dence which would violate the Confucian spirit. This then implies that Wang Yang-ming would hold here the first interpretation as most common and most practicable.

Nature of the *pen-t'i* of Mind: Does It Partake of Good and Evil?

In explaining this Four-Sentence Teaching on the basis of pedagogical expediency, what seems to stand out is that Wang did not directly or sub-stantially explain the "hidden" meaning and consistency of the Four-

Sentence Teaching, at least not from a philosophical point of view. The question remains whether the *pen-t'i* partakes in good and evil; or to put the question another way, whether *pen-t'i* is morally significant, particularly after one affirms that morality is ontologically significant. Wang does provide us with some clues for answering this question in a recorded passage from *Ch'uan Hsi Lu*:

Question: When ancients speak of nature, they have their agreements, but which view is the correct view?

Answer: There is no fixed substance for nature (*hsing*), and there is no fixed substance for theory [on nature]. Since they speak of nature from the view of the *pen-t'i*, some from the view of function (*fa-yung*), some from the view of source; some from the view of consequences. But all in all, there is only this nature, the way to see it being all different is by being shallow or deep. If one clings to one side, he could be wrong. The *pen-t'i* of *hsing* is originally devoid of good or evil. But in its being put to use, it can do good, and it can do evil; its consequences can be definitely good and definitely bad.[10]

This passage makes it quite clear that there are different ways of evaluating and understanding the *pen-t'i*, and none is absolute or complete. It grants in one sense that the *pen-t'i* is without good or evil because it is not applied to things and not related to activities and their consequences. This is the state where mind has not yet been activated by desires, judgments, and perceptions or expectations. This means that good and evil are matters of *yi*, and feelings are states of mind activated which are not entailed by the original substance of mind. What *is* is responsible for the rise of good or evil is the activity of *yi* and the judgmental activities of the mind. This is called the functioning (*fa-yang*) of the *pen-t'i*.

But what is the *fa-yung*? One necessary condition of *fa-yung* apparently is that mind is oriented toward affairs or things of the world so that these affairs or things form the object of mind's desires and feelings. A second necessary condition of *fa-yung* of mind is that what the mind desires or is oriented toward intrinsically involves motivation toward action and therefore it could be said to be the motivating cause of action. As actions bring about good and evil results insofar as they may affect other people, so too mental states of desires and feelings can be said to be good and evil. In this way we may conclude that good and evil become properties of mind when mind is actively involved with things where these active involvements are manifested in desires and feelings oriented toward things and actions resulting from them. The *pen-t'i* of mind is not actively involved with things and actions and therefore cannot be said to be good or evil. Yet the *pen-t'i* of mind forms the basis of the activity of mind; it is the agency and onto-logical base for mind. It therefore contributes to the rise of good and evil even though it does not contain good and evil as its content. Good and evil result from the interaction of the *pen-t'i* with the world and things.

Given the analysis of the *pen-t'i*, we can draw two conclusions. First, the *pen-t'i* or the "substance of mind" can be conceived as a state devoid of desires and feelings.[11] But can the *pen-t'i* be said to be devoid of a sense of awareness? Since Wang identifies *liang-chih* with the *pen-t'i* of mind itself, the answer to the question is that mind is not lacking in awareness. Wang himself says,

The *pen-t'i* of my mind is that which by nature is subtle, pure, bright, and perceptive.[12]

But we might point out that this is the way in which the *pen-t'i* is described from the point of view of a knower. Yet when a knowing situation is involved, it is logically possible to posit the object of knowing, and there is no reason why the object of knowing cannot be described in terms of things other than the knowing mind—in fact, it has been described as *hsing* (nature) or the *t'ien-li* (heavenly principle) or *t'ien-ming* (heavenly destiny). Thus Wang says,

The *pen-t'i* of mind is *t'ien-li*.
T'ien-li is only one.
How is it obtained by way of thinking?[13]
The perfect good is the *pen-t'i* of mind.[14]
The perfect good is the nature.[15]
The nature of *t'ien-ming* is purely the perfect good.[16]

All these passages seem to suggest that the *pen-t'i* of mind can be described in terms other than those of the knowing mind. This indicates that Wang does not really think that there is exclusive ontological identifi-cation of *li* with the knowing mind. He would suggest that reality finds its identity in both mind and nature, but not in mind alone. When he eventu-ally comes to hold that mind is *li*, he does not mean that *li* is only mind. As it is well known, the point of Wang's stressing the mind as defining the quality of *li* is that it is in the mind that one finds ultimacy, unity, definiteness, clarity of *li* and judgments of good and evil. These qualities are opposed to the sense of scatteredness associated with Chu Hsi's doctrine.

The second thing about the doctrine is that the *pen-t'i* of mind is without good and evil, in the sense that it does not involve itself with the orientation of the mind toward an object and a possible action and its consequence, and that it is compatible with the assertion that the *pen-t'i* of mind is indeed the perfect good (*chih-shan*).[17] Wang has himself more often than not held that the perfect good is the same as the *pen-t'i*, which is the same as *hsing*. This we have mentioned earlier. But the question remains about how Wang can maintain that the absence of good and evil is the "substance of mind." How is this compatible with the "perfect good" theory of the *pen-t'i*? The apparent incompatibility herewith apparently caused Huang Tsung-hsi and his teacher, Liu Tsung-chou, to doubt the validity of the Four-Sentence Teaching by Wang. The apparent incompatibility here is no more apparent and may be explained as follows: the perfect goodness of the *pen-t'i* can be understood as objective goodness involving no votive and practical elements. If we can use Plato's doctrine of forms for illustration, this "perfect good" theory of the *pen-t'i* says no more than that the *pen-t'i* is a perfect and ideal form of goodness—a norm and a standard of good which cannot be exactly duplicated or imitated on a different level. On the other hand, the good and evil of desires and feelings in mind are concrete items in life and experience. They are objects of judgments and subjective experiences which are relative to concrete affairs of the world. Thus it becomes clear that we can speak of the perfect goodness of the *pen-t'i* on the one hand, and can speak of good and evil in connection with activities of mind on the other, for it is only when mind has a goal and involves considerations of action and its consequences can we speak of success, satisfaction, harmony of our activities (good), and their converses (evil).

Is the *pen-t'i* of Mind a Buddhistic Notion?

A more serious question in connection with this understanding of the Four-Sentence Teaching of Wang is whether this understanding of the *pen-t'i* conduces to a Buddhist, specifically Ch'an Buddhist, position, or to put it in a more neutral way, whether this position is related to the Buddhist position whereby mind is considered the exclusively ultimate truth, and mind is held to respond to nothing without the clinging desire of illusion if it is enlightened. In fact, Huang Tsung-hsi has expressed this doubt in the following terms:

Since there are no good nor evil, then where are mind, intention, knowledge and things? Finally one would advance to mindlessness, intentionlessness, knowledge-lessness, and thinglessness in order to be perfect. In that case what would be the significance of *chih-liang-chih*?[18]

As good and bad both vanish, one would let one speak of empty, subtle and perceptive *ch'i* (vital force) flow anywhere and have clear bearings; it will not depart from nor will fix on any definite point. How would this view not fall into the trap of Buddhism?[19]

It is clear that Hung Tsung-hsi sees the absence of good and evil in the *pen-t'i* as a sign of Buddhistic tendencies or at least a step toward approaching Buddhism. His argument is interesting in that he seems to see no problem for Buddhists to concentrate on the thesis of the absence of good and evil in the *pen-t'i*, for their enlightenment concern is precisely to transcend life and death and to reach a state of emptiness in which "there is no evil to remove and no good to achieve."[20] But this position is not sound for Confucianists, for Confucianists have their own lifestyle. They live in the world and confront all desires in their daily life. Thus, if they speak of doing away with good and evil, they are in fact to help evil to grow! In this argument Huang Tsung-hsi presents his opposition to the Four-Absence (Nonbeing) Teaching of Wang Chi, because he thinks that this teaching is unsuitable and harmful to the Confucianists. But his anxiety is misplaced, for as we have seen, the absence of good and evil in the *pen-t'i* theory is not logically incompatible with the need and necessity of the judgments of good and evil by the mind.

There is no doubt that the first sentence of the Four-Sentence Teaching suggests a Buddhist connotation and could lead one into Buddhistic conceptions. In fact, there should be no denial that the conception of the *pen-t'i* in the first sentence, as we have analyzed, indeed sounds Buddhistic. But to say this is to say that the very essence of the *pen-t'i* and its understanding do not naturally divest themselves of Buddhist connotations— transcendence, detachment, quietude. The way to understand this could be Buddhistic, for it takes efforts to remove desires and illusions to see it. All these indicate that Wang's theory would reach a point whereby he could communicate with the Buddhists. This also explains how through Wang's theory some of his disciples did reach the Buddhist conception of ultimate experience of reality and even advocated its achievement as the final goal of learning, and thus pushes Wang's original doctrine into the Buddhist camp, as their critics point out. This is indeed true of Wang Chi and Wang Ken. But this is natural for an exhaustive development of a doctrine within a framework.

Thomas Kuhn has pointed out in his book, *The Structure of Scientific Revolutions* (1964), that normal science will solve questions in a given framework, using the same paradigms, until the research exhausts the original system and problems arise which need fresh approaches, and accordingly a revolution takes place. Obviously there were no revolutionary changes in Wang's school after Wang. Wang's disciples push the Four-Sentence Teaching to all extremes or try to keep an equilibrium and balance in his theory. The limitations of this discussion prohibit our pursuing this development in post-Wang school, in reference to such major figures as Wang Chi, Ch'ien Te-hung, Wang Ken, Chou Tung-kuo, Nieh Shuang-chiang, Lo Nien-yen, and the like. It suffices to point out that the original Four-Sentence Teaching shows that one should not stop at understanding the nature of the *pen-t'i* which one discovers or even stop at understanding the way to reach it, but one should move to understanding the functioning of the *pen-t'i* in life and society, for the activation or functioning of the *pen-t'i* is more important than understanding the *pen-t'i* itself. In fact, to understand the *pen-t'i* is for the purpose of the activation of the *pen-t'i*, which means, we may say, to distinguish between good and evil in motive, and to achieve good and remove evil in action as required by the Confucian faith. This is the general meaning of the doctrine of *chih-liang-chih* which Wang has consistently taught throughout his life.

Yi—Activity and Meaning of Good and Evil

Earlier I have tried to explain how the ontology of the *pen-t'i* is compatible with the moral activity of *chih-liang-chih*. What I have done can be said to preserve the consistency of the first sentence of the Four-Sentence Teaching with the remaining sentences of the teaching. I have indicated how the absence of any good-evil distinction in the *pen-t'i* could lead to the presence of just such a distinction when mind comes to respond to things. That Wang Yang-ming assumes that there are things for individual minds to respond to exempts him from being labeled a subjective idealist. He certainly could hold that the *pen-t'i* is universal and gives a unity to all things while at the same time holding that an individual mind will have to interact with things external to it. However, when the individual mind comes to realize its *pen-t'i* and has obtained or retrieved its *liang-chih*, it will judge its activities according to an innate criterion of goodness provided by the ontologically universal mind—the *pen-t'i*.

Now an individual mind is individuated by its thoughts and feelings, and these thoughts and feelings, as bases for action, must be orientated toward objective things. The Chinese word "*nien*" (thoughts) seems to be a good word for characterizing the content which individuates the individual minds. *Nien* literally means the "present mind" (*ching-hsin*),[21] which is an indication of activities and involvements. *Nien* in a sense is to be identified with *yi* (intention) which knows itself in terms of likes and dislikes of the mind. Chu Hsi says that "*yi* is when feelings have a concentrated object."[22] Liu Tsung-chou points out that *yi* is shown in "hating the bad smell and liking the good appearance" in the *Ta Hsüeh* and concludes that *yi* is what masters the mind and is not just a matter of concentration on an object.[23] With this understanding of *yi*, we can safely explain *nien* as the basic constituent of *yi*, and we may say that *yi* manifests itself in terms of moments of mind activities which are *nien*. In fact, what Wang Yang-ming calls "*yi-chih-tung*" (the movements of *yi*) is no more than *nien*. We have pointed out how mind comes to interact with things and affairs and generate states which can be distinguished in terms of good and evil. The presence of this good-evil distinction suggests at least that mind has involvements with things and has a potential for changing things or their relations. That this is possible is due to the activities of mind in terms of *yi* and *nien*. Thus it could be said that the movements of *yi* in mind makes possible the distinction.

Though Wang Yang-ming, and for that matter all Neo-Confucianists, seldom make clear what they mean by good and evil, we may give a meaning to these words through generalizing over things which they normally approve in their life. The basic Confucian values such as the virtues of *jên*, *yi*, *li*, *chih*, *hsing*, *chung*, *hsiao*, *ti*, and so on, are valued for their capacity to preserve basic human relationships so that a harmonious society and an integrated personality will be created. They are values of goodness, and the lack of them and even worse, the tendencies and efforts to oppose them or to adduce converse effects are considered items of badness or evil. Given this basic Confucian criterion, we see that for such Neo-Confucianists as Wang, good and evil are to be judged and reasoned in the Confucian framework and are things not determined independently of human relations or relations to things in the world. Good and evil are not entities in and by themselves. They characterize potential relations among men and states of harmony and integration in a person when he interacts with other persons. Given this understanding of good and evil, we can see that what makes a difference to the mind which feels, desires, and responds to things is the good or evil of its *nien* or *yi*. For it can be further assumed that *yi* and *nien* are initial causes or partial causes which lead to the formation and transformation of a state which is good or bad from an objective view within the Confucian framework. Thus we may say that to understand the second statement of the Four-Sentence Teachers, "to have the good-evil distinction is characteristic of the movements of *yi*," is to understand that *yi* has efficient causal power for generating a state which is good or bad within a framework of basic values of man as set forth clearly by the Confucian doctrine.

To fill out our understanding, we need to repeat that, for Wang Yang-ming as for all major Neo-Confucianists before him, *yi* or *nien* are motives for action and are part of efficient causes for action. Therefore, they are responsible for the effects they bring about. This belief in motive causation for human action is quite natural and is typical of all moral philosophers, East or West. What has yet to be made clear is to what extent consequences of these motives can be assessed and evaluated. But given the present belief, we are already sufficiently warranted to maintain the view that if we control our motives well enough so that we nourish the good motives and at the root cut bad ones—a doctrine of self-cultivation stressed by the *Ta Hsüeh* and Wang Yang-ming in his third and fourth sentences of his Four-Sentence Teaching—we will be sure that good will ensue and bad will cease. At least we could feel exonerated from the responsibility of not vanquishing the evil in its beginning.

The Metaphysical Source of *yi-nien*: An Ontological Observation

A metaphysical question which is closely related to the *yi-nien* doctrine is how an individual mind comes to have occurrences of *yi-nien*, or how it comes to interact with things external to it at all. This question is most important and has received some worthy responses from such Sung Neo-Confucianists as Ch'eng I, Chang Tsai, and Chu Hsi. On the other hand, Wang Yang-ming has not felt particularly interested in clarifying the issue. The particular importance of this question is that its answers are relevant for clarifying the distinction between Confucianism and Buddhism.[24] It seems clear that *yi-nien* occurrences in an individual mind must have a metaphysical basis and must be different or distinct from the *pen-t'i* as we have described. What are *yi-nien* ontologically? The answer is provided by the doctrine of the *li-ch'i* distinction in many of the Sung Neo-Confucianistic theories. According to this distinction, individual mind is made of the ever-moving *ch'i* (vital force) *versus* the eternally stable *li* (principle). Consequently *ch'i* can be said to constitute the ontological base of *yi-nien*. As *ch'i* also dominates over other things, that which we think, feel, and desire through *yi-nien* is a natural result of the basic forms of interaction between our nature of *ch'i* and the worldly thing. These are factual data of life to be recognized, not to be justified. The Confucianists, from Confucius to Mencius to Hsun Tzu, all recognize these facts of life and accept them at face value. Mencius even calls this nature (*hsing*) when he says: "To eat and to have sex is the nature of man."[25] But unfortunately, failing to draw correct moral conclusions from the ontological premises of *ch'i* as an activity and as an individuation principle for both man and things, some Neo-Confucianists wish to eliminate desires in the mind and thus try to reduce humanity to a level of a passive mirrorlike existence while things are still recognized as real. One must recognize the reality of the mind's activities (*yi-nien*) if one recognizes the reality of things. The Buddhists, on the other hand, wish not only to eliminate desires but also to deny the reality of things in the world, and they do this consistently because they see in *ch'i* the common origins of human desires (or *yi-nien* of individual minds) and illusions concerning the existence of external individual objects.

Wang Yang-ming has exposed himself to criticism insofar as he has failed to remind himself of the twofold task of consistently developing a Confucian moral psychology and relating it to its ontological basis. His doctrine of reducing desires is an example. But now we can see that insofar as the distinction between good and evil has meaning, and insofar as occurrences of *yi-nien* in individual minds are natural, we need not worry about elapsing into a Buddhist position. There is good reason to believe that Wang Yang-ming has preserved this basic Confucian view. We might say that there is an ontological force which compels one to move from sentence one to sentence two in Wang's Four-Sentence Teaching.

Difficulties in Relating the Second and Third Sentences: Two Objections from Liu Tsung-chou

Though we have resolved the difficulties between the first and second sentences of the Four-Sentence Teaching, there still remain difficulties concerning the relation between the second sentence and third sentence. The difficulties involve the relation between the "movement of *yi*" (*yi-chih-t'ung*) and the *liang-chih*, and the relation between good and evil in movements of *yi* and the knowledge of good and evil in *liang-chih*. What are these relations? Are "movements of *yi*" prior to the knowledge of *liang-chih* or are they posterior to it? Do good and evil come into existence before knowledge of them by *liang-chih*? Do we need to know good and evil apart from feeling them in "the movements of *yi*"? Are *yi* and *chih* (knowing) two entities or one? Is the distinction between good from evil purely a matter of judgment of mind or is it something which exists independently of such judgments? Various theories by disciples of Wang Yang-ming were developed as results of trying to answer these questions or even to formulate these questions.

Liu Tsung-chou, Huang Tsung-hsi's teacher, has raised these kinds of questions. He has specifically formed two objections to the separation of *yi* from *chih*. In the first place, Liu points out that the third sentence and the second sentence are inconsistent or even contradictory. He says that, "The statements 'There are good and evil in movements of *yi*,' and 'To know good and evil is the goodness of knowledge (*chih-chih-liang*)' can never be consistent." Since *chih* and *yi* appear to be two distinct things, one may ask, "Does *yi* first move and *chih* follow it? Or does *chih* hold first and *yi* succeed? If *yi* first moves and *chih* follows it, then *chih* lags behind and cannot be said to be good (*liang*). If *chih* first holds and *yi* succeeds, then after *chih* has illuminated, where does evil (ghostly existence) stay over? If we get rid of *yi* from the mind (*hsin*), so that we will only have *chih* and *hsin*, then the method should be to remove *yi*, and there would be no requirement of *ch'eng-yi* (to make sincere the intention)."[26]

Apparently for Liu, *chih* and yi cannot be two; if they are two, then there would be difficulties in relating them. The issue here is whether the two statements (the second and third sentences) entail that *chih* and *yi* are two and separate. As a matter of logic, that *chih* and *yi* are two and separate need not follow from these two statements. For there is no reason, when *yi*, as a function of individual mind starts to move, *chih*, as another function of mind, could not immediately discern good and evil of the movements, as objectively good and evil already exist in the movements of *yi*, for in the immediacy of movement there is immediacy of distinction. In this way the question of before or after does not arise, for both *yi* and *chih* occur at the same time, and this is the subtle beginning (*chi*) of *yi*. This is the position which Liu himself holds, and he thought that to discern good and evil at the very movement of *yi* is to make *yi* sincere which is already the efforts (*kung-fu*) of *ke-wu* and *cheng-hsin*, and he thinks that *chih-liang-chih* in Wang is nothing but the effort of making sincere the *yi* in this sense.

Given this interpretation, are the second and third sentences of the Four-Sentence Teaching incompatible or compatible? My suggestion is that they are compatible and need not even be misleading once we know how *chih* stands to *yi* in the mind. They are two aspects of mind and they are united in oneness. Yet *yi*, as we have explained, is a response to the outside world and therefore has initiative in manifesting itself whereas *chih* is an immediate reflection of *yi* once it is formed, as it is also a reflection of all things, and it is in this reflection that good or evil are judged. In this perspective one might then say that *yi*-occurrence could be slightly earlier than *chih*, for *yi* is the agency of *ch'i* and action. Yet why can this be unacceptable? Why might this make *chih* less good (*liang*)? It is good if it distinguishes good from evil. In fact, Wang Yang-ming's doctrine of unity of *chih* and *hsing* (action) holds that *chih* and *hsing* are two aspects of the same thing, and there should be no denial that *hsing* represents the direct result of *yi*. The doctrine could also mean that *chih* and *hsing* should unite and interact to form a single attitude of mind. It involves a command from *liang-chih* to achieve unity, a command leading to Wang's theory of *ke-wu*. In David Hume's *A Treatise of Human Nature*, reason, being distinct from passions, has the function of judging good and evil of passion and need not for this sense become less respectable and less commendable. There is also no reason to exile passions because of the agency of passion. Similarly, there is no reason to exile *yi* from the mind simply because *yi* has the agency of initiating movement within the mind; it is precisely the movements of the mind. The doctrine of *ch'eng-yi* focuses on *yi* as an essential activity of individual minds. To make intentions sincere is to be able to judge good from evil in movements of *yi*, and this is the function of *liang-chih*. Another function of *liang-chih* is to urge and use *yi* itself to get rid of evil and to preserve good. This is as if to let reason guide passions, and this involves the doctrine of *ke-wu* as stated in the fourth sentence of Wang Yang-ming's Four-Sentence Teaching.

The second objection of Liu to the separation of *chih* and *yi* in the second and third sentences of mind is as follows:

> To like something and know that it is evil, to dislike something and know that it is good, only this is the *liang-chih*. Thus to fulfill *chih-liang-chih* is not another item and still to be found in *ch'eng-yi*. If one departs from the roots of *yi*, there would be no *chih-chih* (reaching knowledge) to speak about. I have said that to like the good and to dislike the evil is *liang-chih*. If one gives up the recognition of liking the good and disliking the evil, there is no sense of talking about knowing good and knowing evil. To like is to know the good, to dislike is to know the evil. It is not to say that after knowing the good, then one would like the good, or after knowing the evil, then one would dislike the evil. If this is the case, how could one see goodness of the *chih*? Thus, we know that knowing and desiring (*yi*) are only one unity, and one should not distinguish which one is subtle, which one is crude, which one moves, which one is still.[27]

What Liu Tsung-chou objects to is that one should not separate the activity of *yi* from that of *chih* as the second sentence and third sentence seem to do, for they are not really separable and form a unity. This is demonstrated by the observation that to like good is to know good and to dislike evil is to know evil, and the further observation that to like is to know good and to dislike is to know evil. This position of Liu is, however, in my view, not really contradicted by the second and third sentences, which can be regarded as analytical explanations concerning wherein the activity of *yi* consists and wherein the activity of *chih* consists. The analytical explanation does not rule out the assumption or the presupposition that they are two aspects of the same mind, as I have indicated earlier, or even as two ways of describing the same mind. Indeed, one may even point out that in the first sentence, the substance of mind need not be conceived as totally devoid of relevance for *yi*—it is simply the state of mind in an individual case where *yi* is not yet activated, but remains potential all the same. The *pen-t'i* of mind is also the *pen-t'i* of intending (*yi*) as it is the *pen-t'i* of knowledge (*chih*).[28] When *yi* is not activated, there is equilibrium (*chung*) which can be described as involving neither good nor evil or, equivalently, which can be described as involving only "perfect good" (*chih-shan*), recognizing that perfect food is not exactly good in active form. The worry that Liu has with regard to the understanding of the Four-Sentence Teaching results from mistaking a complete analytical statement of aspects and processes of the same *pen-t'i* in its functioning as indicating a dichotomization of mind which in my view is far from the case.

A correction, however, has to be introduced to Liu's statement of the criterion of knowing the good by liking the good, and knowing the evil by disliking the evil. Do we always know good by liking goodness and know evil by disliking evil? More generally, do we know good by liking something and know evil by disliking something? The answers to these questions cannot be simple. In simple cases we know good by liking good and know evil by disliking evil; and liking and disliking would be the criteria for judging the good or evil or what is being liked and disliked. Yet it is common sense that liking and disliking cannot always be such a criterion. In complex situations, what we like and what we dislike do not guarantee us correct judgments of good and evil.[29] We may trust our intuitions and we may make efforts to sharpen, refine, and refresh our intuitions, still we can be misled and misinformed by our intuitions, and liking and disliking are intuitions. In fact, it has been pointed out by Liu himself that, in reference to the discussion on self-cultivation in the *Ta Hsüeh*, to like something and yet know that it is evil and to dislike something and yet know that it is good, is the capacity of *liang-chih*. The *Ta Hsüeh* does not say that this is *liang-chih*. But if this is *liang-chih*, it is clear that *liang-chih* would merely be a state of simple liking and simple disliking. We must suggest that *liang-chih* as the *pen-t'i* of mind involves more than the activation of *yi* in simple liking and disliking; rather, it involves efforts to rectify one's ideas, to seek correct information, and to broaden one's scope of thinking. It involves all the recommended procedures of learning—broad learning (*po-hsueh*), intense inquiry (*shen-wen*), close thinking (*shen-ssu*), clear distinguishing (*ming-pien*) and sincere practice (*tu-hsing*) as mentioned in the *Ta Hsüeh*. It involves the procedures of "regulation of *li*" (*yueh-li*) and "understanding the good" (*ming-shan*) as taught in the *Analects*. To say this is not to return to Chu Hsi's position. It is merely to avoid an oversimplified understanding of *liang-chih* or *chih-liang-chih*.

If again we take David Hume as an illustration, reason in Hume's philosophy of morality will analyze and reason out what is good and what is evil in the activities of the passions. Reason forsees by reflection and calculation. It is not a simple matter of intuition. Even though reason may start with a simple intuition and reach as its conclusion an enriched intuition, there need not be scatteredness in the reasoning process. The process of reasoning is one, and its premises and conclusions are one. In light of this distinction we may still maintain that *yi* (such as liking and disliking) and *chih* can be functionally and analytically distinctive even though ontologically they are one. One may even suggest that to like something in the concrete is a natural response of *yi*, yet it takes the judgmental rational capacity of the same mind to find out correctly whether what *yi* likes and dislikes is good or evil.

Doctrine of *ke-wu* and Definition of *hsing* (Action)

We come to the last sentence of the Four-Sentence Teaching. I have pointed out that once the *liang-chih* discerns the good and evil of the *yi*-activity, it can arouse *yi* for removing evil and preserving good. As the existence of good and evil pertains to *yi*-activity, to preserve good and to remove evil would pertain to *yi*-activity. But to discern good and evil is a function of *liang-chih* which is the application of the *pen-t'i* to illuminate the things to which *yi* responds. I have explained that this does not mean that *yi* and *liang-chih* must be two things but they could constitute two aspects of the one mind. That they must be two aspects of the mind is shown by the fact that *liang-chih* could determine the good and evil in the inception of *yi*-activity and that it even can, in fact, rectify it so that we can effectively speak of preserving good and removing evil as they are found in *yi*-activity.

Liang-chih is not just a passive thing or just stationary *li* (principle) which merely illuminates, but may have the creative power to effect change. This means that *liang-chih* partakes of *yi*-activity. It is to make the *yi*-activity conform to goodness; that is, it is to realize the *li* (principles) in one's *yi*-activity or in the mind and consequently to realize *li* in things which we focus on in the *yi*-activities. This is what is called *ke-wu* by Wang Yang-ming. This doctrine of *ke-wu* is different from what Chu Hsi understood to be *ke-wu*. Whereas Chu Hsi speaks of *ke-wu* as exhaustively investigating the principles of external things, Wang takes *ke-wu* as a matter derived from the active application of mind in *liang-chih* to things being responded to by *yi*. It is to rectify things of *yi* so as to establish the right principles among things. In Wang's words,

To extend the heavenly principles of *liang-chih* in my mind to affairs and things, then affairs and things all get their principles. To extend the *liang-chih* in my mind is a matter of *chih-chih* (reaching knowledge). Affairs and things all get their principles—that is *ke-wu*: it is to unify mind and principles into one.[30]

That Wang Yang-ming assumes that we can establish *li* among things comes from his conviction that mind is *li* and that once we understand mind, we understand what *li* is in individual things. In this sense mind is the *pen-t'i* of *liang-chih*.[31]

Given this interpretation of *ke-wu*, *ke* is interpreted as "to rectify." It follows then that *ke* is "to rectify" the *yi* (or *nien*) which determines or defines affairs, and this means to get the *yi*-activity on the right path, to assure its goodness and to rid it of evil. It is to realize *liang-chih* in each *yi*-activity.[32] It is in another sense equivalent to the doctrine of *ch'eng-yi* (to make sincere the intentions), for *ch'eng-yi* is precisely an utmost achievement of making *yi*-activity conform to *li* or to what is revealed in mind or *liang-chih*. Thus we reach the conclusion presented by the fourth sentence of the Four-Sentence Teaching: "To do good and to remove evil is *ke-wu*."

The consistency of Wang Yang-ming's thought on *ke-wu* is surprisingly subtle, given Wang's doctrine of *ke-wu*. What has been seldom noted is that his *ke-wu* doctrine sheds new light on his doctrine of unity of *chih* and *hsing* and renders a clearer definition of *hsing* (action). Though Wang discussed the doctrine of unity of *chih* and *hsing* earlier in his career than his doctrine of *chih-liang-chih*, he did not give any metaphysical reasons why *chih* and *hsing* must be one. He merely argued that they should be one, but are they in reality one? Given his *ke-wu* theory, *chih* and *hsing*, in fact, must be one, for *hsing* is no more than the effort to remove evil and to do good by *yi*-activity—*hsing* is the effort to *ke-wu*. Then it follows that *hsing* must entail *chih*. By the doctrine of *Chih-liang-chih*, *chih* must entail *hsing*—namely, the effort to make *yi*-activity conform to goodness. Thus, *chih* and *hsing* are ontologically one. When Wang Yang-ming says that "*chih* is the motive for *hsing* and *hsing* is the effort for *chih*,"[33] that "*chih* is the beginning of *hsing* and *hsing* is the completion of *chih*,"[34] and that "the most real and substantial of *chih* is *hsing*, the most perceptive and discerning of *hsing* is *chih*,"[35] he may have the ideas of *chih-liang-chih* and *ke-wu* in mind. But it is obvious that only when those ideas are made explicit, the doctrine of the unity of *chih* and *hsing* becomes logically intelligible and its ontological import clear.

Concluding Remarks: Four Requirements of *chih-liang-chih*

In the preceding I have explained both the internal consistency of the Four-Sentence Teaching and the consistency of this teaching with Wang's earlier teachings. I have also tried to bring out the philosophical meaning of this doctrine. On the basis of this I want to suggest first that the Four-Sentence Teaching of Wang Yang-ming as reported by his arch disciples represents a mature and systematic view of Wang Yang-ming which is not merely a matter of pedagogical expedience but a matter of deep ontological and moral significance. I have clarified where misunderstandings and objections arise and how they can be met. Secondly, s a whole, the Four-Sentence Teaching, in my view, also represents a complete solution to the problem of *chih-liang-chih*. In fact, it can be said to explicate the meaning of *chih-liang-chih*. However, it need not be regarded as providing a definitive list of terms such as *hsin-chih-t'i* (substance of mind), *yi-chih-tung* (activation of intention), *liang-chih*, and *ke-wu*. Although the forms of these sentences in the teaching may not indicate how these sentences can be explicative of the *chih-liang-chih* doctrine, they can be reformulated in such a way that they would explain and present various steps and aspects of the *chih-liang-chih*. These four sentences can be said to give rise to the following four requirements for *chih-liang-chih*: (1) one should see and realize the substance of mind as devoid of good or evil before it applies to the affairs of things; (2) one should see and realize that good and evil ensue from activities of *yi* in the mind, and there will always be *yi*-activities in the mind; (3) one should see and realize that an internal component of mind always performs the function of seeing and distinguishing good from evil in its *yi*-activities, and this is *liang-chih*; (4) one should also see and realize that after seeing good and evil in *yi*-activities, the mind is capable of removing evil and preserving good because it finds itself obligated to remove evil and to preserve good under the direction of *liang-chih*. These requirements as derived from the Four-Sentence Teaching make quite clear not only the meaning of the *chih-liang-chih* doctrine but also how one may proceed to apply the doctrine to one's life. The doctrine acquires both an ontological and a pragmatic meaning from the Four-Sentence Teaching.

Given the earlier explication of the Four-Sentence Teaching and of the doctrine of *chih-liang-chih* in this connection, we can further see, as a final observation, how immediate followers and disciples of Wang Yang-ming and their own followers and disciples developed doctrines concerning *chih-liang-chih* and concerning the nature of *liang-chih pen-t'i* or the *pen-t'i* of mind. Some disciples, such as Lo Lien-yen and Nieh Shuan-chiang, seem to stress and grasp the essence of the first sentence. Some others, such as Ch'ien Te-hung and Chou Tung-ku, seem to stress and grasp the essence of the second sentence and the third sentence. There are still others, such as Wang Chi and Wang Ken, who seem to grasp and stress the essence of the fourth sentence. What is interesting to note is the fact that one can move closer to Buddhism, particularly Ch'an, by pushing to extremes the importance of the first sentence or the importance of the fourth sentence. It is apparent that Nieh Shuan-chiang becomes Buddhistic by means of the former, whereas Wang Ken becomes Ch'an Buddhistic by means of the latter.[36]

Notes

1. In this sense one may speak of "exhaustively fulfilling one's nature" (*chin-hsing*) in Confucian philosophy.
2. All these and other terms following them have philosophical meanings which cannot be adequately discussed here. But they are mentioned and conventionally translated for providing a context of discussion on the topic of this chapter.
3. A simple observation on the notion of *t'ien* (heaven) in relation to *li* (principle): *t'ien* connotes something about *li*, namely, the naturalness, unity, orderliness, and vitality of *li*; furthermore, *li* connotes something about *t'ien*, namely, the realness, objectivity, rationality, unchangingness, and the necessity of *t'ien*. The classical Confucianists seldom speak of *li* alone just as the Neo-Confucianists seldom speak of *t'ien* alone. Ch'eng Hao's *t'ien-li* (heavenly principle) is a profound term uniting two dynamically rich concepts into one.
4. See *Ming Ju Hsüeh An*, Shih Shuo.
5. See *Lung Ch'i Hsien Sheng Ch'uan Ch'i* by Wang Chi.
6. See *Nien P'u* of Wang Yang-ming by Ch'ien Te-hung.
7. See *Ch'uan Hsi Lu*, Part III.
8. We shall use "*pen-t'i*" to refer to the "original substance of mind" or simply the "substance of mind." Sometimes Wang identifies mind (*hsin*) itself with this *pen-t'i* or *hsin-chih-t'i*. Mou Tsung-shan refers to it as *hsin-t'i*.
9. See *Ch'uan Hsi Lu*, Part III.
10. Ibid.
11. In fact there are passages where Wang Yang-ming admonishes the reduction and extinction of desires for recovering the *pen-t'i*.
12. See Wang Yang-ming, *Ta Hsüeh Wen*.
13. See *Ch'uan Hsi Lu*, Part II.
14. Ibid., Part III.
15. Ibid., Part I.
16. See complete works of Wang Yang-ming, 26, *Shu P'ien*.
17. This is also the view which Ch'ien Te-hung himself holds.
18. See *Ming Ju Hsüeh An*, Shih Shuo.
19. Ibid.
20. Ibid.

21. This entymological explanation is pointed out by Liu Tsung-chou in his *Liu Nien-t'ai Tu Cheng P'ien*; see *Ming Ju Hsüeh An, Chi Shan Hsüeh An*.

22. Liu Tsung-chou quoted Chu Hsi's statement in Chu Hsi's *Shih Hsun Mon Shih*, see Liu Tsung-chou, ibid.

23. See Liu Tsung-chou, ibid.

24. Buddhism rejects the occurrence of *yi-nien* as illusion-producing and as itself being produced by the *alaya*-consciousness.

25. See the *Book of Mencius*, Chapter 7.

26. See Liu Tsung-chou, ibid.

27. Ibid.

28. Just as we may speak of the *hsin-t'i* (substance of mind), we can speak of the *yi-t'i* (substance of intentions).

29. For example, one may like smoking marijuana, but it does not follow from this that we know that smoking marijuana is not harmful. Otherwise, there is no sense to conduct scientific experiments for deciding whether smoking marijuana is harmful.

30. See *Ch'uan Hsi Lu*, Part I.

31. Wang says, "There is nothing outside mind, and there are no affairs outside mind, and no *li* outside mind, no rightness outside mind, no good outside mine." See his *Complete Works*, 4, Wen Lu 1, Letter to Wang Hsun-ku.

32. See Wang Yang-ming, *Ta Hsüeh Wen*.

33. See *Ch'uan Hsi Lu*, Part I.

34. Ibid.

35. Ibid.

36. In this connection we might point out that if one does not have a synoptic vision of the totality of Wang's theory of *chih-liang-chih*, one will be misled or be puzzled about the Four-Sentence Teaching and will also lack understanding as to how latter followers like Wang Chi held views which seem to contradict some central teachings of Wang Yang-ming. All these mistakes are due to a lack of understanding of the development of paradigms and idioms in Wang Yang-ming's mature system and possible limitations and pitfalls inherent in such a system. The development and decline of Wang's school may be conceived as being guided by an inner logic of its own. Due to different understandings of the Four-Sentence Teaching, due to the gradual loss of the original whole vision of its founder, and due to a consequent partiality in developing one idea at the expense of another, the Wang school grew, matured and finally encountered the limits of its life-span.

20. *Li-Ch'i* and *Li-Yü* Relationships in Seventeenth Century Neo-Confucian Philosophy

Introductory Remarks

Two basic facts about Neo-Confucianism are generally recognized by scholars of Chinese philosophy. First, Neo-Confucianism is founded on the classical Confucianism of Confucius, Mencius, and the other Confucian classics, as the Neo-Confucianists understand them; second, Neo-Confucianism arose as a result of attempting to meet the challenges of Chinese Buddhism, which was well-developed since the sixth century. How to make a precise interpretation of these two facts, however, constitutes a problem that is open to further study. But it must be admitted that, in the light of these two facts, Neo-Confucianism has been influenced by Chinese Buddhism and yet is essentially Confucian. The influence of Chinese Buddhism on Confucianism, it might be suggested, comes in two forms: (1) by way of stimulating interest in theoretical constructions and metaphysical speculations; and (2) by ways of taking substantial hints from the Buddhist views.

In Chinese Buddhism there are two major tendencies that clearly affected Neo-Confucian philosophy. The first tendency is toward an irreconcilable dualism between existence and nonexistence or nothingness. This dualism is reflected in various forms of contrast between *fa* (law) and *shih* (fact), *se* (form) and *k'ung* (void), *jan* (polluted) and *ching* (pure) in the Buddhist vocabulary.[1] The second tendency is toward an idealistic interpretation of reality in terms of the mind. This tendency is dominant in the school of *wei-shih* and receives an implicit reinforcement from the development of *ch'an*. The first tendency is reflected in the dualistic thinking of Ch'eng I and Chu Hsi who represent *li* (principle, order, reason) and *ch'i* (vapor, indeterminate reality) as different forms of reality. *Li* is the ultimate substance of all things, it is well-structured and preserved in a static equilibrium. It is furthermore the accomplished standard for judging and regulating individual instances of existence. It is identified finally with the authority of reason and indeed with any authority that can claim reason as its ground. Thus, *li* is a principle of rationality that perceives the world in a fixed order. *Ch'i*, on the other hand, is treated as a principle of imperfection that gives rise to a variety of concrete things and causes change, mutation, and transformation of things. *Ch'i* is not a principle of rationality, but one of dynamic creativity. This principle of dynamic creativity, being essentially an exhibition of both the perfect and the imperfect, was considered merely the basis of life, not the ideal of life.

The disparity between *li* and *ch'i* furthermore is reinforced in the contrast between the morality of *li* and immorality of *ch'i* in terms of *yü*. *Li*, as the principle of rationality, preserves order in society as well as in the individual. But *ch'i*, as the principle of vital existence, causes passivity, desire (*yü*), disorder, and therefore a tendency toward evil. *Li* is contrasted with *yü* (needs, desires), and *yü* is explained on the basis of *ch'i*. In *yü* there is no *li*. The ontological principle of *ch'i* thus gives rise to the demoralizing principle of *yü*. As values, *li* are paradigms of good, for good is identified with order, equilibrium, stability, the status quo, and rationality. On the other hand, *ch'i* is treated as the antipode of *li*, lacking order, rationality, stability, universality, and equilibrium. As moral badness is experienced as disorder, instability, particularity, and acts of corruption and destruction, it is naturally identified with *ch'i* or as a variation of *ch'i*. Hence, we see that the ontological incompatibility of *li* and *ch'i* is concomitant with the moral opposition between *li* and *yü*. As the ontological incompatibility between *li* and *ch'i* is derived from a generalization about substantial existence and the possibility of change and transformation, the world of stability (nirvana) and the world of fluidity (anitya), the contrast between *li* and *ch'i*, and the derivative contrast between *li* and *yü* therefore can be theoretically attributed to Buddhist influences.

The other tendency toward interpreting reality in terms of the mind, as exhibited in the *wei-shih* (mere-consciousness, yogacara) school of Buddhism, influences Neo-Confucianism in regard to the position that Neo-Confucianists generally accord to the mind. Everything in the Ch'eng-Chu school is by no means idealistic, but Ch'eng-Chu considers the mind (*hsin*) as being exclusively fundamental and important. Thus, the statement "mind unifies nature and sentiment" (*hsin-t'ung-hsing-ch'ing*), stressed by the Ch'eng-Chu school, indicates the consciousness of the mind as a dominating concept. In the Lu-Wang school, there is little doubt that the mind plays a role fundamental to the existence of everything, for the significance of everything depends on the mind. The ontological principle of *li* is identified with the mind in the statement "*hsin-chi-li*" (mind is *li*). I have pointed out in an earlier paper that the concept of *li* in Lu-Wang's Neo-Confucianism exhibits the subjectivity of *li* in the mind, whereas the concept of *li* in Ch'eng-Chu's Neo-Confucianism exhibits the opposition of a duality between *li* and *ch'i*.[2]

Given the influences of Buddhism on Neo-Confucianism, it is fair to point out that Neo-Confucianists in general are opposed to Buddhism and are explicitly critical of Buddhist philosophy. Furthermore, they are theoretically committed to constructing Neo-Confucianism in defiance of Buddhist philosophy. Perhaps with the exceptions of Wang Yang-ming, Wang Chi, and Yang Chien, all the other Neo-Confucianists of the Sung-Ming period have shown little true understanding of Buddhism, particularly the Mahayana Buddhism which was well cultivated by the great masters of the T'ang dynasty. This fact certainly is compatible with that of the influence of Buddhism on Neo-Confucianism and the fact that neo-Confucianists are opposed to Buddhism. What is important to note is that the Neo-Confucianists, though professing a Confucian conviction, were not necessarily thoroughly Confucianist in the classical sense. They could have become more Confucian, or more purely Confucian, by ridding themselves of the Buddhist influences just mentioned. There is no reason why this could not have happened, for in a more detached perspective, their Buddhist elements could have been seen more clearly. A true Confucianist, therefore, could choose to reject these elements and restore Neo-Confucianism to a state of greater coherence, with a more strengthened structure.

Throughout the seventeenth century, there was a widespread movement toward critique, reevaluation, and reformulation of Neo-Confucianism as presented by the Sung-Ming masters. Though many cultural or even political factors occasioned this movement among Confucian scholars, the phenomenon nevertheless can be regarded as an internal dialectical development of Neo-Confucianism. By this, I mean that the essentially Confucian mentality had arrived at a state of consistency and perfection and therefore had come to see the weakness of Neo-Confucianism under the conceptual influence of Buddhism. From this point of view, we may regard the seventeenth-century Confucian critique of Neo-Confucianism as a deeper awakening of the Confucian consciousness, which was both a continuation of the great tradition of Neo-Confucianism and an improvement upon it. In fact, even when Neo-Confucianism was at the height of its activities, there was already a trend of antidualistic Confucian thought, with a note of pragmatism, which combated the dualistic, idealistic, and basically unpragmatic thinking of the orthodox. Thus, Ch'en Liang (1143-1194) and Yeh Shih (1150-1223) in Sung times criticized the unpragmatic speculation of the Ch'eng-Chu school. Also Wang Ting-hsing (1474-1544) and Huang Wan (1477-1551) in Ming times criticized Wang Yang-ming with regard to his phenomenalistic-spiritualistic doctrines of *"chih-liang-chih"* (fulfilling innate knowledge of goodness) and *"chih-hsing-ho-yi"* (Unity of knowledge and action).[3] Even in the mainstream of Sung Neo-Confucianism, Chang Tsai already had proved an outstanding figure in developing a philosophy with implicit, if not explicit, undertones of pragmatism, naturalism, and monism, which to a great degree comprehend the spirit of the classical Confucian metaphysics of the *Book of Changes* from a seventeenth century point of view. All these thinkers can be regarded as predecessors to the enlightenment philosophers of Confucianism of the seventeenth century.

It is our purpose in this chapter to accentuate the critical and constructive thinking of the seventeenth-century Confucian philosophers and to make clear our view that the seventeenth century indeed is a highly significant period, which traditionally has been neglected in the study of the development of Confucianism, as well as in the study of the development of Chinese philosophy as a whole. We shall particularly focus on the basic *li-ch'i* and *li-yü* relationships, as areas where the critique of Neo-Confucianism is made and new interpretations in the classical spirit are constructed. We shall see that these two types of relationships represent cores of Confucian thinking, being the metaphysical and moral dimensions of the Confucian system. Our discussion will therefore provide a new perspective for the synthesis of the metaphysical and ethical insights of Confucian thinking. Historically, we hope that this effort will illustrate the true nature of Confucian thinking in the seventeenth century and will shed light on the development of Confucian thinking in the eighteenth century, a major representative of which is Tai Chen.[4]

We shall start with an examination of the *li-ch'i* and *li-yü* relationships in Wang Fu-chih, as Wang was unquestionably the most outspoken, the most productive, as well as the most original thinker in the seventeenth century. We shall then cover Yen Yuan, Li Kung, Huang Tsung-hsi, Ch'en Ch'ueh, Li Erh-ch'u, as well as Fang Yi-chih, whose interpretation of *li* and *ch'i* reflects the influence of Western physical science.

The *ch'i* and *li-ch'i* Relationship in Wang Fu-chih (1619-1692)

Even though most seventeenth century philosophers inherited the Neo-Confucian vocabulary in philosophy, the meanings of many terms were then redefined within the new contexts of the new relationships, established among the terms. Thus the terms "*li*," "*ch'i*," and "*yü*" were old terms, yet they received new meanings in the writings of Wang Fu-chih, precisely because of the new relationships developed between them. Let us now concentrate on the *li-ch'i* relationship in Wang Fu-chih, which gives rise to a new cosmology and a new metaphysics.

In the first place, *ch'i* is considered the most fundamental substance in reality by Wang Fu-chih. It is the prime material from which everything is composed. It is not identified with anything definite, but is considered the source from which definite things (which we call *ch'i* in the sense of utensils and things) are derived. Following Chang Tsai, Wang Fu-chi takes *ch'i* as something pervading the imperceptible space and as capable of every kind of transformation. The basic principles of the transformation of *ch'i* are concentration (*chu*) and dispersion (*shan*). *Chu* is the process of coming into being and assuming a form, whereas *shan* is the process of coming out of being and disintegrating of a form, or simply coming to assume no form. By concentration *ch'i* is being (*yü*), and by dispersion *ch'i* becomes nonbeing (*wu*). Thus Wang said, commenting on Chang Tsai: "The empty is the measure of *ch'i*. *Ch'i* pervades the infinite and does not manifest itself in form. Thus man sees only emptiness, but no *ch'i*. All emptiness is *ch'i*. By concentration it manifests itself. When it manifests itself, it is called existence or being; by dispersion it becomes hidden. When hidden, it is called non-existence or non-being."[5] It is through these two processes of change that species abound and things fall into orders and classes. We shall explain later that *ch'i* as such involves both the momentum of change and transformation, as well as a tendency of necessity toward order, regularity, and reason.

Because *ch'i* is basically formless, even though by concentration it gives rise to form, *ch'i* can be identified with Chang Tsai's "*t'ai-hsu*" (ultimate voidness), a term designating the indeterminate matrix of reality in Chang Tsai's natural philosophy. As "*t'ai-hsu*" always involves a process of change and transformation, the movement of concentration and dispersion mentioned earlier are inherent in the very substance of *ch'i*, and thus form the dynamic potential of *ch'i* for giving rise to a world of things. In other words, *ch'i*, as the foundation of things, is the constant and incessant source of change because of its potentiality. In this sense, *ch'i* is not separated from the process of inherent change that manifests itself in all the forms and is called by Wang Fu-chih "*yin-yun*", which describes the activity of change by way of the concentration and dispersion of *ch'i*. He said: "*Yin-yun* is the original state of the undividedness of the original harmony"; "*Yin-yun* is ultimate harmony. It coincides with *ch'i* and the substance of *yin* and *yang* are all found in it"; "The ultimate voidness is discerned in the original substance of *yin-yun*".[6] *Yin-yun* also is called *"ch'i-hua"* or the transformation of *ch'i* by Wang Fu-chih.

The activity of change in *ch'i* comprehends the process of interchange of the *yin* and *yang* agencies, as described by the *Book of Changes*. In the tradition of the *Book of Changes*, *yin* and *yang* form two phenomenological aspects of the total reality, which are opposite to each other, yet are continuous with each other and complement each other. They are the two observable and yet a priori determinable aspects of things considered as a whole. The reality that makes this whole possible is called *tao*. The dynamic process that exhibits the interchange of rise and decline is *tao* in action. Thus, *yin* and *yang*, in fact, are not separable from *tao*, just as the substance of reality and its function are not separable. These two aspects of *tao* can be said to be the foundation for the concentration in being and dispersion in nonbeing, and movement and rest in the transformation of *ch'i*. It is the very essence of change that continually and eventually gives rise to everything. Wang said:

Yin and *yang* are possessed in the ultimate void of the *yin-yun*. The interchange of *yin* and *yang* are the alternation between motion and rest in *yin-yun* generate a mutual grinding and stirring between the two and manifest their function and capacities at the right time. The fusion and flow of the five elements and ten thousand things, the formation of life in sky and water and on earth displays a pattern of order and is not at random. Thus things have the way of things, spirits and ghosts have the way of spirits and ghosts. We can clearly know about this and can rightly act if we follow our knowledge. All follows this as a principle of course. In this fashion we call the process of *yin* and *yang* the Way.[7]

The activity of change in *ch'i* or the transformation of *ch'i* is, for Wang Fu-chih, a process of creativity, for it gives rise to everything and all life. Therefore, it is a movement of generation and production. It is significant that Wang stressed the notion of creative production (*sheng-sheng*) and its products (*sheng*) in explaining the cosmological and ontological nature of *ch'i*. He considered *sheng* (life, production, generation) as the manifest function of transformation of *ch'i*. The *yin-yang* interchange and their complementation as well as their polarization are to be considered the totality of life. One may even suggest that, for Wang, the creative production of life is the very end of the transformation of *ch'i*.

That change is given the purpose of the production of life is likened to the fact that every person has a nature. Thus he said:

That which makes it comprehend things is its nature; that which generates things is its function. What is light surfaces up, what is deep sinks down; what is dear to the above lifts up; what is dear to the below falls down. What moves and tends to continue is movement; what moves and tends to stop is rest. All are *ch'i* due to the combination and mixture of *yin* and *yang*. [All have] the beginnings of necessary change in being and form a natural state of things. This is like the case where man [by the transformation of *ch'i*] has nature.[8]

The creative activity of *ch'i* is continuous as well as purposive. It is purported to preserve life and to continue life by making the creative activities of life the constant activity of reality. In a sense, even death is a natural process of change that makes new life possible. Wang said: "The dispersion if life entails death; the reconcentration of *ch'i* after death entails life. It is clear that the principle of change involved is consistent."[9] It is on this ground that Wang was opposed to the Buddhist doctrine of generation and annihilation, according to which annihilation means no return to life and total annihilation means complete cessation of life (nirvana without residue). Wang insisted that it is far better to describe reality as coming and going, expansion and contraction, concentration and dispersion, lightening and darkening than as generation and annihilation. Wang suggested that by realizing the transformation of *ch'i* and understanding the nature of ultimate voidness one can be made to fulfill one's nature in a perennial sense and not be bothered by the phenomenon of death in particularity.[10] He said: "What pervades between heaven and earth and flows between them is the process of life generation. Thus it is said, 'The great virtue of heaven and earth is life-generation.' From the void to the real is the process of coming, from the real to the void is the process of going. . . . The *yang* takes life generation as its *ch'i* and *yin* takes life-generation as its form."[11]

The importance of *sheng* (life-generation) lies in the fact that the process of change is not merely a circular interchange of *yin* and *yang* in repetition, but one of interchange without repetition. It is a creative process of realizing the infinitely rich potentiality of the Way or the reality of *ch'i*. For, in the first place, the Way is infinitely rich. One can say that the interchange of *yin* and *yang* is a process of realizing this potentiality of life inherent in the Way. In the second place, the very process of interchange between *yin* and *yang* is a creative one, in the sense that it always brings novel things into being. Both these views may not have been original to Wang, as they easily could have been derived from the *Book of Changes* or Chang Tsai. But Wang was original on a more perspicuous point; namely, the process of change is directed toward a display of a complete variety of things. In other words, the process of change is capable of evolving into a state of the full realization of all things in differentiation. He said: "The Way is born from being and will become complete when the great variety of things is present."[12] In fact, he even suggested that the nature of things is generated everyday and becomes gradually complete everyday (*jih-sheng jih-ch'eng*).[13] He also said that he knew that the Way is rich because it generates new things everyday.[14] In a passage in his commentary on Chang Tsai (*T'ai-ho* chapter), he described how the harmonious *ch'i* combined with the refined five agencies forms human nature and thus explains the nature of people. Even an individual's nature is not permanently fixed, for the nature of one can give rise to new perceptions and new feelings under new circumstances. This nature, which we know through the mind, comprehends the mind in unity, for the mind itself should emerge from nature.[15]

Finally, *ch'i*, as the ultimate reality, is progress in a state of balance and harmony. To designate this characteristic of *ch'i*, Wang adopted the term "ultimate harmony" (*t'ai-ho*), again taken from Chang Tsai. The internal balance and harmony of *ch'i* consists of the potentiality of *ch'i* for realizing and maintaining an infinite order of forms in reality. In fact, it is the hierarchy of forms in its potential state. Only by considering *ch'i* as *t'ai-ho* can *ch'i* be identified with *tao* and the great ultimate (*t'ai-chi*). *Yin-yang* are different, but when interacting in the great voidness, they do not violate each other but instead mutually complement each other. This is the ultimate harmony. After there are concrete things, the original harmony is not lacking. Thus it is called the ultimate harmony."[16] By identifying *ch'i* as both *t'ai-ho* and *t'ai-hsu*, Wang achieved a monistic interpretation of reality. For, according to Wang, in the ultimate harmony there are all the possibilities of change and transformation, and thus *t'ai-ho* becomes the source of creation, just as *t'ai-hsu* is. Similarly, in the ultimate voidness is the infinite potentiality for the relation and actualization of concrete things in order, and thus *t'ai-hsu* becomes the basis of organization, just as *t'ai-ho* is. *T'ai-hsu* represents the creative agency of *ch'i*, whereas *t'ai-ho* represents the organizational agency of *ch'i*. Thus Wang said, "Within *t'ai-ho*, there is *ch'i* and there is *shen* (spirit or the ordering power). The *shen* is nothing other than the principles (*li*) of the two *ch'i*—*yin* and *yang*—in mixture and penetration."[17]

Following Chang Tsai, Wang took *ch'i* as something that can be represented in concrete phenomena (*hsiang*) and *shen* as something inherent in *hsiang*. This is not to say that *shen* is over and above *hsiang*; it simply means that *shen* is the total potentiality for order and organization that cannot be captured in a single phenomena.

To summarize, *ch'i* is the total reality. It is the reality of change between the *yin* and *yang* agencies. Furthermore, it is a creative process of life, which is full of novelty. It is infinite and indeterminate in its potentiality

and yet contains all the possibilities of formation, transformation, and organization. The most important thing we have to bear in mind is that *ch'i* is
both a creative agent and an agent for ordering and organization. One may
therefore say that *ch'i* contains order and organizational principles, but
this can mean only that *ch'i* is the potential order and harmony of things,
for *ch'i* is no less creative and dynamic. The dynamic and creative agency
of *ch'i* is one of ordering and concretization. The order, harmony, and
organization of relations are dispositions in *ch'i* and form what *ch'i* is. They
cannot be considered apart from a context of change and transformation.

At this point, we can now bring in the consideration of *li* (reason,
order, principles) in Wang's metaphysical philosophy. We shall see that for
Wang, as a critic of Sung-Ming Neo-Confucianism, the ultimate proposition
in metaphysics was not "nature (*hsing*) is *li*," as in the case of Ch'eng-Chu,
or the proposition "nature (*hsing*) is *hsin* (mind)," as in the case of Wang
Yang-ming, but rather the more fundamental proposition "*ch'i* is *li* and *li* is
ch'i." We now shall explain this and on the basis of the explanation pave the
way for a correct understanding and appreciation of Wang's antidualistic,
naturalistic metaphysics and its significance as a foundation for his antidualistic, naturalistic ethics, which incorporates the unity of *li* and *yü*.

First of all, we should affirm that for Wang Fu-chih *ch'i* is fundamental
and *li* is derivative. *Li* is derivative in the following senses: (1) In the potential sense, generalized *li* are nothing but ways in which *yin* and *yang* interact and preserve harmony and actualize the world. It can be said that before
the world is actualized, there is the potential harmony of the activities of
yin and *yang*. So in a potential and general sense, *li* is to be understood as
the internal harmony-preserving activities of *ch'i*. This should be clear from
our earlier account of *ch'i* as *t'ai-ho*. In other words, *li* is none other than
the tendency toward the actualization of the world, the ordering of things,
and the presentation of life. (2) *Li*, as the inner tendency toward order and
harmony, has to be brought out as the creative activity of *ch'i*. In this regard,
li depends upon *ch'i* for its realization. In fact, without a process of realization we cannot speak of *li* in an actual sense; *li* is merely a state, mode, or
quality of *ch'i*. When *ch'i* moves and develops, *li*, as a mode of *ch'i*, becomes
actuality. In this regard, *li* is merely a mode of the actualization or realization of *ch'i*. Hence it can be considered the patterning of order and organization as revealed in the activity of *ch'i*. Different activities of *ch'i* give rise
to different *li*. Different degrees of intensity of the activity of *li* give rise to
different degrees of the actualization of *ch'i* in the world of related events.
Thus Wang said: "*Ch'i* is that which *li* depends on. If *ch'i* flourishes, then *li*
reaches its end. The heaven has assembled the strong *ch'i*, therefore it
exhibits the patterning of order in things, and the changes are subtle and

ever new."[18] Here, the so-called heaven (*t'ien*) is the actual movement of *c'hi as seen in everything. The strong ch'i is ch'i* at its height of activity. *Li*, in this context, clearly has no independence but is a matter of the inner manifestation of *ch'i*. It can be said that *li* is the functioning of *ch'i*. "That which makes *li* materialize, on considering their sources, are all fine transformations of the subtleties of heaven and earth. The subtleties of heaven and earth in their movement and interaction do not lose their function of original goodness."[19] The so-called subtleties of heaven and earth are nothing other than *ch'i* in the process of self-transformation.

The ontological state of *li* is undifferentiated from that of *ch'i*. When *li* and *ch'i* are in this undifferentiated state of being, Wang spoke of it as *t'ai-chi*, intended to represent it as a perfect circle, and referred to it as *li-ch'i*. He said: "Even though *t'ai-chi* is void, *li-ch'i* is full. There is no difference between inner and outer, void and fullness. . . . This *li-ch'i* will become square when meeting square; become a circle when meeting a circle. It is either large or small. It changes and transforms and self-interacts and has no fixed substance."[20] From this view, *li* apparently is *ch'i* and *ch'i* apparently is *li*. The different aspects of this totality of reality gives rise to what we have analytically termed as *li* and *ch'i*. Wang said: "Full between heaven and earth is the interacting change and transformation of reality. It is all my original face. Its beginnings of change (*chi*, small things) is *ch'i*. Its ability of realization (*shen*, spirit) is *li*."[21] He sometimes referred to this totality of reality as heaven (*t'ien*). It is the same as the *t'ai-ho* and *t'ai-hsu* of Chang Tsai, and *ch'i* in its primary sense. That *li* is derived from this *t'ai-ho* and *t'ai-hsu* of *ch'i* is held explicitly by Wang. "The original form of heaven is unity and wholeness. Formless, quantityless, objectless, numberless, it is called purity. Void, one and spacious, it is wherefrom *li* comes."[22] The dynamic identity of *li* and *ch'i* is similar to the dynamic identity of *yin* and *yang* in *ch'i*.

(3) We have indicated that *li* is ontologically undifferentiated from *ch'i* and yet cosmologically is a mode of the actuality of *ch'i*, which consists in being the tendency of the *ch'i*-activity toward order and organization. Now we shall advance to the aspect of *li* that depicts the explicit order and organization the *ch'i*-activities achieve and the resulting world that displays this order and organization. Wang asserted that "*Li* is the order conspicuously exhibited by heaven."[23] He said that "*Li* is not something which cannot change and cannot be seen. The pattern and order or *ch'i* are what can be seen in *li*. Therefore in the beginning there is *li*, and this means that one can see *li* in *ch'i*. As *li* obtains, it forms a natural tendency [in *ch'i*] and one can see *li* in the necessity of the natural tendency [in *ch'i*]."[24] When *li* is actually presented in *ch'i*, *li* is to be conceived in concrete terms. It is

no more than the tendency toward order and organization and no more than the very order and organization displayed in things. The concrete patterns and orders of concrete things are based on the general types of order and organization of reality. Though Wang did not provide much discussion on the general types of order and organization of things, he nevertheless indicated that the general types of order and organization are the principles of change in terms of similarity, difference, contraction, expanding, etc. The general view is that, as *ch'i* has different degrees of actualization and types of activity, the realization of *li* also correlates with the *ch'i*-activity on different levels and in different degrees. As *ch'i* will reach a full realization of nature, so *li* as an inherent aspect of *ch'i* also will reach a full realization of order and organization, again on different levels and in different forms.

Now if we concentrate on the relation between *tao* and *ch'i* (utensils, things) in Wang's discussion, we shall be able to see a close relation between the generalized *li* in the general *ch'i*-activity and the particularized *li* in the particular *ch'i*-activity. The actualized world of *ch'i* (vapor, indeterminate reality) is the world of *ch'i* (utensils, things). "*Ch'i*" (utensils, things) has been used in contrast to *tao* in the tradition of the Sung interpretation of the *Book of Changes*. But in Wang's use, *tao* and *ch'i* are related in the following ways. *Tao*, according to him, is the *tao* of *ch'i*, but *ch'i* is not the *ch'i* of *tao*.[25] This position is one of stressing the fundamental importance of *ch'i*, not *tao*. As we have seen, *tao* is merely the tendency toward order and stability in *ch'i*, and *ch'i* in its primordial sense is the basis of *tao*. Thus he asked, "If we have the *ch'i*, should we worry about *tao*?" He asserted that "If there is no *ch'i*, there will be no *tao*."[26] The implications are not merely that if there is such a *tao*, there is such a *ch'i*, but also that given any *ch'i*, its *tao* will ensue as a consequence. He held that there is no case where you have an arrow and bow and you do not have archery, or where you have a carriage and horse, but no charioteering, or where there is son but no *tao* of the father, or where there is a younger brother but no *tao* of the elder brother. He sees the possibility that some *tao* may possibly exist, but does not actually exist, simply because there is no corresponding *ch'i*. To say that *tao* may possibly exist means simply that the potentiality of achieving *li* is always inherent in the *ch'i*-activity.

By making *tao* dependent on *ch'i*, Wang showed that *li* (whose total presentation is *tao*) is dependent on *ch'i* (vapor, indeterminate things) and must realize itself in concrete objects (*ch'i*). *Li* will not be *li* in the actual sense until it has full concretization in the world of *ch'i*. One may say that *ch'i* (utensils, things) is the result of the *ch'i*-activity, with its tendency toward order and organization. Thus Wang concluded that the Way of the superior person is nothing other than exhausting the possibility of making *ch'i* possible. He spoke of this with the intent to urge people to develop *ch'i* in order to develop *tao*, or to fulfill the potentiality of *ch'i* (vapor, indeterminate reality) in order to understand *li*. *Li* is a post-*ch'i* production and cannot be grasped in spite of or before the understanding of concrete things.[27] To reinterpret Wang, Wang held that one cannot understand *li* apart from *ch'i*, or *tao* apart from *ch'i* (utensils, things).

(4) A final important aspect of the *li-ch'i* relationship is related to the nature and mind of human beings. The formation of the human mind results from the highest degree of the activity of *ch'i*. It is the realization of the subtle potentiality of the ultimate reality. The existence of an individual therefore exhibits the most valuable potential of reality and yet is related to everything else in the process of change and transformation. This is a Confucian position that all Confucianist philosophers, including the Neo-Confucianists of Sung-Ming, hold in common. For Wang, what is significant is that the nature and mind that distinguish an individual as human are not alienated from the primordial reality of *ch'i*. They are not something that have an independent substance over and above *ch'i*. On this basis, Wang was skeptical about Ch'eng Yi's claim that "mind, nature and heaven are just one *li*."[28] This latter statement, in light of the centrality of *li* in Ch'eng-Chu's philosophy, often has been understood as indicating the fundamental nature of *li*. But for Wang, the human mind and nature share with heaven and *li* the fundamental base of *ch'i* (vapor, indeterminate reality), for they are regarded as derived from *ch'i*. He said, "For to speak of mind, nature, heaven, and *li*, we must speak of them on the basis of *ch'i*. If there is no *ch'i*, there are none of them."[29]

Furthermore, the human mind is considered to be an embodiment of *li*, for the mind is made possible by the transformation of *ch'i*. Wang even seemed to define *li* as that which is realized in the human mind, just like that which is realized in heaven is defined as phenomena (*hsiang*), and that which is realized in things is defined as numbers (*shu*) and patterns.[30] On the basis of this given point, *li* is the recognition of the patterns and orders of things in the mind. This is further evidenced by the statement: "The ten thousand things all have fixed functions and the ten thousand affairs all have natural regularities. The so-called *li* are the *li* of these. They are what man can necessarily know and practice. There is no other *li* in that which man cannot know and practice. Possessing this *li*, man's knowledge is not obscured and man's action will not be dubious. This is the so-called mind. *Li* is the substance of the human mind, and the mind is where *li* is deposited and stored."[31] In the light of this, *li* now can be considered a conscious understanding of the order and regularities of nature and the mind. It is a matter of knowledge and a principle of reason. In fact, it is in regard to the mind that *li* can now be identified with reason in the proper sense. *Li* thus receives a subjective specification apart from its objective characterization in terms of order. On this level, Wang would have agreed with Wang Yang-ming on saying that mind is *li*. But he would not have taken "is (*ch'i*)" as indicating identity, but merely as indicating that the mind is *li*, while many of the things are *li* as well. He would have qualified this further by saying that many other things are *li* because *li* is fundamentally *ch'i*; namely, the activity or the result of the activity of *ch'i*. Wang explicitly held that "what the human mind obtains before experience, from the sage to the common people, are the good capacities [of the mind] due to the activity of *ch'i*."[32]

Wang also seemed to have no reason to disagree with the view that nature is *li*, if it is understood that the nature of human beings and other things reveal an order that humans can understand and yet is not the unique and exclusive area where *li* is to be found or the unique and exclusive level on which *li* is to be identified. At the same time, *li* again is understood as derived from *ch'i*. The fallacy of "*hsin* (mind) is *li*," or "*hsing* (nature) is *li*" is twofold from this point of view: (1) *li* is identified with the narrow area identified with *hsin* or *hsing*; (2) the fundamental nature of *li* is taken for granted. Given the interpretation of *li*, *hsin*, and *hsing* in terms of *ch'i*, Wang could accept the proposition "*hsin* is *li*" and the proposition "*hsing* is *li*" without committing the fallacy that Wang Yang-ming and Ch'eng-Chu respectively committed. Apart from the fact that *li* and *hsing* are commonly derived from *ch'i*, *li* and *hsing* are related furthermore in the relation specified by the proposition that *hsing* is the *li* of *sheng* (living and life-activity). Nature is what is endowed in an individual, but it is also the order of living proper to an individual. It defines the concrete process of living and its characteristics. Now, to say that *hsing* is the *li* of *sheng* is to say that: (1) *li* is derived from *hsing*, just as the pattern of a concrete object is derived from the object; (2) *li* is recognized by the mind and the mind is derived from *hsing*. Wang said: "*Li* generated from *hsing*, and desires develop from material forms."[33] "*Hsing* generates knowledgeability and knowledgeability knows nature, converges in the center of the void, and is unified in the oneness of mind. From this we have *hsing* as *hsin*."[34] "What is natural of the *li* of heaven, being the comprehensive capacity of the *ch'i* of *t'ai-ho*, is nature, fixed in man and folded in form. The function of form which gives rise to the knowing capacity is the mind."[35] Thus we can use mind to exhaust nature, use nature to correlate with *tao*, and use *tao* to sense heaven.

Finally, we note that for Wang nature is continually in the process of growth and generation. It is not something that is absolutely determined, but involves the possibility of change and transformation. This is so because nature is made from *ch'i*, with its inner dynamics of change. Wang said: "*Hsing* is the *li* of *sheng*. Before death an individual is always living, there is always time for the individual to obey necessity and receive nature. When first born, the individual realizes a quantity of nature, and daily it receives the reality of nature."[36] "*Hsing*, is the *li* of *sheng*. It grows everyday and accomplishes everyday."[37] In the light of this dynamic growth of nature, *li* also can be said to grow and change. The unchangeability of *li* in Sung-Ming Neo-Confucianism thus is rejected. Again, the reason is not hard to seek, for *li* is ultimately an aspect of *ch'i* and *ch'i* is change in its nature.

The *li-yü* Relationship, as Based on the *li-ch'i* Relationship in Wang Fu-Chih

As *li* and *ch'i* are opposed to each other in Sung-Ming Neo-Confucianism, so *li* and *yü* are naturally opposed to each other. To put this differently, the dualism between *li* and *yü* was advocated initially, and the ontological dualism between *li* and *ch'i* was developed to provide a basis for the separation between *li* and *yü*. Now, as Wang Fu-chih has developed a doctrine of cosmological and ontological unity between *li* and *ch'i*, it is natural to expect that the relationship between *li* and *yü* in his moral philosophy will be one of unity and complementation as well. In fact, I believe that it is by recognizing the fundamental unity between *li* and *ch'i* in metaphysics that one can have a correct understanding of the *li-yü* relationship in the philosophy under discussion. In light of this it is clear that *li*, when applied to humankind, should have at least two senses: First, *li* is the order and pattern naturally realized in human nature. It is the natural reason of human beings. Second, *li* should be the recognition and understanding of the order and organization of things in the objective world. Both senses of the term are found in Wang. The references to the generalization of nature, mind, and the knowing capacity of the mind amply testify to these points.

There are two more senses in which *li* can be applied to human existence. These two further senses of *li* are directly related to the ontology of *ch'i*, as well as bearing on the existence of *yü*. They were not made explicit by Wang, but they are important for explaining why there are *yü* and why *yü* should be conceived in unity with *li*. First, *li*, in human nature, is essentially a manifestation of the *ch'i*-activity, being the most refined *ch'i*. In this sense, *li* is an active principle similar to *yü*, as *yü* is no less a creation of *ch'i*. *Li* and *yü* therefore are mutually transformable on the level of the *ch'i*-activity in metaphysics. Second, *li* is the general potential that is directed toward the perfection of nature. It is a principle that should relate an individual to other individuals and to the total reality for the full development of the individual. In this sense, *li* can be understood as a result of the creation of the conditions for such an attainment of perfection. It is, in fact, the practice of virtue that will satisfy the individual.

We can say that the preceding four senses of *li* as applied to humankind correspond to the four metaphysical senses of *li* in the last section. In understanding *li* in these four senses, we can then clearly see that *li* is in no way opposed to *yü*, when *yü* is properly understood, but instead can be understood as the embodiment of *yü*, just as *yü* in a proper sense can be understood as an embodiment of *li*.

Let us therefore concentrate on Wang's understanding of *yü*. In the first place, Wang considered *yü* as a natural activity of life. Insofar as *yü* is natural, it forms a pattern and an order and constitutes the existence of *li*. In fact, by the abstraction principle of *ch'i* (utensils, things), the existence of *yü* should be already a display of *li*. *Yü* (desires), such as those for food and sex, are nothing undesirable in themselves; they are matters of the natural realization of life. One cannot talk of *li* apart from *yü*; for, given any *li*, it must be embodied in the actual actions of life. As *yü* is the activity of life, *yü* must be found for the very understanding of *li*. Hence, Wang held that "*li* and *yü* are both natural."[38] "*Li* and *yü* mutually transform each other. If there is *yü*, there must be *li*. *Li* and *yü* go together even though they are different in quality. But *li* is endowed in *yü*."[39] The question here is how *li* and *yü* go together, can mutually transform, and yet can differ in quality. One answer is very simple. For Wang, *li* in all senses can be *yü*, but *yü* can be *li* only in the first and the third senses of *li*. *Yü* is itself a natural manifestation of life, but not a reflection of the mind on life, as *li* can be considered. As such, *yü* differs from the *li* of the mind or the knowing capacity. But, *yü* also can be different from *li* in another sense; namely, *li* can be formed as a desire (*yü*) tending toward the realization of an individual in the whole reality, whereas *yü* is simply a desire without such a tendency. In other words, *li* is *yü* universalized or universalizable in regard to all people, but *yü* is more or less localized in a person without such universalization.

In insisting that for every *yü* there is one *li*, Wang did not ignore the phenomenological difference between *li* and *yü*. His stress on the identity of *yü* and *li* is to be understood in the fundamental sense of metaphysics, as well as in the sense that *li* and *yü* can be made to realize each other. What is significant for him is that he believed that such a mutual realization was not only possible, but necessary for life. He said: "The sage has desires. His desires are the *li* of heaven. Heaven has no desires, *li* is the *yü* of man. A learning man has both *li* and *yü*. To exhaust *li* one will conform to the desires of man. To extend *yü* one will conform to the *li* of *t'ien*."[40] This passage clearly indicates that the *li* of ontology is precisely the natural human desires and that a thorough understanding of *li* will lead to the affirmation of the importance of *yü*.

This last point can be further developed, for it indicates how *yü* and *li* can be mutually transformed. They are mutually transformable, because to universalize *yü* would be to achieve *li*, and to seek *li* to the utmost will lead to affirming *yü*. This is clearly an implicit criticism bearing on Sung-Ming Neo-Confucianism, in that it had advanced the opposition between *li* and *yü*, simply because it did not see *li* in totality and did not face *yü* in actuality. According to the very principle just cited, for Wang, the only way to realize the *li* of the whole world is to fulfill *yü* for each individual. This is not saying that *yü* should be fulfilled merely as such; but it should instead be fulfilled in the total network of *yü*, which is fulfillment in others and in everyone. This is the very way to achieve political order, social harmony, familial stability, and individual well-being. Thus Wang said, "On this basis, we see that man's desires respectively obtain and this is the great unity of heaven's *li*. The great unity of heaven's *li* is not different from the individual desires respectively fulfilled. To govern people there is a way, and this is the way. To obey the superior there is a way, and this is the way. To deal with friends there is a way, and this is the way. To be filially pious to parents there is a way, and this is the way. To realize one's person there is a way, and this is the way."[41] On this basis, Wang argued for the unity of principle or the Way in Confucius. The unity, in other words, is achieved by universalizing *yü* and therefore by transforming *yü* into *li* (and vice versa) in reality.

It is puzzling that, although denouncing the Buddhists for abandoning worldly duty and demolishing life, the Sung-Ming Neo-Confucianists themselves also looked down upon the *yü* of life. Perhaps, what they sought to denounce were the partial desires or the desires that were not or could not be universalized. But in denouncing these desires, because of their *ch'i* background, they would thereby denounce all desires. Wang did not denounce them, because he saw them as a manifestation of nature and saw their satisfaction as a perfection of nature. The very ordering of life in terms of *li* (rites) depends on the realization and fulfillment of *yü*. Thus he said: "Even though *li* is purely the patterns of order of the heavenly *li*, it must be embodied in human desires in order to be seen. Even though we remain in rest and do not have the regularity for feeling or commitment, one has to manifest the function of [life] through *yü* on the occasions of change. Then, there cannot be heaven apart from man and cannot be *li* apart from *yü*."[42] *Yü* embodies *li*, just like *ch'i* embodies *tao*. We may even extend the metaphysical principle that we have to create *ch'i* (things) in order to fulfill *tao*, to the case of *yü*; we have to create *yü* in order to fulfill *li*. We also can say that *li* is the *li* of *yü*, and *yü* is not the *yü* of *li*, as Wang said that *tao* is the *tao* of *ch'i*, but that *ch'i* is not the *ch'i* of *tao*. *Yü* is the subject, *li* is a characteristic of the subject. There could be characteristic of a subject in separation from the subject. Wang thought that Buddhism was mistaken simply because it believed that there was such a subjectless characteristic called *li*. This criticism applies to some Neo-Confucianists as well.

To say that *li* is not separable from *yü* is not to imply that every kind of *yü* has a *li* that is conducive to the good of life. In discussing the *li-yü* relationship in Wang, it is important to understand that the ultimate *li* of life (which is nature) is that one should search for a full development of the potential in others, which also constitutes a basis and a justification of one's own development of the potential in oneself. Thus, the universalization principle is the basis for fulfilling one's desires, as well as the principle for fulfilling one's *li*.

We may now suggest a distinction between desirable and undesirable desires. The desirable desires are those we naturally experience and apply to everyone, whereas the undesirable desires are those we do not naturally have but instead are caused by external circumstances and, therefore, do not apply to every situation or person. Wang implicitly made this distinction. In his doctrine of "where there is a *yü*, there is *li*," he held as a theoretical consequence of his metaphysics of *li-ch'i*, that any *yü* or any kind of *yü* should be fulfilled in the name of its *li*. Rather, he would hold that if there is a *yü* or a type of *yü* that has its *li* and that can be universalized, it should be fulfilled. We have suggested that the universalizable *yü* are desires that everyone can experience naturally. Wang stated, "Thus in [desires of] sound, color, smell and taste, one will openly see the common desires of the ten thousand things and see it in the *li* of the ten thousand things."[43] In other parts of his commentaries on the Four Books, Wang always stressed this point; namely, that to fulfill the natural desires is to reach the public *li* of heaven, and that there is no incompatibility between private natural desires and the public *li*.[44] He also said: "Availing my heart of self-love, I can reach the *li* of loving others. For I and others share the same feelings and thus share the same *tao*. The universality of human desires is the ultimate righteousness of the *li* of heaven."[45]

We may summarize our conclusions on the *li-yü* relationship in Wang Fu-chih in the following theses:

1. In every *yü* there is a *li*.
2. In the universalizable *yü* there is the heavenly *li* of life.
3. To denounce *yü* is ultimately to denounce life (*sheng*).
4. To fulfill a *li* or reason, one has to fulfill the corresponding *yü*.

5. A well-cultured person should be able to see *yü* everywhere in life
and see *li* everywhere in life.

We have discussed and made clear 1, 2, and 4. We should now say something
about 3 and 5 as the final characteristics of the *li-yü* relationships in Wang.
As we noted, Wang opposed the Buddhist doctrine of the extinction of life,
as life for him was nothing but the movement of the world (*t'ien-hsia-chih-
tung*), which in the human case constituted the reality of *yü*. He said that
"desires develop because there are forms."[46] But there must be forms, and
the inherent goal of the *ch'i*-activity is to fulfill, preserve, and develop them.
Thus, *yü* has the great significance of actually exhibiting the forms of life,
not simply reflecting them (as in mind). *Yü* thus is the foundation of the
reality of human existence. To denounce it is to denounce the living reality
of humanity and to relapse into the views of the Buddhists and Taoists.
Wang said: "Thus to look down upon forms [of life] is to look down upon
the natural feelings (*ch'ing*) [of life]. To do so would be to look down upon
life. . . . To separate from life must involve saying that emptiness is real, and
life is illusory, thus promoting the doctrines of the Buddhists and Taoists."[47]

Finally, human nature is realized in the activities of the mind that constitute *li* in a certain sense, as well as in the natural activity of needs and
desires (*yü*). There is a unity between *yü* and *li*, as there is an ontological
unity in nature (*hsing*). The unity can be understood as one of consciously
identifying *yü* with *li* in experience as well as in knowledge. One needs
cultivation to do this, for it is a metaphysical fact that requires comprehension and concentration of the mind. Wang believed that by understanding
reality as such, one would be able to come to see *yü* as *li* and *li* as *yü*
everywhere in life. He held that this is true of Confucius and Mencius. He
said, "Mencius inherits learning from Confucius. He sees desire everywhere
in life and this is to see *li* everywhere in life."[48] The point of this passage, we
may note nevertheless, is that we must be creative in making *li* an achievement of *yü* and *yü* an achievement of *li* both ontologically acceptable and
justifiable in the *ch'i*-activity of life.

The *li-ch'i* and *li-yü* Relationships in Yen Yuan (1635-1704) and Li Kung (1659-1753)

In my opinion, Wang constituted the stronghold of the seventeenth-
century antidualistic naturalism in both Confucian metaphysics and morality. The philosophy of Wang Fu-chih not only formed a basis for a critique
of Sung-Ming Neo-Confucianism, but also provided a foundation for a new
reconstruction of the Confucian doctrines. This tendency was reinforced

by Yen Yuan, and was given a clear and powerful expression in the eighteenth century writings of philosophers such as Tai Tung-yuan and Chiao Hsüen. For the purpose of making clear the major trend of thinking in Confucianism during the seventeenth century, we shall take Wang as our model. Our detailed statement and analysis of his position on *li-ch'i* and *li-yü* is made in light of this general reflection on the seventeenth-century Confucian rethinking.

In general, Yen Yuan subscribed to the same antidualistic naturalism in moral and metaphysical philosophy as did Wang Fu-chih. On the one hand, he did not possess the metaphysical bent of Wang, nor was he as interested in formulating a metaphysics of *li-ch'i* and *li-yü* with the refined sophistication of Wang. But, on the other hand, he was more explicitly critical of the Sung-Ming Neo-Confucianism and Buddhism than was Wang. Furthermore, he was distinguished by his great stress on pragmatic action and the living practice of the Confucian arts as a way of cultivating the Confucian life. We shall see that this pragmatic stress provides a more realistic and clearer basis for achieving the unity of *li* and *yü* in life than did the other seventeenth century philosophers, including Wang Fu-chih.

We shall first focus on the *li-ch'i* relationship in Yen Yuan. Yen was opposed to Neo-Confucianism in the Sung-Ming period, for he regarded it as an artificial conformity to the Confucian form, without the Confucian substance. He regarded both the Ch'eng-Chu school and the Lu-Wang school as deviating from the authentic practice of the Confucianism of the pre-Ch'in period and as faintly mirroring Buddhist quietism and Ch'an artificiality. According to him, the Neo-Confucianists in Sung-Ming shared with the Taoists and the Buddhists the belief that the natural human endowments (*ch'i-ping*) were evil and that nonbeing was better than being. He feared that the prevalence of this belief would lead people down blind roads and destroy their true life and true character. Because of this fear, he wrote the essays "Preserving Learning" and "Preserving Nature." The former was intended to explain that *tao* consists not in empty speculation nor in the pedantic accumulation of scholarship, but in the actual observance of virtues and the practice of the arts and rites useful for life. The latter work was intended to clarify the positions that *li* and *ch'i* are both ways of heaven, that nature and form are both mandates of heaven, and that human nature and human destiny, though differing in different temperaments, are both good. "Temperaments and natural endowments are functions of the nature and destiny of man and cannot be called evil."[49] From this perspective, it is clear that the primary goals for Yen's thinking of the *li-ch'i* relationship are to justify the goodness of *ch'i-chih* or the human natural endowments so that individuals could develop them fully in action.

Though he considered *li* and *ch'i* as being equal to *t'ien-tao*, he particularly held *ch'i* to be more fundamental than *li*. Like Wang Fu-chih, he accepted a *ch'i*-cosmology, and on this basis explained all the kinds of things and changes in the world in terms of the activity of *ch'i*. He spoke of *ch'i* as the true *ch'i* of the cosmos (*yu-chou-chen-ch'i*) and as "the living of the cosmos" (*yu-chou-sheng-ch'i*).[50] *Ch'i* is not separate from life-activity, for the very characteristic of *ch'i* is that it is the basis for life-generation. Of course, it is not as clear as in Wang whether *ch'i* has this life-generating creativity. But overall, Yen took the very phenomenon of life-generating life (*sheng-sheng*) as a basic reality in which *ch'i* is involved. He said:

Heaven and earth interact and interchange and generate the ten thousand things. The number of classes of living things in the sky, land and water are beyond detection. The subtlety of the combination of forms is beyond exhaustion. All are natural manifestation of heavenly *li*. All that gives life is called male. All that accomplishes [life] is called female. Male and female conjoin and coalesce and there is no ceasing of life-generating. Life-generation [depends] on *ch'i*, which is the *ch'i* of heaven, and the form which is the form of earth. In life generation, the *ch'i* of heaven is assimilated and the form of earth absorbed. Heaven and earth are therefore the great parents of the ten thousand things. Parents are those which transmit the change and transformation of heaven and earth. Man is the only existent which receives the complete ingredients of heaven and earth, and thus is the most refined among the ten thousand things.[51]

In this passage, it is clear that Yen has identified *ch'i* and form (*hsing*) with heaven and earth. Thus, as heaven and earth are the parents of all things, *ch'i* and form should be considered the originators of all things.

Given *ch'i* as the fundamental basis of all things, *li* has no independent ontological nature apart from being the patterns of order in the things generated by *ch'i*. In *Commentary on the Four Books (Shih Shu Chen Wu)*, Yen Yuan explicitly pointed out that "*Li* is the pattern of organization in wood, and in wood there are originally patterns of organization."[52] Conceived in this fashion, *li* is not separate from *ch'i*, and is to be realized only in the objects produced by *ch'i*. They are the characteristics, such as length, shortness, etc., of the objects. In particular, the *li* of humankind is precisely what is revealed in the organization of humankind as a natural product of heaven and earth. Thus he said, "The true *li* of the human mind is the life-generating *li* of the human mind."[53] Furthermore, the *li* of humankind is the natural human disposition that calls the nature (*hsing*) of humankind, and that is developed from *ch'i* and the powers of heaven and earth. He said, "The two *ch'i* [*yin and yang*] and four powers [metal, wood, water, earth] are man not coalesced; man is the two *ch'i* and four powers already coalesced."[54] Because the *li* of humankind is nature and nature is made of primordial *ch'i*, human nature can give rise to the feelings that are the basis for virtues.

At this point we may mention Yen's criticism of an inconsistency in Ch'eng-Chu's thinking. To show this inconsistency he quoted Cheng-I's statements that "In talk of nature (*li*) and *ch'i*, to make two of them is not right," and that "Some are good from childhood; some are bad from childhood. This is so because of natural endowments." He also quoted Chu Hsi's statements that "The moment there is *t'ien-ming*, there is *ch'i-chih* (natural endowments). They cannot be separated" and that "There is *li*. How can there be evil? The so-called evil is only *ch'i*." These statements are apparently incoherent and inconsistent, for it is clear that: "If one says that *ch'i* is evil, then *li* is evil; and [if one says that] *li* is good, then *ch'i* is good. For *ch'i* is the *ch'i* of *li*, and *li* is the *li* of *ch'i*. How can one say *li* is purely good and *ch'i-chih*, whereas the brightness of seeing is nature (or *li*), and in order for eyes to see, they must have both. Both eyeballs and the brightness of seeing are heavenly endowed (*t'ien-ming*) and there is no need for separating the nature of heavenly appointments and the nature of *ch'i-chih*. Yen then inferred that "We can only properly say that heaven has determined the nature of eyes, that the brightly seeing of eyes is the goodness of the nature of eyes and that what we actually see is due to the goodness of the feelings of nature. As to how far or how close, how detailed or how loose one can see, that is a matter of one's ability. There is no evil in it."[57] Of course Yen admitted that eyes could see wrong colors, but it is not a wrong of the *ch'i-chih* of the eyes alone; it has to do with the nature of the eye. If one attributes the wrong to the *ch'i-chih* of the eyes, we would have to do away with the eyes. This, concluded Yen, is a doctrine of Buddhism. The total effect of Yen's criticism, however, is a result of his antidualistic naturalism of *ch'i*. As he from the very beginning rejects the bifurcation between *ch'i* and *li*, he could not see how Ch'eng-Chu could make their points about making the bifurcation between *ch'i* and *li* an ontological principle.

We now come to the *li-yü* relationship in Yen Yuan. Like Wang Fuchih, Yen regarded *yü* as a form of nature and a form of *li*, and thus as a natural way of realizing value and *li*. But more than this, Yen emphasized the continuity of all virtues and the need to satisfy the basic human needs (*yü*). In his essay, "Preserving Man," he questioned whether one could speak of human nature as having *jên* (benevolence) and yet in real life not love one's parents and not wish to continue life. He strongly criticized the Buddhists for their attempt to abolish ethical relations and life's efforts to continue life. He thought that it is impossible to do this and at the same time speak of *jên* and *yi* as the original human nature. *Li*, for him, is something that consistently exhibits itself in all natural feelings and desires. Because there are natural desires, such as sex, one has to face them and satisfy them in order to develop one's nature and fulfill one's potential. This is a way to fulfill the *li* of life. This argument, though only implicit, nevertheless clearly is present in Yen's writings; such as the essay of "Preserving Man." In that essay, Yen called to Buddhist and Taoist monks to return to the secular and practical life. He also called to meditators, foreign monks, philosophers of mere speculation on nature and *ming*, and men of other deviated beliefs to do the same. He said: "Man is the finest among the ten thousand things and how can he alone have no feelings. Thus the attraction between sexes is the great desire of man, and is thus the true feelings and ultimate nature [of man]." Then he asked the monks: "How could you not be moved by these [natural feelings and desires]? I believe that your wish to return to ethical life is a natural inclination."[58]

It is clear that because individuals have desires and needs, the ethical human life is possible and the concrete pragmatic world of actions is possible. For Yen, nothing is more directly related to the fulfillment of *li* than leading an ethical life and participating in the world of actions. He said summarily: "If there is no *ch'i-chih* (the basis for *yü*), there is no nature, and if there is no *ch'i-chih*, nature cannot be seen."[59] Furthermore, in light of the relationship between *hsing* (or *li*) and the use of *hsing* in *ts'ai* (talents), as indicated earlier, Yen held that: "The six actions are the faculty of my nature; the six arts are the capacities of my nature. Since appearances are the discoveries of my nature, the nine virtues are the achievements of my nature. To formulate rites and create music, to harmonize *yin* and *yang*, and to realize an actual universe, are an expansion of my nature. That the ten thousand things are like themselves, earth becomes peaceful, heaven becomes completed, and the cosmos is full of ultimate harmony, is the function of my nature."[60]

Yen naturally asserted that "To realize one's nature to the utmost, one has only to reflect on one's self. To reflect on one's self is to concentrate on reflection, and on the movement and action to be seen in the ten thousand things."[61] He further pointed out that, that the self has a body is a function of my nature, if that one body is not effective, then one function of nature will be missing. From this it is clear that for Yen, *yü* and *shih* (affairs) are parts of *li* and *hsing*, which are exhibited in the functioning of *yü* and *shih*. Thus *li* and *yü* ultimately are related in the relationship of a substance to its functions. The distinguishing mark of Yen's doctrine is that the functions of the substance (*li* and *hsing*) have to be discharged in the form of the pragmatic cultivation of one's virtues. The metaphysical justification of the functional relationship between *li* and *chi*, however, was the same for Wang as for Yen, as was already made clear.

Li Kung, Yen Yuan's close disciple, followed Yen in promoting the thesis that there is no *li* apart from *ch'i*, and *ch'i* comes before *li*. In his commentary on *Lun Yu*, he stressed that there are no *li* and *tao* beyond the activity of *yin* and *yang* and the ethical relationships and actual affairs of people. He held strongly to the principle that *li* is an a posteriori characteristic of *shih* (affairs), for it is only when there are the affairs of heaven, people, and things, that there are the *li* of these. He said: "These affairs have patterns of order and this is the *li* which is in the affairs."[62]

The *li-ch'i* and *li-yü* Relationships in Huang Tsung-Hsi (1610-1695), Ch'en Ch'üeh (1604-1677), Li Erh-chu (1627-1705), and Fang Yi-chih (1611-1671)

Huang Tsung-hsi, as an intellectual historian and a thinker with deep concerns for his time, contributed to the formation of the philosophical opinions of the seventeenth century through his activities and writings, which include his great work, *Philosophical Cases of Ming Confucianists.* Even though Huang had lineage in the school of *hsin-hsueh* (the philosophy of mind of Lu-Wang), he made objective criticisms about the disasters of *hsin-hsueh* in the Ming era. In the first place, he suspected that the idealistic doctrine of the pure perceptive mind as the basis of reality is very close to the Buddhist view. He said "[When "*hsin-hsueh*" comes to [Wang] Lunghsi, *liang-chih* (innate faculty of moral goodness) is regarded as the Buddhanature, and one hopes for the awakening air, and thus ends up in mere games [of ideas]."[63]

In general, Huang Tsung-hsi was sympathetic to Wang Yang-ming's philosophy of mind, yet opposed to conceiving ultimate reality in an absolutely void mind, independent of one's experience of self. He stressed the efforts of self-cultivation for the attainment of truth. He furthermore attempted to reinterpret Wang Yang-ming's statement that the ultimate reality of the mind is without good and evil as meaning that when the ultimate reality of the mind has no good or evil intentions, it is not good nor evil.[64] The point of this reinterpretation is a very profound one. It consists in making a distinction between the ultimate reality of the mind and the mind, a distinction that Wang Yang-ming failed to make. The ultimate reality of the mind is not necessarily the same as the mind; for, unlike the mind, it may have no good and evil intentions. Yet, it is not independent of good or evil. If we take good and evil as a relation and an activity, then this implies that in Huang Tsung-hsi the ultimate reality of the mind bears upon the relationship and activity of life that can be judged as good and evil.

At this point, one may query, what is this ultimate reality of the mind and how it is relation to the relationship of *li-ch'i*? Even though we have no explicit and systematic answer to this question, we have good reason to believe that Huang could take this ultimate reality of the mind as being fundamentally *ch'i* and derivatively *li*. In the first place, Huang praised his master-teacher Liu Tsung-chou's doctrine that there is no *li* apart from *ch'i*, as a matter of resolving the doubt of ten thousand years.[65] Of course, the doubt of the ten thousand years is how *li* and *ch'i* are related and whether *li* comes before *ch'i*.[66] According to this view, the ultimate reality of the mind apparently is nothing but *ch'i*. Huang concluded that, separated from *ch'i*, there is no so-called *li*; and, separated from the mind (flow of *ch'i*), there is no *hsing*.[67] In his preface to Liu's collected works, Huang further said: "For full between heaven and earth, there is merely nature of *ch'i-chih* (natural endowments), and no nature of *yi-li* (righteousness and reason). If one holds there being nature of *yi-li* without falling into nature of *ch'i-chih*, he simply makes no sense."[68] Furthermore, Huang was sympathetic to Lo Chin-shun and stressed Lo's statement that, throughout heaven and earth and throughout ancient and present times, there is nothing but *ch'i*.[69] In his record of the Wang Yang-ming school in Che-tung, he criticized Chi Pen for contrasting *li* as the way of *yang* with *ch'i* as the way of *yin*. In his view, the great transformation (*ta-hua*) is only one *ch'i*: the ascending tendency of which is *yang*, and the descending tendency of which is *yin*. Thus he concluded that *yin* and *yang* are merely *ch'i*, and the only *li* is the *li* of *yang* and *yin*, which naturally cannot be separated from the activity of *ch'i* itself.[70]

In the second place, Huang held that there is no *li* apart from *ch'i*, in the sense that *ch'i* changes whereas *li* should not remain unchanged. For him, *li* changes in relation to *ch'i* and is merely a characteristic of concrete things. From this point of view, he criticized Hsieh Hsuan, who, though holding that there is no *li* without *ch'i*, said that *ch'i* could accumulate and disperse, whereas *li* could not. Hsieh advanced the following example to explain this point:*Li* is like sunlight, whereas *ch'i* is like flying birds. The birds can fly everywhere, but sunlight stays the same.[71] Huang retorted that given this analogy, one can say that there could be sunlight but no flying birds and there could be flying birds but no sunlight. Thus, this analogy to show the relation of *li* to *ch'i* is not a good one. Huang explicitly commented that consequently: "Speaking from the point of view of the unity of the great virtue, as *ch'i* has no limitation, so *li* has no limitation. Thus, not only *li* has no concentration and dispersion, *ch'i* also has no concentration and dispersion. From the point of view of the diversity of small virtues, [*ch'i* and *li*] renew themselves everyday; [we cannot take] the bygone *ch'i* as *ch'i* just coming, [nor can we] take the bygone *li* as *li* just coming. [Thus], not only *ch'i* has concentration and dispersion, *li* has also concentration and dispersion."[72] It is clear from this that Huang would regard *li* and *ch'i* not only as coextensive in scope, but as qualitatively the same in terms of change. What is significant to note is that in, this context, *li*, for Huang like for Wang Fu-chih, has no initial claim to unchangeability or independence from concrete things. There could not be any reason for this other than the ontological conviction that *li* is only a characteristic of *ch'i*.

In light of his naturalism about the unity of *li-ch'i*, it is natural to expect Huang to hold the unity of *li-yü* in human self-realization. This generally is true in Huang, but this aspect of the *li-yü* relationship is perhaps better represented in Ch'en Chueh (1604-1677), who was Huang's fellow student under Liu Tsung-chou (1578-1645). Like Huang, Ch'en was highly critical of Ch'eng-Chu, to the extent that Ch'en even argued that *Ta Hsueh* (the *Great Learning*) is not a classic of the Confucian tradition, as Ch'eng-Chu held. Ch'en was opposed to the view of resting at supreme goodness in *Ta Hsueh*, to which Ch'eng-Chu subscribed. Ch'en further was opposed to the multiple separation of *hsing*, *ch'i*, *ts'ai* (capabilities), and *ch'ing* (feelings) and held, like Yen Yuan, that "the heavenly *li* is just to be seen in human desires, where desires exactly fit is where *li* of heaven is."[73] It can be noted, that in some way, Ch'en's view on *li-yü* reflects Liu Tsung-chou's philosophy, just like Huang's view on the *li-ch'i* relationship reflects Liu Tsung-chou's philosophy.

Among all of seventeenth century thinkers, Li Erh-ch'u (1627-1705), perhaps, was the most conservative, at least as shown in his attempt to preserve the idealistic philosophy of Wang Yang-ming by way of assimilating the doctrines of *ke-wu* (investigating things) together with the *chih-chih* (reaching and extending knowledge) of Ch'eng-Chu. But, nevertheless, he exhibited the seventeenth century's philosophical spirit of pragmatism in advocating the importance of social action and the practice of virtues. He further stressed the inseparability of *ch'i-chih* and *hsing*. This, of course, implies the *li-ch'i* unity thesis. In general, he took *ch'i* in specific cases as a means for realizing the goodness of *hsing* (or *li*).[74] In this regard, he was not as strong and explicit in spelling out the unity between *ch'i* and *li* and neglected the ethical application of this principle to the unity of *li* and *yü*. But he was significant in that, even though he was under the strong influence of Sung-Ming Neo-Confucianism, he did not try to follow its instructions on the duality of *li* and *ch'i* and the desirability of eliminating *yü*.

Finally, we wish to mention a seventeenth century philosopher, Fang Yi-chih (1611-1671), whose views have been scarcely recounted. Fang was important in advancing some novel ideas in regard to the understanding of *li* and its relationship to *ch'i*. He was under the influence of the scientific knowledge brought to China by the Jesuits in his time. Indeed, we may say that the most remarkable contribution in the seventeenth century rationalism and naturalism of the *li-ch'i* relationship was achieved by Fang's efforts to explicitly relate *li* to scientific study, as shown in his unique book *Small Insights into Principles of Things* (*Wu Li Hsiao Shih*).

Fang held without ambiguity that between heaven and earth are physical things (*wu*), which include mind, nature, and necessity.[75] He said: "Heaven and earth are one *thing*. Mind is one *thing*. Only mind can understand heaven and earth and the ten thousand things. To know the origin of heaven and earth and the ten thousand things is to fulfill one's nature to the utmost."[76] To say that the mind is one thing is to say that it is not essentially different from all of the things in the world, even though the mind does have its own qualities such as the capability of understanding.[77] Then comes the question, what is *li* and how is it related to *ch'i*? In this picture, three things can be said in answer to this question.

First, Fang affirmed that there is no *li* apart from things. *Li* is the physical characteristics of concrete things, and it is also what the mind knows when the mind seeks to know external things. As things in general, including the mind, are transformations of *ch'i*, *li* must be a resulting transformation of *ch'i*. It is the regularity of things. He said, "All are made from *ch'i*. The void is filled by *ch'i*. Things have regularities. The void also has its regularity. From what is manifest we know the hidden and there is not a trace of amissness, because there is regularity. *Li* is capable of being identified in experience. That is how knowledge of the mind is possible."[78]

Second, to confirm our view that, for Fang, *li* is a physical characteristic of things, we must identify things with physical objects. This is what Fang precisely did in *Wu Li Hsiao Shih*. For him, everything comes from *ch'i* and *ch'i* is explicitly described as a physical entity. In his discussion, he pointed to the vapor that one can see in the sunlight or in wintertime as an instance of *ch'i*. He also pointed to the vibration from sounding a drum as another instance of the substantiality of *ch'i*. In this case *ch'i* is identified with air. Perhaps, under the influence of Western science from the Jesuits, he held a special discussion on light and water[79] and treated them as the result of the transformation of *ch'i*. He said, "*ch'i* condenses into shape and then gives rise to light and sound."[80] "When *ch'i* warms up and moves and meets the *yin* (wet), then there is water. Rain comes the same way."[81] In general, he developed the traditional doctrine of the five powers to the point that he considered all physical powers to be due to the workings of *ch'i*.

Besides recognizing the principles that *ch'i* condenses in shapes, stores to give light, and vibrates to give sound, he held that many *ch'i* are not yet condensed, released, or provoked in any form.[82] Thus, if we identify his *ch'i* with matter-energy in modern physics, his view will bear a very close resemblance to modern physical theory. There is no artificiality and difficulty in making such an identification, particularly in light of his general discussion of the relationship of philosophy to scientific studies.

Fang conceived human learning in terms of three fields of study. There is, first of all, the study called "comprehending the fundamental beginnings" (*t'ung-chi*), which consists of tracing the origins of complicated principles of things at rest and in motion. In this sense, *t'ung-chi* is a philosophy in general and metaphysics in particular. Then, there is the study called "inquiry into the natural characters of things" (*chih-ts'e*), which consists of investigating the qualities and tendencies of concrete things and in forecasting the regularity of their changes, on the basis of empirical evidence. Thus, *chih-ts'e* corresponds to the modern theoretical and practical sciences, and covers, as Fang himself recognized, acoustics, optics, medicine, mathematics, and astronomy. Finally, there is the study called "inquiry into principles of government" (*ts'ai-li*), which consists of understanding principles of government, education, ethics, and social ethics and can be said to correspond to the modern social sciences in both their theoretical and practical dimensions. Now, according to Fang, *t'ung-ch'i* is contained in *chih-ts'e*.[83] This means that philosophy and metaphysics are contained in the study of science. The relevance of this point to *li-ch'i* relationships is that there could not be an independent, metaphysical study of *li* apart from the actual study of concrete principles in concrete things. Thus, the study of *li* must begin with the study of concrete cases of *ch'i*. This is the third point in answer to the question regarding the nature of *li* and the relationship of *li-ch'i*.

Not only is *ch'i* more fundamental than *li*, but there is no study of *ch'i* apart from its concrete natures studied in the sciences. Fang, in his time, had the insight to suggest that the *chih-ts'e* in the West then was not complete and that one could make further advances in the study of it. He was aware that the Confucianists, in general, are experts in *ts'ai-li* but weak in *ch'i-ts'e*. In focusing on the importance of *chih-ts'e*, Fang had done his job of denouncing *li-ch'i* dualism and the empty speculation on *li* and *ch'i* in Sung-Ming Neo-Confucianism. He also opened in *chih-ts'e* the road for study of *li* and *ch'i*. Though Fang did not touch on the *li-yü* relationship, it is clear that, in general, he would be in sympathy with the main trend in seventeenth-century thinking on this problem; that is, the trend that *li* and *yü* should not be separated in ethics and instead should be considered a unity in which to realize *yü* is the only way to save and achieve *li* in life.

Conclusion

In the preceding we discussed the *li-ch'i* and *li-yü* relationships in the writings of Wang Fu-chih, Yen Yuan, Li Kung, Huang Tsung-hsi, Ch'en Ch'ueh, Li Erh-chu, and Fang Yi-chih. All have addressed themselves to the *li-ch'i* relationship problem. Most have also discussed the *li-yü* relationship on the basis of the *li-ch'i* relationship. In our analysis, all these philosophers have demonstrated, within degrees of variation, an opposition to Sung-Ming Neo-Confucianism in a framework of antidualistic naturalism in both metaphysics and moral philosophy. The antidualistic naturalism in metaphysics consists of holding principles of the ontological primacy of *ch'i* and the inheritance of *li* in the development of *ch'i*. The antidualistic naturalism in morality consists of holding principles of the inseparability of the fulfillment of *li* from the fulfillment of *yü* and of the intrinsic righteousness and goodness of natural *yü*. We have presented Wang Fu-chi as a standard of the seventeenth-century Confucian antidualistic naturalism, who evidenced every aspect of an an antidualistic naturalistic philosophy, both metaphysical and moral. Then we have compared others with this standard in an attempt to define similarities and differences between Wang and others. All these other philosophers appear to be outstanding in developing or improving on Wang's nondualistic, naturalistic model of reality and humankind. In particular, Yen Yuan adds a pragmatic note to the doctrine and Fang Yi-chih gives the *li-ch'i* relationship a scientific outlook.

We must admit that we have not covered every significant thinker in the seventeenth-century enlightenment atmosphere. Notably, we ignored Ku Yen-wu (1613-1682), Chu Chih-yu (1600-1682), T'ang Chen (1630-1704), Lu Shih-yi (1611-1672), Fu Shan (1607-1682), and Pan Ping-ke (?). All of them have been critical of Sung-Ming Neo-Confucianism in regard to its bifurcation between *li* and *ch'i* and in regard to its idealistic tendencies. All have emphasized the primacy of *ch'i*, or *ch'i* (utensils, things), or *shih* (affairs, events) over *li* and *tao*, and their interconnectedness in a process of development. Some of them, such as T'ang, have further stressed the pragmatism of action over speculation. We should also mention Liu Tsung-chou (1578-1645), a philosopher in the early seventeenth century whose thinking has naturalistic and antidualistic tendencies and whose influences in regard to the problems of *li-ch'i* and *li-yü* relationships, as noted, have been properly manifested in his disciples, Huang Tsung-hsi and Ch'en Chueh. We have not thoroughly traced the seventeenth-century antidualistic naturalism to earlier ages nor sought their impact on later times. But it is not improper to mention, as a final note, that, mainly due to the efforts of Wang Fu-chih, Yen Yuan, and others like them in the seventeenth century, we have the later evolution of the more systematic doctrines of *li-ch'i* and *li-yü* in Tai Chen (1734-1771) and Chiao Hsuen (1763-1820), whose contributions bring new life to Confucian thinking.

Notes

1. In the Madhyamika school, one may say that it is because of the recognition of the irreconcilable contrariness between "is" and "is not" that one must transcend both or go beyond both and do this continually without end.
2. Cf. my paper, "The Neo-Confucian *Li*: Its Conceptual Background and Ontological Types," presented at the Columbia University Colloquium on Oriental Thought and Religion, May 9, 1969.
3. See Wang Wan's work *Ming Tao Pien* (*Essay on Clarifying Tao*); and Wang Ting-hsiang's works *Shen Yen* (*Deliberate Words*) and *Ya Hsu* (*Elegant Statements*).
4. In the light of this writing, we can regard the seventeenth-century philosophers under discussion here as spiritual tutors and forefathers of the antidualistic and naturalistic philosophy of Tai Chen. Furthermore, we hope that this discussion will point out the basic issues involved in Confucian thinking in general and open roads for the contemporary reconstruction of Confucian philosophy.
5. See Wang Fu-chih's *Commentary on Chang Tsai's Cheng Meng, t'ai-ho p'ien*.
6. Ibid.
7. Ibid.
8. Ibid.
9. Ibid.
10. Ibid.
11. See Wang Fu-chih's *Outer Commentary on Chou Yu*, on *hsi-t'zu*, Section 6.
12. Ibid., Section 7.
13. Ibid., Section 5.
14. Ibid., Section 6.
15. From Wang Fu-chih's *Commentary on Chang Tsai's Cheng Meng, t'ai-ho p'ien*.
16. Ibid.
17. Ibid.
18. From Wang Fu-chih's *Ssu Wen Lu* (*Record of Thinking and Questioning*), inner chapters.
19. Ibid.
20. Ibid.
21. Ibid.
22. Ibid.

23. From Wang Fu-chih's *Commentary on Chang Tsai's Cheng Meng, Ch'eng-ming p'ien*.

24. From Wang Fu-chih's *Tu Ssu Shu Ta Ch'uan Shuo (On Reading the Complete Works of the Four Books)*, Book 9.

25. From Wang Fu-chih's *Outer Commentary on Chou Yi*, on *hsi-t'zu*, Section 12.

26. Ibid.

27. Here Wang Fu-chih was strongly opposed to the Taoist principle that one can forget concrete things if one can get the truth in language and one can forget the truth in language if one can get the meaning of truth. *See* ibid., Section 5.

28. Chu Hsi quoted this statement from Chen Yi in his work *Meng Tzu Chi Chu (Assembled Commentary on Mencius)*.

29. From Wang Fu-chih's *Tu Ssu Shu Ta Chuan Shua*, Book 10.

30. Ibid.

31. From Wang Fu-chih's *Ssu Shu Hsun Yi (Explanation of Meanings in the Four Books)*, Section 8.

32. From Wang Fu-chih's *Ssu Wen Lu*, inner chapters.

33. From Wang Fu-chih's *Outer Commentary on Chou Yi*, on *t'un*.

34. From Wang Fu-chih's *Commentary on Chang Tsai's Cheng Meng, tai-ho p'ien*.

35. Ibid., *Ch'eng-ming p'ien*.

36. From Wang Fu-chih's *Ssu Wen Lu*, inner chapters.

37. From Wang Fu-chih's *Shang Shu Yin Yi (Extensions of Meanings in the Book of Documents)*, on *t'ai-chia*, Section 3.

38. From Wang Fu-chih's *Commentary on Chang Tsai's Cheng Meng, Ch'eng-ming p'ien*, Book 3.

39. Ibid.

40. From Wang Fu-chih's *Tu Ssu Shu Ta Chuan Shuo*, Book 4.

41. Ibid.

42. Ibid., Book 8.

43. Ibid.

44. Wang Fu-chih said: "In the private desires of man reside the *li* of heaven" (*Tu Ssu Shu Ta Chuan shuo*, Book 26); and "the expansion of heavenly *li* is not opposed to the desires of man" (ibid., Book 6).

45. Ibid., Book 3.

46. From Wang Fu-chih's *Outer Commentary on Chou Yi*, on *t'un*. We of course note that *yü* and *ch'ing* are basically forms of Wang Fu-chih; for *yü* are the natural human feelings and the natural human feelings are the concrete facts of the human needs and desires.

47. Ibid., on *ta-yu*.

48. From *Tu Ssu Shu Ta Chuan Shuo*, Book 8.

49. From Yen Yuan's *Essay on Preserving Learning*, "Letter to Tai-ch'ang Lu Fu-t'ing hsien-sheng."

50. From *Hsi Chai Chi Yu*, Book 1, "*lieh-hsiang chi-hsu.*"
51. Ibid., Book 6, "Essay on Man."
52. From Yen Yuan's *Ssu Shu Cheng Wu* (*Rectifications on Misinterpretation of the Four Books*), Book 1.
53. From *Hsi Chai Chi Yu*, Book 1, "*lieh-hsiang chi-hsu.*"
54. From Yen Yuan's *Essay on Preserving Nature*, Book 2, "*wang-chien-tu.*"
55. From Yen Yuan's *Essay on Preserving Nature*, Book 1, "On Refuting (Doctrines) of the Badness of the Nature of *ch'i-chih.*"
56. Ibid.
57. Ibid.
58. From Yen Yuan's *Essay on Preserving Man*, "Call to Monks."
59. From Yen Yuan's *Essay on Preserving Nature*, "Comments on *hsing* and *li.*"
60. Ibid., "Illuminating Illustrious Virtues."
61. From Yen Yuan's *Essay on Preserving Man*, "Call to Monks."
62. From Li Kung's *Lun Yu Ch'uan Chu Wen* (*Queries into Commentaries on the Analects*), "Tzu-chang 19."
63. From Huang Tsung-shi's *Ming Ju Hsueh An* (*Philosophical Cases of Ming Confucianists*), "*Ssu-shuo.*"
64. Ibid., "Philosophical Case of Yao-chiang (Wang Yang-ming)."
65. Ibid., "Philosophical Case of Chi-shan (Liu Tsung-chou)."
66. Liu Tsung-chou's view is that "full between heaven and earth is *ch'i*. What is in the human mind is the flow of the one *ch'i.*" Ibid.
67. Ibid.
68. From Huang Tsung-hsi's *Nan Lei Wen Ting*, "Preface to the Collection of Essays of my Former Teacher Chi-shan *hsien-sheng.*"
69. From Huang Tsung-hsi's *Ming Ju Hsüeh An*, "*Chu-ju hsüeh-an*, Section 1."
70. Ibid., "*Che-chung Wang-men hsüeh-an.*"
71. Ibid., "*Ho-tung hsüeh-an.*"
72. Ibid.
73. From Ch'en Ch'ueh's essay, "*Ku-yen, wu-yü tso-shen p'ien*," cited in Huang Tsung-hsi's epitaph on Ch'en Ch'ueh.
74. From Li Erh-ch'u's *Ching Chiang Yu Yao*.
75. From Fang Yi-chih's *Wu Li Hsiao Shih*, "Self-Preface."
76. Ibid., "General Discussion."
77. According to Fang Yi-chih, humankind was born the finest thing in the world. He held that human life resides in the body and the human body resides in the world. See ibid., "Self-Preface."
78. From Fang Yi-chih's *Wu Li Hsiao Shih*, book 1, discussion on *ch'i*.
79. Ibid., discussion on light and water.
80. Ibid., discussion on light.
81. Ibid., discussion on water.

82. Ibid., discussion on four powers and five powers.
83. Ibid., "Self-Preface."

21. Categories of Creativity in Whitehead and Neo-Confucianism

I

After becoming familiar with Whitehead's philosophy, particularly as embodied in Whitehead's book *Process and Reality*, many Chinese philosophers have made the suggestion that Whitehead's philosophy resembles Chinese philosophy to a great measure and therefore is highly comparable to Chinese philosophy.[1] What these Chinese philosophers have in mind when they assess the resemblance between Chinese philosophy and Whitehead's philosophy is that Whitehead had developed a system based upon the fundamental notion of reality as a process of change which has always been the fundamental notion of Chinese philosophy, beginning with the *Book of Changes* (the *I Ching*). I shall point out one more comparable feature between Chinese philosophy and Whitehead's on the basis of methodological considerations.

Any philosophy should be an organic process and an organic unity. It cannot be simply regarded as a system of objective and rigid concepts detached from life. Both Confucianism and Taoism, two indigenous traditions in Chinese philosophy, are intended to provide the means of transforming and cultivating the human mind and life, besides representing an ideal norm of life. In the case of Whitehead, even though he explicitly defines speculative philosophy as the attempt to frame a "coherent, logical, necessary system of ideas" to "interpret experience," his metaphysics of organism as a system of ideas should possess ontological significance of agency and efficacy and should form an important ingredient for the constitution of the world and life. Given this organic view of philosophy, it is clear that both Whitehead's philosophy and Chinese philosophy have more than conceptual resemblance: both would agree that philosophy is real, not merely conceptual. As real entities both philosophies can be regarded as admitting development and creative change as reality itself. Thus the resemblance between Chinese philosophy and Whitehead's philosophy is not a matter of static comparison, but a matter of dynamic interaction. It is not a matter of accomplished actuality but a matter of actuality in the making or a matter of potentiality to be fulfilled. It is possible that all potential differences between Chinese philosophy and Whitehead's philosophy could be resolved in a larger system of interpretation in which all ideas as data of experience have their proper place. The comparison of Chinese philosophy with Whitehead's philosophy therefore becomes not a simple occasion for establishing conceptual resemblances but an opportunity for establishing a richer, more comprehensive, and more meaningful framework in which differences should enrich one another rather than contradict one another.

In suggesting this line of comparison, we do not wish to be dogmatic and blind to the historical conceptual differences between Chinese philosophy and Whitehead's philosophy, especially when we realize that Whitehead's philosophy is a complicated structure of many facets having its roots in ancient Greek tradition, whereas Chinese philosophy involves many schools and authors over a span of 2,000 years. Perhaps we may distinguish a retrospective (historical background) point of view from the prospective point of view which is described above. According to the retrospective view, a philosophy has its roots in intractable historical facts. As historical facts are different, the philosophies which grow from them must be different. In this regard, Chinese philosophy and Whitehead's philosophy are bound to have contents which are different and unrelated insofar as they are respectively related to different experiences in historical contexts. For example, one might point out that the notion of the Primordial Nature of God as a transcending entity is something derivable from Platonism which has no correspondence in Chinese philosophy. One might also point out that the Whiteheadian view that the existence of God is "the ultimate irrationality,"[2] which cannot itself be explained but which should explain the apparent irrationality (non-necessity) of the finite world, is a position derivable from Aristotelian metaphysics which again has no exact correspondence in Chinese philosophy. It is quite plausible that differences between Chinese philosophy and Whitehead's philosophy may interpenetrate and 'interprehend' (to invent a term in the spirit of Whitehead), and form a basis for generating a novel view.

In this chapter I intend mainly to explore parallel conditions of creativity in Whitehead's philosophy and Neo-Confucianism (as provided primarily by Chou Tun-i [1010-1073] and Chu Hsi [1130-1200] as representing two closely related systems of categories of creativity for explaining the phenomena and our experiences of change and novelty.

In saying that these two systems are closely related, I do not intend to suggest that they correspond to each other as mirror images, but rather that they share the same purpose (namely, that of understanding concrete facts of change) and the same intended comprehensiveness of scope (namely, that of covering everything in the world), and approximate to the same orientation in reaching an organic image of life and reality. I believe that we shall see many resemblances in concepts and structures in the cosmological and metaphysical philosophies of the two systems; but we are also interested in revealing essential subtle differences in the definition, orientation, and explanation or analysis of the categories of creativity in the two systems. These differences should warrant our conclusion that, even though these categories resemble each other, they still belong to two different systems. Though we shall not be able to explain why there are such differences, we will be in a position to assess plausible merits and plausible difficulties of the two systems in light of these differences. What I wish to stress is that the closeness of ideas and their implications between the categories of creativity in the two systems should not mislead one into ignoring the subtle differences between the two. I shall therefore explore these two systems of creativity and I shall specifically focus on the central notions of creativity in these two systems. I shall begin with the Whiteheadian category of creativity. Then I shall advance to the Neo-Confucian category of *t'ai-chi* in search of subtle conceptual and ontological differences between the two philosophical systems.

II

Whitehead describes creativity as follows:

Creativity is the universal of universals characterizing ultimate matter of fact. It is that ultimate principle by which the many, which are the universe disjunctively becomes the one actual occasion, which is the universe conjunctively: it lies in the nature of things that the many enter into complex unity.[3]

As an ultimate principle of metaphysics, creativity can only be understood through intuition. That is, one has to intuit the universality of creativity in concrete experiences. Though Whitehead only mentions creativity as the principle of creating one from the many,[4] it is clear that it is also the principle of creating many from the one. It is in this sense we can speak of 'creative advance' of the universe. It is in this sense in which creativity exhibits both the unity and plurality of the universe.

Whitehead also holds that creativity is the principle of novelty; namely, the principle by which novel entities which did not previously exist, come into existence. It is the activity underlying the creation of actual entities, the process referred to as concrescence. Whitehead stresses that "the many become one and are increased by one."[5] This means that any creation of an actual entity is a new event in the universe which exemplifies some quality which is not found existing in past occasions. Since there is no end to the creative process, there is no end to increasing novelty in the world. As part of his explanation of the incessant creative advance of things, Whitehead introduces the category of eternal objects which are infinite in number and which provide a basis for introducing novelty into the changing world. Eternal objects are timeless essences, potentialities to be actualized in time. They cannot be completely exhausted or realized in the process of time or change. But they ingress into the process of change and provide "forms of definiteness" for the formation of concrete entities. That they ingress into the process of change or creation is to be made possible by what Whitehead calls "conceptional prehension" by actual entities. In their first ingression these potentialities are conceptually, not physically, assimilated in the formation of new actual entities. Once they have been conceptually assimilated they can be physically assimilated.

Because of the existence of eternal objects one may see that creativity includes (efficient) causality but that causality does not exhaust creativity; for one may reach a clear distinction between the two. Causality (i.e. efficient causality) is limited to creativity of "physical prehension," whereas creativity also involves "conceptual prehension" of eternal objects, so that what had been merely possible becomes actualized.

To generalize about creativity, we may say that creativity involves two aspects. There is in the first place the presence of all possibilities of ideas, forms, and structures; secondly, there is the power to actualize some of these possible orders, forms or qualities in an actual occasion, and this power is inherent in any actual entity. These two aspects explain why there is novelty and continuous novelty in the world. But with regard to the question why there is any actuality or actual entity at all, creativity in the Whiteheadian metaphysics means the *ultimate* necessity of transforming pure possibilities into actualities. It is the actualizing and determining agency in the unlimited and undetermined realm of order, structures and qualities. It is eternal unity of permanence and flux. Whitehead has called the envisagement of all possibilities the Primordial Nature of God and has called the all-inclusive physical prehension of all evolving actuality the Consequent Nature of God. Since God is one, could we not say that possibility of actualization and actualization of possibility are one? I want to suggest that we could think of Whitehead's "God" as no more than a convenient name for the ultimate principle of creativity involving the beginningless and endless process of open change in which causality is no more than a mode of self-formation of actual entities. In so doing, I will be modifying Whitehead's explicit views in favor of what I consider to be a more profound meaning implicit in his position.

Since the notion of actual occasion (or actual entity) is crucial in Whitehead's philosophy for explaining change, including causation, we may note several basic features of actual occasions. In the first place, an actual occasion is a unit of experience. It is a subject of experiencing, a subject which is constituted by its experiencing. Experience is nothing other than grasping or assimilating other actualities and possibilities which contribute to the formation of the actual entity. In Whitehead's terminology, to experience is to prehend and to prehend is to relate and to be constituted by things related. Thus, actual occasions or actual entities are centers of prehensions and experiences. As an actual occasion defines itself in terms of what it experiences, anything which is an actual occasion must be able to constitute itself as a subject of experience, even though these experiences need not be articulated consciously in terms of the human mind and human emotions.

Whitehead has another way of conceiving actuality: an actual entity is a "growing together" of details of experience into a unity. The actual entity becomes and concresces. It is the formation of a unified organized entity in terms of experience. But here we must note that experience cannot be objectively specified. An experience is always some organizing, living center of force or agency. This center of force or agency which is the subject of experience and unification of what it experiences must be given as a basic fact of ontology. Indeed Whitehead approaches a monadological view of reality except that monads in his universe are centers of becoming and are formed from creative open acts of relatedness and prehension, rather than being closed, windowless substances as in Leibniz's monadology.

From the above, it is clear that, although the category of creativity for Whitehead is ultimate, for achieving rational explanation of experiences it nevertheless requires complementation by the Categories of Existence — especially actual entities and eternal objects. One might also say that creativity is not separable from the other two aspects of the Category of the Ultimate: the one and the many. One might even suggest that oneness is the definitive principle of actual entities and multiplicity is the definitive principle of eternal objects. In this sense both actual entities and eternal objects can be said to partake in the intimacy of metaphysical understanding, and creativity can be understood as the principle of achieving a dynamic unity of one and many so that it can generate one from many and produce many from one. One may then conclude that one and many are two aspects of creativity and are manifested simultaneously in our experience of the unison of becoming.

Accordingly, when Whitehead speaks of the Primordial Nature of God as the envisagement of all eternal objects and of the Consequent Nature of God as the prehension of all past actual entities, could we not conceive the Primordial Nature of God as many and the Consequent Nature of God as one, and thus conceive God as creativity itself? In so far as one and many cannot be actually separated, God is a unity of two natures—the primordial multiplicity and the consequent oneness. Of course, there is no reason why the Primordial Nature of God may not have its oneness and the Consequent Nature of God may not have its multiplicity. As one and many interpenetrate each other in creativity, the Primordial Nature and Consequent Nature of God should also interpenetrate each other in God. This should explain how the world of actual entities exists and evolves as the very consequence of our understanding of the world. The world does not begin from God. Its existence is not to be derived from some ultimate source; it is an ultimate itself in so far as it exhibits creativity and creative advance of things. Therefore without the world of actual entities and the world of eternal objects, creativity cannot be adequately explained.

In analyzing the concept of creativity in Whitehead, it becomes clear that there cannot be three separable independent aspects of the Category of the Ultimate. There should be only one ultimate, the ultimate of creativity which exhibits the becoming of one into the many and the becoming of the many into one. The Categories of Existence in Whitehead can be regarded merely as an explication of creativity and modes of its realization as revealed in experience. They are in this sense derived from the ultimate of creativity. Actual entities are concrete presentations of creativity. Eternal objects, on the other hand, are potential forms of creation inherent in the process of creativity. As eternal objects provide forms of many and one, they are determinate and constitutive of many and one, and therefore inhere in the given ultimate of creativity. Similarly, propositions "as matters of facts in potential determination" must be inherent in the process and agency of creativity which is given. Since prehensions and subjective aims are ways in which actual entities become actual entities in the creative advance; they are modes of creativity for actual entities. The Category of Prehension is therefore both a principle for a specific application of creativity to cosmological experience and a principle subsumed under the universal ultimate of creativity.

As for the remaining Categories of Existence, those of Nexus, Multiplicity, and Contrast, they must be considered as modes and ways in which eternal entities stand to one another relative to some given context of actual occasions. It is clear that the Category of Nexus is intended to apply to the conjunction of related actual occasions in a group, just as the Category of Multiplicity is intended to apply to the disjunction of diverse actual entities. They are therefore contrasted with each other as two modes of referring to complex situations. Finally, the Category of Contrast is a way of relating differences in actual entities which add to the depth and meaningfulness of the world as we know it. In fact, the contrast or opposition as a mode of existence can be said to be illustrated in the relatedness of the Category of Nexus to the Category of Multiplicity itself.

In light of the above, all the Whiteheadian Categories of Existence could be said to exhibit creativity in its actualization; they only reveal an actual richness which is potentially present in creativity itself. It can be said that all the Categories of Existence are logical explications of the content and form of creativity. It is not that creativity creates things and modes described in terms of these Categories of Existence. The agency of creativity becomes concretized in these Categories of Existence.

We may indeed conclude that there should be an organic unity in all the Categories of Existence which are explicable in the aspects of the Category of the Ultimate which again form an organic unity of one. Unfortunately, Whitehead has not presented a clear picture regarding their relationships. There even seems to be a tendency in Whitehead to treat them as concepts logically independent of one another. But in fact they all apply to the same thing—the principle of creativity or creative advance. When we come to see this unity and interdependence of these categories, we will find a certain simplicity in Whitehead's philosophy. We will further perceive cogency, even necessity and consistency, in all these categories, which would not be possible if they were derived from an experience of the ultimate simplicity and unity in creativity—the ultimate experience which we intimately embody. We further recognize that Whitehead's system is as much ontological as it is cosmological. It is cosmological in intent as it applies to experience, but it is conceptually ontological. The Category of the Ultimate does not evolve into the Categories of Existence. It explains the Categories of Existence and is explained by them. Utilizing Whitehead's terms, we may thus reach a representational diagram (see next page).

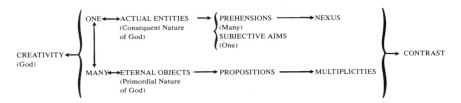

III

When Whitehead is interpreted in the above way, his position seems to approximate to the position which the great Neo-Confucianists from Chou Tun-i to Chu Hsi generally held. Specifically, Whitehead can be understood as reaching a position represented in the well-known *Discourse on the Diagram of the Great Ultimate* (*T'ai Chi T'u Shuo*) as developed by Chou Tun-i and generally accepted by Chu Hsi and other Neo-Confucianists. In the following I shall expound the metaphysical ideas as embodied in the Neo-Confucian doctrine of *T'ai Chi T'u Shuo* and in Chu Hsi's writings, in an effort to compare and contrast them with Whitehead's metaphysical views of creativity and its categories. I shall first explore the significance of the notion of the Great Ultimate (*t'ai-chi*) and other related notions of creativity in the Neo-Confucian system, in search of categories of creativity and parallel correspondences between Whitehead's and the Neo-Confucian categories of creativity.

It must be pointed out from the start that the Neo-Confucianists are extremely conscious of the need for organic unity of their concepts. Needless to say, this is because they have a primordial sense of organic unity of cosmological-human experience as a whole. Therefore, all the basic concepts are more' or less consciously described as more inherently and organically interrelated than in Whitehead's philosophy. All the basic concepts form a network of unity of interpenetrating and interdependent elements which, though differentiated, remain dialectically fluid and open so that they can enrich and support, and not exclude or alienate, one another. They are all derived from a central experience of unified wholeness and they are intended to cultivate and reinforce that primordial sense of wholeness and unity in practical life—a side which Whitehead has generally paid little attention to, as he regards metaphysics (cosmology) as chiefly speculative, but not obviously practical.

In the *T'ai Chi T'u Shuo*, Chou Tun-i has the following vision and understanding of reality as process or process as reality. He says:

The Ultimate of Non-Being and also the Great Ultimate (*t'ai-chi*)! The Great Ultimate through movement generates *yang*. When its activity reaches its limit, it becomes tranquil. Through tranquillity the Great Ultimate penetrates *yin*. When tranquillity reaches its limit, activity begins again. So movement and tranquillity alternate and become the root of each other, giving rise to the distinction of *yin* and *yang*, and the two modes are thus established.

By the transformation of *yang* and its union with *yin*, the Five Agents of Water, Fire, Wood, Metal, and Earth arise. When these five material forces (*ch'i*) are distributed in harmonious order, the four seasons run their course.

The Five Agents constitute the system of *yin* and *yang*, and *yin* and *yang* constitute one Great Ultimate. The Great Ultimate is fundamentally the Non-Ultimate. The Five Agents arise, each with its specific nature.

When reality of the Ultimate of Non-Being and the essence of *yin*, *yang*, and the Five Powers come into mysterious union, integration ensues. *Ch'ien* (Heaven) constitutes the male element and *K'un* (Earth) constitutes the female earth. The interaction of these two material forces engenders and transforms the myriad things. The myriad things produce and reproduce, resulting in an unending transformation.[6]

This short treatise contains all the basic categories and foundations of a Neo-Confucian speculative philosophy which is necessary, consistent, and systematic. The basic categories of the Neo-Confucian speculative philosophy are *t'ai-chi*, *wu-chi*, *tung-ching*, *yin-yang*, *ch'ien-k'un*, *wu-ch'i* (*wu-hsing*), *ch'i*, *sheng*, *hsing*, and *wan-wu*. It is clear that in the whole Confucian tradition beginning with the *I Ching*, *t'ai-chi* is the most important of all these cosmological-ontological categories. I shall argue that *t'ai-chi* is indeed the metaphysical primitive from which everything else is derived. In this sense it corresponds with Whiteheadian creativity. Yet, in the development of the notion of *t'ai-chi*, we shall see that it contains many ideas which should illuminate the nature of creativity and provide clues for resolving the difficulties in interrelating categories in Whitehead's metaphysics.

Whitehead indicates that creativity is an ultimate that cannot be explained. Can we similarly conceive *t'ai-chi* as unexplainable? The answer is that the initiator of the term '*t'ai-chi*' in the *I Ching* did not intend it to be explained in the context of a proper understanding and experiencing of change (*i*) in nature and life. It is a rhythmic movement of alternative polarities. It involves novelty and is revealed in the concretion of things and affairs. It is the essence of time as time is the essence of creativity. It is, at the same time, simple and complex, easy and difficult. Yet it is experienced that the complex always begins with the simple and returns to the simple, that the difficult begins with the easy and returns to the easy. It does have a structure, but the structure it has is not to be statically defined; rather, it is to be grasped in reference to individual things and remains open. It is most comprehensive, most widespread, most penetrating, most firm, most obvious, most subtle, and most exhaustive. It completes things and affairs and yet is dynamically and dialectically incomplete and incompletable. It is finally where goodness manifests and nature realizes itself. It is identified with life, living as well as the potentiality of life and living, which means everything which constitutes, defines, and enriches life and living.

With this concept of understanding and experiencing change, *t'ai-chi* denotes the creative force, process, and nature of change. Therefore *t'ai-chi* satisfies the demand of explanation and description and conforms to the principle of creative change from the simple to the complex. Thus *Hsi Tzu Ta Chuan* says: "Therefore the *i* has *t'ai-chi*, which produces two norms. The two norms produce four images, four images produce eight trigrams." The two norms are *yin-yang* or *ch'ien* and *k'un* (the principle of opening and the principle of closing); the four images refer to the four patterns generated from the combination of the two norms. Finally the eight trigrams indicate doubly differentiated patterns generated from the four images. By further differentiation of eight trigrams sixty-four hexagrams can be generated, as one can see from the text of the *I Ching*. It is in the same spirit that Chou-Tun-i considers *t'ai-chi* as the ultimate of becoming and the ultimate principle for all changes and orderings of things.

Next, there exists a metaphysical context for understanding *t'ai-chi*. It consists in recognizing the following conditions: (1) *t'ai-chi* includes order and creativity; (2) *t'ai-chi* includes determination and indetermination; (3) *t'ai-chi* is inexhaustible and infinite in content and sustains production of novelties; (4) *t'ai-chi* is not separable from reality of individual things and events; (5) though *t'ai-chi* is not to be identified with any specific entity, any specific entity derives order from and has its place in *t'ai-chi* as conceived as both the ultimate origin and the ultimate ground of all things. It is not simply a cosmological beginning, but the everlasting and everpresent being-in-becoming and becoming-in-being. To say that it is an ultimate (*chi*) is to say that beyond it there is nothing else and there is no other ground and source of being and becoming.

Chou Tun-i makes one important contribution toward making the notion of *t'ai-chi* even more intelligible and more envisionable than what the *I Ching* (*Hsi Tzu Ta Chuan*) has done. He introduces the term *wu-chi* (the ultimateless or ultimate of non-being) to indicate the other side (aspect) of *t'ai-chi* which also explains why *t'ai-chi* is *t'ai-chi* in the sense given above. Beyond *t'ai-chi* there is no ultimate, but there being no ultimate, there is precisely *t'ai-chi*. This is the meaning of "*wu-chi erh t'ai-chi* (being Ultimateless yet becomes being the Great Ultimate),"[7] which is the beginning sentence of *T'ai Chi T'u Shuo*. Chu Hsi interprets this sentence in the following way: "*T'ai-chi* is not a thing and there is no place to put it. Therefore

Chou Tzu says: 'The ultimateless becomes the great ultimate.' This is where his statement has merit."[8] But Chu Hsi's interpretation of *wu-chi* is also limited. For if it is as Chu Hsi suggests, Chou would have to say "*T'ai-chi erh wu-chi* (being the Great Ultimate becomes being the Ultimateless)." It is not simply because Chou worries about other people treating *t'ai-chi* as an object that he speaks of the *wu-chi*. It is also apparent that *wu-chi-erh-t'ai-chi* indicates that *t'ai-chi* is a primordial potential creative agency (impulse) which is not derived from any existing object but is given in the very nature of the formlessness and indeterminateness of *t'ai-chi*, which is conveyed by the term '*wu-chi.*' *Wu-chi* is the absolute formless indeterminate potential which always *becomes* the actuality essential for motion and rest and everything else. *Wu-chi* therefore indicates a primal unity of being and becoming before we can conceive anything. But since it can also be conceived as capable of realizing reality, it becomes *t'ai-chi*—the beginning of self-actualizing reality. The important thing to note is that Chou's statement indicates the self-creating nature of *t'ai-chi* and the identification of *t'ai-chi* with the realization of a process of change.

There is a final context for explaining *t'ai-chi*. Chu Hsi suggests that "*T'ai-chi* is the Principle (*li*) of Heaven and Earth and the ten thousand things."[9] Neither the *I Ching* nor Chou Tun-i uses *li* to interpret *t'ai-chi*. *Li* is a category which Chu Hsi inherits from the two Ch'eng Brothers, Ch'eng Hao (1032-1085) and Ch'eng I (1033-1107). It refers to the intelligibility and rationality of things in the world. It can be further explained as the *well-placedness* of a thing in the totality of things. It is therefore a term implying external patterning and internal organization and obviously should be understood as presupposing an organic unity of reality.

Conceived as an organic unity of reality, *t'ai-chi* is therefore to be identified with the *yin-yang* movements as Chou Tun-i indicates in his *T'ai Chi T'u Shuo*. To conceive this identification is to conceive *t'ai-chi* as a center of creativity which realizes itself in creatively evolving into basic and primary forms of productive powers of concrete reality by the alternation of the *yin-yang* process. The Five Agencies are more and more differentiated concrete forms of productive powers than the process of *yin-yang*; but they are evolved from *yin-yang* and thus derived from *t'ai-chi*. It is noteworthy that the Five Agencies are, on one hand, highly visible forms of reality but, on the other hand, they are not specifically determinate particulars. They are amorphous forces of qualitative differences which serve as immediate material for the formation of individual objects or events. Thus they are not to be taken literally as types of things or stuff, but are to be treated as differentiated forces ready to be formed into things. They are also organically interrelated, as they interact and mutually influence and interpenetrate for the realization of particularized phenomena. As a whole they are a manifestation of the *yin-yang* process which is a manifestation of *t'ai-chi*. The *t'ai-chi* and the Five Powers are therefore one.

That which enables *t'ai-chi* to move in the *yin-yang* modes and to differentiate into the Five Powers belong to the nature of *ch'i* or vital force. The Neo-Confucian position that *ch'i* is immanent in *t'ai-chi*, and perhaps constitutes the essence of *t'ai-chi*, testifies strongly to the conclusion that creativity after all is not different from, and is in fact co-extensive and co-temporal with, the concrete totality of changing events. *Ch'i*, an ancient term referring to the indeterminate substance which generates and forms any and every individual thing in the cosmos, no doubt has a rich content. It is formless, yet is the base of all forms. It is the source of everything and the ultimate into which formed things will eventually dissolve. It is non-stationary and forever in a state of flux. It might be conceived as the fluid state of becoming which reveals itself in actualization of natural events and natural objects. But it is best conceived as the indeterminate unlimited material-in-becoming which, through its intrinsic dynamics of alternation and interpenetration of the *yin-yang* process, generates Five Powers, and through their union and interaction generates the ten thousand things.

We must note several important things about *ch'i*. First, *ch'i* starts as pure homogeneity and indetermination and gradually becomes differentiated and heterogeneous. Second, the agency of transformation and change in *ch'i* is intrinsic to *ch'i* itself and is not derived from an external source, as there is nothing external to *ch'i* itself. Third, the process and product of *ch'i*-creativity toward differentiation and heterogeneity does not exhaust nor replace the original and natural state of indetermination and homogeneity of *ch'i*-creativity. In view of the first feature, *ch'i* is identical in agency with *t'ai-chi*; in view of the second feature, *ch'i* is the essence of creativity in its two modes of *yin-yang* and in terms of the Five Powers; in view of the third feature, *ch'i* permeates concrete actualities with indetermination and homogeneity which sustain and preserve the continuous creative change. Thus Ch'eng I says:

Empty and Tranquil, and without any signs, and yet all things are luxuriantly present. The state before there is any response to it is not an earlier one; the state after there has been response to it is not a later one. It is like a tree one-hundred feet high. From the root to the branches and leaves, there is one thread running through all.[10]

That emptiness and tranquillity are intrinsically identical with the creative advance and concretion of things and events in reality is a most important insight of Neo-Confucianism, which in a way recalls the Mahayana Buddhistic theory of the identity of *sunyata* and causality as advocated in the T'ien T'ai and Hua Yen Schools. But for the Neo-Confucianist, the point is that creativity and eventuation of actual entities are no less real than the indeterminate source and agency of creativity. They are in fact to be regarded as inextricably interpenetrated and interwoven in the polaristic unity of *yin-yang*. Unlike the Buddhists, Neo-Confucianists uniformly hold that the essence of this unity is creativity and creative presentation of things and life. On the other hand, they do insist that there is no hindrance nor distance between the formless and the form, which are totally submerged into one another. This is why I say that the evolution of *t'ai-chi* into the Five Agencies via *yin-yang* is not only a cosmological process, but also an ontological structure of pattern, which Whitehead fails to stress in his cosmological speculation.

IV

We have earlier mentioned that Chu Hsi has identified and explained *t'ai-chi* as *li*. We have also explained *li* as structure and order in consistency with human understanding (reason), as well as in unison with general facts of life and nature. If *t'ai-chi* is to evolve into *ch'i* or activities of *ch'i*, it is clear that *li* and *ch'i* must be also closely interlocked as two sides of the same thing. This is fundamentally the position of Chu Hsi and Ch'eng I with respect to the relationship of *li* to *ch'i*, or between *t'ai-chi* and *li* and between *t'ai-chi* and *ch'i*. Chu Hsi says: "Under Heaven there is no *ch'i* without *li*; also there is no *li* without *ch'i*."[11] "If there is this *li*, there is this *ch'i* . . . if there is this *ch'i*, there is *li* therein."[12] Though Chu Hsi maintains the thesis of interdependence of *li* and *ch'i*, he fails to stress explicitly the fundamental unity and oneness of *li* and *ch'i*. In fact, he has the tendency to treat them as separate entities and as constantly conjoined. He even feels inclined to accord some priority to *li* over *ch'i* and therefore makes *ch'i* a consequent creation of *li*. He says: "After there is this *li*, then there is *ch'i*."[13] "First there is the heavenly *li*, then there is *ch'i*."[14] "There is indeed no temporal order between (them), but if we must infer where they came, we must say there is first *li*."[15]

The priority of *li* over *ch'i* may be merely relative to our rational way of understanding; but Chu Hsi could be thought to conceive *li* as also in some sense ontologically prior to *ch'i*. This is, however, a position basically inconsistent and incompatible with the *T'ai Chi T'u Shuo* of Chou Tun-i, where he explicitly maintained that "Five Agencies are one *yin-yang*. Yin-Yang are one *t'ai-chi*. T'ai-chi is originally *wu-chi*." So if *ch'i* is created from *li, ch'i* is *li* and *li* is *ch'i*; and they cannot be necessarily united as one, since they are always one with concrete reality of life and nature. There may be good reason for Chu Hsi to separate *li* as ideal order from *ch'i* as natural and given actuality in the formation of man and mind, so that one can make an effort to improve oneself and so that the imperfection of evil can be explained. But there is no good reason to discriminate against *ch'i* in the formation of things in general in the world. The world is a structure as well as simultaneously a process. The process of change never remains structureless nor does structure ever stand apart from the concrete process of change. Therefore, there is no duality of *li* and *ch'i* except in the creative unity of both. This the beginning and end of change.

The great Neo-Confucianist Chang Tsai (1020-1077) perhaps comes closer to the understanding of the original creative unity of *ch'i* and *li* than Chu Hsi. He explicitly holds that *ch'i* is the ultimate of reality which always manifests alternation of *yin-yang* as two modes of creativity. Chang Tsai even does not refer to *li* as cosmologically prior to *ch'i*. For he called the Great Ultimate the Great Voidness (*t'ai-hsu*). He says: "The floating *ch'i* is the pervading and unorganized. But when it produces the myriad of things and men, [it] has two ends—the *yin* and the *yang* which circulate without ending and this is the way and norm of Heaven and Earth."[16] *Li* is not to be imposed upon *ch'i* to create things. Things naturally concretize and become open to rational understanding and analysis. *Li* is therefore at most inherent in *ch'i* as restraining, ordering, and patterning force. But the notion of *t'ai-chi* becomes highly significant in so far as *t'ai-chi* is conceived to acquire dynamical quality through the natural movements of *ch'i*.

Now let us ask how *li* and *ch'i* in the unity of *t'ai-chi* introduce and produce a rich variety of sensible qualities inherent in that unity; namely, how the simple beginning of *t'ai-chi* leads to the abundant differentiation of types and particulars in the world. The answer is that *t'ai-chi* has unexpectedly developed into various genuine entities, new and old. *Ch'i* absorbs variety and could produce particular variety under the right circumstances. To produce the ten thousand things there are in the universe, we must recognize that *t'ai-chi* contains subtle beginnings of all things which are to be evolved in the creative process of *yin-yang* movements. But to say this is not to say that variety of all things is completely determinate in *t'ai-chi* or that *t'ai-chi* contains all the forms of definiteness (namely, the Whiteheadian eternal objects) in its existence or movements. On the contrary, the Ultimatelessness of the Great Ultimate means that nothing is determinate in its beginnings, and determination only comes gradually through the dynamical movements of *t'ai-chi*. To move from indetermination to determination is what creativity means. There is no ingression of forms but simply concrescence of actual occasions from the indeterminate *ch'i*. In so far as determination of actual entities does not effect or exhaust the original and natural indetermination of *t'ai-chi*, this being the permanent nature of the Ultimateless in *t'ai-chi*, there will always be novelty in the creative change of things. Each determination and formation of things is a complete evidence and vivid illustration of the creativity of *t'ai-chi*. Hence, Chu Hsi says: "Everything has a *t'ai-chi*."[17] We may indeed call the principle which governs the relation between determination and indetermination the Principle of Ultimate (or General) Creativity.

The specific mode of determination of all things in the world for the Neo-Confucianist, as for the Chinese philosopher in general, from the beginning is always considered to be the polaristic and reversive movements of *yin-yang* (*tung-ching*) as we have described earlier. *T'ai-chi* is nothing other than the permanent union of the moving forces of *yin-yang* which therefore exist not as simple *aspect de situ* of *t'ai-chi*. *Yin-Yang* movements are immanent in *t'ai-chi* and are immanent in each other. *Yin-yang* movements again are not mechanical nor cyclic. It is the very process of creative advance which involves differentiation and specification as well as concrete actualization of types and kinds of things. Thus this process yields Five Agencies which, when acting and developing under the movement of *yin-yang*, come to produce all things in the world. We must again note that this process of differentiation, specification, and concrete actualization of life-creativity is not an arbitrary and random matter. It has its intrinsic hierarchical order and structure which are unfolded or realized in the process of generating concrete things.

Specifically, the order and structure of individual things follow the basic rule of development from the easy to the difficult and from the simple to the complex. The differentiation is accompanied by integration, the specification is accompanied by generalization, and the actualization is accompanied by potentialization (negative creation or deconcretion). Each creative movement has *yin* and *yang* momenta as constituting elements. The *I Ching* symbolism of trigram and hexagram system is intended to present and illustrate the creative process of the world, the creation of things, and the eventualization and hierarchical ordering of the primal *yin-yang* movements. That process in the *I Ching* shows that, no matter how complicated and how individually unique a human or natural situation (event) in the world is, it is to be derived or generated from simple beginnings and conforms to the movements of *yin-yang*, as well as possesses a structure understandable in the total system of change of *t'ai-chi*. Again we must note that the differentiation of *t'ai-chi* for the creation of the actual world does not exclude the non-differentiable unity of *t'ai-chi* nor introduce new elements, such as eternal objects, from a transcendental source. Differentiation and integration are simply ways and modes for expressing and fulfilling the inner richness of *t'ai-chi*. This principle governing the mode of creativity of *t'ai-chi* can be called the Principle of Relative or Specific Creativity.

The *I Ching* has paid equal attention to both the *process* of creativity and the *structure* of creativity. It has structurally illustrated the sequence of change according to certain empirically meaningful principles as embodied in the presentation and interpretation of hexagrams,[18] even though it does not systematize these principles nor specify the determinate structure and interrelational order of concrete situations. It is not until the development of the Neo-Confucian philosophy that systems revealing the inner structure and the outer order of the process of change are developed. Shao Yung (1011-1077), for example, has a highly sophisticated and insightful system of this sort. The important point that we wish to focus on in this connection is that the creativity of *t'ai-chi* in *yin-yang* has its inner structure and outer order in consistency with rationality and is capable of human understanding. Specifically, concrete entities and their production have within them a form and structure which may be said to determine what they are. In this sense we come to appreciate the importance of the notion of Neo-Confucian *li* (principle). *Li* is explained as the *well-placedness* of a thing in the totality of things. What makes a thing *well-placed* in the totality of things is precisely its structure or form. Chu Hsi attaches extreme importance to *li* for understanding the process of change, as we have observed. Though *li* can be ontologized as the basis of change, again (as we have pointed out) it is not separate from *ch'i* and should form with *ch'i* in organic unity in *t'ai-chi*.

As Chu Hsi maintained, everything has its *li*. One might therefore suggest that *li* functions like eternal objects which determine the form of a thing. But we must reply to such a suggestion with two important observations:

(A) *Li* could be said to give form and structure to a concrete thing. It is however not separable from *ch'i*, of which things are creatively made. *Ch'i* no less than *li* has the characteristic of eternal objects. For, as the principle of indetermination, *ch'i* contains all the possibilities of actualization. But again we might note that both *li* and *ch'i* have characteristics resembling actual occasions, since both have creative agency which actualizes things and situations. Therefore, the suggestion that *li* alone resembles eternal objects is basically misleading. A better suggestion perhaps is that *li* combines the form-giving power and the power of the Whiteheadian subjective aim for the actualization (*ch'i-hua*) of a thing. Considering its organic structure, it forms the reason for saying that anything having *li* is a subject-superject in the Whiteheadian sense.

(B) *Li* is fundamentally related to rational understanding. It is given ontological significance by the Ch'eng Brothers and Chu Hsi. *Li*, in this sense, is the structure and form of a thing as reached in a retrospective rational understanding. The principle of *li* requires that everything has *li*. To say this is to say that everything is *well-placed* in a system of reality open to rational understanding. Ontologically, this is equivalent to saying that everything has its roots in *t'ai-chi*, together with its movements, and that everything can be traced to a mode of differentiation and integration of *ch'i*. In this sense, the principle of *li* is like the Ontological Principle of Whitehead, which makes the organic unity of things and its rational understanding possible. We may indeed call the principle of *li* inherent in the creative process of *t'ai-chi* the Principle of Rational Creativity.

In the above, we have explained how the Neo-Confucianists understand creativity and how essential categories for understanding creativity are dialectically and organically interrelated and, indeed, unified into a totality. No category in this totality is external and requires explanation other than in reference to the totality, namely, the *t'ai-chi*. The above three principles should provide a ground for the understanding of the generation of the ten thousand things from *t'ai-chi* without introducing categories other than those embodied in the metaphysics of Chou Tun-i and Chu Hsi.

We may indeed present the process of creative change conceived by the Neo-Confucianists in a diagram.

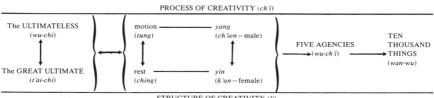

The double arrow on the diagram indicates mutual immanence and reciprocal transformability and the single arrow indicates creative advance in terms of particularization and differentiation which is also a process of generalization and integration in another perspective. Both differentiation and integration are essential to creativity and are co-extensive and co-temporal with each other. The unity of all these internal moments of creativity is indicated by the overall unity of *li* and *ch'i* which as a whole embody novelty and reason, change and permanence, being and becoming, in a comprehensive hierarchy of orderly understanding and ultimate life experience.

V

At this point we may raise questions concerning how the Neo-Confucian system of categories of creativity compares and contrasts with the Whiteheadian system of categories of creativity. Without reiterating what we have said about the resemblances between Whiteheadian and Neo-Confucian categories of creativity, we may point out some salient points of contrast and difference between the two regarding the nature of creativity, which should be topics of fruitful discussion and exploration.

(1) It seems clear that creativity in the Neo-Confucian system is much more radical than in the Whiteheadian system. *T'ai-chi* as the Great Ultimate of creativity contains all possibilities and yet it is fully identical with the process of creative advance as we experience it. Differences, variety, particularity, and forces of determination are evolved and created from the creative nature of *t'ai-chi* in a natural and spontaneous manner. On the other hand, Whitehead has to introduce the notions of 'One' and 'Many' into the Category of the Ultimate and the Category of Eternal Objects as forms of determination distinct from, and perhaps transcending, the creative agency, even though he seems to suggest a unity of eternal objects and actual entities in his notion of God. But the internal dynamics and immanent nature of creativity are not stressed by Whitehead as in the Neo-Confucian *t'ai-chi*.

(2) To account for the generation of novelty and the variety of ten thousand things, the Neo-Confucian philosophers appeal to the process of differentiation and integration as the source and agency of generation. Multiplicity or many are not to be regarded as given, as derived from the Primordial Nature of God, but simply to be considered as a mode of actualization of the Primal One—the *t'ai-chi*. This view has the natural consequence that all things in the universe are mutually interrelated. They are organically derived from the same process of creativity by rationally intelligible principles of production in conjunction with the Principle of Ultimate Creativity. *T'ai-chi* preserves novelty and simplicity as well as order and multiplicity at the same time. There is no need to appeal to eternal objects as a ground of novelty whose ontological status remains rather vague and whose existence in fact depends on existing actual configurations of things.

(3) A special reason for the continuous creativity of *t'ai-chi* is the polaristic structure of the creative process. Everywhere in the Neo-Confucian system there is the explicit and direct mention of the creative agency and creative achievement of the interpenetration of two opposite polarities as shown by the preceding diagram. One might suggest that the Neo-Confucianists recognize polaristic change in spiral ascendancy as the most

simple, yet most logically clear, picture of creativity in action. Even though Whitehead recognizes the importance of "Ideal Opposites" for explaining creativity, he does not establish a central set of paradigms for analyzing and explaining creative change in terms of interrelating opposites which are real and concrete. There is, of course, in Whitehead the contrast between eternal objects and actual entities, between permanence and flux, between the Primordial Nature of God and the Consequent Nature of God, between the one and the many, between order and change, between novelty and familiarity, between disjunction and conjunction, between freedom and necessity, between joy and sorrow, between good and evil, between God and world. There is, however, no stress and little suggestion regarding the ultimate unison and mutual transformation of those contrasting opposites. What is lacking is not a "unison of becoming among things in the present," but "a unison of interpenetration and becoming among all things in the world, past, present and future." This means we need a unison of indetermination and determination as we find in the becoming of *t'ai-chi*.

(4) Given the unison of becoming and interpenetration of all things in *t'ai-chi*, it is clear that a human being specifically can be conceived as a unison and harmony of creative forces evolving from *t'ai-chi*. It is also clear that there is a primordial unity and affinity between humanity, the universe and the ultimate reality. In so far as we can understand human experience in each moment as an actual entity in terms of the creative unity and process of the universe, we should be able to understand the universe in terms of the creative unity and process of human experience. Indeed, as *t'ai-chi* has not created anything else in the actual world nearly as active and complex as humans, to explore humans in order to understand the creative forces of *t'ai-chi* has its ontological validity in *t'ai-chi* as a totality. On the other hand, human beings can learn to cope with their own individual problems or problems of a community of persons by assimilating the creative vision of *t'ai-chi* as a totality. Specifically, human beings can develop and perfect themselves by responding to and participating in the creative advancement of *t'ai-chi*, rather than being satisfied with simply being a product of such creative advance.

The interaction and interpenetration between humans and the larger cosmos is a creative illustration of the creativity of *t'ai-chi* to be experientially and intimately realized in a human being, who is always a cosmological entity. Neo-Confucian philosophers, following the early tradition of the *I Ching*, have elaborated on the philosophy of the human being as a creative entity in the creative totality of *t'ai-chi*. Many categories of human creativity are developed, such as evidenced in the constant use of terms referring to *hsing* (human nature), *ch'ing* (human feelings), and *hsin* (mind). Though there is no time to discuss the meanings of these terms, it may be said that Whitehead lacks this human concern; and this reflects a one-sidedness of his system of creativity and an implicit lack of appreciation of the internal richness of creativity itself.

(5) Finally, the Neo-Confucian system of creativity presents categories relevant for understanding creativity which are mutually defining and mutually supportive. As we have explained, even the category of *t'ai-chi* and the categories of processes and individual things (or the world of individual things) support and presuppose one another for intelligibility and serve as the rationale of being and becoming for each other. As we have seen, there is obviously a strong conceptual interdependence among other basic categories of metaphysics in Neo-Confucianism. In fact, most Neo-Confucian philosophers seem to hold that reality receives different names in different areas of application for different purposes of explanation. There is always a fundamental unity weaving together all different philosophical terms in the metaphysical language of creativity. This is equally true of early Neo-Confucianists and of later Neo-Confucianists such as Wang Yang-ming (1472-1529), who holds that all basic terms in philosophy metaphysically point to the same ultimate truth.[19] Thus a philosophical system becomes an organic unity, directing and manifesting the organic unity of the world and reality of which it is a symbolic representation.

The organic unity among the Neo-Confucian categories we do not seem to find in Whitehead's system of creativity. It appears that all the Whiteheadian categories are given in conjunction and there is no specific effort explicitly to demonstrate or to assess their interdependence. There is no becoming or merging or enmeshing of one category in another in Whitehead as we see in the Neo-Confucian system. There is instead a conscious effort to relate one category to the other in terms of deductive or logical relation, without pointing to a context of wide experience of change and creativity. The concrete facts of life and mind are therefore treated abstractly and placed in a rational order of concepts. Thus, when one reaches the categories of the Ultimate, one faces an inexplicable non-rationality or irrationality. Perhaps Whitehead aims too strenuously to achieve logical clarity, conceptual precision and systematic detail in speculative philosophy, which by nature should remain richly imprecise and ambiguous and yet dynamically meaningful. Thus Whitehead's insights into the reality of process sometimes lapse into rigidity and invite questions which exploit his conceptual definiteness for opposition and inconsistency.

Notes

1. See works by Chinese philosophers such as Thomé Fang, Tang Chun-i, Hsieh Yu-wei, etc. It can be shown that in the light of Whitehead's notion of creativity a creative-organic explanation of causality is suggested. This new view of causality is very close to the traditional Chinese view of causality, basically because the Chinese view is based on a comprehensive philosophy of creativity. This illustrates the closeness of ideas and their implications between Whitehead and Chinese philosophy. See my paper, "Model of Causality in Chinese Philosophy: a comparative study," in *Philosophy East and West*, 26 (January 1970): 1-18 [Chapter 2 of this book].
2. See A. N. Whitehead, *Science and the Modern World*, New York, 1925.
3. See A. N. Whitehead, *Process and Reality*, New York, 1957.
4. Whitehead says, "In their nature, entities are disjunctively many in process of passage into conjunctively unity." Ibid., p. 32.
5. See *Process and Reality*, p. 32.
6. See Wing-tsit Chan, *A Source Book in Chinese Philosophy*, Princeton, N.J., 1963, p. 463.
7. Wing-tsit Chan, however, translates the sentence as "The Ultimate of non-being and also the great ultimate," as we have quoted from his translation earlier. This translation, as I have pointed out elsewhere, ignores the dynamic force of *erh*. See my review of Wing-tsit Chan's translation of *Reflections on Things at Hand* in *Philosophy East and West*, 20, 4 (October 1970): 623-627.
8. See *Chu Tzu Lu Lei*, Chapter 75.
9. Ibid., Chapter 1.
10. See Chu Hsi and Lu Tsu-ch'ien's *Reflections on Things at Hand*, trans. Wing-tsit Chan, New York, 1967, pp. 25-26.
11. *Chu Tzu Lu Lei*, Chapter 1.
12. *Reflections on Things at Hand*.
13. Ibid.
14. Ibid.
15. Ibid.
16. See Chin Ssu Lu, Chapter 1; also compare Wing-tsit Chan, ibid., p. 30.
17. *Chu Tzu Lu Lei*, Chapter 1.

18. See *Hsu Kua Chuan* in the *I Ching*.
19. See my paper, "Unity and Creativity in Wang Yang-ming's Philosophy of Mind," *Philosophy East and West*, 23, 1/2 (1973): 49-72 [Chapter 16 in this book].

Glossary (Introduction)

Ch'an 禪
Ch'eng I 程頤
Ch'eng Hao 程灝
ch'i 氣
ch'ien-hsing 踐形
ch'ien-wu 漸悟
ch'i-wu 齊物
Chang Tsai 張載
cheng-ming 正名
chih 知
chih-chih 致知
chih-hsing 知性
chih-liang-chih 致良知
chih-t'ien 知天
ching (reverence) 敬
Ching Ssu Lu 近思錄
chin-hsing 盡性
chiung-li 窮理
Chou 周
chou-pien-han-yung 周遍含容
Chu Hsi 朱熹
Chuang Tzu 莊子
Chung Yung 中庸
chun-tzu 君子
fa 法
fu (display) 賦
Han Wu-ti 漢武帝
Han Fei 韓非
Hsi Tzu 繫辭
Hsien-liang-tui-tse 賢良對策
hsin 心
hsin (arousing) 興

559

hsing 性
hsing 形
Hsi-Ming 西銘
Hsun Tzu 荀子
Hua Yen 華嚴
I 易
I Ching 易經
jen 形
kan-ying 感應
ke-wu 格物
Kung-sun Hung 公孫弘
Kung-yang Chun-chiu 公羊春秋
Lao Tzu 老子
li (principle) 理
li 禮
liang-chih 良知
liang-yi 兩儀
li-hui 理會
Lu 魯
Ming Ju Hsueh An 明儒學案
ming 命
pen-hsin 本心
pi (analogizing) 比
pu-tsa-pu-li 不雜不離
Shang Shu 尙書
shang-ti 上帝
Shao Yung 邵雍
shen 神
sheng 聖
Shih Chi 史記
Shih Ching 詩經
shih (consciousness) 識
shih-chung 時中
shih-chu-chiao 四句教
shih-hsiang 四象
Ssu Ma-chien 司馬遷
Sung, Ming 宋明
t'ai-chi 太極
t'ien 天
T'ien Tai 天台
t'ien-ming 天命

t'ien-ming-chih-wei-hsing 天命之謂性
t'ien-tao 天道
ta 大
Ta Hsueh 大學
tao 道
Tao Te Ching 道德經
te 德
Tung Chung-shu 董仲舒
tun-wu 頓悟
Wang Yang-ming 王陽明
Wen Yen 文言
wu-lun 五倫
wu-wei 無為
yang 陽
yi (intention) 意
yi 義
yin 陰
yi-li-sha-jen 以理殺人

Glossary (Chapter 1)

Ch'an 禪
chih 知
Chuang Tzu 莊子
Chung Yung 中庸
chun-tzu 君子
fu 復
hsin 心
hsing 性
Han Fei Tzu 韓非子
Hsun Tzu 荀子
Hua Yen 華嚴
jen 仁
kung 公
Lao Tzu 老子
li 禮
liang-chih 艮知
ming 命
nei-sheng-wai-wang 內聖外王
sheng 生
sheng-jen 聖人
Sung-Ming 宋明
tao 道
ti 帝
t'ien 天
T'ien T'ai 天臺
te 德
Tu Shun 杜順
yi or i 義
yin–yang 陰陽

Glossary (Chapter 2)

chien 簡
Chu Hsi 朱熹
Chuang Tzu 莊子
Chung Yung 中庸
Huai Nan Tzu 淮南子
i 易
I Ching 易經
Lao Tzu 老子
li 理
Lu Shih Chun Chiu 呂氏春秋
sheng-sheng 生生
Ta Chuan 大傳
tao 道
Tao Te Ching 道德經
t'ien 天
t'ien-jen-ho-yi 天人合一
Tung Chung-shu 董仲舒
Wang Chung 王充
Wang Pi 王弼
wu 無
wu-hsing 五行
wu-wei 無為
yin–yang 陰陽

Glossary (Chapter 3)

Ch'an 禪
ching 靜
Chi Wu Lun 齊物論
hsüeh 學
kung 空
kung-an 公案
tao 道
tao-shu 道術
t'ien-ni 天倪

Glossary (Chapter 4)

Chang Tsai 張載
Ch'eng I 程頤
ch'eng 誠
chi 寂
ch'i 氣
chien 踐
chih-chih 致知
chih-hsin-ho-yi 知行合一
chih-liang-chih 致良知
chih-shan 知善
ch'ing 情
ching 靜
Chou 周
Chu Hsi 朱熹
Chung Yung 中庸
fa 發
han-yang 涵養
hsiao 孝
hsin 心
hsin-chi-li 心即理
hsin-tung-hsing-ching 心統性情
hsing 性
hsu-ling-ming-chueh 虛靈明覺
jen 仁
ke-wu 格物
kung-fu 功夫
li-hui 理會
liang-chih 良知
liang-neng 良能
ling-chao-ming-chueh 靈昭明覺
ming 命
mou-lian 磨鍊

sheng 聖
shu 熟
ssu-yi 私意
ssu-yü 私欲
ta-jen 大人
tao 道
te 德
ti 悌
t'i-yen 體驗
ts'un-yang 存養
Wang Yang-ming 王陽明
Wu 武
yang 養
yi 義
yi 意

Glossary (Chapter 5)

Ch'ien 乾
Chung Yung 中庸
Hsi Tzu Ta Chuan 繫辭大傳
hsiang 象
hsing 性
Hsü Kua Chuan 序卦傳
i 易
I Ching 易經
K'un 坤
pien 變
pien-hua 變化
pu 樸
Sho Kua Chuan 說卦傳
su 素
tao 道
Tao Te Ching 道德經
wu 無
yang 陽
yin 陰

Glossary (Chapter 6)

bodhi 菩提
ch'an 禪
Chang Chih-tung 張之洞
Chang Tsai 張載
Cheng Meng 正蒙
ch'i-chih-chih-hsing 氣質之性
chi–jen 己人
Chi Wu Lun 齊物論
chih–hsing 知行
chin-shih chih-yung 經世致用
chiung-li 窮理
Chou Tun-i 周敦頤
Ch'üan Hsüeh P'ien 勸學篇
Chün Chiu Fan Lu 春秋繁露
chü-ching 居敬
chung 終
chung–ho 中和
fa–li 法禮
fan 反
fu 復
Han Shu 漢書
ho 合
Hua Yen 華嚴
Hsi Ming 西銘
hsing–hsüeh 性學
hsing 性
hsing-erh-shang hsing-erh-hsia 形而上 形而下
hsiu-shen chih-kuo ping t'ien-hsia 修身治國平天下
Hsiung Shih-li 熊十力
I Ching 易經
jen-che hui-jan yu wu t'ung-ti 仁者渾然與物同體
Jen Shuo 仁說

jen–yi 仁義
Kung Chih-chen 龔自珍
Kung Yang 公羊
li–ch'i 理氣
Li Kung 李琠
li–yi 禮儀
li–yü 理欲
liang-chih 良知
Liang Shu-ming 梁漱溟
Lu Hsiang-shan 陸象山
Lung Shu 龍樹
mou 末
Mou Tsung-shan 牟宗三
nei–wai 內外
pen 本
prajna 般若
sheng-sheng-chih-wei-hsing 生生之謂性
shih 始
shih-hsueh 實學
Shu Ching Ssu Lü 續近思錄
ssu-yü 私欲
Ta Hsueh Wen 大學問
ta-jen-che yi t'ien ti wan-wu wei yi-ti 大人者以天地萬物為一體
Tai Chen 戴震
t'ai-chi 太極
T'an Ching 檀經
T'ang Chun-yi 唐君毅
tao 道
tao–ch'i 道器
Tao Te Ching 道德經
te 德
ti–yung 體用
t'ien–jen 天人
t'ien-jen ho-te 天人合德
t'ien-jen ho-yi 天人合一
t'ien-li 天理
T'ien Tai 天臺
Tui-chiao-hsi-wang-yueh-ta-fu pi-te-wei-jen 對胶西王越大夫不得為仁
t'ung–ching 動靜
Tung Chung-shu 董仲舒
tzu-jan 自然

Wang An-shih 王安石
Wang Fu-chih 王夫之
Wang Yang-ming 王陽明
wen–chih 文質
wu-chi 無極
wu-chi erh t'ai-chi 無極而太極
wu-hsing 五行
yang 陽
Yen Yuan 顏元
yi–li 義利
yi-li-chih-hsing 義理之性
yi-yin yi-yang chih-wei-tao, chi-chih-che shan yeh, ch'eng-chih che-hsing-
    yeh 一陰一陽之謂道, 繼之者善也, 成之者性也
yin 陰
yü 欲
Yu Lu 語錄

Glossary (Chapter 7)

ch'eng 誠
cheng-hsin 正心
cheng-ming 正名
ch'eng-yi 誠意
ch'i-chia 齊家
chih-kuo 治國
chih 智
chih-chih 致知
chih-pen 知本
Chung Yung 中庸
hsiu-shen 修身
jen 仁
ke-wu 格物
li 禮
ming-ming-te 明明德
p'ing-t'ien-hsia 平天下
Ta Hsüeh 大學
yi 義
yung 用

Glossary (Chapter 8)

chang-jen-chih-chang 長人之長
Ch'en Chung-tzu 陳仲子
Ch'en Ta-ch'i 陳大齊
chih 氣
chung-shu 忠恕
Chung Yung 中庸
hao-jan-chih-chi 浩然之氣
Hsien Wen 憲問
jên 仁
Kao Tzu 告子
li 理
liang-chih 良知
liang-neng 良能
pu-tung-hsin 不動心
tao 道
Tzu Han 子罕
Tzu Lu 子路
wen-jen 問仁
wen-yi 問義
wu-ko-wu-pu-ko 無可無不可
Yang Ho 陽貨
Yen Yuan 顏淵
yi 義
Yung Yeh 雍也
yu-so-pu-wei 有所不為

Glossary (Chapter 9)

Book of Mencius 孟子
ch'eng 誠
chen hsin 正心
Ch'eng I 程頤
chiao 教
chi-chih 自棄
chih 知
chih 志
chih-chi 致知
chih-ching-yeh, chih-shih-yeh, chih-to-yeh, chih-chu-yeh, chih-hsing-yeh,
    chih-tzu-yeh 自禁也, 自使也, 自奪也, 自取也, 自行也, 自止也
chih-pao 自暴
chih-tao 知道
ching 靜
chueh 覺
chung 中
chung-chieh 中節
Chung Yung 中庸
fang 放
ho 和
hsin-chih-tao, jan-hou-ko-tao 心知道, 然後可道
hsing 性
hsu 虛
hua 化
Hsun Tzu 荀子
I Ching 易經
kan 感
ke-wu 格物
kuan 官
Li Chi 禮記
liang chih 良知
ming 明

pen-hsin 本心
pi 蔽
sheng 聖
sheng-sheng 生生
shih 失
ssu 思
ta-ching-ming 大清明
Ta Hsüeh 大學
tao 道
t'ien 天
t'ung 同
wei-fa 未發
yi 意
yi 一
yi-fa 己發
yin–yang 陰陽

Glossary (Chapter 10)

chih 知
chih-chi 知己
chih-jen 知人
chih-liang-chih 致良知
chih-sheng 知生
chih-yi 知義
chiung-li 窮理
chung 中
hao-jan-chih-chi 浩然之氣
ho 和
huo 惑
hsin 心
hsing 性
hsing 行
hsueh 學
jen 仁
li 理
li 立
liang-chih 良知
ming 明
ssu 思
te 德
t'ien 天
t'ien-ming 天命
tui 推
wu-min-chih-yi 務民之義
yen 言
yung 用

Glossary (Chapter 11)

Analects 論語
ch'eng 誠
Cheng I 程頤
chih 知
ching-wen 金文
Chu Hsi 朱熹
ch'uan 權
Chung Yung 中庸
hsing 性
hua 化
I Ching 易經
jên 仁
li 禮
ling-ming 令命
Lu Hsiang-shan 陸象山
Mencius 孟子
ming 命
pu-tzu 卜辭
sheng-hsing 生性
shih 時
Shih Ching 詩經
Shu Ching 書經
Ta Chuan 大傳
Ta Hsüeh 大學
Tai Chen 戴震
tao-te 道德
te 德
t'ien-ti 天帝
wei 位
yi 義
yü 育

Glossary (Chapter 12)

ch'eng 誠
chih 知
chung 中
fa 法
ho 和
hsiao 孝
hsing 性
hsueh 學
I Ching 易經
jen 仁
li 禮
shan 善
sheng 聖
tao 道
te 德
ti 悌
yi 義

Glossary (Chapter 13)

ai-jen 愛人
ch'an-fa 戰法
cheng 政
ch'eng 誠
chieh-chü-chih-tao 絜矩之道
chieh-chü 絜距
chih-shen 自省
ching 敬
chuan 權
chün-tzu 君子
fa 法
fa-chi 法紀
fa-chia 法家
fa-shu 法術
fa-tu 法度
fa-yi 法儀
feng 分
hsing 刑
hsing 形
hsiu-chi 修己
hsiu-sheng 修身
jen 仁
ju 儒
kung-yi 公義
li 禮
li 利
li-fa 禮法
ping-chun-chih-fa 平準之法
shih 詩
shih-chieh-ta-t'ung 世界大同
shu 書
tien 典

578

t'ien-hsia-wei-kung 天下為公
tse 則
tzu-hsing 自省
wang-che-chih-chih 王者之制
wang-che-chih-fa 王者之法
wu-hsing-chih-fa 五刑之法
yang 養
yi 義
yüeh 樂

Glossary (Chapter 14)

ch'eng 誠
ch'eng-che 誠者
ch'eng-chih-che 誠之者
ch'eng-jen 成仁
cheng-ming 正名
ch'i 氣
ch'ien-i 簡易
ch'ien 乾
ch'ien-k'un 乾坤
chih 知
chin 盡
chi-shih 亟時
Chung-kuo che-hsüeh fan-ch'ou ch'u-t'an 中國哲學範疇初探
Chung Yung 中庸
chün-tzu pu-ch'i 君子不器
Han Hsüeh Yen Chiu 漢學研究
ho 合
Hsi Tzu 繫辭
hsing 性
hsing 行
Hsun Tzu 荀子
hua 化
i 易
I Ching 易經
jen 仁
kua 卦
k'un 坤
li 禮
li 理
Li Chi 禮記
li-ming 立命
ming 命

nei 內
pi 闢
pien 變
pien-tung 變動
pien-t'ung 變通
pien-i 變易
pu-i 不易
sheng 生
sheng-sheng 生生
shih-ch'eng 時成
shih-chung 時中
shih-yi 時意
shih-yung 時用
sui 隨
shun-shou-ch'i-cheng 順守其正
t'ai-chi 太極
tao 道
Tao Te Ching 道德經
t'ien 天
t'ien-ming 天命
Tuan 彖
Tuan Chuan 彖傳
t'ung 通
wai 外
yang 陽
yi 義
yin 陰
yin-ch'i-shih-erh-t'i 因其時而惕
yu 育
yu-fan 憂患
yu-shih-chieh-chi 與時偕至
yu-shih-chieh-hsing 與時偕行

Glossary (Chapter 15)

Ch'eng Hao 程顥
cheng-shih 正事
Ch'eng I 程頤
ch'i 氣
ch'ien 乾
ch'ien-hsing 潛形
chih-chih 至知
ch'ih-chih 持志
chih-hsing 知性
chih-jen 知人
chih-tzu-chih-hsin 稚子之心
chin 盡
chin-hsin 盡心
Chin Ssu Lu 近思錄
ching 敬
ching-hsüeh 經學
ch'iung-li 窮理
chü-ching 居敬
Chu Hsi 朱熹
chu-wan-li 具萬理
chüan 卷
ch'üan-li 全理
chung 中
Chu Tze Yu Lei 朱子語類
fang-fa 方法
han-yang 涵養
ho 和
hsia-hsüeh-era-shang-ta 下學而上達
hsing-li 性理
hsüan-chih 學知
huo-jan-kuan-t'ung 豁然貫通
ke-chih 格致

ke-wu 格物
ke-wu-chih-chih 格物致知
k'un 坤
li 禮
li 理
li-hsing 力行
liang-chih 良知
Lu Tsu-ch'ien 呂祖謙
Meng Tzu Chi Chu 孟子集注
pen-hsin 本心
pen-t'i 本體
shen-ming 神明
shou-yi 守義
Ssu Shu Chi Chu 四書集注
Ta Hsüeh 大學
Ta Hsüeh P'u Chuan 大學補傳
t'ai-chi 太極
tao 道
tao-t'i 道體
t'ien-li 天理
ts'un-yang 存養
wang-hsing 妄心
Wang Yang-ming 王陽明
wei-hsüeh 為學
wu-chu-cheng 無助長
wu-wang 無忘
yang 陽
yin 陰
ying-wan-shih 應萬事
yung-ching 用敬

Glossary (Chapter 16)

ch'eng-hsin 誠心
ch'eng-yi 誠意
ch'i 氣
chih 智
chih 知
chih-chih 致知
chih-chung-ho 致中和
chih-hsing-ho-yi 知行合一
chih-liang-chih 致良知
ch'ing-hsing 情性
chiung-li 窮理
chung 中
chung-ho 中和
fa 發
hsin 心
hsin-chih-fa-tung-ch'u 心之發動處
hsin-chi-li 心即理
hsin-chih-pen-t'i 心之本體
hsin-hsüeh 心學
hsing 性
hsü-ling-ming-te 虛靈明德
i 易
jen 仁
ke-wu 格物
le 樂
li 理
li 禮
liang-chih 良知
liang-chih-pen-t'i 良知本體
ling-chao-ming-te 靈照明德
ming 命
ming 明

ming-te 明德
pen-t'i 本體
pen-t'i-chih-hsin 本體之心
piao-te 表德
shen 身
shih 事
t'i 體
t'ien 天
Weng Yang-ming 王陽明
wei-fa 未發
wu 物
wu 無
wu-shan-wu-o 無善無惡
yi 義
yi 意
yi-fa 己發
yung 用

Glossary (Chapter 17)

Che-tung 浙東
Ch'en Liang 陳亮
ch'eng 誠
ch'eng-shih-li-yeh 誠實理也
ch'eng-shih-shih 誠是實
cheng-te 正德
Ch'eng I 程頤
chi-shou-wu-yung 寂守無用
ch'i 氣
ch'i-chih 氣質
Chiang hsi 江西
chih 智
chih 知
chih-chih 致知
chih-hsing-ho-yi 知行合一
chih-liang-chih 致良知
chin-shih 進士
chin-wen hsüeh-p'ai 今文學派
ching-t'ien-chih 井田制
ching-tso 靜坐
Chou Kung 周公
Chou Li 周禮
Chu-chih-p'ing-fu-ti-fang-yi-t'u-chiu-an-shu 處置平復地方以图久安疏
chu-ching 主敬
Chu Hsi 朱熹
Chu-hsüeh 朱學
chu-yi 主意
chung 中
feng-chien 封建
fu-ch'i-chiu-hsing 復其舊性
fu-kuo-ch'ieng-ping 富國强兵
Han 漢

Hou Wai-lu 侯外廬
hsi 習
Hsi-yu 西域
hsiao 孝
hsin 心
hsin-hsüeh 心學
hsing 性
hsü 虛
hsüh-ku hsüeh 訓詁學
hsüeh 學
jen 仁
K'ang Yu-wei 康有為
kao-huan 高幻
k'e-chü 科舉
ke-wu 格物
ku-wen hsüeh-p'ai 古文學派
Kuang Hsi Ssu T'ien 廣西思田
kung 功
k'ung 空
kung-fu 功夫
Kung Tzu-chen 龔自珍
Kung-Yang hsüeh 公羊學
li 禮
li 理
li-hsüeh 理學
li-yung 利用
liang-chih 良知
liu-fu 六府
liu-hsing 六行
liu-te 六德
liu-yi 六藝
Lu Ling 廬陵
ming 名
ming-te 明德
Nan Kan Hsiang Yüeh 南贛鄉約
Nan K'ang 南康
Pien Wu Shu 邊務疏
san-shih 三事
Shang Shu 尚書
she 射
Shen Hao 宸濠

sheng-hsüeh 聖學
shih 事
shih-chi 實績
shih-hsing 實行
shih-hsüeh 實學
shih-t'i-shih-yung 實體實用
shih-wei-t'ien-ti 實位天地
shih-wen-shih-yung 實文實用
shih-yu-wan-wu 實育萬物
shu 書
shu 數
Shun 舜
Sung-Ming 宋明
Ta Hsüeh 大學
tao 道
t'i 悌
Ts'un Hušeh P'ien 存學篇
Tung Chung-shu 董仲舒
Wang Yang-ming 王陽明
wen 文
wu 物
Wu Shen Feng Shih 戊申封事
Yao 堯
yeh 野
Yeh Shih 葉適
Yen Fu 嚴復
Yen Yuan 顏元
yi 藝
yi 義
Yi Ch'uan 伊川
yi-li 儀禮
yu 御
yuan-sheng 原生
yüeh 樂
Yung Chia 永嘉
Yung K'ang 永康

Glossary (Chapter 18)

ch'eng 誠
ch'eng-ming-so-chih-nai-t'ien-te-so-chih 誠明所知乃天德所知
ch'i 氣
chih 智
chih-ch'eng 至誠
chih-chih 致知
chih-liang-chih 致良知
chih-yu-chih-shen 止於至善
chih-hsing 盡性
ch'in-min 親民
ching 敬
ch'iung-li 窮理
chü-ching 居敬
chu-yi 主一
han-yang 涵養
hao-jan-chih-ch'i 浩然之氣
hsin 心
hsin-t'ung-hsing-ch'ing 心統性情
jen 仁
kan-t'ung 感通
ke-wu 格物
li 禮
li 禮
lieng-chih 良知
ming 明
ming 命
ming-ming-te 明明德
pen-hsin 本心
pien-hua 變化
shen 神
shen-ming 神明
sheng-wu-ch'i-hsiang 生物氣象

shih-fei-chih-hsin 是非之心
t'ai-chi 太極
t'ai-ho 太和
tao 道
tao-t'i 道體
t'ien 天
t'ien-ming 天命
T'ien Ti 天帝
wu-chi 無極
wu-shih 無適
yi 義

Glossary (Chapter 19)

Ch'an 禪
Chang Tsai 張載
cheng-hsin 正心
ch'eng-jen 成仁
Ch'eng I 程頤
ch'eng-yi 誠意
chi 幾
chi-yi chien-hsing 集義　踐形
ch'i 氣
ch'ieh-ssu 切思
Ch'ien Hsü-shan 錢緒山
Ch'ien Te-hung 錢德洪
chih 知
chih 智
chih-ch'eng 至誠
chih-chih 致知
chih-chih-liang 知之良
chih-ch'ü 致曲
chih-chung-ho 致中和
chih-hsing 知性
chih-jen 知人
chih-liang-chih 致良知
chih-ming 至命
chih-shan 至善
chih-t'ien 知天
chih-yen 知言
chin-hsin 今心
chin-hsin 盡心
chin-hsing 盡性
ch'iung-li 窮理
Chu Hsi 朱熹
Chuan Hsi Lu 傳習錄

591

chung 中
chung 忠
Chung Yung 中庸
fa-yung 發用
hsiao 孝
hsin 心
hsin 信
hsin-chi-li 心即理
hsin-chih-tung 心之動
hsing 性
hsing 行
Hsün Tzu 荀子
Huang Tsung-hsi 黃宗羲
I Ching 易經
jen 仁
ke-wu 格物
kung-fu 功夫
li 理
li-ming 立命
liang 良
liang-chih 良知
liang-chih-pen-t'i 良知本體
liang-neng 良能
Liu Tsung-chou 劉宗周
Lu Hsiang-shan 陸象山
Luo Nien-an 羅念庵
ming-pien 明辨
ming-shan 明善
Nie Shuang-wang 聶雙汪
Nie Shuang-chiang 聶雙江
nien 念
pen-t'i 本體
po-hsüeh 博學
shen-wen 審問
ssu-chu-chiao 四句教
Ta Hsüeh 大學
t'i 悌
t'ien-li 天理
t'ien-ming 天命
Tsou Tung-kuo 鄒東廓
tu-hsing 篤行
Wang Chi 王畿

Wang Ken 王艮
Wang Yang-ming 王陽明
wei-fa 未發
wu 物
yang-ch'i 養氣
yi 意
yi 義
yi-chih-tung 意之動
yi-nien 意念
yüeh-li 約體

Glossary (Chapter 20)

Ch'an 禪
Chang Tsai 張載
Che-tung 浙東
Ch'en Ch'üeh 陳確
Ch'en Liang 陳亮
Ch'eng I 程頤
chi 即
ch'i 器
ch'i 氣
ch'i-chih 氣質
ch'i-hua 氣化
ch'i-ping 氣稟
Chiao Hsün 焦循
chih-ts'e 質測
chih-chih 致知
chih-hsing-ho-yi 知行合一
chih-liang-chih 致良知
ching 淨
ch'ing 情
Chu Chih-yu 朱之瑜
chü 聚
fa 法
Fang Yi-chih 方以智
Fu Shan 傅山
hsiang 相
hsin 心
hsin-chi-li 心即理
hsin-hsüeh 心學
hsin-t'ung-hsing-ch'ing 心統性情
hsing 性
hsing 形
Huang Tsung-hsi 黃宗羲

Huang Wan 黃綰
jan 染
jen 仁
jin-sheng jih-ch'eng 日生日成
ke-wu 格物
Ku Yen-wu 顧炎武
k'ung 空
li 禮
li 理
li-ch'i 理氣
Li Erh-ch'u 李二曲
Li Kung 李㻛
liang-chih 良知
Liu Tsung-chou 劉宗周
Lu Shih-yi 陸世儀
Lu-Wang 陸王
P'an P'ing-ke 潘平格
san 散
sa 色
shen 神
sheng 生
sheng-sheng 生生
shih 事
shu 數
Ssu Shu Cheng Wu 四書正誤
Sung-Ming 宋明
Ta Hsüeh 大學
ta-hua 大化
Tai Chen 戴震
t'ai-chi 太極
t'ai-ho 太和
t'ai-hsü 太虛
T'ang Chen 唐甄
tao 道
t'ien 天
t'ien-hsia-chih-tung 天下之動
t'ien-ming 天命
t'ien-tao 天道
ts'ai 才
tsai-li 宰理
t'ung-chi 通幾

Wang Fu-chih 王夫之
Wang Lung-hsi 王龍溪
Wang T'ing-hsiang 王廷相
Wang Yang-ming 王陽明
wei-shih 唯識
Wu Li Hsiao Shin 物理小識
wu 無
wu 物
yang 陽
Yeh Shih 葉適
Yen Yuan 顏元
yi-li 義理
yin 陰
yin-yun 絪縕
yu 欲
yu-chou-chen-ch'i 宇宙真氣
yu-chou-sheng-ch'i 宇宙生氣

Glossary (Chapter 21)

Chang Tsai 張載
Ch'eng Hao 程顥
Ch'eng I 程頤
chi 極
ch'i 氣
ch'i-hua 氣化
ch'ien-k'un 乾坤
ch'ing 情
Chou Tun-i 周敦頤
Chu Hsi 朱熹
Hsi Tsu Ta Chuan 繫辭大傳
hsin 心
hsing
Hua Yen 華嚴
i 易
li 理
Shao Yung 邵雍
sheng 生
t'ai-chi 太極
T'ai Chi T'u Shuo 太極圖說
t'ai-hsü 太虛
T'ien T'ai 天臺
tung-ching 動靜
wan-wu 萬物
Wang Yang-ming 王陽明
wu-chi 無極
wu-ch'i 五氣
wu-chi-erh-t'ai-chi 無極而太極
wu-hsang 五行
yin-yang 陰陽

Index

Confucianism 504
enlightenment 78
hsin (heart-mind) 77
Hua-yen 75ff
Hui-neng 75
idealistic tendency 504ff
irreconcilable dualism 504ff
kung (sunyata) 77
language 78, 119
logic of denial in Madhyamika 75
Madhyamika 75
nirvana 78, 505
T'ien-tai 75ff, 77
wei-shih (mere-consciousness) 505
Yogacara 75ff
Chinese ontology 126
Chinese Philosophy 2, 3, 81
art 3
cultural creativity 3
holistic unity 2
humanism 80
immanentization 17
inter-subjectivity 3
intrinsic vs. extrinsic humanism 80
medicine 3
natural relationship 2
organic totality 2
real process 2,
two levels 2
unity of experience and thinking 2
unity of man and nature 126
Chinese Marxists 211, 213
dialectics of conflict 213
dialectic of harmonization 211, 213
Chisholm, Roderick 391
and Chu Hsi 390
coherence theory of truth 393
self presentation 392
theory of knowledge 391
Chomsky, N. 35
concept of internal grammar 35
logical/linguistic analysis 36
Chou 13, 24, 320
Chou Li (Rites of Chou) 426

Chou Tung-ku 501
Chou Tun-i 50, 55, 57
I Ching 546
t'ai-chi (the great ultimate) 546
T'ai Chi T'u Shuo (Discourse on the Diagram of the Great Ultimate) 544, 549
wu-chi (the ultimateless) 546
chou-pien-han-yung (all-inclusive and comprehending) 17
in Hua Yen 17
in Neo Confucianism 17
in T'ien Tai 17
Chu Hsi 20, 27, 47, 61n, 148, 207, 210, 289, 409, 481
and Ch'eng I 145, 270
and Lu Hsiang-shan 126
and Wang Yang-ming 54, 126, 148
and Western philosophy 390ff
Buddhism and Taoism 432, 433
Ch'an 481
Ch'eng brothers 391
Ch'eng I 481
chi 431
ch'ien-wu (gradual enlightenment) 55
chih (knowing/knowledge) 51
chih (wisdom) 462
chih-chih (extending knowledge) 435
chih-chih (reach for knowledge) 145, 389
ch'ih-sou (holding and abiding) 389
ching (serious-mindedness) 385ff
Chin Ssu Lu 49, 389
ch'iung-li (exhaustingly fulfiling principles) 385ff
chu-ching (holding to serious-mindedness) 385ff
Chu Tzu Yu Lei (Classified Conversations of Chu Hsi) 385, 387, 389
Doctrine of the Mean 389
four sentence teaching 53
full knowledge of total truth 392

hsing (nature) 398, 399

hsing (nature)/hsin (mind) 53, 141, 142, 396

hsing (nature/human nature) 27, 154, 397

hsin-hsueh (mind learning) 396, 440, 441

hsin-t'i-pen-t'i (original substance of mind) 400

Hsu Ai 404

hsu-ling-ming-ch'ueh (vacuity, intelligence, perceptiveness and sensitivity) 137, 400

jên (benevolence/love) 398

ke-wu (investigating things) 144, 147, 410, 411ff, 483, 498, 499

kung-fu (efforts) 140

liang-chih (innate knowledge of good) 52, 137, 138, 140-3, 146-148, 152-555, 397, 400, 406-407, 441

liang-chih-pen-t'i (the original substance of the innate knowledge of good) 398, 402

li-hui (thoroughly understand) 148

ling-chao-ming-chueh (intelligent clarity and illuminating perception) 137, 400

li (propriety) 27, 52, 54, 143, 147, 148, 154, 397

Li Yen-ping 415

Lu Hsiang-shan 483

Mencius 273, 417

mind of sincerity 404

ming (enlightenment) 403

ming (mandate/destiny) 399

ming-ming-te (illuminating bright virtues) 412

Ming period 210

moral psychology 494

nature of reality 483

onto-hermeneutical circling 53

ontology 151

organic and integrated understanding 469

ought/is 404

pen-hsin (original mind) 52

pen-ti (the original substance) 20, 53

pen-t'i (the original/ultimate reality) 398, 400, 401, 411

philosophy of mind 52, 396ff

p'iao-te (manifest virtues) 397

Pien Wu Shu (Memorial on Border Affairs) 445

pi-yu-shih-yen (there must be specific engagement of the mind) 402

self-reflective knowledge 401

sheng (physical body) 399

sheng-hsueh (learning of sagehood) 442

shih (affairs) 403

shih-hsueh (practical learning) 438

shu (very acquainted with) 148

ssu-yi (selfish intentions) 141, 410

ssu-yu (selfish desires) 141, 410

standard of goodness 144

tactical acumen 446

ta-jên (great man) 152

tao (the way) 152, 412

t'ien (heaven) 397, 399

t'ien-li (heavenly principle) 401, 403

ti-nien (deeply experience) 148

t'i (ruler/supreme lord) 399, 400

t'i (substance/the ultimate reality) 400

t'i (substance)/yung (function) 400

tsen-yang (preserving and nourishing) 141

unity and creativity 397, 399

unity of knowledge and action 442

unity of ontology and morality 53

unity of theory and practice 53, 57, 83, 274, 397, 404, 412

wu (things) 402

wu-shan-wu-o (without good and without bad) 416

yang (nourish) 148

yi (intentions) 402, 410